THE HISTORICAL BIGFOOT

THE HISTORICAL BIGFOOT

EARLY REPORTS OF WILD MEN,
HAIRY GIANTS, AND WANDERING
GORILLAS IN NORTH AMERICA

SECOND EDITION

CHAD ARMENT

COACHWHIP PUBLICATIONS
Greenville, Ohio

ACKNOWLEDGMENTS

Loren Coleman, Paul Cropper, Rod Dyke, Paul Grzybowski, Gary Mangiacopra, and Richard Muirhead.

Contents

EYE-WITNESSES SEE BIGFOOT

1958 was the year newspapers began using "Bigfoot" in their headlines.

Introduction

This book attempts to gather and arrange alleged Bigfoot reports of a specific type—those historical accounts that pre-date the cultural development of Bigfoot, which, whether or not it actually exists as an undescribed species, is a recognizable ethnoknown creature within North America. The following accounts range from the early 1800s to the 1950s. ('Bigfoot,' as an epithet for this creature, began to be used in 1958.)

Native American mythology, except as related to actual sighting accounts, is not included in this volume. It would require a book, or more, just to begin exploring legends and stories of snow-walkers, stone giants, and tribes of Others, let alone attempt to discern a physical creature within the supernatural-natural intersections of such lore. I recommend Kathy Moskowitz Strain's (2008) *Giants, Cannibals & Monsters: Bigfoot in Native Culture,* if you wish to delve in that direction.

Before the term Bigfoot was applied to such a creature (or even before J. W. Burns popularized the name Sasquatch), towering, bipedal, hairy manlike-apes were reported all the same, but under a wider variety of monikers. Wild Man, Gorilla, Yahoo, What-Is-It, and Nondescript were commonly applied. Regional folklore sometimes hid reports under Dwayyos and Jabberwockies. When apelike characteristics were emphasized, the terminology often focused on fugitives from escaped menageries. (For brevity, I'll use Wild Man throughout the book as a generic term for the historical Bigfoot.)

Obviously, this chaotic linguistic scheme was ripe for confusion, and mistaken identifications clearly took place. After all, perception (the mental image) of a creature was based not only on witness descriptions, but also on societal pressures and biases regarding outsiders, conformity (or not) to recognized norms, and the extent of scientific progress. On the one hand, for example, there was a tendency to emphasize apelike characteristics in humans who lived outside "decent" society or in the poorest classes, and so infuse Wild Man reports with "crazy" hermits and degenerate fugitives.

At the same time, even in the late 1800s, the influence of "scientific progress" was strong enough for some newspaper editors to dismiss outright the possibility of non-human primates as the root cause of Wild Man sightings. After all, gorillas and other tropical apes would not survive long in temperate North America, certainly not over winter, so consecutive years of similar gorilla-like sightings must be pure bunk.

As will become evident, not all of the reports in this book can be traced to what we refer today as Bigfoot (either as biological entity or folkloric motif). While I did aggressively cull numerous Wild Man reports that were obviously just human beings, some remain for which that or other commonplace explanations are most reasonable. I also include certain misidentifications and hoaxes that have been previously published in Bigfoot literature as legitimate accounts. What particularly interests me is that while explanations abounded in early accounts, some were clearly based on cultural bias, particularly in terms of the Savage, or a being living in wild places without the aid of advanced tools. The Savage was perceived as either a reversion to bestial nature (thus opposing law and order), or as throwing off materialistic trappings to live freely in nature (the Noble Savage concept). This relates to both historical and modern Bigfoot sighting descriptions, as an individual's perception may color the eyewitness account. (When someone describes the creature as having a malignant or peaceful expression, does that tell us more about the animal or the witness?) The Noble Savage was always in perfect condition in sightings where he vanishes into the forest, but when captured, usually turned out to be a shell of his former glory, scrawny and dirty, subsisting on what scraps he could scavenge in the wild.

The following explanations were suggestions by newspapers, governing officials, and witnesses for early Wild Man reports. Some explanations are feasible for certain accounts, while others are un-likely for any account.

1. HUMAN BEINGS
   a. *Hermits:* living alone in the woods, often found with a cabin or rudimentary shelter
   b. *Mentally Disabled:* escaping from asylums or familial care
   c. *Mentally Afflicted:* short-term insanity, some-times recoverable, person behaves like an animal
   d. *Tramps:* itinerant wanderers
   e. *Outlaws and Deserters:* fleeing from the law, military service, or military draft
   f. *Fugitive Slaves*
   g. *Immigrants:* displaced foreigners
   h. *Refugees:* fleeing from military action
   i. *Indians:* cultural perception regarding Native Americans
   j. *Lost Tribe:* cultural perception by Native Americans
   k. *Lost Children:* growing up feral

A typical "wild man" hermit
(Casper, WY, STAR TRIBUNE, April 3, 1922)

"Orab," Who Recently Arrived from Africa, and Who Is the Only Living Gorilla in the United States.

**A fake gorilla (showman's hype),
actually a young chimpanzee**
(Buffalo, NY, Courier, July 19, 1903)

2. KNOWN ANIMAL
   a. *Bear:* walking on hind feet, causing misidentification
   b. *Gorilla, Orangutan, Chimpanzee, Baboon, or other Wild Primate:* menagerie escapee

3. HOAXES AND STORIES
   a. *Newspaper Hoax:* to fill up space, entertain readers, or spark sales
   b. *April Fool's Hoax*
   c. *Practical Jokes:* especially by juveniles
   d. *Campfire Tales:* stories by woodsmen, may or may not be true, but often exaggerated
   e. *Rumors:* spread through towns, sometimes picked up by newspapers
   f. *Showman's Hype:* story created to attract crowds to an exhibit
   g. *Social Control:* stories spread to scare and manipulate people

4. UNKNOWN OR UNRECOGNIZED SPECIES
   a. *Unknown Ape:* American 'gorilla' or other
   b. *Primitive Man:* Neandertal or other

Over the years, many enthusiasts and investigators have collected historical Bigfoot accounts. Those who have actively compiled and disseminated these stories include Gary Mangiacopra, and the late John Green, Ray Crowe, and George

Haas. They provided a strong foundation for research into Bigfoot as a historical, and not merely recent, phenomenon. While a historical Bigfoot does not in itself confirm the presence of an unrecognized species, it does answer the critic who claims that the absence of historical reports supports a folkloric explanation rather than a biological one.

Early compilations of historical Bigfoot accounts were limited by technology, of course. An individual might spend hours, days, weeks on end, diligently searching through microfilmed newspapers without finding anything useful. When an article was discovered, it was a treasure, and eventually found itself reprinted in various books and newsletters.

The advent of digital newspaper archives has allowed for greater depth and scope in this type of research. When I wrote the first edition of *The Historical Bigfoot,* I noted that the number of known historical Bigfoot accounts would likely quadruple over the next twenty years. That was 2006, and the book was just under 350 pages. This edition, at the end of 2019, is over 1000 pages. We likely have the majority of stories that were published via wireservice, but local newspapers that haven't yet been digitized probably hold a number of interesting sighting accounts. One area that requires serious investigation is in historical

French-language newspapers, books, and journals from Quebec and other parts of Canada.

Even with a wide range of historical Bigfoot reports presented here, I am strongly disinclined to make any sweeping generalizations, pro or con, about a historical Bigfoot—yet there is a need for realism in investigations. Take those Wild Man accounts, for example, that involve a creature wearing rags or skins. Certainly, a witness may include such descriptives subconsciously, if human-like characters are being emphasized. (We see a similar bias toward humanlike characteristics when sticks and rocks are described as clubs and tomahawks.) I may even consider an ape mimicking a human possible. (Unlikely, but within the realm of possibility.) But for the vast majority of reports, if clothing is prominent in the story, a human being is the source of the account. (Some researchers suggest that in certain remote regions, Bigfoot encounters are rooted in surviving Neandertals; whether that is viable or not, I don't think anyone has suggested that ragged-clothed Neandertals are roaming the entire continent.) A desire for more evidence should not tempt us into accepting faulty assumptions. It is not quantity of reports that helps us, but quality, and even then, the primary purpose of any collected sighting is to point toward regions where present-day field work might be productive.

Objectivity requires us not only to be wary of wishful thinking, but also of the credulity rampant within debunking methodologies. Shoemaker (1990) attempted to deconstruct the historical Bigfoot in an article for *Strange Magazine*. (This is, still, to the best of my knowledge, the only substantive critique of the historical Bigfoot concept.) He limited his case studies to the oldest reports (pre-1900), assuming they were less tainted than those in the modern era, which 1) influence witness' perception of Bigfoot's description and behavior, 2) are more sophisticated in what is plausible in science, and 3) provide more opportunities to make money on a hoax.

I have difficulty believing that anyone who has spent much time at all reading historical newspaper accounts would consider these assumptions correct. These same "modern" influences were very much present before 1900. Wild Man reports, complete with standardized newspaper descriptions, were transmitted throughout the country, and certainly influenced stereotypes of what a Wild Man was or how it behaved. Scientific plausibility during this period included the ongoing discovery (and pseudo-discovery) of great ape species, which one would expect to directly influence the feasibility of unknown species in uncharted North America. We certainly can't say that hoax opportunities were fewer in the nineteenth century.

Far from it. Extravagant stories were bread-and-butter for showmen to lure a paying crowd (and a 'wonder tale' to titillate readers was beer money for an enterprising journalist). Thus, there's little reason for limiting an examination of the historical Bigfoot to just nineteenth century cases.

Shoemaker's summaries for the cases he presented were hit or miss. Several cases he just wasn't able to properly investigate due to lack of material, while others were dismissed for not fitting his perceived stereotype of what Bigfoot must look like. (Or, even, how Bigfoot must look like to someone in the nineteenth century.) He did offer useful information in the article, but this was overshadowed by serious mistakes in the method of analysis. Shoemaker attempted to connect Wild Man reports to potential influences in the media. He discovered that a "curiously co-incidental" article about a baboon in India was published in newspapers in May 1838, prior to the August 1838 report of a whistling "wild boy." A theater troupe with monkeys was publicized a few days prior to an 1856 Arkansas Wild Man report. A story of a zoo monkey being killed by its cage-mates preceded publication of an aggressive 1891 Michigan creature. (As Shoemaker noted, "The 'coincidence' of a monkey killing a monkey and a Bigfoot killing a dog is highly suggestive, to say the least.") The problem is that these are classic *post hoc* fallacies. Shoemaker attempted to mitigate the obvious flaw by claiming, "The influence would not operate, as debunkers of the CSICOPian sort would have us believe, by inducing people to see things that are not there, but rather would work in tandem with a real stimulus such as a wild man dressed in skins, leading the observer to interpret the man as something hairy and sub-human." In reality, though, connections and influences are subtler and less contrived than Shoemaker presented. Yes, outside influences may lead to mistaken perceptions, but the methodology that Shoemaker uses makes it impossible to identify sightings of an actual Bigfoot species, assuming one exists. After all, early newspapers are filled with stories of natural history, with exotic animals and strange natural phenomena. We could easily manipulate connections to "triggering" stories, especially with as vague a determination as Shoemaker offers. Take his comments on the 1818 Ellisburgh, New York, report, where he suggested that because a letter to the Sacket's Harbor *Gazette* warned of seeing ergot in the rye fields, "We may legitimately wonder whether this natural hallucinogen, unknowingly eaten at a meal, induced a mild hallucination in the witness." Reasonable likelihood? I don't think so.

While historical Bigfoot accounts must always be approached with caution, and uncertainty is guaranteed unless and until physical confirmative evidence of a North American primate is found, I think there is room for enjoying the search. If I had to choose a favorite among the accounts to follow, it would be the 1891 series of California sightings. I'm willing to bet there are more sightings from that region and time period that are waiting to be uncovered. I would be very interested in hearing about other historical Bigfoot reports, and can be reached through my website, StrangeArk.com, or the StrangeArk Facebook page.

Technical Note

I originally attempted to reprint newspaper articles close to original spelling and wording. Some words, particularly in the earliest accounts, will occasionally be misspelled. (For example, *gorrilla* was a common misspelling for *gorilla*.) Having gone over so many versions of different stories for this second edition, it is possible that I've corrected a few spellings here and there. You may view the originals on various digital archives.

Readers should note that placenames may change spelling over the decades, and some early locations may not longer exist under those names. Maps will show general localities for main sighting accounts, though obvious hoax locations are not usually included.

AMUSEMENTS.

GREGORY'S FIFTH ST. MUSEUM.

GALA HOLIDAY ATTRACTIONS !

WILD MAN	CHE-MAH	TEXAS GIANTS

--HAIRY--   WILD MAN   CHE-MAH   TEXAS GIANTS   --FOUR--

THE

FAT

GIRL !

During Holiday Week the Museum and Stage Features will be augmented to an extent never before attempted by any similar place of amusement in this country.

THE

WHITE

MOOR !

SIGNOR ETANO'S PERFORMING BIRDS.

Japanese

Jugg'ing

and Balancing !

The Wild Man is confined in strong cage and securely chained to floor. His entire body is covered with full, heavy growth of hair. He was captured in Russia.

Funny

Character

Impersonations !

New Ventriloquial Acts, Songs and Dances.

STEVENS AND MAXWELL.	BIRDIE AND GOLDIE RINEHART.	LIEUT.
	EDDIE LESLIE.	ALLEN.

A thorough change in stage bill. A highly proper and amusing resort for Ladies and Children. Open from 1 to 10 p. m. On Christmas and New Year's from 10 a. m. till 10 p. m. One Dime admits to all departments.

An 1883 advertisement
for a dime museum
with a "wild man" act

Hoaxes and Misidentifications

Without a doubt, the vast majority of Wild Man reports found in early newspapers are men or women who found themselves outside of society, fending for survival in the wild. Misidentification of human beings as half-human creatures, or even gorillas, may seem strange, but fear of the unknown and shifting cultural recognition of what defines man or beast both played their part. Many accounts of feral humans are readily identifiable in hindsight, but there were also misidentifications of native or exotic animal species or even deliberate hoaxes. Bears, for example, are the source behind some reports, though that explanation has been used inappropriately in certain cases.

Deliberate hoaxes are less common, but can be found. These may involve tracks, strange sounds, and/or disguises. The Wild Man hoax is an offshoot of the Big Snake hoax, or any number of Snallygaster, Dwayyo, or other folkloric creatures used to effectively frighten persons in a community. While sometimes done for fun, many cases had a purpose: either to control access to property (berry patches, locations of stills, etc.), or to manipulate behavior in children and others. Shoemaker (1990) noted that racist tactics are the possible explanation behind some hoaxes.

Investigators should be aware that modern hoaxers have create supposed "classic" Bigfoot cases. Chorvinsky (1990) analyzed the deliberate hoaxing, probably by a certain self-proclaimed skeptic, of a "captured wild man" photograph that was claimed to have been published in a 1912 Idaho newspaper. That photograph was determined to be a still from a 1914 movie, *The Miser's Reversion*.

These next cases are a sampling of misidentifications or hoaxes involving wild men and hairy apes.

1. MISIDENTIFICATIONS

Wellsboro, Pennsylvania, *Agitator,* August 29, 1894

—It is stated that the "giant wild man" who appeared in the woods at several times in the West-branch region, was captured last Friday by a large party of citizens who set out to hunt for him. It turns out that he was no giant at all but of medium size, his body covered with hair and his beard and head a matted shock of long hair. His name is Bodine Brooks, and he is about 45 years of age.

He is described as a half-witted specimen
of humanity whom his brothers and sisters
have kept under lock and key in a hovel in
the woods, half starved and neglected. His
escape and prowlings caused a all the excitement about a "giant." The case is no doubt a
proper one for the State Board of Charities
to investigate.

Atlanta, Georgia, *Constitution,* August 28, 1905

A wild man who recently terrorized the residents of Moultrie, Fla., and who was described as "a tall, ape-like creature, hideous,
with long, bristly hair, and giving forth wild,
blood-curdling cries," proved to be, when captured, a Boston, simple life enthusiast who
was trying innocently to get close to mother
nature.

Danville, Virginia, *Bee,* August 14, 1926

They captured the "gigantic wild chimpanzee," loose in tame New Jersey. Mothers have
kept their little boys indoors, ladies have
wondered what they would do if they met
the rampaging Darwinian ape. That monster, caught, turns out to be the modest little
monkey, about as big as a household cat. So
it is with most of our fears in this world.

Titusville, Pennsylvania, *Herald,* January 25, 1929

FRESHMAN WITH FUR COAT.

Meadville, Jan. 24.—(AP)—A "great hairy beast" that left strange tracks in the snow on the Allegheny college campus has been found to be a man who walked around in the snow in his bare feet to relieve chilblains, and a freshman with a fur coat. Co-eds reported seeing the "ape man" or "gorilla" and tracks were found which appeared to prove that something out of the ordinary had invaded the campus. Girls asked the night watchman to escort them home. He did so and then tracked the "monster" to a nearby residence, where he found the chilblain sufferer. Further investigation disclosed that a freshman with the collar of his fur coat turned up provided the "hairy" dimension.

2. PRANKS (JUVENILE AND OTHERWISE)

Humeston, Iowa, *Advocate,* September 4, 1903

HUMESTON BUSINESS MEN
ON CHASE OF A WILD MAN

They are telling a good one on two or three of Humeston's prominent business men in connection with the attempted capture of a supposed wild man on a farm about a mile out in the country Wednesday.

Word was telephoned to town by some children who were alone on the farm that a crazy man was hiding in the hay mow and accordingly the gentlemen mentioned above set out to capture him. After a cautious and futile search in the barn it was concluded that the crazy man or terrible monster, whatever it might be, had escaped, but while the searchers were debating what next to do there arose on the still air a horrible, indescribable noise, not unlike a human voice,— the kind of noise that makes each separate hair on one's head to rise.

To make a long story short the gentlemen found after a short search, in a hollow in a field some distance away, a steam thresher to which was attached a "devil's screecher", or a whistle with a sliding scale which ranges from deep bass to extremely shrill treble and is apparently designed to scare the daylights out of unsuspecting humans and skittish horses.

Kansas City, Missouri, *Star,* December 30, 1936

SPOOK IDENTIFIED

The far-famed mysterious animal that had caused bad cases of jitters among farmers in the vicinity of Erie has at last been identified as a young farmer near there, who rigged up an empty barrel and a rosined string.

Modern youth, with their picture shows, dances and nickel games wouldn't recognize the contraption if they saw one, but years ago "smart alec" boys would rig up a tin can and a rosined string which would produce weird howls when the string stretched taut was rubbed. And the quietness of summer nights in the little country towns of long ago was frequently disturbed in this manner. And so the famous Erie mystery is solved! What a disappointment to the dozens of farmer youth who have scoured the countryside in vain the last few weeks with their trail hounds and shotguns!—Ben. S. Hudson in Fredonia Herald.

Minneapolis, Minnesota, *Star Tribune,* September 25, 1944

'BORROWED' APE-MAN
RESCUED BY POLICE

St. Paul police Sunday night nipped an ape-man scare when they apprehended five boys, 13 to 16 years old, who had "borrowed" a stuffed chimpanzee which was the property of Hamline university.

The boys were discovered while walking down an alley with their trophy. They had planned, they said, to put it up to windows at night "to scare people."

Hartford, Connecticut, *Courant,* July 20, 1947

BOY ACCUSED OF CREATING GORILLA SCARE

Police Saturday studied reports that a gorilla, or a man resembling a gorilla, had caused a near-panic on Henry Street late Friday night. The monster was "thick-shouldered, had bushy hair, long dangling arms, a heavy set body and fangs," according to reports.

But under orders to appear in Juvenile Court is a 13-year-old boy, and police are inclined to think that he will prove to be the cause of it all.

The excitement in the Henry Street area started when a figure lunged from a clump of bushes into the path of two young boys, who were considerably frightened. Later the same figure, wearing a "gorilla" mask again, ambushed a group of youngsters, whose shrieks and screams brought residents from their homes with sticks and clubs to repel the invader.

Police summoned to the area conducted a bush-beating search for the quarry. They listened to fearsome descriptions of the invader. Long after they abandoned their search, residents congregated in front of their homes discussing the episode.

Saturday morning Captain Jere Grady of the Juvenile Division learned the identity of the youth suspected of having perpetrated the prank and notified him to appear in court. The boy reportedly told the captain, "It was all a joke." He was "having fun," he said.

Captain Grady commented: "Too many movies." Lieutenant Paul B. Beckwith of the Detective Bureau, looking over the reports, observed: "Gorilla: now I've heard everything."

3. Scare Tactics

Fort Wayne, Indiana, *Daily Gazette,* June 13, 1870

HOW TO GET RID OF THE BOYS.

From the Boston Advertiser.

The mystery of the huge footprints seen in the sand at Babble Brook, Caledonia, has at last been solved and a laughable solution it is. It seems that McNaughton, the song writer, was tormented with mischievous boys depredating in the woods and making it vocal with unusual music. By a comical ruse he got rid of them. He moulded in the sand giant footprints two feet in length and paces eight feet apart, as if entering the thicket.

The next day the whole neighborhood was "gathering in hot haste" to see the steps of a live "Cardiff," the boys tremblingly clutching their fathers' hands, and mothers nervously pressing their babies to their bosoms. One glance at the huge footprints and the long pace (ex pede Herculeur!) was enough. A puffing stampede, away from the lair of "Cardiff" was the order—mothers and daughters are hurrying home, and furtively glancing back to see if pursued by the giant of the thicket. Our informant, a jolly Dutchman, says, "der poys stay away from Pable prook any more preddy soon quick already!"

Atlanta, Georgia, *Constitution-Sun*, May 16, 1880

Mr. W. Thornton and Wm. Strickland, while hunting in the swamp on the Altahama river, three miles below Clark's bluff, last week, met a strange animal. It resembled a bear standing on its hind legs, had no head, but had large red eyes in its breast. The thing asked them what they were doing there and ordered them off. They left the place, but went back next day with four more men. The animal appeared again and threatened to kill them if they did not leave. They became frightened and retreated. One of the party lost his gun.

Atlanta, Georgia, *Constitution,* June 11, 1888

From the Jackson, Ga., Argus.

In going over my plantation a few days ago
I saw some cow tracks. The tracks were in a
place, strange to say, that a cow could not
possibly have gotten into. Moved by curiosity I followed the tracks, and directly I came
upon a—I don't know whether you would call
it a wild man or a beast. It had hoofs like a
cow, hair like a cow, a short tail something
like a deer, hands like a man and extra large
red eyes. It walked like a man bent half forward. On getting a scent of me it gave a peculiar whistle like a deer, raised its head
and dashed away. I was greatly excited; but
as soon as I recovered sufficiently I went to
see my neighbor, Joe Wright. He asked me
not to say anything about it, as he thought
he could get a large steel trap with wings
like a partridge net for a hundred dollars,
and catch the creature. In case this plan
failed Mr. Wright said he would offer a $500
reward for it alive, or $150 for its hide. Mr.
Wright already has a circus wagon and says
that if we could get this curiosity our fortune
would be made. Neighbor Wright is a married man and didn't move fast enough for me,
for honestly, I am afraid to move about my
premises. I went to Marshal Malone, but he

didn't give me much encouragement. Then I went to Marshal Coon. He said that he was "no detective, and did not consider it his business to tackle a wild man in the woods, but if it came to town and cut up any devilment he would carry it before the mayor." I spoke to the sheriff about it and he said he would do all in his power to capture it, and with this object in view, has ordered a fine blood hound. He wants 150 men to meet him in Jackson on the fourth Sunday this month, but as for myself I am going to stay at Neighbor Ball's till that animal is either caught or run out of this country. I think it will be very dangerous for black folks to gather blackberries until it is caught or killed.

"Bill," the Gopher.

Warren, Pennsylvania, *Evening Mirror,* June 28, 1909

The Mystery Solved—According to the Meadville Messenger, the mystery, surrounding the "wild man" who has been lately made the hero of many tales of marvelous supposition, has been solved. The "wild man" proved to be not a cousin of the "wild man of Borneo," not the ghost of the "Last of the Mohicans," not a convict escaped from Riverside, Sing Sing, Newgate or the sulphur mines of Russia, not a lunatic from Warren, not a prodigal son, who had wandered from his father's side in his days of delayed adolescence, nor even, did he prove to be Leon Ling, the personified embodiment of the Yellow Peril, but a mere, ordinary unassuming and perfectly guiltless man whose heart had been touched at the sight of some children shooting birds. At the cruel sight this man was indignant and when chiding words were of no avail he used the goblin method of obtaining obedience and saving the life of the birds. Dressed in fantastic garb, which critics very much mistakenly claimed was no garb at all, he appeared suddenly to the youthful law breakers, with the desired effect. But, alas; he was seen by jokers, who reported the '"wild man" story to a Conneaut Lake reporter. The bait was taken. Hence the catch.

Oakland, California, *Tribune,* April 3, 1926

APE MAN SCARE SAID
TO BE LAND DEAL PLOT

North Stonington, Conn., April 3.—Taugwank's "ape man," is a plain human being in fur coat and trousers. A game warden has come to that conclusion after a thorough search of the Horace D. Miner farm in Taugwank.

Further, he declared his belief that the man was attempting to frighten Muriel, 19, and Mildred Miner, 16, orphans, into selling the farm. The ape man has variously been reported by the girls and neighbors as a hairy creature of terrifying mien, that slipped along in the manner of an ape, and jumped about with considerable more agility than a human being.

4. EXHIBITION HOAX

Ludlow, Vermont, *Tribune,* April 20, 1883

A VERITABLE WILD MAN

[FROM THE DENVER TRIBUNE]

Probably the greatest curiosity in the shape of a human being ever seen by Denver people is on exhibition here now. The story of the wild man and the wild woman from the mountain fastnesses of the Pueblos is not entirely a myth. It is said that these singular beings were captured in a cave near Los Crusis about two months ago by Captain Lovett, who has them in charge. Captain Lovett tells a strange story of their capture. For many months he had known of their existence and resolved to capture them. With a party of

three others he discovered their hiding-place
in a cave. Relying upon his great physical
strength, he entered the place with the intention of dragging the little people from their
bed, when the man pounced upon him like a
tiger. A desperate struggle ensued, and had
not his comrades come quickly to the rescue,
Capt. Lovett would have been killed. So badly
was he hurt that he was confined two weeks
to his bed. Though the man will not weigh
more than 85 pounds, he is said to be a creature of great strength. After this encounter
it required the combined strength of the rest
of the party to conquer the little giant. When
found, both were naked and utterly devoid
of intelligence. Though they could communi-
cate with each other in a guttural chatter
resembling that of a monkey, there was not
an articulation that in any wise assimilated
a word in any language of earth. A few days
ago they were brought to Denver and placed
on exhibition. They seem to be utterly devoid of sense, but have become tractable by
constant association with their keeper. They
have the color of the Indian, and are both
hideous in appearance. Whether the story of
their wild life be true or not, they are idiots,
and probably belong to the Pueblo tribe.

5. Newspaper Hoaxes (April Fools', etc.)

Lima, Ohio, *Daily News*, April 1, 1890

WHAT IS IT?

A Question That is Agitating the People of Auglaize Township.

Capture of a Creature Half Man, Half Beast

Sets the Whole Township

Wild with Excitement

Nothing Like It Ever Seen

or Heard of Before

A Correct History of the Whole Affair

The greatest excitement prevails in the southern part of Auglaize Township.

A capture was made yesterday that has taken a heavy burden from the minds of the farmers of that region. Fond mothers are hugging their children closer to their bosoms as they reflect in a frightened manner on what might have been.

Word was received at this office yesterday afternoon by special messenger of the capture, near the village of West Newton, of a frightful creature that was neither man nor beast.

A representative of the Times left at once for the scene of the capture, returning with Mr. Perry, a farmer. From him it was learned that for some time there have been all manner of depredations going on in that section

of the township lying on the northern slope
of what is known there as the Backbone. At
first they were scarcely noticeable and the
occasional absence of a pig or a sheep from
some farmer's flock was attributed to acci-
dents or to dogs.

These mysterious disappearances were
first noticed over a year ago, but they were
given little thought till in the past few
months when they became so common as to
create alarm. Instead of an occasional death,
it became a general slaughter. A farmer
would awaken in the morning to find every
pig in his possession lying dead with its neck
broken or half his flock of sheep dead.

They became half crazed with their fear
and losses continued. They never knew when
they closed up their sheds for the night how
they would find things in the morning. Investigations were made and mass meetings
held to compare notes to try and get a clew
to the perpetrator of the outrage. The farmers were completely mystified and the fact
that no noise was ever heard, no trace left,
led them to fear it was a visitation of Divine
Providence.

Strange as it may seem it was decided at
their first meeting to hold secret sessions
and not mention their peculiar misfortunes

till the mystery had been cleared up or they found there was no hope of doing so. For this reason the matter has never before reached the public through the press.

About the first of March, Mr. H. C. Lemmon was wakened from his slumbers by a violent disturbance in his barn. Hastily dressing himself, he ran out to ascertain the cause. Opening the door he saw by the rays of light from his lantern a sight that made his blood run cold. Struggling in the last throes of death were his two fine horses. Carefully examining them he found that each had its neck broken.

At the first break of day, he spread the news among his fellow farmers and it struck terror to their hearts. Were their teams and cattle to suffer the same fate as their smaller stock? A close vigil was set and for a time all was quiet.

Last week, however, the mischief began again, but a clew was gained that led to yesterday's capture. Two young men were returning home late last Sunday evening and while passing a barn that stood along side the Bellfontaine road on which they were traveling, they saw what looked to be a giant man coming out of the building. They quietly hid in a corner of the fence and watched.

Instantly the thought flashed through their minds that they had fathomed the great mystery. And they had. By the moonlight, they were able to get a good view of the destructive monster as he passed near them.

The alarm was given as soon as the thing had passed out of hearing, and in an hour after the discovery fifty men, some on foot and others on horseback, were on the trail. It was the opinion of the young men that they were hunting a ferocious animal, and when about noon yesterday his capture was effected, their surmise proved to be correct.

The party had completely lost the trail and were about to give up in disgust when someone noticed a small opening in the hillside under the roots of a bushy tree that stood just to the right of the party. Monster foot steps led to it. There was no need to look further. Here was their game, but how to get it? All sorts of suggestions were offered, but none were practicable. No one was brave enough to enter.

It was at last decided to smoke the creature out. First a rope was secured and a noose so arranged that the moment it came out, the rope could be pulled taut about his body. A fire was then built near the opening and the wind being favorable, the smoke soon began in pouring in in great clouds into the cave.

Not long did they have to wait. Dan Cook, one of the young men who had seen the creature on Sunday evening, held the rope, suddenly the head and shoulders of the creature peered out of the opening, and gasping and choking, it made a dash for liberty. A quick pull of the rope tightened the noose, and in a trice it was landed with its arms pinioned to its side, right in the midst of the party. The struggle and bellowing of the maddened being were said to be frightful and it is doubtful if had its arms been free it could have been held. It was finally bound tightly round and round from head to foot, and carried to a strong room in West Newton where it was viewed last night by the reporter. It had the form of a man, but is covered from head to foot with hair that is coarse and matted. Its nails are long and sharp, while its muscles are like iron. The teeth are big and yellow and the mouth has a horrid appearance. The eyes are black and fierce, and altogether the huge captive is a ferocious looking object. The only sound he has muttered, for it is evidently a man, since his capture, has been an occasional groan. He eyes everyone fiercely that comes within the range of his vision, and seems to be entirely bereft of reason.

The society that was organized to effect his capture, have him in care and are charging an admission of twenty-five cents to see the monster. People are flocking in from all points to which the news has spread and it begins to look as if the proceeds of admission would be sufficient to repay the members for their losses, that being the object of the society.

The excitement is so great at present over the almost incredible circumstances of the capture of the wild man and his character that no one seems to know what will be done with him in the future.

It is possible he may be placed on exhibition in Lima and an effort will probably be made to dispose of him to some showman.

Medical attention will also be directed to this freak of nature, and an effort made to diagnose his case.

It is the opinion of the Times that in his capture Allen county has produced one of the greatest freaks the world has ever known.

(This being April first, all fools day, the above article will be appreciated.)

Leadville, Colorado, *Herald Democrat,* April 6, 1922

GIRL STOLEN BY MONSTER

STRANGE ANIMAL WITH HEAD OF ALLIGATOR AND BODY OF GORILLA SPREADS TERROR AMONG FARMERS IN ILLINOIS

Chicago, April 5.—A state of terror reigns among the farmers along Lake Michigan from Highland park to Waukegan, towns almost suburban to Chicago. A monster said to resemble a gorilla with a head like an alligator is roaming the lake front and committing depredations at will, no one having the temerity to attack the monster. . . .

[Lengthy story follows, ending in *April Fool!*]

6. Notice of Escaped Apes

Not necessarily hoaxes, but a reminder that such events did sometimes occur. Though sometimes, a "loose gorilla" might be a publicity stunt to drive attention to a circus.

Ogden, Utah, *Herald,* September 16, 1887

A GORILLA AT LARGE.

Last night a number of men were seen in the lower part of town running around with torches, peering over fences and around houses, as if in search for something. On inquiry it was learned that a gorilla had got loose from the circus which is now exhibiting on Union Square. At a late hour the animal had not been found.

Burlington, Iowa, *Evening Gazette,* August 16, 1904

BIG APE AT LARGE.

Hammonton, N.J., Aug. 16—"Esau III.," a large ape belonging to a circus that exhibited here, escaped, and is at large in the woods in the vicinity of Ancora. The superintendent of the show has hunted the ape all day with dogs.

Until captured the ape will be a dangerous animal to meet. As soon as he grows hungry, his owners fear, he will make his way to some farmhouse and kill whatever suits his fancy.

Lubbock, Texas, *Morning Avalanche,* July 6, 1929

BABOON AT LARGE.

Dallas, July 5. (AP)—A big fluffy-headed baboon that chases little boys and scares the celebration out of negro picnics is at large in Dallas.

For several weeks the animal has been reported in the vicinity of the Marsalis zoo here and has frightened many. Zoo keepers have sought the animal, which they declare is not theirs. They have expressed wonder whence he came.

Newspaper Reactions to "Wild Man" Reports

Newspaper reactions to Wild Man or "gorilla" reports varied widely, but a few trends are noticeable. Generally speaking, the initial report within the newspaper of origin was matter-of-fact, whether positive in tone (e.g., conveying emphasis of a witness' veracity) or mildly sceptical. As these stories were reprinted in other parts of the country, however, (through copy-trading, independent telegraph systems, and the early wire services), objectivity often disappeared. Newspaper rivalries or simple disbelief produced insinuations of drink or fever, whimsical jabs at politics, and increasing reliance on scientific facts already known, with little recognition of what might still be undiscovered. Wild Man accounts gave reporters opportunity to wax poetic (seriously and comically) on the nature of humanity. Wild Men also became common characters in newspaper story fiction.

In many cases, an original report initiated legend-making by suggesting unlikely causative agents (children who disappeared in the woods decades past, menagerie escapees from distant towns, etc.). The description of the creature may also have been homogenized, sculpting details to fit a preconceived notion (or mental image) of the being's true aspect. (More on legend-making can be found in my previous text, *Cryptozoology: Science & Speculation*.) This concept of a Wild Man, in particular, was influenced by medieval literature (often alluded to by using the name Orson, referring to a feral human from early European folk tales), the discovery of the gorilla and consequent widespread interest in the natural history of anthropoid apes, as well as newspaper reports of "wild" people in Asia and Africa (including the Ainu of Japan). Detailed travelers' tales (often inaccurate) were published as entertainment and "education."

I'll start off with a selection from paragraphists—editors often set aside a section of the newspaper for brief remarks on news coming in from other parts of the state or country. This commentary was usually humorous or sarcastic, but sometimes held a gem of truth. These can be particularly useful in pinpointing areas previously unknown for potential Bigfoot sightings. Following the paragraphs are a selection of essays and stories that illustrate the perspectives (on both home-grown and foreign Wild Men) found in historical newspapers—perspectives that certainly influenced the readers.

Dubuque, Iowa, *Herald,* June 1, 1873

The paragraphist must rack his brain for
some other fund of information outside of
those public characters who have been considered fair game for the last five years. . . .
The wild man, big snake, sea serpent, wonderful cave, musical prodigy, learned dog and
learned pig have had their day, and any new
lies about them can hardly break the monotony of hot weather.

Marion, OH, *Daily Star,* June 25, 1879

They come, they come! Already the sea serpent has been seen twice off Newport, a bear
came out of the woods at Catskill, and the
wild man ran naked out of a swamp in Texas,
and bit a whole porterhouse steak out of a
man before help arrived. And last Saturday
night, at the last stroke of twelve, a dark
figure with upraised arms stood on the porch
of the Burlington court house and said, "Ha!
ha! ha!" in sepulchral tones. He was taken
along and fined $3.85.

Placerville, California, *Mountain Democrat,* November 8, 1879

The people of Franklin county, Iowa, have
been seeing a wild man, naked, with bushy
hair and a huge knife. And yet that has the
reputation of being a temperance county.
Where did they catch 'em?

Bismarck, North Dakota, *Tribune,* June 22, 1883

Ohio papers are discussing a terrible creature supposed to be a jabberwock which is
now roaming through the woods of that state.
Run it down and see if it isn't Nickerson fleeing from the wrath to come.

Lafayette, Louisiana, *Advertiser,* March 1, 1890

With the progress of science a whole race
of men has disappeared, the so called "wild
men," in whose existence the most learned
firmly believed a few decades ago, and who
still live in the imagination of many who are
unacquainted with recent investigations.
The wild man was supposed to be a peculiar
creature, half man and half beast, forming
the connecting link between the human species and the apes. The belief in his existence
is to be ascribed, without doubt, to erroneous
observations and reports of travelers.

Chippewa Falls, Wisconsin, *Herald Telegram,* December 8, 1891

Two reputable citizens of Michigan recently
discovered a hairy wild man seven feet tall,
who leaped twenty-three feet at a bound.
These gentlemen need to investigate the
Keeley treatment.

Stephens Point, Wisconsin, *Journal,* March 7, 1896

Prof. Garner, the expert on monkeys, claims to have discovered in the interior of Africa what is really a gorilla man. These discoveries are not always trustworthy. Occasionally they are made to sell books or lecture tickets.

Atlanta, Georgia, *Constitution,* November 10, 1924

Since the lull in politics, stories of "wild men of the woods" are with us again. The alleged "wild men" are doubtless the defeated candidates.

Camden, South Carolina, *Weekly Journal,* April 5, 1853

THE WILD MAN CAUGHT AT LAST

It has been the custom of certain Arkansas editors, when they run out of the usual supply of "tremendous excitement," "horrid murders," "desperate affrays," &c. &c., to trump up a "wild man of the woods," and chase him round from one editorial tripod to another, until he finally becomes lost amid the vast and impenetrable swamps that abound in those wild regions. . . .

Lancaster, Pennsylvania, *Examiner,* December 22, 1858

A Wild Man—The appearance of a thing like a man, but hairy as a bear, has been creating a great sensation in some parts of Lancaster county. It has not been captured.

The above item of *news* is traveling the rounds of the press, and exciting the wonder of the credulous. The "great sensation in some parts of Lancaster county," we opine, existed only in the muddled brain of the itemizer. It proves, however, the old adage,—if you want to hear news go from home.

Kansas City, Missouri, *Star,* September 20, 1907
"WILD" MEN ARE FUGITIVES
CRIMINALS BEREFT OF REASON,
SAYS A TERRITORY DEPUTY.
MANY REPORTS OF THESE CREATURES
OF THE FURRED BRAND IN THE NEW STATE,
BUT THE MINIONS OF THE LAW UNDERSTAND.

Muskogee, I. T., Sept. 20.—Little credence is given stories to wild men these days, yet every now and then there comes a persistent rumor from some remote part of Indian territory, usually a mountainous section, that a "wild man" has been sighted.

A deputy marshal who has been in the service in Indian territory for the last twenty years has advanced an explanation for these stories. He says that the so-called "wild men" are simply fugitives from justice, who have been driven to close hiding in the wilds of the territory by pursuit of officers after some crime had been committed, and that after an enforced existence in the woods, they remained there partly from inclination, and partly from a fear of capture and punishment that had made such an impression on their minds that they were in a sense deranged.

It was only a short time ago that a "wild man" was seen in the wild section of country surrounding Antlers. After the people there had been terrorized for some time, the man was finally run down and found to be a harmless fellow who had remained in hiding in the woods so long that his mind had become practically a blank. He had taken on the habits and instincts of a hunted beast.

In every instance of this kind the one indisputable evidence of reason is that the "wild men" use fire and that their food, some of the time at least, is partly cooked. How they manage to keep fire is a mystery. The fact that they usually have some sort of ragged clothing also indicates that they steal such things as they can find without coming too close to civilization, for there has never been an instance in which one of these creatures has been seen actually nude.

Buffalo, New York, *Express*, September 18, 1869. Written by
Mark Twain. Reprinted, *The Curious Republic of Gondour,
and Other Whimsical Sketches*, 1919.

THE WILD MAN INTERVIEWED

There has been so much talk about the mysterious "wild man" out there in the West for
some time, that I finally felt it was my duty
to go out and interview him. There was something peculiarly and touchingly romantic
about the creature and his strange actions,
according to the newspaper reports. He was
represented as being hairy, long-armed, and
of great strength and stature; ugly and cum-
brous; avoiding men, but appearing suddenly and unexpectedly to women and children;
going armed with a club, but never molesting
any creature, except sheep, or other prey;
fond of eating and drinking, and not particular about the quality, quantity, or character of the beverages and edibles; living in
the woods like a wild beast, but never angry;
moaning, and sometimes howling, but never
uttering articulate sounds.

Such was "Old Shep" as the papers painted him. I felt that the story of his life must
be a sad one—a story of suffering, disappointment, and exile—a story of man's inhu-
manity to man in some shape or other—and I
longed to persuade the secret from him.

"Since you say you are a member of the press," said the wild man, "I am willing to tell you all you wish to know. Bye and bye you will comprehend why it is that I wish to unbosom myself to a newspaper man when I have so studiously avoided conversation with other people. I will now unfold my strange story. I was born with the world we live upon, almost. I am the son of Cain."

"What?"

"I was present when the flood was announced."

"Which?"

"I am the father of the Wandering Jew."

"Sir?"

I moved out of range of his club, and went on taking notes, but keeping a wary eye on him all the while. He smiled a melancholy smile and resumed:

"When I glance back over the dreary waste of ages, I see many a glimmering and mark that is familiar to my memory. And oh, the leagues I have travelled! the things I have seen! the events I have helped to emphasise! I was at the assassination of Caesar. I marched upon Mecca with Mahomet. I was in the Crusades, and stood with Godfrey when he planted the banner of the cross on the battlements of Jerusalem. I—"

"One moment, please. Have you given these items to any other journal? Can I—"

"Silence. I was in the Pinta's shrouds with Columbus when America burst upon his vision. I saw Charles I beheaded. I was in London when the Gunpowder Plot was discovered. I was present at the trial of Warren Hastings. I was on American soil when the battle of Lexington was fought when the declaration was promulgated—when Cornwallis surrendered—When Washington died. I entered Paris with Napoleon after Elba. I was present when you mounted your guns and manned your fleets for the war of 1812—when the South fired upon Sumter—when Richmond fell—when the President's life was taken. In all the ages I have helped to celebrate the triumphs of genius, the achievements of arms, the havoc of storm, fire, pestilence, famine."

"Your career has been a stirring one. Might I ask how you came to locate in these dull Kansas woods, when you have been so accustomed to excitement during what I might term so protracted a period, not to put too fine a point on it?"

"Listen. Once I was the honoured servitor of the noble and illustrious" (here he heaved a sigh, and passed his hairy hand across his eyes) "but in these degenerate days I am become the slave of quack doctors and newspapers. I am driven from pillar to post and hurried up and down, sometimes with stencil-plate and paste-brush to defile the fences with cabalistic legends, and sometimes in grotesque and extravagant character at the behest of some driving journal. I attended to that Ocean Bank robbery some weeks ago, when I was hardly rested from finishing up the pow-wow about the completion of the Pacific Railroad; immediately I was spirited off to do an atrocious, murder for the benefit of the New York papers; next to attend the wedding of a patriarchal millionaire; next to raise a hurrah about the great boat race; and then, just when I had begun to hope that my old bones would have a rest, I am bundled off to this howling wilderness to strip, and jibber, and be ugly and hairy, and pull down fences and waylay sheep, and waltz around with a club, and play 'Wild Man' generally— and all to gratify the whim of a bedlam of crazy newspaper scribblers? From one end of the continent to the other, I am described as a gorilla, with a sort of human seeming about me—and all to gratify this quill-driving scum of the earth!"

"Poor old carpet bagger!"

"I have been served infamously, often, in modern and semi-modern times. I have been compelled by base men to create fraudulent history, and to perpetrate all sorts of humbugs. I wrote those crazy Junius letters, I moped in a French dungeon for fifteen years, and wore a ridiculous Iron Mask; I poked around your Northern forests, among your vagabond Indians, a solemn French idiot, personating the ghost of a dead Dauphin, that the gaping world might wonder if we had 'a Bourbon among us'; I have played sea-serpent off Nahant, and Woolly-Horse and What-is-it for the museums; I have interviewed politicians for the Sun, worked up all manner of miracles for the Herald, ciphered up election returns for the World, and thundered Political Economy through the Tribune. I have done all the extravagant things that the wildest invention could contrive, and done them well, and this is my reward—playing Wild Man in Kansas without a shirt!"

"Mysterious being, a light dawns vaguely upon me—it grows apace—what—what is your name."

"Sensation!"

"Hence, horrible shape!"

It spoke again:

"Oh pitiless fate, my destiny hounds me once more. I am called. I go. Alas, is there no rest for me?"

In a moment the Wild Man's features seemed to soften and refine, and his form to assume a more human grace and symmetry. His club changed to a spade, and he shouldered it and started away sighing profoundly and shedding tears.

"Whither, poor shade?"

"To dig up the Byron family!"

Such was the response that floated back upon the wind as the sad spirit shook its ringlets to the breeze, flourished its shovel aloft, and disappeared beyond the brow of the hill.

All of which is in strict accordance with the facts.

M. T.

Phoenix, Arizona, *Arizona Republican,* June 3, 1903

GRAND CANYON WILD MAN

The people of Arizona duly appreciate the fact that they have in the Grand Canyon the greatest attraction for tourists that the world affords, but they have silently mourned the absence of exciting features in connection with the wonderful gorge. Every little

Jim-crow seashore resort has its sea serpent but the Grand Canyon has been under a serious handicap in having nothing but its own scenery wherewith to thrill visitors. This shortage has been remedied, however. The Canyon has a wild man. We know it harbors a wild man, for the San Francisco Examiner is authority for the story, and the Examiner never lies—at least it does not always admit that it is lying. And, anyway, people are hard to please who insists upon an affidavit with each story that appears in the Sunday supplements of the yellow journals. Our own citizens, who visit the Canyon this summer, should not fail to take along a camera for protection against the wild man. But here is the story. . . .

Wisconsin Rapids, WI, *Daily Tribune*, September 8, 1928

A WAY OF ESCAPE

By Bruce Catton

If you have the idea that the world is pretty well explored, cultivated and tamed by this time, consider the task that Senor J. Tozzi Calvao, Brazilian engineer, has set himself.

Senor Calvao is going to lead an expedition far up into the steaming jungles of the Amazon, along a torrential river that has never yet been seen by white men.

He is looking for lots of things; but chiefly he wants to find out about the "Pe de Garrafa" that the back-country Indians tell about.

"Pe de Garrafa" is called, in English, the bottle-footed monkey. It bears this odd name because its footprints, in soft mud, look exactly like the mark that is made by pressing the butt end of a bottle into the ground. And, if the legends are true, it is a fearsome beast.

According to reports, this member of the monkey tribe is a man eater. It is very large, very powerful and very fierce, and is so tough and hardy that a well-placed bullet from the most powerful rifle often will not knock it out. Hunting tigers, apparently, could be no more dangerous than hunting this animal.

One is compelled to wonder, at times, why men set themselves such tasks as Senor Calvao has chosen. The senor is a man of means and position; the world can be quite an entertaining place for such a man, with many ingenious devices to provide amusement and interest. Why should he voluntarily go up into the remote Amazon country looking for a fabulous ape that eats men?

Perhaps it is the very security and ingenuity of modern civilization that makes a man undertake such a quest. Danger, in itself, can be a great spice for the monotony of life;

and in this particular case there seems to be something more involved. There is an outlandish, bizarre quality to the whole thing that might make a strong appeal to a resident of a modern city.

Senor Calvao has been living in New York. While there are, in all conscience, outlandish people and things enough there to satisfy anyone, they are all the artificial products of modern society. Up in the headwaters of the Amazon, where man-eating apes prowl through damp, suffocating jungles, is nature in her most savage and demoniac mood. If Senor Calvao is not able to find his escape from civilization there, he will never find it anywhere.

Washington, District of Columbia, *Post*, January 30, 1909

JERSEY MONSTERS.

New Jersey seems to be the breeding ground of other predatory things than the octopuses which have come out of that progressive State to plague meticulous legislators throughout this broad land. It was only two weeks ago that south Jersey was infested with hysteria by the appearance of a ferocious monster—a flying, crawling, jumping terror, with eyes, ears, and several mouths, not to mention flopping, bat-like wings, and hoofs like those of the evil one himself. It swam and soared and croaked. All, even the puling infants, knew it wasn't a new species of octopus, for those leave the State at birth to prey upon the innocents of other commonwealths, if the tens of thousands of trust-busters outside of Jersey are to be credited.

Hardly had the terror over this monster subsided when in north Jersey was discovered a wild man, or diabolus, which runs on all fours, has a beard, the growth of centuries, and "bays like a hound." Reports are overdue as to the bulldogs, bloodhounds, and children in hundreds which have fled from this new menace of the octopus State. The raising of blood-curdling, man-eating freaks is a new industry in New Jersey, but what could that up-to-date Commonwealth do when the last crop of octopuses was almost a failure? Go ahead, Jersey, and supply the country with freaks! Old superstitions have nearly disappeared, and it is well to have on hand something which will feed the imagination and keep us home at night.

The Fort Wayne, Indiana, *Gazette* had an occasional contributor, A. W. Hoffman, who would describe his imaginative exploits in various parts of the globe. In the June 17, 1883, issue, Hoffman wrote a story about a wild beast that terrorized the Lafayette area, eventually captured, which turned out to be a "regular 'gorilla,'" "seven feet high and weighs 300 pounds, and has red hair." Not long after this fictional beast was described, Indiana had a real Wild Man account, or rather a Wild Woman, described in the section on Indiana reports. Upon that sighting, Hoffman threw together another imaginary expedition, reprinted below.

Fort Wayne, Indiana, *Sunday Gazette,* July 15, 1883

THE WILD WOMAN.

MR. A. W. HOFFMAN, THE GAZETTE'S
SPECIAL EXPLORER, RIDS THE WABASH
VALLEY OF ANOTHER TERROR—
THE SAD FATE OF AN EDITOR.
THIS LATEST MONSTER FOUND TO BE A
MATE TO THE GORRILLA RECENTLY
CAPTURED—HOW IT WAS MISTAKEN FOR A WOMAN
THE CHASE THROUGH KOSCIUSKO COUNTY—
CHLOROFORMED AND BOUND—
SICKENING NARRATIVE BY THE PEOPLE—
IT IS NOW ON EXHIBITION WITH ITS MATE.

A few days ago the Lafayette papers contained a vivid account of the appearance of a monster in that locality which was thought to be a wild woman. We sent the narrative to A. W. Hoffman, esq., of Roann, the special explorer attached to the Gazette staff, and telegraphed him to leave at once for the scene of action. He went and the wonderful story of his adventures is graphically told.

Your telegram came to hand in due time and harvest being in full blast and all other business dull, I at once set about to look up the "Wild Woman." While I was laying my plans and getting ready for the fray, I received a message from Samuel V. Hopkins, editor of the North Manchester Journal, that he would be down on the next train, and that he had something of importance to tell us. He soon came, rushed into our place of business with large drops of perspiration standing on his forehead, while a very large drop dangled from his prominent nose, and as soon as he could he began to tell us that the wild gorilla which I had caught, and was now at Manchester, had a mate that was playing havoc in the vicinity of the Wabash valley, and that the Lafayette folks had told him to see us and have us come down. While we were yet talking,

In Rushed A Man

from Fulton county, perspiring as freely as Hopkins did. He broke in on our arrangements and said he was just from Akron, and that a horrible human being had been seen near that place and the people thought it was another gorilla, and that he had been committing depredations in and about the little hamlet.

That large broods of young chickens had been devoured in their coops; that pigs and lambs were eaten every day, and that the citizens had sent an earnest request for us to attend, and, if possible, capture the invader without any further ceremony. We concluded it had taken the same route that the former one had, and we at once proceeded to Akron. Mr. Hopkins was very enthusiastic. He made us promise that we would not write up our experience, but that he would have all the matter copyrighted and then he would use it in the Journal only. We suggested that he had better inform Mr. Snook, editor of the Akron Signal, before he published our doings. He sought out the venerable editor, whom he found in Akron's only saloon, and told him he had come to hunt down the lone gorrilla.

A Few Hot Words

passed between the quill drivers but nothing serious happened, as when we appeared upon the scene we adjusted the matter by agreeing that the editor of the Signal might accompany us in our hunt after the human-like devil that we had determined to take. While we were thus talking a messenger arrived from Rochester, which is an old dilapidated town on the banks of Lake Manatau. He told us that the object of our search had been seen swimming in Lake Manatau that morning and that he was certain that it could now be found in the vicinity of the lake or in the extensive marshes that were so numerous in that country. We at once hired a team and us three started for the scene of action. We were well armed and ready for any emergency that might occur. When we arrived we divided up in three companies, one in each, and started in pursuit. Soon after this a very funny incident occurred. The editor of the Signal became hot and tired, he resolved to go in the water bathing. After he had been in the water for some five minutes Mr. Hopkins came that way and took him to be the gorrilla and actually ran and catched him and bore him to shore. Despite the struggles of Mr. Snook he then tied him and left him lay on the sandy beach in the hot sun until we came up. Mr. Snook plead most piteously for mercy and done all he could to assure his captor that he was not a gorrilla nor any other kind of a wild man. We were soon convinced that a mistake had been made and assisted in turning Mr. S. loose. Mr. H. still had some doubts for the resemblance by the description given was striking, and well calculated to deceive most any one. but after he put on his linen he began to look natural, and Mr. H. was then sorry for what he had done. We again renewed our search, but this time with more care, so that a like mistake might not again occur. We soon found where the

Fiend Had Eaten

up a poor fisherman, leaving the ghastly looking skeleton to bleach in the sun. The sight was so sickening and looked so heartless like, that both editors fainted quite away, and we brought them to only by the aid of some spirits, which they both took to with much relish, after which they went to Rochester, both quite sick and much fatigued. They stayed there until the next day and then went home. We, by this time, had learned that the object of my search had gone north toward Argos, and when we got there we found that it had been seen near Plymouth and was heading for Warsaw. We were now certain that it would strike Fort Wayne before we could. So we chartered a special train at Plymouth, which took us to Warsaw at a breakneck speed over the Pittsburgh, Fort Wayne & Chicago railroad. We arrived just in time to learn that our game had left the railroad and started in the direction of Palestine, a small town among the lakes of Kosciusko county. By this time we were very tired, but we sought out our friends Chaplin, the book agent, Prosecuting Attorney Green and William Fraser, who are all men of bright intellect and herculean endurance. They three and myself proceeded to Palestine and found the inhabitants of the little village in the wildest confusion. It was fully thirty minutes before we could get an intelligent account of what was the matter, but they at last told us that a monster in human form had just passed through, walking or leaping on all fours, going faster than any horse could run; that near the edge of the village it had grabbed up a child and

Tore It From Limb To Limb

and ate it, ran right there, and then crushed its head between its ponderous knees, and then sucked out its brain. This sickening narrative given by these poor people made us resolve that the dastardly deed should not be repeated, and we pushed forward in hot haste. We found that the demon had gone in the direction of Yellow Creek lake. We hastened there, and as we neared the beach we heard a loud splash and saw the gorilla swimming amidst the high grass and grinning in the water. Mr. Green fired four shots at him, but without effect. He now took to the deep water, and swam with great rapidity. We watched him and saw him land nearly two miles away. We rode leisurely around to his landing place and soon found traces. By this time it was nearly dark, and we were obliged to look up a place to stay. We found comfortable lodging in a farm house, where we were well treated and had a good night's rest. After breakfast in the morning we saddled our horses, and again set out. We were not long in tracing the game to Silver Lake. Here we met a large and excited crowd of all ages and sexes. The monster had passed right through the business part of the town, walking remarkably upright, while the

Long Silken Hair,

with which the body is covered, waved in the breeze. Its looks had so terrified a few women and an attorney that they swooned away, and could scarcely be restored. The attorney, whose name is Conner, is now quite low with spinal meningitis brought on by fright. We felt quite sure that our chase would soon terminate; no animal could stand the fatigue long as this one had stood it. We now followed more carefully, hoping that our game might be found napping. From Silver lake it went eastward, and soon came in contact with another large lake, which it swam, but we could see that its strength was failing, and we hastened around thinking that we might intercept its landing. We got to the beach near the same time it did and secreted ourselves in a thicket without being observed. We saw it enter the thicket and lie down for a rest. We waited impatiently for a half hour, and then going quietly up close to it, we saw that it was sound asleep. Our first impulse was to shoot it on the spot, but that seemed

Too Much Like Murder.

We held a short consultation and decided that we would put a kerchief on a long stick and have it well saturated with chloroform and then hold it to the creature's nose. Mr. Green volunteered to do this, and accomplished the feat with marked ability. In less than ten minutes the loud snoring of the Gorilla might have been heard for more than a mile; indeed it sounded like distant thunder. When we became satisfied that he was under the influence of the drug, we went up to him with ropes and chains and bound him hand and foot, fastened him to some small trees, then sat down some fifty feet away to await the result. He lay perhaps three hours in that stupor before he began to show signs of waking. We sat and trembled, fearing the result. It was quite awhile before he began to realize his situation, and when once fully convinced that he was chained the scene was one not easily described. He writhed

Like A Bound Snake,

and the most unearthly yells came from our captive monster. We began to think that he never would get quiet but after a struggle of four long hours he became calm and quiet as a lamb, when we unbound him and led him to North Manchester, where the other one was. They seemed to know each other and were glad that they had met. Many prominent men have called to see the almost human pair. Mr. Snook came over from Akron and at once recognized the Gorrillas and said that he had seen them in Canada during the war. Mr. S. thinks them about fifty years old as they were full grown when he was acquainted with them from 1862 until 1865. There is now no longer any doubt but these creatures are genuine African gorrillas and have broken away from some menagerie. It seems strange to us that no one has ever looked after them. They have been in the vicinity of Lafayette for years. They stayed in the caves of Howard county, near Kokomo, for a long time, but became frightened and ran further west. They are both males, but one seems to be of a feminine nature; finer boned and of neater build. Our reflections on this

Wild Freak Of Nature

can be imagined but not well told. Mr. Frazier made a neat speech to the large assembled crowd at Manchester. His extensive knowledge of history makes him familiar with the profound works of nature. While he was holding the audience spell-bound our mind was carried off to Africa, where those poor creatures roamed unmolested and lived off the spontaneous products of that tropical clime. Here they were born and loved each other as the highest order of man does. No wonder that the great book of nature says the Diety's ways are past finding out. We believe that this capture will now rid the Wabash valley of its worst plagues. The twin gorrillas can now be seen any day at the Journal office in North Manchester. They are now quite docile and can be approached without the least danger. I am now holding myself in readiness and should another turn up we will do our best to catch him. We now consider ourselves masters of the art, and poor Snook owes his freedom to us, for had it not been for us he today would be held as captive, and cruelly named a wild beast.

A. W. H.

Petersburg, Virginia, *Index*, April 29, 1871

THE WILD MAN—WHAT IS HE?

[FROM THE N. Y. TIMES.]

As most of our readers are probably aware, there is at present roaming over the United States, and for aught we know, making occasional excursions into British America and Mexico, a singular creature known as the "Wild Man." We have before commented on his eccentricities, which are many and various. At regular intervals of time he appears in different parts of the country, creating always great excitement in the neighborhood, and a vast deal of discussion in the local Press. With one exception, which we shall presently mention, accounts uniformly agree as to his appearance. He is preternaturally hirsute and ferocious, swift, and strong. He has flaming eyes, and generally speaking, a horrent and uninviting aspect. The few rash mortals who have approached him near enough for conversation aver that he speaks an uncouth and unintelligible gibberish. So far the received descriptions of him are unanimous. The apparent discrepancy with regard to his stature, which varies in different narratives from about four feet to ten, is easily accounted for by the mental agitation under which those observations of his person must necessarily be made. Or he may have the power of extending or contracting himself at will. This would not be so strange as the faculty which gives rise to the exception above referred to, of changing his sex, so that after horrifying Alabama as a wild woman, he will immediately plunge Oregon into consternation as a wild man.

His seeming ubiquity is another perplexing attribute of this strange being. Superior to time and space, he thinks nothing of being seen simultaneously at points hundreds of miles apart. Quite as extraordinary is his peculiar power of eluding capture. Usually, all the able bodied inhabitants of the district turn out en masse to hunt him with guns and dogs, but we have never heard of his being taken. After keeping up this game of hide and seek in one locality for a few days, he departs for another, with the same result. In all his wanderings, however, it is observable that he keeps aloof from the settlements, confining himself, for the most part, to that border of civilization where contact with nature keeps the imagination fresh and vivid, undulled by the prosaic realities of city life. After flitting about the continent in this manner for a while, he suddenly vanishes into impenetrable obscurity, where he rests quiet perhaps for months. Then he reappears, and the programme is renewed as before.

We have been led to return to this subject by the recent appearance at once of the real and a bogus wild man in Tennessee and Michigan respectively. The Michigan monster is, in some respects, eruditably prepared and shows ingenuity in its inventors. Its appearance is well calculated to deceive. To begin with, it is "fearfully deformed"—a sufficiently obvious trick, but still effective. Then its "hands are covered with long coarse hair, face grown full of rank whiskers," while its eyes "look like those of a wolf." These details, it must be admitted, show skillful handling, and only a practiced eye could detect the deception. But the one infallible test of the true wild man is here wanting—his defiance of pursuit. If his more than mortal speed fails to outstrip his would be capture, he either subsides into the ground, or simply exhales into thin air before their wondering eyes. So, after hearing that the Michigan prodigy was caught by the paltry and commonplace device of hunting him out of a swamp with two dogs, we are not unprepared to learn that he is only a wretched lunatic. And it is, on the whole, not surprising that the excellent persons who caught him should

have vented their natural disappointment
by chaining him in an out-house, and permitting the dogs and boys of the neighborhood
to worry him. It must be not only admirable
sport, but adapted to make him as near a
copy of the genuine wild man as need be desired.

The Tennessee report, on the other hand,
bears all the intrinsic evidence of authenticity. This wild man, according to the Jackson
Whig, gives the impression of a "strange and
frightful being," which is, in itself, almost
conclusive. "He is said to be seven feet high,
and possessed of great muscular power."
Conviction deepens as we proceed. "His eyes
are unusually large, and fiery red; his hair
hangs in a tangled and matted mass of jet
below his waist, and his beard reaches below
his middle." What skeptic desires more? Yet
this is not all. "His entire body is covered
with hair, and his aspect is most frightful."

"He shuns the sight of men, but approaches
with wild and horrid screams of delight every woman who is unaccompanied by a man.
He sometimes with great caution approaches houses; and should he see a man he runs
away with astonishing swiftness, leaping the
tallest fences with the ease of a deer, defying
alike the pursuit of men and dogs. He has

frightened several women by attempting to carry them off, as well"—adds the judicious chronicler—"as by his horrid aspect, and the whole country around Sobby is in consternation. The citizens are now scouring the woods, and are determined either to capture or drive off the monster."

Of course, we know that the determination of the citizens will be in vain, and that the monster will be neither captured nor driven of until it suits his wish. But, in the meantime, while the good people are furtively scouring their woods, would it not be well for naturalists to investigate the interesting wonder? Perhaps the wild man is a remnant of those unknown and prehistoric races who once ruled this continent, for the memory of man can scarcely recall a period when he was not. Or may he not be—we offer the suggestion with diffidence—may he not be that lost link for which Mr. Darwin is looking?

Girard, Kansas, *Press,* October 13, 1870

GORILLA.

A wild man, gorilla, or what-is-it, was lately seen by a goodly number of our citizens, near Iowa City. The citizens of Cox's creek will recollect the bold appearance of one of those most wonderful specimens of animated nature in 1868; but this one, for boldness,

daring, and eccentricity of instinct, excels
any of its predecessors. It very nearly resembles a man in appearance, at a distance; but
when you take a microscopic view of it it is
said to prove to be of the orang-outang species. Its face is almost covered with hair; its
eyes are black; its complexion swarthy and
dark; its hair long and brown; and it is supposed to be about five feet, ten inches high,
when walking upright, although sometimes
it goes on all fours; it smokes a pipe, and
makes raids on the settler's tobacco patches; it makes a bellowing, guttural sound, not
much unlike the human voice, and has really
some knowledge of the English language; like
a well trained pall parrot, it knows almost
the whole catalogue of popular epithets, and
when at a safe distance does not hesitate to
defiantly hurl the vilest of calumny against
all who cross its path, or tread on the ground
of its favorite haunts; its lower extremities
partially resemble the African baboon, its
head and shoulders that of a wild Brazilian
jackass. It is thought to be of a carnivorous
nature, and it is supposed to have escaped
from one of the menagerie that is recently
passed through this county.

Can any of the experts in obstetrics tell
from whence this most wonderful living specimen of animated nature? Baker.

Biloxi, Mississippi, *Daily Herald,* December 17, 1937

CRAB-OLOGY

THOSE PANTHER STORIES

The stories in The Herald one day last week were a little surprising to us. We had suspected that there might be some tigers of the blind variety down in those woods but never had thought about panthers infesting the country that near to the Coast. We had a panther scare up here on Flint Creek about a year ago, that caused considerable excitement, and caused the more timid of our citizens to stay pretty close around their firesides after the sun went down of evenings, but the varmint passed on to fields and pastures new and it may be our panther has moved down to Gulfport. We are inclined to believe that a panther, or a tiger of the right kind in a community is a good thing and serves a useful purpose. One squall from a panther will keep more men at home at night and from prowling around trying to get into some devilment than all the deputy sheriffs and rural police in the country. Over in Southeast Perry County a few years ago some white men put out a story that a very large gorilla that had escaped from a circus had taken up in Whiskey Creek swamps a noted fishing stream and had already caught and devoured a turpentine negro that was fishing in the creek. The object was to break up so much fishing among the negroes from a nearby turpentine camp. The story did its work, and gave the fish a chance to grow.

NEWSPAPERS AND FOLKLORE

The bulk of this book consists of newspaper accounts of sighting events, whether sole reports or "flaps" (multiple sightings over a set period of time, sometimes in different parts of a state or region). Newspapers can be repetitious, but different accounts may offer varying, even contradictory, details. They may also point to sightings we haven't yet uncovered. (Not all newspapers are yet digitized; some may never be.)

One point that can't be overemphasized is that they show folkloric patterns (recurring descriptive details, origin rumors, etc.). Folklore is, essentially, information that is shared within a culture, how it develops and how it is expressed. Newspapers shape stories: they choose what to include, what not to include, what tone to take, and the explanations they think readers should consider. The contemporary Bigfoot researcher needs to understand how this played out in historical newspapers in order to adequately evaluate that data.

1 Bear Creek (Marion Co.)

2 Rocky Creek (Butler Co.)

3 Anniston and Choccolocco (Calhoun Co.)

4 Refuge/Clanton (Chilton Co.)

Alabama

1880s: Bord & Bord (2006) noted the report of a fisherman near Bear Creek who found himself being watched by a large creature which jumped into the creek and fled when noticed.

Montgomery, Alabama, *Weekly Advertiser*, October 11, 1888

A TERRIBLE ENCOUNTER.

Mr. S. B. Brown Attacked by a
Half Human Monster in a Cave

Rocky Creek, Ala., Oct. 6.—The long supposed but heretofore undiscovered cave, which was, before the war, the rendezvous of deserters and escaped slaves has at last been discovered by a gentleman from Greenville, Mr. S. B. Brown. While traveling the road from Monterey to Rocky Creek, and passing through the lime hills, which are familiar to all old settlers, he discovered, while looking for a spring to get water, the entrance to a cave. The gentleman, whose curiosity was excited, determined to explore the cave, and dismounting he entered, and upon advancing forty or fifty feet into the cave it enlarged into a cavern fifty by eighty feet wide, the floor of which was covered with skeletons of supposed human beings. While gazing in amazement upon the spectacle, his attention was attracted by a snarling, rasping noise, which seemed to come from another quarter of this cavern, and upon looking, he saw approaching a hideous monster, half human and half savage, about four and a half feet high, with arms three feet long, whose head was level with its shoulders, and the entire upper portion of its body was covered with kinky hair of a motley color, the lower portion of its body being entirely bare, the skin having a rough callous appearance, its feet being formed with claws like an eagle. Its face was full and resembled a gorilla. It approached Mr. Brown in a stealthy manner and when within ten feet of him it sprung, with a blood-curdling howl, upon Brown's shoulders, and fortunately Mr. Reynolds and Dr. Jarrett were passing, and upon hearing the noise rushed to the rescue of Brown and succeeded in overpowering the demon. Brown is seriously lacerated about the neck and breast, his clothing being entirely torn off. The monster was left in the cave and Brown carried to Cheatham's house, near by, and cared for by his good lady and the doctors. A posse of young men formed themselves into a body and captured the animal and killed it, and it can now be seen at Serman's gin house.

Several men have been missing around here for the last ten years, and this accounts for it. But for Mr. Brown using his knife with effect, he probably would have been killed before assistance arrived. I will keep you posted on this matter if anything more should happen. Brown is getting along alright at present. Yours, A. G. Traweek.

Several negroes left this section to work on railroads around Birmingham and have never been heard of since, and the description of a jeans coat tallies with one described by the mother of a missing boy. A. G. T.

Oshkosh, Wisconsin, *Northwestern*, April 15, 1938

HAIRY WILD MAN SOUGHT IN SWAMP

Anniston, Ala.—(UP)—A wild man who runs on all fours, chases dogs and frightens farmers is being sought in a dense swamp in the Choccolocco valley.

Sheriff W. P. Cotton led a posse in search of the strange beast which, farmers insisted, was accompanied by a woman and a child—both as savage in appearance and actions as the man.

Rex Biddle, a farmer, told Sheriff Cotton that the man approached his home walking on all fours in the manner of an ape.

"He was about five feet tall, and had hair all over his body," Biddle said. "He was unclothed. Despite his beastlike appearance, his nose and other features indicated he was human."

Biddle said he reached for his gun but didn't shoot because "I didn't know whether that would be legal."

Roy Storey, another farmer, said the creature followed him for a time and then "dropped to all fours and chased my pet dog into the swamp."

Residents of the district petitioned the sheriff to "catch this thing or we are moving out."

Hammond, Indiana, *Times*, April 15, 1938

SWAMPS OF ALABAMA SAID TO SHELTER MAN, WOMAN AND CHILD

Anniston, Ala., April 15—(INS)—Through the soggy, mud-ridden swamps of Choccolocco, at the foot of Choccolocco mountain, sheriff's deputies, neither believing or disbelieving, today searched for a "wild man" and "wild woman" and a child.

The strange hunt started when reports reached Sheriff P. W. Cotton that folk by the mountain had been frightened and whole flocks of livestock had stampeded at the sight of this family that wore no clothes.

Rex Biddle, a farmer, brought the first word of the strange family. The trio, he said, approached his home and then, apparently frightened, fled.

Officers, revealing the tale given them by Riddle, said the farmer didn't know whether to shoot or not as he didn't know whether it was "legal."

Piecing together the various tales given them, officers gave this description of the man:

He walked stooped like a gorilla.

He roared like a lion.

He wore no clothes but he had more hair than humans.

The child, they said, was "animal" like.

But where the strange family came from, no one knew, unless driven from an abode in the swamp by high flood waters.

San Mateo, California, *Times*, April 15, 1938

SHERIFF FAILS TO
FIND GORILLA FAMILY

Anniston, Ala., April 15.—(UP)—Sheriff W. P. Cotton dismissed a posse of "wild man" hunters today and reported that an all-day search for a strange gorilla-like family in a valley swamp was in vain. Cotton led a group of farmers and citizens into the swamp after rural residents reported seeing a man, woman, and child whose bodies were covered with hair and who at times walked on all fours.

Clanton, Alabama *Union-Banner,* May 28, 1953

Is there a booger in Refuge Community? Some children were playing in the wooded part of Tom Minor's pasture Sunday afternoon, and gave forth alarm that a funny creature had been seen "walking almost upright." Several men with guns went to the scene, but were unable to see anything. The largest child that saw the thing is about 8 or 9 years old. Some smaller children said they saw it also. The alarm kindled the memory of others in the community who had seen a weird-looking animal in the woods nearby. Bernie Clyde Minor, the 18 year old son of Dewey Minor, said he saw something resembling a gorilla last fall while he was squirrel hunting. He shot at it several times, but to no avail. Cary Easterling says he has seen tracks like those of a bear in his bottoms near the woods. Now, the question is, what is it?

Alaska

1900: Small hairy creatures from east of Thomas Bay were described by a witness, Harry D. Colp, in a short booklet posthumously published in 1953, *The Strangest Story Ever Told*. As the manuscript wasn't discovered until after the author's death, it is unknown for what purpose it was written. It does appear to have elements of a fantasy adventure (reminding me of Algernon Blackwood or Hyatt Verrill), and may very well have been intended for one of the fiction magazines, though it is not a single cohesive story. "Swarming up the ridge toward me from the lake were the most hideous creatures. I couldn't call them anything but devils, as they were neither men nor monkeys, yet looked like both. They were entirely sexless, their bodies covered with long coarse hair, except where the scabs and running sores had replaced it. Each one seemed to be reaching out for me and striving to be the first to get me. The air was full of their cries and the stench from their sores and bodies made me faint." A scanned booklet is available for reading at the HathiTrust website.

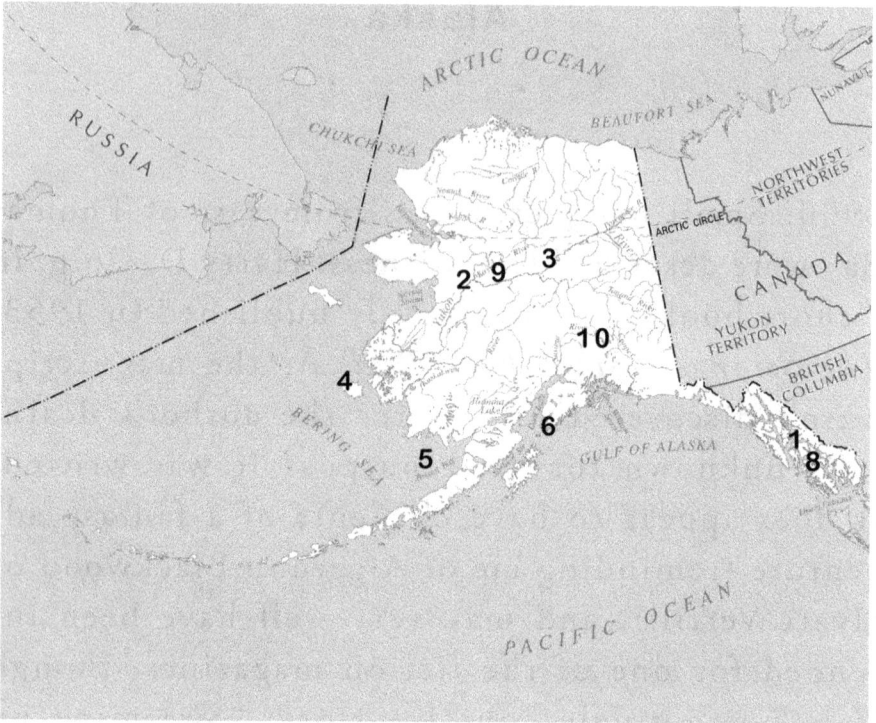

1 Thomas Bay

2 Nulato (Yukon-Koyukuk)

3 Rampart (Yukon-Koyukuk)

4 Nunivak Island

5 Bristol Bay

6 Portlock (Kenai Peninsula)

7 Kaluka (ghost town, unknown location)

8 Wrangell Narrows

9 Ruby (Yukon-Koyukuk)

10 Yellowjacket Creek

c. 1920: Green (1978) noted the report of Albert Petka, of Nulato, who was attacked on his boat by a "bushman." His dogs drove the creature off, but Petka later died of the injuries.

c. 1930s: Cobb and Sasser (2000) homesteaded in the Rampart area. While there, they learned about the 'Bushman' clan, a hairy people who had been known to steal children and raise them as their own. Cobb met one old native woman who had been taken from a berry patch when she was a young woman. The woman claimed that they had taken her because a young one was ill, and the Bushman people thought the humans had magic powers. She said they lived in a cave, didn't bathe, and were slowly dying off. She said they communicated with here through her mind. After the young one got better, they let her go after she promised not to tell other humans where they lived.

c. 1930s: Lincoln (2018) recorded the story of three hunters visiting Nunivak Island, who were bunking in an abandoned sod house in an old fish-camp. Awakened by their dogs (tied up outside), they realized that something was trying to break into the sod house but was too big to fit through the small doorway. It gave up and walked away; the hunters looked out and saw a tall, silver-colored creature heading off, walking upright.

Newark, Ohio, *Advocate*, January 19, 1935

PROSPECTORS SAY WILD MAN RULES ARCTIC KINGDOM.

Anchorage, Alaska, Jan. 19.—(AP)—Out of the isolated district north of Bristol bay comes a tale of "the wild man of the Nashagak" —a nebulous terror jealously guarding an empire which, even on the larger maps, is an unexplored white patch with dotted lines for streams.

Charles J. Dumbolton, sourdough prospector of many years in Yukon and Klondike valley camps, told the story today after arriving by plane from a season of prospecting 125 miles from the nearest settlement.

The wild man is believed in so firmly by the few men in the area, that they have drawn a voluntary boundary to their northern trips. While he has made no effort to investigate the wild man's authenticity, Dumbolton said he found trappers feared to venture beyond their own established frontier, the King Salmon river.

He said the wild man, perhaps some man crazed by loneliness, has been reported seen several times, and is blamed for the disappearance of several men who have ventured into the region of the upper Nashagak and its tributaries during the last several seasons.

The wild man's empire is a vast region between the south-flowing Upper Nashagak and the westward-flowing middle course of the Kuskokwim.

1940s: Green (1978) noted that the cannery village of Portlock, Alaska, on the Kenai peninsula was abandoned in 1949 because of ongoing tales of eighteen-inch footprints while tracking moose. There had also been stories of hunters going into the hills and disappearing, or being found mutilated in ways unlikely for bear attacks. A 1973 *Anchorage Daily News* article noted that the town was still abandoned and former residents refused to spend a night there.

c. 1940: Bord & Bord (2006) noted a report collected by John Green regarding a female black-haired creature that was captured near Kaluka. It fed on raw fish, but became ill and died.

1942: Green (1978) noted that Bob Titmus saw an upright ape on the coast, possibly near Wrangell Narrows. Titmus "refused to believe his eyes" at that time.

1943: Green (1978) noted that a man, John Mire, living at DeWilde's camp, near Ruby, was attacked by a hairy man, before dogs drove it off. Mire died of injuries sustained in the attack. Green is skeptical of both this and the Petka account, though noting they are not impossible.

Unknown date: Sanderson (reprinted in Patterson 1966), located a 1963 story in *Sports Afield* about a mountain man, Tex Cobb, who spent years in Alaska and Canada. While camping near Yellow-jacket Creek, on the Nelchina Plateau, Cobb and Russell Annabel met up with a group of Denna (Dineh), who told them that one of the Gilyuk (cannibal giants) was in the area. They showed a sign of the creature's presence, a birch sapling with a four-inch diameter that had been twisted apart. The Denna chief, Stickman, was later found missing, his tattered clothes found next to the lake's edge. All believed he had been taken by the Gilyuk.

Arizona

The following story is sometimes given as an early sighting of the Mogollan Monster, but has all the earmarks of early newspaper fiction:

Albuquerque, New Mexico, *Morning Journal*, May 16, 1903

WILD MAN IN GRAND CANYON

COLORADO MAN TELLS THRILLING STORY
OF ADVENTURE WITH STRANGE CREATURE.

Many strange stories have been told of the "wild man" of the Grand [Canyon] of the Colorado, and while some persons have credited these weird tales, they have for the most part been regarded as the ingenious inventions of imaginative travelers, and have passed into tradition as such. But according to I. W. Stevens of Cedar, Colo., the "wild man" is not a myth, and he gives a thrilling account of an encounter he had with the creature.

"Two years ago," says Mr. Stevens, "I had business in the northwestern part of Arizona that took me in the neighborhood of the extreme lower end of the Grand [Canyon] of

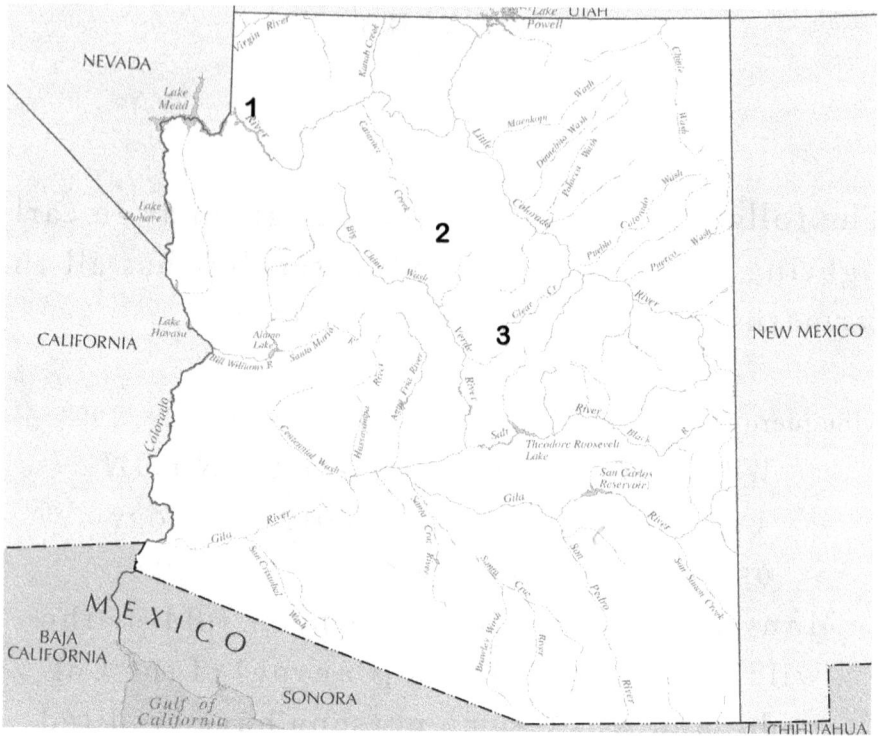

1 Mohave County

2 Flagstaff

3 Tonto Creek / Mogollon Rim

the Colorado river, in Mohave county, Arizona. Having the misfortune of getting my arm broken, I took a trip to the river to kill time and catch a few beaver. I constructed a skiff, with the aid of a friend, and when my arm got strong enough I took a trip up the [canyon] as far as I could go with a boat. A few miles above the entrance I hauled my boat upon the sand and got ready to examine the rock walls.

"The first thing that attracted my attention was the imprint of bare feet in the sand. Thinking the tracks had been made by some Indian, perhaps a Piute or a Hanlipi, I began looking the gorge over with much interest. Going down stream a short distance I found more tracks.

"The third day of my stay I saw the head of a man on a bench of rocks on the north side of the river. Evidently he was seated on the edge of a cliff some distance above my camp. I rowed up stream a little above where I saw the man's head and part of his shoulders above the greasewood brush. Climbing up to the bench, I had some difficulty in finding a place that I could get over the ledge and be on a level with my strange neighbor.

"I finally succeeded in approaching closer to the point. I saw sitting on a large boulder a man with long white hair and a matted beard that reached to his knees. The creature was unaware of my approach and I gazed upon him for some moments unobserved. He was about fifty yards away and in full view. He wore no clothing, and upon his talon-like fingers were claws at least two inches long. A coat of gray hair nearly covered his body, with here and there a spot of dirty skin showing. I had found the 'wild man' of the rocks!

"At that moment a rock, loosened by some animal, came rolling down. The creature turned his face toward me. Horrors! What a face! It was seared and burned brown by the sun, with fiery green eyes. With a wild whoop and a leap he was off up over rocks and cliffs like a mountain sheep for about seventy-five yards. Then he stopped. He was armed with a queer-shaped club, large enough to fell an ox. Brandishing this bludgeon, he shrieked and chattered for a moment, then started toward me, roaring and still flourishing his weapon. Faster and faster he came and my hair began to stiffen.

"I am a poor runner, so I stood my ground. When the creature was within about fifteen yards of me I raised my rifle to fire, thinking to cripple him. As I glanced along the barrel I heard a deep growl just above the

wild man. Looking up I saw a she cougar
and two half-grown cubs. The mother cougar
crouched, with tail lashing, ready to spring
on the wild man. He also had heard the growl
and he braced himself for the shock.

"I drew a hasty bead on the cougar and
pressed the trigger. When the smoke had
cleared away the mother cougar lay dead
where the wild man had stood. The man himself had disappeared. The two young cougars
were still on the rock, apparently frightened
by the report and echoes of my old Sharp's
rifle.

"Reaching hastily for a cartridge, I found
I had neglected to buckle on my belt when
leaving camp, so I hastily retreated to the
boat, where I found everything as I had left
it. I shoved the boat off and drifted toward
camp, which was near the cougars. There lay
the old cougar where she had fallen. The wild
man was standing over the two cubs, which
also were dead, he having beaten the life out
of them with his club. He stood a moment
[gazing] on the carcasses, then got down on
his hands and knees and drank the warm
blood as it flowed from the death wounds.
The sight sickened me.

"I stood up in the boat and yelled. The
man sprang to his feet, took a long look at

me, and then fled up from ledge to ledge until he reached the fourth ledge, where he
stopped. Here he flourished his club again
and screamed the wildest, most unearthly
screech I ever heard, then turned and sprang
onward up the craggy wall of the canyon.

"Not fancying my wild neighbor, I packed
my outfit into the boat and drifted down and
out of the [canyon] before I made camp for
the night. That was the strangest adventure
of my life.

"Tradition records that years ago hostile
Indians captured three men, bound them to
logs far up the canyon and cast them adrift
upon the swollen river. It may be that this
wild creature is one of those unfortunate
men, who, by chance, freed himself and
escaped death, but was made insane by his
awful experience."

1924: Green (1978) noted the report of a woman
who claimed that, while living near Flagstaff, she
and her mother saw a seven-foot-tall, light-haired
creature raiding their garden. Their ranch was at
the foot of the San Francisco Peaks.

1940s: Don Davis (n.d.) told how he had seen a
Bigfoot from just a few feet away, in the moonlight, while on a boy scout trip to Tonto Creek, in

the Mogollon Rim area north of Payson, Arizona. "The creature was huge. Its eyes were deep set and hard to see, but they seemed expressionless. His face seemed pretty much devoid of hair, but there seemed to be hair along the sides of his face. His chest, shoulders, and arms were massive, especially the upper arms; easily upwards of 6 inches in diameter, perhaps much much more. I could see he was pretty hairy, but didn't observe really how thick the body hair was. The face/head was very square; square sides and squared up chin, like a box."

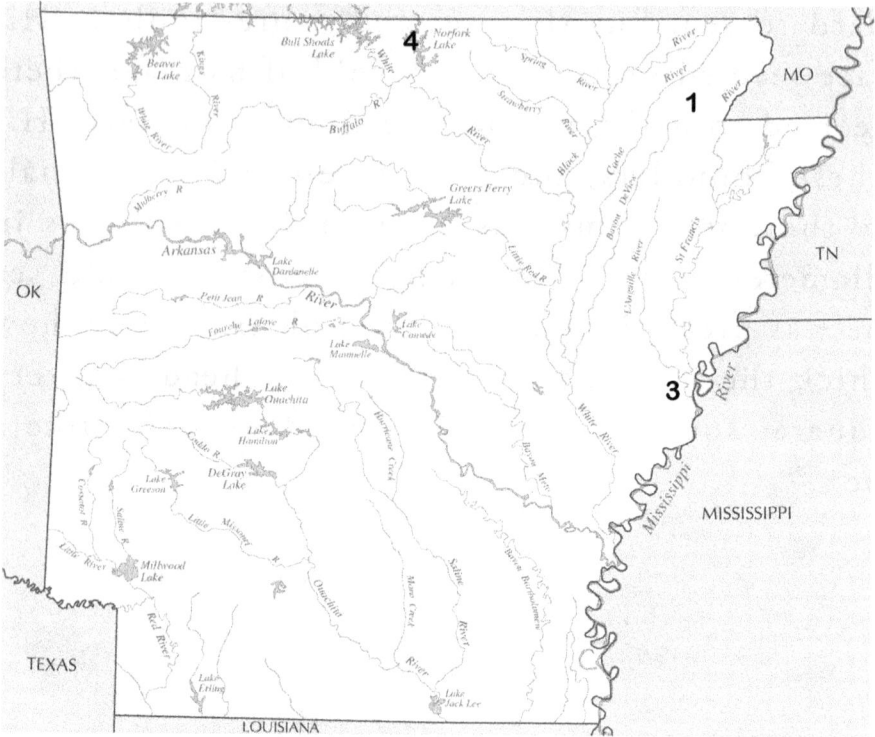

1 Greene County

2 Brant Lake and Sun Flower Prairie (could be
  anywhere along Arkansas/Louisiana border)

3 Helena

4 Baxter County

Arkansas

Scientific American 1:27 (March 1846): 3

A Wild Man.—A wonderful account is given of the discovery of a monstrous wild man, in the swamps about the Arkansas and Missouri line.—His track is said to measure 22 inches; and his toes as long as a common man's fingers. We are of the opinion that either the "wild man," or the man who raised the story, is a *great monkey*.

Baltimore, Maryland, *Sun,* March 13, 1846

A Wild Man.—A man in a wild state, it is said, has been seen in the swamps near [Creoles'] Ridge, about the Arkansas and Missouri line; his track measures 22 inches; his toes are as long as a common man's fingers; and in height and make, he is double the usual size.

Gettysburg, Pennsylvania, *Adams Sentinel and General Advertiser,* June 2, 1851

A WILD MAN OF THE WOODS.

The Memphis Inquirer gives an account of a wild man recently discovered in Arkansas. It appears that during March last, Mr. Hamilton, of Greene county, Arkansas, while out hunting with an acquaintance, observed a drove of cattle in a state of apparent alarm, evidently pursued by some dreaded enemy. Halting for the purpose, they discovered, as the animals fled by them, that they were followed by an animal bearing the unmistakable likeness of humanity.

He was of gigantic stature, the body being covered with hair, and the head with long locks that fairly enveloped his neck and shoulders. The wild man, after looking at them deliberately for a short time, turned, and ran away with great speed, leaping from twelve to fourteen feet at a time. His footprints measured thirteen inches each.

This singular creature, the Inquirer says, has long been known traditionally in St. Francis, Greene and Poinsett counties, Ark., sportsmen and hunters having described him seventeen years since. A planter indeed saw him very recently, but withheld this information lest he should not be credited, until the account of Mr. Hamilton and his friend placed the existence of the animal beyond cavil.

A great deal of interest is felt in the matter, by the inhabitants of that region, and various conjectures have been ventured in regard to him. The most generally entertained idea appears to be that he was a survivor of the earthquake which desolated that region in 1811. Thrown helpless upon the wilderness by that disaster, it is probable that he grew up in his savage state, until he now bears only the outward resemblance of humanity.

So well authenticated have now become the accounts of this creature, that an expedition is organizing in Memphis, by Col. David C. Cross and Dr. Sullivan, to scout for him.

Helena, Arkansas, *Southern Shield*, May 1, 1852

The Wild Man Again.—We are credibly informed by a gentleman of this city, that the "wild man" has been seen again in the swamps of Arkansas. He derived his information from two gentlemen, who were out hunting, and approached as near as twenty paces to him. His appearance was so frightful that they did not attempt to approach nearer. He is described by them as being about 7 feet 2 inches high, and covered completely with black hair, interspersed now and then with gray. The story or the representations of him as last seen, published in some of our papers, they pronounce untrue. He has no claws to his hands and feet, nor is he eight or nine feet high: still he would be a curiosity worth seeing. We understand it is the intention of some of our citizens to capture him if possible. In the way of shows, he would be the "wild mare," with the "hippodrome" thrown in. *Memphis Express.*

Little Rock, Arkansas, *Arkansas Whig*, June 17, 1852

The Wild Man of the Woods of Arkansas.— From the following paragraphs, it would seem that this distinguished but very mysterious individual has gone to New York and become an editor. Who would have thought it was Greeley, the [—] and Free Soiler, who had astonished the natives across the river!

"Every now and then we see it stated in the Western papers that a wild man is roaming through the great Mississippi bottom in the State of Arkansas. Numerous travelers and hunters have asserted that they have seen him, but none have ever been able to get near enough to give particulars concerning the strange being. The story is just revived again. The creature is said to be unmistakably a human being, over 7 feet high, but with all the shyness and habits of a completely wild animal.—*N. Y. Courier and Enquirer.*

It's strange how soon people forget! We remember when that wild man was first caught and brought to this city. He was kept for several months on Graham diet, then tamed and made editor of the Tribune.—*N. Y. Day Book.*

Madison, Wisconsin, *Weekly Argus and Democrat,* January 8, 1856

A Wild Giant in Arkansas:—A wild man, seven feet high, is said to be roaming through the great Mississippi bottom, in the State of Arkansas. Numerous travelers and hunters have asserted that they have seen him, but none have ever been able to get near enough to give particulars concerning this strange being.

Madison, Wisconsin, *Patriot,* May 10, 1856

THE WILD MAN AGAIN.

A correspondent of the Caddo Gazette writing under date of the 28th ult from [Paraclifta], Arkansas, on Upper Red River, states that the cold during the present winter has been in that region the severest within the memory of man.—The rivers were frozen solid, the plains presented an unbroken sheet of snow.—The writer relates the following story of an attempt to capture the famous wild man, who has been so often encountered on the borders of Arkansas and Northern Louisiana:

"In my travels I met a party from your country in pursuit of a wild man. They had struck his [trail] at a cane brake bordering on Brant Lake and the Sun Flower Prairie. I learned from one of the party that the dogs ran him to an arm of the lake which was frozen, but not sufficiently strong to bear his weight which consequently gave way. He had, however, crossed, and the dogs were at fault.

One of the party, mounted on a fleet horse, coming up, encouraged the dogs to pursue, but found it impossible to cross with his horse, and concluded to follow the lake round until he could ascertain the direction taken by the monster of the forest. On reaching the opposite side of the bend, he was surprised to see something in the lake like a man breaking the ice with his arms, and hastened under cover of the undergrowth to the spot where he expected him to come out. He concealed himself near the place, when he had a full view of him, until he reached the shore where he came out and shook himself. He represents him as a stout, athletic man, about six feet four inches in height, completely covered with hair of a brownish cast about four to six inches long. He was well muscled and ran up the bank with the fleetness of a deer.

He says he could have killed him with
his gun, but the object of the party being to
take him alive, and hearing the horns of his
comrades and the howling of the dogs on the
opposite bank of the lake, he concluded to ride
up and head him, so as to bring him to bay
and then secure their prize. So soon, however, as the wild man saw the horse and rider,
he rushed frantically toward them, and in an
instant dragged the hunter to the ground and
tore him in a most dreadful manner, scratching out one of his eyes and injuring the other
so much that his comrades despair of the re-
covery of his sight, and biting large pieces
out of his shoulder and various parts of his
body. The monster then tore off saddle and
bridle from the horse and destroyed them,
and holding the horse by the mane broke a
short piece of sapling, and mounting the animal, started at full speed across the plains
in the direction of the mountains, guiding
the horse with his club. The person left with
the wounded man informed me that the party
was still in pursuit having been joined by a
band of friendly Indians, and thought that
if they could find a place in the mountains
not covered with snow, or a canebrake in the
vicinity to feed horses, they might overtake
him in a day or two."

Memphis, Tennessee, *Daily Avalanche,* January 4, 1859

CORRESPONDENCE OF THE *AVALANCHE*

Messrs. Editors: Since I addressed you at the pleasant young City of Helena, I have had the privilege of traveling over a portion of Arkansas, and will now give you a brief sketch of what I have seen. Helena is located at the foot of a range of hills that run through several counties in this State, and this is the only place where the highlands come to the Mississippi river. This range of hills divides the St. Francis and White Rivers, and so far as my observation has been made these highlands are rich, and as proof of this they produce the gigantic beech tree, which I believe is a sure indication of a productive soil.

There is a circumstance that occurred on the Northwestern region of this range of hills that I will relate. About eight or ten years since there was discovered a wild man of gigantic [stature], who had hid in the caves of these hills. The whole country was set on fire with excitement and curiosity to see the wild man of the forest, and he was represented as being eight or nine feet high, and his whole muscular system was proportionably developed; at his usual walking gait he stepped from eight to nine feet, and looked to be moving slowly, but an ordinary man would have to go in a fast trot to keep up with him. Notice was given that the settlers in that portion of Arkansas would on a specified day go in search of the wild giant, for the purpose of capturing him; he had been chased on horseback, but he could distance their swiftest horses. At the appointed day the arrangements were made, and men stationed at stands, as the huntsmen do in deer-driving, to head and surprise the untamed man. He was forced out of his concealment and pursued on horse, and as he approached where the men were stationed, one of them threw himself in the course of the escaping giant, at which he became angry and struck the horse on the neck with his fist, breaking his neck, and the rider fell from the horse, rejoiced to escape with his life. The wild giant kept on and has not been seen since, and is now probably spending his summers on the craggy peaks of the Rocky Mountains with the mountain sheep, and his winters in the dark caves, and has for his companions the grizzly bears, free from molestation of the white man. . . .

Frederick Gerstäcker, a German traveler/writer, spent many years exploring the Americas, and eventually other parts of the world, recounting his adventures in books and periodicals. His skill in observation and ability to describe culture and natural world made him a favorite with his readers. The following is from a piece eventually collected in an English anthology, *Western Lands and Western Waters,* where Gerstäcker (1864) describes the manner in which certain Arkansas natives perceived exotic primates in a traveling menagerie. Obviously, their recognition of a native Wild Man is of particular interest, though unfortunately it only provides a possible region in which further research is needed.

> The Frenchman, whose object it was to have the marvels of his show spread about the forest as quickly as possible, decided on delighting the two backwoodsmen with a sight of the ape, just as he had shown Stewart the catamount on the road, and he therefore suddenly drew back the curtain which had hitherto covered the barred prison of a large chimpanzee, the most valuable specimen in his menagerie.
>
> "Darn my buttons!" Both men exclaimed on noticing the marvel, "if that don't blow the lid off the pot."
>
> "Jimmy! where did you catch it?" Stewart shouted, employing the first name that

occurred to him, while he bent down before the cage, and put his elbows on his knees, to have a better look at the monkey. "Is it eatable?"

"By this and by that, if it isn't a wild man!" Wilson interposed. "He was caught down there in the Cash swamps. Prince was after him twice, but couldn't come up with him."

"And there's no fall in the trap," Stewart said, now examining the cage carefully on all sides. "I should like to know how he got in."

"It is a monkéh—an ape," the little Frenchman remarked, revelling in the amazement of his spectators—"comes from India, lives in a very hot country, very warm, and has much ressemblance with men."

"Much what?" Stewart said, gazing at the stranger with open mouth.

"Much ressemblance," the latter continued; "much, much like you; comprenez?"

"Ahem!" Wilson said; "he can climb up trees?"

"Yes, climb up trees; and many other animals here—extraordinary beasts."

"Well, out with 'em, old fellow," Stewart encouragingly said—"out with 'em; I am much inclined to pass them in review." "Non, non!" the little Frenchman said, stepping before him as he prepared to examine another cage; "not this evening; no more; to-morrow evening, grande entrée—grand exhibition in Francisville—see all when all in order; this evening see nothing, for nothing in order." . . .

Wilson and Stewart now went back to the hotel, for they soon found that the little Frenchman was not inclined to make further concessions to them. But the whole conversation in the little town that evening, irrespective of the court-day and the coming election, turned solely on the stranger's collection of traps; and the most improbable suppositions and conclusions were arrived at as to why the strange man took the beasts about the country—whether he wished to eat then, or show them to the people, in the hope of receiving commissions to catch more. Stewart and Wilson had a bet of a deer-skin as to the place where the Frenchman caught the "wild boy;" Stewart asserting that he had been brought from Leckie's Elbow—a curve in the Mississippi, far down in Tennessee, where one was said to be living in the swamp—while Wilson insisted he was nailed, in some way or other, in the Cash Swamps; and he should himself have captured him on one occasion, had not his foot slipped and plumped him headforemost into one of the numerous bayous there.

1938: Hall (1993) noted that George Haas recorded a sighting of a creature seen in July, 1938, in Baxter County. A 15-year-old boy was walking home after an evening church social, when he found himself followed by a seven-foot-tall creature. It chased him until reaching a barbed-wire fence. Over the next few weeks, neighbors reported hearing "blood-curdling screams" after nightfall.

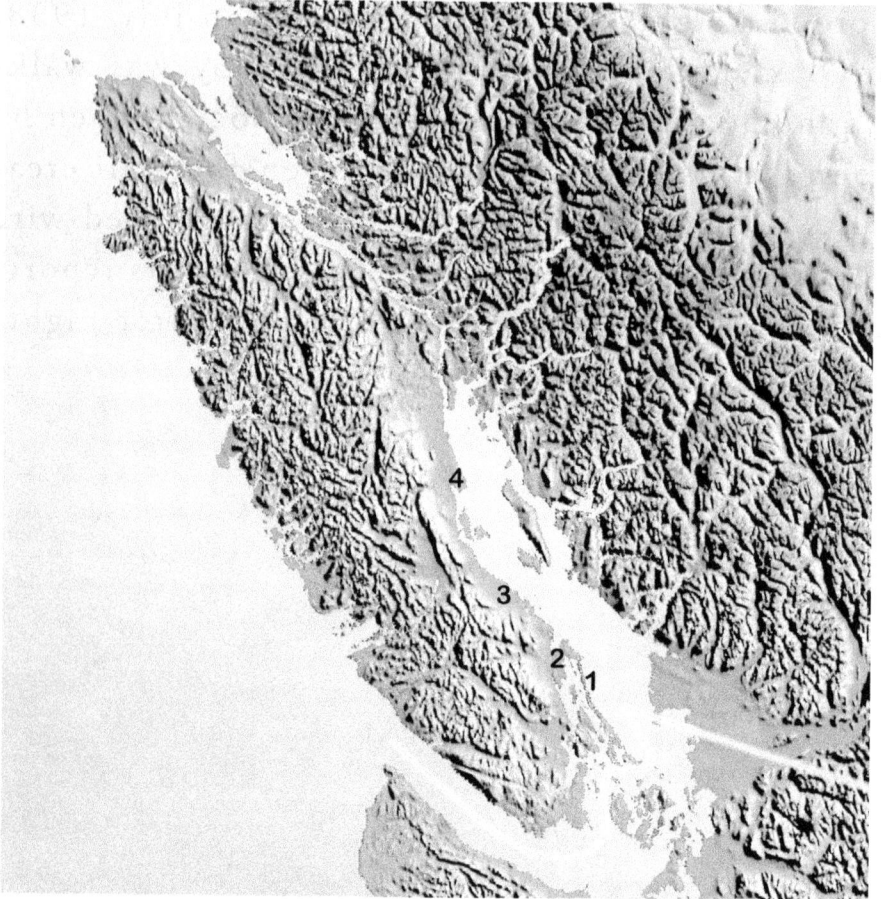

Vancouver Island

1 Valdes Island

2 Nanaimo

3 Qualicum

4 Comox

British Columbia

1846: Sanderson (1961) noted that Mr. Alexander Caulfield Anderson, surveying for the Hudson's Bay Company, (incorrectly noted as 1864) "reported just such hairy humanoids as having hurled rocks down upon him and his surveying party from more than one slope." This particular report is likely false, as John Green and Sabine Sanderson (1975) noted that the hand-written report by Anderson in the B.C. Archives mentions no such story, though Anderson was shown a large "footprint" in stone.

1871: Sanderson (1961) noted that J. W. Burns collected a report from a Native American woman who claimed to have been abducted by a hairy creature when she was 17, and kept for a year until she was able to escape. In a 1957 letter to the Chilliwack (BC) *Progress,* Burns noted that the woman was a member of the port Douglas Indians, and was abducted in June 1871 while picking berries near the Harrison River. Burns said: "The Sasquatch and the girl swam across the Harrison

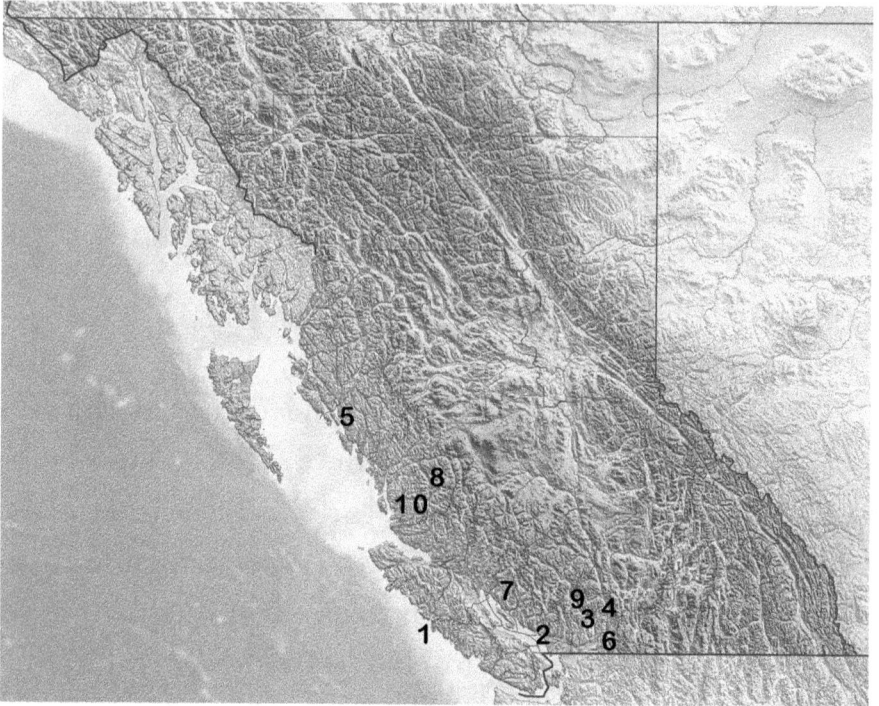

(CC BY-SA) NordNordWest

1 Vancouver Island

2 Vancouver

3 Harrison Lake

4 Yale

5 Bishop's Cove (15 miles north of Princess
   Royal Island, mouth of Gardner Canal per
   WRIGLEY'S B. C. DIRECTORY)

6 Greendrop Lake

7 Toba Inlet

8 South Bentinck Arm (bay)

9 Port Douglas

10 Rivers Inlet

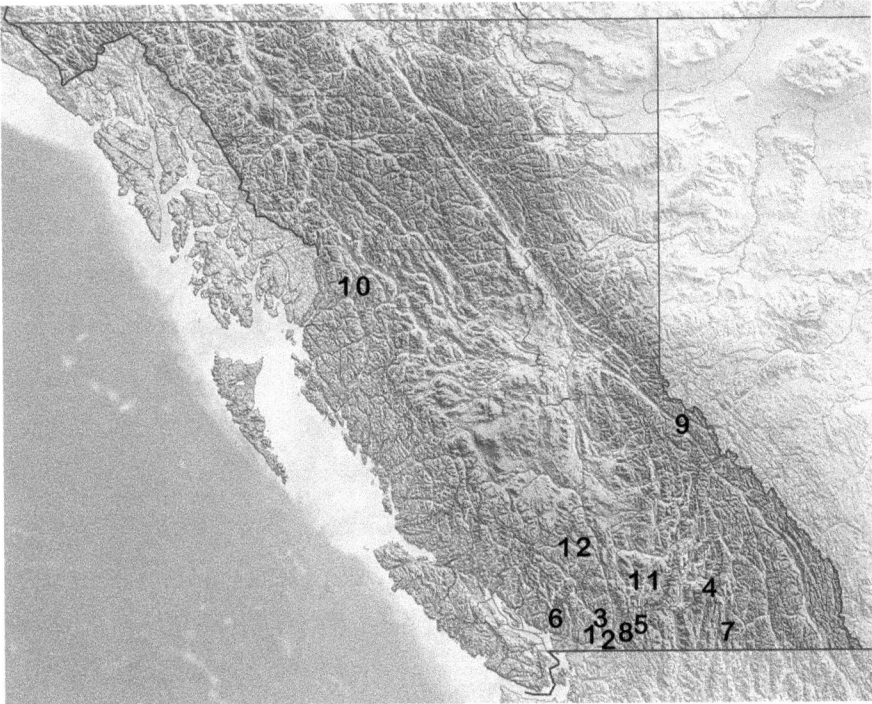

(CC BY-SA) NordNordWest

1 Harrison Mills

2 Agassiz

3 Chehalis

4 Vernon

5 Hope

6 Pitt Lake

7 Bridesville

8 Ruby Creek

9 Tête Jaune Cache

10 New Hazleton

11 Spuzzum

12 Lillooet

to the south side, where the Chehalis range is on the north side of the river. It is well known to the Chehalis Indians that Sasquatch had their home on the south side of the Harrison as well as in the Chehalis mountains. . . . [The] Sasquatch, she said, was very kind to her. But she made life so miserable for the Sasquatch that he and his aged parents were glad to get rid of her. After saying with them for about a year, her abductor returned her to the Chehalis village, where she recounted her experience." She was known to Burns personally, and he spoke to her just a few years before she died in January 1940. ("Sasquatch bride story re-told," Chilliwack, British Columbia, *Progress*, May 8, 1957.) Other accounts published in the same period noted a Sasquatch-abducted woman's name as Serephine Long, with mention of a child born (eg, "Mainly About People," by Sir Michael Bruce, Vancouver, British Columbia, *Province*, March 4, 1957), which may or may not be a folkloric variation of the same story.

1884: John Green (1978) was sent a newspaper clipping detailing the capture of an apelike creature, now well-known in Bigfoot lore as Jacko. (Jacko, sometimes Jocko, was a generic pet name often given to monkeys or apes.) This clipping has created some controversy over its credibility. Green's investigation into the newspaper article (with Sabine Sanderson, 1975) noted that looking through a number of newspaper issues from British Columbia, they only found two other mentions of the account. One was a skeptical paragraph from a competing newspaper, and the other stated that a group of citizens went to the local jail to view the creature, without finding it there. In a later article, Kinne (1976) pointed out that competing newspapers may not be the most objective parties, and that is certainly recognizable in any number of Wild Man incidents noted in this book.

Based on what was previously known and what has been unearthed since, however, expanding the newspaper accounts discussing the alleged creature, the Jacko story appears to have been a simple prank on readers (and intentionally or not, a few locals). We'll probably never know what instigated the story, though the letter from J. B. Good that follows certainly shows that folklore of such creatures was not unknown in the region.

Victoria, British Columbia, *Daily British Colonist,* July 4, 1884
WHAT IS IT?
A STRANGE CREATURE CAPTURED ABOVE YALE.
A BRITISH COLUMBIA GORILLA.
(CORRESPONDENCE OF THE COLONIST)
YALE, B. C., JULY 3RD., 1884.

In the immediate vicinity of No. 4 tunnel, situated some twenty miles above this

village, are bluffs of rock which have hitherto been unsurmountable, but on Monday
morning last were successfully scaled by Mr.
Onderdonk's employee on the regular train
from Lytton. Assisted by Mr. Costerton, the
British Columbia Express Company's messenger, and a number of gentlemen from Lytton and points east of that place who, after
considerable trouble and perilous climbing,
succeeded in capturing a creature which
may truly be called half man and half beast.
"Jacko," as the creature has been called by
his capturers, is something of the gorilla
type standing about four feet seven inches in
height and weighing 127 pounds. He has long,
black, strong hair and resembles a human
being with one exception, his entire body,
excepting his hands, (or paws) and feet are
covered with glossy hair about one inch long.
His fore arm is much longer than a man's
fore arm, and he possesses extraordinary
strength, as he will take hold of a stick and
break it by wrenching or twisting it, which
no man living could break in the same way.
Since his capture he is very reticent, only
occasionally uttering a noise which is half
bark and half growl. He is, however, becoming daily more attached to his keeper, Mr.
George Tilbury, of this place, who proposes

shortly starting for London, England, to exhibit him. His favorite food so far is berries, and he drinks fresh milk with evident relish. By advice of Dr. Hannington raw meats have been withheld from Jacko, as the doctor thinks it would have a tendency to make him savage. The mode of capture was as follows: Ned Austin, the engineer, on coming in sight of the bluff of the eastern end of the No. 4 tunnel saw what he supposed to be a man lying asleep in close proximity to the track, and as quick as thought blew the signal to apply the brakes. The brakes were instantly applied, and in a few seconds the train was brought to a standstill. At this moment the supposed man sprang up, and uttering a sharp quick bark began to climb the steep bluff. Conductor R. J. Craig and Express Messenger Costerton, followed by the baggageman and brakesmen, jumped from the train and knowing they were some twenty minutes ahead of time immediately gave chase. After five minutes of perilous climbing the then supposed demented Indian was corralled on a projecting shelf of rock where he could neither ascend nor descend. The query now was how to capture him alive, which was quickly decided by Mr. Craig, who crawled on his hands and knees until he was about forty feet above the creature. Taking a small piece of loose rock he let it fall and it had the desired effect of rendering poor Jacko incapable of resistance for a time at least. The bell rope was then brought up and Jacko was now lowered to terra firma. After firmly binding him and placing him in the baggage car "off brakes" was sounded and the train started for Yale. At the station a large crowd who had heard of the capture by telephone from Spuzzum Flat were assembled, each one anxious to have the first look at the monstrosity, but they were disappointed, as Jacko had been taken off at the machine shops and placed in charge of his present keeper.

The question naturally arises, how came the creature where it was first seen by Mr. Austin? From bruises about its head and body, and apparent soreness since its capture, it is supposed that Jacko ventured too near the edge of the bluff, slipped, fell and lay where found until the sound of the rushing train aroused him. Mr. Thos. White and Mr. Gouin, C. E., as well as Mr. Major, who kept a small store about half a mile west of the tunnel during the past two years, have mentioned having seen a curious creature at different points between Camps 13 and 17, but no attention was paid to their remarks as people came to the conclusion that they had either seen a bear or stray Indian dog. Who can unravel the mystery that now surrounds Jacko? Does he belong to a species hitherto unknown in this part of the continent, or is he really what the train men first thought he was, a crazy Indian?

Victoria, British Columbia, *Daily British Colonist,* July 9, 1884

INDIAN TRADITIONS.

THE RECTORY, NANAIMO, JULY 6TH, 1884.

To the Editor:—In reference to the capture of Jacko on the Frazer canyon bluffs above Yale, as given in your issue last week, I may be able to furnish the public with some particulars connected with my late superintendence of the Lytton Indian Mission that may throw additional light upon this strange event, and at the same time confirm some mysterious rumors that were current amongst the entire tribe in that locality during our residence among them.

On three different occasions in successive years, and in entirely different points of observation, the most startling reports were circulated far and wide, that when camping out for purposes of hunting, fishing, gathering wood and berries, certain of our Indians had been visited in the dead of night by something that seemed half man half-beast, which had come into the tents whilst sleeping or prowled around their encampment, producing the greatest consternation and amazement.

The idea prevailed that certain wild men of the woods were at large in the less frequented parts of the country, and were exceedingly dangerous and might one day invade the settlements.

We, at the time, laughed at their fears and pooh-poohed the matter, considering the reports in question here on par with their traditional stories about certain lakes and special spots being haunted and that numbers of their tribe had been found dead upon venturing to pass a night on these dreaded haunts of mysterious and unearthly visitants.

It may appear, therefore, that there was more truth about some of these tales than was dreamed of in our boasted enlightened philosophy. That Jacko is destined to point a moral or adorn a tale, viz: that truth is stranger than fiction, and facts are stubborn things, specially Jacko.

Yours, &c.,

J. B. Good.

Mainland, British Columbia, *Guardian*, July 9, 1884 (from Green
and Sanderson 1975)

The 'What Is It' is the subject of conversation in town, this evening. How the story
originated, and by whom, is hard for one to
conjecture. Absurdity is written on the face
of it. The fact of the matter is, that no such
animal was caught, and how the 'Colonist'
was duped in such a manner, and by such
a story, is strange, and stranger still, when
the 'Columbian' reproduced it in that paper.
The 'train' of circumstances connected with
the discovery of 'Jacko' and the disposal of
same was, and still is, a mystery.

REX.

Yale, B.C., July 7, 1884.

New Westminster, British Columbia, *British Columbian*, July 11,
1884 (from Green and Sanderson 1975)

The Wild Man—Last Tuesday it was reported
that the wild man, said to have been captured at Yale, had been sent to this city and
might be seen at the gaol. A rush of citizens
instantly took place, and it is reported that
not fewer than 200 impatiently begged admission into the skookum house. The only
wild man visible was Mr. [Moresby], governor of the gaol, who completely exhausted
his patience answering enquiries from the
sold visitors.

Port Moody, British Columbia, *Gazette*, July 12, 1884

The "Colonist" may become—infamous. The story of the gorilla taken near Yale was a strange sample of rant, a low practical joke. On Sunday last the same journal, in that sickening column that contains "What some people say," announces "that the wild man captured above Yale has arrived, and can be seen at the post-office."

Does the editor of the "Colonist" suppose that the readers of that journal are all gorillas? It appears that rant suits them better than reason. A newspaper edited by a lunatic would circulate in the capital as fast as a scandalous report. The taste of the modern editor is not good taste, but he must please the palate of the uneducated.

Victoria, British Columbia, *Daily British Colonist*, July 13, 1884

"WHAT IS IT" IN JAIL.

The Columbian says it was reported last Tuesday that the supposed gorilla, stated to be captured at Yale, was in New Westminster goal. The citizens immediately made a stampede for that institution, and drove the gaoler, Mr. [Moresby], nearly crazy with enquiries, but the wild man wasn't there.

New Westminster, British Columbia, *The British Columbian,*
August 23, 1884

A Chilliwhack correspondent sends us a letter relating to Jacko, the wild man, who, he
says, has been brought down for exhibition
at Centresville. We suppose there is a good
point in this joke, but we are really not able
to discover it, and we are afraid our readers
might be equally unfortunate.

Victoria, British Columbia, *Daily British Colonist,* August 24,
1884

The Yale Wild Man.—A gentleman from Yale
called on us yesterday to deny the story that
the capture of the wild man above Yale was
a fact. He had been credited with being its
keeper, and has since been in receipt of letters from zoological gardens and circus proprietors in various parts of the continent asking his price for its disposal. He feels kind
of mad about it—mad because he has not the
wild man in stock—and wishes to inform the
curiosity hunting public that he is not open
for any offers.

One additional Jacko theory, suggested by Dr.
Grover Krantz (1992), was that the creature may
have been purchased by Barnum, to be exhibited

as Jo-Jo, the Dog-Faced Boy. Krantz pointed out that there were differences in sketches and images of Jo-Jo in 1884 and 1885, suggesting that the original Jo-Jo had died and was replaced by a human impersonator. I'm including here a copy of the 1884 newspaper description of Jo-Jo. Assuming that the newspapermen actually witnessed and described the boy correctly, it appears that the 1884 Jo-Jo was not Jacko. Jo-Jo was capable of speaking several languages and writing his name.

New York, New York, *Times*, October 13, 1884

A HUMAN SKYE TERRIER.

THE DOG-FACED PASSENGER
OF THE CITY OF CHICAGO.

The passenger who attracted the most attention during the voyage of the Inman steamer City of Chicago, from Liverpool to this city, was Theodor Jo Jo, a boy of 10, whose face resembles that of a Skye terrier. Jo Jo held an informal reception in the Astor House after his arrival yesterday, during which he submitted gracefully to a good deal of pulling about and inquisitive handling by reporters and other invited guests. His face is covered with a long wavy mass of silken hair, which in color is between light red and silver gray. It hangs upon his brow down to the eyes, parting in the centre and waving off to either side like that of a fancy terrier. It droops from his cheeks in long wavy locks, grows from the nostrils, and hangs from both ears. The length of this luxuriant growth of hair varies from 2 to 4 inches, and it is so thick that the skin beneath is visible only in scattered spots. The eyes of this dog-faced boy also resemble very closely those of a terrier. They are slightly bluish in color, almost perfectly round, and the whites are visible entirely around the pupils. His mouth is furnished with only the two canine teeth above and two incisors below, and all four are thin and sharp, resembling miniature tusks rather than human teeth. The entire body is covered with a growth of thin light hair, but the thick heavy locks are found only on the face. It is said that Jo Jo snarls occasionally like a dog, but he was perfectly tractable yesterday, allowing his visitors to pull his hair and satisfy themselves that it was not fastened on by artificial means, and to examine his teeth as they would have investigated the molars of a horse on exhibition. He speaks Russian and German tolerably well, and a few words of English, and took great pride in showing that he could write his name by signing it to the back of his pictures in large, flowing characters.

The dog-faced boy was captured in the forests of Kostroma, in the centre of Russia, about 11 years ago, with his father, who is described as a wild man, with the same peculiar face which the boy now possesses. Jo Jo was then little more than a baby, and his face was comparatively hairless. The father was exhibited all over Europe until three years ago, when he died. Mr. Bailey, of Barnum, Hutchinson & Bailey's Biggest Show on Earth, succeeded recently in securing the boy by giving heavy bonds to return him safe to Russia, and Nicolas Forstet was sent over with Jo Jo as an agent of the Russian Government to accompany him and see that he was protected according to the terms of the contract. The boy has been secured from Mr. Bailey by Hager, Campbell & Co., of Philadelphia, but he will be placed on exhibition in a museum of this city to-day, where he will remain for a season.

1880s: Standwood (1957) noted that Capilano Chief August Jack told Rene Dahinden that he had seen a nine-foot-tall female Sasquatch captured in the 1880s. She was "caged and exhibited 'for 10 cents a peek'" in New Westminster, then taken to Victoria for exhibition where she died, as she refused to eat.

1901: Sanderson (1961) noted that prospector Mike King explored an isolated northern section of Vancouver Island alone because local guides refused to accompany him. After a few days, he encountered a large humanoid creature covered in reddish brown fur. It was washing roots in a stream, then piling them up. The animal ran off— "His arms were peculiarly long and used freely in climbing and bush-running." King investigated its tracks, stating that it left a "human foot but with phenomenally long and spreading toes." The following accounts add a few details.

Windsor, Ontario, *Evening Record*, August 30, 1904

WILD MAN OF VANCOUVER.

The Indians tell of a wild man on Vancouver Island, and now a Caucasian, Michael King, relates that he has seen what looked like a half-man, half-ape.

King told his story at a camp fire to the accompaniments of a chattering mountain brook and the whispering pines towering to a starlight sky. He was on one of his solitary cruises for timber on the island, and had not seen a human face for days. A strange cry of mingled surprise and fear, very human in its quality, brought him to a sudden halt, rifle in hand, and eyes straining everywhere for an explanation.

This was quickly forthcoming in a manner to try even the nerve of so superb a woodsman as this veteran of the forests. Within 100 yards appeared a thing, large, completely covered with hair, with long arms hanging below the knee, penetrating eyes under a mass of unkempt hair—certainly a man, said Mr. King, but yet such a human as no nation, tribe, or country knows.

As he saw this striking object in his path Mr. King's memory went back to the stories told by Indians who had refused to enter that part of the island with him. They had said that a fearsome thing lorded over the country, and, in their superstitious terror, they had said it was a god of the Spaniards, the descendant of a great chief who had left his ship at Nootka and mated, by force, with a princess of the tribe.

But while he thought these things, King's hand was on the trigger of his rifle. He was prepared for the wild man, or the ape, or whatever it might be. But the wild man was in no mood to meet the man with the stick that talked in thunder. After a moment's scrutiny of the pathfinder it decided on flight, and plunged into the forest wilderness, where it was quickly lost to sight. No further meeting with the wild man fell to King's lot.

Hist story, of course, has been received with sarcastic comment on the coast, but it is curious to note that Otto Scheen has just come in from the northern end of Vancouver Island bringing a tale of having seen footprints such as are made by no wild animal that ranges the forests of this continent. While apparently made by a human being they are those of neither Siwash nor white man.

Perhaps the hairy monster seen by King has retreated further north with the object of flying from contact with real humanity.

Kansas City, Missouri, *Star*, August 6, 1924

THE WILD MAN OF VANCOUVER

That report of apelike giants in the interior of the state of Washington, with a reference to other hairy giants in the interior of Vancouver Island, has recalled to C. H. Gibbons, a former British Columbia newspaper correspondent and writer, a story he once heard from a veteran timber cruiser.

"The Seeahtiks," said the dispatch from Kelso, Wash., "made their home in the heart of the wilderness on Vancouver Island and on the Olympic range. The Seeahtiks are seven to eight feet tall, with hairy bodies like bears. They are great hypnotists, and also have a gift of ventriloquism, throwing their voices great distances."

Michael King was the timber cruiser who told Mr. Gibbons of the strange contact he had years ago with the wild man in the wild interior of Vancouver Island, in the vicinity of Campbell River.

"I was dropping down a hillside to a likely spot for water," said King, "when I heard a shout. I don't know that you'd call it a shout, either, or a scream, or a yell exactly—sort of mixture of all three. Wasn't any sort of animal I ever heard of. I know 'em all pretty well. Of course I stopped dead in my tracks and stood maybe two minutes listening, but there was not another sound.

"Then I caught a glimpse of him. He was running uphill across the draw, legs and arms all working, four or five feet tall, I'd judge, and plenty hairy—sort of reddish brown, like a bright bay horse. I dropped by 30.30 on him as he climbed, when, all of a sudden, he stopped short, pretty near the top, and turned round and stared at me. 'Course he saw me. Wasn't more than eighty yards. I couldn't a' missed him, but then I couldn't shoot somehow. Looked too much like a man—

"Well, we stands there sizing each other up. Looked like we were trying to see which

could stand it the longest. I never felt so
queerlike before or since. Finally I starts
on down hill. I hadn't taken two steps and
he was on his way, howling t' beat th' band.
Fear, it was plain this time, and I felt a heap
easier. He was into the bush like a flash,
traveling fast and regardless. You could tell
by the noise he was making. I kept on to the
waterhole, where I knew it would likely be.
And what d'yeh think I found?

"Down there by this little spring, to one
side, was a pile of lachamas—the wild onion
the Siwashes are so stuck on—just as it had
been pulled out by the roots, with the dirt
and all sticking. And a bit away was another
pile, clean, white roots. He'd been pulling
and washing them at the spring when I came
along. Ain't that human-like?

"That was the last I saw of him, though
he must a' circled round and round me fifty
times that night. In the soft spots he'd left
his prints, a foot big enough for a No. 12,
toes spread wide apart, and the drag of a
long claw on each."

Vancouver, British Columbia, *Province,* December 14, 1904
(excerpt, from Green 1978)

A. R. Crump, J. Kincaid, T. Hutchins and
W. Buss, four sober-minded settlers of

Qualicum, are the new witnesses and there is not the slightest deviation or variation in detail in the stories they tell with an earnestness that defies ridicule. They were out hunting in the vicinity of Horne Lake, which lies mid-way between Great Central Lake and Comox Lake, in an uninhabited and little explored section of the interior of Vancouver Island, when they came upon the uncouth being whom they describe as a living, breathing and intensely interesting modern Mowgli. The wild man was apparently young, with long matted hair and a beard, and covered with a profusion of hair all over the body. He ran like a deer through the seemingly impenetrable tangle of undergrowth, and pursuit was utterly impossible.

Decatur, Illinois, *Herald,* January 3, 1905

VANCOUVER WILD MAN.

A correspondent at Vancouver, B.C., sends out this story: The Vancouver island wild man, whose existence has been persistently prominent in the traditions of the northern island tribes and who has been vouched for by Mike King, the most famous backwoodsman and timber cruiser of British Columbia, has again made his appearance, and this time there were four credible witnesses.

A. B. Camp, J. Kinkaid, T. Hutchins, and
W. T. Buss, four sober-minded settlers of
Qualicum, are the new witnesses, and there
is not the slightest variation in the detail
of the stories they tell with an earnestness
that defies ridicule.

They were out hunting in the vicinity of
Horne's lake, which lies almost midway between Great Central and Comox lakes, in
an uninhabited and little explored section
of the interior of Vancouver island, when
they came upon the uncouth being on the
lake shore, whom they describe as a living,
breathing and intensely interesting Mowgli.
He ran like a deer through the seemingly impenetrable tangle of undergrowth, and pursuit was utterly impracticable. The wild man
was apparently young, with long and matted
hair and beard, and covered with a profusion
of hair all over the body.

It was four years ago that Mike King came
across the strange being which (according to
his description) comes as near to the missing
link as any one could well imagine. Mr. King
was at the time making one of his solitary
tramps, prospecting the timber country inland from the head of the Campbell river, his
Indians having resolutely refused to go beyond a certain landmark which they referred

to as the boundary of the country of the "massache ikta"—literally "the bad thing." It was
drawing toward evening, and the man-beast
was surprised in the act of bending over a little water hole, washing certain edible grass
roots which he had disposed in two neat little
piles, the one cleaned and the other awaiting
cleaning.

Utters Cry Very Human.

At the sound of Mr. King's approach the creature uttered a cry very human in its quality, of mingled terror, astonishment and defiance, then running half way up the hillside,
where he stood for possibly five minutes, curiously regarding the intruder, who kept him
covered with his rifle. Mr. King's description
was very similar to that given by the Qualicum quartet, and their meeting place with
the savage was in approximately the same
territory.

Mr. King made an effort to approach the
remarkable creature, which dashed through
the thick underbrush. He did not see the
man-beast again, although his weird cries
were heard at intervals during the night,
and Mr. King (who sat the night out by a big
fire, rifle in hand) was thoroughly convinced
that the wild man slipped back silently to
inspect him at long range during his vigil.
He says that the body was covered with

reddish-brown hair and that the arms were peculiarly long and used freely in climbing and bush running, while the trail showed a distinct human foot, but with phenomenally long and spreading toes.

The Indians through northern Vancouver Island shun what has since time immemorial been set apart by them as the country of the "massache itka," and no money or persuasion will induce them to go into it with hunter, trapper, timber cruiser or prospector. Their tradition is to the effect that at the time of the coming of the Spaniards to the west coast an immense monkey (presumably an ape or orang-outang) escaped from one of the vessels and took refuge in the forest wilderness. Several months later it appeared suddenly at the Muchalat village, and, the Indians running from it in terror, it caught up and carried away with in a girl of 15. The natives allege that two wild children resulted, but that one was years afterward found dead in a rude hut beyond the headwaters of Campbell river, leaving at least one other lonely creature to roam and dominate the woods. Mr. King himself saw in the unexplored country shunned by all the Indian tribes a hut that seemingly had been built for shelter by some semihuman denizen of the forest.

Seen As Far Back As 1865.

Old prospectors also tell of reported glimpses of the wild man, as far back as 1865, when
a mining man named Brown (now employed
in Victoria, B.C.) contributed to the Victoria
Colonist a two-column account of his adventures through the desertion of his Muchalat
Indians in terror during an ascent of Gold
river, they having seen the wild man and one
of their number having his eyes picked out
by the nomadic savage. It is the tradition of
all the west coast Indians that loss of sight
is the penalty enforced against any Indian
venturing into the territory of the "massache
ikta."

The Qualicum settlers say that half a
dozen times during the past few years reports have come to the settlements of such a
creature being seen, but as the truth of the
encounter depending upon one or, at the
most, two witnesses, they have been universally scouted. Mike King is a man whose
word on anything in his business or pertain-
ing to the woods is a law throughout British
Columbia. He knows the wilderness of this
province perhaps better than any other living
man, white or red, never drinks, and never
sees phantoms. On the subject of the wild
man he is ready to make sworn attestation at

any time, although he has been reluctant to discuss the matter.

There is a new theory evolved at Qualicum which connects the wild man with remembrance of the fact that nine years ago a child was lost from the settlement, straying into the forest and never again emerging therefrom. They incline to the belief that this child has lived, succored perhaps by the beasts in Mowgli fashion, and is the wild man of today. Indeed, so strongly has this theory impressed the little community that the father of the long-lost child, with others, is now out with an expedition for the capture of the unhappy being.

Another theory is that the wild man is a hunter of Englishman's river, lost twenty-six years ago when, having shot and wounded a wolf, he followed its trail into the forest and was by the forest forever swallowed up. It is held that he may have met with some accident depriving him of reason, and has since roamed the woods.

Pittsburgh, Pennsylvania, *Press*, December 19, 1905

HAIRY GIANT IN THE WOODS

According to arrivals from Comox today by the steamer City of Nanaimo, the residents of Valdez [Valdes] Island, near Comox, B.C., have been terrorized of late by visits from Vancouver Island's now famous "Mowgli." A rancher from Valdez Island reported that the wild man of Vancouver Island is at present on Valdez, and by the description of the creature which he solemnly asserts he saw, including the corroboration of half a dozen others, the "Mowgli" is undoubtedly the same as seen near Horne Lake two months ago.

A family named Pitcock, residing on Valdez, last week was frightened one night about 10 o'clock while sitting at supper by seeing a ghastly face looking through the window into the room. The face was covered with long black coarse hair, only a small portion of the skin being visible. Directly the creature saw he was noticed he uttered a diabolical scream, which was heard by ranchers nearly a mile away and vanished.

A number of young farmers with rifles searched the vicinity next day without success. Large prints of feet upon the soft earth of a flower bed under the window was the only sign of the monster who, according to those who have seen him, is nearly seven feet tall.

Twice during the next night the family heard a scream similar to that uttered by the wild man. All that day a careful watch was kept, but there were no signs of the "Mowgli," although there were a number of footprints corresponding with those seen before, which were found along the creek that passed the Pitcock household.

The boys, however, determined to capture the individual that has created a panic among the female residents and the next night a dozen well-armed men concealed themselves near a stack of hay where the footprints of the "Mowgli" were traceable. About 10:30 p.m. horrible yells were heard in the direction of the creek and after waiting for an hour some of the posse determined to go in that direction. They had gone up the stream about half a mile when the light of a lantern carried by the "Mowgli" came into view. Hiding behind a tree the posse had a splendid chance to view this denizen of the woods. They describe him as very tall and powerfully built and with the exception of a few rags hanging from a belt at his waist he was entirely naked. His body was covered with long black hair and the face, which presented a most hideous appearance, was identified as the same as that seen at the Pitcock home the evening previous.

The men, after recovering from their fright, broke from cover and one raised his rifle, but before he could find range the "Mowgli," who had by this time discovered the farmers, threw himself into the icy waters and swam for the other side of the creek.

Nothing more has been seen of him around the Pitcock residence, although two half-breeds of Alert Bay claim to have seen the same man a few days after.—Nanaimo (B.C.) Cor. Seattle Times.

Winnipeg, Manitoba, *Morning Telegram,* May 2, 1905

WILD MAN DISCOVERED

INDIANS OF BRITISH COLUMBIA
SAY ONE IS IN THEIR MIDST

Victoria, May 1.—(Special)—Captain Owen, pilot, reported today that Indians had seen and shot at the wild man, previously reported to have been seen near Qualicum. The creature, which was naked and covered with hair, was engaged in digging clams with his knife when Indians came, and thinking him a bear, shot at him and wounded him. The man ran away shrieking. The Indians returned to Union, much frightened, and reported having wounded the wild man. Search parties sent to look for the creature have failed. Residents of Union and that vicinity firmly believe in the existence of the wild man. Some allege they saw the young man who disappeared twelve years ago.

Van Wert, Ohio, *Daily Bulletin*, October 28, 1905

BRITISH COLUMBIA MOWGLIS

TRIBE OF WILD MEN ROAMING
WOODS AND FRIGHTENING PEOPLE.

James Johnson, a rancher living near Comox, seven miles from Cumberland, B. C., reports several Mowglis, or wild men, who have been seen in that neighborhood by ranchers, says a Nanaimo (B. C.) correspondent of the San Francisco Call. Johnson asserts that they were performing what seemed to be a sort of "sun dance" on the sand. One of them caught a glimpse of Johnson, who was viewing the proceedings from behind a big log. The Mowglis disappeared as if by magic into a big cave.

Thomas Kincaid, a rancher living near French creek, while bicycling from Cumberland, also reports seeing a Mowgli, whom he describes as a powerfully built man, more than six feet in height and covered with long black hair. The wild man upon seeing Kincaid uttered a shriek and disappeared into the woods. Upon arriving home Kincaid wrote Government Agent Bray of Nanaimo, inquiring if it would be lawful to shoot the Mowgli, as he was terrorizing that vicinity.

The government agent replied that there was no law permitting such an act. It is reported that on a recent hunting expedition up the Quailicum river an Indian saw a Mowgli and, mistaking him for a bear, shot at and wounded him. During the past month no less than eleven persons coming to Nanaimo from Cumberland have seen the wild men. Parties have been organized, and every effort is being made to capture the Mowglis.

Lincoln, Nebraska, *Evening News,* January 1, 1906

HAIRY GIANT IN WOODS.

HE IS A "MOWGLI" IN REAL LIFE AND TERRORIZES AN ISLAND.

Nanaimo (B. C.) Cor, Seattle Times. According to arrivals from Comox today by the steamer City of Nanaimo, the residents of Valdez Island, near Comox, B. C., have been terrorized of late by visits from Vancouver Island's now famous "Mowgli." A rancher from Valdez Island reported that the wild man of Vancouver Island is at present on Valdez, and by the description of the creature which he solemnly asserts he saw, including the corroboration of half a dozen others, the "Mowgli" is undoubtedly the same as seen near Horne Lake two months ago.

A family named Pitcock, residing on Valdez, last week was frightened one night about 10 o'clock while sitting at supper by seeing a ghastly face looking through the window into the room. The face was covered with long black coarse hair, only a small portion of the skin being visible. Directly the creature saw he was noticed he uttered a diabolical scream, which was heard by ranchers nearly a mile away and vanished.

A number of young farmers with rifles searched the vicinity next day without success. Large prints of feet upon the soft earth of a flower bed under the window was the only sign of the monster who, according to those who have seen him, is nearly seven feet tall.

Twice during the next night the family heard a scream similar to that uttered by the wild man. All that day a careful watch was kept but there were no signs of the "Mowgli," although there were a number of footprints corresponding with those seen before, which were found along the creek that passed the Pitcock household.

The boys, however, determined to capture the individual that has created a panic among the female residents and the next night a dozen well-armed men concealed themselves near a stack of hay where the footprints of the "Mowgli" were traceable. About 10:30 p.m. horrible yells were heard

in the direction of the creek and after waiting for an hour some of the posse determined
to go in that direction. They had gone up the
stream about half a mile when the light of
a lantern carried by the "Mowgli" came into
view. Hiding behind a tree the posse had a
splendid chance to view the denizen of the
woods. They describe him as very tall and
powerfully built and with the exception of
a few rags hanging from a belt at his waist
he was entirely naked. His body was covered
with long black hair and the face which presented a most hideous appearance, was identified as the same as that seen at the Pitcock
home the evening previous.

The men, after recovering from their fright,
broke from cover and one raised his rifle,
but before he could find range the "Mowgli"
who had by this time discovered the farmers,
threw himself into the icy waters and swam
for the other side of the creek.

Nothing more has been seen of him around
the Pitcock residence, although two half-
breeds of Alert bay claim to have seen the
same man in a few days after.

Walla Walla, Washington, *Evening Statesman*, February 12, 1906
SEE WILD MAN IN HIS CAVE
Nanaimo, B.C.—Feb. 12.—James McLay, of
Gabriola Island, the rediscoverer of Malispina

Gallery, has made another remarkable discovery on the island. The Vancouver island wild man, strange and weird tales of whom have been reported from different parts of the island from time to time, has been seen by Mr. McLay. Several days ago, in company with a trapper, Mr. McLay was hunting in the northeast end of the island. Hearing noises and mumblings, as if proceeding from some strange animal, they started to investigate.

A few feet up the side of a precipice they perceived a cave, from which the noises seemed to emanate. Creeping carefully up, they were rooted to the ground with astonishment to perceive the wild man in the cave rocking himself to and fro with folded arms and mumbling in a strange language, in which the trapper recognized broken phrases of French, which, translated ran something like this:

"Damn! Damn Johnnie Bull and Wolfe. They kill me people in Quebec."

The description they give of the wild man's appearance is practically the same as that told by Mike King, of Victoria, and others who have seen this strange creature, differing only in this particular—that on this occasion the "mowgli" had a girdle of leaves around him. When seen before he was always absolutely naked. He is a giant in size, very

powerful looking, and covered with long hair
all over his body many inches in length. From
the fact that the only intelligible words he
uttered are French, it is presumed that he is
a French Canadian. What connection there
is between "Johnnie Bull" and Wolfe, in Quebec, and the man is hard to say. Wolfe captured Quebec in 1754, and it may be possible
that some of his ancestors fell while defend-
ing the city at that time.

While the two were gazing at him he suddenly looked up, discovering their presence.
For a few seconds not a movement was made
on either side, until the trapper reached to
lean his gun up against a rock, which action
the wild man evidently interpreted as a hostile movement, for, giving vent to his usual
half-man-like, half wild-beast-like shrieks,
he leaped fully 10 feet from the cave into
the water and swam outwards, using a stick
rudely paddle shaped at either end to help
him in his progress, kicking his feet and paddling at the same time, progressing through
the water with the speed of an average canoe.
Going up the shore line a short way, where
Mr. McLay and his badly frightened companion could not follow him, the wild man made
for shore and disappeared with the alacri-
ty of a deer through the dense underbrush.

Although vigilant search has been made by different parties since he was seen last week, no more sight or tidings have been received of the wild man.

Vancouver, British Columbia, *Daily World,* July 30, 1906

ISLAND MOWGLI IS SEEN AGAIN

The Mowgli of Vancouver Island, has been seen again. A gentleman who came over from the island today, and who is stopping at the Leland, says that four days ago two prospectors dropped right on the wild man on the shores of Horn Lake, Alberni District. Horn Lake is what by most people would be called a marshy or rushy pond.

The wild man was clothed in sunshine and a smile except that his body was covered with a longish growth of hair of a brownish color, much like the salmon berry-eating bears that infest that region. The wild man ran as soon as the prospectors came within the range of vision.

The prospectors found the wickiup in which he had been sheltering, and also many traces of where he had been gathering roots of the reeds along the lake bank for sustenance. The World's informant says that once more it has been absolutely proven that the wild man is no figment of the imagination.

Vancouver, British Columbia, *Province,* March 8, 1907 (from
Green 1978)

A monkey-like wild man who appears on the
beach at night, who howls in an unearthly
fashion between intervals of exertion at clam
digging, has been the cause of depopulating
an Indian village, according to reports by
officers of the steamer Capilano, which
reached port last night from the north.

The Capilano on her trip north put in to
Bishop's Cove where there is a small Indian
settlement. As soon as the steamer appeared
in sight the inhabitants put off from the
shore in canoes and clambered on board the
Capilano in a state of terror over what they
called a monkey covered with long hair and
standing about five feet high which came out
on the beach at night to dig clams and howl.

The Indians say that they had tried to
shoot it but failed, which added to their superstitious fears. The officers of the vessel
heard some animals howling along the shore
at night but are not prepared to swear that
it was the voice of the midnight visitor who
has so frightened the Indians.

Victoria, British Columbia, *Daily Colonist,* October 20, 1907
IMMENSE FOOT MARKS FOUND
Vernon, Oct. 19.—With a human footprint
nineteen inches long, the big toe alone

measuring five inches, it is left to the imagination to fill in the superstructure of this huge monster that has frightened the inhabitants of this smiling valley. Men, women and children have turned out to look with awe and wonder at the mysterious and enormous "hoof." It is a naked human foot in all the essentials, and its partner is at the other side of a six-foot creek, giving some idea of the prehistoric stride of the creature.

A resident was calmly sawing timber when a gentleman of the neighborhood came up to him and sprung the yarn on him so suddenly that he thought he had somebody from the New Westminster institution to deal with. But the informant was perfectly sane, and produced a stick with the pedal particulars carefully marked. The footprint was down the hill there for anybody to see. No one certainly ever heard of the fertile Okanagan producing stray giants, but an old Indian gives color to the theory by averring that forty years ago there were what he terms giants who stole children and things. Perhaps this may be the last of the Canadian mound dwellers.

The reservation folks have certainly had a genuine scare and have called up all the whites round about to help them out. Rifles are all loaded and lanterns flit about in the darkness, so that it is unsafe for a stranger to loom up into view too suddenly when the least crash in the bush is sufficient to excite the tense nervous system. Some have gone on the trail on horseback with magazine guns, but few men even with a Maxim under each arm could stand the ordeal of confronting a hairy monster some thirteen feet high, judging by the feet. Besides, the possession of the creature alive would be as good a financial "spec" as a valuable quarter section of Okanagan land. As there are no people around here to hoax and the Indians are too grave and occupied to manufacture footprints for sport, the story and the evidence are just as stated, the Indians themselves being the most concerned and serious over it.

1915: Sanderson (1961) noted the sworn testimony of Charles Flood, who along with two companions was prospecting at Green Drop Lake near the Holy Cross Mountains. While exploring near Cougar Lake, they saw an eight-foot-tall hairy manlike creature eating berries.

1924: In 1957, Albert Ostman wrote a letter to newspaper reporter William Roe, who was covering the Harrison Hot Springs (B. C.) interest in a Sasquatch hunt. Ostman claimed that in 1924, he had been kidnapped by a Sasquatch family. After talking to several reporters, he eventually was interviewed by John Green, Ivan T. Sanderson, and others interested in the question of Bigfoot. Ostman remained remarkably consistent with his story over the years. The following is his story in his own words.

Agassiz-Harrison, British Columbia, *Advance,* Friday, May 5, 1961 (from Patterson 1966, reprinting an article from *True Magazine* by Ivan T. Sanderson, 1960)

KIDNAPPED PROSPECTOR LIVED SEVERAL DAYS WITH GIANT FAMILY

I have always followed logging and construction work. This time I had worked over one year on a construction job, and thought a good vacation was in order. B.C. is famous for lost gold mines. One is supposed to be at the head of Toba Inlet—why not look for this mine and have a vacation at the same time? I took the Union Steamship boat to Lund, B.C. From there I hired an old Indian to take me to the head of Toba Inlet.

This old Indian was a very talkative old gentleman. He told me stories about gold brought out by a white man from this lost mine. This white man was a heavy drinker—spent his money freely in saloons. But he had no trouble in getting more money. He would be away a few days, then come back with a bag of gold. But one time he went to his mine and never came back. Some people said a Sasquatch had killed him.

At that time I had never heard of Sasquatch. So I asked what kind of an animal he called a Sasquatch? The Indian said:

"They have hair all over their bodies, but they are not animals. They are people. Big people living in the mountains. My uncle saw the tracks of one that were two feet long. One old Indian saw one over eight feet tall."

I told the Indian I didn't believe in their old fables about mountain giants. It might have been some thousands of years ago, but not nowadays.

The Indian said: "There may not be many, but they still exist."

Late one day I found an exceptionally good campsite. It was two good sized cypress trees growing close together and near a rock wall with a nice spring just below these trees. I intended to make this my permanent camp. I cut lots of brush for my bed between these trees. I rigged up a pole from this rock wall to hang my pack sack on, and I arranged some flat rocks for my fireplace for cooking. I had a really classy setup. I shot a grouse just before I came to this place. Too late to roast that tonight—I would do that tomorrow.

And that is when things began to happen.

I am a heavy sleeper, not much disturbs me after I go to sleep, especially on a good bed like I had now.

Next morning I noticed things had been disturbed during the night. But nothing missing that I could see. I roasted my grouse on a stick for my breakfast—about 9:00 a.m. I started out prospecting.

That night I filled up the magazine of my rifle. I still had one full box of 20 shells in my pack, besides a full magazine and six shells in my coat pocket. That night I laid my rifle under the edge of my sleeping bag. I thought a porcupine had visited me the night before and porkies like leather, so I put my shoes in the bottom of my sleeping bag.

Next morning my pack sack had been emptied out. Some one had turned the sack upside down. It was still hanging on the pole from the shoulder straps as I had hung it up. Then I noticed one half-pound package of prunes was missing. Also my pancake flour was missing, but my salt bag was not touched. Porkies always look for salt so I decided it must be something other than porkies. I looked for tracks but found none. I did not think it was a bear, they always tear up and make a mess of things. I kept close to camp these days in case this visitor would come back.

I climbed up on a big rock where I had a good view of the camp, but nothing showed up. I was hoping it would be a porky, so I would get a good porky stew. These visits had now been going on for three nights.

I intended to make a new campsite the following day, but I hated to leave this place. I had fixed it up so nice, and these two cypress trees were bushy. It would have to be a heavy rain before I would get wet, and I had good spring water and that is hard to find.

This night it was cloudy and looked like it might rain. I took special notice of how everything was arranged. I closed my pack sack, I did not undress, I only took off my shoes, put them in the bottom of my sleeping bag. I drove my prospecting pick into one of the cypress trees, so I could reach it from my bed. I also put the rifle alongside me, inside my sleeping bag. I fully intended to stay awake all night to find out who my visitor was, but I must have fallen asleep.

I was awakened by something picking me up. I was half asleep and at first I did not remember where I was. As I began to get my wits together, I remembered I was on this prospecting trip, and in my sleeping bag.

My first thought was—it must be a snow slide, but, there was no snow around my camp. Then it felt like I was tossed on horseback, but I could feel whoever it was, was walking.

I tried to reason out what kind of animal this could be. I tried to get out my sheath knife and cut my way out, but I was in almost a sitting position, and the knife was under me. I could not get hold of it, but the rifle was in front of me. I had a good hold of that, and had no intention of letting go. At times I could feel my pack sack touching me, and could feel the cans in the sack touching my back.

After what seemed like an hour, I could feel we were going up a steep hill. I could feel myself rise for every step. What was carrying me was breathing hard and sometimes gave a slight cough. Now I knew this must be one of the mountain Sasquatch giants the Indians told me about.

I was in a very uncomfortable position— unable to move. I was sitting on my feet, and one of my boots in the bottom of the bag was crossways with the hobnail sole up across my foot. It hurt me terribly, but I could not move.

It was very hot inside. It was lucky for me this fellow's hand was not big enough to close up the whole bag when he picked me up—there was a small opening at the top, otherwise I would have choked to death.

Now he was going downhill. I could feel myself touching the ground at times and at one time he dragged me behind him and I could feel he was below me. Then he seemed to get on level ground and was going at a trot for a long time. By this time, I had cramps in my legs—the pain was terrible. I was wishing he would get to his destination soon. I could not stand this type of transportation much longer.

Now he was going uphill again. It did not hurt me so bad. I tried to estimate the distance and directions. As near as I could guess we were about three hours traveling. I had no idea when he started as I was asleep when he picked me up.

Finally, he stopped and let me down. Then he dropped my pack sack. I could hear the cans rattle. Then I heard chatter— some kind of talk I did not understand. The ground was sloping so when he let go of my sleeping bag, I rolled over head first down hill. I got my head out, and got some air. I tried to straighten my legs and crawl out, but my legs were numb.

It was still dark. I could not see what my captors looked like. I tried to massage my legs to get some life in them, and get my shoes on. I could hear now there were at least four of them. They were standing around me, and continuously chattering. I had never heard of Sasquatch before the Indian told me about them, but I knew I was right among them.

But how to get away from them, that was another question. I got to see the outline of them now, as it began to get lighter, though the sky was cloudy, and it looked like rain, in fact there was a slight sprinkle.

I now had circulation in my legs, but my left foot was very sore on top where it had been resting on my hobnail boots. I got my boots out from the sleeping bag, and pulled them on. I tried to stand up. I was wobbly on my feet but had a good hold of my rifle.

I asked: "What you fellows want with me."

Only some more chatter.

It was getting lighter now, and I could see them quite clearly. I could make out forms of four people. Two big and two little ones. They were all covered with hair and no clothes on at all.

I could now make out mountains all around me. I looked at my watch. It was 4:25 a.m. It was getting lighter now and I could see the people clearly.

They looked like a family, old man, old lady and two young ones, a boy and a girl.

The boy and girl seemed to be scared of me. The old lady did not seem too pleased about what the old man dragged home. But the old man was waving his arms and telling them all he had in mind. They all left me then.

I had my compass and my prospecting glass on strings around my neck. The compass in my left hand shirt pocket and my glass in my right hand pocket. I tried to reason our location, and where I was. I could see now that I was in a small valley or basin about eight or ten acres, surrounded by high sides. There was a V-shaped opening about eight feet wide at the mountains, on the southeast bottom and about 20 feet high at highest point—that must be the way I came in. But how will I get out? The old man was now sitting near this opening.

I moved my belongings up close to the west wall. There were two small cypress trees there, and this would do for a shelter for the time being, until I find out what these people want with me, and how to get away from here. I emptied out my packsack to see what I had in the line of food. All my canned meat and vegetables were intact and I had one can of coffee. Also three small cans of milk— two packages of hard tack and my butter sealer half full of butter. But my prunes and macaroni were missing. Also my full box of shells for my rifle. I only had six shells beside what I had in the magazine of my rifle. I had my sheath knife but my prospecting pick was missing and my can of matches. I only had my safety box full and that held only about a dozen matches. That did not worry me—I can always start a fire with my prospecting glass when the sun is shining, if I got dry wood. I wanted hot coffee but I had no wood, also nothing around here that looked like wood. I had a good look over the valley from where I was—but the boy and the girl were always watching me from behind some juniper bush. I decided there must be some water around here. The ground was leaning towards the opening in the wall. There must be water at the upper end of this valley, there is green grass and moss along the bottom.

All my utensils were left behind. I opened my coffee tin and emptied the coffee in a dishtowel and tied it with the metal strip from the can. I took my rifle and the can and went hunting for water. Right at the head under a cliff there was a lovely spring that disappeared underground. I got a drink and a full can of water. When I got back the young boy was looking over my belongings, but did not touch anything. On my way back, I

noticed where these people were sleeping.
On the east side wall of this valley was a
shelf in the mountain side, with overhanging
rock, looking something like a big undercut
in a big tree about 10 feet deep and 30 feet
wide. The floor was covered with lots of dry
moss, and they had some kind of blankets
woven of narrow strips of cedar bark, packed
with dry moss. They looked very practical
and warm—with no need of washing.

The first day not much happened. I had
to eat my food cold. The young fellow was
coming nearer me, and seemed curious about
me. My one snuff box was empty, so I rolled
it towards him. When he saw it coming, he
sprang up quick as a cat, and grabbed it. He
went over to his sister and showed her. They
found out how to open and close it—they
spent a long time playing with it—then he
trotted over to the old man and showed him.
They had a long chatter.

Next morning, I made up my mind to leave
this place—if I had to shoot my way out. I
could not stay much longer. I had only enough
grub to last me till I got back to Toba Inlet.
I did not know the direction but I would go
down hill and I would come out near civilization some place. I rolled up my sleeping
bag, put that inside my pack sack—packed

the few cans I had—swung the sack on my back, injected a shell in the barrel of my rifle and started for the opening in the wall. The old man got up, held up his hands as though he would push me back.

I pointed to the opening, I wanted to go out. But he stood there pushing towards me—and said something that sounded like Soka, Soka. Again I pointed outside. He only kept pushing with his hands saying Soka, Soka. I backed up to about 60 feet. I did not want to be too close, I thought if I had to shoot my way out. A 30-30 might not have much effect on this fellow, it might make him mad. I only had six shells so I decided to wait. There must be a better way than killing him in order to get out from here. I went back to my campsite to figure out some other way to get out.

If I could make friends with the young fellow or the girl, they might help me. If I only could talk to them. Then I thought of a fellow who saved himself from a mad bull by blinding him with snuff in his eyes. But how will I get near enough to this fellow to put the snuff in his eyes? So I decided next time I give the young fellow my snuff box to leave a few grains of snuff in it. He might give the old man a taste of it.

But the question is, in what direction will I go, if I should get out. I must have been near 25 miles northeast of Toba Inlet when I was kidnapped. This fellow must have traveled at least 25 miles in the three hours he carried me. If he went west we would be near salt water—same thing if he went south— therefore he must have gone northeast. If I then keep going south and over two mountains, I must hit salt water some place between Lund and Vancouver.

The following day I did not see the old lady till about 4:00 p.m. She came home with her arms full of grass and twigs of all kinds from spruce and hemlock as well as some kind of nuts that grow in the ground. I have seen lots of them on Vancouver Island. The young fellow went up the mountain to the east every day, he could climb better than a mountain goat. He picked some kind of grass with long sweet roots. He gave me some one day—they tasted very sweet. I gave him another snuff box with about a teaspoon of snuff in it. He tasted it, then went to the old man—he licked it with his tongue. They had a long chat. I made a dipper from a milk can. I made many dippers—you can use them as pots too—you cut two slits near the top of any can— then cut a limb from any small tree—cut down back of the limb— down the stem of the tree—then taper the part you cut from the stem. Then cut a hole in the tapered part, slide the tapered part in the slit you made in the can, and you have a good handle on your can. I threw one over to the young fellow, who was playing near my camp. He picked it up and looked at it, then he went to the old man and showed it to him. They had a long chatter. Then he came to me, pointed at the dipper then at his sister. I could see that he wanted one for her too. I had other peas and carrots, so I made one for his sister. He was standing only eight feet away from me. When I had made the dipper, I dipped it in water and drank from it, he was very pleased, almost smiled at me. Then I took a chew of snuff, smacked my lips, said that's good.

The young fellow pointed to the old man, said something that sounded like "Ook." I got the idea that the old man liked snuff, and the young fellow wanted a box for the old man. I shook my head. I motioned with my hands for the old man to come to me. I do not think the young fellow understood what I meant. He went to his sister and gave her the dipper I made for her. They did not come near me again that day. I had now been there six days, but I was sure I was making progress. If only I could get the old man to come over to me, get him to eat a full box of snuff that would kill him for sure and I wouldn't be guilty of murder.

The old lady was a meek old thing. The young fellow was by this time quite friendly. The girl would not hurt anybody. Her chest was flat like a boy—no development like young ladies. I am sure if I could get the old man out of the way, I could easily have brought this girl out with me to civilization. But what good would that have been? I would have to keep her in a cage for public display. I don't think we have any right to force our way of life on other people, and I don't think they would like it. (The noise and racket in a modern city they would not like any more than I do.)

The young fellow might have been between 11 and 18 years old about seven feet tall and might weigh about 300 lbs. His chest would be 50-55 inches, his waist about 36-38 inches. He had wide jaws, narrow forehead, that slanted upward round at the back about four or five inches higher than the forehead. The hair on their heads was about six inches long. The hair on the rest of their body was short and thick in places. The women's hair was a bit longer on their heads and the hair on the forehead had an upward turn like some women have—they call it bangs, among women's hair-do's. Nowadays the old lady could have been anything between 40-70 years old. She was over seven feet tall. She would be about 500-600 pounds.

She had very wide hips, and a goose-like walk. She was not built for beauty or speed. Some of those loveable brassieres and uplifts would have been a great improvement on her looks and her figure. The man's eyeteeth were longer than the rest of the teeth, but not long enough to be called tusks. The old man must have been near eight feet tall. Big barrel chest and big hump on his back—powerful shoulders, his biceps and upper arm were enormous and tapered down to his elbows. His forearms were longer than human's, but well proportioned. His hands were wide, the palm was long and broad, and hollow like a scoop. His fingers were short in proportion to the rest of his hand. His fingernails were flat like chisels. The only place they had no hair was inside their hands and the soles of their feet and upper part of the nose and eyelids. I never did see their ears, they were covered with hair hanging over them.

If the old man were to wear a collar it would have to be at least 30 inches. I have no idea what size shoes they would need. I was watching the young fellow's foot one day when he was sitting down. The soles of his feet seemed to be padded like a dog's foot and the big toe was longer than the rest and very strong. In mountain climbing all he needed was footing for his big toe. They were very agile. To sit down they turned their knees out and came straight down. To rise they came straight up without help of their hands and arms. I don't think this valley was their permanent home. I think they move from place to place, as food is available at different localities. They might eat meat but I never saw them eat meat, or do any cooking.

I think this was probably a stopover place and the plants with sweet roots on the mountain side might have been in season this time of the year. They seemed to be most interested in them. The roots have a very sweet and satisfying taste. They always seem to do everything for a reason, wasted no time on anything they did not need. When they were not looking for food, the old man and the old lady were resting, but the boy and girl were always climbing something or jumping. The boy's favorite stunt was to take hold of his feet with his hands and balance on his rump, then bounce forward. The idea seems to be to see how far he could go without his feet or hands touching the ground.

Sometimes he made 20 feet.

But what did they want with me? They must understand I cannot stay here indefinitely. I will soon be out of grub and so far I have seen no deer or other game. I will soon have to make a break for freedom. Not that I was mistreated in any way. One consolation was that the old man was coming closer each day, and was very interested in my snuff. Watching me when I take a pinch of snuff. He seems to think it useless to only put it inside my lips. One morning after I had my breakfast, both the old man and the boy came and sat down only ten feet away from me. This morning I made coffee. I had saved up all dry branches I found and I had some dry moss and I used all the labels from cans to start a fire.

I got my coffee pot boiling and it was strong coffee too, and the aroma from boiling coffee was what brought them over. I was sitting eating hardtack with plenty of butter on, and sipping coffee. And it sure tasted good. I was smacking my lips pretending it was better than it really was. I set the can down that was about half full. I intended to warm it up later. I pulled out a full box of snuff, took a big chew. Before I had time to close the box the old man reached for it. I was afraid he would waste it, as I had only two more boxes. So I held on to the box intending him to take a pinch like I had just done. Instead he grabbed the box and emptied it in his mouth. Swallowed it in one gulp. Then he licked the box inside with his tongue.

After a few minutes his eyes began to roll over in his head, he was looking straight up. I could see he was sick. Then he grabbed my coffee can that was quite cold by this time, he emptied that in his mouth, grounds and all. That did no good. He stuck his head between his legs and rolled forwards a few times away from me. Then he began to squeal like a stuck pig. I grabbed my rifle. I said to myself, "This is it. If he comes for me I will shoot him plumb between his eyes." But he started for the spring; he wanted water. I packed my sleeping bag in my pack sack with the few cans I had left. The young fellow ran over to his mother. Then she began to squeal. I started for the opening in the wall—and I just made it. The old lady was right behind me. I fired one shot at the rock over her head.

I guess she had never seen a rifle fired before. She turned and ran inside the wall.

I injected another shell in the barrel of my rifle and started downhill, looking back over my shoulder every so often to see if they were coming. I was in a canyon, and good travelling and I made fast time. Must have made three miles in some world record time. I came to a turn in the canyon and I had the sun on my left, that meant I was going south, and the canyon turned west. I decided to climb the ridge ahead of me. I knew I must have two mountain ridges between me and salt water and by climbing this ridge I would have a good view of this canyon, so I could see if the Sasquatch were coming after me. I had a light pack and was making good time up this hill. I stopped soon after to look back to where I came from, but nobody followed me. As I came over the ridge I could see Mt. Baker, then I knew I was going in the right direction.

Vancouver, British Columbia, *Province,* May 7, 1957

SASQUATCH MAY LIVE IN CITY PARK

. . . A Sidney woman has written The Province suggesting her sister saw one in 1925, only 100 feet from a small wading pool.

Mrs. Dorothy Bailey writes: "Back in 1925 or 1926 my mother had taken my sister and I to the wonderful playground in Stanley Park.

"We were playing near the edge of the playground by the bushes when she let out a scream and grabbed me to run to mother.

"In her description, she had seen a gorilla-like man standing up, towering over the bushes. It was standing still, watching us play.

"To this day I have often wondered if anyone else may have seen the same thing.

"With so much talk about the Sasquatch lately, it makes me wonder if that could have been a Sasquatch, and if they inhabited Stanley Park years ago when it was much denser forest than it is now."

Vancouver, British Columbia, *Daily Province,* January 16, 1928

"DRIFTWOOD YARNS"

By Leo Bates

Caesar August was fat, black-haired and he waddled, rather than walked, down the rock-strewn beach to give me welcome. The sun was dropping fast, behind the green hills bordering the lakes, and its dying glare flooded the eastern ridges, and painted a blood-red splash on the tapering tower of the Indian church.

"Hello, Caesar, paying a visit?"

This was the busy fishing season, and Caesar's home was a good hundred miles from this sprawling, lake-side village.

"No, sir, no visit—this is my home now—stay all the time."

I remembered the substantial log house and barn, set in a velvet green meadow, beside the tumbling swirl of Lost Child River, and wondered at Caesar's desertion of that abode of plenty.

Squatting on a half-buried log, he sensed my wonderment, and proceeded to haltingly enlighten me.

"That place no good any more—me scare all the time," and he screwed his fat face into a comical expression of despair.

Further questioning elicited more vague replies, but light finally dawned.

"Stick Indians," blurted Caesar, at length, "every night they come my place. Me, my wife, my family, everybody all scare—go away."

Here was opportunity to gather definite information regarding the Indian equivalent to the white man's ghosts. Caesar, sensitive to ridicule, required careful handling, but tact brought results.

"Yessir, every night they come my place—scare my dogs—four dogs I got—every night, run away back into bush an' hide."

"You see Stick Indian, Caesar?"

He laughed uncertainly, and cleared his throat.

"No—no see, but every morning I find tracks—see footmark and place where he sit around in the grass—sure."

"How many come?"

"Oh, I dunno—'bout ten, I guess—sure, maybe ten, twelve, I dunno."

"Do they steal anything? What do they come for?"

"No steal nothing—just scare me that's all. Wanta make me go away, I guess. Lotsa feller see Stick Indian. You ask 'em," and he gestured towards the clustered groups around the village huts.

Suddenly he brightened. "My gal, she see him. You stay here. I fetch her," and he waddled off, shouting loudly.

Sophie was thirteen, intelligent, and shy. She hung her head, giggling, while Caesar vigorously prompted.

"One night," she finally whispered, "I see, before dark. Big tall man, all dressed in black. He hide behind tree when he see me. Black scarf over his face. No, he never speak, just stand behind tree."

This haunted home of Caesar's was surrounded by virgin forest, remote from any other settlement. One of those scattered holdings, handed down from immemorial years and chosen originally for their strategic and hunting and fishing value. No unwanted stranger could lurk around such an isolated place, without being hunted out by the ever-hungry Indian dogs—but the dogs were scared, too, Caesar had said.

Growing braver, Sophie volunteered further. "My little brother, he see too. One night he went out when the dogs bark. He saw a whole lot sitting in the grass, behind the barn. No, they never talk. Just sit—Stick Indians—bad men."

Caesar looked triumphantly vindicated, and I gave it up in despair. Insanity, or imagination run wild? Perhaps if the hallucination had been confined to Caesar. But Sophie was clearly in her right mind, and then there was her little brother too. Sufficient that fear of these unexplainable, "Stick Indians," had driven Caesar and his brood from a natural paradise, to seek shelter in an already overcrowded village.

It comes to mind, reading the last account, that the term "Stick Indians" likely derives from "Seeah-tik Indians."

1928: Byrne (1976) was told the story of Muchalat Harry by a priest, Father Anthony Terhaar, at the Mt. Angel Abbey in Oregon. Father Anthony had been a missionary priest on the west coast of Vancouver Island for many years, and knew Muchalat Harry to be a strong, fearless trapper in that region. Unlike others in his tribe, Harry would travel alone into the forests of inland Vancouver Island. In the Autumn of 1928, he canoed to the head of the Conuma river, hiked upstream about twelve miles, then set up camp. One night, while wrapped up in his blankets, Harry was picked up and carried a few miles into the hills. He found himself surrounded by a group of perhaps twenty hairy creatures. They regarded him mostly with curiosity, though Harry, noticing large bones in their camp, thought they might be planning to eat him. Later that day, as their interest waned and many of them left the camp, Harry took off running all the way back to his cached canoe, not bothering to pick up his gun or supplies at his campsite along the way. He paddled all through the night, before being found by Father Anthony and the other Benedictine monks. It took three weeks to nurse Harry back to health and sanity. Muchalat Harry never went trapping again.

1928: Bord & Bord (2006) noted a report collected by John Green, where a trapper, George Talleo, shot at a Sasquatch and fled. This happened along the South Bentinck Arm, near Bella Coola.

Vancouver, British Columbia, *Province,* June 3, 1928

AND THE PARTY RETURNED WITHOUT FINDING RACE OF HAIRY GIANTS ON VANCOUVER ISLAND, BY B. A. MCKELVIE

In an effort to sort out from the contradictions and mysteries that surround this [Sasquatch]—the strangest story in the Western world—the basis on which the belief was founded, a small expedition was recently organized in Vancouver under the direction of Jason Ovid Allard, 80-year-old adventurer, historian, and [—] of the native lore of British Columbia. Himself a lineal descendent through his mother, of the [—] of T'shoshia, and thus entitled to [—] and homage due to one [—] veins courses the blood of [—] rulers of ancient days, he is qualified, above all others, for such an undertaking. But after weeks of work, and after a mass of information was obtained—the story is still one of mystery. . . .

Jorg Totsgi, an educated Indian, writing on the subject, describes the Seah-tiks:

"Oregon and Washington Indians," he says, "agree that the Seeah-tik Indians are not less than seven feet tall and some have been seen that were fully eight feet in height. They have hairy bodies like a bear. This is to protect them from the cold, as they live entirely in the mountains. They kill their game by hypnotism. They have great supernatural powers. They also have the gift of ventriloquism, and have deceived many ordinary Indians by throwing their voices.

"Oregon and Washington Indians differ in regard to the Seeah-tiks' home. The Oregon Indians assert they make their home in or near Mount Tacoma, while the Puget Sound Indians say they live in the heart of the wilderness of Vancouver Island, B.C."

Mr. Allard, likening his search to that of the first Jason who sought the Golden Fleece, carried his investigations across the border, and there he heard the strange story of Henry Napoleon of the Clallam tribe, who claimed to have come into actual contact with the Seeah-tiks on Vancouver Island:

"I had been visiting relatives near Duncan, B.C.," said Napoleon, "and while there I had been told many stories of the Seeah-tiks by the Cowichan tribe of British Columbia, and was warned by them not to go [far out] into the wilderness. However, while following a buck I had wounded, I went in farther than I expected. It was almost twilight when I came across an animal that I believed to be a big bear, but as [—] at it with my gun, the creature looked up and spoke to me in my own tongue. It was a man about seven feet tall, and his body was very hairy. As he invited me to sit down, he told me that I had come upon him unawares, and that his mind was projected to distant relatives, otherwise I would not have seen him.

"The giant Indian then invited me to meet the tribe. We followed a trail and just at twilight we entered an underground trail. Finally this led us to the home of the See-ah-tik tribe. They treated me with every courtesy while in their home.

"'During the winter,' the Seeah-tik said, 'we sleep like the bear, then when the spring comes we make our regular trip along the Sgv-eeay-nut (or mountain ranges) and come out by Tacobut (Mount Tacoma). Then we go to the Squay-ch (Mt. St. Helens), and sometimes we go down the mountains and return around by the Olympics and back home again.' . . .

"The next night I was escorted back to the village where I was staying with my relatives."

Another Washington Indian who is willing to give his views on the subject of Seeah-tiks, Mr. Allard found, was Peter J. James, a man who is highly respected among the Northwestern natives and has acted as their

representative in conferences with the officials of the United States. He is of the Lum-
mi tribe, and recalls hearing of the fight between the Duwamish tribe and the Seeah-tiks
from his mother who, it is said, witnessed
the struggle. According to the story the Seeah-tiks, who were also referred to as "the Indians of the night," formerly raided the coast
tribes, stealing women and children. The Duwamish warriors retaliated and killed some
Seeah-tiks. Then down from the mountains
came the giants and seized young men and
with their bare hands tore them asunder. . . .

Again, there is a story current about Comox that the Puntledge tribe, once a powerful band, but now numbering so few that
they have been merged with the Comox by
the Indian department, were practically
wiped out, only one or two families escaping,
about seventy-five years ago, by the invasion
in the night of a war party of strange, unknown natives who swarmed down from the
mountain heights of what is now known as
Forbidden Plateau, a few miles from Courte-
nay. Today Coast Indians can not be induced
to venture to this scenic wonderland where,
beneath towering peaks, luxuriant grasses
and beautiful wild flowers grow beside cool
lakes that swarm with trout. . . .

[Allard went on to Duncan and several other Vancouver Island locations to track down the basis for the story Harry Napoleon told, but was unable to locate anyone would could tell him about hairy giants.]

Burns (1929) collected several stories from the Chehalis Reserve:

Peter Williams lives on the Chehalis Reserve. I believe that he is a reliable as well as an intelligent Indian. He gave me the following thrilling account of his experience with these people.

"One evening in the month of May twenty years ago," he said, "I was walking along the foot of the mountain about a mile from the Chehalis reserve. I thought I heard a noise something like a grunt nearby. Looking in the direction in which it came, I was startled to see what I took at first sight to be a huge bear crouched upon a boulder twenty or thirty feet away. I raised my rifle to shoot it, but, as I did, the creature stood up and let out a piercing yell. It was a man—a giant, no less than six and one-half feet in height, and covered with hair. He was in a rage and jumped from the boulder to the ground. I fled, but not before I felt his breath upon my cheek.

"I never ran so fast before or since— through brush and undergrowth toward the Statloo, or Chehalis River, where my dugout was moored. From time to time, I looked back over my shoulder. The giant was fast overtaking me—a hundred feet separated us; another look and the distance measured less than fifty—then the Chehalis and in a moment the dugout shot across the stream to the opposite bank. The swift river, however, did not in the least daunt the giant, for he began to wade into it immediately.

"I arrived home almost worn out from running and I felt sick. Talking an anxious look around the house, I was relieved to find the wife and children inside. I bolted the door and barricaded it with everything at hand. Then with my rifle ready, I stood near the door and awaited his coming."

Peter added that if he had not been so much excited he could easily have shot the giant when he began to wade the river.

"After an anxious waiting of twenty minutes," resumed the Indian, "I heard a noise approaching like the trampling of a horse. I looked through a crack in the old wall. It was the giant. Darkness had not yet set in and I had a good look at him. Except that he was covered with hair and twice the bulk of the average man, there was nothing to distinguish him from the rest of us. He pushed against the wall of the old house with such force that it shook back and forth. The old cedar shook and timbers creaked and groaned so much under the strain that I was afraid it would fall down and kill us. I whispered to the old woman to take the children under the bed."

Peter pointed out what remained of the old house in which he lived at the time, explaining that the giant treated it so roughly that it had to be abandoned the following winter.

"After prowling and grunting like an animal around the house," continued Peter, "he went away. We were glad, for the children and the wife were uncomfortable under the old bedstead. Next morning I found his tracks in the mud around the house, the biggest of either man or beast I had ever seen. The tracks measured twenty-two inches in length, but narrow in proportion to their length.

The following winter while shooting wild duck on that part of the reserve Indians call the "prairie," which is on the north side of the Harrison River and about two miles from the Chehalis village, Peter once more came face to face with the same hairy giant. The

Indian ran for dear life, followed by the wild man, but after pursuing him for three or four hundred yards the giant gave up the chase.

. . .

On the afternoon of the same day another Indian by the name of Paul was chased from the creek, where he was fishing for salmon, by the same individual. Paul was in a state of terror, for unlike Peter he had no gun. A short distance from his shack the giant suddenly quit and walked into the bush. Paul, exhausted from running, fell in the snow and had to be carried home by his mother and others of the family.

"The first and second time," went on Peter, "I was all alone when I met this strange, mountain creature. Then, early in the spring of the following year, another man and myself were bear hunting near the place where I first met him. On this occasion we ran into two of these giants. They were sitting on the ground. At first we thought they were old tree stumps, but when we were within fifty feet or so, they suddenly stood up and we came to an immediate stop. Both were nude. We were close enough to know that they were man and woman. The woman was the smaller of the two, but neither of them as big or fierce-looking as the gent that chased me. We ran home, but they did not follow us.

One morning some weeks after this, Peter and his wife were fishing in a canoe on the Harrison River, near Harrison Bay. Paddling round a neck of land they saw, on the beach within a hundred feet of them, the giant Peter had met the previous year.

"We stood for a long time looking at him," said the Indian, "but he took no notice of us—that was the last time," concluded Peter, "I saw him."

Peter remarked that his father and numbers of old Indians knew that wild men lived in caves in the mountains—had often seen them. He wished to make it clear that these creatures were in no wise related to the Indian. He believes there are a few of them living at present in the mountains near Agassiz.

Charley Victor belongs to the Skwah Reserve near Chilliwack. In his younger days he was known as one of the best hunters in the province and had many thrilling adventures in his time. . . .

"The strange people, of whom there are but few now—rarely seen and seldom met—" said the old hunter, "are known by the name of Sasquatch, or, 'the hairy mountain men'.

"The first time I came to know about these people," continued the old man, "I did not see anybody. Three young men and myself were picking salmonberries on a rocky mountain slope some five or six miles from the old town of Yale. In our search for berries we suddenly stumbled upon a large opening in the side of the mountain. This discovery greatly surprised all of us, for we knew every foot of the mountain, and never knew nor heard there was a cave in the vicinity.

"Outside the mouth of the cave there was an enormous boulder. We peered into the cavity but couldn't see anything.

"We gathered some pitchwood, lighted it and began to explore. But before we got very far from the entrance of the cave, we came upon a sort of stone house or enclosure; it was a crude affair. We couldn't make a thorough examination, for our pitchwood kept going out. We left, intending to return in a couple of days and go on exploring. Old Indians, to whom we told the story of our discovery, warned us not to venture near the cave again, as it was surely occupied by the Sasquatch. That was the first time I heard about the hairy men that inhabit the mountains. We, however, disregarded the advice of the old men and sneaked off to explore the cave, but to our disappointment found that boulder rolled back into its mouth and fitting it so nicely that you might suppose it had been made for that purpose."

Charley intimated that he hoped to have enough money some day to buy sufficient dynamite to blow open the cave of the Sasquatch, and see how far it extends through the mountain.

The Indian then took up the thread of his story and told of his first meeting with one of these men. A number of other Indians and himself were bathing in a small lake near Yale. He was dressing, when suddenly out from behind a rock, only a few feet away, stepped a nude hairy man. "Oh! He was a big, big man! . . . He looked at me for a moment, his eyes were so kind-looking that I was about to speak to him, when he turned about and walked into the forest."

At the same place two weeks later, Charley, together with several of his companions saw the giant, but this time he ran toward the mountain. This was twenty years after the discovery of the cave. . . .

"I was hunting in the mountains near Hatzie," he resumed. "I had my dog with me. I came out on a plateau where there were several big cedar trees. The dog stood before one of the trees and began to growl and bark at it. On looking up to see what excited him, I noticed a large hole in the trunk seven feet from the ground. The dog pawed and leaped upon the trunk, and looked at me to raise him up, which I did, and he went into the hole. The next moment a muffled cry came from the hole. I said to myself: 'The dog is tearing into a bear,' and with my rifle ready, I urged the dog to drive him out, and out came something I took for a bear. I shoot and it fell with a thud to the ground. 'Murder! O my!' I spoke to myself in surprise and alarm, for the thing I had shot looked to me like a white boy. He was nude. He was about twelve or fourteen years of age."

In his description of the boy, Charley said that his hair was black and woolly.

Wounded and bleeding, the poor fellow sprawled upon the ground, but when I drew close to examine the extent of his injury, he let out a wild yell, or rather a call as if he were appealing for help. From across the mountain a long way off rolled a booming voice. Near and more near came the voice and every now and again the boy would return an answer as if directing the owner of the voice. Less than a half-hour, out from the depths of the forest came the strangest and wildest creature one could possibly see.

"I raised my rifle, not to shoot, but in case I would have to defend myself. The hairy creature, for that was what it was, walked toward me without the slightest fear. The wild person was a woman. Her face was almost negro black and her long straight hair fell to her waist. In height she would be about six feet, but her chest and shoulders were well above the average in breadth.

Charley remarked that he had met several wild people in his time, but had never seen anyone half so savage in appearance as this woman. The old brave confessed he was really afraid of her.

"In my time," said the old man, "and this is no boast, I have in more than one emergency strangled bear with my hands, but I'm sure if that wild woman laid hands on me, she'd break every bone in my body.

"She cast a hasty glance at the boy. Her face took on a demoniacal expression when she saw he was bleeding. She turned upon me savagely, and in the Douglas tongue said:

"'You have shot my friend.'

"I explained in the same language—for I'm part Douglas myself—that I had mistaken the boy for a bear and that I was sorry. She did not reply, but began a sort of wild frisk or dance around the boy, chanting in a loud voice for a minute or two, and, as if in answer to her, from the distant woods came the same sort of chanting troll. In her hand she carried something like a snake, about six feet in length, but thinking over the matter since, I believe it was the intestine of some animal. But whatever it was, she constantly struck the ground with it. She picked up the boy with one hairy hand, with as much ease as if he had been a wax doll." . . .

"She pointed the snake-like thing at me and said:

"'Siwash, you'll never kill another bear.'"

The old hunter's eyes moistened when he admitted that he had not shot a bear or anything else since that fatal day.

"Her words, expression, and the savage avenging glint in her dark, fiery eyes filled me with fear," confessed the Indian, "and I felt so exhausted from her unwavering gaze that I was no longer able to keep her covered with my rifle. I let it drop."

Charley has been paralyzed for the last eight years, and he is inclined to think that the words of the wild woman had something to do with it. . . .

The old man said that she spoke the words "Yahoo, yahoo" frequently in a loud voice, and always received a similar reply from the mountain.

The old hunter felt sure that the woman looked somewhat like the wild man he had seen at Yale many years before, although the woman was the darker of the two. He did not think the boy belonged to the Sasquatch people, "because he was white and she called him her friend," reasoned Charley. "They must have stolen him or run across him in some other way," he added.

"Indians," said Charley, "have always known that wild men lived in the distant mountains, within sixty or one hundred miles east of Vancouver, and of course they may live in other places throughout the province, but I have never heard of it. It is my own opinion since I met that wild woman fifteen years ago that because she spoke the Douglas tongue these creatures must be related to the Indian."

At Agassiz near the close of September, 1927, Indian hop-pickers were having their annual picnic. A few of the younger people volunteered to pick a mess of berries on a wooded hillside, a short way from the picnic grounds. They had only started to pick, when out of the bush stepped a naked hairy giant. He was first noticed by a girl of the party, who was so badly frightened that she fell unconscious to the ground. The girl's sudden collapse was seen by an Indian named Point, of Vancouver, and as he ran to her assistance, was astonished to see a giant a few feet away, who continued to walk with an easy gait across the wooded slope in the direction of the Canadian Pacific railway tracks.

Since the following paragraph was written, Mr. Point, replying to an enquiry, has kindly forwarded the following letter to the writer, in which he tells of his experience with the hairy giant:

"Dear Sir: I have your letter asking is it true or not that I saw a hairy giant—man— at Agassiz last September, while picking hops there. It is true and the facts are as follows: This happened at the close of September (1927) when we were having a feast. Adaline August and myself walked to her father's orchard, which is about four miles from the hop fields. We were walking on the railroad track and within a short distance of the orchard, when the girl noticed something walking along the track coming toward us. I looked up but paid no attention to it, as I thought it was some person on his way to Agassiz. But as he came closer we noticed that his appearance was very odd, and on coming still closer we stood still and were astonished—seeing that the creature was naked and covered with hair like an animal.

We were almost paralyzed with fear. I picked up two stones with which I intended to hit him if he attempted to molest us, but within fifty feet or so he stood up and looked at us.

"He was twice as big as the average man, with hands so long that they almost touched the ground. It seemed to me that his eyes were very large and the lower part of his nose was wide and spread over the greater part of his face, which gave the creature such a frightful appearance that I ran away as fast as I could. After a minute or two I looked back and saw that he resumed his journey. The girl had fled before I left, and she ran so fast that I did not overtake her until I was close to Agassiz, where we told the story of our adventure to the Indians who were still enjoying themselves. Old Indians who were present said: the wild man was no doubt a 'Sasquatch,' a tribe of hairy people whom they claim have always lived in the mountains—in tunnels and caves."

1930s: Green (1978) collected a report from a retired insurance broker who claimed that he and another man had seen a creature with "a human face on a fur-clad body" while on a weekend trip to Pitt Lake.

Oshkosh, Wisconsin, *Northwestern*, March 3, 1934

TERRIBLE SASQUATCH
ABROAD IN THE LAND

Harrison Mills, B. C.—(AP)—Indian children clung to their mothers' apron strings today for the terrible sasquatch—a giant hairy and horrid—is on the prowl again.

For hundreds of years the sasquatch has been a fearsome "bogeyman" to the northwest Indians. It may be male or female, but it always is hairy and malicious.

None had been reported for 30 years, but horror swept the lodges of the primitive Chehalis tribe today, as word was whispered that the hairy wild one had returned.

Frank Dan was first to report sighting the monster. He went out into the night to see why his cur-dog was barking so furiously and he came face to face with a hairy giant, tall, muscular and nude.

"He was covered with black hair from head to foot, except around the eyes," Dan said.

The sasquatch and scores of other demons are very real to the Chehalis. They are things of horror, dwelling in caves, on the borders of lakes and in mountain fastnesses, emerging to "snatch" an Indian into the unknown and to devour babies.

Brainerd, Minnesota, *Daily Dispatch,* March 5, 1934

GIANT WILD MAN ROAMS VANCOUVER

Montreal—A giant wild man who has been terrorizing residents of Harrison Mills, near Vancouver, has caused revival of legends of a vanished race of "hairy mountain men," according to dispatches here today.

The wild man, described as "huge, hairy and nearly nude," has been seen three times in as many months according to the reports. The last person he frightened was Frank [Dan] of Harrison Mills.

[Dan] was aroused during the night by barking of his dog. He stepped out of the door of his cabin and saw, in clear starlight, a huge hairy man who advanced at him growling. [Dan] leaped back inside his cabin and barred his door. Tracks in the snow next day showed the wild man had prowled around the cabin and later gone into the bush.

Detroit, Michigan, *Times,* May 13, 1934

TOWN SHUDDERS AS
APE-MAN SCARE IS REVIVED

The weird reports of the mysterious, long-haired ape-men that have been said to live in caves of the Rocky Mountains in Western Canada were interestingly revived recently. The newest reported appearance comes from a little settlement in British Columbia about sixty miles east of Vancouver. Three times lately it is claimed that residents of Harrison Mills have seen one of the hairy ape-men from the neighboring wilderness.

The latest definite statement came from Frank Dan, a mill worker, who describes the visitor as a huge, hairy, naked, wild man, a giant in size and ferocious in appearance. When Mr. Dan saw him the creature was prowling on all-fours near his home. Since his reported experience all the homes in the little Canadian mill town have been locked and barred at night and children have been closely guarded.

Aroused late one night by the continual barking of his dog, Dan went out into the back yard to investigate. It was a bright moonlight night and as he stepped outside the gate Dan says he clearly saw the wild man, crouching near the fence. It stood erect as he approached it and when Dan saw the giant size of the creature and heard it snarling he dashed back into the house to get a rifle. When he came out again the wild man had disappeared.

For a number of years British Columbia residents have caught occasional glimpses of wild men who are believed by Indians of the Chahalis tribe to be the survivors of a ferocious, animal-like race which lived in the mountains. These wild men are frequently mentioned in Indian tribal lore and are referred to as "Sasquatch" or "the hairy mountain men." They live, according to the Indians, in caves and caverns on the borders of Rocky Mountain lakes and are savage when cornered and fight like animals. Some of them, the Indians say, have long animal fangs instead of eye-teeth and use these fangs to deadly advantage when fighting animals or humans. They live like animals, eating raw flesh and vegetable roots and seldom approach the centres of civilization. They have always been greatly feared by the Indians.

Just a few weeks prior to Dan's encounter with the wild man a British Columbia hunter startled Harrison Mills residents with a story of how he had met a hairy, ape-like creature in the woods while he was returning from a day's duck shooting.

"I was carrying a bag of ducks when I met this man-monkey," the hunter said. "It was so close to me I did not have a chance to use my gun or make a run for it. The monster snatched the ducks away from me and darted into the woods and though I searched for it for some time afterwards I am unable to find any trace of it. It was like a hairy man, was completely nude and was much taller than any man I have ever seen. I was so frightened I suppose I wasn't very observant and didn't notice many details about it. It didn't speak or make any sound, just grabbed the ducks and dashed into the woods."

A few days after Dan related the story of his encounter with the wild man, a report came from an Indian fisherman, who said that while he was fishing on the Harrison River, not far from the mill town, he was attacked by one of the wild men. The Indian was gliding along in his canoe, when, without warning, he said, a rock was thrown from the top of the cliff, plunging into the water within a foot of the canoe. The boat was almost swamped.

The startled Indian glanced upwards and asserts that he saw a huge, hairy man bounding down the side of the cliff, like some wild animal, and carrying under his arm another huge rock. As the Indian struggled to swing his canoe out into mid-stream, the wild man paused and hurled the second rock at him, missing the canoe by inches. On missing the boat a second time, the monster "swung his arms wildly and rand down to the edge of the river, snarling and half-shouting, half-screaming," the frightened Indian reported. The Indian paddled away as quickly as he could and returned to the reservation to tell his terrifying tale.

Although perhaps a dozen of the wild men have been reported to have been seen during the past twenty years in British Columbia only one of them has ever been kept "in captivity." Known as Kill-Ith-Ka, this ape-man was supposed to have been discovered as an infant in the mountains and was brought up by an Indian couple on the Chahalis Reserve as their own child. It developed all the characteristics of the dreaded mountain men and was much feared by the other Indians although its foster parents continued to care for it until they died.

For many years Kill-Ith-Ka occupied a kennel on the reserve, living with the dogs owned by the Indians. It never learned to walk on two legs, but spent its entire life on all-fours, eating its meals out of a dish placed on the ground. Kill-Ith-Ka also developed two long fangs instead of eye-teeth and used them as weapons when threatened by dogs or teased by Indian children.

The general opinion in the neighborhood was that the monster was the child of Indian parents born during the time when the Indian villagers were terrified by a series of attacks by ravenous mountain wolves and that the mother's fright during the prenatal period had "marked" the child as half-man, half-animal. But this old-fashioned idea that the fright of a mother can "mark" the unborn child had long since been exploded by science. Scientists who visited the creature concluded that it was the child of an Indian mother, and one of the long list of strange human monsters which history has recorded. The infant might have been deserted by its parents and picked up by members of another tribe or the family that took care of the creature might have been its own parents. The skull of the unfortunate is now in the Vancouver Museum.

Some of the older Indians say they can recall the days when the hairy mountain men were seen fairly frequently and when every Indian encampment kept watch for attacks by these ferocious, prowling creatures. In the records of early, British Columbia settlers, too, there are numerous references to strange wild creatures that lived in the mountain caves and ate the flesh of other animals.

The mention of a 'wolf-man' in this last account leads us to a rather unfortunate story. The individual's name was actually Kilm-ith-ka, and first received notice in 1922 (e.g. McHenry, Illinois, *Plaindealer,* September 14, 1922, "Discover a Freak Wolf-Man"): "A strange wolf-man has been discovered living with the Hesqualt [Hesquiaht] Indians on the west coast of Vancouver island, B.C., Canada. . . . The wolf-man is called Kilm-ith-ka, which means wolf-man in the Indian tongue. He is a wolf in all except form and is said to be about seventy years old. He resembles an old man walking on his hands and feet; he has never walked after the human fashion. He cannot make any human sound, but growls like a wolf. He eats like one and where human beings have eye teeth he has canine fangs. When the wolf-man sits erect he is four feet and a half-inch tall. He subsists on raw or cooked meat and lives in a kennel in the rear of the house of a keeper appointed by the tribe. The keeper feeds him and keeps clothes on him as much as possible, and except for occasional disrobings, Kilm-ith-ka is fairly tractable and accepts semidomestication which is about his only human trait." A. W. (1934) wrote that Kilm-ith-ka was born within the community, but as a child, "Kilm-ith-ka ran about on all fours as agile as a puppy. He had no desire for the human companionship of other children. He ate like a wolf

and growled menacingly over his food. He never
articulated a human word and never attempted to
stand erect. . . . Kilm-ith-ka outlived many of his
generation and several keepers—for only recently, about two years ago at the reputed age of 100
years, did nature call the wolfman back to the vale
of mystery."

KILM-ITH-KA, "THE WOLF MAN."

Vancouver, British Columbia, *Province*, March 23, 1934
HAIRY GIANTS ARE AT IT AGAIN
By J. W. Burns
Harrison Mills, March 23.—Narrowly escaping death when two huge rocks were hurled
by a giant Sasquatch at his canoe in which

he was fishing was the experience of a Harrison River Indian a few days ago.

The Indian was fishing for trout at Morris Creek, a tributary of the Harrison. The canoe was gliding along the sluggish mountain stream close to the rocky, terraced bank, when without warning a rock was thrown from the shelving slope above, falling with a splash within a foot of the canoe, almost swamping it and drenching the unsuspecting occupant, who was busy with his fishing tackle. The fisherman, hurriedly looking round, beheld with fear a hairy creature bounding down a steep declivity with the agility of a cat and carrying under his arm a bulky object which proved to be another big rock. This the wild man deliberately hurled with terrific force at the canoe, missing the frail craft by inches.

Believing that the monster, who was swinging his arms in the wildest manner, was about to leap into the water and attack the canoe, the frightened fisherman let his lines go and paddled out of the danger zone.

. . .

The Sasquatch may be reduced in numbers, but there is abundant evidence that they are not extinct and that they are not merely a superstition or an exaggeration. When an intelligent young woman such as Emma Paul of the Chehalis declares that she saw one of them by the house one evening last summer, it would be an injustice to suspect her of romanticism.

"I saw the Sasquatch," said Emma, "a few yards from the house. I was standing by the door at the time. He was watching me closely and I had a good look at his face. He was big and powerful in appearance. Other members of the family were present who also saw him. We bolted the door and he prowled about the house for some time. We have often heard one of them at night since then and one used to rub his fingers over the window panes. It was only last night that a Sasquatch was outside trampling loudly about the house. We all heard it and so did the white carpenter who lives next door. The one I saw was not so ugly as the one seen by Frank Dan last week."

Tradition has it that the Sasquatch return to the sites occupied by their ancestors for a few days once every score or so years, and that prior to their coming these elusive mountain folk send out scouts over the land, preparing a suitable rendezvous for the men, women and children of the scattered bands.

For scores of years back Chehalis Indians have accurately noted the recurrence every

fourth year of a light for three or four consecutive nights on one of the highest peaks of
the Chehalis range about the middle of July.
The phenomena has been associated with the
Sasquatch, who by this method of communication keep in touch with one another across
the mountain ranges, according to the Indians.

The light as described by an eyewitness
who saw it on two occasions, was of a reddish
tint and rose to a great height. The flame
was sometimes suddenly extinguished to rise
again straight and in spirals.

Brainerd, Minnesota, *Daily Dispatch,* July 10, 1934

HAIRY TRIBE OF
WILD MEN IN VANCOUVER

Vancouver, B. C.—Reports that survivors of
the tribe of wild men known as "Sasquatch,"
a race of ferocious hairy giants, who dwelt
in caves in British Columbia years ago, still
are roaming the rocky wilds near Vancouver,
have been revived here.

The tribe was believed to have become extinct 30 years ago, but during the last year it
frequently has been reported that survivors
have been seen prowling near scattered settlements around Vancouver. The wild men
are described as "hairy giants, nine feet tall,
with a ferocious appearance and demeanor."

Seen by Woman

Mrs. James Caufield, living on a farm near Harrison, B. C., is the latest to report seeing one of the giants.

Mrs. Caufield relates that she was washing clothes in a river when she heard a buzzing sound similar to that made by a humming bird.

"I turned my head," she said, "but instead of a bird there stood the most terrible thing I ever saw in my life. I thought I'd die for the thing that made the funny noise was a big man covered with hair from head to foot. He was looking at me and i couldn't help looking at him. I guessed he was a Sasquatch so I covered my eyes with my hand, for the Indian says that if a Sasquatch catches your eye you are in his power. They hypnotize you. I felt faint and as I backed away to get to the house I tripped and fell. As he came nearer I screamed and fainted."

Screams Brought Husband

Mrs. Caufield's screams brought her husband running out of the house just in time to see the giant run off into the bush. On another occasion two canoeists reported that the giant saw them paddling down a river and started hurling rocks at them.

Lincoln, Nebraska, *Star,* July 29, 1934

ARE THEY THE LAST CAVE MEN?

BRITISH COLUMBIA STARTLED BY THE
APPEARANCE OF "SASQUATCH,"
A STRANGE RACE OF HAIRY GIANTS

By Francis Dickie

It is peculiarly in keeping with this topsy-turvy year of violently varying weather, universal human unrest, droughts, grasshopper plagues and other phenomena that there now comes from various eyewitnesses the report of seeing some of the "Sasquatch," those weird hairy men reported for twenty years to dwell in the tremendous and unexplored mountain region of British Columbia Canada.

Their reported return is particularly in keeping with this unusual year, so remarkable for the number of appearances of various startling monsters sighted from Scotland to the Caribbean, from the Pacific to the Mediterranean, the reality of which is affirmed by scores of eyewitnesses. Moreover, the statements of some of these people, in so far as curious denizens of the ocean are concerned, have been borne out, for within a short time of each other, at a dozen places on the European coast, the remains of incredible monsters of the deep have been cast up.

Of all these mysterious earthly visitants, perhaps the "Sasquatch" is the least known, by reason of the rarity of their appearance and the reluctance of those who have seen them to talk.

The existence of a troglodyte race inhabiting the mountains of British Columbia in many of the vast caves is a tribal legend among the Chehalis Indians of those of the Skwah Reservation, near Chilliwack, in the Harrison Lake district, about a hundred miles east of Vancouver. Among the Indians the race has been known for centuries by the name "Sasquatch," or hairy men.

But reports of these creatures being seen frequently at various times over a period of the last twenty years, and more frequently in recent weeks, have caused a number of people to raise the question if these strange creatures may not be more than an Indian legend of the past, and that some of this race of cavern dwellers are still living in the unexplored fastnesses of British Columbia.

The Sasquatch have been seen, according to the statements from both white men and Indians. The wild, hairy men have mostly been reported in the Harrison Lake district, but also as far east as the mountainous region of Yale, on the main line of the Canadian Pacific Railway.

The repeated reports of eyewitnesses of seeing one or more of the huge hairy men in recent years, and more particularly in the last month, and the mounting number of the reports of eyewitnesses now seem to point strongly that the old tribal legends, long contemptuously flouted by the white man, is true, and that at least a few of this mysterious race may still inhabit the solitudes nearby where once they were numerous. The possibility of this is further borne out when it is recalled that the remains of a giant race of men recently have been unearthed in the mountainous region of Mexico.

The chief difficulty, in fact the whole task of an investigator, in matters of such phenomena as Sasquatch or sea serpents, is, of course, the credibility of the witnesses. If untruthful, what motive lies behind their story? In the case of the Sasquatch, the element of credence is heightened because in most cases the witnesses have been reluctant ones, some of them not revealing their stories for years.

From a careful comparison of all eye-witness statements to date, all are closely in agreement as to the following facts: The Sasquatch are gigantic men, varying from six and one-half to seven feet in height. One, and only one, witness states the nose of them to be very broad, and the arms long, reaching below the knee. All but one are agreed as to the hideousness of the face.

However, as in most instances the Sasquatch were not seen close up, it is natural the descriptions remain very general. Those people who have been close were so terror-stricken that their accounts are vague. Yet, aside from one of the most recent happenings, in only two other cases have the Sasquatch shown themselves hostile.

The fact that some of these strange people have just been reported close to civilization at this time accurately compares with dates noted by the Chehalis Indians. The Indians have oral records covering three generations. According to these, members of the tribe have seen in the Springtime every fourth year the light of a great fire on one of the highest peaks in the Chehalis Range. The fire burns for four nights, rising in a very high, thin column. Sometimes it is suddenly extinguished, to rise again a little later. That this is some periodic mark of a return to a certain place of worship at some ancient shrine, or a communication with members in some remote mountain fastness, are possible conjectures.

These periodic returns to some ancient gathering place do bring these people close to what are now civilized areas.

A few days ago, a middle-aged Indian, Tom Cedar, was trout fishing from his canoe on Morris Creek, a tributary of the Harrison. He was near a rocky terraced bank. Suddenly a large rock struck the water so close to his canoe that he was drenched by the splash. Looking up, he saw with amazement a huge hairy man above him just as he threw another rock. This also barely missed the canoe. Cedar paddled rapidly upstream to the settlement.

By way of noting an odd coincidence, this particular stream, now called Morris Creek, was known as Saskakau when the white man first arrived, and is so called on old maps. Nearby are caverns which were investigated by Captain Warde, forty years a resident in the district. He states they bear evidence of habitation. Upon the walls are some crude drawings. In this region, according to the Indians, two large bands of Sasquatch fought a long time ago until both were brought almost to extermination.

The other evidence of hostile intention of some of these creatures dates back twenty years and consists of the statements of two Indians, Peter and Paul Williams of Chehalis. The following is a very much condensed resume:

"On an evening in May," states Peter, "I was about a mile from the reserve, near the foot of the mountain, when what I first took to be a bear rose up in the underbrush. It was a man between six and seven feet tall, covered with hair. I turned and ran through the underbrush to my dugout. The hairy man came after me. I paddled across the stream, which is not very deep, and the man waded after. I reached the house where my wife and child were inside. I bolted the door. Presently the hairy man arrived. It was growing dark. He prowled around, grunting and growling, but after a little while went away."

About the same time Paul was chased from a creek where he was fishing. But the giant did not run after him very far, and apparently the action was only to drive the man away to get the fish he had taken. On another occasion in the next year, Peter and another man came upon two giants so close as to distinguish a man and a woman. Though the Indians ran, they were not pursued.

Charley Victor, now living at Chilliwack, relates that he and a little group of companions, while bathing in a mountain lake [near] Yale, suddenly looked up to see a huge man, naked and hairy, looking down upon them from among the trees.

"His big eyes looked very kind, and I was about to speak to him when he drew back into the trees," related Charley.

Here we have the only witness who gives a favorable reaction to sight of the mysterious race.

This took place many years ago and at a point about a hundred miles from where the majority of the Sasquatch have been reported seen in recent times.

The next account of which any fully recorded evidence is now to be seen deals with September, 1927, near the little mountain town of Agassiz, which is very near the points at which all the other Sasquatch have been reported. A party of hop-pickers were picknicking here. On their way to this a man, named Herbert Point, and a girl, Adaline August, were walking when they saw a strange creature approaching. "He was twice as big as the average man, with hands so long they nearly touched the ground, and his nose seemed spread all over his face. His body was covered with hair like an animal. He stopped within fifty feet of us. We ran away as fast as we could." The lines in quotes are excerpts from a letter written by the man in answer to a query of what he had seen.

Within recent weeks Emma Paul and Millie Saul, two other members of the Chehalis Reserve, saw one of the Sasquatch near their home on the fringe of the woods. Several nights later he was heard prowling around the home of Millie Saul, and once rubbed his hand over the window pane.

To date, the last report was from Harrison Mills, a small hamlet on the Harrison River.

The woman, on hearing a humming noise, looked up to see a big man covered with hair on the edge of the clearing. She was frightened. Taking a backward step, she fell into one of the half-full laundry tubs at which she had been working. When she had extricated herself and looked again, the man had disappeared.

Such, in brief, are the legendary and eyewitness stories regarding the Sasquatch.

The scientific board connected with the Museum of Vancouver is skeptical regarding the existence of any such remnant of a race that once might have roamed the forested regions.

An objection that the climate is too rigorous for a naked race, no matter how hairy, might be answered by pointing to the Fuegians, who live in a much more inhospitable one.

The eyewitness reports have always been reluctantly given. There may be many more. The chief objection among the natives to telling white inquirers is fear of ridicule. This sensitiveness is much stronger among natives than whites.

Here, for the present, the matter must rest. Perhaps further witnesses may be heard in the future. Remembering, however, in judging the possibilities of the existence of the Sasquatch, how many people have seen sea serpents and that remains of strange creatures have been recently washed on various shores, it is quite within the bounds of probability that just as there are unknown forms of life in the boundless depths of the ocean, equally so may there be in the enormous wilderness stretches of British Columbia wild hairy men roaming.

Eau Claire, Wisconsin, *Leader*, October 12, 1935

REPORTS TELL OF CANADIAN MONSTER MEN

HAIRY GIANTS DESCRIBED BY SETTLERS NEAR VANCOUVER

Vancouver, B.C., Oct. 11—(UP)—Sasquatch men, remnants of a lost race of "wild men" who inhabited the rocky regions of British Columbia centuries ago, are reported roaming the province again.

After an absence of several months from the district of Harrison Mills, 50 miles east of Vancouver, the long, weird, wolf-like howls of the "wild men" are being heard again and two of the hairy monsters were reported seen in the Morris Valley on the Harrison River.

Residents in the district tell of seeing the two giants leaping and bounding out of the forest and striding across the duck-feeding ground, wallowing now and again in the bog and mire and long, waving swamp grasses.

Reported Agile as Goats

The strange men, it was reported, after emerging from the woods, came leaping down the jagged rocky hillside with the agility and lightness of mountain goats. Snatches of their weird language floated on the breeze across the lake to the pioneer settlement at the foot of the hills.

The giants walked with an easy gait across the swamp flats and at the Morris Creek, in the shadow of Little Mystery Mountain, straddled a floating log, which they propelled with their long, hairy hands and huge feet across the sluggish glacial stream to the opposite side. They had abandoned the log and climbed hand over hand up the almost perpendicular cliff to a point known as Gibraltar and disappeared into the wooded wilderness at the top of the ridge. They carried two large clubs and walked round a herd of cattle directly in their path.

Indian's Story Retold

The return of the giants to the legendary stronghold of the Sasquatch monsters recalls the narrow escape of an Indian at the same spot last March. A huge rock narrowly missed his canoe while he was fishing and looking up, he said he saw a huge and hairy monster stamping his feet and gesticulating wildly. The Indian escaped by cutting his fishing tackle and paddling away. The same Indian declares the Sasquatch twice have stolen salmon which he tied in a tree outside his house out of reach of dogs.

The latest appearance of the monsters was peaceful. They avoided the trails usually used by the people of the valley and molested neither cattle nor human beings.

People who have reported seeing the giants on their rare appearances described them as "ferocious looking wild men, nine feet tall and covered from head to toes with thick black hair."

1937: Green (1978) collected a report from Mrs. Jane Patterson, living on a ranch near Bridesville. While visiting an abandoned house on the ranch property, she encountered a large monkey-like animal sitting by a tree. It was larger than her, and covered in light brown hair.

Vancouver, British Columbia, *Province*, February 26, 1938

GIANT CRUSHES BEAR (HE SAYS)

By J. W. Burns

Harrison Lake, Feb. 26.—A terrific struggle for life in which prodigious strength was
matched against savage ferocity, ended last
week in the strangling of bruin after ten
minutes of wild struggle. A hairy giant of
the Sasquatch, the "wild man of the Chehalis
hinterland," crushed him.

The story of this unusual drama of the
wilderness was told by three Harrison River
Indians who were spectators of the singular
incident one evening, as they were walking
along Chehalis River, close to the canyon.

"It was a skookum (strong) fight," said
Jimmy Craneback, "and as we had never seen
a hairy giant of the Sasquatch in a fight before, I'm telling you we got the biggest kick
of our lives."

Asked how they came to witness the unusual battle, Jimmy said: "We were on our
way home after an all-day unsuccessful hunt
in the Chehalis mountains. We had just
crossed the government road at the Chehalis
River—a mile or so north of the Indian village—when, all at once, we heard a roar in
the forest ahead of us that shook the firs and
cedars.

"We stopped to listen. Down the old trail ahead of us, we could hear groans, growls, thuds, and the snap and crack of rotten branches, as if Old Nick himself had gone off his noodle and was running amuck through the dark forest.

"In awe we stopped dead in our tracks. In the fading twilight and shadowy forest, we first thought we were looking on two bears fighting each other to death. As we stood beside a log, twenty yards away, we could see the great struggle of strength.

"There was a crunching of bones as the monsters in their rage came to grips with each other and tumbled and tossed about in their fury on the forest floor, within a few feet of the Chehalis. But there was something about one of the monsters that puzzled us.

"We wouldn't have raised our rifles when we did," explained Jimmy, "but it looked as if they were about to roll over the bank into the river any moment and we didn't want to lose such big game. But then we never shot, for, as we raised our rifles we were startled by a yell—it had in it something human and came from one of the combatants, which to our astonished ears sounded like 'poo-woo-uoo.'

"'Gosh, gosh,' said Ike Joe as we lowered our rifles, 'boys, it's a Sasquatch and a bear—

we'll take the side of the giant, it's well to be on their side. He's put up a good fight—let's step in and help him.'"

The boys were in a sweat, but happy the Sasquatch gave a "pooh-woo," which timely utterance had no doubt saved his life.

"Finally," said Jimmy, "the giant got his powerful hairy arms around the bear's neck. It must have been a humdinger of a hold, for the bear began to gasp for breath, and gasping, pawed the air, and his tongue was hanging out. The wild man had won the fight."

Canandaigua, New York, *Daily Messenger,* May 23, 1938

INDIANS PAY HOMAGE TO IMAGINARY GIANT TRIBESMEN, SERPENT

Harrison Hot Springs, B. C. (AP)—Indians of British Columbia—home of the Ogopogo, legendary lake-dwelling water snake, and his terrifying, salt-water cousin, the sea serpent—paid homage today to Sasquatch, the hairy ones.

An estimated 2,000 from tribes in the territory and Washington State converged on a gaily decorated Indian village here, bringing grotesque native masks and costumes. It's Sasquatch Indian day, and no place for skeptics.

You either take the Sasquatch or leave them alone. There is no middle course.

Many Indians take them straight. To hear tell, the Sasquatch were great hairy legendary creatures that maintain their reputation with an occasional present-day swoop from the mountains to peek in windows or smack down a lone tribesman.

1939 or 1940: Green (1978) collected a report from about 14 miles up Silver Creek, near Harrison Lake. The witness and four other prospectors watched several large dark-colored creatures wrestling in a valley. They were not close enough to get good details, but watched for about half an hour, and the witness did not believe they were bears. They did not appear to be wearing clothes, and moved around on two legs.

Winnipeg, Manitoba, *Free Press,* August 24, 1940

CAVEMEN ROAM THE ROCKIES?

By Edgar D. Smith

Canada, despite the advent of the airplane and other modern transportation facilities, remains one of the least known and certainly one of the least explored parts of the world. And in this great dominion the biggest mysteries are still sealed up securely in the vast Canadian enigma—the Rocky Mountains.

Lake Okanagan in British Columbia is reported to be inhabited by a second Loch Ness monster—the Ogopogu. Alberta is supposed to have a tropical forest. And now, again from British Columbia, comes the strangest and weirdest tale of all—that of the troglodites, the gigantic and prehistoric cave-men who dwell in the loneliest mountain ranges.

A number of years ago, near the town of Agassiz, a young man and his girl were strolling towards their favorite rendezvous. Suddenly the man stopped and listened. He said he heard footsteps as if someone was following them. He turned to look about him. A second later, both he and his companion were almost shocked out of their wits.

Only a few feet behind the two, stood— something. 'It' glared at them and snarled from a hideous, gargoyle face. Its arms, dangling from hunched, powerful shoulders, touched the ground. The monster, naked, was covered only with its own heavy, rank-smelling hair. It began to shamble menacingly towards them. They ran before it and escaped. But, when they told of their experiences to the folks in Agassiz, they were not believed. And no wonder.

An Indian was paddling his canoe when a huge boulder hurtled alongside, drenching him. Terrified, thinking it might be an avalanche, he looked up. There, high on the cliff, glaring down at him like some obscene demon, stood a grisly apparition. The monster, with a roar that resounded over pine forest and distant crag, prepared to plunge into the water and grab him. The Indian, reversing his sodden canoe, paddled away in hysterical panic.

More recently, a housewife went out of her tiny cabin beside the railway to hang the washing on the line. Suddenly she heard a deep growl. A bear? But no bear, she knew, growled like that. She turned and almost swooned. A huge, enormous monster was glaring at her from the edge of the clearing. But it made no effort to molest her. Instead, it turned and vanished.

These are all actual witnesses. Many more similar testimonies could be compiled. For, according to report, the cave-men have been noticed quite often during the last thirty years. And yet the idea of a Neolithic race of troglodites infesting that region is scoffed at by most people. One explanation given is that the so-called monsters are in reality only bears, bigger brutes than usual, that have come down from some of the remote ranges. And bears, the skeptics point out, often rear up on their hind feet with the front ones dangling. A bear, doing this, might quite easily be mistaken for a huge man under certain circumstances. Especially by impressionable or nervous people.

But, ridiculing this 'bear theory' comes the opinion of the archaeologists. They say there is no doubt that such a tribe of semi-human giants could exist. Traces of just such another race of huge monsters have been discovered in other parts of the world, notably in the highest peaks of the Himalayas and in northern Mexico where guides take the curious to caves and point out various and absolutely undeniable proofs. The archaeologist's task is to prove that a similar race of giants dwell in the Rockies.

According to those who have seen the cave-men, the creatures are enormous, twice the size of the average man and varying in height from seven to nearly eight feet—each monster having the most terrifying, repulsive and savage expression. And so established has the fact of their existence become that they are now referred to as the Sasquatches, (Hairy Ones.)

The Indians have their own ideas about them. They believe that the Sasquatches are a Neolithic tribe of mountain troglodites who inhabit only the loftiest and remotest peaks of the Canadian Rockies and who congregate in vast reunion every fourth year. And they dig back into folk-lore and tell how Chief Calling Loon of the Lonely Pool warned his people, many, many months ago, even before the white man came, of the trolls who infest the slimy depths of lonely lakes (might these legends account in part for the Ogopogu?) and of the bad Manitou who dwells on that solitary snow-cap. The presence of these troglodites has long been a source of pow wow—fact or fable—around Indian teepees. One tribesman, it is said, suggested that a special totem pole should be raised to placate the anger of the creatures.

However, despite the testimony of archaeologists, of the Indians and of those witnesses who swear to having seen the monsters, the Vancouver museum discredits the whole idea and in so doing has aroused much criticism. The scientific staff has been urged to at least make some investigation of the rumors. For many people firmly believe that something should be done. As a popular English magazine once commented about the vast, unexplored regions of Canada: ". . . the possibility of a Sasquatch tribe living is very great."

If the tourist should ever visit this part of Canada, he should be sure to look for smoke

on the mountains—thin, wraithlike spirals
emanating from the summits of the most distant and loneliest ranges. These fires, the
guide will inform him, are those of the Sasquatches. Everyone in those parts has noticed
them before—often. Another tip. The visitor
should not go roaming in certain parts of the
forest after night has fallen—not unless he
is with someone else who knows the country.
And, each would be much safer if he carried
a high calibre gun.

Men have disappeared in the Rocky Mountains. They have vanished and no trace has
ever been found of them again. If marauding
animals had attacked them, the question of
their fate would be easily answered. Therefore, it is asked, were Sasquatches responsible?

Most of the Rocky Mountains is yet an
impregnable barrier, a mighty, unsolved secret. What lies in some of those deep gorges,
in some of those lonely valleys—awesome
abysses, chasms and mist-wrapped mountain peaks? Not to speak of the silent depths
of verdant forests. Will their impenetrable
mysteries ever be made known to men?

Finally, there is the last witness. The hermit who, cleaning his gun late one night in
his mountain shack, heard a weird, wild cry

that echoed over precipices and chasm and which brought him hurriedly to the door. But when he looked around, all was quiet and still. Only the last echoes of that fearful howl, ringing bleakly from scarred cliff to towering crag, disturbed the tranquility of midnight.

"It was not an animal," said the hermit. "No animal could have made a noise like that."

A Sasquatch then? Only the Rocky Mountains know the answer. And they are strict guardians of a secret.

Long Beach, California, *Independent,* November 28, 1941

SASQUATCH RETURN FRIGHTENS INDIANS IN BRITISH COLUMBIA

Vancouver, B. C.—(TP)—The Sasquatch is back again.

All through the Harrison river valley Indians are excitedly discussing the reappearance of the legendary hairy giant of the mountains.

Three canoes of Indians arrived terror-stricken at Harrison Hot Springs after a flight from Fort Douglas at the head of the lake. They announced that the Sasquatch is on the rampage.

Jimmy Douglas and his family were among those who say they saw the monster. They claimed that the Sasquatch was at least 14 feet tall, about twice as tall as the average member of his so-called "species."

Prof. J. W. Burns, who has made a study of Sasquatch lore, believes that it is quite possible that the giant was the same one who was sighted a week previously at Ruby Creek, 40 miles away.

The Indians are very sure that it wasn't a big bear they saw. They said the creature walked on two legs like a man.

Cullman, Alabama, *Banner,* April 16, 1942

INDIAN STORY OF MONSTER 'APE MEN' AGAIN IS SPIKED

BIG GRIZZLY BEAR ON PROWL
FITS INTO LEGEND OF HAIRY GIANTS.

Vancouver.—A giant, marauding grizzly bear may explain the revival of the strange story of a tribe of "hairy monsters that look like men" who supposedly roam the wilds of southern British Columbia spreading terror among the Indians.

The story was revived after Mrs. George Chapman of Ruby Creek reported that a "hairy giant," 10 feet tall and "having the shape of a man covered with shaggy brown hair," had chased her and her four children from their home in the woods near Ruby

Creek, 100 miles east of here. It was the third time in two years that the "monster" was reported to be "on the prowl."

News of the appearance of the giant spread terror among the Indians in the area—until they closely examined the tracks left by the "thing" and decided—with a sigh of relief—that it was probably a bear after all.

Children Scream Warning.

Mrs. Chapman had reported that her four children were playing in the back yard when they saw the "monster" approaching and fled screaming into the house.

"I looked to see what had frightened the children and saw a huge hairy man about 10 feet tall coming from the direction of the barn," she said. "We fled to the woods and stayed there in the pouring rain for three hours before we dared go back to the house."

By that time, she said, the "giant" had gone, leaving his tracks in the soft ground on the bank of the Fraser river and in the woodshed, which it almost wrecked, apparently in search of food.

Mrs. Chapman said that the tracks left by the monster were 16 inches long and five inches across the heel and eight inches at the broad part of the foot.

Tracks Like Bear.

White settlers and Indian leaders, recalling previous stories about the mysterious giants, came to examine the tracks, however, and agreed they could have been made by a giant bear that had come out of the mountains to forage for food.

The Indians believe that a strange tribe of "susquash" or "giants" inhabit the country north of Deroche and Harrison lake and leave their cave homes periodically to roam over a wide area, never stopping long at any one place. The Indians say they have seen the "monsters" twice before in the last few years—once on Seabird island and once near Chehalis.

Vancouver, British Columbia, *Province,* January 15, 1944

WILD MEN OF B.C.?

By Arthur P. Woollacott

From time to time the Indians of British Columbia tell their white brethren curious tales of hairy wild men they have met in the mountain solitudes and other lonely places of the west. Most old-timers have heard such stories and have dismissed such yarns without further thought.

Persistent reports of this nature come from the neighborhood of Harrison Hot Springs on the C.P.R. main line 70 miles from Vancouver. The Indians know these mysterious creatures as Susquatch.

An Indian woman of the Harrison Lake tribe, while engaged in domestic duties, turned suddenly and saw standing a few feet away a giant hairy wild man different from any human creature she knew of. He made a step toward her, with muscular arms ready to clutch her, but abruptly changed his mind and fled with great bounds, making vocal noises which she said, sounded as if he were both amused and fearful.

In another case an Indian entering a log cabin was knocked down by a creature that rushed out and away. The hunter scrambled to his feet and raised his gun to shoot, only to lower the weapon with wonder and fear, when he saw not an animal rushing away, but a gigantic hairy wild man. The creature walked quickly in a sort of half-trot towards cover, glancing over his shoulder at the trembling figure in the doorway.

On another occasion two natives, passing along a trail, were startled by big stones thrown on the path in front of them from a cliff above. On looking up they saw two Susquatch leering at them over the edge of the cliff. One of the natives, a more than usually intelligent man, thought that the Susquatch were trying in a half fearful, tentative way to make advances toward getting acquainted.

Retreating hastily, the Indians looked back to note the non-plussed attitude of the wild man, whose gestures seemed to be an invitation to return.

In all cases the Susquatch took the Indians unawares, showing that they were more alert than the natives and knew something of their habits.

When the Indians first saw monkeys they immediately said that the wild men they had seen were "big monkeys." Among several of the northern tribes, notably the Tsimpseans in the neighborhood of the Skeena River and Prince Rupert, these wild men are known as buckwus, the Indian name for monkey. . . .

Vancouver, British Columbia, *Province,* January 29, 1949

STREET CORNERS, JOHN GRAHAM

SASQUATCHES GET HUNGRY, TOO

I've just been chatting with Chief Andy Paull about Sasquatches and he can relate numerous instances of Indians meeting the hairy men. His own brother-in-law ran into one on a deserted road near Agassiz one night not long ago as he and other members of a lacrosse team were on their way home. But they didn't get a very close look; the eight-foot giant plunged into the bush the moment he spotted the approaching Indians.

On another occasion, only a few years ago, three or four young Indian hunters ran spang into one on a mountain near Agassiz. Terrified, the lads fired and fled, with the big man hard on their heels. They got away in their canoe safely, leaving the furious Sasquatch screaming at them from the shore. And one aged friend of Andy's tells him how the shy giants used to creep through the woods to watch loggers clearing land near Sapperton in the early days. And when the loggers departed, the Sasquatches would come out of hiding and playfully imitate the workers they had been watching. But they didn't chop down the trees; they pushed them over. Just like Paul Bunyan.

Vancouver, British Columbia, *Province,* July 4, 1951

TALK OF THE TOWN

. . . Surprised, also, was Ray Sobinsei of Richmond. Walking on the sands near [Port] Douglas on the holiday, he took a double take and sure enough, "they" were footprints, 18 inches long and boasting but three toes . . . Shades, or shapes, of the Sasquatch Indians! . . .

Chilliwack, British Columbia, *Progress,* May 9, 1956

SASQUATCH SIGHTED?
SEARCH GIVEN IMPETUS

. . . Stan Hunt, Vernon auctioneer, . . . claims to have sighted two of the creatures near Hope on a recent Friday morning.

Mr. Hunt described them as being seven feet tall and walking like a bear. Complexions were gray, like the color of a horse. But the creatures weren't stocky like a bear—"gangly" was the adjective he used.

It was near Flood, this side of Hope, and Mr. Hunt was travelling between 45 and 50 miles an hour when he saw the two weird creatures—one crossing the road from the river side, the other already in the bushes, from which Mr. Hunt could only see the top of its head.

The one crossing the road was walking upright. Mr. Hunt is reported as having thought at first it was a big bear "only it wasn't that big around." The hair, too, was thinner—"not matted like an animal."

Mr. Hunt didn't stop to investigate further but continued on his trip to Vancouver.

Vancouver, British Columbia, *Province,* April 23, 1957

HUNTERS SPOTS SASQUATCH GIRL:
'JUST COULDN'T SHOOT HER'

By Don Lory, Province Staff Reporter

Surrey—A veteran hunter who never heard of the Sasquatch until he read about them in The Province drew a bead on one but didn't have the heart to shoot it.

"It looked almost human," says William Roe, 66, of 5085 Pacific Highway, Cloverdale. He claims to have sighted what may have been a Sasquatch in October, 1955, while he and his wife were living at Tete Jaune Cache, about 70 miles west of Jasper, Alta.

Mr. Roe, who worked part time on the provincial highways and part time as a logger, said he was hunting near the old Mica mine at the time.

"I was about the timberline," Mr. Roe said, "when I came to a clearing and noticed some movement in the bush on the opposite side.

"At first I thought it was a grizzly bear, so I hid behind a clump of brush. What ever it was it had brown and black hair with the ends sort of silvery, like an old grizzly.

"It was about 75 yards from me, and when it stepped into the clearing I drew a careful bead on it—just in case. Then I noticed it wasn't a bear, or any other animal for that matter.

"Whatever it was, and I'm not claiming it was a Sasquatch, it was about 6 feet tall, with a complete well-proportioned female figure, and must have weighed about 300 pounds. From head to toe it was covered with fur.

"It walked absolutely upright, and I couldn't help but notice the strange feet. They were about 18 inches long, narrow at the heel—like the average foot—but widened out to about 6 inches at the toes.

"She walked almost directly towards me. Then stopped beside some small shrubs about ten feet away and squatted down to eat. I remained absolutely still and just watched.

"The fur around her mouth was all green from the leaves and vegetation she had eaten. Her teeth were pure white—which probably indicates she was in the prime of life.

"And they were just a little larger than average teeth. She had no tusks.

"Her hands were perfectly formed, except much larger than the average person. The ends of her fingernails were broken and chipped. And they were not claws—they were fingernails. She had a wide flat nose, shiny black eyes, slightly smaller than a person's, and had a short thick neck.

"Her mouth was unusually wide, her complete body was covered with hair about half-an-inch long.

"I watched her about 10 minutes while she grabbed handfuls of leaves and pushed them into her mouth. From my experience in the bush, I am satisfied she was a vegetarian.

"All of a sudden she stared in my direction, then stood up and started backing away, still chewing as she went. I stood up when she was about 50 feet away and she made a noise that was neither an animal cry nor a language.

"She backed up and went around some brush, then rounded down towards Rocky Creek. Just before I lost sight of her, she turned her head again and made that strange noise.

"I honestly don't know what she was, except she was no animal. I'd say she was a cross between a human and a bear.

"I had my gun aimed right between her eyes three times, but I just couldn't shoot. She looked more human than animal, and I would never have felt right about it if I had." . . .

Victoria, British Columbia, *Times-Colonist,* April 26, 1957

INDIAN MET SASQUATCH
FACE TO FACE: 'HAIRY GIANT
THREW TREES AT ME'

By Humphry Davy

. . . The dramatic and hair-raising encounter with the hairy giant was related by 84-year-old Jimmy Fraser, grandson of Chief Cheatchlatcht, a highly respected resident of the Songhees Reserve.

"His eyes glowed like the noonday sun, and the hair on his body was like moss on the rocks," was the old Indian's description of the giant. "His voice sounded like the roar of surf from a heavy sea."

Jimmy's sincerity is not to be doubted as he enjoys an honorable reputation of being the Indian band's historian. . . .

In telling his story, Jimmy at the same squelched the claim that Sasquatch exist in the vicinity of Harrison Lake or Agassiz.

The people of Harrison Lake, he said, had confused Sasquatch with two timber giants which roam the hills of the north Fraser Valley. . . .

"Sasquatches have always lived on Vancouver Island," he said. "You will find them now deep in the hills where the mountain flowers grow." . . .

He related that in his youth he was pursuing a young deer up a mountain slope near a lake in East Sooke. On reaching the summit he could find no trace of the deer. He was about to re-trace his steps when he heard a deafening roar.

"At first I was like a frozen man," he said. "Even the rocks trembled."

"I looked up and there not far away was a hairy man—maybe 18 feet high—as tall as the mountain tree, he held the deer."

Jimmy recalled that his guardian spirit is the wolf who has endowed him with a pair of fleeting legs.

"I turned and ran like the wind," he said. "The giant hurled trees after me. The trees can still be found rotting on the slope of the mountain."

Jimmy said he never went near the mountain again. His description of the mountain where he saw the Sasquatch seems to indicate that it is Mount Matheson, near Rocky point.

The old white-haired Indian took great pains to explain that hairy giants do not go out looking for trouble. They shun people, he said.

"They are only dangerous when they run into people," he said. . . .

1940s: In a letter to the editor, Mrs. Gladys McNutt of Egmont told a story of her brothers fishing in Rivers Inlet about ten years prior. While tied up at the Kildala Cannery dock, a boat with several teenage Indian boys came into dock, calling excitedly for relatives to come and bring their guns. After they returned from a fruitless hunt, they said that they had seen something moving among the brush that they first took for a bear. Shouting at the animal, "To their utter amazement a strange looking creature rose up on its hind legs and in this erect position made off into the woods. . . . It was agreed that the thing was covered with hair and one boy insisted it had a bushy tail—like a wolf, he said. The thing that impressed them most was that it walked erect." ("Was it a Sasquatch that they saw?", Vancouver, British Columbia, *Province,* May 18, 1957.)

Vancouver, British Columbia, *Province,* June 21, 1957

B.C. NORTH ALSO HAS SASQUATCH

. . . Frank Luxton, foreman of the department of highways here [New Hazelton] believes he saw one of the hairy, ape-like creatures four years ago.

He said he was driving near here at dusk when he saw what looked like a large bear standing on its hind legs.

"I slowed down to take a better look," he said. "Then the huge creature, about eight feet tall, started running like a human being into the bush. I could see his large head well above the poplar trees until it fled out of sight."

Chilliwack, British Columbia, *Progress,* February 4, 1959

WHAT DID INDIAN CHIEF
SEE BY MYSTERY LAKE?

By Miss Annie York

. . . High up near the mountain ridge this creek finds its source in a timbered region where a small lake lies in a peculiar horse-shoe or curved form. From this lake it is only a short distance to begin the steep descent down to the Anderson Creek on the other side. . . .

Many years ago an old hunter from the Indian Band of Spuzzum, "Chief Dick" ended up at this lake while out on a one-man hunting expedition. Approaching the spot deep in the timber silently and with musket primed he paused to listen and adjust his vision to the darker surroundings.

Chief Dick's eyesight was unfailing and his nerves were solid as a boulder and he wasn't a man given to imagination, but he stared in amazement and terror at the great manlike creature that reared up from the plants and bushes at the wateredge.

The animal, human or whatever it was, appeared to sense the presence of the hunter. This did little to pacify his fears and for full minutes, "Chief Dick" prayed and pondered whether to retreat or shoot. Despite his great anxiety and agitation he noted that the other being resembled a human or man with generally gray medium hair covering it from head to feet and displaying a massive width of shoulders with long powerful arms. The face, he states, was hairy and wide and the eyes piercing and searching in their probing

efforts to locate his position. A slight movement on the part of the hunter climaxed the
suspense and as Chief Dick watched as he
never had before, the great creature faded
silently from sight and was soon lost among
shadows of the timber. On recovering his
composure his own retreat from the place
was no less hasty and on returning home to
the reservation at Spuzzum he related the
whole story to his brother-in-law, who later
became "Chief Paul."

It was decided to form an armed party and
return to the scene in order to investigate.

On arrival at the mystery lake Chief Dick
and his companions found humanlike footprints on the water's edge which they said
appeared to be half again as long as their
own.

Nothing of the creature was ever seen
again by people in the district although certain events in the area of Anderson Mountain around this period startled berrypickers
so badly they sought safety in numbers and
relied on roaring nightfires and watchdogs
after dark.

The old people laid no claim to any unnatural or dramatic happenings out of their
experiences such as is often told in stories of
the "Sasquatch" and neither do they relate

anything like hostility on any side. . . . They
furthermore had no desire to discuss these
events with outsiders and to a certain extent attached some reverence and respect for
what they never quite understood.

SASQUATCH SKELETON FOLKLORE

In a 1956 article by J. W. Burns, Rene Dahinden
and Wanja Holmstrom claimed that "the skeleton
of one of the giants was accidentally discovered
some years ago by a white man and his wife, whom
this writer [Burns?] interviewed and got documen-
tary proof from them, which we still have. The
skeleton was found in a shallow grave in a good
state of preservation. The discoverers were amazed
because of its huge size, measuring 7 feet 6 inches
in height. The head was enormous. The teeth were
in perfect condition, but twice as large as those of
either white or Indian. Some 50 Indians who saw
the skeleton, declared it was a Sasquatch. There
was a deep dent in the skull, apparently the result of a heavy blow, which Indians thought was
the cause of death. The skeleton was crated on
the spot by the discoverers, and unfortunately
shipped to a museum outside Canada, where I
believe, it is still preserved. The curator of the
museum, commenting on the skeleton, declared
it had the largest head of either man or beast he
had ever seen." ("Explorers on Mighty Sasquatch

Trail," by J. W. Burns, Chilliwack, British Columbia, *Progress,* February 1, 1956.)

The following year, an article provided slightly
different details regarding this alleged Sasquatch
skeleton. Floyd Dillon told a reporter that twenty
years prior, near Lillooet, he had dug up the skeleton of a giant. It was nearly eight feet tall, with a
skull twice the size of a normal man's. It also had
an eight-inch tail bone. Although he and his wife,
Frances, had put together the pieces of the skeleton to turn over to a museum, some local youngsters apparently stole pieces, so that only the skull
and a few other bones remained. Dillon claimed
that these bones were sent to the provincial museum in Victoria. The reporter checked with the
museum, who said they never received any such
bones. Anthropologist Wilson Duff stated that
they found correspondence from that period, but
no bones were sent. ("Bony relics disappear," by
Alex MacGillivray, Vancouver, British Columbia,
Sun, April 5, 1957.)

In another 1957 article, J. W. Burns noted that
he once received a letter from an Ontario lawyer,
S. A. Wallace, who claimed that 10 years prior a
cave with 40 Sasquatch skeletons had been discovered in a good state of preservation. ("'Nothing
monstrous about Sasquatch,' says their pal," by
Alex MacGillivray, Vancouver, British Columbia,
Sun, May 25, 1957.)

California

TRUEly Yours (letters to the editor), *TRUE Magazine*, March 1960 (from Smith and Mangiacopra 2003)

MOUNT SHASTA

My grandfather prospected for gold in the eighteen fifties throughout the region described as being home of the Snowman. Upon grandfather's return to the East, he told stories of seeing hairy giants in the vicinity of Mount Shasta. These monsters had long arms, but short legs. One of them picked up a 20-foot section of sluiceway and smashed it to bits against a tree.

When grandfather told us these stories, we didn't believe him at all. Now, after reading your article, it turns out he wasn't as big a liar as we youngsters thought he was.— John M. Weekes.

New Orleans, Louisiana, *The Times Picayune,* April 5, 1851

The Wild Man of California.—Thomas Mc-Cauley, who took Mr. Gaines to see the wild man of California, and swindled him out of

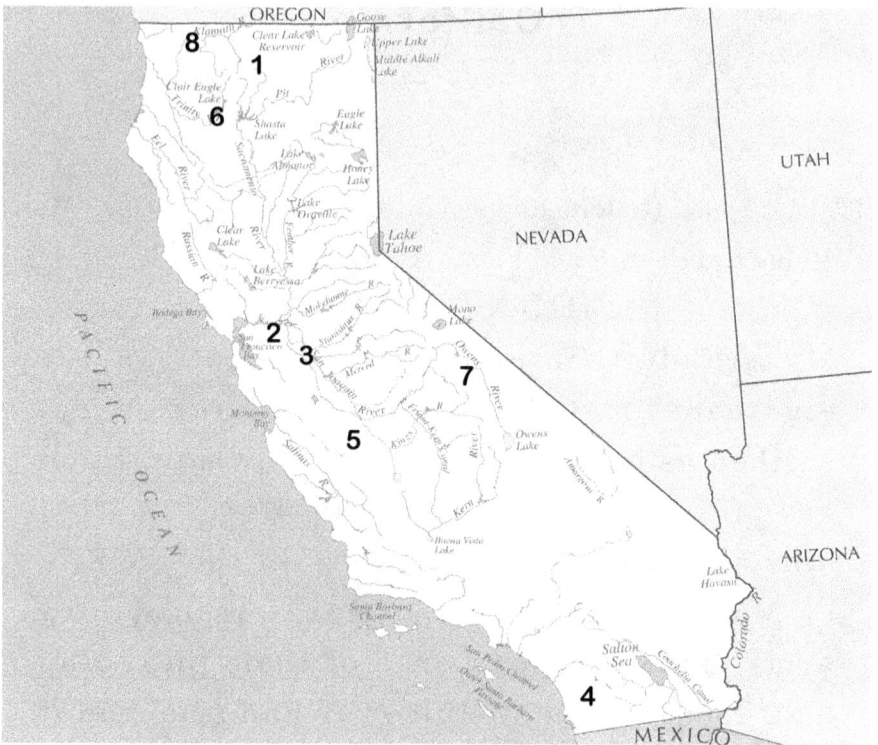

1 Mt. Shasta

2 Mt. Diablo

3 Stanislaus County

4 San Diego County

5 Fresno County

6 Mt. Bally (Shasta Bally)

7 Round Valley (Inyo County)

8 Happy Camp (Siskiyou County)

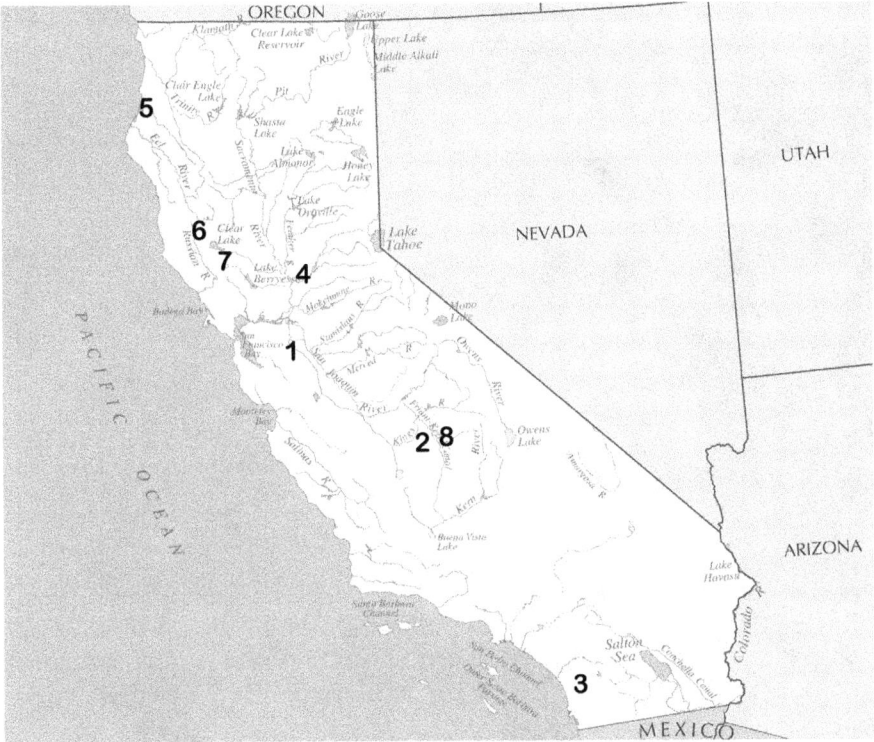

1 Grayson (Stanislaus County)

2 Visalia (Tulare County)

3 Los Penasquitos Canyon (preserve)

4 American River

5 Eureka (Humboldt County)

6 Rumsey (Yolo County)

7 Capay (Yolo County)

8 Three Rivers (Tulare County)

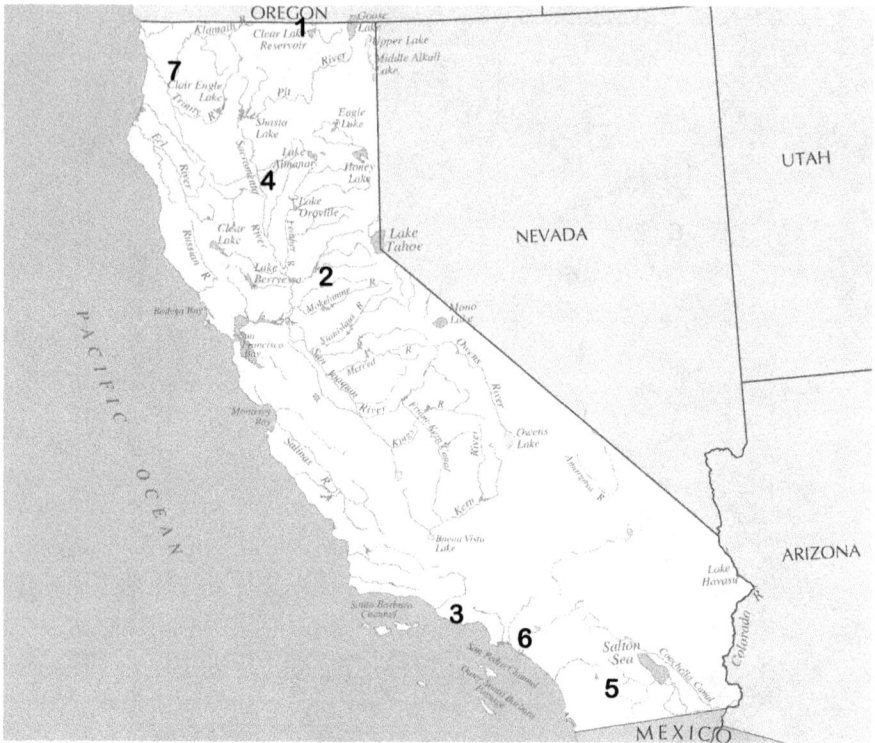

1 Tulelake (Siskiyou County)

2 Prairie City / Folsom (Sacramento County)

3 Point Dume (Los Angeles County)

4 Chico (Butte County)

5 Jamul (San Diego County)

6 Stanton (Orange County)

7 Bluff Creek (Humboldt County)

$40, was, after examination yesterday, sent before the First District Court.

San Joaquin, California, *Republican,* September 19, 1870 (from Green 1978)

Wildman—We learn from good authority that a wild man has been seen at Crow Canyon, near Mount Diablo. Several attempts have been made to capture him, but as yet have proved unsuccessful. His tracks measure thirteen inches.

Oakland, California, *Daily Transcript,* September 27, 1870 (from Green 1978)

An item appeared in the San Joaquin Republican the other day stating that a wild man had been seen in some part of San Joaquin county, and we afterward noticed the statement copied into several other papers, with brief comments indicating disbelief in the report. We must confess to a want of credulity on our part also as to the exact correctness of the item at the time, but we were yesterday placed in possession of certain information which leads us to believe that there may be some foundation for the report. As our columns are somewhat crowded this morning, we will give the reports as we received them and as briefly as possible.

F. J. Hildreth and Samuel De Groot, of
Washington Corners, in this county, while
out hunting on Orias Timbers Creek in Stanislaus county about three weeks ago, discovered footprints along the bank of the creek
resembling the impressions of a human being's feet. Mr. Hildreth, who gave us this
information, states that the tracks were like
those of a human being with the exception
that the impressions of the toes were much
larger. Hildreth afterward became separated from his companion, and upon proceeding
some distance up the creek, saw a few yards
ahead of him what he believed to be gorillas.
If the description Mr. Hildreth has given us
of these animals is true, he is certainly warranted in believing them to be of that species
of animal. Mr. De Groot also reports that he
saw the same objects and is positive that
they are gorillas. The appearance of these
strange animals in that neighborhood is
notorious and that they are gorillas is firmly believed by a great many people in that
vicinity.

A number of old hunters have started out
to capture them, and we are promised whatever further facts may occur as soon as the
party returns. The above we gathered from
various parties, and whether true or not,

there are many persons in the neighborhood of the Washington Corners who firmly believe that the animals referred to are veritable gorillas.

Titusville, Pennsylvania, *Morning Herald,* November 10, 1870

THE WILD MEN OF CALIFORNIA

A correspondent of the Antioch Ledger, writing from Grayson, California, under date of October 16, says: "I saw in your paper, a short time since, an item concerning the 'gorilla' which is said to have been seen in Crow Canyon and shortly after in the mountains of Orestimba Creek. You sneered at the idea of there being any such 'critters' in these hills, and were I not better informed I should sneer too, or else conclude that one of your recent prospecting parties had got lost in the wilderness, and didn't have sense enough to find his way back to Terry's. I positively assure you that this gorilla, or wild man as you choose to call it, is no myth. I know that it exists, and that there are at least two of them, having seen them both at once not a year ago. Their existence has been reported at times for the past twenty years, and I have heard it said, that in the early days an ourang-outang escaped from a ship on the southern coast; but the

creature I have seen is not that animal, and
if it is, where did he get his mate? import her
as the Web-foot did their wives? Last Fall I
was hunting in the mountains about twenty
miles south of here, and camped five or six
days in one place, as I have done every season for the past fifteen years. Several times
I returned to my camp, after a hunt, and saw
that the ashes and charred sticks from the
fire-place had been scattered about. An old
hunter notices such things, and very soon
gets curious to know the cause. Although my
beddings and traps and little stores were not
disturbed as I could see, I was anxious to
learn who or what it was that so regularly
visited my camp, for clearly the half-burnt
sticks and cinders could not scatter themselves about. I saw no track near the camp,
as the hard ground, covered with dry leaves,
would show none. So I started on a circle
around the place, and 300 yards off, in damp
sand, I struck the track of a man's feet, as I
supposed—bare, and of immense size. Now I
was curious, sure, and resolved to lay for the
bare-footed visitor. I accordingly took a position on a hill side, about sixty or seventy feet
from the fire, and securely hid in the brush.
I waited and watched. Two hours or more I
sat there and wondered if the owner of the

feet would come again, and whether he imagined what an interest he had created in my
inquiring mind, and finally, what possessed
him to be prowling about there with no shoes
on. The fire-place was on my right, and the
spot where I saw the track was on my left,
hid by bushes. It was in this direction that
my attention was mostly directed, thinking
the visitor would appear there, and, besides,
it was easier to sit and face that way. Suddenly I was startled by a shrill whistle, such
as boys produce with two fingers under their
tongue, and turning quickly, I ejaculated,
"Good God!" as I saw the object of my so-
licitude, standing beside my fire, erect and
looking suspiciously around. It was in the
image of man, but it could not have been human. I was never so benumbed with astonishment before. The creature, whatever it
was, stood full five feet high, and dispropor-
tionately broad and square at the shoulders,
with arms of great length. The legs were very
short, and the body long. The head was small
compared with the rest of the creature, and
appeared to be set upon his shoulders without a neck. The whole was covered with dark
brown and cinnamon-colored hair, quite long
on some parts, that on the head standing in
a shock and growing close down to the eyes,

like a Digger Indian's. As I looked, he threw
his head back and whistled again, and then
stooped and grasped a stick from the fire.
This he swung round and round, until the
fire on the end had gone out, when he repeated the manoeuvre. I was dumb, almost,
and could only look. Fifteen minutes I sat
and watched him, as he whistled and scattered my fire about. I could easily have put
a bullet through his head, but why should I
kill him? Having amused himself, apparently all he desired, with my fire, he started
to go, and having gone a short distance, he
returned, and was joined by another—a female, unmistakably—when they both turned
and walked past me, within twenty yards of
where I sat, and disappeared in the brush. I
could not have had a better opportunity for
observing them, as they [were] unconscious
of my presence. Their only object in visiting
my camp seemed to be to amuse themselves
with swinging lighted sticks around. I have
heard this story many times since then, and
it has often raised an incredulous smile; but
I have met one person who has seen the mysterious creatures, and a dozen who have come
across their tracks at various places between
here and Pacheco Pass."

Stockton, California, *Daily Evening Herald,* May 30, 1873

WHAT IS IT.

[FROM THE VISALIA *DELTA.*]

PORTERVILLE, MAY 24, 1873?

Editor, Delta: I spent a few days in Visalia this week, and speaking to some one in regard to the wild man you gave an account of having been seen in the mountains, found they had doubts as to whether such creatures had been seen.

Three years ago last November, as near as I can recollect, I was in the mountains after lumber; when I came home I was told the following story: One morning my eldest son, Alexander, then a boy 14 years old, went out ¼ of a mile from the house after a cow. He heard a strange noise in the direction of Deer Creek; looking he saw what he supposed to be an Indian. It came towards him half bent in a trot, the boy was not afraid of Indians, so he waited till it came up to him. It came close enough to shake hands. Of course the boy did not offer his hand, as it was an awful looking creature, as described by the boy. After he recovered sufficiently from his fright, he described it as follows: five feet high, hair from head to heel; on the body, 3 or 4 inches long; on the head and face longer, say 10 or 15 inches; had long nails on hands and feet, no hair on cheek bones; partly bare

on hands and feet. After standing and looking first at the boy, then at the cow, then
at some hogs that were near, and over the
plains at the homes, it took from its back
a redwood splinter, something in the shape
of a large knife, and made motions as if it
would strike the boy. He then stooped down
to get a stone to defend himself, when the
creature gave a kind of whoop and ran off,
the boy said faster than any dog, going half
bent. I give the boy's story as he told it at the
time, which I am inclined to believe, for his
sister saw the creature standing by him, and
said to her mother that Cornelius Gibones
was out there with Alex. I give this as near
as the boy told it as I can. I don't know what
the creature was. I told the boy at the time I
guessed it was the devil, but I don't think it
now.—Wm. Thompson.

Fort Wayne, Indiana, *Weekly Sentinel*, August 27, 1873

THE WILD MAN SEEN AGAIN

Tulare (Cal.) *Times*, August 3: The wild man
who has been seen so often in the mountains
east of here for the last three years, and who
has incorrectly been stated to be a species of
gorilla, was seen again recently near Snow
Valley. He was engaged in picking thimble-
berries, and was perfectly naked. He is covered

all over with long black hair, and had long gray whiskers. He is a white man, large and powerful, and at least six feet high; his finger nails have grown out several inches in length. Downing was within twenty feet of him when he raised up from picking berries. He stood perfectly still and looked at Downing for some time, and then turned and started to run. Downing was sitting down picking berries himself, when this wild creature raised up out of the low bushes near him. He had not seen him before. He is a gentleman of undoubted veracity. Many others of our citizens have at different times caught sight of this monster. William Arnold, an old and well-known citizen, saw him some time ago sitting on the top of a large rock, engaged in the highly romantic, and to him no doubt delightful, occupation of scratching himself. He is the constant terror of the Indians in the mountains eastward, who all have either seen him or know of his existence. They tell the most marvelous stories of his performances. They think he is either the devil or some dead white man, whose ghost has come to annoy them. There can be no doubt of the reality of this wonderful wild man, as he has been seen so often by the most credible witnesses. A short time ago Mr. John G. Knox, our

efficient Deputy County Clerk, while driving
rapidly in a buggy above the Ash Spring Hill,
overtook a man running as though frightened
almost to death. On inquiring the cause, the
man told him he had just encountered a terrible wild man or the devil, and that it was
"enough to frighten anybody." Mr. Knox took
the man into his buggy, and on telling the
story at the next house, the gentleman said
he himself had seen the same creature. Many
persons resident in the vicinity have seen
him at various times. We suggest that an effort be made to capture him. His range is
pretty well known, and his capture could no
doubt be effected without a very great effort.

San Francisco, California, *Bulletin*, October 2, 1873

That Wild Man.—The *Tulare Times*, of September 27th, has the following: The "wild
man," of which so many accounts have been
published, has at last been captured, as
Charles Converse informs us. It turns out to
be a species of nondescript very like a bear,
although it entirely lacks arms or forelegs,
and walks upright like a man. Converse
thinks it is a deformed bear. Shaft (or Shaffe)
and Johnson, who captured him, will be
in town to-day. They propose to sell their
"catch" to Woodward, and will telegraph to

that gentleman in regard to the *lusus natu-rae* they have secured. They had to shoot and wound him before catching him. Converse came down from the mountains on horseback, and passed the captors of the "What is It" on the way down with a team. When they arrive we shall be able to learn the full particulars in regard to this new wonder of the Sierras.

Eugene, Oregon, *Oregon State Journal,* Nov. 22, 1873

The SAN DIEGO WORLD of the 24th of Oct. has the following:

Yesterday afternoon a man named Horace Orten arrived in San Diego from Julian and put up at the Occidental Hotel. He tells a story whose truth we have no reason to doubt.

A Wild Man or Gorilla?

Some miles above Captain Johnson's residence at Penasquitas there is a gulch that leads down to Pagnay [Paguay?], and at some point in this ravine there is an old abandoned mill. Our traveler was riding along leisurely when, casting his eyes upon the ruin, he saw emerging from it a horrid creature about five feet high. He was perfectly naked. He was squat and strong of build, with heavy arms and thighs, and straight lower leg, with very little calf. He was covered from head to foot with matted hair. His head was large and round, with enormous neck, indicating muscular force. This creature advanced upon him with inarticulate noises and violent gesticulations, and at a rapid pace.

The Flight—He Shoots at the Monster

Mr. Orten confesses that he did not like the appearance of this monster, so he put his horse to the trot. He soon found that this pace did not serve for the savage, wild man or gorilla, whichever he was, kept steadily gaining upon him. He now forced his horse into a gallop, and still he put no distance between him and pursuer. His situation was, as he thought, becoming critical. Not caring to come to close quarters with the monster, he drew his revolver and fired at him. One shot failing of effect, he discharged three additional balls in succession, the last having evidently told, for the monster abandoned pursuit. Mr. Orten did not take time to examine the damage done to his pursuer, but rode on into San Diego.

What is to be Done about It?

Mr. Orten is a respectable man, and is entirely persuaded of the truth of the story told by him. He is anxious to organize a party to go out and look for this wild man of the

Pagnay Gulch. There is every possibility that the creature, if not wounded too severely to admit of it, will put in an appearance to other travelers, with perhaps a different result. What is to be done about it? Is he to be allowed to wander at large?

Helena, Montana, *Independent,* April 25, 1876

THE MISSING LINK.

INTERVIEW OF A CALIFORNIA HUNTER
WITH A GORRILLA-LIKE WILD MAN.

A correspondent of the San Diego (Cal.) Union writes as follows concerning a "wild man" recently seen in the mountains in that county. "About ten days ago Turner Helm and myself were in the mountains about ten miles east of Warner's ranch of a prospecting tour, looking for the extension of a quartz lode which had been found by some parties some time before. When we were separated, about a half a mile apart—the wind blowing very hard at the time—Mr. Helm, who was walking along looking down at the ground, suddenly

Heard Somebody Whistle.

Looking up he saw 'something' sitting on a large boulder about fifteen or twenty paces from him. He supposed it to be some kind of an animal and immediately came down on him with his needle gun. The object immediately rose to its feet and proved to be a man. This man appeared to be covered all over with coarse black hair, seemingly two or three inches long, like the hair of a bear; his beard and the hair of his head were long and thick; he was a man of medium size, and rather fine features— not at all like those of an Indian, but more like an American or Spaniard. They stood gazing at each other for a few moments when Mr. Helm spoke to

The Singular Creature

first in English, and then in Spanish, and then in Indian, but the man remained silent. He then advanced toward Mr. Helm, who not knowing what his intentions might be, again came down on him with the gun to keep him at a distance. The man at once stopped as though he knew there was a danger. Mr. Helm called to me, when

The Wild Man

went over the hill and was soon out of sight and made good his escape. We had frequently before seen this man's tracks in that part of the mountains, but had supposed them to be tracks of an Indian. Mr. Helm is a man of unquestioned veracity.

Millheim, Pennsylvania, *Journal*, June 22, 1882

A WILD MAN ON THE
CALIFORNIA COAST.

FROM THE SAN FRANCISCO *CHRONICLE*.

While hunting for deserters from a ship at Guaymas, a few days ago, the searchers discovered a man covered from head to foot with long shaggy hair, of a reddish color. On their approaching him he commenced to run, and they chased him, followed him for a distance of a mile or more to the beach, where he jumped from rock to rock with the agility of a chamois and was soon lost to sight behind a jutting point. . . .

This last story is included here because it may confuse researchers who encounter it. Guaymas is on the coast of the Gulf of California in Mexico.

1882: Bord & Bord (2006) noted the report of a "large, shaggy beast roaming the foothills of Round Valley." One witness shot at it, causing the creature to turn on him. The witness' horse broke two legs and the witness was bruised in the encounter, and the creature disappeared.

Del Norte, California, *Record,* January 2, 1886 (from Byrne 1976)

I do not remember to have seen any reference to the "Wild Man" which haunts this part of the country, so I shall allude to him briefly.

Not a great while since, Mr. Jack Dover, one of our most trustworthy citizens, while hunting saw an object standing one hundred and fifty yards from him picking berries or tender shoots from the bushes. The thing was of gigantic size—about seven feet high—with a bull dog head, short ears and long hair; it was also furnished with a beard, and was free from hair on such parts of its body as is common among men. Its voice was shrill, or soprano, and very human, like that of a woman in great fear. Mr. Dover could not see its footprints as it walked on hard soil. He aimed his gun at the animal, or whatever it was, several times, but because it was so human would not shoot. The range of the curiosity is between Marble mountain and the vicinity of Happy Camp. A number of people have seen it and all agree in their descriptions except some make it taller than others. It is apparently herbivorous and makes its winter quarters in some of the caves of Marble mountain.

Galveston, Texas, *Daily News*, March 25, 1888

A WHAT-IS-IT

THE STRANGE ANIMAL THAT FRIGHTENED
A CALIFORNIA WOODSMAN

F. Burns, who resides near Brighton, was in the city yesterday, and says that a few days

since a man in his employ named Brooks was
at work in the willows, near the American
river, when he was suddenly confronted by
an animal of strange appearance, which was
about four and a half feet in height, walked
erect, and was covered with long, black hair.
Mr. Brooks was of course considerably startled at the appearance of the strange being,
which retreated into the dense thicket skirt-
ing the American river. Mr. Brooks says the
animal appeared to be a large ape or gorilla.
He believes it to be an escape from a menagerie, or possibly some human deformity. Mr.
Burns says he proposes to instigate a hunting party in a few days to find out if possible
what the mysterious creature is. [Sacramen-
to Bee.]

Butte, Montana, *Weekly Miner,* August 31, 1889

A STRANGE ANIMAL ROAMING
THE WILDS OF EUREKA

The "Sentinel" gives the following description of a strange animal roaming in the vicinity of Eureka: It has a resemblance to an
animal combining the forms of a monkey and
a bear, a part of its body being covered with
long shaggy hair and the balance perfectly
smooth and hairless. It is probably a species
of the wonderloo, description of which may

be found in natural history, but how it happened to be in this section is a conundrum.

Woodland, California, *Daily Democrat*, April 9, 1891

WHAT IS IT?

AN UNHEARD OF MONSTROSITY SEEN
IN THE WOODS ABOVE RUMSEY.

Mr. Smith, a well known citizen of Northern
Capay Valley, called on us to-day and tells us
the following strange story which we would
be loth to believe if it were not for the fact
that he is an old acquaintance of this office,
and has always borne a spotless reputation.
Several days ago, Mr. Smith together with a
party of hunters, were above Rumsey hunting. One morning Mr. Smith started out early
in quest of game, he had not gone far when
his attention was attracted by a peculiar
noise that seemed to come from an oak tree
that stood near by. Looking up, Mr. Smith
was startled to see gazing at him what was
apparently a man clothed in a suit of shaggy
fur. Having heard of wild men, Mr. [Smith]
naturally placed upon his guard, but thinking that he would see "what virtue there was
in kindness," he called to the supposed man
to come down, as he was filled with nothing
but the kindest motives. This speech did not
have the desired effect, rather the opposite,

for the strange thing gave grunts of unmistakable anger. Believing that discretion was
the better part of valor, our informant stood
not upon the order of his going, but went at
once in a bee-line for the camp. After placing some distance between himself and the
strange creature, the hunter turned around
just in time to see it descend the tree. Upon
reaching the ground, instead of standing upright as a man would, it commenced to trot
along on the ground as a dog or any other
animal would do.

Smith then realized that it was no hermit
he had seen, but some kind of monstrosity,
such as he had never heard of, much less
seen before. The hunter stood amazed and
spell-bound for a moment, but soon gathered his scattered sense again and was soon
making his best speed to camp, where in a
few breathless words, was telling his companions of what he had seen.

They were disposed to laugh at him at
first, but his sincereness of manner and his
blanched cheeks soon proved to them that he
had seen something out of the usual order of
things.

A hasty council was held, and the party
decided to go in search of the monster, so
taking their guns and dogs they were piloted

by Mr. Smith to whom they soon came in
sight of the unnamed animal. In the meantime it had commenced to devour the contents of Mr. Smith's game bag that he had
dropped in his hasty retreat. The creature
would plunge its long arms or legs into the
bag and pulling forth the small game that
was in it, transferred it to its mouth in a
most disgusting manner. An effort was made
to set the dogs upon it, but they crouched
at their masters' heels and gave vent to the
most piteous whines. The whines attracted the attention of the nondescript, and it
commenced to make the most unearthly yells
and screams, at the same time fleeing to the
undergrowth, some half a mile distant, upon
which the whole party immediately gave
chase. They soon gained upon the strange
beast, and it, seeing that such was the
case, suddenly turned, and sitting upon its
haunches, commenced to beat its breast with
its hairy fists. It would break off the great
branches of trees that were around it, and
snap them as easily as if they had been so
many toothpicks. Once it pulled up a sapling
five inches through at the base, and snapping it in twain, brandished the lower part
over its head, much after the same manner a
man would sling a club. The hunters seeing

that they had a creature with the strength of a gorilla to contend with, beat a hasty retreat to camp, which soon broke up, fearing a visit from their chance acquaintance.

Mr. Smith describes the animal as being about six feet high when standing, which it did not do perfectly but bent over, after the manner of a bear. Its head was very much like that of a human being. The trapezie muscles were very thick and aided much in giving the animal its brutal look. The brow was low and contracted, while the eyes were deep set, giving it a wicked look. It was covered with long, shaggy hair, except the head, where the hair was black and curly.

Mr. Smith says that of late sheep and hogs to a considerable extent have disappeared in his vicinity and their disappearance can be traced to the hiding place of the "What Is It." Among those who have suffered are Henry Sharp, Jordan Sumner, Herman Laird, and J. C. Trendle.

Here is a chance for some energetic young man to start a dime museum and acquire a fortune within a very few years. Anyone wishing to learn more about this peculiar monstrosity can do so by calling on our informant who will no doubt take a delight in piloting them to the dangerous vicinity of the late scene of action.

Woodland, California, *Daily Democrat,* May 6, 1891

John and Dave Lowry were down from Rumsey Saturday. They say the strange and mysterious animal still sojourns in that vicinity and has frequently been seen by hunters. Many sheep have lately been devoured in the locality and the depredations are attributed to the "What-is-It." It is generally believed that the daring intruder is nothing more or less than a gorrilla. It will be remembered that some time last fall a circus train was wrecked and burned up north and many of the animals escaped. Among the number was a gorrilla and it is thought the animal has followed down the Coast and is now the object of so much curiosity in the neighborhood of Rumsey.

Woodland, California, *Daily Democrat,* May 13, 1891

THE "WHAT IS IT?"

STILL AT LARGE AND DEVOURING EVERYTHING WITHIN ITS WAKE.

We have received a communication from Mr. James E. Martin of Casey's Flat, giving us additional information regarding the strange animal seen in that vicinity some weeks ago. Mr. Martin is one of the best known citizens in this county and is well known in this city. At present he is homesteading a quarter section above Rumsey. Much of his spare time

Mr. Martin spends in trapping, and of course if any one would know anything of the "wild man of the woods" it would be him.

But to his story: About the sixth of this month, some of Mr. Martin's horses strayed from his premises. While out looking for them, he suddenly came across a trail showing that some kind of a dead animal had been dragged through the brush. The gentleman's curiosity was excited at such a large animal being made away with, so he followed it as fast as the jagged rocks and matted brush would allow him. Proceeding slow and cautiously, with keen eyes and steady nerves, he felt as though he was about to have a hand encounter with the beast that had done the killing. After going some distance, he came upon the partly devoured remains of a two-year-old heifer, which he recognized as the property of Mr. John W. Clapp. After the monster had satisfied himself on a large portion of the flesh, he had covered the dead carcass over with brush and dirt and had departed. Mr. Martin measured the tracks of the beast, and found them to be sixteen inches long and eight inches broad, with long claws, with which it had torn up the earth that covered the slain heifer.

Our informant is not a coward by any means, but he suddenly remembered that he always felt better about that time of the day if he had his trusty Winchester with him, so, making his way homeward, he took his gun, and, mounting a horse, proceeded to Mr. Clapp's, where he told him what he had seen. Mr. Clapp returned with him, and together they proceeded to the spot. To say that Mr. Clapp was grieved at the loss of his fine bovine, now torn limb from limb, would be putting it mildly.

Late that night, as Mr. Marin lay asleep, he was aroused by the piteous whines of his dogs, which are blood thirsty and ferocious animals. On opening the door, the dogs rushed in and skulked under the bed, where they shivered with fright and fear, and from which place they could not be driven either by threats or entreaties. Stepping outside to see what was the matter, Mr. Martin heard something moving away from his cabin, at the same time giving vent to some most unearthly screams that echoed from crag to mountain, and which finally died away in the lonely canons. The gentleman asks for aid in capturing of this unknown creature, and says that if he can but secure the necessary help, he will not stop until he has captured it dead or alive.

Here is a chance for some of our local braves to make a name for themselves.

In the late 1890s, according to an article published in *Many Smokes, National American Indian Magazine,* fall 1968, by Tawani Wakawa, Wakawa's grandfather had several encounters with large hairy creatures known as "Matah Kagmi." This was in the Tulelake, Siskiyou County, region (Crowe 1993).

Woodland, California, *Daily Democrat,* June 25, 1891

"THE WHAT IS IT"

SEEN ONCE MORE—IT HAS NOT REFORMED YET. Once more the wild and woolly "What Is It" has been seen. It does not seem to have reformed as yet, as it is as frisky as ever. This time the person who saw it was a Mr. Herman Gilbert, who was up in the head of Capay Valley looking for a suitable piece of government land that he might homestead.

He says that he was near Rumsey, where he was stopping with some friends. On last Monday morning he started out with his brother-in-law, expecting to be gone a day or so, as he wished to combine business with pleasure. They came to a nice little valley about half a mile long on Tuesday afternoon, and as it was cool, well watered and full of nice green grass, they determined to pitch their tent there. This they did, and about half an hour later Mr. Gilbert went to the spring near by to water the horses, and was surprised to see around it tracks very much resembling that of a man, but thought nothing of it. Incidentally, when he returned, he mentioned it to his brother-in-law. He then, for the first time, heard of the terror, and suggested that the two return and track the mysterious animal to his lair. This they did, and as they followed the foot prints, they found that they led to the other end of the valley. Just as they came to the end of the defile and were about to turn down the mountain side, they heard a peculiar cry, half human and half bruitish, and quite near them. As may be supposed, they wended their way very carefully and slowly. Before they had gone half a mile, they came upon a path. The gentlemen were too sharp to walk in it, and followed the direction it took by walking in the underbrush near by.

Just as they reached the bottom of the mountain, they came upon a deep ravine and there, walking up and down, could be see "his nibs" himself. Mr. Gilbert says that the beast seemed to be mad at something and would beat its breast, which was covered with gore, and the sound made thereby was like distant thunder. It had lost some hair since last seen, so the gentleman should judge, for the cuticle was plainly discernable and was of a dark color, much like that of a horse.

Near by was a crude cave where the anomaly lived. About it could be seen bones from which flesh had been eaten. The stench arising from the decaying matter was horrible. The muscles of the creature were very powerful, and the animal made an exhibition of its strength once by lifting a huge rock that would weigh at least three hundred pounds and throwing it, without any apparent effort, a hundred feet.

After watching the "What Is It" for some time the gentlemen crept quietly back, and as soon as possible left the locality, determined not to make any closer acquaintance with the Capay curiosity.

Oakdale, California, *Graphic,* August 31, 1892

Prairie City is excited over a wild man scare, and the shepherds are all reported to be leaving the range at the back of the town. Nobody seems to be able to supply a minute description of the ogre.

Fresno, California, *Weekly Republican,* August 4, 1893

THAT JABBERWOCK.

A KERN COUNTY JOURNALIST TELLS WHAT IT IS.

The author of the frozen man, the pterodactyl

and the tree-climbing clam stories has "got in big work again," and regales The Fresno Republican with a blood curdling account of some strange, uncouth creature that is ranging the wilds of that county. This wonderful animal "resembles a human being, beats his breast with his long, powerful arms, and gives utterance to loud, gutteral roars that make the air shiver as well as the spectators."

The probabilities are that Bully Foote and Eugene Deuprey are taking their summer outing in the mountains, and have been seen by some frightened campers who are not acquainted with the court room manners of those gentlemen.—Kern County Californian.

Fort Wayne, Indiana, *News,* November 18, 1908

WILD MAN OF THE MOUNTAINS

ROBS TRAPS OF PREY AND COMMISSARY OF SUPPLIES.
PECULIAR FOOTPRINT LEFT BY THE MAN-ANIMAL
AS HE FLEES FROM HIS WOULD-BE CAPTOR.
SPECIAL CORRESPONDENCE.

Santa Monica. Nov. 18.—Is there a wild man roaming the mountains of the Santa Monica range? There is, according to the story told by Bertrand Basey, who has just come down from the vicinity of Point Dume, where he has been acting as commissary for the contractors who engaged in the construction of the Malibu-Rindge railway.

Basey says that there were frequent losses from the improvised store house. At first, these were attributed the thieving proclivities of coyotes and mountain squirrels, but as it was found to be impossible to trap any of these animals further investigation was made, with the result of learning that the theft was due to some cunning hand whose movements were directed by a reasoning mind. He kept a strict lookout and was soon rewarded by the sight of a brown being fashioned after the form of man, approaching the tent. The thing was on all fours, was devoid of clothing or such covering as might have been provided by the skins of animals, and had a face covered with hair.

Basey was about to fire at the intruder when he was deterred by the close resemblance of the uninvited visitor to a man. Thinking it might be a railroad laborer in disguise, he made a noise as if to frighten the thief away. Suddenly the wild thing gave forth a guttural yell, rose upright on its hind legs and disappeared in the underbrush. Nothing more was seen or heard of the mysterious half-human beast, although the railroaders who went to the beach for a bath that morning are still wondering what manner of animal had been there before them to leave peculiar tracks in the sand. The tracks which they photographed were not unlike those that would have been left by the hands and feet of a man were he provided with long claw-like nails for each of the five toes and the four fingers and thumb.

Carson City, Nevada, *Daily Appeal,* March 5, 1918

ANOTHER CALIFORNIA WILD MAN

Chico, March 5.—George Bushwell of Chico, returning from the Deer Creek country today, reported finding the footprints of another "Ishi" at a spot a couple of miles from where "Ishi" was captured several years ago. A party from Chico was started out to find the "second Ishi." "Ishi" was a wild man, who startled university scientists a few years ago.

THE MYSTERIOUS FOOTPRINTS

Tulare, California, *Advance-Register,* October 28, 1926

THREE RIVERS IS ALARMED

GORILLA BELIEVED IN HILL COUNTRY

NIGHT CRY BRINGS OUT POSSE

Harassed and terrorized by the blood-curdling screams of a mysterious nocturnal marauder, residents of the Three Rivers district are now up in arms and making a determined effort to solve and put an end to the disturbing visits of the phantom, believed by some to be a large monkey or gorilla.

According to word brought here by residents of the section, the weird screams were first heard several days ago, but attracted only passing notice. However, the marauder has since appeared quite close to several farm houses and frightened the occupants with sudden and plaintive outbursts in the still of the night. Several residents report having caught fleeting glimpses of the phantom in the darkness and agree that it looked much like a large monkey or gorilla.

Other old timers suggested that the shrill cries are much like those of a panther. Still others are inclined to believe that it is an animal which might have escaped from a traveling circus.

In any event, the neighborhood is considerably "riled up" over the repeated occurrences and last night a posse of armed men was formed to scour the district, but as yet no report has reached here of the result of the search.

Eureka, California, *Humboldt Times,* 1960 (from Green 1978)

[This account took place in 1934, near Mount Bally.]

Two miles above the timberline, [Dave] Zebo ran into strange tracks in the snow. There was no animal or human to be seen within range. He stated, "I have never seen anything like these indentations of tracks before or since." The tracks were deep and heavy, but the spacing was what especially drew his interest. The tracks were from 4 to 6 feet apart. Too far for the stride of a normal man, but they were single tracks of a two-footed person or creature.

Pointing to the human element, Zebo said, was the fact that an animal will meander. A human, usually takes a straight path (and sometimes the hardest way) to his objective; while an animal is known to meander to find the easiest direction.

The footprints in the snow, of which Zebo was so curiously engrossed that he took photos of them, went from the bottom of the mountain to the top, from west to east; there was no deviation at all.

"I followed the old trail, and as far as I could see I saw the tracks, making the single line," Zebo said. "There were no other tracks around and I stayed the night in the lookout and came back down the next morning. A heavy snow fell during the night and covered the tracks."

The photos gave Zebo proof that the experience really had happened, and upon returning to Weaverville, he had the pictures developed. He showed these to a number of persons in the vicinity.

Speculation ran high, but no one came up with a solution, or among those contacted, had anyone ever seen such an incidence. The forest personnel were among those contacted, with no better luck at a solution. Everyone was interested and intrigued, and discussed the event for days without solving the mystery. "In those days," Zebo said, "we had not heard of Bigfoot." He has since wondered if Bigfoot was the answer to the puzzle.

To summarize the experience: The big tracks were definitely there. They were single, as a human's would have been, but too wide apart in stride (they never hesitated but went energetically up the mountain, as if made by a creature with gigantic strength) for an average man's. . . .

Lima, Ohio, *News,* October 2, 1938

SIMIAN BANDS ON THE LOOSE

San Diego, Calif., Oct. 1—(UP)—There is much monkey business in the back country of San Diego-co these days as ranchers tell strange tales of a band of simians which are running wild in the vicinity of Jamul, 20 miles east.

Conflicting reports of the renegades makes it impossible to determine their number, species or size. One thing is assured; there are wild monkeys in San Diego-co, and Luke F. Pace, Jamul rancher, has the hand of a full-grown female to prove it.

Pace shot the animal as she led a band of half-grown macaques on a chicken raiding expedition in Pace's hen coop.

Speculate on Origin

There is considerable speculation as to the band's origin. Mrs. Belle J. Benchley, executive secretary of the San Diego Zoological society, suggest they escaped their owners and have propagated during the passing years.

Another report is that a motion picture company turned them loose eight years after filming a picture in the vicinity of Jamul. Others contend they never were domesticated but wandered north from Central American jungles years ago.

The leader, a big black fellow, is the most elusive and cunning of the band. Many have reported seeing it swinging from the limbs of the giant oak trees in the late evening, but at the sight of humans, it scuttles away into the deep canyons where it is impossible to trail the creature.

Farmers in the region argue that the male is not a monkey but an ape, and those who have glimpsed him agree that he is of near-man size.

Sought by Hunters

Hunters by the score have sought the evasive colony, but always have been thwarted by the jungle-like undergrowth and rough terrain which makes hunting impossible.

So until a "bring 'em back alive" expedition succeeds in outwitting the black leader and his band, the chickens will continue to disappear, cats, ranch tools and small articles along with them, children will run home fearful of the "hairy men," and weird screaming and chattering will resound from the tall oaks to awaken the good people on Jamul on moonlit nights.

September 1942: "San Juan folks read about the latest exploits of the 'strange, giant creature—half man and half ape—that has been seen walking with a lumbering gait near Stanton." (Hallan 1987)

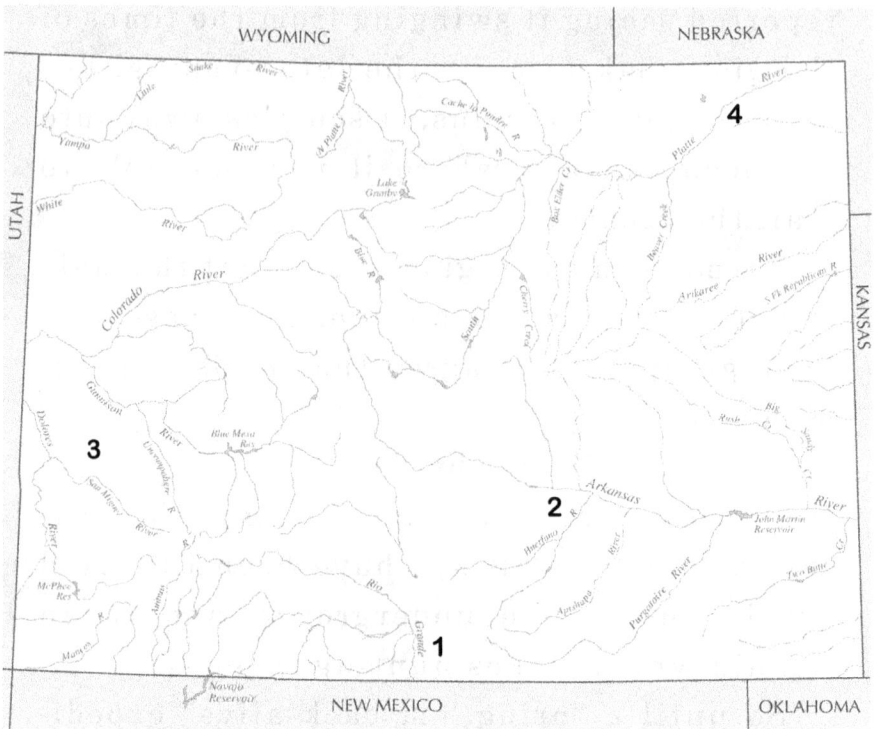

1 Sangre de Cristo Mountains

2 St. Charles River (Pueblo County)

3 Naturita (Montrose County)

4 Sterling (Logan County)

Colorado

Colorado Springs, Colorado, *Gazette,* March 30, 1878

A few days since, says a correspondent of the Rosita Index, a party of prospectors arrived in town, and gave the description of a terrible wild man which they had discovered in the Sangre de Cristo range. The man is represented as being about seven feet high— very large and strong and clothed in deer pelts. We understand that the party will try to capture this 'wild man' of the mountains this spring.

c. 1881: Green (1978) noted the story of the "Lake Creek Monster" from Grizzly Peak, a creature "resembling a man except for the extraordinary length of its arms, and the long shaggy hair covering the body." There are several peaks called "Grizzly Peak" in Colorado, so the exact location cannot be determined just from this brief note.

Pueblo, Colorado, *Daily Chieftain*, July 23, 1882

WHAT IS IT?

For several days past the people living on the St. Charles, about ten or fifteen miles from Pueblo, have been visited frequently, and at various hours of the day and night by a strange looking animal which has driven terror to the hearts of the more timid and caused the brave and doubting to wonder what can it be, and thirst for more knowledge concerning the strange beast which has so disturbed their usually quiet neighborhood.

The animal is a strange one, and his ways really seem past finding out. By some he is described as resembling a bear, by others a human, and still others as a strange and curious cross between a bear and a human. One gentleman, who claims to have seen the animal, declares that it makes a track like a bear with its hind feet, while its fore feet when used in walking make an impression on the soft, yielding soil on the banks of the stream just like the hand of a man. The animal's body is covered with long, shaggy black hair, while the face is only covered by a thin, short growth of hair, but surrounded by a thick mass of hair, giving the beast a [ghoulish] and uncanny appearance. Sometimes the animal walk on all-fours, but more frequently erect, and moves at a rapid gait, so fast in fact as to distance all pursuers, at least so far nobody has been able to get within shooting distance of the great unknown. The animal seems to be a restless ever moving thing, never seems to tire, and has been seen at so many different places at nearly the same time that by some supernatural qualities are attributed to the monster, while all have begun to wonder and fear the strange being. When walking erect or in a stooping posture as he moves along rapidly the beast seems to be nearly seven feet in height, and of monstrous breadth of shoulders and body and heavy weight. This strange being, be he human or devil, never leaves the bottom lands, and seldom comes from the shelter of the thick undergrowth and timber which borders the stream.

This strange creature first appeared in the locality mentioned about ten days ago, when some dogs scared him from his lair where he was resting, and chased him up the creek. The dogs were no match for him in speed, however, and he soon distanced them all. The next morning several hen coops had been disturbed, and quite a number of chickens were missing, and since then the animal seems to have adopted this mode of obtaining a livelihood. As may be imagined the farmers have become tired of this kind of thing, and propose to put a stop to it. Mrs. McMunn, formerly a resident of Bessemer, was in the city yesterday and informed us that a party was being organized to capture the strange creature. If possible, the animal will be captured alive, but if this proves impracticable or dangerous, then an effort will be made to kill the strange visitor, but this means will only be adopted as a last resort, it being the ambition of one and all to capture the strange creature alive. The attempt at capture was to have been made last night, and we only hope that success will crown the efforts of the ranchmen.

Pueblo, Colorado, *Daily Chieftain,* July 25, 1882
Senator Corder offers [$100] for the St. Charles gorilla alive, and $50 [dead]. This offer will stand good for three days, and as we understand the beast has been caught, no doubt the tempting offer will be accepted by the captors.

Lincoln, Nebraska, *Star,* October 22, 1922
TARZAN COMES TO LIFE ON WESTERN SLOPE OF ROCKIES
Denver, Colo., Oct. 21.—Weird stories of the ravages of a reported "wild man, half man,

half beast" in the Naturita valley in a thinly settled district on the western slope of the Colorado Rockies, reached Denver tonight.

According to the "eye witness" accounts, the strange hairy creature leaps across the waste places on all fours and subsists on the raw flesh of fowls and animals. Its body is gaunt and covered with long hair and the eyes gleam ferociously from under shaggy brows, residents of the valley who claim to have seen the animal, declare.

The reported hybrid has invaded barn-yards, killed chickens, robbed hens' nests and fled on the appearance of any person, the accounts stated.

Ranchers of the Naturita district are said to be planning a hunt in an effort to capture the creature.

Reno, Nevada, *Evening Gazette,* October 18, 1934

BOYS REPORT STRANGE ANIMAL

Sterling, Colo., Oct. 18—(AP)—Stories of a strange creature, unrecognizable as a man or ape, were told about Sterling today by four high school boys.

The young men reported that while they were walking along a dark street last night rustling of leaves was heard and they looked back to see an animal resembling an ape.

Uttering terrifying sounds, the creature
pursued them, the boys said.

Russell Moorman, one of the boys, who
was on crutches, discarded his crutches and
outdistanced his companions in the flight.

The boys organized a searching party
which spent the early part of the night in
unavailing hunt.

Castle Rock, Colorado, *Douglas County News,* May 6, 1954

NORTHERN DOUGLAS COUNTY RECOVERING FROM 'GREEN APE' HOAX OF PAST WEEK

Sheriff John Hammond has unmasked the
'green monster' that had the Plum Creek district in an uproar for the past week and the
curiosity-seekers who, up until Wednesday
were over-running the community near the
Plum Creek school have been disillusioned
and are looking for other 'sights'. Warren
"Buck" Jump, who lives south of Littleton,
was one of three witnesses who reported seeing a strange figure, like a giant green ape,
dancing and performing antics on an Indian
mound. The other two men, aided by the encouragement of Mr. Jump who now admits he
was in on the hoax, "took it a little too seriously", Jump said, and the story started snow-
balling until, with the aid of a front-page

spread in the Littleton Independent last week, the whole community was aroused. The two 'witnesses' to the apparition were Tom F. Sliger of Littleton and Frank Barton of Plum Creek Road.

Sheriff Hammond, pretty badly put out by the whole phony affair, got the thing straightened out Wednesday when Jump admitted that another man in costume and mask was the 'monster' who incidentally was not green at all. The touch of color was added through the processes of imagination so often figuring into such deals. Sheriff Hammond, however, refused Thursday morning to reveal the identity of the masquerader. He said "there's been enough trouble over the incident already." It seems that no one has violated any law, or at least that is the attitude of Sheriff Hammond, so the pranksters came off better than might have been expected. Folks, in the neighborhood of the incident are glad for two reasons. First, those few who fell for the hoax are glad there really is no need for fear. Secondly, they are especially glad that the crowds which were getting pretty annoying have been dispersed by the exploding of the myth.

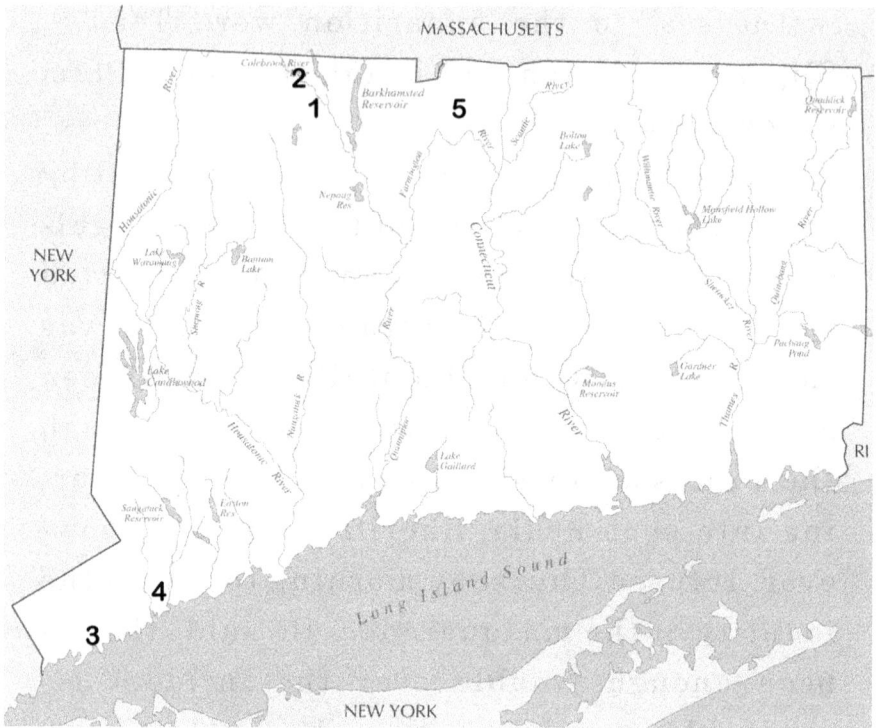

1 Winsted (Litchfield County)

2 Colebrook (Litchfield County)

3 Stamford (Fairfield County)

4 East Norwalk (Fairfield County)

5 East Granby (Hartford County)

Connecticut

In Connecticut, historical Bigfoot reports are practically synonymous with the Winsted Wild Man. Look this up online, and you'll find the story on various sites dedicated to exposing hoaxes. The story goes, Winsted reporter Louis T. Stone was responsible for propagating the hoax (according to Joseph O'Brien (1991), writing the story in 1895), going on to create a number of fantastic humorous phenomena for readers. Research by Michael T. Shoemaker (1993) and Gary Mangiacopra suggests, however, that this is a "hoax" hoax. Shoemaker (who considered a bear the likely culprit for the 1895 sightings) pointed out that Stone's later hoaxes were "little more than whimsies, trifling tall tales such as a tree that grew baked apples and a chicken that laid a red, white, and blue egg on July 4." He did suggest that Stone's earliest known fiction, a 1906 ghost story, may have been roughly modeled on the Wild Man reports. Keep in mind, that Stone was born in 1875, while the first 'gorilla-like' Winsted Wild Man reports began in 1891. It seems unlikely Stone faked the original stories, even if he did instigate or exaggerate the 1895 account.

New York, New York, *Times*, August 30, 1891

"WILD MAN" MAY BE A GORILLA.

Winsted, Conn., Aug. 29.—Passengers on Hall's stage from Colebrook yesterday saw an animal cross the highway, leap a fence, and then stand on its hind legs. As the stage drew near the animal ran into the woods. The passengers say it was a large gorilla, and it was supposed to be the animal that was heretofore reported as a "wild man," as it was seen in the same locality as that where the "wild man" was said to frequent. The gorilla probably escaped from some circus years ago. During last Winter a gorilla inhabited the woods in South Norfolk.

New York, New York, *Times*, September 4, 1891.

SEARCHING FOR THE "WILD MAN."

Hartford, Conn., Sept. 8.—When the Sandisfield stage reached Colebrook, near Winsted, at 10 o'clock this morning, Mrs. Culver ran from her house and stopped the stage driver. She said that the "wild man," or gorilla, whichever it is, spent the night on her doorstep. She was greatly alarmed. Mrs. Culver begged that help be summoned to catch the local terror. Six policemen and a large body of citizens set out from Winsted as soon as the stage reached there, and the country around Mrs. Culver's house will be thoroughly searched for the "wild man."

Barre, Massachusetts, *Gazette*, July 25, 1893

Was It a Gorilla?—A Sportsman Astonished— De Chaillu is wanted in this country just now, to ascertain whether the woods near Stamford, Conn., are inhabited by his famous gorillas. One day last week, while Mr. Cortis Wilbur, a sporting citizen of Stamford, was hunting in the aforesaid woods, he came suddenly upon what he supposed to be a large animal, digging roots. Carefully raising his gun, he took steady aim, and pulled trigger, but the weapon missed fire; whereupon the said animal straightened up, to the size and statue of a seven foot man, covered from head to foot with matted hair, and with an unearthly yell darted deep into the woods, at a speed more than human. As soon as Wilbur recovered from the shock inflicted upon his nerves by the horrible apparition, he turned toward home, and made for the bosom of his family at double-quick, convinced it was a gorilla or the devil. His story was quickly bandied from mouth to mouth;

and on the following day, several who had heard strange cries from the woods, during the night, volunteered to lead a party in pursuit of the wild man. A party was quickly made up; and, with Wilbur as a guide, they started on their errand—taking guns for protection, in case the sylvan gentleman should prove to be a secessionist. They soon discovered footprints similar to those left by a man's bare feet, which led directly from the place where the hunter had first seen the strange creature to a very dense thicket. All search for the "gorilla," however, proved useless; though they could distinctly hear its yells in response to their shouts. The matter-of-fact people in the vicinity believe the "gorilla" to be nothing more than some poor lunatic; and the authorities have taken measures to lure him to his keepers.

Hartford, Connecticut, *Courant,* August 21, 1895 (courtesy Gary Mangiacopra)

A WILD MAN.

HE APPEARS TO SELECTMAN SMITH AND SCARES HIS BULL DOG (WINSTED CITIZEN)

Last Saturday, Selectman Riley W. Smith went up to Colebrook on business. Mr. Smith, while there, went over into the fields and began picking and eating berries from the low brushes in the field.

While he was stooping over picking berries, his bull dog, which is noted for its pluck, ran with a whine to him and stationed itself between his legs. Mr. Smith being in a bent over position picking berries. A second afterwards a large man, stark naked, and covered with hair all over his body, ran out of a clump of bushes, and with fearful yells and cries made for the woods at lightning speed, where he soon disappeared.

Selectman Smith is a powerful, wiry man, and has the reputation of having lots of sand, and his bull dog is also noted for his pluck. But Riley admits that he was badly scared and that his dog was fairly paralyzed with fear.

If any of the readers of the "Citizen" have lost a wild hairy man of the woods, six feet in height, and want to find him, they can go up to Colebrook and when near the "Lewis place" wander around in the woods and fields and perhaps recover their lost property.

North Adams, Massachusetts, *Transcript,* August 23, 1895

BUILT LIKE A HORSE.

Winsted, Conn., Aug. 23.—The wild man was seen again yesterday by passengers on Dodd's stage, en route to Winsted from Sandisfield, Mass. He was in the same tract of brush as when seen last Saturday by Sebastian Smith, which is five miles from here on the old and lonesome highway leading to Colebrook.

The wild man lives in "Injun Meadow," as it is known to the countrymen. He is thought to be one of a family of three wild men seen two years ago. The man seen by Mr. Smith had no clothes, but was covered with hair. The wild man was seen in Canaan mountain a few months ago is thought to be the same person.

Farmers in that section are terrorized and afraid to go out of doors after dark, and the robberies of henneries and mysterious disappearance of calves, lambs, and even Sandisfield and Colebrook farms are

Blamed Upon the Wild Man.

Five hundred men leave here Sunday morning to hunt for the strange character. They will go out in gangs and surround Injun Meadow, and Cobble mountain farmers have given the use of their teams free, while every man of the posse is warned to go armed.

On Saturday, Riley Smith, while coming over the road, stopped to pick a few berries, but no sooner had he commenced to eat than the wild man emerged from the center of a batch of berry bushes. Smith was about scared to death. His dog commenced to whine, and with its tail between its legs sought refuge in Smith's wagon under a pile of blankets.

Mr. Smith described the man as an awful looking sight. He is large in stature and his head is the most conspicuous part of his body, being nearly the size of a horse's head. His teeth resemble those of a horse in size, but are pointed. His hands are extra large.

Scranton, Pennsylvania, *Tribune,* August 26, 1895

WILD MAN SEEN AGAIN.

A BIG HUNT FOR THE MYSTERIOUS CREATURE TO START FROM WINSTED TODAY.

Winsted, Conn., Aug. 25.—The wild man in Colebrook has been seen again, this time by Morris Paefflin, a well-to-do farmer of Colebrook, who owns one of the largest farms in the Litchfield Hills. While on his way here yesterday he saw the wild man eating blackberries in the berry patch near the Holmes farm. Mr. Paefflin got a good view of the hermit and describes his features as did Head Selectman Riley W. Smith, who saw the man in about the same locality a week ago today eating berries. Paefflin's story so terrorized the inhabitants of Colebrook that they came here in groups today and by roundabout ways. They did not dare to leave their homes unless armed. A Colebrook citizen, with an old musket or bull-dog revolver attached to an old army belt is a common sight in Winsted streets.

Some old settlers think the wild man a baboon which escaped from a menagerie here a score of years ago. It is thought the creature lives in a cave in the mountains around Indian Meadow. Hundreds of citizens say they wouldn't go near him for fear of being killed.

More than one party of berry pickers have been shot at from ambush while gathering berries in Indian Meadow in the past few years. Frank Keefe says that while he, in company with Nut Reidy and Al Simons, was berrying at the foot of Colebrook mountain two years ago this summer two frightful looking men emerged from an open place in the ground and ran like deer, shooting as they went. From Smith's description of the man he saw on last Saturday, the boys say they are positive that it is one of the two men that nearly scared them to death two years ago.

The searching party organizing to leave here at 8 o'clock tomorrow morning will number about 500 men. Many members of Company 1, Fourth regiment, Connecticut National Guard, will participate in the hunt. They put in three hours practice work at their rifle range this afternoon. Merchants are selling revolvers as they were never sold before, and if some of the volunteer cracksmen are not killed or fatally wounded by each other in to-morrow's search it will be strange. The spot where the wild man is though to hide in the mountains will be surrounded by squads of men. Justice John F. Simmons threatens to arrest every man seen with firearms tomor-row.

Hartford, Connecticut, *Courant,* August 26, 1895 (courtesy Gary Mangiacopra)

WINSTED'S "MAN HUNT."

(SPECIAL TO THE COURANT.)

WINSTED, AUG. 25.

The Sunday quiet of this inoffensive village was disturbed today by the tramp of armed men. In the early dawn they began to gath-er in front of the Beardsley House and long before the hour appointed to set out on the hunt for the wild man scores of men and youths were lounging about, examining their firearms and talking about the prospective "hunt."

The scene could not be duplicated short of a sortie against the Indians a hundred years ago. The word had been passed around for everyone to come armed, and the injunc-tion had been heeded. It was at once ap-parent that he must be a remarkable wild man who could escape the clutches of these lusty fellows. The display at arms—those of iron not flesh—was something to wonder at. Flint locks of pre-revolutionary days were modern compared with some of the apparatus on exhibition. The firearms market has been "short" over since the wild man was first reported seen and the result was plainly evident in the rusty old carbines, smooth bores and horse pistols that were carried. Some up-to-date young men had Winchesters swung over their shoulders, and tried to look as unconcerned as if this were an every-day occurrence with them. Others boasted finely mounted revolvers slipped in silver-trimmed holsters and had buckled about their waists ammunition belts well filled with cartridges. Some had their pistols in their hip pockets and those there were whose rear pockets were filled with something else. Knives were a favorite weapon, to judge from the number carried. There was a negro or two in the party, and of course they carried theirs in their boots. Others had them tucked away in a jaunty fashion under the belt, or carried them in their hands. Dirks, bowie knives, the bush knife, or machette, big double-bladed jackknives, "pig-stickers" and rapiers were in evidence, and there were several who carried clubs, base-ball bats and sling shots. If a small army of British were to be killed and quartered the party need not have gone out better armed.

Most of the men who started from here belonged in Winsted, although a few came in from out of town and two or three New York newspaper men were in the party. The hour for starting was 8 o'clock sharp and by that time 125 or more were chafing against any further delay. So the start was made, most of the hunters "hoofing it." Several teams joined the procession, a few were on horseback and the genuine "man hunt" that the sceptical had said would never come off, had auspiciously begun.

It is about three miles, as the crow flies, from the Beardsley House, Winsted, to the locality where, if the veracious story of Selectman Smith is to be believed, his nibs, the wild man, was last met. Horse, foot and dragoons, were on the spot in about an hour and the business of the day was ready to be transacted. Along the route and to the place of rendezvous had come a distinctly different class of hunters from those who started out from Winsted. These were the farmers who live in the vicinity of the wild man's domain. They none of them came without weapons and they were of curious and antique design.

One had an old-fashioned blunderbuss and another a brace of horse pistols such as were used in the Mexican war. Many of them said they hadn't had firearms in their hands for thirty years.

It had been said that the farmers in the neighborhood scouted the wild man story as a fake, pure and simple, and to test this statement the "Courant" reporter asked several of them what they thought about it. In eight out of ten cases he found these farmers believed in the genuineness of the wild man. Said one: "Doubt It? No, and I know a man who has lost chickens and sheep as seen him. I sleep with an axe under my bed and a gun in the corner." The opinion in Winsted is about evenly divided.

The party numbered 200 strong when the desolate Losaw place had been reached, horses and teams having been left behind on the main road. This was the farm, which is owned by Selectman R. W. Smith, where a week ago Saturday Mr. Smith claims to have been scared out of a year's growth by a real wild man, naked and hairy, a veritable "Monstrum, horrendum, informe, ingens."

The party divided up into squads of eight or ten, each squad with a leader and started out in different directions, so that the whole neighborhood was patrolled. One party was under the leadership of Michael Langdon, another was led by John Robert Cleveland, and men living in the vicinity took charge of other squads. The search was kept up till sunset. A great many went without food; some went without drink. A few carried lunch, but the zest of the search kept nearly the whole party till late in the afternoon.

What is regarded as the big find of the afternoon was an old cave on the Beardsley farm. Old residents remember this cave to have been the resort, years ago, of a gang of horse thieves, who made midnight raids on the farmers' barns and carried away their horseflesh over the Massachusetts line to swap and sell. The entrance to the cave is overgrown with underbrush, and is so small that one can only enter by crawling on hands and knees. After a little one finds it possible to stand upright, and soon a chamber is reached which a dozen men could occupy comfortably. In this cave were found some comparatively fresh bones and an old shoe. That's all, but it was enough to make many believe that they had found one of the wild man's haunts. And outside there were footprints of naked feet. In the cave was a fireplace and the remain of a fire and one of the party that entered claims to have found a bottle of milk there. The genuineness of the fluid is uncertain.

The most laughable incident of the day was the scare Constable Gillett had. This doughty official of the peace was armed with a revolver and was searching in the underbrush some distance from his companion, when he heard a rustle in the brush and says he thought he saw a human farm. He gave a scream of fright and started (all oblivious of his firearms) on the keen run, only to bring up sharp against a barbed wire fence. He was somewhat cut against the hands and face and had to stand any amount of good-natured chaffing from his friends.

Some persons claim that a man who is suffering with delirium tremens and is confined in an adjacent farm house is responsible for the wild man scare. They say he escaped from the house a week ago and it was two or three days before he was recaptured. When he was found it is said he was stark naked and raving mad. They say this man had only his shirt on when he left the house and soon got rid of that. They think it was this man Selectman Smith saw, but that his imagination played him tricks when he talked about the man's shaggy hair and long finger nails.

Selectman Smith did not join the search today. He said he'd had "enough of wild man" and would let others do the hunting.

WHY NOT HUNT THE HERMIT?

(BY NEW ENGLAND ASSOCIATED PRESS.)

Winsted, Aug. 25.—Some picnickers recently located a small cabin in the Colebrook woods and ran to town saying they had seen the wild man's cabin in the woods. Investigation today showed it to be the present quarters of Mort Pond, a hermit, who has lived in the forest the past twenty years. Searching parties are liable to start out any time. The inhabitants of Colebrook and other small hamlets north as far as Sandisfield, Mass, propose to organize among themselves to hunt the terror.

North Adams, Massachusetts, *Transcript,* August 26, 1895

A FRUITLESS SEARCH.

THREE HUNDRED ARMED MEN SCOURED WOODS FOR THE WILD MAN.

West Winsted, Conn., Aug. 26.—The hunt for the wild man in the wilds of Colebrook yesterday was made by a posse of 300 armed men, but all their scouring was of no avail. The only trace of the wild man to be seen were his footprints.

A hut was also discovered on the Beardsley farm, a half mile south of where the wild man had frightened so man people. A fire-place and a bottle, quarter filled with milk, were all there were to be found within the hut. Farmers think it is one of his homes.

Some picnickers recently located a small cabin, and ran to town, saying they had seen the wild man's cabin in the woods. Investigation yesterday showed it to be the present quarters of Mort Pond, a hermit, who has lived in the forest the past 20 years.

Searching parties are liable to start out any time. The inhabitants of Colebrook and other small hamlets north, as far as Sandisfield, propose to organize among themselves to hunt the terror.

North Adams, Massachusetts, *Transcript,* August 30, 1895
WILD MAN'S IDENTITY.
STRANGE MARAUDER NOW KNOWN
TO BE A FULL-GROWN GORILLA.
HAS BEEN PROWLING AROUND FOR THREE YEARS.
WILL BE FOUND HARD TO SHOOT
AND STILL HARDER TO CAPTURE.

Winsted, Conn., Aug. 30.—The Connecticut wild man, that has divided honors with the sea serpent, is a full-grown gorilla. John G. Hall runs a stage between here and Sandisfield, Mass. While he was passing through Colebrook a large animal crossed the highway

on all fours and leaped a stone wall. Hall
and his passengers at first thought it was
the wild man.

The animal, when the stage approached,
stood erect. Hall drew a revolver. The beast
did not stir. Hall stopped his horses and was
getting a good aim at the brute, when off it
sped on four feet into the "Injun meadows,"
uttering awful cries.

Mrs. Mushone and Miss Sadie Woodhouse
of New York city, who are summering in Colebrook, also encountered the animal while
they were driving in Winsted. The creature,
when they espied it in the "Injun Meadow,"

Was Standing Upright.

They are positive that the "wild man" is the
gorilla. They say that it has large white
teeth, black hair, a muscular form and is
about 6 ½ feet tall.

It is thought the gorilla made its escape
from some circus, and has since made its
home among the Litchfield hills. It has been
heard from in Norfolk, East Canaan, North
Goshen and Sandisfield, Mass.

The gorilla spent last winter in the southeastern part of Norfolk. Charles Benson of
that town saw it jump from a tree. The brute
chased him into the house.

A party of Norfolk people saw it enter a hole in the mountain last spring, and, after closing the opening with huge chains, they went to bed. In the morning they

Found the Chains Broken.

John Williams of West Norfolk met the gorilla three years ago while he was turning home one night. The ground was covered with snow, and the footprints of the animal were traced into the mountains.

A son of Richard Parson, a Sandisfield farmer, saw the gorilla steal one of his rabbits.

Mrs. George Marvin of South Norfolk saw the gorilla robbing her hen roost one morning last winter.

It became so hungry that nearly every farmer in the outskirts of Norfolk saw it prowling about his farm.

Carl Moore and Joseph Bruley shot at the gorilla last winter, but bird-shot had no effect.

New York, New York, *Herald,* September 2, 1895

DANEHY'S AWFUL THREAT

The Gorilla Rushed from His Cave and Put His Hunters to Ungraceful Flight

West Winsted, Conn., Sept. 1, 1895.—Now that the supposed wild man of this place is known to be a circus gorilla, it is not deemed to be such a wicked thing to hunt him on the Sabbath, for there is an ancient prejudice in this vicinity against circus or profane animals, but not against jackasses, as will presently appear.

In a word, the gorilla hunt of to-day might have proved a much more enjoyable affair than that of last Sunday but for the unfortunate bravery of "Scotty" Gibson, Robert McDowell Cleveland, James Paddleford and "Buffalo Bill" Fitzgerald, who camped in the Injun Meadows last night, in the hope of snaring the gorilla.

Long past midnight "Scotty" was awakened by a peculiar noise as though a big fat man were slapping his thighs with the palms of his hands. "Scotty" screamed, and instantly the others awoke, seized their guns and began blazing away.

Shot the Beast.

As soon as the smoke cleared away the men made bold to approach the spot whence the hideous sounds proceeded, and in the darkness it was seen that a strange-looking animal of portentous size was calmly grazing under a tree near by. "Buffalo Bill" fired, and the animal dropped in its tracks, but, as a local authority aptly says:—"When 'Pat' Danehy went after his jackass this morning he found it dead, and 'Pat' Danehy says he will issue warrants for the arrest of the whole party for trespass on his premises."

Notwithstanding this bad beginning of the Sabbath, a posse of fifty citizens left here this morning with every conceivable kind of weapon for the Colebrook woods, determined to bring the gorilla back dead or alive. On the road these were joined by forty farmers, who carried pitchforks, and a large number of picnic parties, of which the village historian says:—"These combined business with pleasure, and ate roasted clams and drank beer in the woods, especially those not acquainted with the dispensers of Sunday rum."

It may have been the smell of the rum or the personal presence of brave Meter Maloney, owner of the yacht Wildwater Lily, but certain it is that footprints were located around 2 o'clock near West Hill Pond leading into the cave, and of course there could no longer be any doubt that the circus gorilla was there.

They Fled in Terror.

Captain Henry S. Terrell, of the Fourth regiment and his crack riflemen are said to have suggested the building of a fire at the mouth of the cave. This may or may not be true, but certain it is that after the fire had burned fiercely for fifteen minutes an immense beast sprang through the opening and so frightened Peter Maloney and his companions that they forgot to discharge their firearms and ran home as fast as they could.

In doing this they lost the chance of freeing this township of the circus gorilla, for that is was he, and that he had in some mysterious way made friends with "Pat" Danehy's jackass, who was shot not far off by "Buffalo Bill" Fitzgerald, there cannot be any doubt.

There were a few scoffers in the store tonight who were saying that the smoked-out beast was a wildcat, but they were in meeting during the hunt, and it is easy work making light of the perils of the brave when you have been under the protection of the church at the hour of stress.

The death of "Pat" Danehy's jackass, however, is likely to put a damper on next Sunday's hunt, for there is a flavor of cruelty to animals in the incident. Meanwhile, nobody ventures within a mile of the gorilla's cave, and there is no use in offering a reward for his death or capture, because there are no Indian fighters around here.

Hartford, Connecticut, *Weekly Courant*, September 5, 1895

THAT LATE WILD MAN.

FIFTY WINSTED PEOPLE HUNT HIM,
BUT DO NOT FIND HIM.
(SPECIAL TO THE COURANT)
WINSTED, SEPT. 3.

Mrs. Culver, mother of Postmaster Culver of Colebrook, stopped Hall's stage this morning, saying that she had seen the wild man a short distance from her home this morning. She was very much excited and asked that a party might be sent out to hunt him down. The chief of police put six officers on the track and a number of citizens joined in the chase. The impression is that the wild man is an escaped lunatic, and that he may be dangerous. All accounts agree that he is a very large man. E. L. Perkins, who saw the wild man two weeks ago Sunday, saw him again this morning about 7:30 o'clock. Mr. Perkins was on the road from Norfolk to Colebrook, and the wild man peeped over the wall and him and then ran off towards a swamp. The party of fifty or more Winsted people who started off the hunt after him at 11 o'clock returned this evening, none of the searchers having a glimpse of the strange object they were pursuing. They were armed with guns and pistols, and carried handcuffs. The party went in a northerly direction, towards what is the wildest section of Connecticut, a region so extensive and so inaccessible that a force of 1,000 men would have hard work to run the wild man down. If he is captured it will be because of some accidental circumstances that places him.

Mrs. Culver and Mr. Perkins agree in the description of the wild man as a large man dressed in very ragged garments, ragged shoes and hat, and with but little semblance of clothes in the rags he wore. His hair hanging on his shoulders and his beard are jet black. He is apparently about 45 years old.

Brattleboro, Vermont, *Phoenix,* September 6, 1895

THE WILD MAN SEEN AGAIN AT COLEBROOK, CONN.

The wild man of Colebrook, Conn., has been seen again. He chased three men employed by M. P. Laeffhin, and they took refuge in a corn house. The wild man crawled under the house and succeeded in tearing off a small board when one of the men struck his hand with a hoe, severing a finger which had a four-inch nail. The wild man hurled himself against the corn house with great force and would have undoubtedly succeeded in destroying it had not Constable Flockton and

a dozen men heard the cries of the three im-
prisoned in the corn house and come to their
rescue. They opened fire on the strange figure, who bounded away. He seemed to be injured, but he distanced all of the pursuers.
The man's body is covered completely with
hair. It is thought by some that the object is
a gorilla which has escaped from a circus.

Philadelphia, Pennsylvania, *Inquirer,* September 22, 1895

A COUNCILMAN'S QUEER FIND

Unless several of the most reputable citizens
of Winsted, Conn., have had optical delu-
sions, a wild man is lurking in the Litchfield
county woods, says the Boston Globe.

Every day some new uncanny story is heard
about him—either a farmer arrives and tells
of depredations in his garden or hen roosts,
or a bicyclist returning from a country jaunt
has come across him.

Much of this information is incredible and
sounds as if it were the offspring and sounds
as if it were the offspring of overwrought
imaginations or a desire to be mixed up in
the sensation of the hour, even at the expense of truth. The story tellers would have
Winsted people believe that this unaccountable creature talks with them, barks at them,
holds up their horses on the wood roads and

milks their cows in the pasture. One of them brought in a pumpkin with the marks of long teeth in it and said the wild man bit it.

He is described as having all sorts of shapes, from a baboon to a mild lunatic with scanty clothing and disheveled hair.

So altogether the grocery stores where the farmers trade are the scenes of go-as-you-please story telling matches.

Selectman Riley W. Smith "discovered" the freak. Selectman Smith takes no part in the cracker barrel symposiums, however. He is inclined to be conservative and doesn't take any stock in most of the wild man talk. He is positive about what he saw and doesn't appear to want to make a sensation out of it.

Selectman Smith is one of the most respected citizens of Winsted, a prominent member in the Congregational church and a Prohibitionist. He never was known to tell a story before that was not entirely plausible.

Relating to his recent strange adventure, he has talked but little about town, not keeping it a secret, but merely telling what he saw in a matter-of-fact way when asked about it. The Globe is the first newspaper to get an interview with Selectman Smith.

On the day of his adventure, four weeks ago Saturday, he was chasing a lost hog.

The chase led him up to a lonely back road between the settlements of Winchester and Colebrook, about two miles north of Winsted. This road is traveled very little. Probably not more than twenty-five wagons pass over it a year. Although it is three miles long there are only two houses on it, and only one of these is inhabited.

Half through this road or horsepath the Selectman saw a clearing and remembered that when a boy he had found blackberries there. The day was very hot, the Selectman felt that blackberries would taste about right, and got out and hitched his horse.

But he had best tell in his own words what then happened.

"I stepped inside the clearing and saw at a glance that the berries were there, as I expected. But almost immediately with my first glance at the place I saw this strange creature. The instant I saw him his back was toward me.

"He was at the other end of the clearing, forty feet away. It was only a small place, you see, which had years ago been a garden, when a house stood on the site.

"His hand was reached out as though he was picking the berries. I think I interrupted him in a feast. He stood around 5 feet 10 inches, I should say, and weighed perhaps 180 pounds. He was naked, and his back and legs were covered with hair, apparently two or three inches long. He had very long, black hair from his head also, reaching down below his shoulders.

"Almost the instant I saw this creature he became aware that I was around. I think I may have stepped on a bush and alarmed him. At any rate, he turned his head just so he could see me over his shoulder, and giving out a sound such as I never heard before, gave one bound over the bushes and disappeared into the woods.

"For an instant I was very much frightened, because the sight was so unexpected. I had a big bulldog along, and he crouched at my feet and whined."

When asked if he had formed any theories in regard to the strange creature, Mr. Smith said:

"I have tried to reason the matter out, and I can't come to any conclusions. I can only believe what I saw. I think it was a man of some sort, however, for it ran like a man and had a human voice."

The scene of Mr. Smith's adventure is in the heart of a very thickly wooded tract. Indeed all the country, from West Winsted to

Sandersfield, twelve miles away, is as wild as could be found in any part of New England. The villages are small and scattering, and the woods between are dense, with very thick underbrush. How wild and uncanny is this region is shown by the game caught there. It is no uncommon thing to get foxes and occasionally a specially daring huntsman will bring in a wildcat. There are miles of hills unvisited by any human being year in and out.

This is not the first rumor of a wild man in this town. Several children a generation ago told stories of an ugly apparition.

Captain Henry Tirrell, a resident, who runs a little steamer on Highland Lake, says that twelve years ago when he was a boy he saw just such a creature as Selectman Smith describes. It was one day when he was returning from fishing and the hairy man ran away from him. Tirrell told his parents about it at the time, and they made sport of the story, crediting it to his "being afraid of the dark."

Another man named Phelps, now dead about four years, once reported in Winsted village that he had seen a hairy man in the woods.

If there are any two men in these parts capable of making a wild man tale believed they are Selectman Smith and Tirrell. Both stand very well in the community and some of the most influential people have been heard to remark: "If it had come from anybody else but Riley Smith I wouldn't have believed it."

Of course there are exceptions. They say that most everybody in Winsted has a morbid love for weird things, and that this will soon be branded the fool town of Connecticut because of the stories of wild men and wild cats and other bugaboo yarns that originate here.

It has been many times shown that some people in the borough are rather gullible. A few years ago Colonel Horn of this town, who was then practicing law, but is now one of the State labor commissioners, succeeded very easily in fooling his neighbors. Weston, the famous pedestrian, had been scheduled to pass through Winsted on a walk from San Francisco. Colonel Horn, who delights in practical jokes, went into one of the downtown hotels on the morning Weston was expected, and reported that Weston would be in West Winsted in two hours. The colonel then went home, dressed to impersonate Weston, and walked through the village street with hundreds of his townspeople on either side. He intended it merely as a burlesque, but he found everybody took the thing seriously.

They invited him to stop and take dinner in the place, and made him gifts, and the deception was carried on for more than an hour, until the colonel took off his hat, unbuttoned his coat and announced himself.

However, in spite of sceptics, the wild man story seems to have some credence with the police officials.

About ten days ago Chief of Police Stephen C. Wheeler and Deputy Sheriff Chester Middlebrooks, with two officers and a party of citizens, spent all day hunting the woods for the man. They went through a very large tract of woods, known as Indian meadow. The day before Edmund Perkins, of Norfolk, had seen a strange person enter the Indian meadow woods on the Colebrook road. This was Perkins' second sight at the supposed wild man. The day after Selectman Smith saw him Perkins was visiting his brother in Colebrook. He went out to the barn, he says, and passed within a few feet of a curious looking person.

Perkins' wild man had on a torn coat and a hat without any rim. His hair was very long. He carried a pail, which looked as though it had been over the fire. He pointed to Colebrook Center, and asked: "What's that place over there?"

Perkins went into the house to call his brother out, and when they returned the individual was gone.

The woods around the Perkins farm come very close to the house, and it would have only taken a second for any one to disappear in the brush.

Previously, however, potatoes have been missed from the place, and several times it was thought the cow which pastures close to the woods had been milked.

Nearly 150 people lined up around Indian meadow on the day of the hunt, but only eight cared to venture into the woods. These made an eight-mile circuit. They found places where the ferns were broken and trampled and the remains of a rude oven.

Many people who believe that there is a wild or demented man in the woods think that the search should be conducted stealthily.

Deacon Manchester, the famous prohibitionist of the town, has suggested to Mr. Smith that they two prepare a tempting layout, which shall include a quantity of whiskey, somewhere in Indian meadow. He hopes to get the wild man intoxicated and capture him alive, and make $10,000, to divide with Mr. Smith, by selling the animal to a museum.

Naugatuck, Connecticut, *Daily News,* June 29, 1898

What terrible nightmares some people have. The four Danbury men who claim to have seen a wild man nine feet tall and weighing about 500 pounds in the woods between High Rock grove and Naugatuck sometime between 11 and 12 o'clock, one night last week, must have had some terrible dreams that night. They should consult a physician at once and undergo a treatment for their malady. Another such dream might prove fatal.

Stamford, Connecticut, *Daily Advocate,* December 29, 1905

GORILLA IN NORWALK WOODS

AMBITIOUS HUNTERS [ENDEAVOR]
TO CAPTURE A BIG MONKEY

There is a real live gorilla at large in the woods near the big farm of Dr. Charles G. Bohannan, on the Rock Spring road, East Norwalk, and yesterday a party of men from that section engaged in an effort to capture the animal.

Herbert Silcox and Fred Carr, with several others, taking a walk, were surprised to see on the ridgepole of Dr. Bohannan's barn what appeared to be a human being. A closer inspection showed that it was not a human being, but a large monkey or gorilla, and that it was eating an apple with every evidence of satisfaction.

They threw some stones at the animal, and it came down from the barn and took to the woods. Several of the young men remained and watched the gorilla, while the others went back home and secured dogs. On their return the gorilla was properly 'treed' and the dogs were stationed at the foot of the big oak to prevent the gorilla getting away.

The animal was perched on a limb about thirty feet from the ground, and chattered in an angry manner. Herbert Silcox climbed the tree, but the gorilla attacked him, and forced him to descend hurriedly to save his life, as the powerful brute was much more at home in the tree than he.

The young men stayed around the tree until a late hour, and when they left the dogs remained at the foot of the tree watching for a chance at the strange animal.

Where the gorilla could have come from is not known, but the boys who saw it state that it is much larger than the average monkey, and believe that it has escaped from Barnum's winter quarters in Bridgeport, or from some zoological garden in New York.

Portland, Maine, *Press Herald,* August 6, 1949

GALLOPING WHATSIS—WITH CLAWS—TERRIFIES LITTLE CONNECTICUT TOWN

UNEASY RESIDENTS OF EAST GRANBY
STILL TRYING TO SPOT MYSTERY CRITTER

East Granby, Conn., Aug. 5. (AP)—Bear? Gorilla? Horse? Or is it some weird mysterious animal?

Uneasy residents in the Lake Basile section of this town asked those questions today after reports got around that there as a strange animal in the neighborhood.

The best description they could give as that it gallops like a horse and has the claws of a bear.

No one has seen it. Some have heard it. But there for all to see were its clawprints on the soft dirt road.

Morgan J. Horne was among those who reported hearing it—at ten minutes past midnight.

"It was nothing like I have ever heard before," he said. "My wife had a horrified look on her face."

The animal's breathing, he reported, was "terrific, almost unbelievable" and a lot heavier than that of a horse.

"When we heard this galloping noise and the heavy breathing, our English shepherd dog, Buddy, went crazy," said Horne. "He almost went through the screen.

Maybe the animal was two animals.

An examination of the prints by Detective Anton M. Nelson of the state police suggested that.

He said there were two sets of prints side by side, one large and one small.

Sportsman Ronald I. Miller opined, "Must be either a bear or a gorilla."

He used to do a lot of hunting when he lived in Maine.

If it's a bear, said Miller, it's a big one— more than six feet tall.

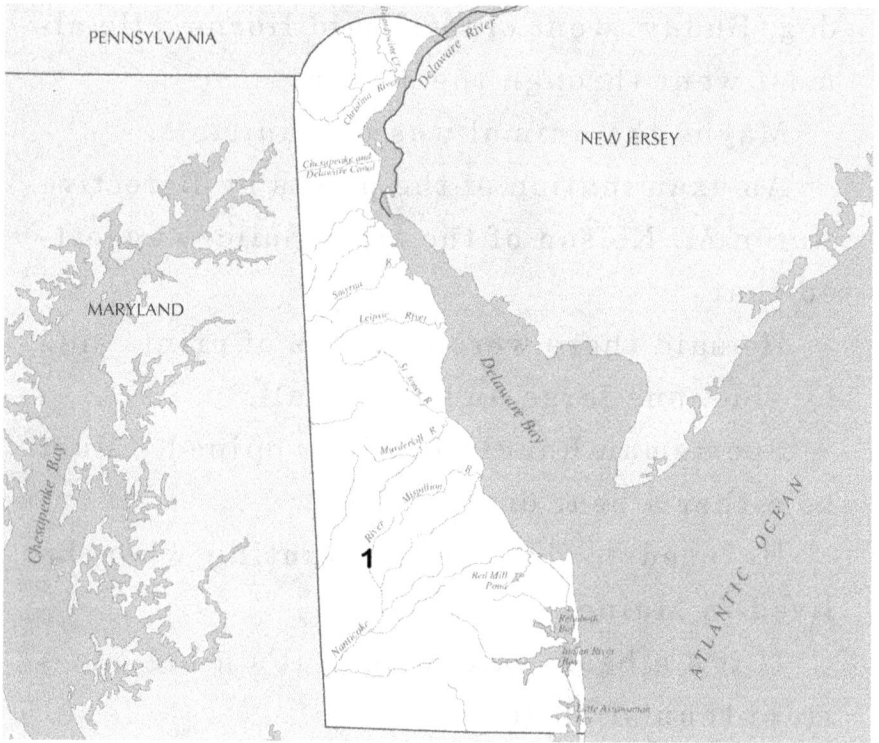

1 Bridgeville (Sussex County)

Delaware

Philadelphia, Pennsylvania, *Inquirer,* November 21, 1901
ATTACKED BY A GORILLA.

Bridgeville, Nov. 20.—Frank Biles, colored, was nearly killed last night by a gorilla near Bethel camp ground, eight miles from here. It is said the gorilla escaped from a circus menagerie at Seaford.

Biles was riding a wheel to Cannon's when he was attacked. It threw him from the wheel and dealt him a heavy blow with its fist. The man in some manner pulled his revolver and shot twice, making his escape to Cannon's. Upon reaching Cannon's he was unable to speak for some time. A crowd gathered about the man, his clothing was in shreds and he had an ugly wound over the ear.

A posse of about fifty men was formed to capture the animal.

(See MARYLAND for related accounts.)

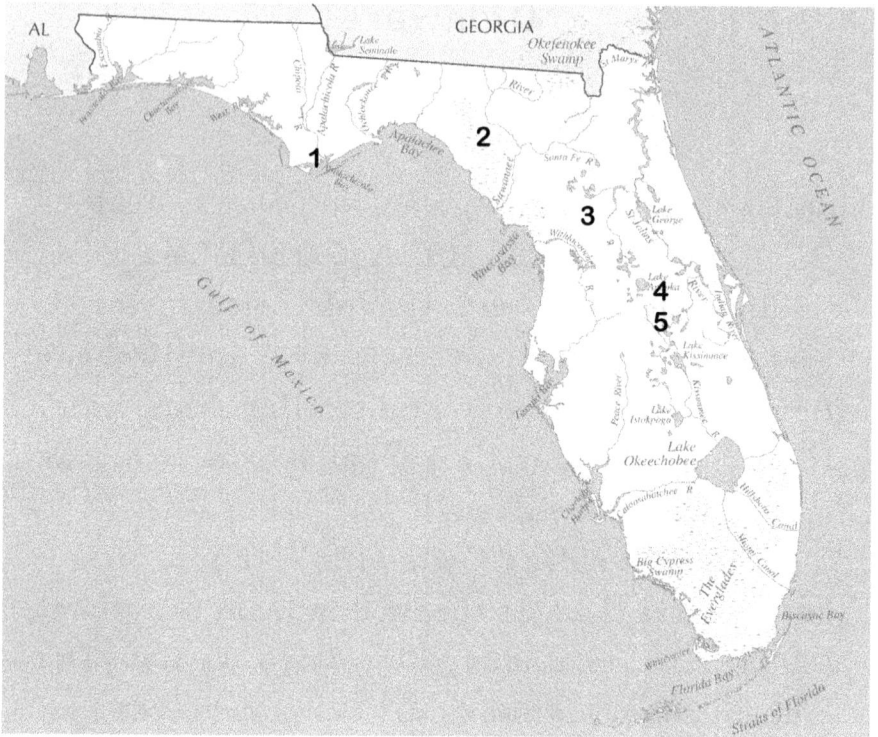

1 Apalachicola (Franklin County)

2 San Pedro Bay (swamp)

3 Ocala (Marion County)

4 Orange County

5 Kissimmee (Osceola County)

Florida

Lodi, New York, *Freeman and Messenger,* May 7, 1840

The Apalachicola Gazette states that the habitation of some unknown animal has just been discovered in the upper part of that city, which has given rise to many strange conjectures. The animal at the time of discovery was in it, but made its [escape]. It is said by those who saw it to resemble somewhat the baboon, and from the size of the nest it is judged to be five feet in height, and of a carnivorous description, as many bones were found about the premises. The nest was nicely made of loose cotton between several bales.—Ib.

Augusta, Maine, *Daily Kennebec Journal,* July 12, 1872

A wild man has been seen at San Pedro bay, Fla. He is said to be entirely covered with hair, and as wild and fleet as a buck. When first seen he was feeding on whortleberries, but as soon as made aware of the presence of a person, ran into the swamp. He is supposed

334 THE HISTORICAL BIGFOOT

to be some fellow who deserted during the war and sought shelter in the swamp.

Columbia, South Carolina, *Daily Phoenix,* May 17, 1873

A wild man has been discovered two miles from Ocala, Fla., in Scott's Cave. He is about six feet high and covered with white hair of bristle stiffness. It is not exactly known whether he is a man, beast or devil.

Newport, Rhode Island, *Daily News*, June 3, 1881

THE JIM-JAMS IN FLORIDA

Florida, Orange county, is greatly excited about a mysterious beast which is said to make nocturnal raids around the neighborhood. There is only one person—a negro—who will swear that he has seen the strange animal, but there are scores of persons who claim to have seen evidences of his depredations on adjacent farms, and to have heard his unearthly screams when startled by the approach of men. The Negro says that he suddenly met with it at the mouth of a cave on the farm of a Mr. Green, and that it stood erect to the height of seven or eight feet and screeched so loudly that it frightened him so badly that he fainted. When he regained his senses the animal had gone. Parties have explored the mouth of the cave on Green's farm, and while they claim to have discovered evidences of the whereabouts of some strange animal they have failed to come up with it. Tuesday it is said that a dead dog, with its back broken, was found near the mouth of the cave, and part of a sheep's skin and entrails were also close to the entrance. A party is being organized to search for and kill the strange animal, but the Negro will not be of the party.

Davenport, Iowa, *Daily Leader,* September 28, 1900

BLOODHOUNDS FEAR.

PART OF FLORIDA TERRORIZED
BY SHAGGY CREATURE.
IT WEARS CLAWS AND RIDES A RAIL—
WHEN FIRED UPON IT ROARS A ROAR
THAT MAKES ONE SHIVER—
BRAND OF WHISKY NOT STATED.

Kissimmee, Fla., Sept. 28.—Great excitement exists about here over the fact that a wild-man is roaming through the woods, and not a woman or child will venture out at night, nor half the men, excepting in company.

One day last week Mrs. Arthur Shiver, who lives a mile from town, saw a strange creature skulking about near the house. It had the figure of a man about four feet high. It was without clothing and was covered with short, shaggy black hair. Its skin was red and the hair on its head was black and hung below its shoulders. It walked on its feet in a crouching attitude, and held between its legs a sort of stick, which it rode, as children do, dragging one end on the ground. Its arms were long and the fingers looked like claws.

Mrs. Shiver called to neighbors who were at the house and tried to catch the creature, but it bounded into a ditch and disappeared. They tracked it up the ditch to a swamp, where it was seen crawling into a big bunch of palmettos. Search was made, but no further sign of it was seen.

The creature's track was plainly seen along the hard bottom of the [d]itch. It was about six inches long, with a deep imprint of the ball of the ball of the foot and a claw mark showing that the nail of the big toe was an inch long at least. The other toes protruded and left imprints like sharp claws. All the way up the ditch was the trail of a stick or something clearly marked in the hard sand.

Three bloodhounds were put on the trail. Two of them paid no attention to it, but one, an old hunting hound, bristled up, showing acute symptoms of fear and refused to follow.

Before the monster took to the ditch Mrs. Shiver's daughter, while trying to cut it off at a fence came within a few feet of it unexpectedly and had a good look at it, and she said it growled at her and shook the club.

The general opinion is that it must be a wild Indian. At the time it was seen there was a party of fifteen Indians at Lake View, not far off, but it is not supposed that the wild creature has any connection with this party.

Several times dogs have found the trail near the town, but after following it a short time have returned with signs of fear and trembling, and no urging could set them on again.

Reports have come in that the creature attempted an attack upon Bill Went's house, near Canoe Creek, and that Went shot at it several times before it left. It was heard to utter a kind of roar and seemed in a great rage when fired upon. A hunting party will set out this week in search of the monster.

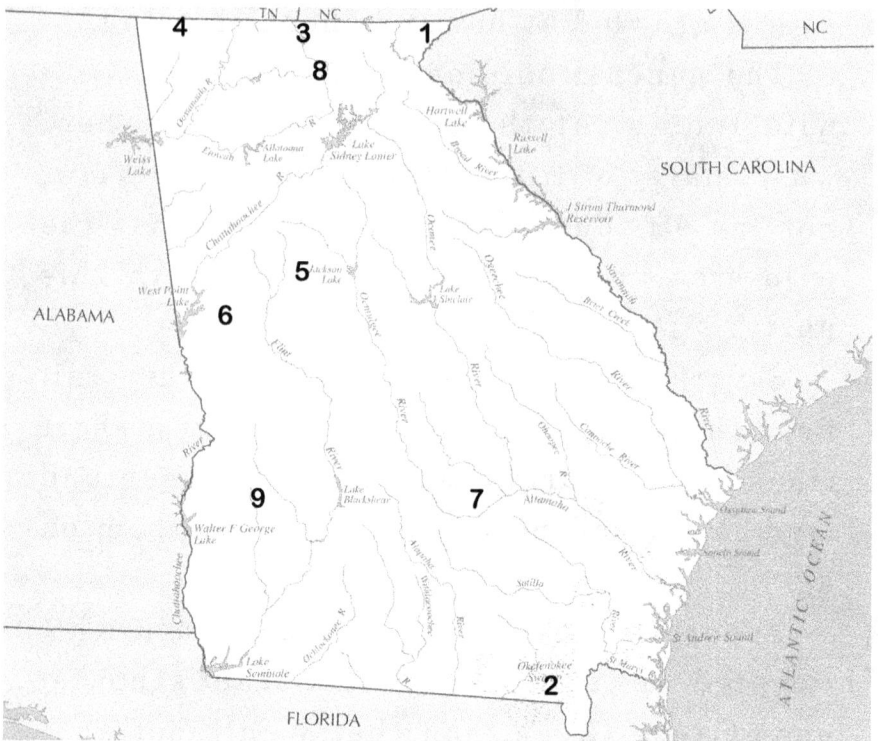

1 Rabun County

2 Okefenokee Swamp

3 Fannin County

4 Lookout Mountain (Walker County)

5 Jackson (Butts County)

6 Greenville (Meriwether County)

7 Satilla River Swamp

8 Little Mountain

9 Dawson

Georgia

Delphos, Ohio, *Daily Herald,* May 14, 1901

AN EARLY GEORGIA MONSTER.

In the fore part of August, 1812, a party of hunters found in a mountainous region now known as Rabun county, Ga., a being nearly eight feet high covered with bluish hair and having a human face adorned with immense ears resembling those of an ass. The creature was stone deaf and on that account seemed wholly unconscious of the approach of the men. This monster seems, from old accounts, to have been seen upon several occasions during the next four years.

In 1816 a number of adventurers from Virginia, most of them surveyors working up the unexplored portions of Georgia and the Carolinas, formed themselves into a party for the express purpose of capturing the uncanny being if possible. They scoured the hills and valleys for several days and at last returned unsuccessful to the starting point.

The many tales told of this extraordinary being seem to have created quite a stir all along the Atlantic coast. A printed circular issued by a land company in 1815 says, "The climate of Georgia is exceedingly mild, the soil productive, and the danger of attack from uncouth beasts which are represented as being half beast and half man are fairy tales not worthy of consideration."

Hagerstown, Maryland, *Torch Light and Public Advertiser,* March 19, 1829

A GIANT STORY.

FROM THE MILLEGEVILLE (GA.) STATESMAN.

There is a tradition among the Creek Indians, that there is, in the trackless gloom of the Okefenokee Swamp, an island of enchanting beauty, more blissful than any spot on earth. While it is generally thought that this murkey fen—this black sea of Avernus, contains nothing higher in the order of being than countless armies of mosquitoes, snakes, frogs and alligators; the Indians say that in the terrestrial paradise on this island there dwells a race of mortals of super-human dimensions and incomparable beauty. This island, tho' sometimes seen, is represented as inaccessible from the attribute which it possesses of locomotion; thus eluding approach—

or from the ever varying labyrinth of fens
and bogs, by which it is entrenched, and in
which the bold invader is confounded who
ventures too near this enchanted spot. Thus,
lost in inextricable sloughs, a few intrepid
hunters were once saved from perishing, by
a company of women from this island, of surprising form and beauty, whom they denom-
inated the daughters of the Sun, or children
of the Great Spirit. Having kindly supplied
them with refreshments, and pointed out to
them a way for a retreat, they admonished
them to fly for safety, for that their husbands
were fierce men, and cruel to strangers.

This legend we have hitherto regarded as
fabulous; but Mr. John Ostean, residing on
the borders of this swamp, in Ware County,
and some of his neighbors over the line in
Florida, have become satisfied from ocular
reality, and they so aver, that it is mainly a
matter of fact! We has a their statement in
writing, tested by a respectable witness, who
has put the paper in our hand containing the
following facts—we beg the gentleman's par-
don— truths we should say.

Not long ago, two men and a boy, in the
vicinity of this swamp, like our friend Paul
Fry, "had a curiosity to know, you know,"
what could be seen by two or three weeks

pilgrimage into the inaccessible regions of this dismal empire. The season being unusually dry, they pushed their exploration far into the interior, and at the end of a little more than two weeks, found their progress suddenly arrested at the appearance of the print of a foot-step, so unearthly in its dimensions, so ominous of power, and terrible in form, that they were at once reminded of the legend we have mentioned above, and began seriously to apprehend its solemn reality. The length of the foot was eighteen, & the breadth nine inches. The monster from every appearance, must have moved forward in an easy or hesitating gait, his stride, from heel to toe, being but a trifle over six feet. Our adventurers had seen enough, and began to think of securing a retreat, without waiting to salute his majesty, not doubting but the other part of the story might also prove true—of his fierceness and cruelty. They happily effected their escape, returned home, and related the history of their adventures, and what they had seen, of the "Man Mountain." A company of Florida hunters, half horse and half alligator, nine in number, determined, a few months since, to make this gentleman a visit to ascertain if he had a family, and his manner of living. Following, for some days, the direction of their guide, they came at length upon the tract first discovered, some vestiges of which were still remaining; pursuing these traces several days longer they came to a halt on a little eminence, and determined to pitch their camp, and refresh themselves for the day. The report of their rifles, as one or two of them were simultaneously discharged at an advancing and ferocious wild beast, made the still solitudes of these dismal lakes reverberate with deafening roar. Echo beyond echo took up and prolonged the sound, which seemed to die away and revive in successive peals for several minutes. The report had reached and startled from his lair the genius of the swamp, and the next minute he was full in their view, advancing upon them with a terrible look and ferocious mien. Our little band instinctively gathered close in a body, and presented their rifles. The huge being, nothing daunted, bounded upon his victims, and in the same instant received the contents of seven rifles. But he did not fall alone, nor until he had glutted his wrath with the death of five of them, which he effected by wringing off the head from the body. Writhing and exhausted, at length he fell, with his hapless prey beneath his grasp. The surviving four had opportunity to

examine the dreadful being as he lay extended on the earth some time, wallowing and
roaring.

His length was thirteen feet, & his breadth
and volume of just proportions. Fearing lest
the report of their rifles, and the stentorian
yells of the expiring giant should bring suddenly upon them the avengers of his blood,
they betook themselves to flight, having first
secured the rifles of their headless comrades,
and returned home with this account of their
adventures.

The story of the report, as related above,
is matter of fact, and the truth of it is ac-
credited, we are told, by persons living an
the borders of this swamp, and in the neighborhood of the surviving adventurers.

Morristown, Tennessee, *Gazette,* May 28, 1873

A MONSTER AT LARGE.

FROM THE CLEVELAND BANNER.

Editor of the Banner—Dear Sir: The horrible
sight of a hairy man has been seen in Fannin
county, Georgia. He is wild and monstrous—
he has been seen in houses carrying off wom-
en and children. He is eight feet high and is
covered all over with a black curly hair. He
started from a house lately with a woman in

his arms, but by the approach of two men she was released. The settlement was alarmed and pursuit given on horseback. After a hard ride the monster was overtaken and a terrible fight ensued, in which a man by the name of John Haircrow was killed, and a horse had his tail torn off, and the pursuers were forced to retreat and leave the field in possession of the monster. The settlers are arming themselves with guns and watching for him. He makes his appearance just before or in time of a rain.

Yours truly, David A. Ballew, Jr.

Wolf Creek, Cherokee co., N.C.

Fort Wayne, Indiana, *Daily Gazette,* March 25, 1884

It is reported by a man who lives on one of the spurs on Lookout Mountain that there is a wild man roaming about who is of giant size and as hairy as a Newfoundland dog and as well as he can guess, about nine feet high and will weigh near five hundred pounds— his eyes giving light equal to the moon—an appearance of the most frightful nature and growls equal to the lion, causing the people in the section to remain home of nights with closed doors and well fastened.

Atlanta, Georgia, *Constitution*, June 11, 1888

A STRANGE CREATURE.

FROM THE JACKSON, GA., ARGUS.

In going over my plantation a few days ago I saw some cow tracks. The tracks were in a place, strange to say, that a cow could not possibly have gotten into. Moved by curiosity I followed the tracks, and directly I came upon a—I don't know whether you would call it a wild man or a beast. It had hoofs like a cow, hair like a cow, a short tail something like a deer, hands like a man and extra large red eyes. It walked like a man bent half forward. On getting a scent of me it gave a peculiar whistle like a deer, raised its head and dashed away. I was greatly excited, but as soon as I recovered sufficiently I went to see my neighbor, Joe Wright. He asked me not to say anything about it, as he thought he could get a large steel trap with wings like a partridge net for a hundred dollars and catch the creature. In case this plan failed Mr. Wright said he would offer a $500 reward for it alive or $150 for its hide. Mr. Wright already has a circus wagon and says that if we could get this curiosity our fortune would be made. Neighbor Wright is a [married?] man and didn't move fast enough for me, for honestly, I am afraid to move about my premises.

I went to Marshal Malone, but he didn't give me much encouragement. Then I went to Marshal Conn. He said that he was "no detective, and did not consider it his business to tackle a wild man in the woods, but if it came to town and cut up any devilment he would carry it before the mayor." I spoke to the sheriff about it and he said he would do all in his power to capture it, and with this object in view, has ordered a fine blood hound. He wants 150 men to meet him in Jackson on the fourth Sunday in this month, but as for myself I am going to stay at Neighbor Ball's till that animal is either caught or run out of this country. I think it will be very dangerous for black folks to gather blackberries until it is caught or killed.

Atlanta, Georgia, *Constitution,* February 4, 1889

A WILD MAN IN WALKER.

The wild man has again made his appearance. He was seen last week near High Point by a reliable gentleman, who was searching along the spurs of Lookout Mountain for mineral indications. On arriving at the head of the hollow, just above Mrs. Oliver's, his attention was attracted by thrilling screams on the side of the high spur that he had just passed along the trail below. He looked in the direction from which the noise came. What should he see but the wild man. When his fright cooled down, he discovered that the old fellow was not making any move towards him, but was standing erect and shaking his fist at him and showing signs that were not favorable to a human being. Therefore, get away was thought about immediately, but before starting he thought he would examine the wild gentleman more minutely. He was about 100 yards from him, but could distinctly see his teeth, nose and eyes, and describes him thus: Was about 7 or 7 ½ feet high, hairy as an old bear, and would weigh, from his looks, 400 pounds; had a pole in one hand that looked to be ten foot long, which he handled as easy as a stout, healthy man would a pipestem. His name was asked, and the answer came in the shape of a large stone, which weighed at least 100 pounds, which was hurled at the inquisitive gentleman. This being done there was no time left for any further inquiry, consequently he tried the working speed of his legs and feet, which worked most excellent until he arrived at Frank Carter's shop, almost breathless. As soon as he could narrate his story a crowd was collected which started in search of the wild man of Lookout Mountain.—Walker County Messenger.

Atlanta, Georgia, *Constitution*, March 16, 1889

THE WILD MAN ABROAD AGAIN.

Ringgold, Ga., March 15.—[Special.]—Walker county is torn up over the reappearance of the celebrated wild man of Lookout. He was seen a few days since, and if descriptions are correct, he is a most remarkable being. His hair and beard are described as flowing to the waist, his fingers and toe nails are long, giving the hands and feet a resemblance of claws. He wears a trunk of bear skin with a bear skin robe thrown over his shoulders. He carried an ugly bludgeon, and persistently avoids coming in contact with anybody.

Macon, Georgia, *Telegraph*, March 25, 1889

In the moonlight last Monday night, at the Muse bridge across Walnut creek, five miles east of Greenville, a singular wild beast was seen by Mr. Chipman. The strange quadruped was first observed in an erect position walking on its hind feet. In this attitude it appeared to be about four feet high. It was the size of an ordinary dog and was covered with a long, thick coat of hair. On discovering Mr. Chipman it became frightened and scampered away on all its four legs. What it is and where it hailed from no one has any idea. In the day it lurks in the jungles of the creek swamp. At night it steals forth and stalks on two feet along the highway.

Atlanta, Georgia, *Constitution,* June 4, 1895.
Another wild man has been discovered in the Satilla river swamp. He is described as being about six feet high, very black and flees at the sight of a white man. He has been seen by different parties.

1943: Berry (1993) noted the highly questionable story of a 7- to 8-foot-tall hairy manlike creature that was killed at Little Mountain and paraded around in the back of a pickup truck before being buried somewhere under a pile of rocks.

1955: The Georgia Bureau of Investigation determined that a "hairy ghost" in Edison, Georgia, was simply a farmer who dressed in a sheet to scare trespassers from his private lake ("'Hairy Ghost' is just an irate landowner," Logansport, Indiana, *Pharos Tribune,* August 6, 1955). At the same time, another strange report occurred in Dawson, Georgia, about thirty miles away, which newspapers unfortunately attempted to connect:

Long Beach, California, *Independent,* August 4, 1955

CREATURE STALKS WOODS: 'HAIRY GHOST' SEEN BY FOREST WORKER

Dawson, Ga. (UP)—The "hairy ghost of Edison" has shifted his haunting grounds about 30 miles and "attacked" a state forestry worker, the still shaking "victim" reported Wednesday.

Joseph Whaley, 20, told his employer, Forest Ranger Jim Bowen, of a terrifying encounter with the "creature" and repeated the story under oath.

Bowen said he went into the woods where Whaley said he was set upon by the six-foot apparition and found "very definitely a trail there."

"Very definitely something was there that looked like a large object," Bowen said.

Whaley said he went into the woods in the Bronwood Road section between Dawson and Americus last Monday to cut grass with a sling blade.

"I walked to the edge of the woods and heard the bushes rattle," he said. "I saw a strange creature coming toward me. It was six feet high, gray in color and built something on the order of a man.

"It reminded me of a gorilla. The creature walked toward me, I swung at him with the

blade and missed. I swung a second time and
hit it on the right hand or paw. I hit him
again on the hand and then in the chest. I
saw I wasn't doing any good so I broke and
ran to the jeep and tried to call the ranger
tower on the radio.

"Then something hit me on the left shoulder, tore my shirt and left three scratches on
my shoulder."

Whaley said he then jumped out of the
other side of the jeep, ran around it and got
enough space between him and the "creature"
to get cranked up and away from the scene.

Whaley's description tallied closely with
that of the Edison "ghost" which has reportedly been operating about 30 miles east of
this woodsy southwest Georgia section. The
Edison apparition was said to be capable of
vaulting over six foot fences.

On ones such leap it left a patch of white
hair which Wayne Dozier sent to the state
crime laboratory in Atlanta for analysis.

Crime Doctor Herman Jones reported
Tuesday the "ghost hair" was human.

The people of Edison, a small community in the southwest corner of Georgia, have
dubbed the apparition the "hairy ghost" because "witnesses" agree it is covered with
scraggly hair, variously described as gray,
white or platinum blonde.

Idaho

Brooklyn, New York, *Daily Eagle,* May 3, 1867

A gorilla has been seen in Idaho.

Newnan, Georgia, *Herald,* May 18, 1867

Idaho Gorilla. We are informed that one of these wild beasts in human shape, has taken his abode in Boise valley, near Snake river. He is represented as being from six to seven feet high, and covered with a heavy coat of hair. He is swift on foot, outrunning horses with ease. Several parties now in pursuit corraled him once, but he foiled them by gnawing the rope which had been thrown over his head. His tracks represent those of a human being, except the toes are longer and appear by the tracks made in the snow to be hoofed. He has taken to the hills. Parties are still in pursuit, and when captured we predict a valuable addition to Barnum's family collection.—*Idaho Times.*

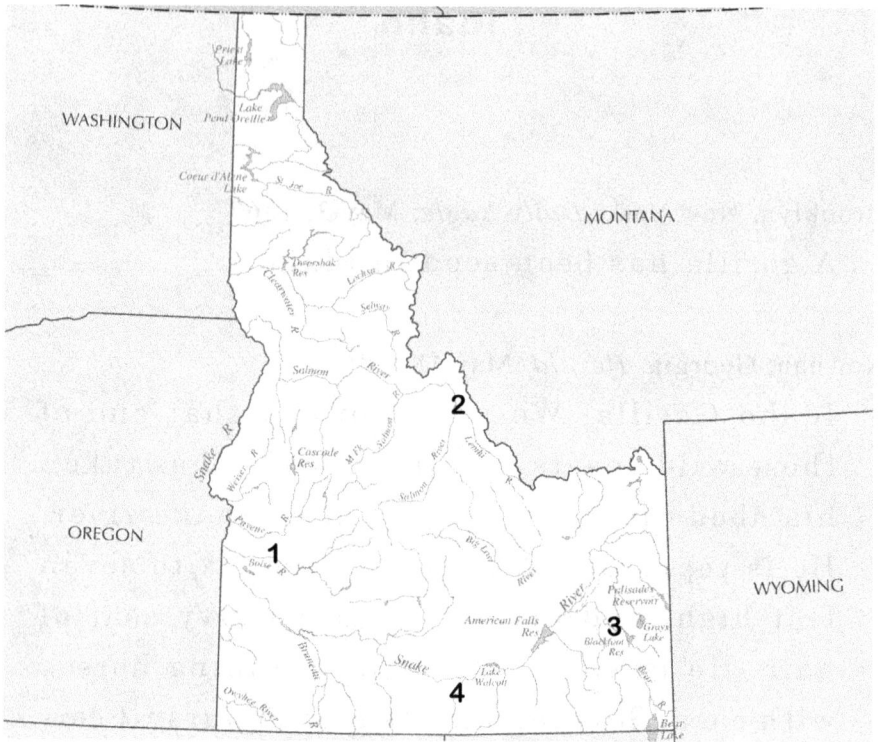

1 Boise (Ada County)

2 Mountains dividing Salmon River forks from Wisdom River (now Big Hole River)

3 Chesterfield (Caribou County)

4 Oakley (Cassia County)

1882: Peck (1977) and Varley (2010) both noted that newspaper publisher T. E. Picotte of the Hailey, Idaho, *Wood River Times* created a series of newspaper stories about a hairy wild man who roamed the plains and mountains north of the Snake River, calling it "The Wild Man of Camas" and describing it as having "a body thickly covered with hair, a tusk protruding from each side of his mouth, sharp claws for nails and presenting a most horrible appearance." In 1883, a reporter for the rival newspaper, the Bellevue *Sun*, wrote an article killing off the character; an angry Picotte noted that the wild man had been "ruthlessly killed by the Noodle of the Sun."

Helena, Montana, *Weekly Herald*, October 19, 1882

A WILD MAN IN IDAHO

Two Veracious Cow Boys See and Chase the Solitary Savage of Snake River.

[Hailey Times.]

Two cowboys who just came in from Camas Prairie relate an experience which will probably go a great way toward reestablishing the popular faith in the wild man's tradition. On the first day of this month two cowboys searching for cattle lost in the story passed over some lava crags, and were startled by suddenly seeing before them the form so often described to them. They were so terrified that they sat upon their horses, looking at it in dread. Mustering courage and drawing their revolvers they dismounted and gave chase, but the strange being skipped from crag to crag as nimbly as a mountain goat. After an hour's pursuit both young men were so utterly worn out that they both laid down—seeing which the wild man gradually approached them and stopped on the opposite side of a gorge in the lava, from which point he regarded the cowboys intently. The latter would not shoot, as they considered it would be unjustifiable, though they kept their pistols ready for use, while carefully returning the compliment in thoroughly inspecting the phantom of Snake River.

The wild man was considerably over six feet in height, with great muscular arms which reached to his knees. The muscles stood out in great knots, and his chest was as broad as that of a bear. Skins were twisted about his feet and ankles, and a wolf-skin about his waist. All parts of his body to be seen were covered by long, black hair, while from his head the hair flowed over his shoulders in coarse, tangled rolls, and mixed with a heavy beard. His face was dark and swarthy, and his eyes shone brightly, while two tusks protruded from his mouth. His fingers were the shape of claws, with long, sharp nails, and he acted very much as a wild animal would which is unaccustomed to seeing a man. The boys made all kinds of noises, at the sound of which he twisted his head from side to side and moaned—apparently he could not give them any "back talk;" so, wearying of eyeing him, the two boys fired their revolvers, whereupon the wild man turned a double somersault and jumped fifteen feet to a low bench and disappeared, growling terribly as he went.

It is supposed that this is the same apparition that has so often been seen before. The man, no doubt, does as the Indians did for subsistence, and lives on Camas roots, which grow wild by acres, and he no doubt kills young stock as many yearlings and calves disappear mysteriously, and nothing but skeletons of them are ever found.

The boys at the stock camp are arranging to go out on a scout again to overtake him, when, being provided with lariats, they will lasso him and bring him to Hailey, to deliver him up to the county authorities.

Idaho City, Idaho, *Idaho Semi-Weekly World,* February 20, 1883

We learn from a reliable source that the big story, in a recent issue of the Bellevue Sun, of the killing of the "Wild Man of

Camas," was made of whole cloth. Picotte, of the Times, had been in the habit when items were scarce, of writing up yarns about this imaginary personage. The Sun, in order to head him off, and spoil his chance for a big item when most needed, concluded to slay the Wild Man. One of the Sun reporters did it with his little pencil. "For ways that are dark and tricks that are vain," the Wood River papers are peculiar.

The next story, recorded by Theodore Roosevelt (1893), is well-known to Bigfoot enthusiasts, though there is some debate over whether it actually involves a Bigfoot-type creature. Disregarding the third-hand nature of the report, the controversy centers on the aggressive nature of the animal. I'll just point out that there are many reports of aggressive Bigfoot, some presented in this text, and that such attacks are often said to follow a shooting or other harassment.

Frontiersmen are not, as a rule, apt to be very superstitious. They lead lives too hard and practical, and have too little imagination in things spiritual and supernatural. I have heard but few ghost stories while living on the frontier, and those few were of a perfectly commonplace and conventional type.

But I once listened to a goblin story, which
rather impressed me. It was told by a grisled,
weather-beaten old mountain hunter, named
Bauman, who was born and had passed all
of his life on the frontier. He must have believed what he said, for he could hardly re-
press a shudder at certain points of the tale;
but he was of German ancestry, and in child-
hood had doubtless been saturated with all
kinds of ghost and goblin lore, so that many
fearsome superstitions were latent in his
mind; besides, he knew well the stories told
by the Indian medicine men in their winter
camps, of the snow-walkers, and the spec-
tres, and the formless evil beings that haunt
the forest depths, and dog and waylay the
lonely wanderer who after nightfall passes
through the regions where they lurk; and it
may be that when overcome by the horror of
the fate that befell his friend, and when op-
pressed by the awful dread of the unknown,
he grew to attribute, both at the time and
still more in remembrance, weird and elfin
traits to what was merely some abnormally
wicked and cunning wild beast; but whether
this was so or not, no man can say.

When the event occurred, Bauman was
still a young man, and was trapping with a
partner among the mountains dividing the

forks of the Salmon from the head of Wisdom
River. Not having had much luck, he and his
partner determined to go up into a particularly wild and lonely pass through which ran
a small stream said to contain many beaver.
The pass had an evil reputation because the
year before a solitary hunter who had wandered into it was slain, seemingly by a wild
beast, the half-eaten remains being afterwards found by some mining prospectors who
had passed his camp only the night before.

The memory of this event, however,
weighted very lightly with the two trappers,
who were as adventurous and hardy as others
of their kind. They took their two lean mountain ponies to the foot of the pass where they
left them in an open beaver meadow, the
rocky timber-clad ground being from there
onward impracticable for horses. They then
struck out on foot through the vast, gloomy
forest, and in about four hours reached a little open glade where they concluded to camp,
as signs of game were plenty.

There was still an hour or two of daylight left, and after building a brush lean-to
and throwing down and opening their packs,
they started upstream. The country was very
dense and hard to travel through, as there
was much down timber, although here and

there the somber woodland was broken by
small glades of mountain grass.

At dusk they again reached camp. The
glade in which it was pitched was not many
yards wide, the tall, close-set pines and firs
rising round it like a wall. On one side was
a little stream, beyond which rose the steep
mountains slope, covered with the unbroken
growth of evergreen forest.

They were surprised to find that during
their absence something, apparently a bear,
had visited camp, and had rummaged about
among their things, scattering the contents
of their packs, and in sheer wantonness destroying their lean-to. The footprints of the
beast were quite plain, but at first they paid
no particular heed to them, busying themselves with rebuilding the lean-to, laying out
their beds and stores and lighting the fire.

While Bauman was making ready supper,
it being already dark, his companion began
to examine the tracks more closely, and soon
took a brand from the fire to follow them up,
where the intruder had walked along a game
trail after leaving the camp. When the brand
flickered out, he returned and took another,
repeating his inspection of the footprints
very closely. Coming back to the fire, he stood
by it a minute or two, peering out into the

darkness, and suddenly remarked: "Bauman, that bear has been walking on two legs." Bauman laughed at this, but his partner insisted that he was right, and upon again examining the tracks with a torch, they certainly did seem to be made by but two paws or feet. However, it was too dark to make sure. After discussing whether the footprints could possibly be those of a human being, and coming to the conclusion that they could not be, the two men rolled up in their blankets, and went to sleep under the lean-to.

At midnight Bauman was awakened by some noise, and sat up in his blankets. As he did so his nostrils were struck by a strong, wild-beast odor, and he caught the loom of a great body in the darkness at the mouth of the lean-to. Grasping his rifle, he fired at the vague, threatening shadow, but must have missed, for immediately afterwards he heard the smashing of the underwood as the thing, whatever it was, rushed off into the impenetrable blackness of the forest and the night.

After this the two men slept but little, sitting up by the rekindled fire, but they heard nothing more. In the morning they started out to look at the few traps they had set the previous evening and put out new ones. By an

unspoken agreement they kept together all
day, and returned to camp towards evening.

On nearing it they saw, hardly to their
astonishment, that the lean-to had been
again torn down. The visitor of the preceding day had returned, and in wanton malice
had tossed about their camp kit and bedding,
and destroyed the shanty. The ground was
marked up by its tracks, and on leaving the
camp it had gone along the soft earth by the
brook, where the footprints were as plain as
if on snow, and, after a careful scrutiny of
the trail, it certainly did seem as if, whatever the thing was, it had walked off on but
two legs.

The men, thoroughly uneasy, gathered a
great heap of dead logs, and kept up a roaring
fire throughout the night, one or the other
sitting on guard most of the time. About midnight the thing came down through the forest
opposite, across the brook, and stayed there
on the hill-side for nearly an hour. They could
hear the branches crackle as it moved about,
and several times it uttered a harsh, grating,
long-drawn moan, a peculiarly sinister sound.
Yet it did not venture near the fire.

In the morning the two trappers, after discussing the strange events of the last thirty-
six hours, decided that they would shoulder

their packs and leave the valley that afternoon. They were the more ready to do this
because in spite of seeing a good deal of game
sign they had caught very little fur. However
it was necessary first to go along the line of
their traps and gather them, and this they
started out to do.

All the morning they kept together, picking up trap after trap, each one empty. On
first leaving camp they had the disagreeable
sensation of being followed. In the dense
spruce thickets they occasionally heard a
branch snap after they had passed; and now
and then there were slight rustling noises
among the small pines to one side of them.

At noon they were back within a couple of
miles of camp. In the high, bright sunlight
their fears seemed absurd to the two armed
men, accustomed as they were, through long
years of lonely wandering in the wilderness,
to face every kind of danger from man, brute,
or element. There were still three beaver
traps to collect from a little pond in a wide
ravine near by. Bauman volunteered to gather these and bring them in, while his companion went ahead to camp and made ready
the packs.

On reaching the pond Bauman found three
beavers in the traps, one of which had been

pulled loose and carried into a beaver house. He took several hours in securing and preparing the beaver, and when he started homewards he marked, with some uneasiness, how low the sun was getting. As he hurried toward camp, under the tall trees, the silence and desolation of the forest weighted on him. His feet made no sound on the pine needles and the slanting sun-rays, striking through among the straight trunks, made a gray twilight in which objects at a distance glimmered indistinctly. There was nothing to break the gloomy stillness which, when there is no breeze, always broods over these somber primeval forests.

At last he came to the edge of the little glade where the camp lay and shouted as he approached it, but got no answer. The campfire had gone out, though the thin blue smoke was still curling upwards. Near it lay the packs wrapped and arranged. At first Bauman could see nobody; nor did he receive an answer to his call. Stepping forward he again shouted, and as he did so his eye fell on the body of his friend, stretched beside the trunk of a great fallen spruce. Rushing towards it the horrified trapper found that the body was still warm, but that the neck was broken, while there were four great fang marks in the throat.

The footprints of the unknown beast-creature, printed deep in the soft soil, told the whole story.

The unfortunate man, having finished his packing, had sat down on the spruce log with his face to the fire, and his back to the dense woods, to wait for his companion. While thus waiting, his monstrous assailant, which must have been lurking in the woods, waiting for a chance to catch one of the adventurers unprepared, came silently up from behind, walking with long, noiseless steps, and seemingly still on two legs. Evidently unheard, it reached the man, and broke his neck by wrenching his head back with its fore paws, while it buried its teeth in his throat. It had not eaten the body, but apparently had romped and gambolled around it in uncouth, ferocious glee, occasionally rolling over and over it; and had then fled back into the soundless depths of the woods.

Bauman, utterly unnerved and believing that the creature with which he had to deal was something either half human or half devil, some great goblin-beast, abandoned everything but his rifle and struck off at

speed down the pass, not halting until he
reached the beaver meadows where the hob-
bled ponies were still grazing. Mounting, he
rode onwards through the night, until beyond reach of pursuit.

Salt Lake City, Utah, *Deseret Evening News,* January 27, 1902

AN IDAHO MONSTER AT LARGE.

QUEER STORY OF PEOPLE SAID TO
HAVE BEEN FRIGHTENED BY A LONG-
HAIRED CREATURE IN HUMAN FORM.

SPECIAL CORRESPONDENCE.

Pocatello, Ida., Jan. 26.—A letter from Chesterfield, Idaho, Jan. 14, contains a startling
rumor of having been visited by an eight-
foot-all-hair covered human monster, while
a party of young people were skating on
Portneuf river in the field of John Gooch.
The creature showed fight and flourishing
a large stick and giving vent to a series of
yells attacked the skaters, but it being slow
of movement, they regained their wagons
and got away in safety. A party of young men
returned armed and got a good view of the
monster warming himself by the fire they
had left. The beast was at least eight feet
high, covered with long reddish brown hair,
the face was hidden by immense bushy whiskers, and no part of the naked skin was to

be seen except a small spot above the eyes. The boys concluded not to bag the game that night. Measurements the following morning showed the tracks to measure [over twenty inches] long, by seven and one-quarter inches broad, with the imprint of only four toes. The stockmen report having seen similar tracks along the range west of the river, but as far as known no one has ever before seen the animal, who was trekking westward. The people feeling unsafe while this beast is at large, have sent some twenty men on its trail to effect its capture. Interested parties are referred to John Gooch, who was on the scene from the appearance to the disappearance of the monster.

Anaconda, Montana, *Standard,* January 29, 1902
IDAHO'S WILD MAN.

Eight feet tall, covered with hair, possessing the semblance of humanity and fierce with the fierceness of a wild beast—that is the description of Idaho's newest wild man, according to the veracious Deseret News. An associated press dispatch from Salt Lake yesterday gave the tale in full. There is a familiar note in the story is it comes, an intangible something that recalls to mind those always thrilling and delightful little yarns

the New York Sun used to print from New
Jersey about wild men. But, of course, since
the Deseret News is a church paper and filled
with piety, the slightest insinuation that the
thrilling item from Idaho is not founded on
fact is entirely out of place.

The Idaho wild man, according to those
who have seen him, is a regular, old fashioned
bogy man, the materialization of that awful,
hideous, soul thrilling thing that formed the
subject of a little ditty in "Sinbad." When the
party of skaters on the Port Neuf river saw
him approaching perhaps they were minded
of the words of that ditty, for certainly he
tried to catch them. That he failed was due
to the fact that they beat him to the wagons.
No one can blame them for their fright. Even
an Idaho man is not willingly going against
an eight foot monster which leaves a footprint twenty-two inches long and six inches
wide. One well directed blow from a foot like
that can put a man out more completely than
several drinks of Galena street whiskey.

A peculiar feature of the Idaho Wild man's
track is that it shows only four toes, the
number now affected by Carrie Nation since
her distressing accident of several days ago
when her new tomahawk amputated a pink
one from her right foot. Four toes, according

to a scientific gentleman who has been gazing into the future, is the number that will be fashionable on each human foot several centuries hence. It cannot be that the creature is the new man, a human placed upon earth in advance of his proper era. Idaho is a progressive state, but that she has leaped ahead several ages without the rest of the world being aware of it is hardly probable. The four toes do not prove the existence of a new man. More likely a closer examination of the track would reveal that what appears to be the mark of four toes is the imprint of a cloven hoof. If in the snow behind a faint line is traced, as if a forked tall had been dragged along, the identity of the monster is established. The twenty men from Chesterton who are in pursuit would best beware, else all that is left of them on the earth will be a smell of brimstone and a fond remembrance.

1930s: Matthews (2017) noted that Oakley *Herald* editor Charley Brown had a lot of fun speculating about what was behind stories of what one rider in nearby Birch Creek Canyon described as "a gorilla-like creature, unclothed, (and) hairy" in 1932. Sightings of the creature appear to have continued even after the *Herald* ceased publication.

Illinois

Wheeling, West Virginia, *Daily Intelligencer,* January 2, 1891

A STRANGE CREATURE

Chicago, Ill., Jan. 1.—Maywood has a mystery, and through it that usually peaceful little suburb bids fair to become quite notorious.

Something over a week ago a rumor was started in Maywood that a bear or some animal very much resembling one, had been seen on the Desplaines river bank, just below the village.

Christmas day the Desplaines river was crowded with skaters. They covered the ice from Harlem to Turner Park, and were as happy as they were numerous. In the crowd that kept close to the Northwestern railroad bridge, between River Forest and Maywood, was a party of young people from North Clark street. Charles Gardner, a clerk on the Board of Trade, was one of the number, and as he was anxious not to miss the next train he went ashore below the railroad

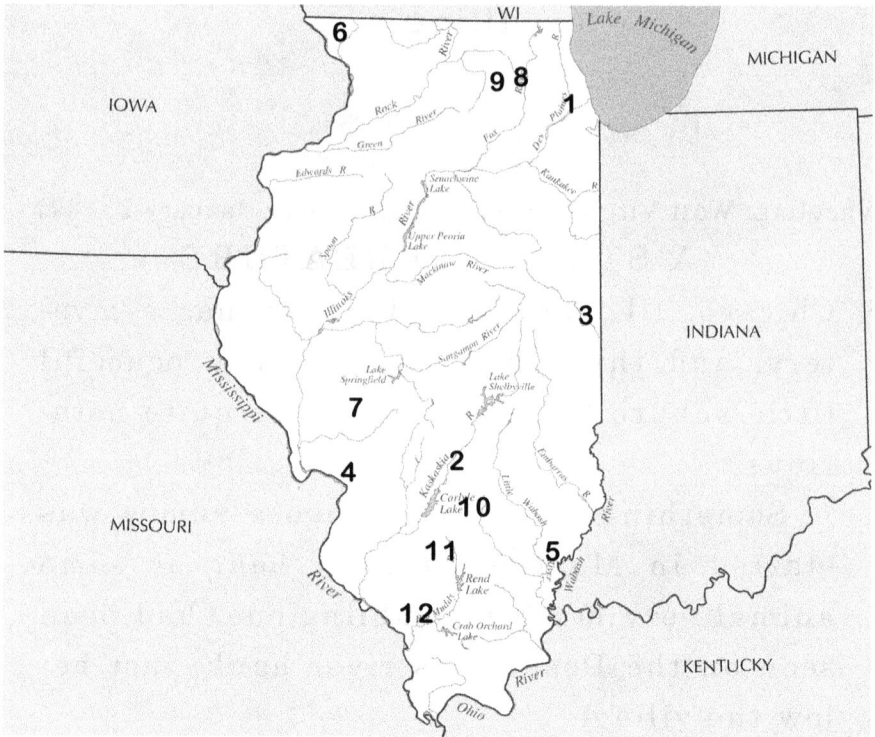

1 Maywood (Cook County)

2 Vandalia (Fayette County)

3 Danville (Vermilion County)

4 Madison (Madison/St. Clair Counties)

5 Carmi (White County)

6 Elizabeth (Jo Daviess County)

7 Carlinville (Macoupin County)

8 Virgil (Kane County)

9 DeKalb County

10 Mt. Vernon (Jefferson County)

11 Du Quoin (Perry County)

12 Carbondale (Jackson County)

bridge, removed his skates and commenced
to pick his way along a small path which led
toward the Maywood Park. This was through
a very thick undergrowth, and led directly
to a small bridge on First avenue, spanning
a ravine which runs the entire length of the
park, running into the river about two hundred feet from the small bridge.

As Gardner approached the bridge, he was
startled by hearing what sounded to him like
a moan or growl. Looking up he saw at the
foot of one of the piers of the bridge something which he at first took to be a man. The
figure was seated on a projecting rock and
was partially concealed behind the thick
weeds that surround the spot. It was peering
through the tops of the weeds, and the face,
as the startled man saw it, was that of a
monster. It had a low heavy brow, over which
hung hair that was coarse and matted. Its
eyebrows were heavy and long, and the head
seemed to be set low down on the chest, so
high and massive were the huge shoulders.
The entire face was covered with bushy hair,
and as Gardner looked in fright and wonder,
a huge arm was lifted to grasp the wall as
the creature rose. That was all the young
man wanted to see. He tore his way up the
steep bank, rushed to the depot nearly half

a mile away, and boarded his train just as it was about to leave.

Again Seen.

In the meantime the mysterious creature had been seen and heard by other people. John Haberlein, Hans Mouns and Sam Harburg, three Germans living near Turner park, had heard from some boys that some wolves or bears were prowling up and down the river. Friday they started out with guns and dogs and carefully scoured both banks of the river from Turner Park almost to Harlem, but they saw nothing alive, although in the sand, on the river bank near Harlem, they ran across some strange-looking footprints, which led from the ice to the bank of the river. These tracks resembled somewhat those of a bear, but the peculiar imprints of the toes at once proved that they were not made by any bruin in existence.

Late last Saturday night, Henry Phillips and R. A. Lewis, two young men who board in River Forrest, went over to Maywood to call on some young ladies. They were walking home after their visit, and when on the West Lake street wagon bridge, stopped to look at a passenger train that was crossing the railroad bridge just below. They saw the train pass, and then looked up and down the

river. The moon was shining brightly, and
the reflected glitter from the ice made the
picture a pretty one.

As the two young men watched the ice
they saw a movement on the icy surface at
the bend. Without being aware that the other
was looking at the moving object each
watched the figure until they both broke out
at the same instant with a remark that some
fellow must like skating very well to be out
alone at that time of the night.

They both laughed, and as they did the
figure drew away from the bend and made its
way down the river toward the two watchers.
It came very slowly and appeared to be carrying something. As it approached the bridge
the young men could see very distinctly that
it was not a skater. It took long, regular, but
very slow strides, and at each step a clacking
sound could be heard as if some souse shoe
sole was coming in contact with the smooth
ice at every step.

The reflection from the ice threw its rays
on the features of the strange looking midnight marauder, and as it came nearer and
nearer to the young men they were almost
horror-stricken at its appearance. The figure
was that of a man, big, brawny and muscular,
but whether covered with hair or clothes was

hard to discern. It wore no hat, and its white
hands, as one hung by its side and the other
grasped the burden on its shoulder, were in
great contrast to the dark face, black hair
and peculiar looking body. The head seemed
scarcely higher than the shoulders, and as
the creature moved along, a peculiar hissing
sound came from it, as if it were breathing
through its teeth.

Frightened Watchers.

When it halted under the bridge, or a little to
one side of it, and directly in full view of the
watchers, it dropped its burden. It seemed to
be fearful of something, and looked around in
every direction. The young men crouched on
the floor of the bridge and peered cautiously
over the edge of the rail. The Thing hissed
and mumbled as it stood there, and Lewis
became so badly frightened that he almost
yelled outright, and was only stopped by the
strong hand clasp of his friend.

In a few moments a movement was heard
on the ice. They saw it pass under the railroad bridge and watched it move on down toward Harlem until it was lost to view around
the bend of the river just below.

Just as Lewis and Phillips had reached the
end of the bridge on their homeward way, and
were discussing the strange sight they had

seen, they were again startled by hearing a
loud cry. They concluded that they had seen
enough for one night, and agreed that the
sound they had just heard had been made by
some night-bird or animal. They were quite
nervous anyhow, and as Lewis was especially
anxious to go to his home, it was with difficulty that his friend could persuade him to wait a
few moments to see if anything would appear.

They did not wait long. From under the
railroad bridge shot the same figure they
had just lost sight of. It was moving rapidly,
and was without the burden it had carried
when last seen. It rushed to the center of
the space between the two bridges and sat or
crouched on a small rock that showed above
the surface of the ice, where it remained for
a few seconds, hissing through its teeth and
waving its long arms around as if to ward off
some pursuer or enemy. Only for a few seconds did the mysterious creature remain in
this position. Then it arose and slowly moved
toward the west bank of the river.

The young men at once started for their
homes, and the next morning told their story.
Young Gardner was found by the reporter,
and a visit to Maywood disclosed the fact
that many prominent persons had heard of
the mysterious figure.

Chicago, Illinois, *Inter Ocean*, December 8, 1891

DIDN'T FIND THE "WILD MAN."

Vandalia, Ill., Dec. 7.—Special Telegram.— News reached here today that the wild man hunt came off at the prescribed time and place in Louden Township Saturday. The party hunted over an area of ground about four miles in circumference, but failed to sight the man. It is now believed by many of the people of Louden that the supposed wild man is no more nor less than a citizen of their own township, who more than once during blackberry season played the wild man act and frightened the berry pickers.

Bennington, Kansas, *Ottawa County Democrat*, January 29, 1892

A dispatch from Vandalia, Ill., says: The wild man of Louden township is still at large, the searching party thus far having been unable to sight him. It is now believed by the people of that neighborhood that he is a full-blooded Indian, and almost a cannibal for the way he devours raw flesh. Several farmers have lost fat shoats of late, and it is thought they have been killed and eaten by the wild man, as several carcasses have been found with the flesh stripped clean. Another searching party is being organized at St. Elmo, with a view to aiding the other party in capturing him if possible. Many people along Beck's

creek are afraid of the so-called wild man,
and will not venture out any distance from
their houses after dark.

Springfield, Illinois, *Daily Illinois State Journal,* April 20, 1892
A wild man whose body is covered with long
thick hair is said to be in hiding in the woods
around Danville.

Woodland, California, *Daily Democrat,* February 14, 1894
A WILD BOY CAUGHT.
The authorities of Madison, Ills., have a wild
boy, who they believe hails from St. Louis. He
was captured in the woods near that town and
in many respects resembles the "wild man of
Borneo" found in the side shows of traveling
circuses. His finger and toe nails have grown
to immense length, hair has sprung out over
nearly his whole body, and he has well nigh
lost his ability to talk, merely uttering inco-
herent howls and screams instead. He was
brought in by a party of townspeople who
had been disturbed by the reports of the wild
creature prowling in the vicinity of their
homes.—St. Louis Globe-Democrat.

Chicago, Illinois, *The Inter-Ocean,* July 23, 1894
TO RUN DOWN A WILD MAN.
Vandalia, Ill., July 22.—Special Telegram.—
In Louden Township, in the northwestern

part of this county, there is said to be at large a wild man. He has been seen twice by the inhabitants along Beck's Creek, and two hunts have been organized to capture him, but they failed each time. This wild man was seen again last week, and now the residents of that locality are organizing with a view of running him down.

Chicago, Illinois, *Tribune*, July 23, 1894

LOUDON WILD MAN SEEN AGAIN.

A PARTY OF VANDALIA CITIZENS WILL MAKE AN EFFORT TO CAPTURE HIM.

Vandalia, Ill., July 22.—[Special.]—The wild man who is said to live along Bick's Creek in the northeastern part of this county and is known as the Loudon wild man was seen again last week. The wild man is said to resemble a negro in appearance and is extremely large. Twice before hunts were organized to capture him but without success. Another party of men will try it again.

Evansville, Indiana, *Journal,* August 26, 1928

APE SEEN AGAIN NEAR CARMI; SCARE GROWS

Carmi, Ill, Aug. 25.—(Special)—Uneasiness of the people of this city caused by widespread reports of a huge ape at large, grew to proportions of almost a community terror here today when the sheriff's office received substantial evidence that there is a huge monkey, that may be either a baboon or a gorilla, prowling about in this vicinity.

Many women here today became so frightened that they refrained from going shopping unless their husbands would escort them.

The scare was intensified this morning after it had become known that "Mollie" Sefried, farmer living about a mile northwest of Carmi reported to the sheriff's office that he had seen the ape in a cornfield across the road from his house.

Sefried's daughter also saw the beast when her father called her to look across the road, she told the officers. When the sheriff and one of his deputies scanned the soft ground in the cornfield where Sefried said he saw the ape, they found footprints that resembled bare human footprints and measured 10 to 12 inches from toe to heel.

May Form Posses

The officers searched the cornfield at length but were unable to find the mysterious simian.

Community uneasiness may force the organization of posses to hunt out the animal, if such it is, within the next few days, it was indicated here tonight.

A big ape escaped from a zoo at Maywood more than a week ago, and it is believed that the animal may have come to this city.

Carbondale, Illinois, *Daily Free Press*, August 31, 1928

REPORT APE ROAMING WOODS NEAR CARMI

Carmi, Ill., Aug. 29.—A posse of 50 Carmi men and boys staged an unsuccessful hunt Monday night for the large ape that is reported to be roaming the vicinity of the city, when about dusk, William Pratt, who lives below Shipley Hill about a half mile northwest of the city, reported seeing the elusive animal.

The ape has kept the people of Carmi in more or less consternation for the last week or more. When Pratt saw the ape in the field near his house, he went after his shotgun, only to find that the much sought animal had evaded him. Then he telephoned to a local pool room.

A posse of about 50 was quickly recruited from among the younger and sporting element of the city. Armed with pool cues, clubs and flashlights, they combed the underbrush in vain. They reported, however, seeing the ape's footprint.

Freeport, Illinois, *Journal-Standard*, July 25, 1929

REPORTS FROM JODAVIES COUNTY INDICATE WILD APE IS ROAMING ABOUT THAT SECTION AT NIGHT

(SPECIAL TO JOURNAL-STANDARD)

Elizabeth. Ill., July 25.—A report which has spread through this section of the country during the past few days with great rapidity tells that an ape was seen in the woods near the highway in Derinda township a few miles south of this city recently.

According to the story, a young man who is employed on a farm in that part of the county was going home late the other night and as the car approached a thick woods the young man saw an ape leave the road and dash into cover in the trees. So vivid did the animal appear that he saw its shape, its tail and other characteristics of such an animal.

While a great many of the people in this locality felt there must be some mistake about an ape in this part of the country, there were many who still expect that the animal may again put in its appearance. It is said that a searching party was organizing to rid the country of what might be a menace to the locality, but so far as can be ascertained no other persons have yet reported getting a glimpse of the ape.

It was reported that although the searching party did not locate the animal, they will
continue their efforts. Many of the residents
of this vicinity, especially the women, were
much aroused over the story, fearing that the
wild animal might carry away their children
or do harm to the adults of the community.

The fact that only one person is said to
have seen the animal there are still many
who believe in the yarn and are anxiously
awaiting further developments.

It should be noted that one earlier article on
the Carmi "ape-man" suggested it "dressed like a
workman, but acts in every way like a gorilla or ape.
It has long arms that swing in front of his body as
he walks, opposite to the way a man's arms swing."
No witness names are given. "City terrorized
by strange ape-man," Evansville, Indiana, *Press,*
August 24, 1928.

Middlesboro, Kentucky, *Daily News,* July 26, 1929.

ILLINOIS VILLAGE NOW ENGAGED
IN BIG GORILLA HUNT

Elizabeth, Ill., (UP)—This community was
engaged in a great gorilla hunt today.

Posse of farmers searched the countryside for a huge Simian. The "big boy" first
observed in a patch of woods just outside of

this town late yesterday, is believed to have escaped a carnival at Savanna, twenty miles from here.

He was wandering about aimlessly, reports here stated. Housewives barricaded their doors as men folks sought the unwelcome guest.

Port Arthur, Texas, *News*, July 26, 1929

MOONSHINE MONKEY GIVEN BLAME FOR ALLEGED GORILLA

Freeport, Ill., July 29—(AP)—The terrible gorilla which yesterday, had Elizabeth, Ill., agog, astir and aghast had shrunk today to a monkey, if even that.

The farm women who locked themselves indoors, and their men folk who went forth with guns and grim determined faces were breathing more easily. The "gorilla" they wanted was the one who started the story.

Freeport police said the gorilla was a combination of monkey and moonshine. A carnival lost some monkeys while showing here recently. The police hold that some person suffering from sunshine and moonshine saw a monkey and translated it into a gorilla. As one astute officer explained, even good whiskey has been known to produce an entire horde of pink elephants.

Freeport, Illinois, *Journal-Standard*, July 31, 1929

JO DAVIESS COUNTY APE NOT AN APE AT ALL BUT BILLY GOAT, DERINDA MAN SAYS

(SPECIAL TO JOURNAL-STANDARD)

Stockton, Ill., July 31.—After hundreds of Jo Daviess county people, especially women and children, had been terrified by the reported presence of an ape roaming by night among the canyons, hills and timber lands of the northwest portion of Illinois a week ago, residents of this section are becoming more at ease as later reports are seeping out and gradually circulating throughout this community.

Whether the ape was small of stature or large was a question which puzzled residents of this section for the past week, as many farmers, armed with shotguns, searched in vain for the animal which spread terror throughout this region, especially in the vicinity of Elizabeth, where the ape was first supposed to have been seen.

Reports which are fast gaining circulation in the vicinity of Stockton indicate the ape was not an ape at all but a whiskered "Billy" goat, prowling around by night, hopping fences, nibbling trees and dodging in and around the underbrush. Whether this is a solution to the question which has perplexed thousands all over this section of the country is as yet undetermined. However a few people in this community have offered a clew which might be of assistance to those who may be desirous of continuing the search for the beast.

Information "leaked out" here, today to the effect that Archie Ehler, a resident of Elizabeth, owns a goat. The same "authority" expressed the belief that the owner of the goat pastures his whiskered pet on the Moffett farm in Derinda township each summer, and it was in this section of the county that the ape was first reported prowling around.

Further investigation may reveal the identity of the ape and probably solve the perplexing problem.

Murphysboro, Illinois, *Daily Independent,* December 17, 1936

SEARCH FOR APE-LIKE CREATURE THAT FRIGHTENS GIRL

Carlinville, Ill., Dec. 17—(UP)—An ape-like animal or man which has frightened Lenora Rhodes, 14-year-old daughter of Mr. and Mrs. Jim Rhodes, on her way home from Carlinville high school, was sought today by an armed posse.

Residents of Macoupin station and the surrounding vicinity joined in the search for the mysterious figure yesterday. They concentrated on a wooded hill section which is sparsely settled.

The girl rides from Macoupin station on a bus to Carlinville high school each day. On the return trip at night Lenora and other students ride on the bus to Macoupin station and then walk the remaining distance to their respective homes, but Lenora walks alone the last half mile to her home.

She told authorities that while walking along this last half mile during the past week she has frequently been frightened by guttural mutterings, ending in a scream, in a nearby woods. Her parents at first believed the noise was made by a screech owl.

Tuesday, however, the thing came closer than before and almost emerged from the woods, Lenora said. She became frightened and ran to the home of neighbors, who started a search. Sheriff A. S. Henry also began an investigation.

One resident reported to the sheriff that he had seen an ape-like figure crashing through the underbrush in the woods near Macoupin creek. The report sent residents of the area on a determined search.

Freeport, Illinois, *Journal-Standard,* September 23, 1937

THEY'RE HUNTING GORILLA
NEAR VIRGIL, KANE COUNTY

Elgin, Ill., Sept. 23.—What is it that has hair all over, rides a cow and waves its arms?

That's what they're wondering about these days in the locality of Virgil in Kane county since Engineer Maas, of Chicago, reported seeing the strange animal last Thursday afternoon while on his run on the Chicago Great Western railroad.

It was daylight and other members of the crew are said to have seen it, too.

Maas is certain that what he saw was an ape, chimpanzee, baboon, or baby gorilla. He said the animal was covered with hair, about four feet high, dark, probably jet black. It was at first moving slowly in a pasture but later became playful and with a wild leap landed on a cow's back. Then it stood up and waved its arms in wild circles.

Authorities of Kane county couple the tale with that of the one going the rounds of a so-called escaped tiger near Morrison.

If it isn't some sort of ape, authorities believe the only solution is that it was a boy who may have acquired a play suit resembling a chimpanzee. If it is a boy, they reason, then he must be exceedingly agile to leap on a cow's back in the rig and ride around a pasture standing up.

Henry, Illinois, *News Republican,* November 11, 1937

PLAYFUL BABOON
FROLICS AMONG HOGS

A mysterious "Hound of the Baskervilles" was identified as a playful baboon by Deputy Sheriff Lyman Sebree of DeKalb County recently as the animal frolicked among the hogs on the Sam Thorgerson farm near DeKalb.

Hundreds of motorists who had seen the strange animal as they drove past the farm described it in a variety of weird forms. It became a phantom about the countryside until Deputy Sebree sped to the Thorgerson farm.

They found the baboon riding the backs of hogs and cows, leaping from one to another, and alternately feeding them from an ear of corn. It was no stranger to Thorgerson, who said it had been gallivanting around his place for several weeks.

Although he had been unable to get close enough to the baboon to capture it, he regarded the visitor as a pet. It had made friends with his stock, sometimes sleeping in his barns, or in the trees about the farm. A collar and bell the baboon wore when it arrived seemed to indicate the jungle beast was the property of a hurdy gurdy man or circus, and had escaped its owner.

So far as Thorgerson could learn, the hogs didn't seem to mind the stranger in their midst who obliged by digging out fleas and other bothersome pests in true monkey fashion.

Carbondale, Illinois, *Free Press,* March 26, 1942

MASS HUNT FOR MYSTERIOUS WILD ANIMAL PLANNED

A mass hunt for a mysterious wild animal will be held Sunday in the Gum creek bottoms of Spring Garden near Mt. Vernon.

Men of the community will beat the thickets and scour the deep woods in search of a beast described by eye witnesses as probably an unusually large monkey or baboon whose shrill screams are frequently heard at night.

. . .

The animal was first seen late last summer by the Rev. Lepton Harpole who was squirrel hunting. It jumped from a tree, narrowly missing the hunter who struck at it with his gun barrel when it approached on its hind feet. He fired two shots to frighten it away. He believed it was an escaped circus animal.

A few nights ago the animal killed a dog which a Bonnie farmer had set on its trail after hearing its terrorizing screams. It has been heard at rural schools and its tracks seen frequently by hunters.

Centralia, Illinois, *Sentinel,* March 28, 1942

JEFFERSON COUNTY MASSES FOR ATTACK ON 'WHAT-IS-IT'

Mt. Vernon, Ill., Mar. 28 (AP)—They won't know what their quarry is but nimrods of Jefferson county are expected to turn out by the score tomorrow to comb Gun Creek bottoms for a strange animal whose screaming has brought fear to that area.

The "what-is-it" first made its appearance by jumping from a tree to attack a squirrel-hunting Mt. Vernon preacher on the closing day of the hunting season last October. The pastor used his gun as a club to fend off the animal and then scared it away by firing the weapon.

Since then its nightly screaming, comparable to the cry of a wildcat, has been heard frequently.

Last week a man who heard the screaming set his dog into the woods and later found the dog dead, apparently clubbed.

Some believe the strange animal is a monkey escaped from a circus or carnival. Its tracks are described as similar to those of a raccoon but about four times as large. Sometimes two tracks have been found, sometimes four.

J. R. Reed, a merchant, organized the expedition which will begin beating the thickets and woods in search of the animal at 11 a.m. Sunday. Members of the Jefferson County Sportsmen's club will participate.

Freeport, Illinois, *Journal Standard,* March 30, 1942

MYSTERY OF GUN CREEK BOTTOMS STILL MYSTERY

. . . Not even 1,500 southern Illinois hunters could flush the mysterious animal with a "wildcat's scream" and "paws like a huge raccoon" yesterday, although they combed the bottoms with shotguns and rifles on the ready. . . .

The affair wasn't without results, however. Merchant, J. R. Reed, who organized the hunt, sold out his candy bar, soda water and lunch meat stocks. Some hunters shot a large hoot owl and several cows. . . .

Leonard (1975) looked back on this story, providing additional details:

It wasn't a little green man. Nobody even said it was a little red man. Somebody compared it to a very hairy 10-year-old boy and it may have been some kind of large monkey with a short tail. Whatever, there was something out there that attacked Lepton Harpole.

Most agree on that. Lepton always held to his story and his brother, who's a minister, believed him. Folks around Bakerville Bottoms put importance on endorsements like that and so the story became gospel.

It was 1942 and Harpole was hunting rabbits south of Mt. Vernon where the I-57 bridge is now. Exactly how successful a hunter he was is not remembered, but local citizens still recall that something was hunting Lepton that afternoon. He had stopped to rest when it sprang from behind a tree and he beat it off with his shotgun. It was about three feet tall, covered with brown hair and moved on two feet. No question that it was more animal than human, but for some reason Harpole did not kill it. After three unsuccessful assaults it fled into the bush, limping.

Whatever happened to whatever it was is not known but about 10 days later something killed a dog over at Gun Creek and the tracks looked like a raccoon, only they were four times larger. That got about a thousand residents to take part in a big game hunt that only turned up some crows and a large owl. Which is the end of the story at Bakersville Bottom.

But not the end of the little red men. Throughout the years, they've been sighted near Vandalia and along the Big Muddy and Sangamon Rivers. And when one looks beyond Illinois, he discovers reports in Kentucky and down the Mississippi Valley. In fact some believe our state may be the northern extreme of an annual migration that winters in Louisiana. . . .

Carbondale, Illinois, *Free Press*, September 30, 1942

CITIZENS REPORT SEEING MYSTERIOUS ANIMAL ROAMING DU QUOIN STREETS DURING NIGHT
(DU QUOIN CALL)

It's from seven to 12 feet tall; it walks erect like a man; and it has tremendous strength— that's the only description of the mysterious animal which has been reportedly been prowling about Du Quoin that can be gleaned from the variety of unverified tales circulating here today.

What few persons claim to actually have seen the animal maintain they were so scared they didn't take time to gather a good description.

There is no indication that it's the same creature which has been reported roaming the country side in Washington county—but stories of its escapades are just as many and varied.

Thus far police have had but one report concerning the animal which some believe (if it exists) is an escaped gorilla.

A resident of the West Side excitedly informed state police earlier in the week that the creature had been scratching on his screen door. When patrolmen rushed to the scene to investigate, however, they found no trace of the "monster." They hinted that perhaps some of the gentleman's friends had been playing pre-mature Hallowe'en pranks.

Apparently Worden Pyle, an employee of the Woodside tavern on South Division street, is the latest person who claims to have actually seen the beast.

According to Mr. Pyle it was meandering about a pasture in the southern part of the city about 10 o'clock last night while Pyle was en route home from work.

When he caught a glimpse of the creature, Pyle said, he suddenly remembered he was in a hurry and neglected to study its build.

It was, however, about seven feet in height, he said, and he understood a young bull belonging to a resident in that area was killed later in the night.

But Pyle's version of the beast's appearance differed from that of one of Coach John H. Rauth's Indian football players who reported [he] met up with the "thing" near the First Baptist church Sunday night. Although he left the scene faster than he ever moved on the gridiron, the athlete maintained the creature walked on its hind feet and was about 12 feet tall.

Other favorite street stories are how one man fired (some say three, others say nine—choose your own figure) at the animal and "didn't even phase it" and how the creature killed three pet cats in the area around Sunfield Sunday night.

As yet mothers haven't been advised to keep their children off the streets at night.

Murphysboro, Illinois, *Independent,* September 30, 1942

DU QUOIN SEEING THINGS AT NIGHT, BARTENDER, TOO

Du Quoin, Ill., Sept. 30.—(UP)—State police today presumed the "silver monster" had left Perry county, but were not certain he had been here at all. . . .

Tales of a monster marauding through Perry county mirror similar reports to Sheriff Henry Anderson, Nashville, that a seven-foot man-like creature was terrorizing Washington county [*sic?*] last week.

Police believed the monster to be an escaped circus or zoo ape.

Carbondale, Illinois, *Free Press,* October 2, 1942

OFFICERS SEARCH FOR 'GORILLA' NEAR BIG MUDDY RIVER BRIDGE

Tales of persons in scattered parts of southern Illinois seeing a large, gorilla-like animal running loose are rapidly developing into actual facts with the beast reported just north of Carbondale about 10 o'clock last night by a Tennessee motorist.

Chief of Police Floyd Jones reported this morning that a man, driving an automobile with Tennessee license plates, rushed into the police headquarters in the City Hall Building here about 10 o'clock last night, and in great excitement, told the authorities that he had seen some strange monster run across the highway in front of his automobile just after he had crossed the Big Muddy River Bridge four miles north of the city limits.

The motorist described the animal—he was not sure what it was—as being about seven feet tall and weighing some 400 pounds. He said that it could have been a gorilla but he admitted that he was unable to get a clear picture of the mysterious animal from the brief glimpse that he had had as the beast ran across through the distant reflection of the headlights.

Local police with several highway patrolmen immediately started a search of the area where the animal was reported by the motorist, but no trace of the beast was uncovered.

Earlier this week reports from Du Quoin indicated that a mysterious animal—described as being at least 12 feet tall—had been seen within the city limits. Everyone who reported seeing the strange sight said that they fled from the scene without a second look.

Reports from Coulterville of a similar and unidentified monster have also added to the mystery. A rural school was reported to have been closed near Coulterville after stories of the monster in the neighborhood.

From all the stories told, it is apparent that most of the persons who have chanced to meet the beast believe it to be a gorilla. However, gorillas are few and far between and had one of the captives escaped from some zoo, the fact would have been widely

publicized, leaving most people in doubt as
to the strange tales. However, last night's
report by a total stranger to the area and a
man who said he knew nothing of previous
tales, makes the persons doubting the stories think twice before branding the idea as
complete nonsense.

We would not attempt in these columns
to endorse the story that a gorilla is running
loose, nor would we call the stories false. It is
entirely possible that some animal has been
seen but we are hoping that someone takes time
enough to definitely establish the identity of
the beast the next time it appears in public.

Murphysboro, Illinois, *Independent,* October 5, 1942

"THE THING" SEEN IN THIS COUNTY, CROSSING "SLAB"

"The Thing," a towering, ape-like creature
that stalked first through St. Clair county,
then visited Washington and Perry counties
in nocturnal prowlings, made its most recent
reported appearances at Big Muddy bridge
several miles north of Carbondale in Jackson
county.

Floyd Jones, police chief at Carbondale,
told Saturday how a frightened motorist ran
into police headquarters and said "an animal

weighing about 400 pounds, had crossed the highway in front of his car."

But the ruffled scene of all is at Colp, a mining community made up largely of colored people. The Thing, according to Enoch Franklin of Colp, "has lived in this region, I'd say a year. Last winter we followed its footprints, but snow covered them before we found it." Colp folks did not get far from home at night when The Thing stalks.

Some coal belt newspapermen said: "Of course we didn't believe rumors of such a beast until we inspected his footprints. They measured eight inches across and were V-shaped—unlike anything we've seen."

State police at Du Quoin earlier this week searched Perry county for the "Silver Monster" that had frightened a Du Quoin policeman and a bartender. They failed to find anything.

Some persons who profess to have seen The Thing declare it is "eight feet high and must weigh about 400 pounds."

Some years ago a tall story went the rounds that a tiger had escaped from a circus train in the Gorham vicinity. That story, however, was later run down as a gag to frighten a night railway depot telegrapher.

But The Thing reportedly remains abroad and for that reason children are advised to remain out of the woods unless accompanied by their parents.

It is suggested that the American Fox Hunters association with hundreds of members in southern Illinois, loose their hundreds of hounds on the monster, take him alive, sell him to the exhibitors, and donate the returns to the Salvation Army.

—. 1946. "Strange Beast Stories." *Hoosier Folklore Bulletin* 5:19. (from Sanderson 1961).

Another type of story that is of much more concern to us here in Southern Illinois nowadays is the "strange beast" legend. . . . Every few years some community reports the presence of a mysterious beast over in the local creek bottom.

Although it is difficult to determine just where a story of this sort has its beginning, this one seems to have originated in the Gum Creek bottom near Mt. Vernon. During the summer of 1941, a preacher was hunting squirrels in the woods along the creek when a large animal that looked something like a baboon jumped out of a tree near him. The preacher struck at the beast with his gun barrel when it walked toward him in an upright position. He finally frightened it away by firing a couple of shots into the air.

Later the beast began to alarm rural people by uttering terrorizing screams mostly at night in the wooded bottom lands along the creeks. School children in the rural districts sometimes heard it, too, and hunters saw its tracks. . . . By early spring of 1942, the animal had local people aroused to a fighting pitch. About that time, a farmer near Bonnie reported that the beast had killed his dog. A call went out for volunteers to join a mass hunt to round up the animal.

The beast must have got news of the big hunt, for reports started coming in of its appearance in other creek bottoms, some as much as 40 or 50 miles from the original site. A man driving near the Big Muddy River, in Jackson County, one night saw the beast bound across the road. Some hunters saw evidence of its presence away over in Okaw. Its rapid changing from place to place must have been aided considerably by its ability to jump, for, by this time, reports had it jumping along at from 20 to 40 feet per leap.

It is impossible to say how many hunters and parties of hunters, armed with everything from shotguns to ropes and nets, went out to look for the strange beast in the various creek bottoms where it had been seen, or its tracks had been seen, or its piercing screams had been heard. Those taking nets and ropes were intent on bringing the creature back alive.

Usually this strange beast can't be found, and interest in it dies as mysteriously as it arose in the beginning. . . . About 25 years ago, a 'coon hunter from Hecker one night heard a strange beast screaming up ahead on Prairie du Long Creek. Hunters chased this phantom from time to time all one winter. Their dogs would get the trail, then lose it, and they would hear it screaming down the creek in the opposite direction. It was that kind of creature: you'd hear it up creek, but when you set out in that direction you'd hear it a mile down creek.

Indiana

Baltimore, Maryland, *Niles Register,* December 21, 1839

WILD CHILD

It is stated in the Michigan City, Indiana Gazette of the 4th instant as a current and generally believed report, that a wild child or lad, is now running among the sand hills round and in the vicinity of Fish Lake. It is reported to be about 4 feet height, and covered with a light coat of chestnut colored hair. It runs with a great velocity and when pursued, as has often been the case, it sets up the most frightful and hideous yells and seems to make efforts at speaking. It has been seen during the summer months running along the lake shore, apparently in search of fish and frogs, and appears to be fond of the critters, for it will plunge into Fish Lake, and swim with great velocity all the time whining most piteously.

Fort Wayne, Indiana, *Daily Gazette,* November 15, 1870

Newton county in this State, boasts of a wild man seven feet high. He was probably

1 Fish Lake (LaPorte County)

2 Newton County

3 Lafayette (Tippecanoe County)

4 Kouts (Porter County)

5 Eckerty (Crawford County)

6 Vernon (Jennings County)

7 Chestnut Ridge, near Greenville (Floyd County)

8 Bourbon (Marshall County)

invented to scare children with. Why did they not make him ten or twelve feet in height, and have a good thing of it?

Fort Wayne, Indiana, *Daily Gazette,* July 10, 1883

THE WILD WOMAN.

THE FEARFUL BEAST OR HUMAN BEING THAT IS TERRORIZING THE WABASH VALLEY AND MOVING UP THIS WAY.

A wild woman or perhaps the mate of the gorrilla which our special correspondent, A. W. Hoffman, esq., recently captured, has appeared near Lafayette and is terrorizing the people. Mrs. Frank Coffman, the wife of a well known farmer, saw it the other day and thus describes it in the Courier:

Mrs. Coffman was passing through the timber when she suddenly saw to her right a hideous creature formed like a woman with long black hair floating in the wind, and the whole body covered with short gray hair. The creature was breaking twigs from a sassafras bush and eating the bark. The noise made in breaking the bush prevented its hearing Mrs. Coffman's approach. Frozen with horror the farmer's wife stood and gazed on the remarkable creature before her. Suddenly the wild woman turned and facing her civilized sister, glared at her with the baleful light of

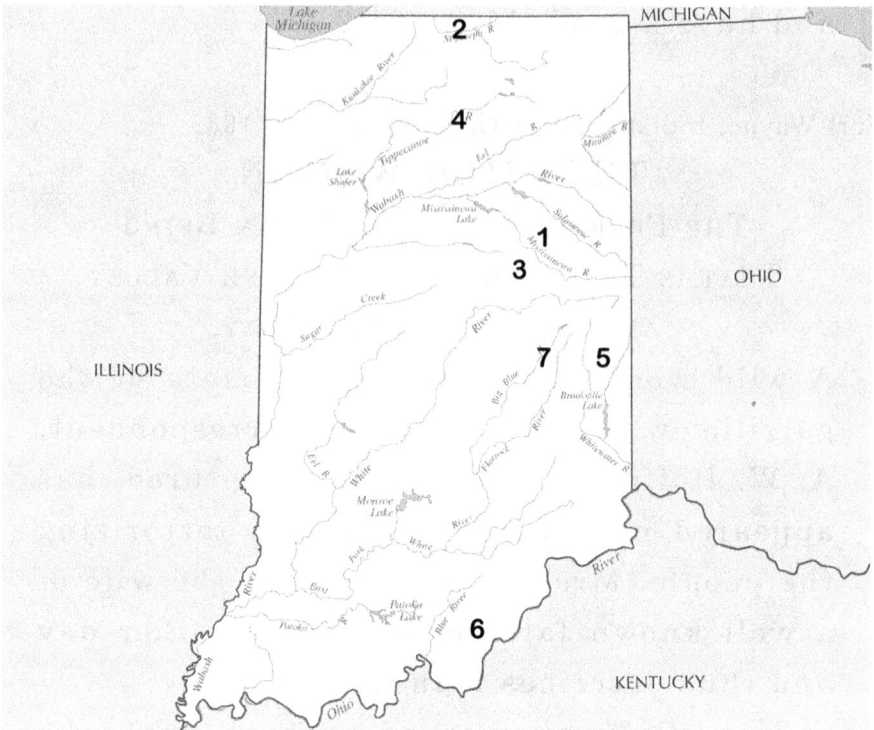

1 Gilman (Madison County)

2 Elkhart (Elkhart County; Sailor is said to be
   seven miles NE of Elkhart, which could be
   either Michigan or Indiana. It appears to be a
   dead placename.)

3 Pendleton (Madison County; Menden was just
   south of this town, and appears to be a dead
   placename.)

4 Macy (Miami County)

5 Richmond (Wayne County)

6 Galena (Floyd County)

7 Newcastle (Henry County

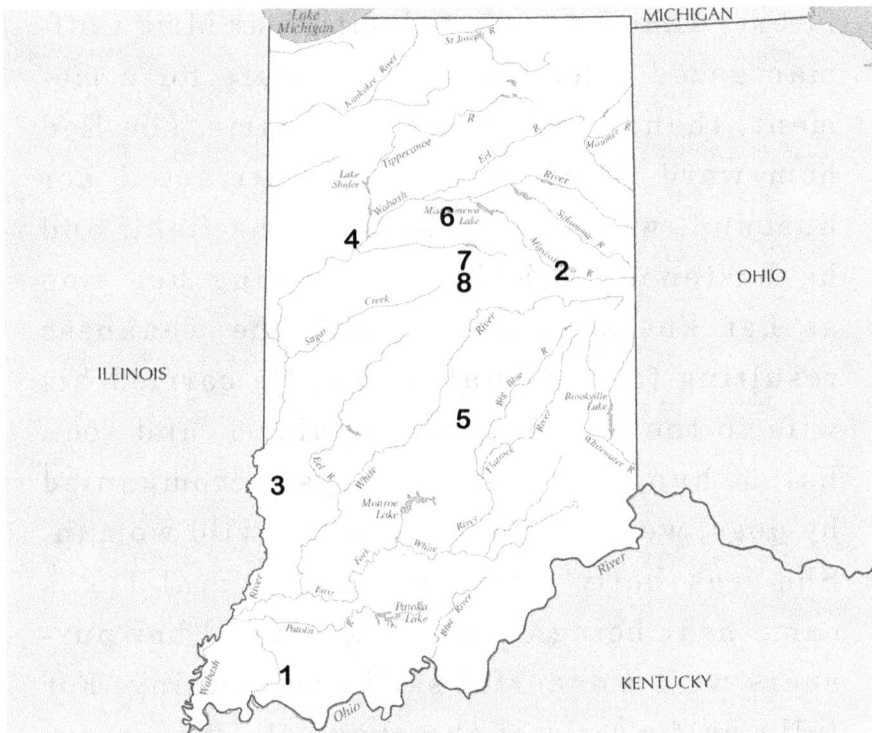

1 Cypress Beach, near Boonville (Warrick County)

2 Anderson (Madison County)

3 Sullivan (Sullivan County)

4 Thorntown (Boone County)

5 Edinburgh (Bartholomew, Johnson, and Shelby
    Counties)

6 Tipton (Tipton County)

7 Arcadia (Hamilton County)

8 Cicero (Hamilton County)

hate. Raising her long hairy arms she gave an unearthly shriek and darted away into the forest. Almost paralyzed with fear Mrs. Coffman gazed after the wild creature for a moment, then, with agonized screams, she fled homeward. Her cries of fear attracted her husband, who was at work in the field, and he hastened toward her, reaching her side as her knees gave way with the weakness resulting from mortal terror. He carried his wife to the house, gave the alarm, and soon half a hundred men and boys, accompanied by dogs, were on the trail of the wild woman. She was hotly pursued, and several times came near being caught, but eluded her pursuers with wonderful skill and cunning. For fully half a mile of the chase she was never out of sight. Her feet touched the ground but seldom. She would grab the underbrush with her long, bony hands, and swing from bush to bush and limb to limb, with wonderful ease. She seemed only endeavoring to keep just beyond the reach of her pursuers, until coming to a swamp, she disappeared as suddenly and effectually as an extinguished light, and no searching served to ascertain her whereabouts.

We have telegraphed Mr. Hoffman, at Roann, to go to the field, but as he may have some scruples about tackling women, we do not know whether he has left for the scene of action.

Logansport, Indiana, *Pharos*, October 2, 1886

A STRANGE APPARITION.

A telegram says that the people in the vicinity of Kouts, a station on the Panhandle half way between Logansport and Chicago, are living in terror of a strange apparition seen by several people. Some describe the strange being as a man covered with hair over a foot long, and when he travels he strides along at a wonderful pace. He steps or jumps, as they call it, over ten feet, and with apparently no effort. He is described further by other people as a sort of half man and animal, having a tail which drags the ground behind him when he is on the run. He is never seen excepting coming out of the swamps, and whenever anybody approaches he turns back and runs faster apparently than any race horse. Lately, however, he has been seen at a house in the vicinity of the marsh sitting down near the barn, tearing and eating a chicken from which life had scarcely departed. His mouth and fingers were covered with the feathers and blood of the chicken, and when aroused he darted off with a low shriek.

Several hunting parties have gone there, and we expect to give a better description when they return.

Pittsburg [sic], Pennsylvania, *Dispatch,* September 19, 1889

A GORILLA AT LARGE

A STRANGE CREATURE FRIGHTENING
THE NATIVES OF SOUTHERN INDIANA

Eckerty, Ind., September 18.—A naked, hairy creature, from which descriptions given by reliable persons who have seen him, must be a young gorilla, was seen recently by various persons in the woods and cornfields six miles south of here. Mrs. Kate Knight and Oscar Grant, besides others, are the names given as eye-witnesses, and each person named saw him on different occasions.

Robinson's show is on the river between New Albany and Evansville, and it is supposed a gorilla escaped from them.

Phoenix, Arizona, *Arizona Republican,* May 3, 1891

A WEIRD CAVERN.

IT WAS ACCIDENTALLY DISCOVERED AND
FOUND TO BE OCCUPIED BY A WILD MAN
OR A GORILLA—WHICH ONE IS IT

Vernon, Ind., April 30.—This is one of the oldest towns in Indiana, and is surrounded by rock-ribbed hills whose ruggedness render them quite romantic.

Years ago a subterranean cavern was reported to have been discovered by a man residing near here, named Barnes, in which he claimed to have explored a short distance and discovered a large, tall form, somewhat resembling a human in form, but appearing to be naked, and covered with a tuft or growth of hair. Barnes was so frightened that he fled from the presence of the being, whatever it was, and was so ridiculed when he told his story that he carried with him to the grave, a few years later, the secret of the location of this cave. The story has not been revised by a startling discovery made yesterday by Alex. Shepherd, a real estate dealer, who was showing a farm to a prospective purchaser. Going

Up A Deep Ravine,

whose bed is covered with stone for a long distance, they accidentally discovered a small entrance, or hole, behind a large stone, that apparently led into the ground underneath a large hill. Procuring a lantern, they entered the opening with some difficulty, and soon found themselves inside a large and lofty cavern, the rooms glittering with stalagmites and stalactites like other caverns of its character abounding in Southern Indiana. After wending their weary way through

numerous apartments, each more elaborate
and beautiful than the one first gone through
with, they stopped to gaze on the magnificent
spectacle that greeted them on every hand;
but suddenly their awe-inspired admiration
turned to horror, and their hair stood on end
as they discovered only a few feet from them
the huge form of what seemed to them to be a
gorrilla, or some human-shaped being resembling a wild man, naked, and covered with
apparently a coat of grizzly brown hair. After gazing on the intruders for a moment it
gave a

Low, Guttural Sound,

and went ambling off into the deep, impenetrable darkness of the cavern. It appeared to
be over six feet in height.

After this strange being disappeared, the
explorers turned to the right and discovered
what appeared to be a store room, which was
found to contain piles of potatoes, corn and
wheat and bones of fowls, and in another
room, adjoining this one, were found numerous bones, dry with age.

For a long time, almost nightly, strange
noises have been heard in the locality of the
deep wood surrounding this subterranean
cavern and all attempts to fathom the mystery proved a failure. No one could ever see

the source of the noise, and dogs refused to follow its trail. Farmers in the locality were losing their products almost nightly, and no one knew where they went. It seemed that in making its nightly incursions, it always followed the stony pathway of the stream leading to the cavern and this accounted for their failure to trace him to his hiding place. Years ago there was a wild man, or a similar object to this being, who inhabited Trimble county, Ky., and later Jefferson county, this State, adjoining this (Jennings) county, and for some years now no trace of him has been known. This being is believed to be the same one by some.

The discovery has created a great neighborhood excitement and a large party is being organized to explore the labarynthe of this mysterious cavern and fathom the mystery of its occupant.

Regarding this last story, a New Harmony, Indiana, *Register* version from April 10, 1891, places the story on April 4, suggesting it may be an April Fool's newspaper fiction.

Logansport, Indiana, *Journal*, July 25, 1891
BETTER THAN A SNAKE STORY.
Chestnut Ridge, near Greenville, in Floyd county, is the scene of a tremendous sensation.

While Prof. J. W. Sturn, a teacher, and W. M. Martin were picking blackberries, they became separated, and Mr. Martin suddenly found himself confronted with a singular looking beast, possibly four feet in height, with broad shoulders, head and face much like that of an ape, color black, fur long with a bunch of long stiff hair covering the back and top part of the head. It stood with its head thrown over its left shoulder, holding a short stick in its claws. Mr. Martin started to run, but stumbled and fell, and when he regained his feet the animal had disappeared. The alarm was given and the neighborhood rallied with dogs, guns and pitchforks, but no trace of the singular creature was found. Mr. Martin is regarded as a gentleman of unquestioned integrity and his story is credited.

Richmond, Indiana, *Item,* January 24, 1894

THE WILD MAN SEEN AGAIN.

Bourbon, Ind., Jan. 24.—While passing through a dense thicket near here last evening two young men, who were hunting, claim to have had an encounter with the "wild man" who has created great excitement of late in this county. They found him lying on a log asleep, like a panther. He woke as they approached and viciously attacked one of them, Harry Shull, striking him in the face and burying his long nails in Shull's flesh. The other hunter struck the man on the head with his gun, whereupon he made his escape. He is described as six feet high, of immense build, and covered with long hair. A searching party is out after him.

Newark, Ohio, *Daily Advocate,* January 1, 1896

MAY BE THE "MISSING LINK."

[Gilman], Ind., Jan. 1.—The populace here are greatly excited over the appearance of some strange wild beast in the woods near here. It resembles a baboon.

Elkhart, Indiana, *Weekly Truth,* April 29, 1897

A STRANGE ANIMAL

RESIDENTS NEAR SAILOR AROUSED
BY ITS REPORTED APPEARANCE

The residents in the neighborhood of Sailor, a hamlet about seven miles northeast of this city, are aroused over the reappearance of a strange animal in the woods belonging to H. Rines. Reports on the appearance of the creature have more than once for the past two or three years come from that locality but heretofore those who reported having seen it were merely laughed at.

Ed Swinehart and Adam Gardner both profess to have seen it last Saturday evening. The previous evening it was seen by Miles Chamberlain. Probably the best description yet secured is that given by Chamberlain.

He said that the beast walked on its hind feet and had every appearance of a man save that the body was covered with hair instead of clothing. When on its legs it stood nearly as high as an average-sized man, but when making its retreat from Mr. Chamberlain dropped onto its hands or front feet and disappeared at great speed in bounds something after the fashion of a rabbit.

When Chamberlain first came upon the mysterious animal it was sitting at the trunk of a tree near the edge of the woods. He approached within probably fifty feet of it before it jumped and started for the thick portion of the forest. The animal ran rapidly on its hind feet for several rods before it dropped on its hands.

On the following evening the beast was seen by Messrs. Swinehart and Gardner and the description given by them tallies in part with that given by Mr. Chamberlain. Gardner had a revolver with him at the time and claims that he shot the animal.

The wound did not take sufficient effect, however, to prevent the escape of the creature. Gardner attempted a second time to discharge his revolver but the weapon refused to act.

It is said that arrangements are being made to form a searching party to hunt for the mysterious animal.

Elkhart, Indiana, *Weekly Truth,* May 27, 1897

WILD ANIMAL AGAIN.

The mysterious animal that was seen in the neighborhood of Sailor recently has made its appearance in [Osolo] township and stricken terror to the hearts of at least a dozen young people. The monster was seen, or supposed to have been seen, on Sunday night.

Three young ladies whose names are given as Misses Minnie Bickel, Mabel Swartz and Libbie White were returning from church, it is said, in company with their escorts. Presently the couple in the front buggy saw a huge animal moving across a neighboring pasture. It looked like a gorilla, they said, and was making for the other side of the field from that on which the road was situated.

The occupants of the two succeeding buggies were not long in seeing the same animal and fright came down and sat upon the whole crowd with the rapidity of well-lubricated

lightning. The composure of the three young
men, it is said, was soon regained, however,
and they immediately decided to give chase
to the mysterious creature.

The young ladies were accordingly in-
structed to get in one buggy and the trio of
escorts started in quixotic strides over the
field. On ahead of them the great mysterious
animal was taking an easy course in the direction of a friendly wood. The soft sixteen
to one beams of the rising moon were dropping gently on the dew-bathed grass of the
pasture and the meadow looked more like a
silvery lake than a mere herding place for
sheep and cows or a place where strange and
mysterious animals would think to roam.
But the beast itself unconsciously added to
the aquatic picturesqueness of the scene,
for when it glided across the watery field in
the shadow of the moon beams the long dark
shadow it cast caused it to look peculiarly
like a ship.

While the young ladies quaked with fear
in the buggy the young men are said to have
moved bravely on. They found that their pace
was too slow to gain headway on the animal
and with that began to run.

At this point it is said, some unusual
noise cause the animal to look back and see
that it was being pursued. But it did not stop

or show inclination to fight. In fact, this is said to be one of the strongest proofs that the beast is the same one seen near Sailor for the general deportment of the two corresponds so closely.

As soon as the beast became aware that it was not alone it began an undignified flight and in far less time than it requires to tell it, it is said, was at the edge of the woods. The young men are reported to have run very fast until they, too, reached the edge of the woods when the thoughtfulness of one of them reminded him that the young ladies had been left alone in the buggy.

Then it was, it is said, that unadulterated fright seized the young men for the first time since they began the pursuit. They were horrified to think of the possibilities of the animal making a flank movement and attacking the buggy with its fair occupants.

"What if it should get back and eat up the girls and the horses before we get there," one of the young men is reported to have said.

The remark caused all three to hasten their pace in the direction of the buggies and it was not long before they reached the roadside.

They found their friends alive and safe. But the same fear had taken hold of the young women and they are reported to have been terribly frightened, too. Their fright may be said to have been two-fold, both because they were afraid they might be taken unawares and bodily by the strange creature and because of the possibility that their escorts might not return and they would be forced to carry the sad story to friends and relatives.

The pleadings of the young ladies are said to have prevented the young men from returning to the search though the latter were very anxious to scour the woods then and there for the strange beast.

Indianapolis, Indiana, *State Journal*, January 26, 1898

A TERRIBLE VARMINT

INFESTS THE NEIGHBORHOOD
OF MENDEN, EAST OF HERE

Pendleton, Ind., Jan. 20.—Reports from the Menden neighborhood, south of this town, bring information of a panic among the people there on account of a ferocious wild animal which has made its appearance there. The daughter of Mel Russell was the first to see the beast and she describes it as looking like a baboon or gorilla. It is too large for an ordinary monkey. Charles Patterson, a well-to-do farmer, saw its tracks in the snow and he says it had toe-nails fully eight

inches long. Others who have seen the tracks
corroborate Patterson's story. John Brough,
who saw it at night in a tree, where his dogs
had tracked it, says that when he approached
the animal easily swung to the ground and
that his dogs fled and he after them as he
was not armed. The animal disappeared in
the darkness unmolested. These stories have
been coming in for several days and people
here are beginning to believe some ferocious
beast has actually taken up its haunts in this
locality. Dogs will trail it, but no amount of
urging can prevail on them to "close in" and
give it fight. Some say it is a monkey while
others think it a crazy man, and still others
a panther. Whatever it is it is creating considerable terror in the Menden neighborhood
and the men are preparing to "hunt it down"
if for no other purpose than to quiet the
alarm of the women and children.

Goshen, Indiana, *Daily Democrat,* February 16, 1898

WILD ANIMALS AT LARGE

Madison, one of the oldest and most thickly
populated of Indiana counties, is greatly
worked up over two wild animal scares. Farmers are arranging a big round up in order to
rid the county of what are claimed to be a big
black grizzly bear and a monster gorilla.

No one knows where they came from but it is claimed by scores of farmers that the bear is in the woods just north of White river and the gorilla is making his home along Fall creek. A great deal of excitement is the result.

Children describe the gorilla as a monkey as big as a man and dogs, which have chased it, lose their courage when it turns on them. It is claimed that the animal has forced its way into outbuildings and stolen small animals.

Logansport, Indiana, *Reporter,* January 25, 1906

SOMETHING IN IT.

PREHISTORIC REMAINS IN CAVE NEAR MACY.

As a sequel to the wonderful find in a wonderful cave near Macy, as reported several weeks ago, the Monitor says that those who think that the account of a wild animal was a myth, may have all doubts set at rest if they will call at Cloud & Son's store. You will find on exhibition there the skull of an animal found in the cave where the strange animal was seen some weeks ago. The skull resembles that of a huge baboon, and has teeth more than two inches in length. A crowd of men, getting the location of the cave from those who were so badly frightened when it was discovered, made an investigation and brought out the skull now on exhibition at Cloud's. It is a ferocious looking thing, and no doubt is the remains of some prehistoric creature.

Columbus, Indiana, *Republic,* September 14, 1929

TO HUNT APE-LIKE ANIMAL
REPORTED TO BE PORCH CLIMBER

Richmond, Ind., Sept. 14. (AP)—Four Richmond youths today held a police permit to search the White water river bottoms for an animal whose actions have alarmed residents of a neighborhood in the south part of the city. No one has obtained a clear view of the creature, which has been prowling about south Fifth street, climbing to second story windows and onto porch roofs.

Raymond Fraze and Charles Robinson reported to police they believe the animal to be some species of ape, probably escaped from a circus or carnival. The two, with Gilbert Brown and Marion Brown, were given permission to hunt the marauder.

Valparaiso, Indiana, *Vidette-Messenger*, February 8, 1929

MAYBE IT WAS A MAN,
THEY'RE UP TO STUNTS

Galena, Ind., Feb. 8—(INS)—Another hunt has been started here for the mysterious

black beast that raided the A. A. Akins farm
just east of here, killed one pig and carried
off in its "arms" another pig weighing 85
pounds, according to Leonard Akins, 20, who
surprised the animal and was forced to flee
for his life.

Posse of farmers, aided by dogs which
tried to trail the black animal, failed to find
it and returned still in doubt as to the identity of the creature.

"I can't imagine what it was unless it was
a cross between a big bear and a hyena,"
young Akins said.

The hunters found one set of tracks that
resembled bear tracks, Akins related, but as
no one in the party was an expert on bears,
the question was left open, he said.

"The critter walked on its hind legs, had
pointed ears and ferocious teeth, I can say
that much," Akins declared.

The youth said he ran into the animal in a
barn on the Akins farm. The beast was killing a 60-pound pig.

"The creature reared up on its hind legs
and started toward me," Akins said. "My
airdale dog, however, dashed ahead and
barked at it and it turned on the dog."

Akins then started to run to his home to get
his gun. In running he glanced around, saw
the animal seize another pig which weighed

at least 60 pounds, take it in its "arms," go across the fence and start for some woods.

"It was as big as a man and walked on its hind legs," the youth asserted.

A canvass will be made of all circuses and zoos in Southern Indiana to determine if any wild beast escaped.

Kokomo, Indiana, *Tribune*, August 26, 1933

REPORT GORILLA SEEN AT NEWCASTLE; POSSE HUNTS STRANGE ANIMAL

Newcastle, Ind., Aug. 26.—(AP)—Residents of the Maplewood section of Newcastle were aroused today over reports of a very strange animal, variously described as a Simian and a large police dog.

The animal was said to have approached the home of Mr. and Mrs. George Smith. Mrs. Smith notified police that she had seen a gorilla. A machine-gun armed police squad made a futile search yesterday.

Today twenty-five men, carrying rifles and shotguns, organized a hunt. Some of them said they believed the animal was a chimpanzee or baboon escaped from a carnival or circus. One man said he had seen what appeared to be an exceptionally large police dog.

Hammond, Indiana, *Times,* August 16, 1937

SOUNDS LIKE A BEAR YARN

Boonville, Ind., Aug. 15.—(INS.)—They're looking for a hairy ape near here today after a monster has terrorized this community.

Persons living near Cypress beach, a few miles south of here, have told tales of encountering a giant beast which specializes in blood-curdling screams in the middle of the night and leaves footprints larger than a human's.

Ralph Duff, a fisherman, first reported the animal about a year ago after his police dog was torn to shreds in an encounter with the beast.

This week-end Mrs. Duff said she heard a terrifying howl late in the night and saw a tower[ing] monster larger than a bear. When she screamed, the beast ran away.

Duff believes that the animal is a huge ape, which lives in one of the caves along the river, and has set a number of bear traps.

Hammond, Indiana, *Times,* August 18, 1937.

SLOTH SCARES THE
BOONVILLE NATIVES

Boonville, Ind., Aug. 18.—(U.P.)—A stranger who declined to identify himself strolled into the newspaper office today and declared that the weird, mysterious beast whose screams and prowlings have terrified residents of the Ohio river valley is simply a giant sloth.

The man said he and his uncle were returning from Mexico two years ago with the sloth, which they had captured on a game hunting expedition. He said they lost it near Evansville and never had found a trace of it since. He was uncertain if it was two-toed or three-toed, but averred that sloths came in both varieties.

When a sloth is hungry and frightened, he said, it will give vent to blood-curdling shrieks and yells such as terrified river valley residents have reported they have heard intermittently since Friday night.

At that time Mrs. Ralph Duff reported she caught a fleeting glimpse of the animal and said it looked like an ape.

Posses, according to reports here, are searching the river bottoms cautiously in the hope of tracking the beast to its lair.

River folk said today that they had seen an empty circus truck in the vicinity, and assumed that animal experts are endeavoring to capture the alleged monster also.

Hammond, Indiana, *Times,* September 13, 1937

MONKEY INTRIGUES FARMERS

Anderson, Ind., Sept. 13.—(INS)—Farmers in the vicinity of the Rose Hill gravel pit northwest of here today were on the alert for a strange animal, believed to be an orangutang, which has been seen a number of times in treetops. It is believed to have escaped from a circus.

Indianapolis, Indiana, *News,* May 16, 1939

SKEPTICAL SULLIVAN OFFICERS HUNT FOR 'APE-LIKE MONSTER'

Sullivan, Ind., May 16 (Spl.)—Sullivan county officers were skeptical, but nevertheless conducted a search through Busseron creek bottoms near here last night after Mr. and Mrs. William Alsop told them they had seen a huge, ape-like monster near the highway as they drove through the bottoms toward Sullivan. The strange creature reared on its haunches and raised hairy forelegs or arms when it saw their car, the frightened couple reported.

Hubert Sevier, deputy sheriff, said the couple was "breathless" when they reached his office to tell their strange story.

The creek bottoms are densely wooded.

Indianapolis, Indiana, *News,* June 15, 1949

NO FISH TONIGHT WITH 250-LB. GORILLA LOOSE

Thorntown, Ind., June 15—Look out for the "gorilla."

A posse here is hunting an animal weighing about 250 pounds, with visible claws and protruding teeth. The posse took dogs along to help hunt down the beast. Efforts were being made to reinforce the posse with a circus animal trainer.

Four fishermen, Homer Birge, Amos Coppas, Erne Fairfield and George Coffman, have reported seeing the animal. Coffman said he saw it at the New York Central Railroad bridge. The other three men reported it near the Barker gravel pit.

Two other anglers, James Robbins and Carl Gant, said they had seen the creature's tracks in the sand near the bank of Sugar Creek.

While the posse is hunting, popular swimming holes are vacant and night fishing is at a standstill.

Edinburg, Indiana, *Daily Courier,* June 22, 1949

GORILLA FRIGHTENS
EDINBURG ANGLERS

A creature described as an ape or gorilla stalked from a brush pile yesterday afternoon about dark and scared the dickens out of J. D. Goldsmith, 21, and Howard Goldsmith, 14, of 410 East Thompson Street.

The boys were fishing near the confluence of Blue River and Sugar Creek on the

Andrew Parmerlee farm a mile and one-half west of Edinburg when the ape or gorilla made its appearance. The boys abandoned minnow seines, fishing tackle, just pushed their boat into the bank, and ran for more civilized parts.

Churubusco and your turtle, make way for a real monster.

The Goldsmith boys reported that the creature made a grunting noise that sounded like Tarzan's companions in his jungle existence.

Indianapolis papers have reported that various persons have seen strange tracks along Sugar Creek and one story previously had persons seeing the ape or gorilla.

Rushville, Indiana, *Republican,* June 28, 1949

MUST BE THE HEAT! THORNTOWN GORILLA AT STATE PARK NOW

Indianapolis, June 28 (AP)—Maybe it's the heat:

A "gorilla," previously reported at Thorntown and Edinburgh, turned up in Spring Mill State Park, near Mitchell. Park attendants Jimmy Flora, 18, and Paul Bell, 27, claim a tusked, hairy animal, 4½ feet tall, took to the bushes when they drove along a

park road. Park Superintendent Leon Montgomery saw the animal, too, but didn't both-
er to look very closely.

Indianapolis, Indiana, *News,* July 16, 1949

SAFARI MIXUP LEAVES
'APE' STILL AT LARGE

By Fremont Power

Thorntown, Ind., July 16—A gorilla that
some folks believe must be a twin or else has
wings was safe for another day here. The big
gorilla hunt scheduled for this morning has
been postponed until tomorrow because of a
mixup in dates.

About 30 farmers showed up for the gorilla
posse this morning but returned home when
they learned of the mixup. According to Ray
LaRue, Thorntown, there'll be about 300 in
the posse tomorrow, 150 from the Thorntown
area and the same number from the Advance
Conservation Club.

Boone County Sheriff Rush L. Robinson
took newspapermen on a tour of the gorilla
area. At Barker's Pit, where the animal was
first seen, Mrs. Marvin Larsh repeated her
opinion that "It's just someone dressed up
like a gorilla."

The mysterious beast was the main conservation topic today, but Ed Rose, town

clerk, grins when you talk to him about it. He says that it's a joke around Thorntown either is a twin or has wings, because reports of a similar animal have been received from near Evansville and from Minnesota.

However, farmers with children in the Sugar Creek area, three miles west of here, are serious about it and resent any scoffing. Those with children are particularly concerned, because of the possible lurking danger.

Mrs. Harley Etter, who lives about 4 miles west of Thorntown, was driving into town about 9:30 a.m. three weeks ago when she saw some bushes shaking.

"We could see the bushes just shaking like that." And she made a shaking motion with her arms. She said "it" was big and black and it had a whitish face.

The animal, if a gorilla, is a small one and has been described as about the size of a large dog. The men who will comb the countryside are all experienced fox hunters and thus danger from indiscriminate shooting will be avoided.

Conservation Department Capt. Charles White, Lebanon Game Warden Robert Perkins and Thorntown Marshal Ralph Davidson will head the posse.

Galveston, Texas, *Daily News*, July 17, 1949

HUNTERS STARTING
'GORILLA' SAFARI

Thorntown, Ind., July 16. (INS)—Scores of hunters armed with shotguns, began a "gorilla" safari in the Sugar Creek wilds near Thorntown today.

State conservation department officers headed four posses searching for a big, hairy beast who has been terrorizing fishermen and keeping Thorntown residents indoors at night.

Witnesses say that the animal weighs about 250 pounds and is "brown, hairy and has protruding teeth."

Nearly 30 Thorntown residents allege that they have seen the beast, including two fishermen, who fled Thursday night when the "monster" surprised them.

Muncie, Indiana, *Star Press*, July 18, 1949

POSSE HUNTS GORILLA
IN BOONE COUNTY

Lebanon, Ind., July 17 (AP)—A posse of about 50 armed men went hunting today for the latest of Boone County's marauding animal demons. This time it was a gorilla.

The hunt ended as did the others when posses stalked the mountain lion, a boa constrictor and other types of wild life. They didn't even turn up an out-of-season quail.

Long Beach, California, *Independent,* July 19, 1949

NAB 'GORILLA,' IT'S A WOMAN

Thorntown, Ind.—(INS). The "gorilla" mystery of Thorntown ended Monday night when a demented woman confessed she was the one who had frightened the countryside for several days.

When Thorntown Marshals Sam Allen and Ralph Davidson seized her, she asked:

"Do you think I have scared them long enough?"

The officers captured the woman, crouching in bushes near Sugar Creek where fishermen had reported seeing a "gorilla." She was wearing a dark dress, her hair was uncombed and her clothing and body were covered with filth.

The authorities said she is about 40 years old, but refused to disclose her name. They said proceedings for her commitment to a mental institution have been started.

Some 40 farmers, armed with shotguns, Sunday engaged in a fruitless safari in quest of the "gorilla."

Tipton, Indiana, *Tribune,* August 1, 1949

MONSTER ATTACKS MAN'S CAR

Sheriff Jesse Owen today was investigating a report of a "wild gorilla" that was alleged to have attacked a car Sunday evening about dusk near the Crooked Bridge, a mile south and one mile east of Tipton.

According to Owen, the call that he received Sunday night from the Cash Cochran farm was the second call in as many nights concerning a monster described as resembling a "wild gorilla." The monster was reported by two men to have been seen near the Tipton County home Saturday night.

"Something"

Owen said he thought that the first report was probably the result of the men "seeing things," but admitted that now the thing was becoming serious that that people were undoubtedly seeing "something."

The sheriff was called at 9:30 p.m. Sunday to the Cash Cochran farm after Mr. and Mrs. John Maness, who reside there, had reported that the "gorilla" attacked their car just as they were approaching the Crooked bridge.

Strikes at Car

The animal came up from under the bridge and struck at the side of the car as the Maness' neared the bridge. According to

Maness, after the monster struck at the car, it slid back down the embankment.

Maness described the "thing" as being more than five feet tall with long rusty brown hair, and as having a slick, shiny head, a black pug nose and teeth more than two inches long. "It had an extra long tusk on each side of its mouth," Maness added.

"Horrible Experience"

Mrs. Maness, who was still obviously frightened today, said that she hadn't been able to sleep last night from fear of the animal and told a reporter from The Tribune that the "thing" resembled a gorilla and gave the same description of the monster as did her husband.

Said Mrs. Maness, "I hope that everyone who doesn't believe that the 'thing' exists, sees it themselves. It was the most horrible experience that I ever had."

Tipton, Indiana, *Tribune,* August 2, 1949

RUMORS FLY . . .
AS 'GORILLA' HIDES

Rumors were a dime a dozen in Tipton and Tipton county today as the hunt for a "wild gorilla" entered its second day. Shortly after noon today an unidentified woman called The Tribune to report that the Omar Bread

truckdriver had seen the monster on highway 19 north of Tipton, and that a posse was
being formed to chase it in a cornfield.

Early this morning huge tracks were reported on South Conde street between Adams
and Jackson street. The tracks which were
about 15 inches in length and seven inches
in width were written off by Sheriff Jesse
Owen as a "hoax," inasmuch as the tracks
grew darker in color instead of lighter as the
"animal" progressed. The tracks were caused
by the "animal" coming off the oily street
onto the sidewalk. Owen believed that the
tracks were made by someone as a trick.

Meanwhile some six persons reported seeing the "gorilla" in the Crooked Bridge area
last evening, giving the same description of
the animal as did Mr. and Mrs. Maness, route
4, who first reported the monster.

The area near the Crooked Bridge was
swamped with automobiles and sightseers
Monday afternoon and evening, with approximately 200 persons arriving at the scene
hoping to catch a glimpse of the "gorilla."
An airplane piloted by Arthur Noble and
Deputy Sheriff Paul Grimme "buzzed" the
wooded area near the bridge, but failed to
catch sight of anything answering the description of the animal.

On the other side of the dense woods away from where the monster was seen on the bridge, it was noted that something had been eating garbage from an area where the city had been dumping garbage on the Joe Mattingly farm and that banana peels, orange peels and apples were strewn along a path leading into the woods.

The hunt goes on . . . and the rumors . . .

Kokomo, Indiana, *Tribune,* August 2, 1949

TIPTON COUNTY
HAS 'GORILLA' SCARE

SEARCH MADE BY PLANE FOR MONSTER

Tipton, Ind., Aug. 2—(Tribune Area Special)—Tipton county's "gorilla" proved to be

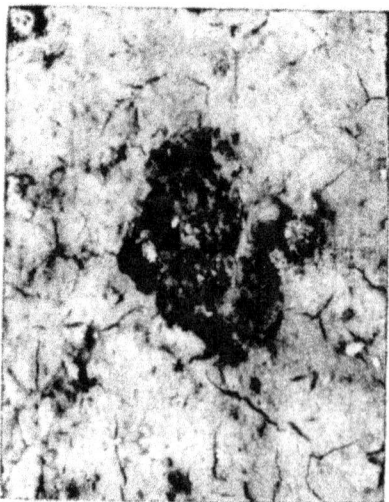

GORILLA TRACK?

The footprint of the "gorilla" was snapped by a Tribune photographer under the Crooked Bridge where the monster was alleged to have struck at a car in which Mr. and Mrs. Maness, route 4, were riding. The track was about 10 inches in length, narrow at the heel, and spreading out at the toes.

as elusive as the turtle of Churubusco today after efforts by local authorities to find
evidence substantiating the report of Mr. and
Mrs. John Manese that a "gorilla" attacked
their automobile Sunday night failed.

The search Monday afternoon was divided
into two branches, the "air posse" with Art
Noble, pilot, and Deputy Sheriff Paul Grimme
canvassing the area in Mr. Noble's airplane,
where the beast was last reported seen.
Ground forces, under the guidance of Sheriff Owen, were delayed by a strong and determined army of flies in "swarm formation"
which circled in and around the sheriff's car.

The "air posse" reported back, "We never
even seen a hare."

Tipton, Indiana, *Tribune*, August 5, 1949

'GORILLA' ONLY GROWLS, BUT SHOWS UP IN HAMILTON COUNTY

The "gorilla" in Tipton suddenly came to life
again Thursday afternoon, from the news
angle at least, although he did not make an
actual appearance.

City police and Deputy Sheriff Jesse Owen
were called to the Henry Tebbe Farm, four
miles north of Tipton on highway 19, following a report that the "gorilla" had been spotted there.

According to the police, Domar Blakely, who is employed on the Tebbe farm, said that he was mowing weeds along a fence row when the incident occurred. Blakely said that he heard noises that sounded like two dogs fighting. The growling got louder and seemed to be coming toward him. Blakely left the scene and reported the matter to the sheriff's office.

No Trace

Police were unable to find any trace of the monster.

Meanwhile, the "mystery beast" has been reported in Hamilton county. According to reports from there, tracks of the animal were seen in the Arcadia community early this week. Then on Tuesday evening "it" was seen by Mr. and Mrs. Ralph Pearce of Riverwood while driving from their home to Cicero near 10 o'clock.

About two miles east of Cicero, near the Morbaugh Farm, Pearce said he noticed two round lights, yellowish-red in color, along the side of the road. At a distance he thought it was an automobile, but as he drove closer he realized it was the reflection of light from an animal's eyes.

"Big Animal"

Just before the Pearce car reached the animal it dropped down on all fours in the ditch at the side of the road. Pearce flashed his spotlight at it and said it looked like a big fur robe thrown over a wash tub—"only bigger."

Pearce rounded up some men and guns and returned to the spot. The animal was gone, but they tracked it through the weeds for a short distance before losing the trail. The men hunted for two or three hours in the vicinity without finding further trace of the beast.

According to the Noblesville Ledger, "It may be the Tipton county gorilla on a visit to this county, or 'it' may be a bear which observer are inclined to think more likely."

New Report

Wednesday evening a farmer near Strawtown reported observing a strange animal crossing a field when he was driving his cows to the barn about dusk. He said he wasn't close enough in the dim light to tell for sure what it was, but that it was walking erect on its hind legs and could have either been a bear or gorilla. He added that he was as close to it as he wanted to be!

Pearce says he believes the animal is a bear, but that it could be a gorilla. However, the tracks of the beast, according to Pearce, resemble those of a bear.

Last night several groups of Hamilton county hunters were making plans to seek "big game" in an effort to locate and capture the beast.

Iowa

New York, New York, *Herald*, August 31, 1869

A Wild Boy In Iowa.—Considerable excitement exists in East Davenport and Gilbert Town, in consequence of a wild boy who has been seen by several veracious individuals prowling about the woods at the back of Judge Grant's farm and on the river's bank and islands. About a week ago a man returning from a shooting excursion saw what he at first took for some wild animal crouching by the bank of the river. It suddenly plunged in and emerged with a fish, which it devoured ravenously. Getting closer to it he saw that it was a boy, apparently about fifteen or sixteen, entirely without clothes, and covered with light sandy hair of a silky appearance. He plainly saw the face, and describes it as revoltingly ugly and brutal in its aspect. He attempted to approach it, but the creature became alarmed, and, taking to the water, swam to a neighboring island and hid in the

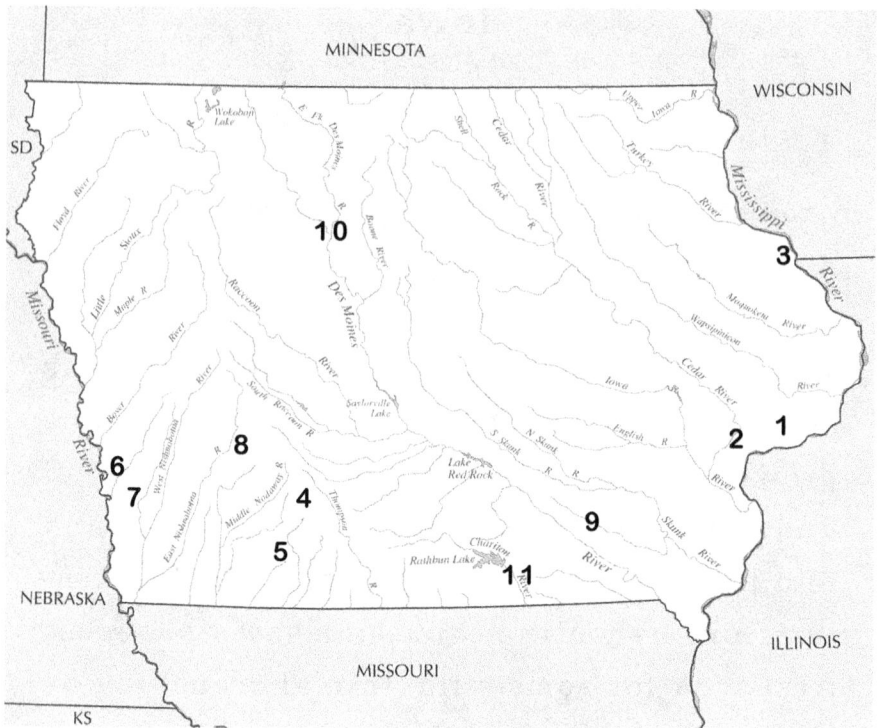

1 East Davenport (Scott County)

2 Muscatine (Muscatine County)

3 Dubuque (Dubuque County)

4 Macksburg (Madison County)

5 Diagonal (Ringgold County)

6 Council Bluffs and Lake Manawa (Pottawattamie County)

7 Glenwood (Mills County)

8 Atlantic (Cass County)

9 Ottumwa (Wapello County)

10 Holiday Creek / Fort Dodge (Webster County)

11 Centerville (Appanoose County)

sedges. On returning home he gave information and a close lookout has been kept. The creature, whatever it may be, has been seen twice since, and this wild boy of the woods will doubtless be shortly captured.

Muscatine, Iowa, *Evening Journal,* May 30, 1872

A "Wild Man" Scare.—Some of the laborers on a division of the Muscatine Western road, near the city, have got up a big scare over the reported appearance of a "wild man," gorilla, devil or some like hideous apparition. A teamster under Col. Horton threw up his situation yesterday, alleging as the reason therefor that same monster in human shape had issued from the woods and appeared several times in the midst of the squad of laborers with which he worked, spreading terror and consternation on every hand and driving them into their cabins in a panic. On one occasion it leaped from a tree upon one of the men and tore a part of his clothing. The only description the man could give of this "What is it?" is that it resembled a gorilla. Col. Horton offered him a carbine if he would return, but he refused to go back for any consideration. Whether the report as made is true, or whether it is partly or wholly the result of a prolific imagination, heightened by fear, we cannot say, not having had time, as yet, to personally investigate the matter. At best, it is a singular story.

Dubuque, Iowa, *Daily Herald,* August 9, 1887

LOCAL NEWS IN BRIEF.

A nondescript animal, a mixture of monkey and baboon, caught on the bluffs in the rear of the brewery, is a curiosity of the four-footed tribe.

Des Moines, Iowa, *Daily Iowa Capital,* September 28, 1899

WILD MAN SEEN AGAIN.

REPORTED TO BE IN THE
NEIGHBORHOOD OF MACKSBURG.
SPECIAL TO THE CAPITAL.

Macksburg, Sept. 28.— The wild man is in this vicinity, or at least was at an early hour Wednesday morning. He was seen by a hired man employed by Capt. Garker while he was in the Grand river timber looking for some stray stock. The man says the mysterious stranger "took after" him and admits that he was so badly frightened that any description he may give of it cannot be relied upon. Sifted from the terrified story teller the facts appear to be about as follows: The wild man was of gigantic stature, covered with hair, either natural or from some wild beast, and looked like a gorilla or large ape. The hired man ran until he found a horse, when he mounted it and rode off. The wild man did not make any effort to follow him. There is a reign of terror in the community and it is probable that there will not be any school until the mystery is solved as the children are unwilling to leave home so long as the wild man is at large. A circle hunt is being organized to search for the mysterious creature. When the first reports concerning this mystery came to Macksburg there was much skepticism and very few people thought there was anything in the rumors but the testimony of Barman and also Mr. Prangle, who saw the object at short range, has satisfied all that there is some object roaming about the country that should be captured and detained. If it is an insane man he should be placed in an asylum, where he cannot harm people nor frighten women and children; if it is a wild animal, it cannot be anything else but a gorilla, one of the most savage animals in existence and extremely dangerous when running at large.

Council Bluffs, Iowa, *Daily Nonpareil,* September 28, 1899

STRANGE MONSTER AT LARGE.

WILD MAN OR BEAST
FRIGHTENS FARMER'S FAMILY.

SPECIAL TO THE DAILY NONPAREIL.

Diagonal, Sept. 27.—A wild man, or wild animal resembling a man, made an appearance
four miles form this place yesterday morning
and later in the day at other places and has
occasioned great excitement. It came first
to the house of Mr. S. Crook. That gentleman was absent at Diagonal, his wife and a
daughter 15 years old being alone at the time,
and an infant was in the cradle. The hairy
monster suddenly entered the house from a
back door. It was of large stature, considerably more than six feet high, and was covered from head to foot with long black hair,
either natural or the skin of beasts. Its color
was very dark, like that of a negro. It did not
appear to be able to speak, but made a growling noise, a sort of suppressed roar, and occasionally beat its breast. Mrs. Crooks ran
away from the house and fainted dead away
just outside the door. The daughter's courage was stronger, and snatching up the baby
she confronted the object, prepared to defend
the little one or sacrifice her life. After it
had thrown open several doors it espied that
of the pantry and seized some food that happened to be in sight. The daughter saw that
it was hungry and placed on the table all
the eatables available, which the wild brute
instantly devoured, using both hands as a

beast does its paws. When it had satisfied its hunger it left the premises and walked toward the timber, distant about half a mile from the house. When he was about half way to the timber some hunters, accompanied by dogs, drove up to the house and were informed by the girl of the circumstances, and the wild man was pointed out to them. They immediately gave chase, but the wild man easily distanced them, and was lost in the timber. They returned to Diagonal to organize a circle hunt for the man or whatever it is.

About noon the children of the Clayburn school saw the same object in the woods near the school house, to which they ran for protection, barricading the door and windows, but it passed on without making any effort to enter.

Later in the afternoon it visited the house of Mr. Frink, about eight miles north of Diagonal, and was seen by that gentleman, his daughter, a girl of 14, and a younger son. The two latter were alone in the house at the time, but Mr. Frink drove up with a load of corn while it was standing in the door. As soon as the wild man saw him it gave a loud roar and jumping a fence without touching it, ran into a corn field.

There is an unconfirmed rumor this morning that the wild man has been seen in Grand river timber southeast of Afton. Mr. Frink feels certain that the thing is not a man, but an immense ape or gorilla. All that have seen it agree that it is of a very dark color, of great size and covered with long black hair.

Sheboygan, Wisconsin, *Press-Telegram,* March 20, 1923

MYSTERY "APE MAN" BRINGS TERROR TO COUNCIL BLUFFS

(BY UNITED PRESS.)

Council Bluffs, Iowa.—A graphic description of an "ape man" who has been terrorizing Council Bluffs' women, attacking fourteen during the past three weeks, was given to police today in a written statement by one of the victims, whose name is being withheld.

"His arms are monkey-like," she declared. "He slinks along in a stooped fashion, arms swinging loosely like those of a monkey.

"His attacks are like those of a wild animal.

"He creeps up behind and snatches at the legs of the girl he has selected for his victim. He tears at her clothing.

"All the girls who have been attacked were nervous wrecks afterwards. I know of one girl whom he dragged between two buildings where she had to put up a fight for her life.

"But he is a coward. When his victims scream and create a commotion he darts off with lightning-like rapidity and disappears behind buildings."

James C. Nicoll, chief of police, said that only six of the alleged attacks had been reported to the police. He said he has had difficulty in getting the victims to talk about the affair.

The entire police force has been out on the alert to try to capture the "apeman" with the football tactics. A civilian committee will be formed if the attacks continue. The police chief advises that young women should not go about unescorted but that if attacked they run to the nearest home for protection.

(BY UNITED PRESS)

Council Bluffs, Iowa.—The women of Council Bluffs were unmolested last night for the first time in a week.

The ape man failed to walk.

The dozen women assaulted during the last week hovered about the police station, ready to identify any suspect.

All of the women were attacked within fifteen minutes of midnight. Violence committees and the police searched the community in the hunt for the ape man.

Chief of Police Nicholl today started an investigation among several circuses who have winter quarters here. He declared that "the thing" may be a monster monkey.

Cincinnati, Ohio, *Post,* March 21, 1923

POLICE ON TRAIL OF APE-MAN

OFFICERS DISGUISED AS WOMEN
STROLL THRU STREETS

[This story recaps the previous article, while noting that the "ape-man" was "a huge, ungainly creature, believed to be but half human, with most of the characteristics of a gorilla." One witness said he was "dark, heavy set and with a small, red face," with long hair that covered his face, hairy arms, and roughly dressed. He prowled an exclusive residential area in the evenings.]

Atlantic, Iowa, *News-Telegraph,* October 6, 1930

GORILLA AT LARGE NEAR RED OAK; SEEN ALSO AT EMERSON

Red Oak, Ia., Oct. 6.—People of this section are going about these days wearing an anxious expression, due to the belief that a gorilla is present in this vicinity.

The "Gorilla" was first said to be seen by a farmer near Glenwood, who was startled by the hairy animal ambling up the runway to a water tank, where it quenched its thirst, and then disappeared hurriedly.

Elmer Larson, night man at the Coggagae garage on highway No. 34, in East Emerson, was the next person to meet the animal. It was 4 a.m. Elmer's keen hearing picked up the pat, pat of a soft foot on the driveway. He caught one glimpse of the hairy animal.

Elmer leaped out of his chair and had a mind to run, but his feet and legs refused to function, he said. There stood in front of the screen a monkey, nay, a hairy animal the size of a small man. The gorilla looked at Elmer for a time, and then cantered away and was lost in the darkness.

Elmer tried to study it all out and remembered that several weeks ago an animal of the gorilla species escaped from a circus at Glenwood.

Atlantic, Iowa, *News-Telegraph,* November 6, 1930

GORILLA ROAMS IN ATLANTIC VICINITY

Atlantic—A gorilla, the largest species of ape known, is roaming the countryside surrounding Atlantic. The hairy man-like monster has been seen a number of times during the last few days and is thought to be the same beast that has been roving over southwestern Iowa for the last year.

Last fall a gorilla was seen by many farmers in west Pottawattamie county and several hunting parties were organized to kill the beast which was terrorizing livestock on the farms, but no trace of the animal could be found by the posses. The gorilla story was almost forgotten until last August, when a giant ape was reported seen at Red Oak and at Emerson. At the latter place, a night watchman at a garage was aroused from his lonesome vigil late at night by the gorilla as it came up to a window of the garage and stood there peering in at him for several minutes and then hurried away into the darkness

Approached Woman in Field

During the last week numerous reports have been heard of the gorilla's visits to farms in the local territory. He was seen first near the Sam Jensen farm on the South Olive street road and last Saturday while she was husking corn with her husband, Mrs. Fred Scheef saw the beast in the corn field. According to Mrs. Scheef, the gorilla came down the corn row and watched her for several minutes, standing first on its hind legs and then flopping down on its forefeet, finally retreating without showing any viciousness.

Monday the gorilla was seen on the Fred Walter farm, northwest of Atlantic, and last

night he was seen about a half mile north of
the Jim Wilkensen farm, a mile and a half
north of Atlantic.

Jumped Over Fence

Fred Ruston and Charles Myers of Kimballton, while en route to the Wilkensen place
in their car, saw the gorilla walking along
a fence. As their car approached the animal leaped over a fence and disappeared in
the Wilkensen field. The young men had not
heard of the gorilla's presence in this territory and they supposed that it was a man
wearing a fur coat that they saw.

When they reached the Wilkensen place,
however, they learned of the gorilla being seen at the Scheef farm, which is located a mile west and a half mile north of the
Wilkensen farm, and they related seeing the
beast along the road. It was about 8:30 when
the Kimballton young men saw the gorilla.

Deputy Sheriff P. H. Edwards expressed
his willingness today to head a searching
party to run down the hairy monster. It is
believed to be one which escaped from a circus near Glenwood a year ago.

Albert Lea, Minnesota, *Evening Tribune,* November 18, 1930

HUNT FOR GORILLA IN RIVER
BOTTOMS AT COUNCIL BLUFFS

Council Bluffs, Ia., Nov. 18.—(AP)—The

Missouri river bottoms around Lake Manawa, two miles south of here, was the scene yesterday of a search for an animal, believed to be a gorilla, which has been seen in that vicinity for the last six days.

C. Williams, a farmer, reported he had seen the animal last night at close range and it was about the size of a man. Tracks of a large foot were found in the mud along Mosquito lake. The animal had been reported seen near Red Oak and Atlantic during recent weeks and previously at Emerson. it is believed to be the gorilla which escaped from a circus near Glen wood, more than a year ago.

Lincoln, Nebraska, *Star*, November 18, 1930

GORILLA REPORTED SEEN ALONG RIVER AT COUNCIL BLUFFS

Council Bluffs, Iowa, Nov. 18—(AP)—Stories that residents in the vicinity of Atlantic, Ia., had seen what they believed was a gorilla were given additional credence today following reports that persons living in the Missouri river bottoms two miles from here had seen the animal.

Tracks of a large foot were seen in the mud and a farmer said he saw the beast, about the size of a man, at close range.

Doubters have pointed out that the tropical animal could scarcely survive the rigors of an Iowa winter. Peace officers have volunteered their aid in seeking the beast, which is believed to have escaped from a circus near Glenwood more than a year ago.

Mason City, Iowa, *Globe-Gazette*, November 20, 1930

HUNTER HOT ON 'GORILLA' TRAIL

STRANGE TRACKS NEAR COUNCIL BLUFFS
THOT TO BELONG TO CIRCUS ANIMAL

Council Bluffs, Nov. 20. (AP)—G. C. Bain, who says his experience with a Colorado sheepmen's organization qualifies him for big-game hunting, today was hot on the trail of an animal, variously described as an ape or gorilla.

The beast, said to have escaped from a wagon circus more than a year ago, has been reported seen or heard by farmers living as far as 50 miles from here during the last three weeks.

Tracks near Lake Manawa, three miles from Council Bluffs, were described by Bain as being unlike any he had seen before. He said he would put baited traps around the lake, and said, "we should have a look at whatever it is in a day or so."

It was reported that parents in Shelby county were accompanying their children to school because of reports of the presence of the "ape."

Mason City, Iowa, *Globe-Gazette*, November 21, 1930

PHANTOM IS NOT "MERE MONKEY"

ANOTHER ADDED TO LIST OF
THOSE WHO HAVE SEEN BEAST.

Council Bluffs, Nov. 21. (AP)—On the side of those who think Lake Manawa's phantom is more than a mere monkey today was aligned J. Miller, farmer, who has been added to the growing list of those who have seen the beast.

While working in the field yesterday, Miller said, his horses started plunging wildly. "I looked toward where the horses were grazing," he said, "and saw something ambling thru the corn rows. It was almost as tall as a man, shaggy and broad, but I couldn't say positively what it was."

Miller's farm borders on the Missouri river where G. C. Bain, Gunison, Colo., trapper, has undertaken a search for the animal, believed to be an ape or gorilla that escaped from a wagon circus in Glenwood more than a year ago. Bain's efforts, tho, came to naught when rain obliterated the beast's tracks. The hunter today resumed his search.

Further credence that the beast is an ape was given by the statement of Dode Bachelor, resident in the willow thickets near the river for more than half a century, that there was in the wilds some creature that "has never been there before in 50 years." Bain quoted the hermit as saying the animal's uncanny wailing "put to shame" the howl of a wolf and sounded "like a woman being murdered." His dogs, Bachelor told Bain, had been restless for two weeks.

Helena, Montana, *Independent*, November 22, 1930

TERRIFYING ANTHROPOID
JUST A WEE MONKEY

Council Bluffs, Ia., Nov. 21.—(AP)—The terrifying gorilla of Lake Manawa flats shrunk to a monkey today.

Many people have reported seeing the anthropoid—described as large as a man—as it roamed about the countryside.

Today, a small boy living near the lake said he saw the animal at close range and that it was a common size monkey.

A Colorado trapper, G. C. Bain, who came here to trap the beast, said he found monkey tracks about the flats yesterday.

Council Bluffs, Iowa, *Daily Nonpareil*, November 23, 1930

COL. "IDAHO BILL" DECLARES
QUEER BEAST IS HIS PET

With G. C. Bain, Colorado trapper, temporarily out of the willow [thickets] south of

Lake Manawa after stating that in his opinion the tracks of the "mystery animal" which he has crossed do not indicate that it is huge enough to be dangerous, "Colonel Idaho Bill" Pearson of Hastings, Neb., was preparing to come to this city from Chicago, Ill., Saturday night intending to claim the animal as a pet.

In a telegram to The Nonpareil Saturday Colonel Pearson stated that the animal was in all probability one which escaped from his truck when it was turned over in an accident three weeks ago.

While he did not classify the creature, the colonel wired that it resembled a gorilla and was not dangerous and he begged hunters not to harm it.

Colonel Pearson is a survivor of the old days on the plains. He still affects the goatee, long hair and buckskin jacket of the old-time westerner.

During his frequent visits to this city and to the home of his daughter in Shenandoah, Ia., he has brought with him an animal in a specially constructed cage at the back of his truck and has offered rewards for any person who can name the beast.

He stated in his telegram that he would get back to Iowa soon to capture his pet.

It should be noted that "Idaho Bill" Pearson was a well-known showman who had no difficulty in spinning yarns. He supplied broncos to rodeos and is said to have roped and captured several bears. In a 1928 story, Pearson was traveling with a large feline, "about twice as large as a mountain lion, with peculiar beard and markings similar to those of a tiger. Its ears resemble those of a gorilla. The colonel expects the animal, which he captured in southern Mexico, will be identified at the zoological gardens." ("Idaho Bill Taking Mammoth Cat to Washington Zoo," Boise, Idaho, *Statesman,* August 18, 1928.) It seems possible that Pearson was taking advantage of the "ape" story to try and capture a new animal for his sideshow.

Carroll, Iowa, *Carroll Daily Herald*, August 24, 1932

WILD GORILLA SEEN

The regular periodical find of a wild animal at large in the fields or wild places of Iowa has again turned up—this time near to the city of Ottumwa. Three men reported to officers that they had seen a wild manlike animal, with fur all over and a white stripe down its back. The animal was jumping about on a large log in the timber. It generally takes a month or two to unravel a mystery like this, but in this case, those on the hunt found Andy Meyers, a farmer, dressed in a horse hair coat and fur mittens, trying to get the honey from a bee tree and leave the bees behind.

Connellsville, Pennsylvania, *Daily Courier,* June 29, 1936

WANDERING APE HUNTED

Fort Dodge, Ia., June 29.—Residents near Holiday Creek are searching for a mysterious chimpanzee, which appeared in the vicinity late last fall. The animal survived the severe Iowa winter and has been seen lately searching for food. The chimpanzee is believed to have escaped from a circus cage.

Cedar Rapids, Iowa, *Gazette,* August 27, 1944

CENTERVILLE POSSE TO HUNT STRANGE ANIMAL IN VICINITY

Centerville (INS)—A posse will start out Sunday hunting a strange animal. It has been described as rather large, looking something like a monkey.

Farmers who have seen it several times, report it is about the size of a large dog, with brown-black body, and grayish-white face.

The last farm on which the strange creature was seen was the Bob Bear's farm where the animal picked some corn and placed it neatly in a pile.

Kansas

Dubuque, Iowa, *Daily Herald,* September 4, 1869
WHAT IS IT?

A GORILLA OR WILD MAN IN KANSAS.

The Arcadia, Kansas, correspondent of the St. Louis Democrat says:

"Aside from the excitement caused by the trouble in regard to the ownership of these neutral lands, we, of Arcadia valley, in the southern part of Crawford county, are having a new sensation which may lead to some new disclosures in natural history, if investigated, as it should be. It is nothing less than the discovery of a wild man, or a gorilla, or "what is it?" It has at different times been seen by almost every inhabitant of the valley, and it has occasionally been seen in the adjoining county in Missouri, but it seems to make its home in this vicinity. Several times it has approached the cabins of the settlers, much to the terror of the women and children, especially if the men happen to be absent working in the fields. In one instance it

465

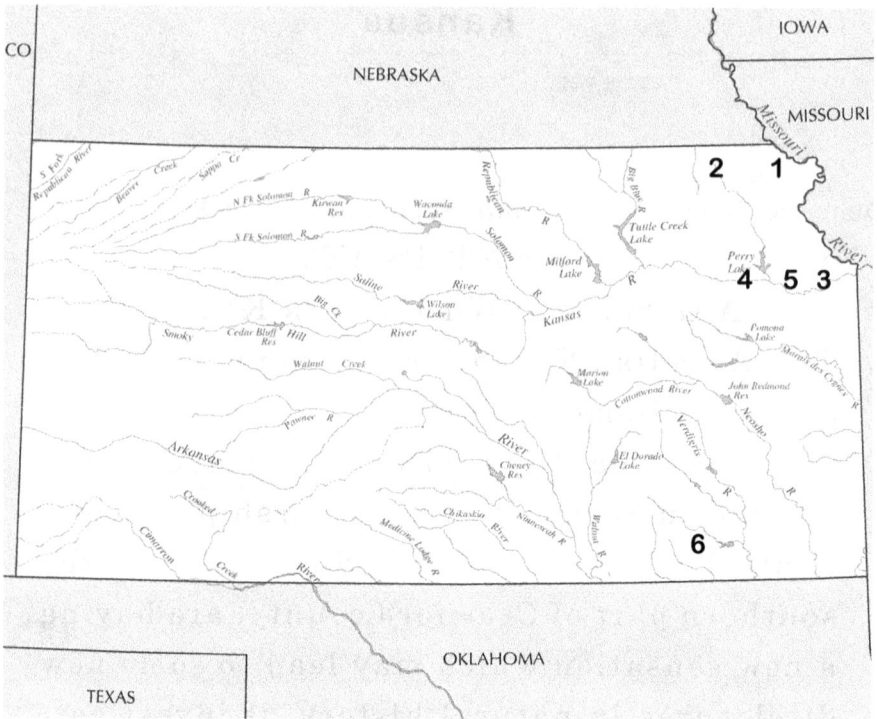

1 Doniphan County

2 Nemaha County

3 Olathe (Johnson County)

4 Quinton Heights, Topeka (Shawnee County)

5 Lawrence (Douglas County)

6 Independence (Montgomery County)

approached the house of one of our old citizens, Wm. Armsworthy, but was driven away with clubs by one of the men. It has so near a resemblance to the human form that men are unwilling to shoot it. It is so difficult to give a description of this wild man or animal. It has a stooping gait, very long arms, with immense hands or claws. It has a hairy face, and those who have been near it describe it as having a most ferocious expression of countenance; generally walks on its hind legs, but sometimes on all fours. The beast, or "what is it?" is as cowardly as it is ugly, and it is next thing to impossible to get near enough to obtain a good view of it. The settlers, not knowing what to call it, have christened it Old Sheff. Since its appearance, our fences are often found down, allowing the stock free range in our cornfields. I suppose Old Sheff is only following his inclination, as it may be easier for it to pull them down than to climb over them. However, as it is, curses loud and deep are heaped on its head by the settlers. The settlers are divided in opinion as to whether it belongs to the human or not. Probably it will be found to be a gorilla or large orang-outang, that has escaped from some menagerie in the settlements east of here. At one time over sixty of the citizens turned out to hunt it down, but it escaped; but, probably, owing to the fright it received, it kept out of sight for several days, and just as the settlers were congratulating themselves that they were rid of an intolerable nuisance, Old Sheff came back again, seemingly as savage as ever. If this meets the eye of any showman who has lost one of his collection of beasts, he may know where to find it. At present it is the terror of all the women and children in the valley. It cannot be caught, and nobody is willing to shoot it."

This story, as explained below, was simply a newspaper joke, ridiculing Mr. Joseph Sheffield, who ended up the target of local settlers because he came down on the wrong side of a convoluted legal battle regarding the sale of land previously owned by the Cherokee, which became known as the "Joy land troubles." A later blurb in the Lawrence, Kansas, *Republican Daily Journal,* January 18, 1870, points to editor J. Speer as the inventor of this story.

Lawrence, Kansas, *Tribune,* September 23, 1868
     [The] Fort Scott Moniter thus disposes of the strange story—"a gorilla at large in Crawford county"—which was published in the

Missouri Democrat and was also printed in
The Kansas Tribune:

The story that has been going the rounds
for some time, under the above heading,
which has been looked upon by some as sen-
sational, and by others as barely possible,
is simply a slur on our old friend, generally
known in this community as the "Yankee
from the neutral lands." His name is Sheffield, and he is a Joy man. Sometime last
winter the settler's on Cox's creek drove Mr.
Sheffield from his home, as he avers, because
he was against the Leaguers; but the settlers
say he is a bad man in the community, and
that he was driven off on general principles.
How this is we are unable to state, but they
have succeeded in perpetrating a huge "joak"
on Mr. Sheffield, that will stick to him as
long as he lives. He will in future be known
by the appellation of "Old Sheff."

The Horton, Kansas, *Headlight Commercial,* July 15, 1920

Item in "Fifty Year Ago Column" [1870] in St.
Joseph Gazette: "A wild man or gorilla has
been seen in the woods and fields of Doniphan county lately. He seems to take a great
delight in tearing down fences and small out
buildings and is supposed to have escaped
from some traveling show."

Sabetha, Kansas, *Nemaha County Republican,* October 6, 1888

ONEIDA ITEMS.

Dr. Hamlin tells us that a farmer came in town the other day and said there was a wild man out on Deer creek, that he had killed a dog for his neighbor, that he looked like a gorilla, had tusks like a hog, and they supposed he was the only one escaping murder by the "injuns" a great many years ago. At any rate he has frightened the people out there we learn. Our proposition was to form a ring hunt and capture him and bring him to Oneida at our earliest moment and people would be attracted to the place thereby in the absence of the newspaper spoken of up above and it might liven up trade a little. Some people seem to think they have the world by the foretop, so to speak, and that it would not move unless they gave it a jerk.

Correctionville, Iowa, *Sioux Valley News,* June 22, 1893

A STRANGE MONSTER.

JOHNSON COUNTY, KANSAS,

PEOPLE CHASING A HAIRY MAN.

Kansas City, Mo., June 21.—The people living along Cedar Creek, in Johnson county, Kan., near Olathe, about thirty miles form this city, are greatly excited over the antics of some strange animal that roams through the woods in that part of the country. Robert Sanders, a colored man, ran into Olathe and said he had been chased over a mile by a hideous monster that appeared to be half man and half devil. The next morning a man employed on the farm of Edward Lane, living half a mile north of Olathe reported having seen the man. Since then several others have described the animal as it appeared to them. All agree upon description and say that it appears to be fully seven feet tall with a heavy covering of brown hair, and perfectly naked. It stands in a half stooping posture, with long arms crossed over its breast, but when startled or in pursuit, it gets over the ground rapidly with a swinging gait. Robert Wilson, who owns a dairy farm two and a half miles northwest of Olathe, reports that the monster had killed two cows and a calf belonging to him. He came to Olathe for assistance, and a heavily armed party of men are scouring the woods in search of the strange beast. Two of the party have returned, and say while they found no signs of the animal's tracks, they found the cows and calf, and say that the carcasses were so torn and mangled that they must have been killed by a most powerful animal. It is thought by many to be an African gorilla that has escaped from some traveling menagerie, and the people fear it will kill human beings before it can be captured or shot.

Glasco, Kansas, *Sun,* September 8, 1893

LOOKS SOME LIKE A FAKE.

Topeka, September 6.—The daily Journal gives publicity to this:

Deputy Clerk Shell Curtis, of the district court, who lives at Quinton Heights, says the people residing in his neighborhood are badly frightened on account of the stories of a gorilla which is said to be in hiding in the woods along the Shunganunga about six miles southwest of the city and gradually working his way towards Topeka. It is said that John Sims, a son of Major William Sims, has seen the animal and reports him to be about six feet high.

Mr. Sims saw the gorilla after night, and the horrible scream or whistle of the animal was said to be hideous. The farmers of that neighborhood have suffered from his depredations on their hog lots, and he is said to have killed several calves, a cow and a horse.

A farmer by the name of Schraver is the only person said to have seen the animal in daylight. He was plowing in the field when it came walking toward him at full gait. Schraver unhitched his team and started for the house at full speed.

Several other persons are said to have seen the animal after night. A gorilla was reported to have escaped from Cook & Whitby's circus at Lawrence a few months ago and was afterwards said to have been seen near Olathe, and this is supposed to be the same animal.

Topeka, Kansas, *Daily Capital,* September 10, 1893

Topeka is now having the gorilla scare which shows that the people there know how to protect their melon patches after seeing the way Lawrence did it.—*Lawrence World.*

Augusta, Kansas, *Journal,* September 15, 1893

The inhabitants of Topeka, especially those of a dusky hue, are in great excitement over a supposed "gorilla" which is alleged to be wandering up and down the poetical Shunganunga and giving vent to terrible roars and other outrageous noises. Nobody has seen it however, and it is dimly suspected to be a shrewd device of some farmer to protect his watermelon patch.

Topeka, Kansas, *Daily Capital,* July 21, 1895

STRANGER THAN FICTION

[This newspaper fiction claims to explain the sightings of a gorilla in Topeka in August, 1893, with the tale of an escaped gorilla that was tracked down and killed by the ministers of an African Emperor.]

Lawrence, Kansas, *Daily World,* July 27, 1897

GORILLA SCARE.

A gorilla which roamed around in the city last summer and caused consernation has again made its appearance, and its nocturnal caterwauling is said to be hideous in the extreme, and caused the blood of the rural residenters to become suddenly clogged and bristles to grow on their backbones. Frank Dimery, while on his way home from out in the country, heard the beast and was so frightened that he ran past his own home and when he recovered from the shock he was hugging a sycamore tree on the river bank near Eidemiller's ice house. An old colored man met the animal in the road last Saturday night and has been as pale as a sheet ever since. Even the brave populist, Randall Doolittle, is afraid of the beast, and cringes when he hears its weird pule. Everybody in the country goes armed to the teeth, as in colonial days, but they say they will not kill the beast until the watermelon season is over, unless it crowds them. Wakarusa is one of the garden spots of Kansas, and nearly every gardener has a melon patch this year. You Lawrence fellows who were contemplating a foraging expedition to Wakarusa during the melon season had better give it up, for the gorilla is abroad in the land, and he has no mercy on a melon thief. Frank Thralls, who has a big patch, will vouch for the truth of this story.

Lawrence, Kansas, *Weekly World,* August 12, 1897
THE GORILLA ONCE MORE.
Lawrence papers state that the gorilla has been seen again. It is reported that last Thursday night a party of colored boys were on their way to Gibson's watermelon patch, up the river, and they saw what they took to be a man of their own color standing in the middle of the Santa Fe track and did not discover their mistake until within a few feet of what proved to be a full-sized gorilla, standing

up with outstretched arms, waiting for them. The boys did not wait for the report of Gibson's shot gun, but made a wild dash for town.

It is also reported by Wm. Hughes, an old reliable farmer of Kaw Valley, that the gorilla was sneaking through Schaake's corn field into Thrall's onion patch, where about fifty-five colored people were picking onions, and the stampede that followed was simply appalling. Those colored people went the four ways of the wind. The Thrall boys say they did not find more than half their baskets, and their "hands." They are now hunting new men to fill their places.

John Moody, a sturdy-going young farmer two miles west of here, interested in the culture of watermelons, sweet potatoes and onion sets, sent his colored man to hoe sweet potatoes. While thus engaged he heard a threshing sound in the weeds behind him followed by a horrible growl; a jack rabbit darted across the patch, closely followed by a terrible looking animal, that proved to be the gorilla. The colored boy was so frightened that he didn't know which way to go, but got in ahead of rabbit and gorilla.— Eudora News.

San Antonio, Texas, *Express*, August 3, 1929

HUGE GORILLA SEEN BY BOY

Independence, Kan., Aug. 2—Embryo big game hunters of the county sheriff's office today vainly attempted to find a "gorilla six feet tall with short feet and long hands," reported by Charles Shepherd, 12, to have been seen south of the city limits.

The boy fled crying to his home after the alleged encounter. He said he met the animal near Rock Creek while en route to a swimming party. The animal was reported to have attempted no violence, but to have followed behind the youth.

Officers failed to find even any footprints. Four days ago a "gorilla" was reported at large at [Nowata], Okla., 50 miles from Independence.

Lawrence, Kansas, *Daily Journal World,* September 2, 1929

POLICE STAGE HUNT IN
NORTH LAWRENCE FOR APE

City police were called to the vicinity of Eighth and Lyons streets in North Lawrence late Saturday afternoon when neighbors reported a large gorilla at large in a field nearby.

An intensive search by the officers failed to reveal any trace of the animal. Several small children reported seeing a large, hairy beast which "looked like a man" and their dog, they said, left for parts unknown when the animal was sighted.

Kentucky

Folklorist Leonard Roberts (1957) collected two tales of "wild people" from Kentucky, one referred to as the Yeahoh. The stories themselves are simply transplanted folk tales from the Old Country, given a Kentucky veneer.

Pittsburgh, Pennsylvania, *Dispatch,* March 31, 1892
A monster resembling a gorilla is said to be terrorizing the people of Brownsville, Ky.

Lincoln, Nebraska, *Herald,* May 7, 1892

A BIG GORILLA

The little village of Brownsville, Ky., the county seat of Edmonson county, is in a condition of strange excitement over a singular marauder. Brownsville is surrounded with knobs and hills, and the whole country around is cavernous. It is in the county of Edmonson that the Mammoth Diamond, Grand Avenue, Proctor's, Hundred Dome and other caves are situated. A gorilla is striking terror to the hearts of the people there.

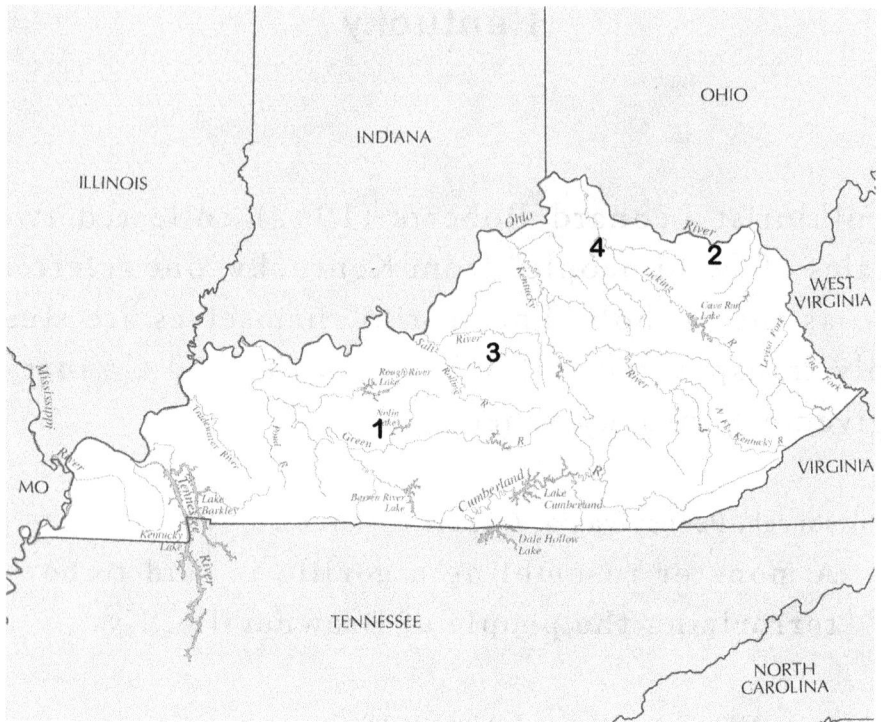

1 Brownsville (Edmonson County)

2 Lewis County

3 Washington County

4 Buena Vista (Harrison County; The news account says it is in Garrard County, but that may be a mistake. There does not appear to be a similarly named town in that county.)

During the day the monster keeps himself up among the neighboring knobs, but when night comes is heard perambulating about the streets of Brownsville, and not a few have seen him.

As soon as darkness comes, so great is the terror of the people, everybody closes securely and bars the doors and windows of his house. The animal probably made its escape from some traveling show.

A posse of citizens will probably soon turn out and seek the capture of the terror or fill its hide with slugs of lead.

New Philadelphia, Ohio, *Ohio Democrat,* August 11, 1892

A MODERN ORSON.

KENTUCKY HAS A GENUINE
WILD MAN IN THE HILLS.

Mayville. Ky., August 2.—Dr. H. W. Dimmit of Vanceburg, says the citizens of Lewis county are much excited over the existence of a genuine wild man who haunts the hills and thickets of the country. He is described as being of gigantic stature, covered with a thick growth of hair and is fierce and untamable. One gentleman encountered the creature in a lonely part of the hills last week and endeavored to strike up a conversation with him. A shower of rocks greeted his first

words and the gentleman made a hasty retreat. Dr. Dimmit says that he saw this modern Orson with his own eyes.

Lincoln, Nebraska, *Evening News,* November 14, 1894

HAIRY MONSTER IN KENTUCKY.

LIVES IN A CAVE, LOOKS LIKE A MAN
AND LIVES BY ROBBING FARMERS.

Over in Washington county, near the line of
Mercer, reigns a being which, man or beast,
mystifies all the neighborhood. For months
the housewives have missed their chickens,
eggs, milk, meat from meathouses and half
grown pigs and young lambs. At first all efforts and schemes to catch the guilty one
proved of no avail. Joseph Ewalt arose one
morning before day and went to the spring-
house, a hundred yards distant from his
dwelling. His wife and son, becoming alarmed
at his continued absence, went in search of
him and found him at the door of the spring-
house in a faint. They restored him to consciousness, and he told them he had seen a
man beast, and that he ran out of the spring-
house as he opened the door; that he had
great, long white hair hanging down from his
head and face that was as coarse as a horse's
mane. His legs were covered with hair, and
the only article of clothing he wore was a

piece of sheepskin over the lower portion of his body, reaching nearly to his knees. When it became noised around that Ewalt had seen a man beast, sober headed men began to set a plan to catch the monster. In the neighborhood, near the mouth of Deep creek, is a cave of considerable proportions, and the natural conclusion was that there would be the place to find their game.

Early Sunday morning Eph Boston and his sons, Tom and James, saw the object of their watch walking in a half gallop, half run for their barn. Notwithstanding the men were armed, they were badly frightened, and after they saw the object enter the barn all three were afraid to enter to try to capture the terrible looking creature. They kept hid and were not seen by the monster, standing in a half erect position nearly 6 ½ feet. His feet were like the paws of a bear or brute, with long claws. His hands also were like those of a feline more than a human. Before the men could come to some action or get over their fright the creature came out of the barn in the same half gallop-run gait and made for the creek. By this time the men started in safe pursuit. Tom Boston foolishly shot at it and the creature half turned and glanced at them, increasing his gait, but never dropping the three large chickens he held in his claws. The Bostons managed to keep in sight of the creature for only a half mile or so, they vowing he ran swifter than a horse. Just as they got to the top of a hill about 500 yards off they were rewarded by seeing the brute man turn, with a wild, scared look, glance around and enter the cave

The men went to the month of the cave, but would not enter. They saw feathers, bones, etc., scattered around the entrance. They returned home and reported what they had seen, and Tuesday they, with a half dozen other men, went to the cave and made a partial survey, proceeding in several hundred yards. They saw fresh indications of habitation by bones, feathers, pieces of calf and sheep skin being strewn around. The passages grew smaller and dwindled, and no one of the party would enter alone, though one, Joe Smith, went in 30 or 40 feet, when the most unearthly yell the men ever heard greeted them. They were good, stout men, but they cowed before that yell and beat a hasty retreat to the main passage of the cavern, but after consultation they agreed it would not do to kill or be killed, and they gave up their search for another time.—Louisville Courier Journal.

Reno, Nevada, *Evening Gazette,* March 27, 1907

HAIRY CREATURE SEEN BY FARM-HAND, AND BOTH ARE SO SCARED THAT THEY PREPARE TO RUN

Lexington, Ky., March 26.—Information has been received here that the people in the country around Buena Vista, a village in Garrard county, are much excited over the reports that a wild man has his haunts in the Kentucky river hills near that place. A party is being organized to explore the cave where the creature is believed to have his lair and attempt to capture him.

Jim Peters, a farm hand employed by S. D. Scott, postmaster at Buena Vista, while working in Bowman's woods, near High Bridge, a short distance from Buena Vista, was attracted by the peculiar actions of his dog, which came running to him from a thicket near by, yelping and showing every evidence of extreme fright. A moment later, Peters says, a creature with the shape of a human being followed the dog and approached within twenty yards of him. Peters says he was too frightened to run. The apparition kept its eyes on the dog until asked what it was doing there, when it turned and disappeared in the woods. Peters says that the creature wore no clothes except a coon skin tied about its loins. Its long black hair streamed down its back and breast in a matted mass, and covered the face so that he could not see whether it had a beard or not. Its body was covered with a coat of soft, fuzzy black hair and its finger and toe nails were long and curved like talons.

Peters hurried home and told his employer, who today organized a party who went to where the wild man had been seen. They found no trace of him in the woods, but in the mud of the river bank they found tracks of bare human feet with claw-like toe nails.

Meanwhile the women and children of the vicinity are afraid to leave their homes. The man is supposed to be an escaped prisoner or lunatic.

Labrador

Ogden, Utah, *Standard,* October 22, 1904

HAS LABRADOR A GIANT RACE?

Quebec, Oct. 22.—Stories of a race of aboriginal giants unknown to white men and dwelling in the unexplored interior of Labrador have come from Indian sources at frequent intervals during the last few years. The late Adirondack Murray had planned an expedition to the far north for the purpose of testing the truth of the oft-repeated rumors, but died before carrying his purpose into execution; and Leonidas Hubbard, Jr., was starved to death in the inhospitable interior of the Labrador islands less than an year ago while endeavoring to make his way to the abode of this strange people.

Ethnologists declare that if any such Indian tribe is now in existence, its numbers must be exceedingly small, and its members represent the only survivors of the once famous Beothics or Red Indians of Newfoundland. The last living representative of the

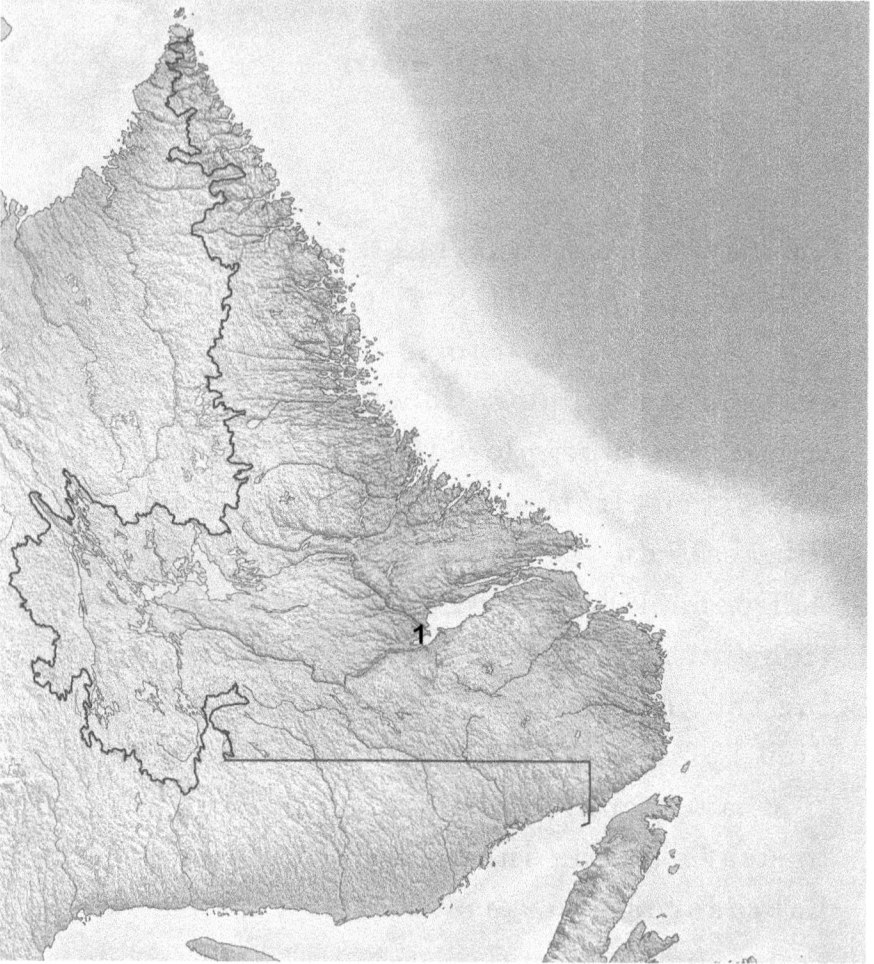

1 Traverspine (now Happy Valley-Goose Bay)

Beothics seen by white men died in captivity at St. Johns, Newfoundland, in 1829, and it is a much motted point with the historians whether the race became altogether extinct immediately after that, or whether as some suppose, a small remnant escaped from the island and crossed by the straits of Belle Isle to Labrador. . . .

Taft (1980), previously published by David J. Hufford in *Fabula* 18(1977): 234-241.

One afternoon a young girl was playing in front of her parents' cabin when she saw a large animal covered with short white fur, walking erect and appearing to have practically no neck, come out of the forest and start toward her. She very reasonably ran screaming into the house where her mother barred the door and the creature went away. However, it returned at night and walked around the cabin beating on the walls, apparently with a branch or other piece of wood. During the following days the men of the area tracked it hoping to shoot it. They claimed to have seen it at a distance several times, but never got a clear shot at it. For some time it continued to come back at night, frightening the inhabitants of the community, and then at length it simply disappeared.

The local people explained it as apparently being a gorilla which had somehow found its way into the local forest.

Bruce Wright, *Wildlife Sketches Near and Far,* Fredricton: University of New Brunswick Press, 1962. (from Green 1978).

About 1913 the little settlement of Traverspine at the head of Lake Melville was visited in winter by two strange animals that drove the dogs to a frenzy and badly frightened the people. They left deep tracks about twelve inches long indicating great weight and they rooted up rotten logs with great strength and they tore them apart as if searching for grubs.

They sometimes stood erect on their hind legs (at which time they looked like great hairy men seven feet tall, and no doubt from this description Merrick got his title of the Traverspine Gorilla), but they also ran on all fours. They cleaned up some seal bones "too big for the dogs", and what is too big for a husky is really big, and many dogs followed them and did not return when they came around the settlement at night. This was a serious loss as dogs were the people's sole means of transportation.

These two strange animals, which the inhabitants called the man and the woman because one was larger than the other, stayed about the settlement despite attempts to trap them or drive them away. One day Mrs. Michelin was alone in her house with her young daughter playing in the edge of the bush behind. Suddenly the child rushed in crying, "It's following me Mummy, it's following me!"

Mrs. Michelin reached for a shotgun loaded with buckshot which she always had near when her husband was away, and stepped out the back door.

"All I could see was the moving bush and the shape of a great animal standing seven feet tall in the alders. It seemed to have a sort of white ruff across the top of its head, I could not make out the rest. I fired into the bushes and I heard the shot hit. I went back into the house and bolted the door. It never came back and there was blood where it had stood when the men from the sawmill came back."

The sawmill closed down and the men turned out in force to look, but they never found it. Similar animals have been reported since and their tracks have been found at intervals, the latest being about 1940.

I asked Mrs. Michelin point blank if this could have been a bear. "It was no bear Mr.

Wright. I have killed 12 bears on my husband's trapline and I know their tracks well. I saw enough of this thing to be sure of that. I fired a shotgun at it and I heard the shot hit."

Eliot Merrick, *True North,* New York: Charles Scribner's Sons, 1933. (from Green 1978).

Ghost stories are very real in this land of scattered lonely homes and primitive fears. The Traverspine "gorilla" is one of the creepiest. About twenty years ago one of the little girls was playing in an open grassy clearing one autumn afternoon when she saw come out of the woods a huge hairy thing with low-hanging arms. It was about seven feet tall when it stood erect, but sometimes it dropped to all fours. Across the top of its head was a white mane.

She said it grinned at her and she could see its white teeth. When it beckoned to her she ran screaming to the house. Its tracks were everywhere in the mud and sand, and later in the snow. They measured the tracks and cut out paper patterns of them which they still keep. It is a strange-looking foot, about twelve inches long, narrow at the heel and forking at the front into two broad, round-ended toes. Sometimes its print was so deep it looked to weigh 500 pounds. At other times the beast's mark looked no deeper than a man's track. They set bear traps for it but it would never go near them. It ripped the bark off trees and rooted up huge rotten logs as though it were looking for grubs.

They organized hunts for it and the lumbermen who were then at Mud Lake came with their rifles and lay out all night by the paths watching, but with no success. A dozen people have told me they saw its track with their own eyes and it was unlike anything ever seen or heard of. One afternoon one of the children saw it peeping in the window. She yelled and old Mrs. Michelin grabbed a gun and ran for the door. She just saw the top of its head disappearing into a clump of willows. She fired where she saw the bushes moving and thinks she wounded it. She says too that it had a ruff of white across the top of its head. At night they used to bar the door with a stout birch beam and all sleep upstairs, taking guns and axes with them.

The dogs knew it was there too, for the family would hear them growl and snarl when it approached. Often it must have driven them into the river for they would be soaking wet in the morning. One night the dogs faced the thing, and it lashed at them with a stick or club, which hit a corner of the house with such force it made the beams tremble. The old man and boys carried guns wherever they went, but never got a shot at it. For two winters it was there.

Smith and Mangiacopra (2005) note that Dr. and Mrs. C. Hogarth Forsythe were interviewed in 1947 about their medical experiences during 15 years in Labrador. In the interview, the couple noted that there were reported sightings of "ape-men" in that region. The couple is quoted, "The stories are based on many reports of giant bare-foot tracks in the snow. Usually they are found by trappers whose living depends on their knowl-edge of tracks. Trappers have traced the tracks to 'nests' under trees in the open." And, "The trail usually runs out on glare ice or in running water. But such trails have been followed as much as 15 miles over rough country. Whatever made them climbed easily over stumps and other obstructions where an ordinary man would have gone around. And whatever it was walked on two feet."

Louisiana

Cincinnati, Ohio, *Daily Enquirer*, July 10, 1868

"Have you seen the wild man" were the first words upon everybody's tongue yesterday. Some answered in the affirmative, and some in the negative. For my part I have not seen him. The people in this community were on the 30th ult. thrown into the greatest excitement by the announcement that a wild man had been seen in the woods by some hunters, distant about one mile west of this town, in Livingston County. The description given by the parties who saw him I obtained second hand and consequently can not vouch for its accuracy. He is described as being about seven feet high, with large, ferocious eyes, his body covered with long black hair, and as being precisely of the shape of a human. It is reported as being bullet-proof, as he has been shot at several times by different parties who have encountered him, without any visible effect. All sorts of stories and considerable speculation have been in circulation

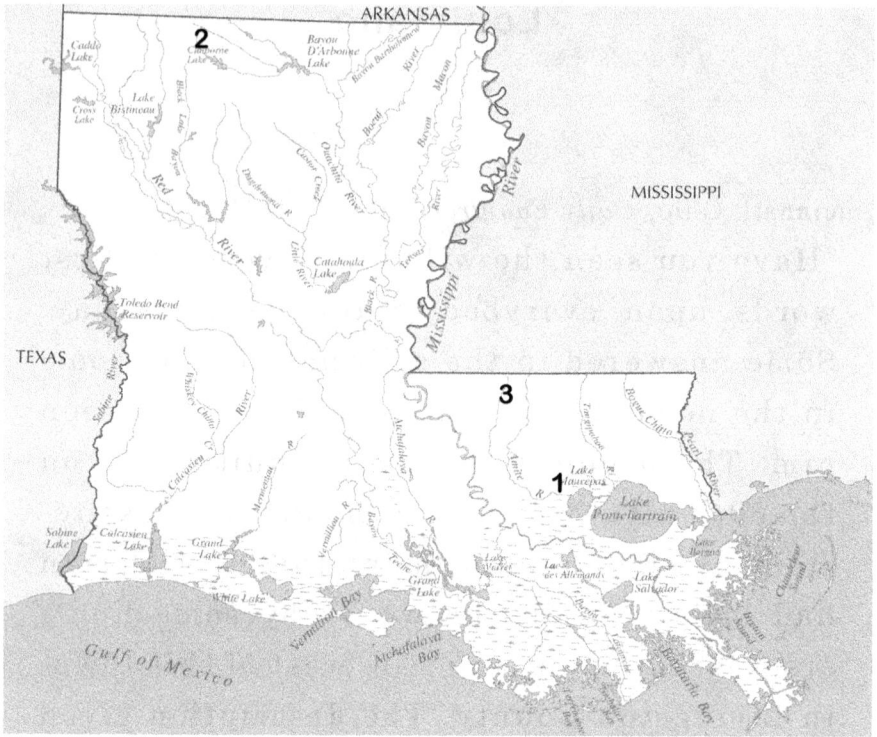

1 Livingston Parish

2 Homer (Claiborne Parish)

3 Cole (East Feliciana Parish)

concerning this singular being. Some positively assert it is the Devil, come for the Radi-
cals and the Negroes; others say it is Christ
come again on earth; while another class insist upon its being a ghost; and still another
and more probable character is given by
others, who are of opinion it is some escaped
animal from a menagerie now exhibiting in
Mississippi. Again, there are others who believe no such thing has been seen at all, it just
being something gotten up for the purpose of
alarming the Negroes. And if the latter be the
case, the object is completely accomplished,
for a more thoroughly alarmed set of beings
never existed than are the negroes here. A
perfect panic has broken out, and yesterday,
as the freight train went north, twenty-four
of these panic-stricken beings leaped on the
flat cars and were carried away. From the inconsistent stories told, I am of opinion that
there is more "scare" than hurt, although one
report says he has killed one man, six dogs,
three horses and five head of cattle. But as
I can trace the rumor to no reliable source, I
give it no credit. A young man named Samuel
Akers, it is reported, shot three times at the
object, and missed it; and after the third
shot he ran to a pile of cross-ties, seized one,

threw it on his shoulder, and jumped thirty
feet up into a pine tree, and then threw the
tie at young Akers, which came very near
hitting him. This is rather too huge a story
to meet with believers.

As far as I can learn this curious animal
(if such it is) was first seen about sixty miles
from here, in the State of Mississippi, and
was driven ten miles across the State line.
This took place about a week ago. The next
seen of it was as before stated, about one
mile from this place. I have tried to find some
one who could give a reliable version of the
affair, but can find no such person. I am inclined to the belief that if there is any thing,
it is either an escaped man monkey from a
menagerie, or a device of the Kuklux to in-
timidate the negroes, as it is known there
are a large number loitering about here, who
live entirely by support of the Freedman's
Bureau, including what they can steal.

New Orleans, Louisiana, *Times-Picayune*, March 20, 1893
Homer Guardian, March 15: For several days
past Homer and vicinity has been infested
with a real, live gorilla, at least in the imagination of some of our people. The monster
was first seen Saturday night near the old

female college grounds. Next it was seen
getting over a fence near the D'Arbonne. At
another place it ran a negro up a tree and
kept him there for some time. At one place
a litter of pigs was destroyed; at another a
calf was killed and partly devoured, and at
still another a negro was killed. And so the
stories grow until at last the gorilla himself
was killed somewhere on the D'Arbonne, but
no one seems to have inspected the remains
any closer than they did while the beast was
alive. The gorilla scare may have kept some
persons indoors after dark.

Alexandria, Louisiana, *Weekly Town Talk*, April 19, 1930

FISHERMEN SEE STRANGE
ANIMAL IN ALLEN PARISH

Oberlin, La., April 14.—(Special)—One night
this week a party consisting of Joe, Ezie and
H. Taylor and Francis and Foster Manuel
went to Calcasleu river near the Cole settlement to fish with set lines. During the night,
while going to the lines they encountered
some strange animal, which they state resembled a gorilla. They say he was standing
with his arms around a tree when they came
upon him. They left for home with much more
reference to speed than to grace, arriving in
town just before daylight, having come afoot

as the car that took them had been sent back. After daylight they armed themselves and returned to the scene, but found only strange tracks, so they report.

Maine

The earliest report from Maine is the Waldoboro' Wild Man, a small monkey-like creature. Reprinted here is the original tale, and a follow-up. The second article may be a bit difficult to understand for modern readers, but for those wondering, a "demijohn" is a large glass or earthenware jug, covered in wicker, that is used to ferment alcohol. Whatever this Wild Man was, it probably has nothing to do with the question of Bigfoot.

Marysville, Ohio, *Tribune,* January 31, 1855

EXTRAORDINARY—A WILD MAN.

—The following communication relative to the discovery of a wild man in Waldoboro', (Maine,) was handed to the editor of the Thomaston Journal by Mr. J. W. McHenri. The Journal says there are several persons who can vouch for the truth of the statements which it contains:

Mr. Editor: On the morning of the 2d of January, while engaged in chopping wood a short distance from my house in Waldoboro',

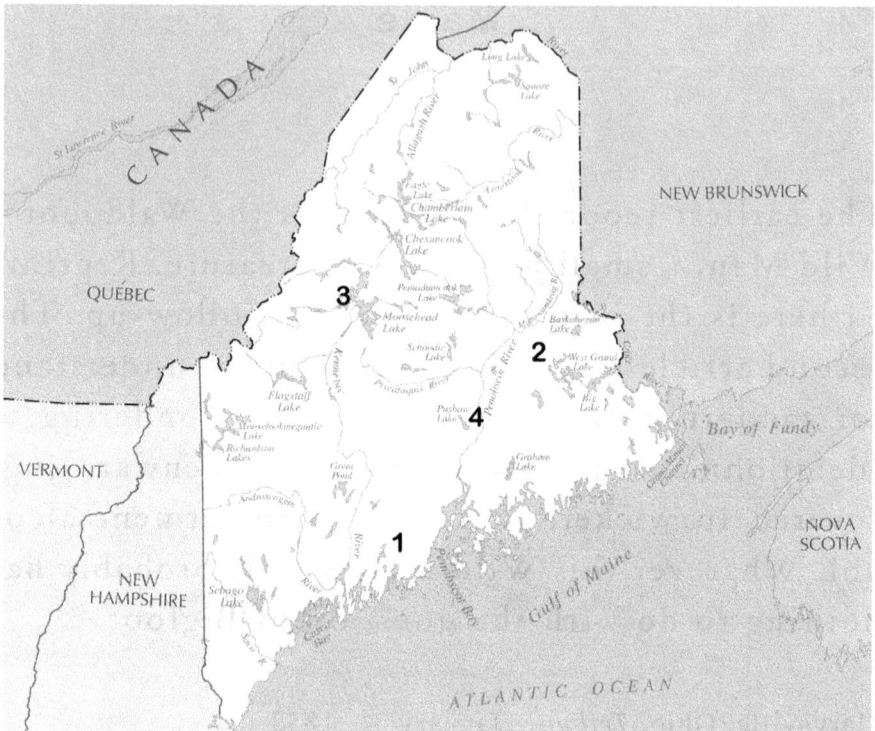

1 Waldoboro (Lincoln County)

2 Springfield (Penobscot County)

3 Moosehead (Piscataquis County)

4 Brewer (Penobscot County)

I was startled by the most terrific scream that ever greeted my ears; it seemed to proceed from the woods near by. I immediately commenced searching round for the cause of this unearthly noise, but after a half hour's fruitless search, I resumed my labors, but had scarcely struck a blow with my axe when the sharp shriek burst out upon the air.— Looking up quickly, I discovered an object about ten rods from me, standing between two trees, which had the appearance of a miniature human being. I advanced towards it, but the little creature fled as I neared it. I gave chase, and after a short run succeeded in catching it. The little fellow turned a most imploring look upon me, and uttered a sharp shrill shriek, resembling the whistle of an engine. I took him to my house and tried to induce him to eat some meat, but failed in the attempt. I then offered him some water, of which he drank a small quantity. I next gave him some dried beech nuts, which he cracked and ate readily. He is of the male species; about eighteen inches in height, and his limbs are in perfect proportion. With the exception of his face, hands and feet, he is covered with hair of a jet black hue. Whoever may wish to see this strange specimen of human nature, can gratify their curiosity by calling at my house in the eastern part of Waldoboro, near the Trowbridge tavern. I give these facts to the public to see if there is any one who can account for this wonderful phenomenon.

J. W. McHenri.

Janesville, Wisconsin, *Free Press,* February 6, 1855

Where is Waldoboro'! The whole thing savors of the "woolly horse" and will pass current as a Barnumism.

Latest from the Waldoboro' Wild Man.— Our readers will recollect that last week we published a communication relating to the discovery of a wild man in Waldoboro' purporting to come from one J. W. McHenri; but the wild man does really exist; there can be no humbug about him. We have been enabled through the kindness of a friend, to obtain his name and pedigree. He is a lineal descendent of the "Striped Pig," a cousin to the "Horse with a snake in his eye," and a distant relative of the "Elephant." He will in a few days, visit this place in charge of Gen. Muggins, Commander-in-Chief of the "Knights of Star Spangled Banner, or Guardians of the Tail Feathers of the American Eagle," when our citizens will have an excellent opportunity to gratify their curiosity in regard to him.

By close examination the hair on his body proves to be very coarse, and very much resembling ratan. Some brute in human form, was so cruel as to seize the little fellow by the nape of the neck, and suck the blood entirely from his body, but by the new French process of resuscitating a dead body, his veins were again infused with blood, and at last account he was in a very healthy condition. We had almost forgotten to mention his name, it is Demi surnamed John. If we learn anything further in regard to this remarkable individual we shall give it to the public.—[Thomaston Journal Jan. 11th.]

Greenville, Pennsylvania, *Shenango Valley Argus*, November 4, 1876

A FRIGHTENED HUNTER

The Calais (Me.) *Times* says: "Samuel Spaulding, of Springfield, while hunting in the vicinity of that town recently, encountered the devil face to face. This he persistently and tremblingly declares. In corroboration of his testimony there is a collateral fact. Whereas he formerly passed a great part of his time in the woods with his gun, he now secludes himself at home, hardly venturing from his premises. All questioners obtain from him the same statement accompanied by a description of his Satanic majesty. For many years the story has been periodically revived of some strange creature in the woods near Springfield, and lumbermen have seen it as far distant as the head of Musquash stream; but Mr. Spaulding is the first man bold enough to declare that it is the devil. If his story is true, and his manner and character are in his favor, he had a very near view and might have bagged the creature, had he not been afraid to fire his gun. If it was really the devil, there are many who will never forgive him his remissness."

Bangor, Maine, *Industrial Journal,* October 8, 1886

A NEW KIND OF GAME.

[WATERVILLE SENTINEL.]

An affrighted Frenchman from over the line has hid fellows in town all by the ears with a story of a gigantic wild man, killed a week or so ago in the dense woods above Moosehead. The Frenchman's story, which is implicitly believed is that three men were camping out in the woods about a hundred miles north of Moosehead Lake. Two of the campers were away from the camp for a week and came back to find the dead body of their companion. They went for help and reinforced by a dozen others searched the woods for the unknown murderer. It proved to be a terrible wild man, ten feet tall, with arms seven feet in length, covered with long, brown hair. The party fired several shots into him and finally succeeded in reaching a vital spot, laying the monster low. The story has caused great excitement among the more ignorant portion of our foreign population.

San Francisco, California, *Call*, November 27, 1895

A TERROR IN THE WOODS

GREAT CONSTERNATION CAUSED
BY THE DEEDS OF A WILD MAN.
UNLUCKY LUMBERMEN SLAIN AND THEIR
BODIES MANGLED IN A SHOCKING MANNER.

Bangor, Me. Nov. 26.—A lumberman who returned to-day from the forest in the north of the State brings the most harrowing intelligence of the doings of a wild man in the lumber region of the west branch. He states that great consternation has been caused and a large number of lumbermen have left the camps and returned to their cities rather than face the monster.

For over two months quite a number of men have disappeared from the camps and when found bore the semblance of having had an encounter with some wild animal, their bodies in every instance having been terribly mangled and torn. A lumberman who returned to a camp a little north of this city a week ago startled all by stating that while at work he had been attacked by this wild man, and it was only by the help of his ax that he had been able to defend himself from the murderous attacks. Since that time he has been seen by the crews several times, but on their approach he fled into the deep woods with the speed of a deer.

He is described as being so nearly like an animal that it is almost impossible to detect him from one. He has a long, shaggy beard, and is covered with a huge, skin coat. The general belief is that he is a sportsman who has become lost in the deep forests, and after wandering around for weeks has gone hopelessly crazy, and already there have been over half a dozen instances of a similar character in the State.

The crews of the lumbering camps are out hunting for the man and hope by shooting him in the leg to effect his capture.

Chicago, Illinois, *Inter Ocean,* October 26, 1902

WILD MAN SCARES THE TOWN.

SPECIAL DISPATCH TO THE INTER OCEAN.

Bangor, Me., Oct. 25.—Much excitement prevails in the settlement of Brewer, close to

the Holden town line, known as Whiting's
Hill district, over the appearance of what is
popularly known as a wild man there. This
man is described as being about six feet in
height, very stoutly built, and his body unclothed except by a great growth of hair. It
is said that he has been seen by several persons. Contrary to the usual habit of these
wild men, reported in the past, this one has
been seen only by men.

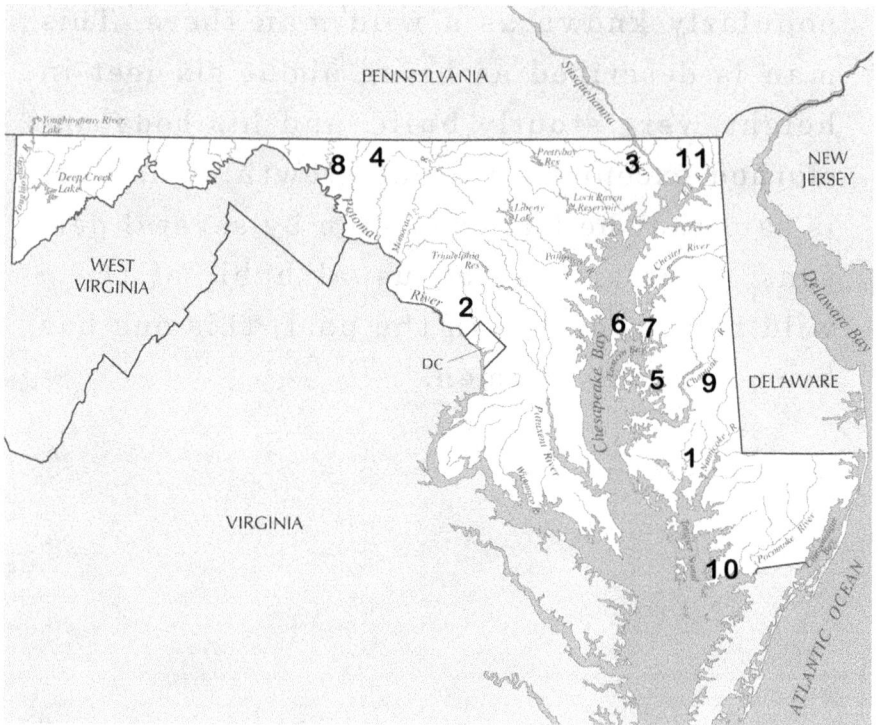

1 Dorchester County

2 Montgomery County

3 Harford County

4 Wolfsville (Frederick County)

5 Miles River Neck (Talbot County)

6 Chester, Kent Island (Queen Anne's County)

7 Queen Anne's County

8 Williamsport (Washington County)

9 Harmony (Caroline County)

10 Crisfield (Somerset County)

11 Cecil County

Maryland

Opsasnick (2004) noted several folkloric creatures from the 1800s and early 1900s that may or may not have relevance to the subject of Bigfoot. Some cases are hoaxes (like the stories of H. L. Mencken, who later boasted about inventing them), others are just stories told for entertainment, but some do appear to represent legitimate sightings of hairy bipedal creatures. A few cases in point: in 1909, (Dorchester County), a farmer, Albert Evans, came across a dark, hairy, 7-foot tall manlike creature standing over dead cows in his pasture. In 1912, sightings of a wild man were reported in Montgomery County. In 1914, (Harford County), a young boy saw a large hairy creature sitting on a log.

Frederick, Maryland, *News*, April 30, 1887
THE JABBERWOCK.
A correspondent at Wolfsville, this county, states that a gentleman of that place had an exciting experience with the now famous and fearful "Jabberwock" on Sunday night last,

on the road leading from Foxville to Wolfs- ville, and rumor has it that his gait would have done credit to the "flying dutchman." The young man's descriptions of the noises he heard are truly fearful and it is thought that he will never be caught on that road be- tween two days again.

1903: Baer (1982) described how, as a young reporter, H. L. Mencken invented a wild man story for a Sunday edition of the Baltimore *Her- ald*. Mencken noted, "I had invented him [the wild man] myself, and no one else knew that he was imaginary save Tom Dempsey, an old-time police lieutenant, who had kindly helped me with the job. . . . The story was spoiled at last when an alarmed magistrate, believing the bogus evidence offered by the cops against a half-wit stranger that they had collared, sentenced him to six months in the House of Correction."

Washington, D. C., *Post,* January 8, 1905

TERRIBLE BEAST WHICH ROAMS AROUND MILES RIVER NECK

SPECIAL CORRESPONDENCE OF THE SUNDAY POST. Baltimore, Jan. 7—The yaho is abroad again in the land, and the people of Miles River Neck are in a state of terror. The wilds in the vicinity of Unionville are the favorite resort of this wild beast or wilder human being. What it really is no one knows for a certainty, for such is the terrible nature of its roar, which approaches a shriek, that would-be investigators flee at its approach. Many colored people are convinced that it is the Old One himself, and the white people are not much behind them in their ideas as to its identity.

Sunday, as a gentleman of Easton was journeying on foot to the home of his mother, on Miles River Neck, he heard the unearthly shrieks of the yaho near Unionville. Thoroughly frightened by the weird cries, which proceeded from a dense wood a few hundred yards away, he did not deem an investigation advisable, but quickened his steps toward his destination, not neglecting to cast an uneasy glance over his shoulder every few feet in the direction from which came the sounds.

After advancing a short distance the gentleman met Robert Jackson, a colored man who had also heard the shrieks, and was in an extremely agitated state of mind. He refused to continue on his trip, which would have carried him past the woods and closer to the source of the mysterious cries, and the two men hurried to Unionville.

The colored people there soon learned of the return of the yaho, and they immediately took steps to guard themselves against a possible attack.

It is solemnly averred that the animal has, upon one or two occasions, attacked parties in vehicles, and in one case made a horse run away and injure its driver.

This is the fifth time within fifteen years that this mysterious animal has made its appearance in the vicinity. Many reputable people of tried veracity, both white and black, testify of having at one time or another heard the soul-piercing screams of the yaho, but, the number who claim to have seen the creature is small. Of this number, no one can give a detailed description of the animal, for none ever stopped long enough to make a close inspection. Indeed, there is doubt whether it is a human being bereft of reason and living the life of a wild beast, or is a dumb animal. Certain it is that the thing is a most uncommon creature, and either seen or heard is sufficient to strike terror to the hearts of the most valiant.

Some people who claim to have seen it say that it is similar to a gorilla, only taller, and has a head twice as large as that of a man,

with long, large, projecting teeth, and that
its eyes are sunken deep into the head. Its
body is covered with a long, thick growth
of hair, and its arms, legs, hands, and feet
correspond in general make-up to those of a
man, except that they are much larger.

Three years ago it made its appearance
in the vicinity of Kirkham, about five miles
from Easton, but it soon found its way back to
its old haunts near Unionville, where it was
heard a number of times during the nights
and days thereafter.

A distinguishing feature of the animal is
its piercing voice, which cannot be imitated.
When it shrieks it sounds much like "Ya-ho!
ya-ho! ya-ho!" It generally makes this cry
three times in quick succession and then remains quiet for some minutes.

Several persons give it as their opinion
that this creature is a wild animal of some
kind that made its escape from the Robinson & Franklin circus that was touring this
peninsula a number of years ago. The circus
train met with a railroad wreck, and several
wild animals were freed from their cages.
many of these beasts were captured, and
others were shot, while a few were never
seen again by the circus people.

A bear, which was believed to have been one that escaped at the time of the wreck, was slain in Chapel district, this county, several years afterward.

The last time the creature made its appearance here, a gentleman from Baltimore, who read an account of it, came to Talbot, and made a vigilant search for it, saying he believed it was his wife's brother, who had become demented, and had disappeared from his home, and they knew nothing of his whereabouts. He was unable to locate the animal, and returned to the city uncertain whether his theory was right or wrong.

The people, especially the colored population, are much wrought up over the affair, and are hoping that some action will soon be taken to hunt it down.

Some of the daring ones are for making organizing a hunting party to make a diligent search for the animal, and this will probably be done.

Among the reputable people who have heard the creature are Wildie E. Todd, William Henry Roe, and Mrs. Sarah A. Todd.

Baltimore, Maryland, *Sun*, January 15, 1907

FLAGMAN DIDN'T WAIT TO SEE

CROUCHING FIGURE CHASED HIM
HALF-MILE ON THE TIES, HE SAYS

It was about midnight and dark as black clouds could make it last Friday night when a Baltimore and Ohio freight train was held up just west of Chester by a wreck ahead.

The train was out on the main track, and Grant Billings, flagman, 1308 Light street, was sent back to protect the train with his lantern and torpedoes.

He picked his way carefully up the track toward Upland, the next station, and when about half a mile away from his train he placed his "caps" on the rail and took his station, with his lanterns, near a bridge.

Just ahead of him was Upland Station, with just a big arclight showing. He stood by with only the distant arc and the warmth of his own lanterns to comfort him, waiting for the order for his train to get under way and the whistle to recall him.

Looking up suddenly he made out in the gloom what looked to be the figure of a man making his way across the bridge on hands and knees. According to a railroad man's way of looking at things, that is a poor way to cross a railroad bridge, and Billings stepped forward to assist the man over.

He was holding out his white lantern, and was about to call out something sarcastic about a man who didn't have the nerve to walk upright, when the figure rose to its full height.

Billings hails from Indian Territory. He has ridden the range, acquitted himself creditably in numerous stampedes, has hunted deer and bear in North Carolina and has generally established a reputation for bravery, but what he saw almost took the heart out of him.

Instead of the normal proportions of a man, the figure that stood up, outlined against the arclight of Upland Station, looked to be about 8 feet tall and its arms reached nearly to the ground. In the dim light that was projected that far from the flagman's lantern it could be seen that long hair covered the body.

Billings outdid Corbett in sidestepping. He looked twice at the strange creature, which, however, did not appear to be after the flagman's blood. One foot back of him, the other extended and his body in a crouch, Billings was ready to run at the first move of the hairy creature. For all he knew, it was the Wild Man of Borneo out for a midnight stroll.

But railroad men are taught to stick to their posts, and Billings was loth to desert.

He was in misery between the longing to run and the determination to stick by and protect his train.

Then came the welcome four whistles recalling the flagman. It was all he asked for. A frightened look around showed him that the stranger was again on all-fours and coming his way, and the manner in which he moved was not pretty to see.

Billings started. He did that half mile of ties, rock ballast and cinder path in time that would put the record for the half-mile run way down in the beginners' class. His were as the winged feet of Mercury. They touched only the places of greatest altitude. It was a great run.

Not once did he look around, and when he reached the caboose it was with a great sigh of relief and a comfortable feeling of safety that he signaled with his lantern. The sound of the couplings as they jerked noisily in response to the engine's pull was like the sweetest of music and the clank and clatter of carwheels tole him that they were putting distance between him and the strange hairy man with the long arms.

"Say, something chased me down the track," he said to the conductor when that dignitary entered the caboose.

"Did, eh?" he replied. "I'll bet it was that gorilla that's been running loose around here for the last two weeks scaring people up."

As the flagman never did hanker after the society of the wild beasts of the jungle, he is not a bit sorry he ran.

Lancaster, Pennsylvania, *Intelligencer Journal*, February 16, 1921

"GORILLA" SEEN IN MARYLAND.

Williamsport, Md., Feb. 16—Declaring that she saw a woolly creature, which walked upright, on the road along the Conoco-cheague Creek near Kemp's Mill, 14-year-old Florence Christ fled in terror to the mill at Kemp's and asked for protection. She said the animal looked like a "gorilla" that had been reported around Pen Mar and other sections recently. George Kemp and several other men, armed with guns and pistols, accompanied the girl to her home, but they did not see the animal.

(See PENNSYLVANIA for related sightings.)

I included an early newspaper's mention of a "gorilla" being kicked to death by a Queen Anne County farmer in a chapter on the early 1920s central Pennsylvania Bigfoot flap in *Cryptozoology:*

Science & Speculation. The following account is further evidence that this Maryland "gorilla" was probably not an ape, though I would like to see a better description. It may just have been a feral dog.

Denton, Maryland, *Journal*, February 26, 1921

GORILLA CAPTURED, THEY SAY.

Locked in a death struggle with a ferocious "gorilla," which for several days had terrorized the colored population of the Willoughby neighborhood, Queen Anne county, William B. Quimby, a prosperous farmer, who resides on the "Walnut Ridge" farm, chocked the creature into insensibility and then kicked it to death, said a Centreville correspondent last Saturday. This is the story the slayer's friends are telling, but Quimby says he shot the animal. Quimby emphatically denied that he had received any offers of contracts from motion picture companies to make a steady business of choking "gorillas" to death. Rumors of the appearance of the "gorilla" in the neighborhood were first heard the latter part of last week. Several negroes told hair-raising stories of escapes. Finally some fox hunters saw the animal. The fact is vouched for by M. W. Beardley, John W. Perry, and other prominent men. The "gorilla" made its appearance at "Walnut Ridge" farm yesterday. Quimby sighted him from a distance and started in pursuit, with the result mentioned. Quimby says he never saw a "gorilla" before and is inclined to believe that the animal might be a cross between bulldog and a Newfoundland instead of a "missing link." Certainly it was a strange and ferocious beast and it is dead. And Quimby is the hero.

Baltimore, Maryland, *Sun*, July 8, 1940

TERROR-SPREADING "VARMINT" IS SEEN

James Wright Believes Mysterious Animal is Big Orangutan

Reports Seeing Creature About 4½ Feet Tall in Woods Near Harmony

[Special Dispatch to The Sun]

Preston, Md., July 7—The "varmint" which has been spreading terror throughout the vicinity of Harmony, about seven miles from here, was this morning identified as an orang-utan.

James Wright, who reported seeing the creature as he drove by a clump of woods two miles from Harmony at 9 o'clock this morning, described it as being about four and one half feet tall and weighing about 250 pounds.

A posse of approximately one hundred persons, armed with clubs, shotguns, knives, etc.; carrying flashlights and lanterns, and accompanied by hounds, searched in vain for the animal last night. The search was continued with renewed vigor today after Wright reported what he had seen.

Aroused by Screeching

Residents of Gainey's wharf section were the first to report the presence of a "mysterious

Shore Posse Ready For "Varmint" Hunt

Some of the scores of persons who scoured the woods near Harmony for "varmint."

creature" when they were awakened by an unearthly screeching followed by a thumping sound as it made off into the woods several nights ago. Since then reports of a similar nature have come from other nearby sections accompanied by proof in the discovery of large, mysterious and unidentified tracks.

The women and children of the area have been staying home at night since the reports spread and the majority of the men have been traveling armed. No organized action was taken, however, until the posse went out last night.

Recalls Ancient Score

To many of the older residents of the area this reign of what might be termed mental if not physical terror brought back memories of a time about thirty years ago when a "werwolflike creature" was reported in the vicinity. Several small animals were actually found torn asunder in the werwolf fashion at the time, but, as far as could be ascertained, the creature escaped and its true identity was never learned.

The present day "man of the woods," as the orang-utan is sometimes called, is supposedly not vicious except when attacked,

but nevertheless the members of the posse
are taking no chances and neither are the
residents until the creature is apprehended.

Cumberland, Maryland, *Evening Times*, July 8, 1940

'VARMINT' REPORTED
SEEN NEAR PRESTON

RESIDENTS OF HARMONY CONTRADICT

STATE POLICE CLAIM CREATURE IS "MYTH"

Preston, Md., July 8 (AP)—Search for a "varmint" which kept residents of Harmony, seven
miles from here, in an uproar over the week-
end lagged today in the face of official claims
the "mysterious creature" was a myth.

At the same time, Harmony citizens con-
tradicted such a finding, pointing to the unearthly screechings, thumphings, and large
unidentified tracks in the woods near Gaf-
ney's Wharf section.

Since these manifestations several nights
ago, women and children in the neighborhood
have been staying home at night and many of
the men have gone armed.

James Wright reported he saw a creature
—he identified it tentatively as an orang-
utan—as he passed a clump of woods two
miles from Harmony Saturday morning. A
posse of about 100 armed men searched the

section vainly Saturday night and again yesterday.

State police who visited the section yesterday reported after inquiries that there was "nothing to" the "varmint" reports. Officers said they appeared to have grown from a rumor, passed around the countryside and improved with each telling.

Baltimore, Maryland, *Afro-American*, August 13, 1949

NEWSBEAT, BY RUFUS WELLS

Something that looks like a beast but walks like a man, is on the loose in Crisfield, Md., and the authorities are more than remotely concerned.

For two weeks now fear-stricken residents have told of seeing "The Thing" and with each report the descriptions become more confusing and alarming.

Last Monday morning, Mrs. George Bradshaw, a white housewife, aroused her son, George, 26, with a scream and said she saw something resembling "a big wildcat that ran as fast as a deer."

Bushes Found Disturbed

Police investigated—they have been doing so faithfully for two weeks now—but located no tracks. They did report finding evidence of an animal having crashed through some bushes, however.

George Ward, a teen aged colored boy, saw The Thing last week and said it "looked like a gorilla." He said it was 6 feet tall, hair-covered and had a face like a man's. It ran, the youth added, slightly sideways on all fours.

Reporter Has Theory

State police and posses have made several efforts to trap The Thing, with no results. They did report seeing tracks that resemble a man's hand.

Some people say it is a "spook," others, a mountain lion; and still others, just someone's imagination. I have a different theory.

Having recently returned from Crisfield, I believe The Thing is Jim Crow. He's all over the Eastern Shore; and if the police can put him out of operation, more power to them.

Cumberland, Maryland, *News*, August 28, 1953

PAPER SAYS "GORILLA-LIKE" ANIMAL SEEN IN "SNALLYGASTER" COUNTRY

Elkton, Md., Aug. 27 (AP)—The Cecil Whig, a 112-year-old conservative weekly published in this town at the head of the Chesapeake Bay "snallygaster" country, lent credence today to reports that a "gorilla-like" animal is roaming the woods nearby.

The paper said an extensive investigation conducted by its staff has shown there is a "definite possibility" a large gorilla-like animal is loose in the heavily wooded hilly area along the Maryland-Pennsylvania line in the northern portion of Cecil County.

It based its conclusions primarily on reports of H. S. Osborne and Ray Potter, two farmers who live at Lombard, just south of the state line, and Joseph Eggers who lives a quarter of a mile from them.

Osborne said he had seen the animal on two occasions, once from about 20 feet. With him that time was Potter. Osborne said it was about 3 p.m., the light was good and when they looked toward the woods, the animal was peering over the fence at them.

Osborne described it as about 6 feet tall, brownish hair all over and a pink ring around its face. It stood erect and had a monkey-like appearance, Osborne said.

The Whig, seeking expert advice, contacted Fred Ulmer, curator of mammals at the Philadelphia Zoo.

Ulmer ruled out the possibility that the strange animal was a gorilla both because of their scarcity and their high value. He said the descriptions of the beast seemed to indicate it was a chimpanzee.

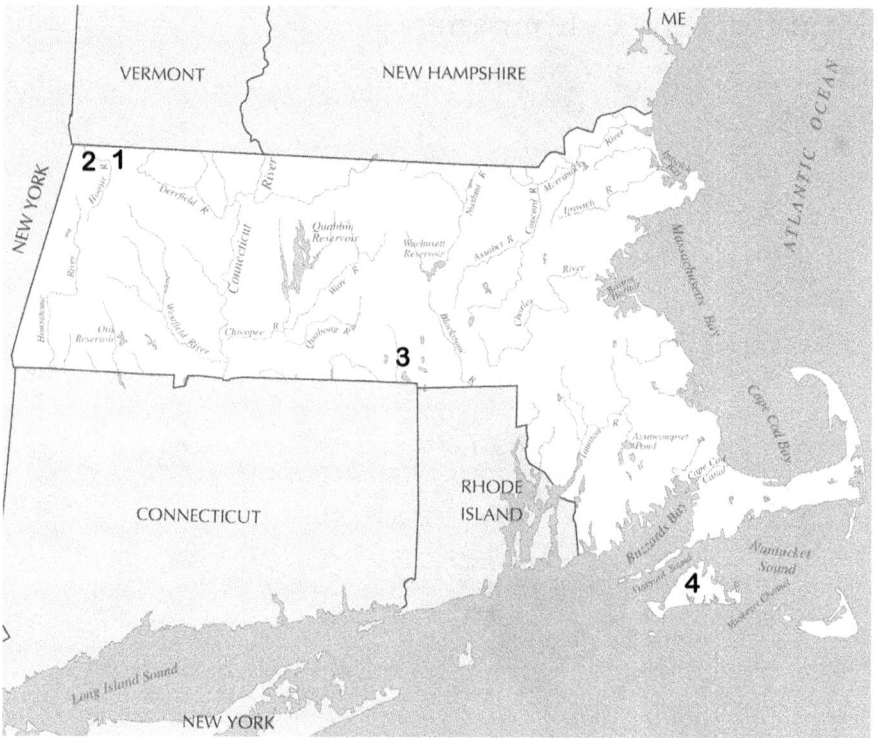

1 North Adams (Berkshire County)

2 Williamstown (Berkshire County)

3 Webster (Worcester County)

4 Martha's Vineyard

Massachusetts

Pittsfield, Massachusetts, *Berkshire County Eagle,* August 15, 1861

BIG HUMBUG.—It is believed that there is a wild man in the woods between North Adams and Stamford. He has been seen several times, and his shrieks at night have been heard. There was a report in North Adams last Monday that the wild man had been captured, and hundreds wended their way to a place where the strange man was said to be confined. Crowds entered the shed and gazed upon the strange being, who was chained and immoveable in the corner, with long beard and glassy eyes. Men went so far as to shut up their stores and discontinue business to take a peep at this celebrated individual, while crinoline from the factories and dwellings crowded the highway in eager haste. After a large number had been humbugged by an image which was got up for the frolicsome students of Williamstown, the hoax leaped out.

Bangor, Maine, *Daily Whig and Courier,* August 19, 1861

It seems that the "wild man of the woods," whose appearance has created so much consternation in North Adams, Massachusetts, and in the adjoining towns across the Vermont line, turns out to be a student at Williamstown, who assumed the gorilla guise in a frolic which might have cost him his life. In Vermont, he was pursued with guns, but so frightened his pursuers by his hideous appearance that they could not shoot straight, and he escaped harm.

(See VERMONT for related sightings.)

New York, New York, *Times,* October 18, 1879

A WILD MAN OF THE MOUNTAINS

Two Young Vermont
Hunters Terribly Scared

Pownal, Vt., Oct. 17—Much excitement prevailed among the sportsmen of this vicinity over the story that a wild man was seen on Friday last by two young men while hunting in the mountains south of Williamstown. The young men describe the creature as being about five feet high, resembling a man in form and movement, but covered all over with bright red hair, and having a long straggling beard, and with very wild eyes. When first seen the creature sprang from behind a rocky cliff, and started for the woods near by, when, mistaking it for a bear or other wild animal, one of the men fired, and, it is thought, wounded it, for with fierce cries of pain and rage, it turned on its assailants driving them before it at high speed. They lost their guns and ammunition in their flight and dared not return for fear of encountering the strange being.

There is an old story, told many years ago, of a strange animal frequently seen among the range of the Green Mountains resembling a man in appearance, but so wild that no one could approach it near enough to tell what it was or where it dwelt. From time to time, hunting parties, in the early days of the town, used to go out in pursuit of it, but of late years no trace of it has been seen, and this story told by the young men who claim to have seen it, revives again the old story of the wild man of the mountains. There is talk of making up a party to go in search of the creature.

Winnipeg, Manitoba, *Daily Free Press,* October 31, 1879
TWO TERRIFIED HUNTERS.
PITTSFIELD, (MASS.) LETTER TO NEW YORK SUN.

Two Vermont hunters, John Simmons and

William Shegan, aver that they met with a strange adventure a day or two since, on the "Pine Grabble" peak, just east of Blackinton village, about four miles north of North Adams. This pine-capped peak was, some years ago, the resort of wild animals, and of late it has been seldom visited. The story of the hunters is that, while hunting in the vicinity of this mountain, they heard a slight noise near a rugged cliff and saw a huge hairy object, apparently half man and half beast, spring from behind the cliff and start for the woods, running with the speed of the wind. Mistaking it for a wild animal, one of the hunters fired at it. The shot appeared to take effect in the arm, for, with a scream of pain, the creature halted, tapped the wound, and, turning, charged its pursuers, who, with empty guns in hand, dared not measure strength with such a foe. Dropping their guns, both sought safety in flight, and stopped only when compelled to do so for lack of ability to run further. The men say that they are positive the creature resembled a man in its general appearance. It was wild-eyed and very fierce in its disposition, judging from the short time they saw it.

The hunter's story revives a long forgotten, but now distinctly recalled yarn to the effect that many years ago a lunatic, then a young man, escaped from his keepers from somewhere near the New York State line, and gained the mountain fastnesses, where he evaded pursuit, and, it is thought, subsisted on berries and the flesh of animals killed through some means best known to himself. Several years later, a strange creature, answering the description of the being recently seen, with the exception of the grizzly beard, was discovered by a party who were berrying on the mountain, and it is thought that this may be the same.

North Adams, Massachusetts, *Transcript*, July 18, 1902

APE WILD IN WOODS

Strange Animal Chased Berry Pickers on Hoosac Mountain Three Weeks Ago Was Seen Again Yesterday Father Dared Not Shoot at Animal for Fear of Hitting His Daughter. Party Organized to Hunt Creature Tomorrow Afternoon

Residents of South Church street and vicinity in the neighborhood of St. Joseph's cemetery are in a state of excitement over the presence of what is supposed to be an escaped ape in the woods south of the tunnel road. The animal has been seen on three distinct occasions, and those who saw it are ready to take oath that it is an ape of unusual size, weighing at least 100 pounds.

Three weeks ago people walking in the woods or on the tunnel road were frequently startled by a peculiar noise coming from among the trees, described as something between a shriek and a squeal. The rumor gradually gained headway that a wild animal of some unusual and unknown variety was making its home in the woods near the cemetery.

Two weeks ago Wednesday Frank Jones, who lives on the tunnel road above the cemetery, was working in his back yard when he saw his daughter, a 16-years-old girl, and a young man with whom she had gone out to walk, running across the pasture towards the house closely pursued by a large black animal. Mr. Jones ran into the house for his gun, but did not dare to shoot for fear of hitting either his daughter or the young man.

When about 50 yards from the house the animal suddenly abandoned the pursuit and made tracks for the woods. Mr. Jones then had time to observe it, and was convinced that it was a large black ape. The young people were badly frightened at their startling encounter. They said they were just passing the edge of the woods when the ape appeared and started to follow them.

Mr. Jones told the story to a number of his neighbors that night and tried to organize a party to hunt the animal down. The neighbors were inclined to be incredulous, and the attempt was not successful. They attributed the pursuit to an unoffending and prosaic Newfoundland dog. One or two who had heard the strange cry in the woods were half inclined to believe Mr. Jones' story, however.

Some days later the report was circulated that the ape had been seen in Briggs' pasture, quite a distance to the south of its alleged familiar haunts. There was nothing definite to substantiate the rumor, however, and it soon died out again.

Nothing further was heard of the ape until one day last week, when Mrs. Jessie Carr, who also lives on the tunnel road, went up into the woods after berries. She had been picking for some time and not paying much attention to her surroundings, when the bushes were parted not 25 feet away from her and the ape peered steadily at her through the opening. She gave one glance and started for home, leaving her berries behind her.

Last Wednesday Mrs. Jane Vaughn, mother of Fred Vaughn, who works in the dye house of the Arnold Print works, wont berrying in the same locality and was badly frightened by the peculiar cry close overhead. She did not see the ape, but says there can be no doubt as to where the noise came from.

And yesterday forenoon the ape was seen again by Mr. Jones. He says he was walking down the tunnel road towards his house, when it suddenly appeared in the road ahead of him.

The animal bounded along in front of him on all fours, and ho got a good look at it. He rushed into the first house he came to to see if he could borrow a gun. He was unsuccessful, and when he came out again the ape had disappeared.

Mr. Jones and Mr. Vaughn have now succeeded in organizing a hunting party, which will go up into the woods tomorrow afternoon and try to kill or capture the strange animal.

The descriptions of those who have seen the ape, agree in nearly every particular. It is large, with black shaggy hair, a good deal of which is worn of around the neck, evidently where it had been chained. The supposition is that it has made its escape from some circus and wandered up into this section of the country.

Woonsocket, Rhode Island, *Evening Call,* July 17, 1908 (from Schaffner 1997-2006)

'WILD MAN' SCARES
WEBSTER PEOPLE

Webster, Mass., July 16—Political, social and business circles here were stirred yesterday by the report that a wild man had been seen up in a berry pasture on the Orchard road.

It is getting to be pretty well established thing for the wild man to show up here once a year. Whether the town is merely one of many on his itinerary or whether he comes out of his hole somewhere nearby once a year is not known.

It is said, however, that every year he gets a bit wilder. This year he frightened Mrs. Paul Lanphiere of West street, her son Paul, Katie Langlois, Wilfred Langlois and Howard Steele, all of whom were picking berries, by suddenly appearing in a bunch of tall bushes and starting toward them with a whoop.

Terror evidently lent wings to their feet. Anyway, the wild man was outdistanced like a selling plater. The town is breathing easier, now that his annual visit is a thing of the past.

Boston, Massachusetts, *Daily Globe*, August 23, 1915

MARTHAS VINEYARD
SEARCHING FOR APE

SPECIAL DISPATCH TO THE GLOBE.

Chilmark, Aug 22—Is there an ape roaming unrestrained through the woods of Marthas Vineyard? It is this question that has thrown a chill over the vacationists on the upper end of the island. Women and children hesitate before they go out on the hills berrying, and every farmer with a dog turns it loose instead of chaining it up at night, as was his custom.

The little colony of cottagers at Menemsha Creek is wondering when the dark form seen scampering across the field of George D. Eustis the other night will come their way.

For, strange and impossible as it may seem, two men have caught glimpses of this big and unwelcome visitor. A track in the sand like the footprint of a young child and the unusual manner in which a turkey nest was despoiled of its eggs point to a visitor of the ape family.

One of the Chilmark Tiltons first encountered the intruder a week ago while he was at work in the woods. At first he thought it was a young bear. Any curiosity Mr. Tilton may have felt was dissipated when the animal turned on him. He fled to his house after a gun and when, with his brothers, he set out again the animal had disappeared.

His description of the creature was somewhat vague and unsatisfactory, but it was enough to prove that the Vineyard had a visitor not native to its soil.

"It was heavy limbed and black," Mr. Tilton said. "Stood I should judge about three

feet in height. The head was big and rounded, his teeth were white and prominent."

George D. Eustis of Hollyholm Farm on
the South Shore noticed that his dogs were
very uneasy several nights. One evening they
suddenly ran into the woods together, apparently in pursuit of something, and after
a brief time came back pretty much out of
breath.

Mr. Eustis thought little of the incident
then, but when he turned out one morning to
find a turkey nest on the edge of the woods
robbed of all its eggs, he became interested.

The robber left a trail of sucked eggs behind him. The animal might have picked up
an armful of eggs and held them against his
breast with his paw while he ambled off toward cover, dropping them as he went.

Then Mr. Eustis saw the creature. A commotion in his henhouse brought him to the
window Thursday night. When he rubbed
sleep out of his eyes a bit he saw a dusky
figure crossing: his field. It lumbered along
with a sidewise motion and as near as Mr.
Eustis could tell was three feet tall. It was
black and hard to see against the woods,
but in its passage across the open space the
watcher had a good view of it.

At the farm brook the beast stopped, bent over and drank. Then it stood erect, turned and went into the woods.

In the morning the family found a footprint like that of a child on the sand. At Valleydale Farm, the Summer place of Dr. C. R. L. Putnam of New York, they have an ape as a pet for the children. It is kept securely in a cage. Mrs. Putnam is authority for the statement that the ape walks on the toes and ball of his feet. Such an impression was that found on the Eustis Place.

Mrs. Putnam is reported to have offered to come down if the ape reappears and attempt to capture it. She is confident that her experience with her own pet will make it possible for her to catch the wild animal.

At first cry an ape on Marthas Vineyard, separated by five miles of water from the mainland, seems most improbable. An ape might easily have dropped over the side of a passing ship and swam ashore.

Fred Luce, the rural carrier, remembers a sailor landed at the Marine Hospital in Vineyard Haven who had a pet ape. This animal was so obnoxious that the authorities killed him and his body was cremated.

"But," Mr. Luce says, "one might just as easily run away and take to the woods."

Michigan

From: *Le Voleur* (Paris, France), August 15, 1862 (noted in Hall 1999, previously in *Bigfoot Bulletin,* Jan.-March 1971, translated by Richard L. Tierney).

There have just come indications, says the Courier des Estats Unis, that in the forests that extend along Lake Saint Claire and Lake Huron there exists a tribe or family of savage beings of a formidable and bizarre appearance, of a phenomenal and unknown species. This is a troop of seven or eight individuals, of which two are men (if it can be said that these beings are human) and one woman or female, and three or four young or small ones. The men are of an elevated stature, slender but strongly muscled; the woman of a height below the medium, and the young ones aged from ten to sixteen years; all are covered with hair, and the woman and the young ones, even as the men, have the face framed with a bristly beard, like those of certain simians of Brazil; one of the men has a bald head and a white beard. The head

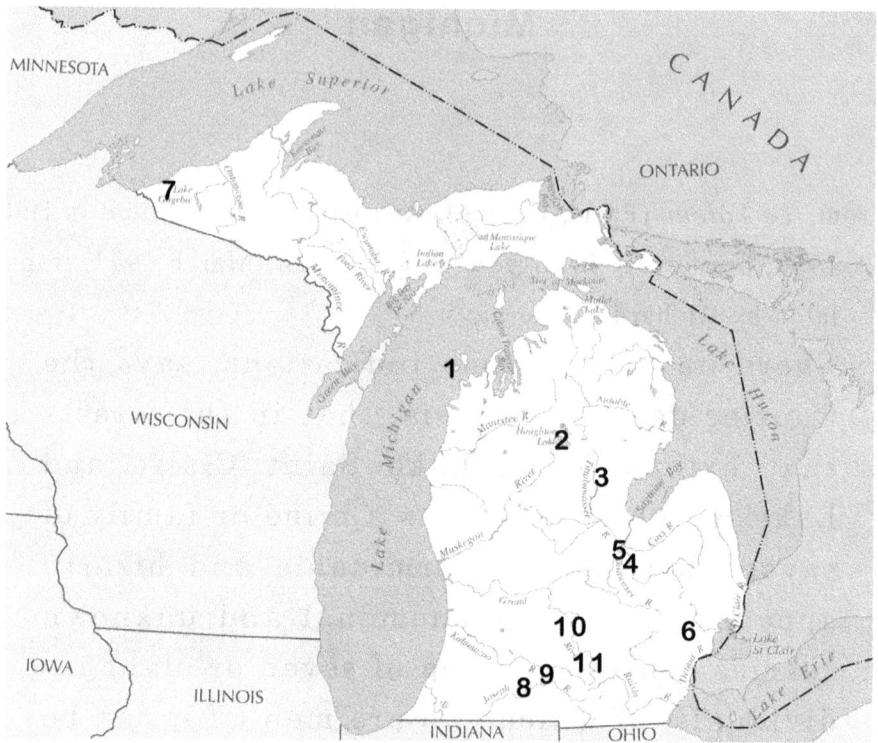

1 Little Manitou Island (now South Manitou Island)

2 Houghton Lake

3 Gladwin County

4 Bridgeport (Saginaw County)

5 Saginaw (Saginaw County)

6 Hamtramck (Wayne County)

7 Ironwood (Gogebic County)

8 Athens (Calhoun County)

9 Burlington (Calhoun County)

10 Eaton County

11 Marshall and Wilder Creek (Calhoun County)

is very large in proportion to the body, the stomach is enormous, the arms inordinately long and the legs are knock-kneed. . . .

St. Joseph, Michigan, *Herald,* July 11, 1868

WILD MAN OF THE MANITOUS.

A wild man has been discovered on Little Manitou Island in Lake Michigan, and efforts are being made to capture him. Mr. J. R. Anderson, who is spending the summer on one of the Manitous, writes to the Cleveland Plaindealer an account of the discovery of the "What is He" or "What is It," from which we take the following: "Some ten days ago one of our party took his boat and started for the Little Manitou, one of our group of islands, about four miles distant from the one on which we are encamped. He returned about 3 o'clock in the afternoon and related that after he had landed upon the island, he heard what he supposed was a man hallooing loudly, as though in distress, that he proceeded to the spot from whence the noise seemed to come, and when within ten or fifteen feet of it he said he saw a form that had an appearance of a man, at least eight feet tall, entirely naked, with his body covered with hair. His face had the appearance of intellectuality, his brow being quite high. His beard descended nearly to his stomach, and his hair was disheveled and coarse. As the monster saw the approach of my informant, he gave a loud shriek, and at once fled. Knowing that it would be impossible to overtake him, my friend returned to his boat, and came home.

"After relating his story, we held a consultation, and decided to make up a party on the next day, return to the island, and hunt the monster up. At ten o'clock we landed on the island, and commenced our search. In choosing our positions I took that which would lead me to the west, on the shore of the lake. I had not proceeded far, when I beheld the unknown sitting upon the beach, washing his feet in the pure water of the lake. I approached him gently, and hoped to be able to capture him without trouble, but when within at least twenty feet of him, he heard me approaching, and at once springing to his feet, commenced to run. I fired upon him with my gun, but failed to bring him down. I then endeavored to overtake him, but my efforts were fruitless. The rest of the party were not able to get sight of him, and it is as yet unknown where he succeeds in hiding. We start out to-morrow again in the hopes of catching him, and, if possible, in finding out who he is. There is a story afloat among the older fishermen of the island that some twenty years ago a woman lost a child here about four years old, that every effort was made to find it, but all the efforts were unsuccessful, and the bereaved mother at last came to the conclusion that her boy had been stolen and carried off by some one of the wandering tribes of Indians then inhabiting the Islands. As I said before, we start out to-morrow in search of the strange character, and I will, as soon as possible, give you the result of our trip."

Jackson, Michigan, *Citizen Patriot,* July 20, 1868

HAVE WE A GORILLA AMONG US— THE WILD MAN OF THE MANITOUS —HE IS FOLLOWED AND PURSUED INTO THE LAKE

FROM THE CLEVELAND *PLAIN DEALER,* 14TH.

A few weeks ago we published a letter from a correspondent on one of the Manitou Islands, giving an account of the discovery of a wild man in one of the discovery of a wild man in one of the islands forming what is known as Manitou Islands, situated in Lake Michigan, between 50 and 60 miles *[sic]* from Sleeping Bear Point. We have lately received another letter from the same correspondent, which we give entire:

Manitou Islands, Lake Michigan, June 31, 1868.

Editors, Plain Dealer—I informed you in my last, dated 10, of the discovery, by one of my comrades, on the Little Manitou, of a wild man, and of the unsuccessful chase we had for him, also of our intention to again visit the island for the purpose of capturing him or learning something of his history, if such a thing was possible—owing to the heavy rains which prevailed until the 18th, our plans were delayed, and not until the morning of the 19th were we able to land upon the shores of the Little Manitou. Our party consisted of six men and two boys, with several dogs to use in case a chase was necessary. On reaching the island we divided into three parties of two each, the boys going by themselves. Signals were agreed upon in case we came upon the strange monster, and we all started with a firm determination to thoroughly explore the island and capture the creature if possible.

It must have been two o'clock in the afternoon when the report of a gun from one of the exploring parties gave us notice that the unknown had been discovered, and we all at once hastened to the spot. I was so fortunate as to be within a short distance of the scene of the discovery, and was soon upon the spot, and found two of our party parleying with something or somebody that they had chased into a tall beech tree. His description tallied exactly with that given in my former letter. It was of a form that had an appearance of a man, at least eight feet tall, entirely naked, with his body covered with hair. His face had the appearance of intellectuality, his brow being quite high. His beard descending nearly to his stomach, and his hair was disheveled and coarse; though I am of the opinion that he could not have been over six feet high, my companions differ with me. His language was perfectly unintelligible, sounding more like the growl of a bear than that of a human being. When we pointed our guns at him he would howl, gnash his teeth, and run like a monkey higher up the tree. After holding a consultation of war, we concluded to adopt peaceful measures, and sending for our basket of provisions, and laying aside our guns, we after an hour or more spent conversing, induced the stranger to descent the tree. He had no sooner struck the ground than one of our dogs started for him, and evidently frightened, he started upon a run, we all following him closely. He gained rapidly upon us, but the dog overtaking him, he turned, and, grasping the animal by the throat, literally tore him to pieces. Throwing the dog's carcass upon the ground with evident disgust, he again started towards the lake, where, as we arrived on the edge of the sand, we saw him throw himself into the blue waters of Lake Michigan. For a time he swam out boldly and gracefully, but while some of our party went in quest of our boat, those who remained to watch him saw him rise several times in the water, as though in agony, and then beheld him sink to rise no more. He was gone. Who he was, what he was, or where he came from, no one will ever probably know. Some person may be able to trace out all the facts of this strange creature's life; I have merely endeavored to give you the facts just as they occurred and just as they are.

Yours, J. R. Anderson.

Indiana, Pennsylvania, *Progress*, November 1, 1877
—A wild man is reported to be in the woods in the vicinity of [Houghton] lake, Michigan, with terrible long nails and as fleet as a deer.

Oshkosh, Wisconsin, *Daily Northwestern*, October 28, 1891
WILD MAN OF MICHIGAN.
AN UNTAMED GIANT, SEVEN FEET TALL,
SEEN IN GLADWIN COUNTY.
Gladwin, Mich., Oct. 27.—George W. Frost

and W. W. Vivian, both reputable citizens, report having seen a wild man on the banks of the Tittabawassee river, in Gladwin county. The man was nude, covered with hair, and was a giant in proportions. According to their story he must have been at least seven feet high, his arms reaching below his knees and with hands twice the usual size. Mr. Vivian set his bull dog on the crazy man and with one mighty stroke of his monstrous hand he felled the dog dead. His jumps were measured and found to be from twenty to twenty-three feet long.

Topeka, Kansas, *State Journal,* January 4, 1897

WILD MAN SCARES A TOWN.

WOODCHOPPERS ENCOUNTER A
GORILLA-LIKE CREATURE IN MICHIGAN

Saginaw, Mich., Jan. 4.—Louis O'Leary and Charles Warner, wood choppers, assert that they encountered a wild man while at work near the Flint and Pierre Marquette railroad tracks in the woods near Bridgeport. After a severe struggle, they say, they were able to drive the gorilla-like object into a retreat. The strange visitor is about the size of an ordinary man, with dark, swarthy hands and face, and appears to be covered from head to foot with a mat of long, curly hair. The women and children of the village are afraid to venture from their homes lest they meet the creature. A posse of men will scour the woods in search of the terror.

Detroit, Michigan, *Free Press,* July 24, 1905

WILD MAN WAS SEEN AGAIN

Another person now comes forward and says he has seen the Hamtramck "wild man." W. H. McKinley, called "Major," a noted character of the village and a grown up man. Heretofore it was only boys who saw the wild fellow. Saturday night, about 9 o'clock, he was passing the woods near North Detroit, where the fellow is supposed to be located, when something jumped from a tree upon his back. He threw it off and, not stopping to see what it was, cut and ran as fast as his legs could carry him.

Yesterday afternoon, Marshal Whelan, Constable Kusch, Justice Gerhard and nearly the whole village turned out and searched the woods, but no signs were seen of the man or animal, whatever it is. The officers think it became scared at the crowd and roosted in some tall tree or sought a safer retreat while the investigation was going on.

Eagle River, Michigan, *Telegram*, February 25, 1917

BLONDE BEAR-MAN
IS A DEER THIEF?

Ironwood, Michigan, Feb. 24th—It looks as if it may be Halloween in February for the Ironwood Sheriff's Department as they are bemused once again by more fantastic reports of the Blonde Bear-Man that people had witnessed walking across Cloverland Drive after a church service last October.

Saturday's report came in from two men who apparently watched from a distance as what they described as a giant man in a blonde fur suit proceeded to steal a deer they had hung from a tree to be gutted. Local officers suggested that it may have been a white bear or timberwolf, while the hunters insisted that the fellow or beastie had indeed quickly dashed off on two feet while it carried their kill away under its arm. The Sheriff's Department commented that should they locate the perpetrator and it is a man in furs, he will be charged with petty larceny for making off with the deer carcass. However, if it should turn out to be a white bear, Sheriff Miller has plans for a new pelt-rug in front of his hearth.

Ludington, Michigan, *Daily News*, July 19, 1926

MYSTERIOUS ANIMAL
DISAPPEARS FROM ATHENS

Battle Creek, Mich., July 19.—(AP)—The animal of uncertain size and origin that haunted the district near the Pine Creek swamp near Athens, for several days about two weeks ago, has made no reappearance recently.

Scores of stories regarding the beast have been started but apparently without foundation, the only actual knowledge that can be gained of the "thing" being its attack upon Harley Inman over two weeks ago; an attack on a dog belonged to Ed Harbaugh and the killing of sheep on the Michaels farm.

Ludington, Michigan, *Daily News*, July 22, 1926

MYSTERIOUS ANIMAL IS REPORTED
RANGING COUNTRY AROUND
BURLINGTON AGAIN

Battle Creek, Mich., July 22.—(AP)—John Henry, 55, rural route mail carrier out of Burlington, reported to the sheriff's department last night that he had been attacked "by the thing," mysterious animal which had previously attacked Harley Inman, Athens township farmer.

Two hours later four Marshal men, staying at Lyon lake, six miles from Burlington, reported they had seen "the thing" in the Lyon lake marsh and secured permission from the sheriff to use shotguns in a hunt for it.

Sheriff Colby came to Battle Creek today to confer regarding offering a reward.

Mr. Henry, the only horse and buggy survivor of the Burlington rural carriers, said he noticed a chicken floundering in the road. He started toward it, he said, and noticed in the brush at the side an animal which he took to be a large dog but which was unusually "skinny." The animal leaped at him, he said, and in throwing up his right hand to protect his face his coatsleeve was caught and torn. He beat the animal back with the butt end of the buggy whip and it came at him again. He again struck, this time hitting the animal squarely on the nose and, with a whine, it departed. Mr. Henry believed that it was a wolf.

The four Marshall men who reported seeing an animal, said that it appeared to be an ape.

Sheriff George Colby today announced a reward of $25 until further notice for each wolf killed or captured in Calhoun county.

He said that the entire sheriff's force organized into a hunting expedition tomorrow
to search in the vicinity of Burlington and
Athens. He said that he did not believe the
story told by Paul Noonan, 18, and Arthur
Cowles, 16, of Marshall, that they had seen
"a large, hairy thing arise from a marsh and
climb a tree," near Lyon lake late yesterday,
but that he had implicit confidence in the
story of Mr. Henry.

Marshall, Michigan, *Evening Chronicle*, July 22, 1926

HUNT FOR APE NEAR LYON LAKE
Two Boys Saw Huge Animal
Hundred Men with Guns Take
Part in Search for Beast

Paul Noonan and Arthur Cowles said they
saw an ape or a large monkey in the swamp
east of M-29 just opposite the driveway that
leads to the cottages on the east side of Lyon
lake at 4:00 o'clock yesterday afternoon. They
reported it to Deputy Sheriff John Harther.

The report spread like wild-fire and headed by Deputy Sheriff Orlo Fish of Tekonsha,
a large crowd of men with rifles, shotguns
and revolvers searched the swamp and way
back into the woods as far as the Fissenden
farm which is located on the east and west
cross roads. But they didn't find any ape nor

any other wild animal. Reports that an ape was shot and that it weighed 180 pounds and that the beast had attacked Ethan Allen were without foundation.

Noonan and Cowles had been swimming in the lake, they said and were starting to walk down the road for home. They looked over to the swamp and standing beside a small tree they said they saw a large animal which looked like an ape standing on its rear foot and waving its fore feet. It was perhaps six rods from the road.

The boys caught a ride into town and then reported the matter. Townspeople flocked to the lake as farmers in the vicinity of the lake gathered for the hunt. There were at least a hundred men with firearms hunting for the animal and the cars were parked for nearly half a mile along the road.

Paul Noonan told his story in the Evening Chronicle. "Art and I were starting for home from the lake and we had been thinking about going huckleberrying when the berries got ripe. I said to Art, 'I wonder if there are any berries in this marsh,; and we looked over and about ten rods from the road we saw the ape. It was standing on its hind legs and waving its hands. We stayed there about two minutes and then we beat it." He said it must have been at least five and one-half or six feet tall and might weight 200 pounds.

Paul was certain it was an ape. He said he could see the brown hair on it. His story was confirmed by young Cowles. Other men who were out there said they saw where the animal had wallowed in the marsh grass and two women who were picking huckleberries said they saw the animal climb up a tree.

An examination of the tree in question revealed that something had certainly climbed it as the bark on the tree was torn in places. The tracks of the animal were plainly visible down to the road and the hunters traced it that far and from there on the trail was lost.

The animal is believed to have been scared away by the commotion and to have made for the woods where it probably lost itself in the trees. While some people are inclined not to believe that there actually was an ape seen, those who were on the ground say that there can be no question about it whatever.

This same animal was seen to cross M-17 about eight miles west of Marshall Sunday night. At the same time came reports from the farm of Mrs. John Paxton that chickens had been killed in that vicinity.

The Evening Chronicle published the first story of a wild animal of some kind attacking people in Calhoun county. Several days ago an Athens man was said to have been attacked by an animal not far from his house. The day following the reported attack, the principal of the Athens high school wrote an article about it and brought it to the Chronicle office.

The Evening Chronicle confirmed it and with a few additional details published it.

Yesterday afternoon was the first time that anyone had actually identified the animal. It must be traveling nights because no one had actually seen it before although a Burlington mail carrier claimed he saw what he took to be a wolf devouring a chicken while on his mail route.

According to Deputy Fish, as Mr. Henry, the mail carrier, was driving down the road with his horse and buggy, he saw an animal in the road and he took it to be a police dog owned by Wm. Platz. As he approached the animal Henry saw it had a chicken in the road which was not yet dead. Mr. Fish says Mr. Henry took out his jack-knife and grabbed his whip fearing the animal might attack him and as he drove up to the animal it left the chicken and Mr. Henry hit it with his whip and the lash on the whip went around the animal's neck but it gave a jerk and got away. Mr. Henry told Deputy Fish he took it to be a wolf.

Deputy Fish took the ape story as a joke this morning. He, however, stated that he understood an ape or monkey with a carnival company got away from its cage when the company was showing in Kalamazoo about a month or six weeks ago and had never been captured to his knowledge.

Marshall, Michigan, *Evening Chronicle*, July 23, 1926

POSSE OUT AFTER WOLF

SHERIFF COLBY SENT OUT TWELVE MEN ON ITS TRAIL TODAY

Sheriff Colby had twelve men out today with John Langridge of Fredonia as leader, in an effort to run down a wolf or dog that is killing sheep in the southwest part of the county. One farmer, whose name Mr. Colby could not recall, has had five sheep killed.

Mr. Colby stated he took no stock in the report about an ape, gorilla, baboon or any other unusual animal having been seen in the vicinity of Lyon lake. "That is just hot air" said the sheriff. Mr. Colby stated he would pay $25 reward for the capture of any wolf, dead or alive that is killing sheep. "Remember it must be a wolf. I'll not pay a cent for an ape or any other animal" said he.

All kinds of reports were in circulation last evening about two expert hunters having killed an ape near Lyon lake. However Jay Bryant, one of the men mentioned, stated he had been in Battle Creek all the afternoon on business. Sheriff Colby says he does not take any stock in the story told by the two boys. "It was a clever story all right," said he.

Mr. Colby stated he did believe the story told by John Henry, the rural route letter carrier from Burlington. "There is either a wolf or stray police dog in that section that is killing sheep and I am willing to help run it down," said Colby.

Mr. Colby says wolves rarely ever travel at night and it is for this reason that he has the posse out today. Deputy Sheriff Eckloff who lived in the upper peninsula when a boy says it is rare that one wolf will attack a man. They are easily frightened.

John Lee said this morning that he saw footprints of an ape in his huckleberry marsh near the Kahance place about three-quarters of a mile from the marsh where Paul Noonan and Arthur Cowles said they saw the ape Wednesday.

Mr. Lee said that the animal had torn down some of the bushes and had evidently gorged on huckleberries. The tracks were identical with those found at the Lyon lake marsh. The animal must have been in there Tuesday, according to Mr. Lee. He doubts however that it is anything more than a good-sized monkey.

Mr. Lee said the monkey is probably traveling nights and that it will be heard from again as it is "staying" in marshes for the most part and huckleberry pickers will see it sooner or later. He doubts if it would molest any one unless angered by an attack.

Marshall, Michigan, *Evening Chronicle*, August 16, 1926

ATHENS POSSE FOILED AGAIN

Athens, Aug. 16—General alarm sounded here Friday afternoon by Glenville Coffman, who announced that he had seen the wild beast which has been reported lurking about Athens for several weeks, sent more than 25 armed citizens into the fields and woods near the Coffman farm home.

The Coffman Home is half a mile west of the brick school house, south and went of Athens.

Tho no trace of any animal was found, the country side was well scoured by the local posse before the hunters returned homo and again stood their shotguns in the corners.

Mr. Coffman declared he could not tell from having seen the animal whether it was an ape or a bear. He pointed out the spot where the beast was, but marks could be found in ground.

"He did not leave any tracks," Mr. Coffman declared. One group of hunters followed a pair of tracks across plowed fields for two miles, thinking they were trailing a bear and found two boys who had gone swimming.

All of the hunters yesterday had either shotguns or rifles except William A. Wilson, garage man, who carried a trusty pitchfork.

Ed Harbaugh, farmer living west of town has exprest the belief that the animal may be lurking about his farm.

"I am confident that this beast is sucking the milk from my cows," says Mr. Harbaugh. "They do not give as much milk now as they did in the spring."

Ludington, Michigan, *Daily News*, August 20, 1926

MYSTERIOUS BEAST AGAIN SEEN NEAR BATTLE CREEK

FARMER DESCRIBES 'THING'

Battle Creek, Mich., Aug. 20.—(AP)—"The thing," mysterious beast, that has caused some persons in this vicinity to become frightened and others to wax sarcastic, made its appearance six miles from Battle Creek last night, according to the report that Floyd Bowman, a farmer, gave the Calhoun sheriff's department.

Undersheriff Peter Hymer, City Detective Jack Cramer and Patrolman James Thayer responded to the call and spent the better part of the night, with dogs, in searching underbrush in the vicinity of St. Mary's lake, where "the thing" was supposed to have lurked.

Mr. Bowman said that he was attracted by his dog, which returned to the house howling, went under the porch and refused to leave. He said he investigated and saw a "black, fur-bearing beast, about four feet high" which disappeared in the underbrush at his coming.

"The thing" is credited with having attacked a farmer near Athens, a rural mail carrier near Burlington and several dogs and to have killed a number of sheep. It has been described in various forms, from an ape to a lynx.

Two Marshall youth claimed they saw it climb a tree. The huckleberry crop around Pine Creek swamp has been practically a failure because people were afraid to go into the marshes to gather them, it was said.

1937: Green (1978) noted an entry in the Folklore Archives at the Indiana University Library: "In the year 1937, Saginaw, Michigan, a fisherman sitting on the banks of the Saginaw River is reputed to have seen a manlike monster climb up the river bank, lean upon a tree and then return to the river. The man suffered a nervous breakdown."

Marshall, Michigan, *Evening Chronicle*, July 13, 1950

SEEK STRANGE, HAIRY
BEAST NEAR CHARLOTTE

Charlotte.—(U.P.)—Sheriff's officers today searched for a strange hairy animal, described as an ape or gorilla, which has been seen by at least five people in western Eaton county.

Jack Haley, 60, a state highway department employe, said an animal, about five feet tall, with long black hair and running on all fours, fled into the woods when he flashed his automobile spotlight at it.

Mr. and Mrs. Charles Rogers of Kalamo and two other motorists reported seeing the creature.

Deputy sheriffs Sherman Beaver and Elwin Smith flew over the area last night but failed to spot the animal. Police are checking all zoos and circuses in the area to determine if any animals are missing.

Marshall, Michigan, *Evening Chronicle,* June 14, 1956

IS THE MONSTER OF WILDER CREEK FACT OR FICTION?

By Sid Cato

Is the Green-Eyed Monster of Wilder Creek fact or fiction?

Most reports of hairy monsters or little men from Mars are laughed at; but authorities caution skeptics, reminding them that the stranger-than-fiction tale of a half-man, half-animal was proven about 15 years ago in this area.

And now comes the present-day story of a 10-feet-tall hairy monster with glowing green eyes "big as light bulbs."

When initial reports of the Wilder Creek monster filtered out nearly a month ago, it touched off whispers which have carried across Calhoun county. The whispers have resulted in a twisting of the original report; the area where "it" allegedly was spotted has been changed; the nationality of the men who were picked up by the snarling beast has been altered, and at least one person wrote the entire tale off as a figment of some child's imagination, spurred by a TV program.

But three Marshall-area young men will swear that their story is not fiction; one was so shocked by the event he broke down and cried.

It happened on a Saturday night about a month ago when brothers Herman and Philip Williams, part-Indian, and their friend Otto Collins, 20, a full-blooded Indian, returned home from dates in Marshall. The three stopped off at a local restaurant for a cup of coffee and then drove their 1949 model car to their home, southeast of Marshall, just past Wilder Creek.

The time was about 11:30 p.m. Philip, 17, stepping outside for a breath of fresh air, saw "something big" and ran to tell the other two. While Herman, 20, searched for a shotgun, Otto and Philip went outside.

"Evidently, it was behind us," Philip said. He told of feeling arms wrapping around him and of thinking it was his friend "fooling around." Then he felt himself being hoisted off the ground.

"We couldn't see it—it was dark. It had big green eyes, that we could tell," he said. "The eyes were big as light bulbs; they were enough to scare you to death!"

Herman, who couldn't find the gun, ran to his car when he heard screams. "I was doing his (Otto's) share of screaming," Philip said, explaining that Otto "couldn't scream: It choked him."

Herman, running out of the building, saw the object toting the two, who have a combined weight of at least 300 pounds, down a dirt road that leads off the Homer road, past the front door of the house and through a "village" of some 22 huts.

He flicked on the car lights and turned the car around. When the lights hit the monster, it veered from the flat stretch of ground surrounding the eastern end of the house, and brushed a table, losing its balance and its grip on Otto (tucked under one arm while the animal covered Philip's face with its other paw), who landed in an upright position.

Philip credited Otto who pushed the beast, causing it to lose its balance again, releasing Philip—with saving his life.

"It stood there and watched us; probably wondered what we were," Philip recalled.

The three described their experience to their employer, who informed sheriff's deputies.

So frightened were the young men that they vacated their three-room residence and now occupy one room. The day after the event occurred, the 22-hut village was deserted.

"I think it just wanted us," Philip theorized. "It could have killed us if it had wanted to."

Do the brothers, who have lived near Marshall for eight years, believe in monsters?

"Heck, no! But we saw something," Herman reported. "I don't know what it was but we saw something," his brother agreed.

The trio took a dog to the area the first part of the week following the incident. It appeared nervous when they kicked at what appeared to be footprints in the grass.

Sheriff's deputies, who might be expected to scoff at reports of monsters, nevertheless sat with sawed-off shotguns in the area for three nights, but found not trace of the green-eyed monster.

Following the first report, a wave of similar stories cropped up. One man told friends in the Wilder Creek area that he too had spotted "something" the previous night; an area farmer told friends his cow had been clawed to death by something mysterious, but investigating officers were unable to locate him.

Is there such a monster? Some may recall a similar tale of a few years back being debunked by Charlotte police who learned that boys had dressed up with an animal skin.

But three young men, who were frightened to tears, are convinced it exists.

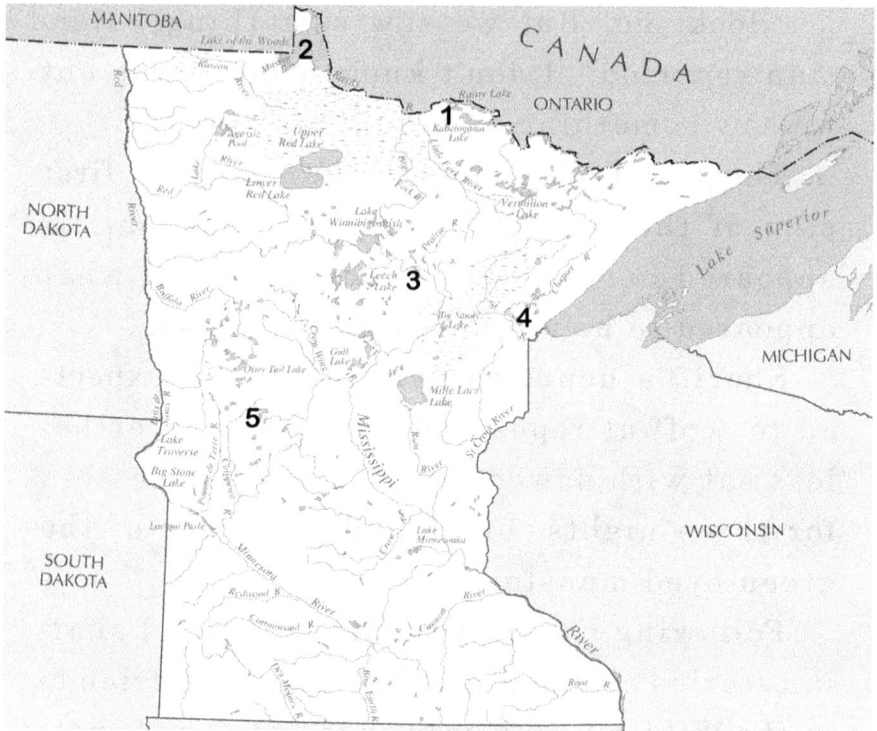

1 International Falls (Koochiching County)

2 Lake of the Woods

3 Remer (Cass County)

4 Duluth (Saint Louis County)

5 Lake Mary

Minnesota

London *Times*, January 4, 1785.

There is lately arrived in France, from America, a wild man, who was caught in the woods, 200 miles back from the Lake of the Woods, by a party of Indians; they had seen him several times, but he was so swift of foot that they could by no means get up with him; till one day, having the good fortune to find him asleep, they seized and bound him. He is near seven feet high, covered with hair, has but little appearance of understanding, and is remarkably sullen and untractable: when he was taken, half a bear was found lying by him, which he had but just killed.

Gettysburg, Pennsylvania, *Star and Republican Banner*, December 10, 1839.

WILD MAN OF THE WOODS.

FROM THE BOSTON *TIMES*.

Robert Lincoln, Esq., Agent of the New York Western Lumber Company, has just returned from the St. Peters river near the head of steamboat navigation, on the Mississippi, bringing with him a Living Wild Man of the woods, with two cubs supposed to be about three months old.

Mr. Lincoln went out in the north-west as agent of the N. Y. Lumber Company, in July last, with a view to establish extensive saw mills, on the pine lands near the Falls of St. Anthony, and he has given us a detail of the operations of the company, and the circum-stances which led to the capture of the extra-ordinary creature mentioned above.

The Company sent out their expedition in July last. The workmen and laborers, with the principal part of the machinery, went by way of New Orleans, and at that city they chartered a steamboat and proceeded up the Mississippi. The whole business was under the direction of Mr. Lincoln. They had on board all necessary tools and saws, together with all the apparatus for a grist mill, horses, cows, a good stock of provisions, arms, ammu-nition, &c. They passed directly up the river, finally reached the St. Peters in safety.

During the winter Mr. Lincoln and several of the workmen made frequent excursions in pursuit of game, which was very abundant, and their camp was one continued scene of festivity. The Indians brought in large quantities of furs, which Mr. Lincoln purchased for a mere trifle, and lines his cabins with them throughout, which rendered his rude huts very warm and comfortable.

About the 14th January, two of the carpenters who had been in pursuit of a gang of wolves that had proved very troublesome, came into the camp and reported that they had seen a huge monster in the forest, on a branch of the Mississippi, having the form of a man, but covered over with long hair, and of a frightful aspect. They stated that when seen he was standing on a log, looking directly at them, they raised their muskets, he darted into the thicket and disappeared. They saw him again in about half an hour, apparently watching them, and when they turned towards him he again disappeared. Mr. Lincoln was at first disposed to think lightly of this matter, believing that the men might have been mistaken about the size and height of the object, or supposing it might have been a trick of the Indians to frighten them— He was informed, however, by some natives, that such a being had often been seen on the St. Peters, and near the falls of the Mississippi, and they proposed to guide a party of workmen to a bluff where they though he might be found.—The men were all ready for an adventure and armed themselves with rifles and hunting knives, they started for the bluff under the direction of Mr. Lincoln and the Indian guides. On the way they were joined by several of the natives, and the whole party numbered twenty-three.

They arrived at the bluff late in the afternoon of the 21st January and encamped in a cave or grotto, at the foot of the hill.— Early next morning two of the Indians were sent out to reconnoitre, and in about an hour returned, and said that they had seen the wild man on the other side of the hill. The whole party immediately prepared for the pursuit. Mr. Lincoln gave positive orders not to fire upon him unless it should be necessary in self defence, as he wished if possible to take him alive. The Indians stated although a powerful creature, he was believed to be perfectly harmless, as he always fled at the approach of men. Mr. L. was giving his men their instructions, when the wild man appeared in sight. He ordered them to remain perfectly quiet, and taking out his pocket glass surveyed him minutely. He appeared to be about eight or nine feet high, and very athletic, and more like a beast standing erect, than a man.—The Indians had provided themselves with ropes prepared to catch wild horses, with which they hoped to ensnare and bind the creature without maiming him.

The instant the company moved toward him he sprang forward with a loud and fearful yell which made the forest ring; the Indians followed close upon him, and Mr. L. and his men brought up the rear. The pursuit was continued for nearly an hour—now gaining upon the object of their chase, and now almost loosing sight of him. He finally darted into a thicket and they were unable to find him.

They then began to trace their steps towards the place of their encampment, and when within a mile of the cavern, the wild man crossed their path, within twenty rods. They immediately gave chase again and accidentally drove the creature from the forest into an open prairie. At length he suddenly stopped and turned upon his pursuers. Mr. Lincoln was then in advance. Fearing that he might attack or return to the woods and escape, he fired at him and lodged a charge of buckshot in his leg. He fell immediately, and the Indians sprang forward and threw their ropes over his head, arms and legs, and with much effort succeeded in binding him fast. He struggled however, most desperately, gnashed his teeth, and howled in a frightful manner.—They then formed a sort of litter of branches of limbs of trees, and placing him upon it, carried him to the encampment. A watch was then placed over him, and every effort that could be devised to keep him quiet, but he continued to howl most piteously all night. Towards morning two cubs about three feet high, and very similar to the large monster came into the camp and were taken without resistance. As soon as the monster saw them he became very furious—gnashed his teeth and howled, and thrashed about until he burst several of the cords, and came very near effecting his escape. He was bound anew, and after that he was kept most carefully watched and guarded. The next day he was placed on the litter and carried down the Hills on the St. Peters.

For two or three days, Mr. Lincoln says, he refused to eat or drink or take any kind of food, but continued to howl at intervals for an hour at a time, at length, however, he began to eat; but from that time his howls ceased, and he has remained stupid and sullen ever since. The cubs took feed very readily, and became quiet, active and playful.

Mr. Lincoln is a native of Boston, and some of the workmen engaged at his mills are from this city. He arrived here on Saturday afternoon, in the brig St. Charles, Stewart, master, from New Orleans, with the wild man and the cubs, and they were all removed from the vessel that evening. By invitation of Mr. Lincoln who is an old acquaintance, we went down to his rooms to examine this monster. He is a horrid looking creature, and reminds us of the fabled satyrs, as we have pictured them to our own mind. He is about eight feet three inches high, when standing erect, and his frame is of giant proportions in every part. His legs are not straight but like those of any other four footed animal, and his whole body is covered with a hide very much like that of a cow. His arms are very large and long, and ill proportioned. It does not appear from his manner that he ever walked on "all fours." The fingers and toes are all bunches, armed with stout claws. His head is covered with thick, coarse black hair like the mane of a horse. The appearance of his countenance, if such it may be called, is very disgusting—nay, almost horrible. It is covered with a lighter and thinner coat than the rest of his body— there is appearance of eyebrows or nose; the mouth is very large and wide, and similar to that of a baboon. His eyes are quite dull and heavy, and there is no indication of cunning or activity about them. Mr. Lincoln says he is beyond doubt carnivorous, as he universally rejected bread and vegetables, and eats flesh with great avidity. He thinks he is of the ourang-outang species; but from what we have seen, we are inclined to consider him a wild animal, something resembling a man.

He is, to say the least, one of the most extraordinary creatures that has ever been brought before the public, from any part of the earth, and we believe will prove a difficult puzzle to the scientific. He lies down like a brute, and does appear to possess more instinct than common domestic animals. He is now quite tame and quiet, and is only confined by a stout chain to one of his legs.

It is Mr. Lincoln's intention to submit these animals to the inspection of the scientific for a few days, in order to ascertain what they are, and after that to dispose of them to some person for exhibition. Mr. Lincoln himself will return to St. Peters in the course of two or three weeks.

An earlier April 12, 1839, edition of this story, from the Woodstock, Vermont, *Mercury*, includes an addendum (foreshadowing Jacko):

April Fool.—The custom of telling large stories and taking liberties of speech and poetical license on the first day of April has not
ceased. The editor of the *Boston Times* has
indulged himself by getting up an account of
the wild man of the woods, taken in the western wilderness of which the foregoing is an
extract. He announced that the animal would
be exhibited at a public house in Boston, on
the first of the present month, and so much
was the keeper of the house annoyed by visitors, that he was obliged to put up a board
with the words 'April Fool' upon it to prevent
further accessions of the curious. One of the
papers say that some of the disappointed repaired to the office of the *Times* and after
viewing the editor, declared themselves as
well satisfied with the curiosity as if they
had seen the wild man himself.

1898: Mike Quast (1990) noted that *Haunted
Heartland*, by Beth Scott and Michael Norman,
includes several Windego tales from 1898 to 1904,
involving a giant white-haired creature. Quast
indicates that though supernatural elements are
associated with the stories, this may just be para-
normalism (invoking mystical qualities for a natural event), as the creature itself does nothing
supernatural.

c. 1910: Mike Quast (2019) interviewed Bigfoot researcher Ed Trimble, who had heard a rumor of loggers in the International Falls area capturing a Bigfoot, keeping it in a cage, but that it escaped before an expert could arrive to examine it. Quast noted that the loggers named it "Jocko," suggesting it may be a confused story with the famed British Columbia case. That is certainly possible, but as noted before, "Jocko" or "Jacko" were very popular names given to primates in the 1800s and early 1900s.

1911: Sanderson (1967) noted the report of a light-haired "human giant" seen by a couple of hunters in the northern tip of the state.

c. 1940s: Mike Quast (2019) interviewed Bigfoot researcher Ed Trimble, who said during this decade he had seen red eyeshine fairly high off the ground while driving near Lake of the Woods.

c. 1942: Mike Quast (2019) noted a vague story of a man picking blueberries in the Remer area who was frightened away by a gorilla-like creature.

c. 1946: Mike Quast (2019) noted a May 13, 1991, *Cook County News-Herald* article which details a rumored accidental release of two Chinese "yetis" in the Duluth area (captured and brought over by a couple of Navy men to sell to Ringling Bros., Barnum & Bailey). A couple of local residents discussed their possible encounters with such creatures in subsequent years.

Late 1940s: Mike Quast (2019) noted an online report of a group of Lake Mary ice fishermen who watched a naked, hairy woman walk out on the ice where they were fishing and steel their catch of eelpout.

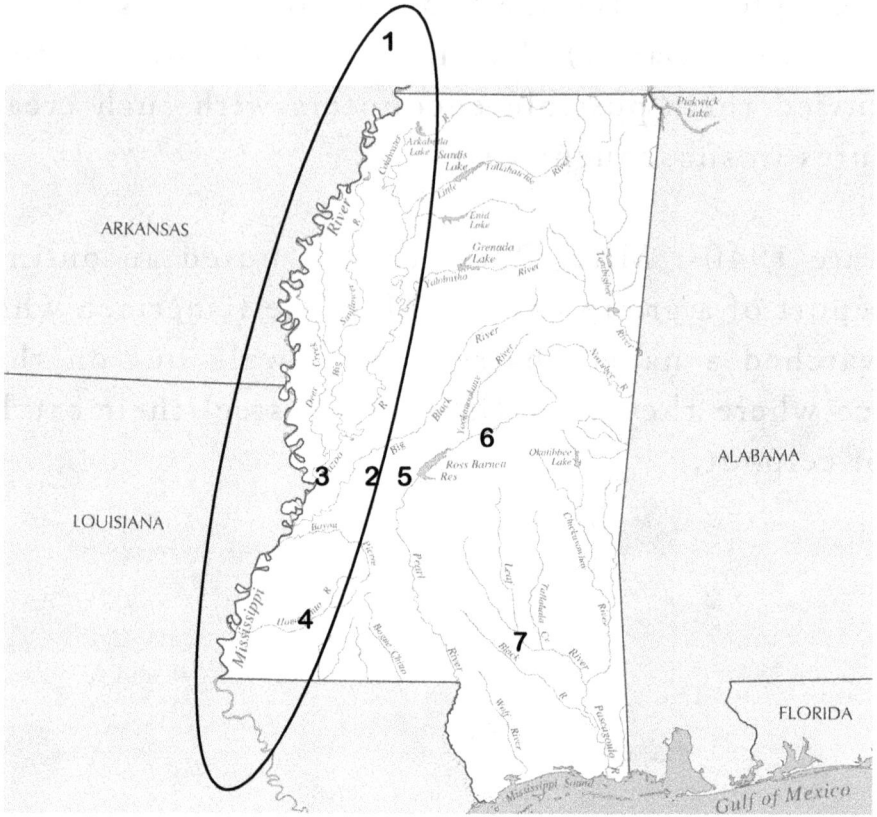

1 Mississippi Delta

2 Bolton's Depot (now Bolton; Hinds County)

3 Vicksburg (Warren County)

4 Meadville (Franklin County)

5 Jackson (Hinds, Rankin, and Madison Counties)

6 Walnut Grove (Leake County)

7 Ralston (Forrest County)

Mississippi

Sanderson (1961) received a letter from an educated woman (with an M. A. in zoology) who said that she grew up hearing stories about the Little Red Men of the Delta. She said they were supposed to be "about the size of a ten year old kid and able to climb like monkeys and to live back from the bayous." She was unsure if they were human or ape.

Vickburg, Mississippi, *Herald,* March 15, 1868

The Southern Star of the 12th says:

A rumor is current in the neighborhood of Bolton's Depot that a human monstrosity inhabits the vicinity. This wild man, a sort of non-descript, between a beast and a human being, has been seen, according to report, by several individuals and on one occasion was pursued by some hunters with a pack of well trained hounds, which brought him to bay in an extensive brake of the swamp, through which it was scarcely possible to proceed. Before reaching the spot the hunters noticed that the 'music' of their pack was being constantly decreased and when they arrived within several hundred yards, one dog only was baying, and shortly after his 'mouth was stilled.' Pushing on to the point whence the baying was last heard, to the surprise of the party, they found their whole pack mangled, and lacerated, not a dog surviving. The limbs of several dogs were found torn entirely off, and cast several paces from the place where the bodies lay.—Others seemed to have been killed by the heavy blows of a club, while the huge barefoot track of a man was plainly visible among other traces of the fight.

We do not vouch for the truth of the story, but only give it as we received it, that our friends in the vicinity of the river may be on the "qui vive."

Waterloo, Iowa, *Courier*, March 26, 1868

THE "WHAT IS IT" OUTDONE

THE WILD MAN OF THE WOODS,

AN EXTRAORDINARY CREATURE DISCOVERED

IN THE FORESTS OF WARREN COUNTY

FROM THE VICKSBURG [MISS.] *HERALD*.

The following extraordinary story, which for want of space we have been compelled to condense—we have received from a perfectly reliable source.—About twenty-five miles from this city, but in this county, is a small stream known as Bear Creek, which empties into the Big Black river. The margin of both these streams, in that vicinity for miles back, is an almost impenetrable swamp, grown up with canebreakers, and wild, tangled vines, but filled up with all kinds of game, including bear, deer, and turkeys.

In pursuit of this game many young men resort to this spot with their hounds. For some time past, strange stories have been told by the negroes of an extraordinary animal seen near these swamps. The negroes, in their usual manner, have graphic and startling descriptions of his appearance, but usually winding up with the declaration that it was the devil which had been seen by them. One peculiarity, as described by the negroes, was that from his tracks he seemed to be going both ways at once. That is, one foot pointed to the front and the other to the rear. These stories were laughed at and derided by the citizens, no one believing in any such statements. This extraordinary creature had often suddenly presented himself among the negroes in the early twilight, causing great consternation among them. He is described by the negroes as being about eight feet high, each eye, in their language, "as large as a hen's egg," with no nose and no upper lip, his two eye teeth as large as a man's thumb, extending down over his chin about eight inches; his right foot points directly to the front and the left one to the rear, and the measurement of the track is just twenty-three inches in length; his finger nails are perfectly hard and solid, and are about six inches long; the hair on his head—which is stiff and wiry—sweeps the ground as he walks, and is parted in the rear and brought down in front on each side of his singularly-formed chest, which is not round nor flat, but is angular like that of a fowl. The hair on the body of this singular being is very stiff and grows to the rear, parting at the angle of the breast bone growing back and uniting with a long stiff growth on his spine, which extends back about one foot like the spinal fin of a fish, or the bristles on the back of a boar—the hair on his arms is parted and grows in the same way, making a long, thick brush on the back of the arms, extending from the shoulders to the point of his middle finger; the same peculiarity is observable on his legs.—

This singular and horrible object, the negroes represent, has been seen by them at different times for several months, and that night has been rendered hideous by the unearthly howlings of this unknown animal. No white person has ever seen him until recently, when he was discovered by a hunting party. Several gentlemen—acquaintances of ours—met on last Thursday week with a view of bear hunting in this swamp; they were accompanied by about fifteen well-trained bear dogs. They prepared for the hunt early in the morning, and, when about commencing, their attention was attracted to an unusually large man track in the soft soil, upon examination it was discovered that the track was constantly being reversed. In an instant the stories of the negroes occurred to the party, and at once it was determined to pursue the creature which had made this track. The dogs were instantly called and encourage to follow the track, which they did promptly. The gentlemen, mounted upon good horses, found but little difficulty in keeping up well with the hounds. In a few minutes an object was presented to their view which sent a chill to the heart of every member of the party. They had unearthed a nondescript. A being—apparently human—suddenly arose from his lair—turned, and for a moment stood in silent inspection of his pursuers, and then, instantly, with a yell truly terrific wheeled, and with the speed of the fastest horse rushed away before the dogs.

This wild and exciting chase was continued for nearly ten miles, when at last the terrible monster, foaming with rage, was brought to bay upon the bank of the Big Black, and turning with a fury unparalleled, it seized the foremost dog with both hands, and by the exercise of super human muscular strength, buried its long talons in the body of the howling brute, and literally tore the dog asunder. Dropping this it instantly seized the next and sent its two immense tusks through the skull of the doomed dog. One of the hunters, becoming alarmed for the safety of the party, drew his revolver and fired twice at the monster, but evidently without effect other than to frighten it by the report, when, turning with a hideous yell, it plunged into the river, diving and remaining under water fully five minutes, when it would suddenly spring high into the air, screaming with the voice of a regiment of soldiers. It finally swam to the opposite side and disappeared in the neighboring forest, since which time it has only been seen twice by white persons. Several attempts have been made to capture it, but, up to the present time without success.

What this strange creature is, no one can conjecture. The gentlemen with whom we have conversed represent it as a black man about six feet high, but in other respects resembling to a great degree the description given by the negroes.

It has broken the negroes from attending loyal leagues at night in that section of country.

Dubuque, Iowa, *Daily Herald,* June 27, 1868

A "WHAT IS IT"
SEEN IN MISSISSIPPI.

A STRANGE AND TERRIBLE CREATURE
PURSUED BY DOGS AND HUNTERS.

CORRESPONDENCE OF THE ST. LOUIS DISPATCH.

A strange visaged creature, apparently one of nature's prodigies, has just been discovered near Meadville, Franklin county, Mississippi, causing much excitement in that usually monotonous village. A letter from a friend residing in the above named village, dated June 4th, says: "M—, at this time, is very much agitated on account of the strange creature seen near here.

It is said to be similar to the one seen near Vicksburg last fall. A Vicksburg paper of a date some few days subsequent to the discovery of this strange creature near that place, gave a full description of it, and the manner in which it was discovered, which, given from memory, is in substance about as follows: Some time in September last, as a party of huntsmen were driving in the swamps some miles from the river, a trail was taken by the hounds and followed up at a brisk pace, leaving the party far behind. In following after the dogs they discovered the tracks of the game in some miry places, which appeared similar to the track of a human foot; and they observed, also, that the toes of one foot turned backward. On coming up with the dogs, who were now baying, they beheld a frightful looking creature, of about the average height of man, but with far greater muscular development, standing menacingly a few yards in front of the dogs. It had long, coarse hair flowing from its head and reaching near its knees; its entire body, also, seemed to be covered with hair of two or three inches' length, which was of a dark brown color. From its upper jaw projected two very large tusks, several inches long. Its head and face, as well as could be determined from the distance of the observers, bore a striking resemblance to that of the negro, except that the chin and cheeks were covered with long hair. On the near approach of the hunters, it fled toward the Mississippi river, and was not overtaken again until within a few yards of the bank. When the party came up with the dogs the second time, the monster was standing erect before them, none of them having yet dared to clinch with it. But when the dogs were urged by their masters, they endeavored to seize it, when it reached forward and grabbed one of them, and taking it in its hands, pressed it against its tusk, which pierced it through and killed it instantly. Becoming alarmed at this display of strength, the hunters fired several shots at the creature, which caused it to leap into the river. It remained under water several minutes, and then rose almost its entire length above the surface, uttering shrieks which almost petrified the pursuers with terror. No similar sound had ever come to the ears of these men, who were familiar with the howl of the wolf, the whine of the panther, and the hoarse bellowing of the alligator. After sinking and rising several times, it swam to the Louisiana shore and disappeared.

This report of the huntsmen created quite a stir, and considerable speculation among theorists, and a much greater amount of fear among the commonality, who looked at the thing in a practical point of view. But, however, as time rolled away, and no new discoveries were made concerning the monstrosity, the excitement died away, and the strange individual had almost ceased to be though of long before its second appearance.

Meadville, where it has last appeared, is about 40 miles east of the Mississippi river, and, I suppose, near one hundred miles from Vicksburg. Throughout Franklin county there are retreats especially adapted to the accommodation of wild beasts, such as the high barren hills, ravines, and the dense, vine-matted swamps of the Homochitto river.

It is highly probable that this is the same creature seen near Vicksburg, and for fear that it is the only living specimen of that genus, some of our scientific men who are ambitious of contributing a mite to natural history, should contrive to become acquainted with its nativity, lineage, characteristics, &c., and give them publicity, that they may take the place of the fear and speculation that are now prevailing.

Jackson, Mississippi, *State Ledger,* July 4, 1884

WILD WIZARD OF THE WOODS.

A VERITABLE WILD MAN MAKES HIS APPEARANCE IN PEARL RIVER SWAMP.

The Inhabitants of Jackson are very much excited over a strange living object seen on several occasions, by various persons, in Pearl river swamp. In shape it represents a human being, walking erect and using his long, upper appendages as arms. This strange freak of nature, made so, evidently, by his long association with the woods, and the absence of all human beings, was first seen about two weeks ago, since which time his frightful visage has appeared several times in different parts of the swamp. It has no certain locality, but the favorite spot seems to be near the lakes back of the Capitol. How he obtains a subsistence is a matter of conjecture, but there is little question but what he lives on such things as can be obtained in the forest. On one occasion he was seen devouring a large fish with demoniacal greed, in a short space of time—between his massive jaws and enormous teeth the bones being crushed as if they were straws. To women or children he does not appear wild or scared, but makes fight at them, and has chased several from the swamps, and, on one occasion, caught an old negro woman and frightened her within an inch of her life, leaving the imprint of his long finger nails in several portions of her body. The sight of a man, however, has an opposite effect, and he flees with almost the speed of the wind. The startling effect produced on parties seeing him renders it somewhat difficult to get a correct description. They are all agreed, however, as to the following, some of them making it much worse: The body is entirely devoid of clothing and is covered with a coarse hair six inches long; head covered with hair reaching to the middle of body, and whiskers of enormous length. Between breaks of whiskers the enormous teeth can occasionally be seen. His finger and toe nails have grown to a point and attained the enormous length of four inches. In regard to this witnesses do not agree. His eyes are bullet shaped, and when excited become very red and look as if they emitted sparks of fire. Nose and ears, if he possesses either, are hidden by the long hair. When near a human being each hair seems endowed with life and stands out separately from the body, his head hair appearing four feet long and standing out from all points. His height is almost seven feet, eight inches. This is supposed to be the same person that created so much excitement in Alabama a few years since, various attempts being made to capture him without avail. He mysteriously disappeared from that section.

A large posse is now being raised to scour the swamp, and if possible secure the strange being.

He has been seen by several reliable persons of this city, and that he is at the present time in Pearl river swamp there can be no question.

Jackson, Mississippi, *Daily News,* February 15, 1917

WILD MAN REPORTED.

Carthage, Miss., Feb. 15—(Special)—What is supposed to be a "wild man" was seen by Mr. Ford Cox who lives near Walnut Grove. While cutting timber in a clearing the top of a tree fell on a brush pile and the object ran out. Mr. Cox says it was about four feet high with a body like a man. Its face was covered with a shaggy beard or hair and its body was literally covered with black hair or it had on a black slicker coat. A few days later it was seen by some negro children while on their way to school. It has so frightened the negroes in that community until the school has been broken up. Some people think it is a [chimpanzee] or a gorilla that has made its escape from some show traveling through the country. Whatever it is has so frightened the negroes that they do not get out at night.

Hattiesburg, Mississippi, *American,* September 8, 1952

HUNT 'GORILLA' SOUTH OF TOWN

Doors were latched tight today in the Ralston community eight miles south of here and parents, both colored and white, kept their youngsters inside, on the strength of a report a gorilla was loose in the area.

The report was made Saturday night by Daisy Burney (colored) and her 13-year-old daughter, Lady, who told this story:

They had gone down to the spring for a bucket of water. It was almost dusk. They had reached their own back yard when "this big something with eyes like a mule's and standing up straight like a man" came at them from out of the piney woods.

Daisy Burney, 45, said she "let out a scream you could hear most anywhere" and the thing, which she believed to be a gorilla, veered off into the bush. "It ran without making no noise."

Another Search Planned

Sunday night a searching party, headed by a white man, Ray McRaney, had no luck in locating the shaggy intruder. McRaney and a white neighbor, John [Tyner], plan to go out again tonight, taking five or six Negroes with them all to be armed with shotguns or rifles.

Sheriff Abb Payne toured the sector this morning investigating the incident without arriving at an official conclusion.

Today the Burney cottage was locked tight, windows as well as doors and while Daisy and Lady worked in the fields with Daisy's husband, Grantham, the latter's 80-year-old mother sat guard in the stiflingly hot kitchen.

The old woman said:

"I'm nelly blind and can't make out nothin'. I heard the jumpin' and pitchin' aroun' out in the yard Sattiday night when they saw the thing. It happened right there twixt here and the hen-house."

She said her name was Eastie Mixon and that if the thing returned and broke in the house she planned "to git under the house an' let him have it."

Ralston community is spread thinly over hills and hollows just off State Highway 24.

Other Comments

A mile down the road from where Eastie Mixon sat in the suffocating kitchen, was Sarah Bass, lolling somewhat tensely on the back porch of her own home: "My pistol's in there where I can get it in a hurry. But if it's a real gorilla—a pistol won't do that no good, will it?"

Sarah said that, come to think of it, Saturday night she heard a commotion down around her hog-pen and that the dogs got after something.

John Parker, a husky Negro logger who lives in the sector, said he was going to give up night-time hunting and scouting around until the mystery was settled. "It kind of makes you think, this go-rilla talk. He might be hungry for a fella."

Parker, asked if in view of his own bulk, he might not give the thing a battle for its money, answered: "I'm big, but you see we don't know what that thing's carryin' to fight with."

At the home of Mary Jane Brown, a half-mile from the Bass place, the mother had her shotgun on the bed in the living room. The shades were drawn and you could see the pale circles of the eyeballs of her three small ink-black children: "I haven't seen anything, but if I do I want to be ready."

Sheriff Notified

Sheriff Payne learned of the situation at Ralston this morning after receiving a phone call from Mrs. Gladys [Tyner], whose husband is a meat-cutter here for Swift's. Said Mrs. [Tyner]: "It makes you feel funny stuck off here in these woods. I mean if there is something like that loose."

Mrs. [Tyner], a neat attractive blonde, added: "They must think there's something to it to round up all those men and guns."

She said she wondered if a gorilla might have escaped from a circus.

The sheriff told her there had been no animal shows in this neighborhood for a long time but that he understood gorilla were very sturdy travelers and could clip off a hundred miles or so without much wear and tear.

Mrs. [Tyner] said since there weren't many gorillas in this country "probably all of them—or most of them—are registered."

The sheriff confirmed this belief, but promised to remain on the lookout nevertheless. And to let her know of he received word that some registered gorilla was at large.

The white woman was calm, but concerned, since she is the mother of two small children and their home is rather isolated: "Half the time if you needed help, you'd find the telephone party-line was busy."

Hattiesburg, Mississippi, *American,* September 9, 1952

TRAFFIC TOO THICK; GORILLA HUNT RECESSES

A searching party armed with rifles and shotguns combed the Ralston community Monday night without seeing hair nor hide of a gorilla.

A Negro woman, Daisy Burney, 45, and her 13-year-old daughter, Lady, reported

Saturday night that a gorilla-shaped animal had leaped at them from the bushes behind their rural home.

Daisy Burney said she had seen enough pictures of gorillas to believe the animal was one. She said when she screamed the shaggy monster veered off and fled into the woods.

The searching party, led by Ray McRaney, a white man, went out just before dark Monday and remained until 10 p.m. But by this time so many curious motorists had moved into the area, intent on having a look for themselves, that the searchers went home and put up their guns.

Mrs. John Tyner, wife of one of the party, said this morning: "The men finally got disgusted. The dust on the road from the visiting cars was awful. And every where you looked there were headlights." . . .

When the public interest dies down a bit the men of the area, both white and Negro, intend to resume the search. They have contacted a man who owns trained dogs and some horses and the hunt will continue on horseback. . . .

Hattiesburg, Mississippi, *American,* September 10, 1952

GORILLA SIGHTED; DOGS
AND RIFLEMEN MISS TRAIL

By Elliott Chaze

The moon sailed white and lopsided as a torn picnic plate against the navy-blue sky and a fall breeze blew against the crest of the hill, so that the shadows of the bushes wavered in odd shapes—gorilla shapes.

I'd never been on a gorilla hunt before.

Neither, for that matter, had the five big coon dogs which now bugled half-heartedly in the hollow. They belonged to District Attorney Lawrence Arrington, who now walked ahead of me, shouldering a .22 automatic rifle.

Arrington wore heavy trousers, a thick jacket, and massive galoshes. He said: "Those coon dogs don't act like they want to be gorilla dogs, do they?"

Sheriff Abb Payne, who carried a single-shot 12-gauge piece of ancient origin, said: "Can't say I blame them. It's a hell of a change for a dog, this switching to gorillas in the middle of the night."

He Saw It

Leading the party was slender Ray McRaney, a mechanic who lives in the Ralston community and knows the woods like the palm of his hand. McRaney's artillery consisted of an old M-1 rifle and three spare clips of ammunition. He had phoned the sheriff five hours earlier with the news. "Sheriff, this is no gag about the gorilla running around here. I wish you'd come out. About 4 p.m. I got a look at

The Thing from no more than 35 yards. It stood up on its hind legs and it was about man-high."

McRaney said it was broad daylight and the [—] coarse hair on the beast was "so dark it sparkled."

He said he let loose with five shots and The Thing did a kind of back flip into a cane brake and began running "on its feet and knuckles like a great ape."

McRaney, who is a calm, sensible man with steady blue eyes and a square jaw, and he'd spent several years in the Pacific with the United States infantry, and he knew the difference between "monkey-looking things and bear-looking things." But until he squared off with The Thing Tuesday afternoon he'd had the feeling the gorilla scare in the Ralston area seven miles south of here was pretty much a joke. . . .

I also felt somewhat on the cynical side until I listened to McRaney's level, unexcited account of the afternoon's happenings; until I'd spent a couple hours last night stumbling around the hills, sidestepping shadows.

With us was C. D. Cole, a cheerful little man with a long rifle in the crook of his arm and a hunter's lamp strapped to his head.

And there was John Tyner, who lives down the road from the Burneys. John was undecided about the existence of the gorilla. But he plainly did not consider the possibility of a gorilla a joke.

We reached a boggy little branch at the bottom of the hill and two of the five coon dogs came puffing and scrambling to us out of the dark. McRaney had said the beast we sought was given to the habit of "beating on his chest" and making "blowing noises." The dogs in the darkness made noises which could have been interpreted in that direction; and I was nervous until their good, plain dog faces showed in the light of the electric lamps. Beyond the light and beneath the pines it was black as all get-out.

"Shine your light this way," McRaney said to Cole, who swiveled the lamp against McRaney's chest. McRaney reached in his jacket pocket and came out with a big pinch of coarse hair, dark brown, almost black. "He left this on that barbed-wire fence after I shot at him."

"What?" I asked.

"The Thing," McRaney said. "After I shot at it it ran a ways and ducked between the strands of that fence just behind you. This snagged on the barbs."

No Bear

I can't very well describe the hair beyond the color and texture since I am not too well acquainted with what kind of hair fits what kind of animal. But I am most certain it was not hair of a bear.

McRaney put the pinch of hair back in his pocket, strode to the two-strand barbed wire fence and studied it. "He went through right here," he said.

He moved off into the blackness, parallel to the fence, and we followed, Arrington yipping occasionally at the dogs, which were still lashing around and baying in the bush. "They're on a cold trail," the district attorney said.

We walked a long time. Cole said the woods were crawling with rattlesnakes. Payne said this was true: "A bird dog of mine was bitten out here near Shelby two years ago. Died before we could do anything with him." McRaney said it was true about the snakes. Tyner said that it was true. I understood Arrington's galoshes. They no longer seemed at all funny to me, not even the way they flapped when he walked.

Only Noise

Suddenly the dogs, the entire pack of them, began raising Cain in the woods to the North of us.

We stopped, frozen by the racket.

"They've really hit something now," someone said.

The yowling gave way to thrashing and cracking in the bushes, angling downwind to us as we waited. Now we heard the separate twigs snapping, the rushing [—] of the leaves. And there was a heavy-footed thumping coming our way fast. The men held their guns at port arms and Cole's lamp cut a clean yellow tunnel into the woods as we waited.

"If it's the ape," McRaney said, "we want to start shooting before he's too close. They take a lot of shooting."

Not twenty yards ahead in the glare of the lamp the bushes and grasses wig-wagged violently and the coon dogs came lumbering into the open, running as thumpingly as horses. There was no gorilla.

"Cold Trail," Arrington said.

"Good old cold trail," I said.

And we went home.

Hattiesburg, Mississippi, *American,* September 11, 1952

GORILLA HUNT: STUDENTS SEE APE, FIND FOOTPRINT

By Elliott Chaze

Here are the latest developments in the gorilla hunt eight miles south of here in the Ralston community:

Bill Brody, a biology major at Mississippi Southern College, said Wednesday afternoon that he had pumped at least one high-velocity bullet into a beast which resembled a great ape.

Charles Gavin, Brody's hunting buddy, and also a student at the college, verified Brody's account and said the animal "ran on its feet and knuckles, swinging its legs between its arms as it sped through the woods."

Gavin said that he and Brody were with Ray McRaney Tuesday afternoon when the latter opened fire on the animal, less than a mile from the cottage of Daisy Burney, the Negro woman who launched the hunt last Saturday night after telling neighbors she had seen a "gorilla."

Finds Print

Brody, who is now working on his master's degree at Southern, said that he found one clear-cut track, about as long as a big man's foot. He said the track had a great thumb instead of the kind of toe humans have.

At least 30 men were in the area Wednesday afternoon, many of them armed with high-powered rifles.

They followed a pack of coon dogs, which did not pick up a hot trail of any sort all afternoon. Nor did anyone see anything in the way of wildlife. Game Warden Manuel Bounds was on the scene and warned against the dangers of "so many guns in the woods." Bounds said when you collect that many armed men at one point you're going "to have a couple who will fire every time a bush wiggles."

No bushes wiggled. There were no shots fired. Bounds remained on patrol in the sector until most of the hunters returned to their homes.

Residents of the Ralston community are, for the most part, sick of the gorilla business. They receive scores of phone calls from townspeople who want to know how to reach the community and where to look for the gorilla.

Gorilla-burghers

Albert Jackson, who runs a roadside restaurant on Highway 11 about a mile from the woodland scene of the hunt, has begun advertising gorilla-burghers. A placard on the front of his place asks in capital letters: HAVE YOU TRIED OUR DELICIOUS GO-RILLA-BURGHERS?

Children around Ralston have become extremely gorilla-conscious, a direct result of the fact their parents no longer allow them to play out in the yards without adult supervision. . . .

Thick Cover

Hence of there is an ape in the woods of the sprawling reservation bordering Camp Shelby, it is managing to elude his pursuers despite inferior mental equipment. The nature of the land would be to its advantage, however. It is rugged and jungley and at points the undergrowth makes visibility zero.

Added to this the woods are studded with slit trenches, foxholes and concrete pill-boxes, used in the training of fighting men during World War II. The concrete boxes are square, six-by-six feet, and would offer acceptable living quarters to an ape who did not mind sharing home occasionally with a rattlesnake.

The climate presents a different problem. There is little possibility that an anthropoid ape, with its need for steady warmth, could survive for any length of time. If, as some suggest, the animal was once a pet of some forgotten Shelby soldier and which escaped while it was a baby and matured in the woods, it would have faced almost certain death during the winter. There have been no animal shows in the area since last winter.

Nor is the sector supplied with ideal gorilla food. And if such an animal ventured into the open plowed fields for vegetables it would most surely leave tracks. No farmer has reported seeing any such tracks.

Indications today are that the gorilla hunt, as an organized program, is on the wane.

But odds are there will be scattered parties in the woods for at least another week.

After all this, the Ralston gorilla hunt petered out. A summary article noted that "at least five persons still argue seriously that they have seen an animal running on feet and knuckles through the tangled undergrowth of the area." Varied rumors in the area included 1) the Hattiesburg newspaper paid a few families to support the gorilla story and increase circulation, 2) moonshiners had fabricated the story to discourage officers from poking around, 3) someone cooked up the story to frighten residents and run them off the land, and 4) witnesses had just seen a 'hog bear' that stood up on its hind legs and waved its front feet like an ape. ("Gorilla hunt: Recess called to let the dust settle," Hattiesburg, Mississippi, *American,* September 12, 1952.)

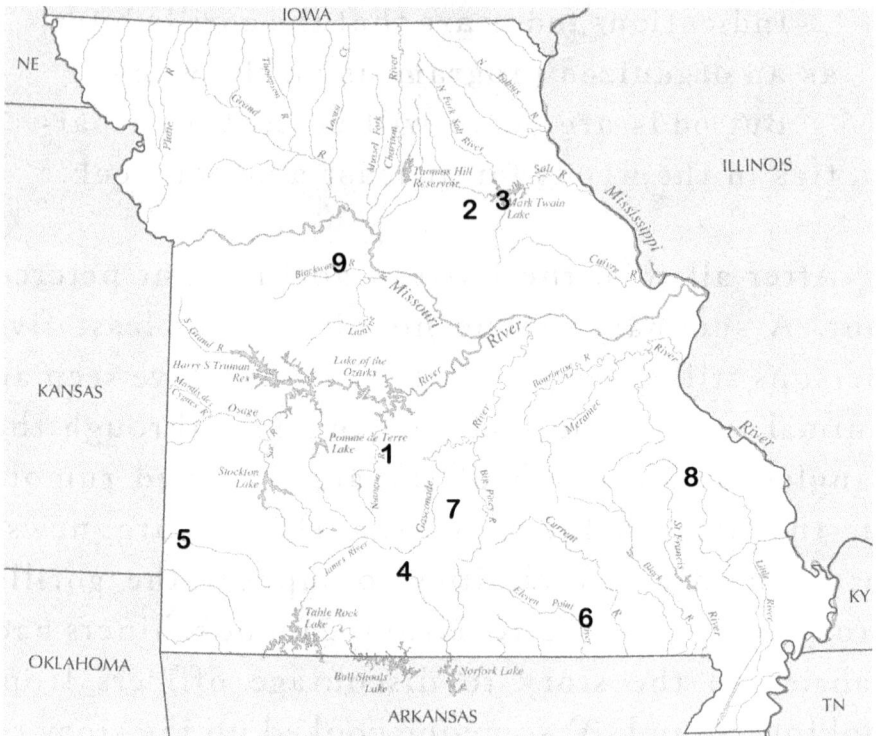

1 Laclede County

2 Hallsville (Boone County)

3 Mexico (Audrain County)

4 Douglas County

5 Joplin (Jasper and Newton Counties)

6 Alton (Oregon County)

7 Houston (Texas County)

8 Frederickstown (Madison County)

9 Beaman (Pettis County)

Missouri

Columbia, South Carolina, *Daily Phoenix,* July 4, 1867

Three beings of the What-is-it race, with human voices, but covered with hair, have been found in Missouri.

Cincinnati, Ohio, *Daily Gazette,* July 9, 1870

The St. Louis Republican says: "Mr. P. H. McDonald reports having seen a wild man in the woods in Laclede county, a short time ago. It had an ape-like head; only two legs, the body and legs covered with a thick coat of hair. The animal ran away very fast. It kept an upright position, and appears more like a human, with the exception of the hair and color, which was a dark brown."

San Francisco, California, *Bulletin*, January 28, 1873

WHAT IS IT?—
A STRANGE, WILD CREATURE

For some weeks past, the people living near the lowlands, or creek bottoms, five miles southwest of Hallsville, in this county, have been seriously alarmed and nearly startled out of their wits, by the sudden and mysterious appearance in the neighborhood at various times, of a strange, ferocious looking creature, resembling a gorilla, which it seems, has its haunt in the deep thickets, and under the shelving rock and caverns that line the creek in that vicinity. What it is or where it came from, no one knows. That it is there, a living reality, many a frightened farmer can attest from the scare it gave him. It appears to be over five feet high, has short crooked legs, a long body and long arms with ugly looking talon like fingers, a short, thick neck, large savage looking head, in which gleams a pair of blood-shot eyes, while its mouth extends from ear to ear, and is filled with long fangish teeth, which it displays when disturbed. Its body is covered with a heavy coat of brownish hair, and its general aspect is absolutely terrible and ferocious, making the stoutest heart quail before it. Thus far, no one has suffered personal injury from it, other than a severe fright, as it never seeks to make a direct attack on human beings, but rather seems to delight in suddenly rushing forth from its lair, and with appalling roars and fearful gestulations chasing all who venture near its haunts. Poultry, shoats, etc.,

have been missed by the farmers, and it is
thought this creature has something to do
with their disappearance. The range of this
wild being is near the farms of W. Winn and
Ollie Barnes, and in that neighborhood. One
person gravely informed us that it was the
devil, as he had tried in vain to shoot it, and
that dogs cannot be induced to go near its
haunts. We gathered the above facts from
reliable parties, while in the neighborhood
last week.—*Centralia (Mo.) Guard*

Centralia, Missouri, *Fireside Guard,* January 1, 1881

A wild animal recently scared several persons
in the vicinity of Mexico and Paris. From the
description we recognize it to be the same
animal which was seen several years ago in
the vicinity of Hallsville, and which was described as resembling a gorilla by those who
obtained a near view.

Kansas City, Missouri, *Star,* June 27, 1915

SAW "BLUE MAN" OF OZARKS.

Famous Creature Was
Observed Again by Woodsman.

Willow Springs, Mo., June 26.—The periodical reappearance of the "Blue Man of Spring
Creek" was reported by tie haulers who
reached this city yesterday from [Douglas]

County. The supposed "wild man" had not been seen at his old haunts since 1911 until about six weeks ago, when O. C. Collins, while searching for two lambs, got a glimpse of the man while he was attempting to capture a hog.

Since then other persons have seen the "Blue Man," according to word brought in by the tie haulers. Jay Taber saw him a week ago, but he ran up the mountainside. Taber told his neighbors that the man's hair is now white, but that he is still powerful looking.

The "Blue Man of Spring Creek" was reported in the wilds of Douglas County as early as 1865. "Blue Sol" Collins, a noted hunter, supposed he was following the tracks of a bear in the snow when he suddenly caught a glimpse of the object of his search. "Blue Sol" said long black hair covered the body of the man and that he wore a breech cloth and shoulder piece made of the skins of wild animals. He also wore moccasins and the thongs which held them together made prints in the snow like the claws of a bear. "Blue Sol" was forced to flee for his life when the "wild man" began hurling huge boulders at him down the mountainside.

He has been reported as having been seen several times since then, a posse of farmers locating his den in 1911. They said the floor was littered with sheep pelts, skins of wild animals and bones left from feasts.

Washington, D.C., *Times,* July 9, 1915

"BLUE MAN" RETURNS TO HIS OZARK HAUNTS

SEARCHING PARTIES IN MISSISSIPPI
UNSUCCESSFULLY TRAIL WILD CREATURE

Springfield, Mo., July 7.—News comes to this city that after an absence of four years the mysterious "Blue Man of Spring Creek" has again appeared in his old haunts and is causing great excitement in the wild and hilly country along the Big North Fork, Indian and Spring creeks, in the eastern end of Douglas county.

It was in the beginning of 1865 that a noted Ozark rifleman and trapper, "Blue Sol" Collins, came across strange tracks in the snow along Spring Creek. He had trailed many a bear, and these tracks resembled a bear's, but this bear must surely be the largest bear in all Missouri. The imprints in the snow were longer and broader than any bear tracks Collins had seen, and along the tracks were queer markings, seemingly made by great claws.

Collins was fearless and followed the footprints, determined to [slay] the greatest bear in the history of the region. Hour after hour he followed the trail. He was toiling up the slope of Twin mountain when he heard a noise on the hill above him. Looking up, he was just in time to leap to one side as a huge bowlder swept past him down into the valley. Another and then another bowlder swiftly followed. When Collins had time to look closely and see what was causing the avalanche of rocks he was terrified.

Saw Gigantic Figure.

On the steep hillside above him stood a gigantic figure. An enormous man, stark naked except for a breech cloth and a shoulder piece of some animal's skin. The huge body was covered in long hair almost black in color, and as thick as that of any wild animal. On the man's feet were rude moccasins of deerskin tied with thongs of leather. The end of these thongs had made the claw-like marks in the snow.

The terrifying figure was armed with a club six or eight feet long. This he had laid aside in order that he might more readily tear the bowlders from the frozen soil. Collins was no coward, but he never denied that after one look at that fearsome figure on the hill he turned and fled.

The Ozarks were a thinly settled region fifty years ago, but several of the scattered families among the hills missed calves, sheep, and hogs, and after long search found discarded hides and clean-picked bones in remote crannies among the hills. Some of them, too, saw the fearsome figure slipping among the woods.

After 1865 the "wild man" disappeared and became no more than a tradition in the remote region. In 1874 he reappeared, was seen by probably a score of men, and was systematically tracked by men skilled in trailing wild animals. But all efforts to capture him were in vain.

During the next sixteen years the "Blue Man" made several trips to his original haunts and on each trip the farmers lost some of their smaller animals. Every incursion was marked by energetic efforts to capture the strange creature now universally known as the "Blue Man of Spring Creek." Why "Blue" no one knows unless the name was given because it was "Blue Sol" Collins who first saw him.

In 1890 it was rumored a party of searchers had captured the quarry so long sought, but this proved false. Evidently, however, they made it too hot for the "Wild Man," for again he disappeared. It was not until 1911 that he again appeared. This time his den was found, but he disappeared.

Not So Fat Nowadays.

Six weeks ago an Ozark farmer noticed two of his lambs did not come home with the rest of the flock. He searched the hills and at last found their bloody pelts in a hollow in a remote part of the woods. The next day he saw the "Blue Man" running down a hog in the woods and since then several other farmers have seen the creature. The wild man is said to be less robust than formerly. His blue-black coat of hair now is iron gray and his limbs are not as well muscled as formerly. Nevertheless, it may be safely wagered that there is not a man among the sturdy Ozark mountaineers who would like to risk combat single-handed with the fearsome creature.

Before the Revolution, while this region was yet under the flag of France, it is said that a French Indian trader came into the Ozarks, bringing with him a beautiful Spanish woman, a native of Florida. Somewhere in the region the trader abandoned the woman or sold her to the Indians. From this poor outcast descended a race of Indian-Spanish half-breeds. One of these in the third or fourth generation may be the "Blue Man of Spring Creek." This was the theory of "Uncle Jerry" Hildebrand, who settled in what is now Douglas county in 1830, and lived there until 1885.

In the course of nature the "Blue Man" cannot be expected to live much longer. Whether he ever will be caught or whether the secret of his long absences and mysterious returns will ever be solved is doubtful.

Kansas City, Missouri, *Star*, October 24, 1915

THE WILD MAN OF THE OZARKS

Terror reigns supreme in the Spring Creek country; fear grips the hearts of those Ozark mountaineers. From Tater hill to Collins Ford and from Blue Buck Mountain to the Ava Crossing, many miles to the west, people are searching for the Blue Man of Spring Creek. No cattle are allowed to graze on the long wild grass; the sheep that range on the hill slopes are watched by herders—silent, determined hill men with long range rifles. Each night all live stock is locked up. Nobody ventures away from his home unarmed. The churches are closed. Probably no attempt will be made to open the schools soon. People, armed with shotguns and rifles, search the woods, over the hills and across the valleys, up the ravines, through glade and glen, anywhere, everywhere, for the Blue Man of Spring Creek.

Some weeks ago the Blue Man was seen on Spring Creek, four miles from Old Horton, the first time he had appeared in this country since May, 1911. Oc Collins had lost two lambs; he went to search for him through the woods and found their pelts in a hollow tree. The next day he saw the Blue Man chasing a hog on the range near the mouth of Spring Creek. Two days later Cap Turner saw him catching fish with his hands in the Big Indian Creek. In the twinkling of an eye he saw Turner, and swinging an immense club wildly, the Blue Man chased the intruder up the steep hillside.

Carried Off A Live Sheep.

One Sunday two boys, who were swimming in Spring Creek near the Collins Ford, saw the Blue Man stealthily creep down the rugged mountain side, grab a full grown sheep from a flock grazing in the hollow and carry it into a nearby cave. The boys at once set out to spread the news. A posse was soon organized. Nearly a score of men were climbing up the mountain to the entrance of the cave when the Blue Man stepped out of the hole, gazed for a full half minute at the posse and again disappeared into the opening. Among the posse was Cal Alsup, a man of extraordinary courage and daring. Taking a short barreled shotgun for a weapon he sprang into the cave den after the terrible Blue Man. The posse heard much commotion inside the cave. They heard Cal Alsup discharge both barrels of his shotgun, then all was quiet. They waited at the mouth of the cave den for a long time, probably two hours. They shouted into the cave, but only the echoes answered. Not one of the posse dared enter the hole in the mountain side in search of their companion. Surely, this awful wild man, who had killed so many of their animals, had made short work of Alsup. But not so, Alsup soon appeared over the crest of the ridge from the opposite side of the divide. He had followed the Blue Man through an underground passage to an opening two miles away. When Alsup first entered the cave the Blue Man showed fight, but when the gun was fired the wild creature fled. His assailant followed, but was soon outdistanced. The darkness was intense, and many times when Alsup groped along he stumbled over objects he knew to be the withered pelts of sheep or the dried-up hides of hogs and calves that long ago had made meals for the Blue Man. None, except this wild creature, had known of this mammoth cave and subterranean passage until Alsup made his exploration. The floor was littered with feathers, pelts, hair and bones. But nothing in the cave indicated the Blue Man had any knowledge of the use of fire.

Since eluding his pursuers so successfully the Blue Man has been seen again. This time at the Ava Crossing on Indian Creek and by a woman, Pamrella Collins. He was catching crayfish from under the rocks in the creek, biting off and eating their tails. He saw the woman, but contented himself by allowing her to do all the running, while he quietly finished his meal.

This is not the Blue Man's first visit to the hills. Indeed, he may be called an old settler. He has been in the Spring Creek country many times during the past half century.

His First Appearance.

One morning in the early spring of 1865— fifty years ago— Blue Sol Collins, who lived on Upper Indian Creek, set out for his daily hunt. Blue Sol was past 60, and had lived in the Ozarks since early youth. He lived by hunting, trapping and fishing. On this particular day he decided to hunt deer far to the west. A light snow had fallen the night before. The woodland was covered with a myriad of tracks, deer tracks, wolf tracks, turkey tracks, rabbit, fox and 'coon tracks, but most noticeable were long, broad tracks with clawlike impressions in the soft snow. Blue Sol had come after deer, but if he could get a bear—and those big tracks with the claw prints were surely the tracks of the biggest bear in the Ozarks—the deer could wait. He set out on the trail. After following the long broad tracks for several hours, Blue Sol was beginning to lose hope. Just before sundown he came suddenly upon the object of his search as he was climbing the north slope of Upper Twin Mountain. Collins looked, jumped out of the path of several descending boulders and ran. He hardly slackened his pace until he had reached his home. On the mountainside above him, a giant figure, unmistakably human, had hurled huge rocks at him. A figure nearly seven feet high—powerful, gorilla-like arms—a mat of blue-black hair covered his body—he wore a shoulder piece and breech-cloth of some animal skin. His feet were covered with deer hide moccasins, held together by thongs of buckskin that made the clawlike appearance in the snow. By his side was a huge club six or seven feet long, which he probably used in hand to hand conflicts.

Blue Sol Collins never saw the wild man again. Five years later, Sol was killed by a wounded buck near Rosin Ridge in Western Howell County.

His Regular Raids.

In 1874 the Blue Man was said to have been seen again. Tom Green had carried a bushel of corn and an empty jug to Dumwright's mill and still house on North Fork. Somewhere on the return trip, he couldn't remember just where, he had seen the Blue Man. According to tom the wild man was carrying a cow; he had acted very vicious and had given vent to his feelings by roaring like a lion and chasing Tom down the trail about half a mile. No credence was given to Green's story.

But the Blue Man was seen many times between 1874 and 1890. During those years he made his home in the Spring Creek Hills, stealing small stock from the different farmers, as he pleased, and nobody paid any particular attention to him.

In time he disappeared and everybody supposed him dead, but in 1911 he came back. A posse headed by Oc Collins raided his den, and finding him gone, they set a large sawtoothed bear trap on the floor of his cave. By some peculiar accident the Blue Man was caught by two fingers. Knowing of no better way to get loose than by giving up his fingers, he pulled them off at the second joints, where the trap had cut them nearly in two.

After losing his fingers the Blue Man disappeared again, this time for four years. He reappeared in his old haunts last May. He is not as robust as he was fifty years ago when he threw boulders at Blue Sol Collins. His once time blue black hair is snowy white; his body is lean and gaunt, but his muscles are not flabby. He is erect and very fleet of foot. He is an old, old man, but powerful withal.

Who Is He?

Who is this wild, hairy giant of the hills? Nobody knows. Two traditions are handed down about him, either of which may be true. According to one story he is of French, Spanish and Indian blood—a descendant of traders who visited this country before the Revolution. One of the traders was accompanied by a beautiful Spanish woman from Florida. He cast her aside somewhere in the Ozarks. She was adopted by an Indian tribe and became the chief's wife. The Blue Man of Spring Creek is their grandson. The Blue Man's mother (a daughter of the Spanish woman) was very beautiful. When only 15 years old she ran away with a young Frenchman. They went to live in the caves of the hills away from the Indians. They were killed by warriors of a hostile Indian tribe when the Blue Man was a mere child. He escaped and remained in the hills which he knew so well. Thus thrown on his own resources he became a wild, man-animal of the forests. Such was the story of Jerry Hildebrand, who settled in Douglas County in the early part of the last century and died there in 1885.

The other tradition about the Blue Man says he is a child of the Lost Camp. Many years before the Civil War a family of pioneers bound for the Far West camped in a fertile valley of Howell County—now known as Lost Camp Valley. Howell County at that time was a dense wilderness. Mighty forests stood on every hand. The wolf and the bear ruled supreme. Some time during the night the movers' 6-year-old son disappeared from the camp. Not until morning did his parents know he was gone. They searched everywhere for him, but to no avail. He was never found. His mother died of a broken heart and his father went on toward the gold fields.

Some folks think the Blue Man of Spring Creek is the same person who, eighty years ago, wandered away from the campfire in his sleep.

Joplin, Missouri, *News Herald*, July 28, 1924

APE ROAMING IN E. JOPLIN; ATTACKS DOG

Joe Frakes isn't inclined to be a drinking man. Therefore it is proper to assume that Joe doesn't "see things." Joe is the watchman at Miners park and the story he relates of the nocturnal visits of a large ape is told without exaggeration.

Frakes has seen the "bugger" as he calls it, and Sunday night his two dogs, which he keeps at the park, got into something of an argument with the visitor as a sprinkling of hair in the grandstand will testify.

According to Frakes, the ape made his escape by running to the top tier of seats in the stand and making a flying leap onto the roof which extends over the entrance. From there he made one leap to the ground and disappeared. His footprints are visible on the roof. Frakes said that he understood the ape had escaped from its owner and was roaming wild, having the "scalp" of one dog to his credit already.

Salamanca, New York, *Republican Press*, February 20, 1925

LEGEND OF "BLUE MAN" TOLD AGAIN IN OZARKS

Ava, Mo.—With renewed reports of depredations by panthers and other animals in the wilds of the Ozark mountains, the older residents of Douglas county are recalling the legend of the "Blue Man of Spring Creek."

This is one of the many legends of the Ozark country, and the pioneer residents declare that it is true. It deals with a huge, manlike creature, more than nine feet high, of a purple color, which is said to have terrorized the countryside nearly sixty years ago. Many of the old residents have declared they saw the creature, and one man asserts he had a hair-raising encounter with it.

Winona, Missouri, *Shannon County Democrat,* June 25, 1925

WHICH IS IT, WILD MAN, APE OR GORILLA?

More or less excitement has been cause the past three or four weeks by reports coming here that a wild man, ape or gorilla, had been seen near Alton, by the farmers out in that neighborhood.

The first report coming in was that a peculiar looking beast crossed the state highway some three weeks ago and was noticed by some of the road hands. A little later, parties northeast of town had seen something in the woods that walked upright like a man that soon disappeared in the thick undergrowth and was lost sight of. However the latest report comes from Lewis Bates, who lives two miles out on Greer road, who says last Wednesday his children first saw it and told him about it, and he went out to where they told him it was, riding a mule, and got within 50 yards of it and was able to see it plainly, and he terms it an animal that walks upright like a man, rather brown hair all over it and had a face something like a monkey. He said when he tried to ride closer it ran and was soon lost sight of in some thick brush.

Several parties living out in the neighborhood where it was seen, got together Sunday and tried to get a look at it but were unsuccessful.—Alton *Democrat.*

Washington, Missouri, *Citizen,* July 10, 1925

FARMERS SEE WILD MAN

A few years ago much excitement was created in Oregon county by a "wampus" which roamed the woods around Rover and Thomasville. Now the excitement in that county is caused by a wild man or animal in the country east and north of Alton. The Alton South Missourian-Democrat says of the excitement: "More or less excitement has been caused in the past three or four weeks by reports coming to Alton that a wild man, ape, or gorilla had been seen east and north of Alton by the farmers out in that neighborhood. The first report coming in was that a peculiar looking beast had crossed the state highway some three weeks ago and was noticed by some of the road hands. A little later parties out northeast of town had seen something in the woods that walked upright like a man that soon disappeared in the thick underbrush and was lost sight of. The last report comes from Lewis Bates, who lives two miles out on the Greer road, who says last Wednesday his children first say it and told him about it. He went out to where they told him it was and got within 50 yards of it, and was able to see it plainly and he terms it an animal that walks upright like a man, rather brown hair all over, and had a face something like a monkey. He said when he tried to ride closer to it, the thing ran and was lost sight of in some thick brush."—Howell County Gazette.

Houston, Missouri, *Herald,* August 5, 1937

Wild Man—Four Houston boys out for a drive Sunday evening report seeing a large hairy man clad in nature's garments and carrying a big club cross the road at a distance in front of them near the Springs Ford north of town. The boys were Frank and Walker Burkhead and two Achen boys. A search was made for the "wild man" Monday without success.

St. Louis, Missouri, *Globe-Democrat,* September 8, 1947

APE-LIKE BEAST TERRORIZES FAMILY IN WILDS OF OZARKS

An "ape-like beast" has been terrorizing a family of six huddled in their farm home in an isolated section of the Ozark foothills near Fredericktown, Mo., for two weeks, a St.

Louisan who participated in an unsuccessful hunt Saturday reported yesterday.

Agnes, 10-year-old daughter of George Slocum, the farmer, first saw the animal which she said "was like an ape I saw at the St. Louis Zoo," according to Oliver B. Ferguson, publisher of the *Democrat-News* at Fredericktown.

The St. Louisan, W. L. Hale, 62-year-old Public Service Company streetcar operator, brought back with him a plaster cast which he said was made of a footprint of the animal.

Hale, who lives at 6828 Magnolia ave., said he joined with four other heavily armed men, accompanied by four dogs, in scouring the area.

"It is one of the wildest, roughest territories in Missouri," Hale asserted. He is a native of Fredericktown and was visiting there on vacation when he read of the "ape" in the *Democrat-News*.

"Slocum said he and his family have heard weird cries from the orchard at night. He said he is terrified because of fear something may happen to his children," Ferguson said.

Slocum's nearest neighbor is about a mile away, Hale said. About 10 families live in the hilly area known as Boswell's Community, about seven miles south of Fredericktown.

Hale said John Lute and his son, Gene, of Fredericktown, both of whom accompanied him Saturday, told him they saw and shot at the beast Labor Day.

Chief Deputy Sheriff E. R. Bayless of Madison County, said authorities are skeptical of the story.

Sedalia, Missouri, *Democrat,* September 5, 1958

FACT OR FICTION? THAT BEAMAN THING POSES BIG QUESTION

[An unknown animal roamed the Beaman area. Strange cries were heard, including a scream "like a child" which was thought might be a wildcat. While driving, a trio of youth saw something "with shaggy brown hair, a big leg and foot disappear in a corn field." One thought it "must be seven or eight feet tall." State troopers and conservation agents looked for it, without luck. The article notes, "These reports bring back reminders of several reports by motorists last spring who saw something resembling either a gorilla or a bear along Highway 65, once south of Carrollton, later between Marshall and Marshall Junction, and a day or two later in the area of Bothwell Lodge."]

Montana

Anaconda, Montana, *Standard,* August 20, 1892

WITH GUN AND FISH POLE

HUNTERS AND ANGLERS LEAVE
FOR STREAM AND FOREST

. . . Some of the old-time hunters and Indian fighters, who are still holding out in the city, should endeavor to find a wild-eyed individual who came in from the mountains this morning. Whether he discovered a new brand of whisky or whether it was the loneliness of this life in the mountains that caused him to see visions and hear sounds is not known, but, whatever the cause, he had told a story that knocks Joe Klaffki's ghost story, attested to by Jack Brennan, completely in the shade. He said that over in the range of mountains which form part of the Wyoming line he had seen evidence of the existence of a creature whose genus was unknown to him. He also claimed to have obtained a glimpse of the "varmit," but always when he was unarmed, and as its appearance

633

**1 Wyoming Line mountainous area (now Yellow-
stone National Park**

was such as not to invite a close inspection
he had never sought to get near enough to
it to see just what it was. He says the animal is covered with hair, but in form it is
not unlike a man, a resemblance that is increased by the creature's habit of rising on
its haunches and walking on its hind legs
after the manner of a gorilla. After having
seen the animal the man said he could account for the existence of the torn and partly
eaten carcasses of several large bears and
also of one mountain sheep that he claimed
to have found in the vicinity of where the
unknown animal apparently makes his headquarters. The stranger says he will return to
the mountain shortly and will pilot anybody
who may desire to visit the locality to the
exact spot where he last saw the monster.

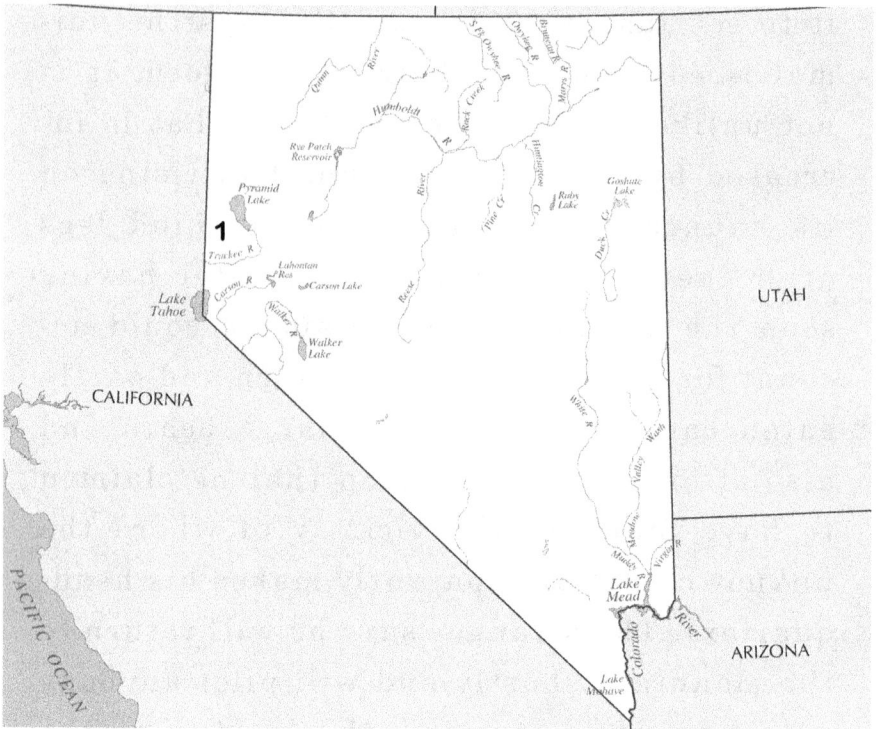

1 Antelope Valley

Nevada

Sacramento, California, *Daily Union,* November 8, 1879
A STRANGE CREATURE.
TWO HUNTERS CHASED BY A WILD MAN
IN THE ANTELOPE MOUNTAINS.

William Shegan, who came in from Antelope
Valley last evening with a load of produce,
tells a Leader reporter a very strange and
startling story of the experience of two men
who were hunting in Antelope valley last
week. He says that Peter Simons and John
Gore had been out all day hunting ducks and
such other game as came in their way, and as
evening came on they took a short cut across
the mountains on their way back to the ranch.
The mountain over which the trail led them
was a very rugged one—in fact, the wildest
place in the Antelope range of mountains—
and a few years ago used to be infested with
the larger species of wild animals. As they
were slowly picking their way around the
edge of a large chasm, they heard a slight
noise near a rugged cliff, and saw a huge,

hairy object, apparently half man and half beast, spring from behind a cliff and start for the other side of the mountain, running with the speed of the wind. Mistaking it for a wild animal, one of the hunters, Gore, fired at it. The shot appeared to take effect in the arm, for, with a scream of pain, the creature halted, tapped the wound, and, turning, charged its pursuers, who, with empty guns in hand, dared not measure strength with such a foe. Dropping their guns, both sought safety in flight, and stopped only when compelled to do so from lack of ability to run farther. The men say that they are positive that the creature resembled a man in general appearance. It was wild-eyed, and very fierce in its disposition, judging from the short time they saw it. Mr. Shegan's story revives a long-forgotten but now distinctly recalled yarn, to the effect that many years ago a lunatic, then a young man, escaped from his keepers in California and gained the fastnesses of the Sierra Nevada, where he evaded pursuit, and, it is thought, subsisted on the flesh of small animals killed through some means best known to himself. Several months ago, says Shegan, a strange creature answering the description of the being recently seen, with the exception of the grizzly beard, was discovered by a party of men who were hunting on the mountain some fifteen miles from Antelope, and it is thought that this may be the same. The hunters say they are positive that it was no optical illusion, but a genuine wild man, and a very fierce one at that. The creature's arms, they say, were long and hairy, and it looked very much like a full-grown gorilla. They aver that it ran with remarkable swiftness, all the time uttering loud cries, as though in pain and enraged. They declare that it was only by their utmost exertion that they escaped their pursuer, and they say that there is not money enough in Nevada to hire them to again venture across its path. Mr. Shegan says there is talk of organizing an armed force in Antelope valley to go in search of this creature.—[Eureka (Nev.) *Leader,* November 1st.]

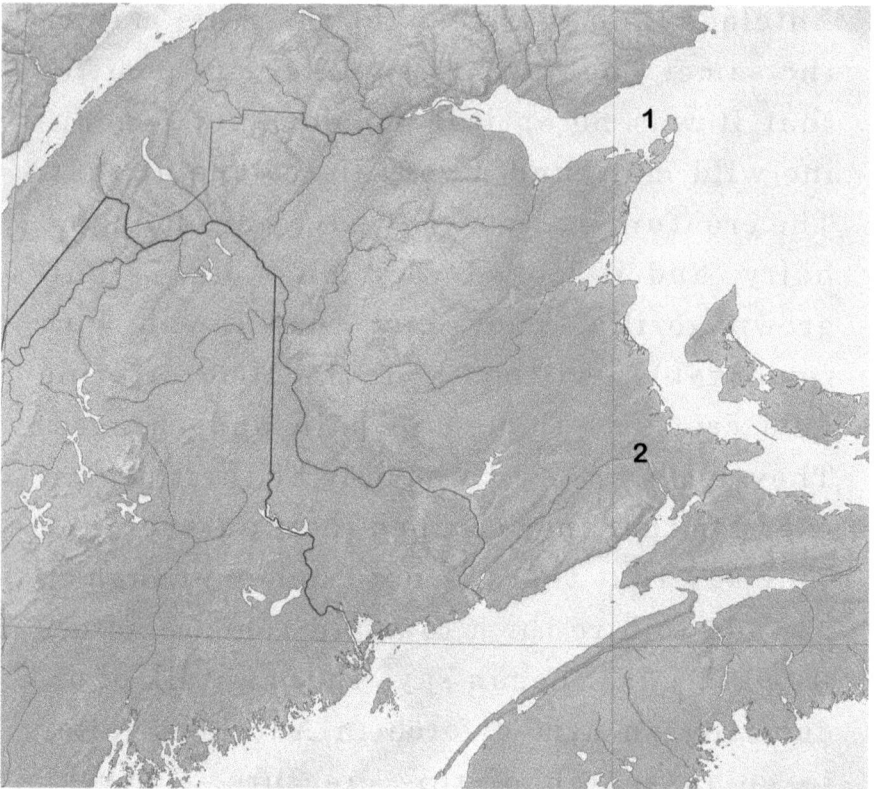

(CC BY-SA) Sémhur

1 Chaleur Bay

2 Moncton

New Brunswick

Samuel de Champlain (1922) collected a Micmac story in the early 1600s that many enthusiasts have cited as relevant to Bigfoot. We don't have enough details on these "horrible noises" to determine if this story truly is applicable, but later iterations of the folkloric being Gougou (or Gugwes, Kukwes, etc.) may be intertwined with accounts of manlike beasts. The (translated) passage notes:

> There is still one strange thing, worthy of an account, which many savages have assured me was true; that is, that near the Bay of Heat [Chaleur Bay], toward the south, there is an island where a frightful monster makes his home, which the savages call Gougou, and which they told me had the form of a woman, but very terrible, and of such a size that they told me the tops of the masts of our vessel would not reach to his waist, so great do they represent him; and they say that he has often eaten up and still continues to eat up many

savages; these he puts, when he can catch them, into a great pocket, and afterward he eats them; and those who had escaped the danger of this awful beast said that its pocket was so great that it could have put our vessel into it. This monster makes horrible noises in this island, which the savages call the Gougou; and when they speak of it, it is with unutterable fear, and several have assured me that they have seen him. Even the abovementioned Sieur Prevert from St. Malo told me that, while going in search of mines, as mentioned in the preceding chapter, he passed so near the haunt of this terrible beast, that he and all those on board his vessel heard strange hissings from the noise she made, and that the savages with him told him it was the same creature, and that they were so afraid that they hid themselves wherever they could, for fear that she would come and carry them off. What makes me believe what they say is the fact that all the savages in general fear her, and tell such strange things of her that, if I were to record all they say of her, it would be considered as idle tales, but I hold that this is the dwelling-place of some devil that torments them in the manner described. This is what I have learned about this Gougou.

1870s: Green (1978) noted a report collected by Loren Coleman regarding a creature, "very squatty, with long arms and with its entire body covered with hair," seen multiple times at the edge of woods near Moncton, New Brunswick.

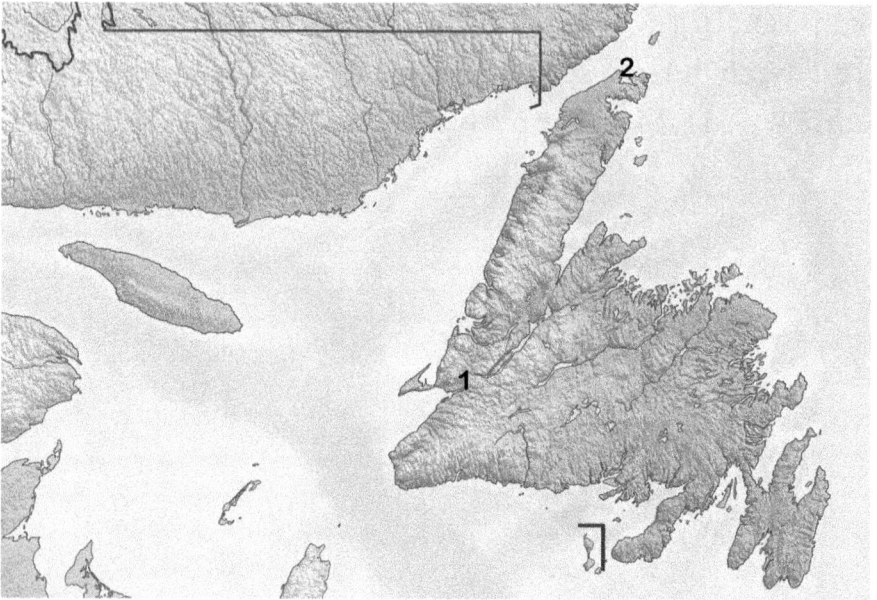

1 Indian Head

2 Pistolet Bay

Newfoundland

Taft (1980) noted several accounts of giant "Indians" who left large footprints. In one account, taken from the mid to late 1800s, a group of men fishing along Indian Head encountered two "Indians," one of which was shot and killed, while the other disappeared into the forest. (Apparently, fishermen in that area often came back to camp to find their gear and equipment destroyed, so they believed these were the culprits.) The "Indian" was "approximately nine feet tall, covered with hair from an inch to an inch and a half. He had on no clothing whatsoever." The body was towed back to town and buried. In another account, during the 1890s, a William Decker was hunting along Pistolet Bay when a giant manlike creature charged him in a marsh. He killed it with three shots, and roughly measured the hair-covered body at ten to twelve feet tall, an outstretched arm-span of fourteen feet, and perhaps weighing one thousand pounds. He left it where it fell.

1 Greenville (Hillsborough County)

2 Sandwich (Carroll County)

New Hampshire

Springfield, Massachusetts, *Republican,* November 3, 1895
ANOTHER WILD MAN APPEARS.
[FROM THE TROY BUDGET.]

The people of Greenville, bordering upon the southeastern boundary of New Hampshire, are excited over what they call a gorilla seen in the woods of that forest section. On Tuesday, a party of young men were out gunning for squirrels. After firing they were startled to see a large beast jump from the brush and disappear into the forest. Their story is vouched for by a reputable New Ipswich man. The same evening a young man who lives a short distance out of town, when nearing the cemetery, heard growling, with noise in the brushwoods. He saw the same figure and started on the run.

A party of men with guns went in pursuit of the gorilla Wednesday, but found no trace of the beast. Another party informs a correspondent that the gorilla was seen in that vicinity some weeks ago. The hardy and brave pioneers of that forest section are greatly excited over affairs, and are determined to make aggressive warfare upon the animal or whatever it may prove to be.

1942: Green (1978) noted a reported sighting in Central Sandwich. The creature was 6 to 7 feet tall and gorilla-like, walking on two legs. It followed the witness for about 20 minutes.

New Jersey

Jersey City, New Jersey, *News,* October 26, 1896
A GORILLA ROAMING FREE.

Somerville, Oct. 26, 1896.—The inhabitants of the Watchung Mountains, six miles north of this place, are greatly excited over the supposed presence of a monster gorilla.

Three weeks ago four strangers drove through the valley in search of the gorilla which they said had escaped from a circus caravan near Morristown. A week later Zipp Wyckoff, a farm hand, encountered the big beast on Round Top Mountain, near Bernardsville. He pelted the beast with rocks until it retreated into the bushes.

Two days after Wyckoff's encounter with the gorilla, it is thought the same beast entered a sheepfold near Round Top and killed three sheep.

New Haven, Connecticut, *Register*, October 20, 1899
Queer Beast in Jersey

Phillipsburg, Oct. 20.—For several days past farmers have reported a mysterious animal

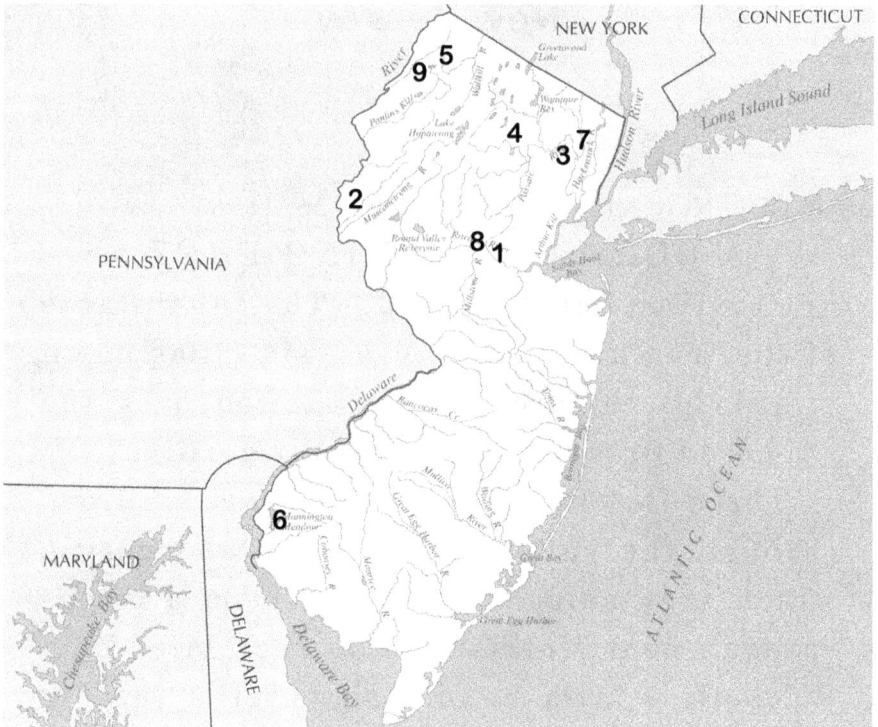

1 Watchung Mountains

2 Phillipsburg (Warren County)

3 Montclair (Essex County)

4 Dover (Morris County)

5 Sussex County

6 Salem (Salem County)

7 Clifton (Passaic County)

8 Berkshire Valley

9 Bear Swamp

on Marble Hill, a few miles above Phillipsburg. It has been described as ranging from
the size of a sheep to that of a cow. No one
claims to have obtained a good look at the
creature, which goes crashing through the
brush when approached. All who have had a
glimpse of or heard the animal report that
it makes a sound like "Hoo-hoo," roared long
and loudly.

Such an animal was reported in the vicinity of Lambertville, in Hunterdon County,
a year ago. The proximity of the animal to
the State Turnpike today caused a wheelman
named Shields to stop and investigate, but
he could find no traces of the beast.

Two chestnut hunting parties were put to
flight by the strange roaring.

Hornellsville, New York, *Evening Tribune,* July 31, 1900

WILD MAN IN JERSEY.

CITIZENS OF MONT CLAIR TERRORIZED
BY AN UNCAUGHT FREAK.

New York, July 31.—Policemen are making
search of the woods on the outskirts of Mont
Clair, N.J., in an effort to find a giant wild
man, with long, streaming hair, who for days
has been spreading terror throughout the
neighborhood of his haunt.

They have found every evidence that a savage being of some kind has been inhabiting

the strip of forest. There are the gnawed bones of animals and fowls which have fallen victims to the prowess of the wild huntsman. In several places were discovered the embers of fires. Near one of the heaps of ashes was a rude club.

The wild man himself cannot be found, although a posse beat the woods carefully. The news that a wild being is at large has thrown the town into a state of excitement.

Reno, Nevada, *State Journal,* February 4, 1909

MAN OR BIG APE; IT'S TERRIFYING

WILD CREATURE IS FUR CLAD, RUNS ON ALL FOURS AND LIVES IN TREES

New York, Feb. 3.—There is a wild man roaming the woods near Dover, N. J., if the stories told by more than one hunter are credited. They say the creature, apparently half man and half monkey, runs part of the time on all fours and part of the time upright. All agree that the man or beast, whichever it is, is powerfully built and is clothed apparently in long brown-gray fur. None of the hunters have been close enough to get a good look at the creature, because it darts away when approached.

John Nee, of Bowlbyville, was the first man to run across the strange prowler. He was out after a fox Tuesday with gun and hound when he heard a strange answering bray to the cries of his dog. At first he paid no attention, but as it came nearer he made up his mind that another hunter was after the same game, and went in the direction of the sound. Suddenly through an opening in the trees he saw the wild man. At sight of Nee's dog the wild man turned and made away through the underbrush at great speed, sometimes running erect and at other times running on all fours. The creature frequently jumped, catching low branches and aiding its flight by long swings.

For an instant the dog hesitated as if debating whether to give chase or flee. Then with a low whine, it turned tail and ran hard for home. Nee, who had stood spellbound, got scared too and followed the example of the dog. So deeply was he affected by his experience that he told no one of it until yesterday, and then he learned that others had seen the creature and were just as timid about telling of it as he. Adventurous persons are about to organize a hunting expedition and hope to capture the strange man or beast.

Kennebec, Maine, *Daily Kennebec Journal,* February 3, 1909

New Jersey claims to have a wild man as yet uncaptured who "gallops on all fours." Unquestionably, he is a gargoyle.

1920: Berry (1993) noted a report by a farmer in Green Township, Sussex County, who tripped over an animal in his pasture at night. He initially thought it was a cow, but it stood up on two legs, was taller than a man, and was covered in fur. The farmer took off running.

New York, New York, *Daily News,* August 29, 1927

WILD MAN HUNTED

Salem, N.J., Aug. 27—After Tommie Smith, 15, told Sheriff J. Enos how a "big hairy man without any clothes" beat him and smashed his bicycle on an isolated road near here, a posse was organized for a wild man hunt here today.

Ashbury Park, New Jersey, *Press,* April 5, 1929

GORILLA SCARE RESULTS
IN CHILDREN'S ESCORT

Clifton, April 5 (AP).—Rumors that a gorilla escaped from a circus train when it passed thru here last week on the way to New York has developed into a scare in this town which today found the streets deserted of children.

Mrs. J. Donovan of Madeline avenue, found a "very large impression of a palm" on a clothes pole in her back yard. She called the police, pictures were taken, and it was decided that a gorilla had climbed the pole.

Word spread quickly thruout the community. Children were escorted to and from school, policemen on beats were ordered to keep a sharp lookout and citizens walked about peering furtively into trees and behind hedges.

1939: Berry (1993) noted a report by a group of coon hunters in the Berkshire Valley. They encountered a large hairy manlike creature that killed several dogs and threw a man who got too near. It ran off into a swamp.

1940: Berry (1993) noted a report by a Native American trapper who saw a 7-foot tall manlike creature walking in Bear Swamp.

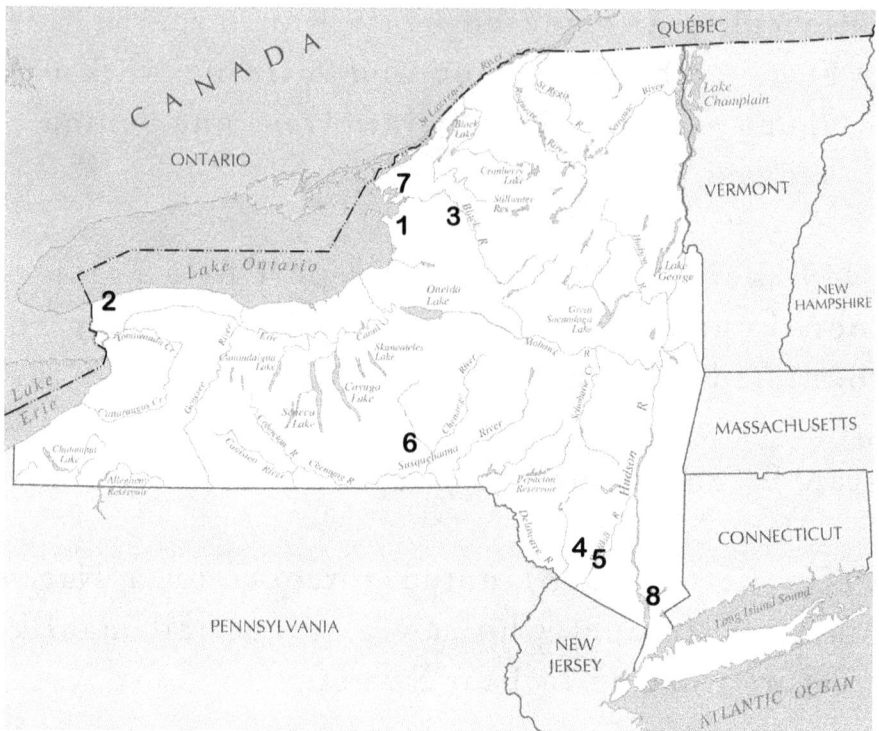

1 Ellisburg (Jefferson County)

2 Niagara County

3 Lewis County

4 New Hampton (Wawayanda, Orange County)

5 Florida and Glenmere Lake (Orange County)

6 Maine (Broome County)

7 Big Run (Jefferson County)

8 Kensico (dead placename, flooded to build reservoir; Westchester County)

New York

Lowville, New York, *Journal and Republican,* August 18, 1921
SACKETTS HARBOR *GAZETTE* DATED OCTOBER 8,
1818.

One particular, interesting advertisement is as follows: "Report says that in the vicinity of Ellisburgh was seen on the 30th ult, by a gentleman of unquestioned veracity, an animal resembling the Yo-ho, or Wild Man of the Woods. It is stated that he came from the woods within a few rods of this gentleman— that he stood and looked at him, and then took his flight in a direction which gave a perfect view of him for some time. He is described as bending forward when running—hairy—and the heel of the foot narrow, spreading at the toes. Hundreds of persons have been in pursuit for several days; but nothing further is heard or seen of him. The frequent and positive manner in which this story comes, induces us to notice it. We wish not to impeach the veracity of this highly favored gentleman—yet, it is proper that

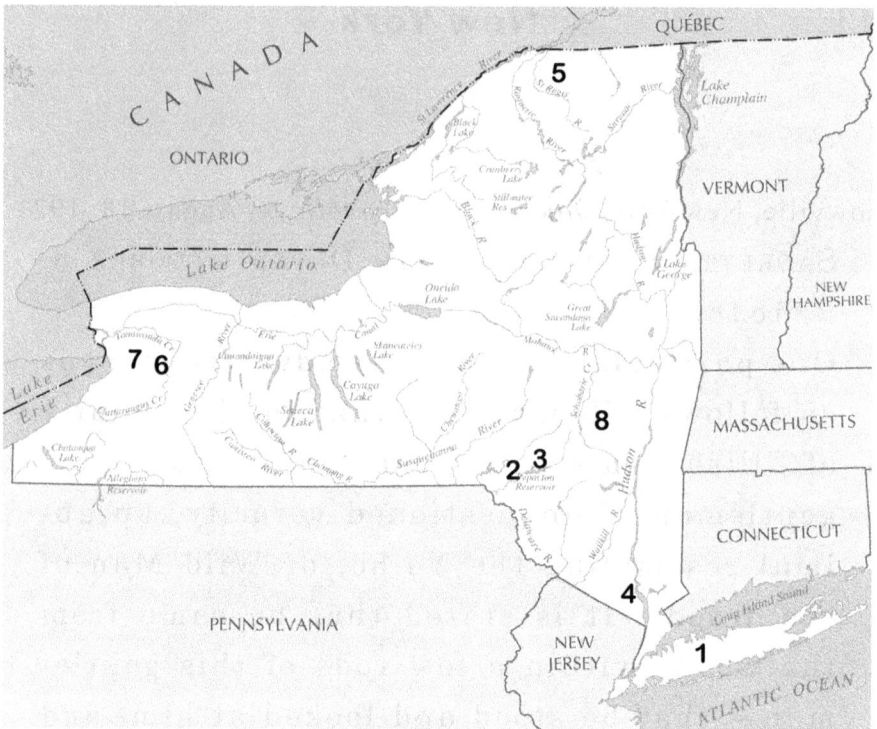

1 Long Island

2 Delaware County

3 Margaretville (Delaware County)

4 Spring Valley (Rockland County)

5 Skerry (Brandon, Franklin County)

6 Wyoming County

7 Alden (Erie County)

8 West Settlement (Ashland, Greene County)

LONG ISLAND

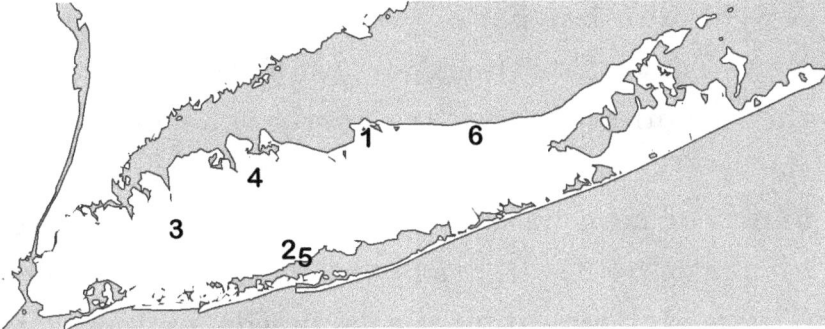

1 Setauket (Suffolk County)

2 Babylon (Suffolk County)

3 Mineola (Nassau County)

4 Huntington (Suffolk County)

5 Amityville (Babylon, Suffolk County)

6 Wading River (Suffolk County)

such naturally impossible events should be established by the mouth of at least two or three eye witnesses, to entitle them to credibility."

Reading, Pennsylvania, *Times,* July 19, 1865

A wild man has been seen in Niagara county, New York. The Lockport Journal says: "If the accounts we get are correct, he is one of the rarest specimens of humanity. Organized bands of men have been out to take him, but hitherto, by his fleetness he has eluded them. Great excitement prevails in the vicinity of his roving ground.

Silver City, Idaho, *Owyhee Semi-Weekly Tidal Wave,* November 5, 1869

A party of coon hunters in Lewis county, N.Y., says the Lowville Journal, consisting of three men and three boys, were recently badly frightened by the appearance of a wild man on the shore of Black lake. He jumped on one of the party, tried to bite him, etc. The men picked up the boys, fled into a corn field and eluded him.

New York, New York, *Times,* August 7, 1870

A WILD MAN DISCOVERED
NEAR NEW-HAMPTON, N. Y.

A wild man has been discovered near New-Hampton, Orange County, who is creating quite an excitement in that vicinity. A few days ago a party of gentlemen were out shooting along the Big Ditch, a stream which flows through the town, when their attention was attracted by a strange being in a nude state, with long hair and a wild appearance, who appeared to be a man who had been running wild for some time, and who probably had been living in the mountains. He was apparently busy in the destruction of frogs and snakes, and when he observed the party he set up a fierce yell and fled for the woods. A small party gave chase, but was unable to ascertain his whereabouts. He has since been seen by several of the citizens of Dolsontown, but he manages to keep always at a distance. It is probable that he is an escaped lunatic.

Helena, Montana, *Independent,* June 12, 1881

A WILD MAN.

THE SINGULAR CREATURE LIVING
IN A NEW JERSEY CAVERN.

Philadelphia, May 29—The *Times* has the following to-night from Newton, Sussex county, N. J.: On the farm of William D. Green on the road from the village of Florida

[NY] to Glen Moor Lake, not far from here, is a cave inhabited by a nondescript, partaking of the human form. Some time ago this animal was seen by two men named Armstrong and Sullivan, who were at work in a field near the cave. It so much resembled a human being, that Armstrong, who was eating his lunch, asked it to take a piece of bread, whereupon it gritted its teeth and fled to the cave, remaining in sight only a few seconds. Several persons have endeavored to entrap it, but without success. All who have seen it described it as being covered with long, shaggy hair. A few days ago, Ira Seybolt, a well known hunter, chanced to pass the cave, and saw the animal lying at length upon a stone wall, when with a mingled cry of pain and rage, it leaped from the wall and fled into the cave. Mr. Green, on whose farm the cave is located, now has a quantity of hair about eight inches long, which was cut from the body of the creature by Seybold's shot. The creature walks upright and prowls considerably at night, making unearthly noises. There are a variety of conjectures as to what the "thing" is. There is not a man in the entire section who could be induced to enter the cave under any circumstances. The entrance to the cave is small but is said to have a very

large interior. Many people believe the creature who inhabits this cave is a wild man,
and a watch is being kept over the mouth of
the "den" to see what manner of creature it
is. The affair has created much excitement
and considerable nervousness in this section,
and the developments are anxiously awaited.
People will not travel the road near where
the cave is located, and Mr. Green could not
sell his otherwise valuable farm at a cent an
acre at present on account of the superstition prevailing among the country people.

Atlanta, Georgia, *Constitution-Sun,* November 25, 1883

HUNTING A WILD MAN.

Binghamton, November 24.—A score of men
are hunting the woods in the vicinity of
Maine, N.Y., for what they believe to be a
wild man. He first appeared in the vicinity
in August last. Before he was seen by any
one, loud and startling cries had been heard
in the woods in different portions of the region. They were believed to emanate from a
panther, and much alarm was felt by bark
peelers and others whose duties called them
into the woods. The berry crop, the gathering
of which has for years afforded a livelihood
for many families in the town, was entirely
neglected in some parts of the neighborhood.

The first knowledge that the cries which
had caused so much terror were those of a
wild man was obtained by a party of berry
pickers in August. He appeared suddenly
out of the bushes and ran rapidly along and
disappeared in the woods, yelling as he ran.
The berry pickers were frightened away. Their
description of the wild man was the regula-
tion one, low in stature, covered with hair,
and running while bent close to the ground.
This description was added to a month later,
by Frank Hayes and John White, employees
of Sherwood's tannery in Maine. They were
loading bark in Lewis's woods, near the Newark Valley road, when suddenly a terrible
shriek came from a clump of bushes near by,
and then the mysterious wild man sprang
out into the opening, where, according to the
tannery men, he repeated his yell, and "ran
off like lightning." He tarried long enough
for the men to see that the description that
had been given was correct, with the additional peculiarity that his arms ended at the
elbows. For some time since then the wild
man seems to have kept himself rather close,
for he was not seen nor heard of until the latter part of October, when William Jennings
met him in the woods about three miles from
here. His shrieks have been heard every

night since, as it is reported from different parts of the township, until last week it
was decided to hunt the mysterious creature
down. Thus far, however, the wild man has
eluded his pursuers.

Brooklyn, New York, *Daily Eagle,* December 2, 1885

THE WILD MAN STILL VISIBLE

DANCING AND SCREECHING
BEFORE PLUNGING INTO THE SEA.

Rockaway Beach is still excited over the mysterious wild man of the sea and last night a
company of New York men went down to the
beach to see the strange creature. They saw
the figure and declare that his body is covered with auburn hair as long as a horse's
mane. John B. Ennis declared this morning
that at eight o'clock last night he met the
wild man near the Atlantic Park. Ennis came
upon the dweller in the sea suddenly. He was
dancing like one deranged, until, catching
sight of Ennis, he gave a peculiar screech
and darted into the sea. Ennis lost sight of
the figure after the first wave broke over it,
and walked the beach for half an hour, pistol
in hand, hoping to see the suspicious person
emerge from the water. Every man on the
beach goes armed, and the women and children do not venture out alone, day or night.

There is a pretty general inclination to shoot the hairy being, as a means of ascertaining whether it is natural or supernatural, but no one will run the risk of being prosecuted if it should turn out that the wild man is only an insane creature.

Brooklyn, New York, *Daily Eagle,* December 3, 1885

THE DEPARTURE
OF THE WILD MAN.

The wild man was not seen on Rockaway Beach last night, having taken his departure for Hoboken yesterday afternoon. The man was an expert swimmer and familiar with the beach, where he as employed last Summer as life saver at Smith & Wainwright's bathing pavilion. He had been hired to create a sensation to attract trade to the beach, but the scheme did not take. He dressed in a buffalo skin, which is on exhibition at the Gem of the Sea.

Maysville, Kentucky, *Daily Evening Bulletin*, November 3, 1886

SCARED BY A BIG GORILLA

A Museum Monster at Large
in Long Island Woods.

New York, Nov. 5.—The villagers of Setauket, L.I., believe there is a gorilla lurking in

the woods which border their town, and they
are fearful of their lives in consequence. The
farmers go armed to their work in the fields
and do not venture out alone after dark.
Their wives would as soon defy an army
of mice as leave the shelter of their home,
and the children are afraid to go to pasture
for the cows, and in some cases have to be
escorted to and from school. The nutting
season is at its height, but the children dare
not venture near the woods. The colored
natives, many of whom go nightly to Stony
Brook, two miles distant, to buy rum, now
make the trip in groups armed with axes and
pitchforks.

Selah Strong is a farmer of Setauket, who
has a fine flock of Southdown sheep. Two
weeks ago the pick of his flock was found
one morning dead in the field with its throat
horribly mangled. There were marks of claws
in the flesh, and [in] a spot of soft ground
near by was an almost human footprint. The
sheep was skinned, and then it was found
that its back was broken. Farmer Strong was
puzzled. A man, he argued, might have broken the animal's back and left the footprint
in the soft ground, but he could not have torn
the flesh about the throat and left the claw

marks. He finally concluded that a man had started the job and that later a beast had finished it.

Two nights afterward Jacob Satterlee, who lives about a mile from Farmer Strong, heard a fearful squeaking in his chicken house. He loaded a double-barreled shotgun and went forth. The chickens had quieted down, but on the floor beneath the roost were three fat hens whose heads had been literally torn from their bodies. There was nothing to indicate who or what had been guilty of the slaughter.

The "bloody butcher," as the unknown trespasser came to be called, remained veiled in mystery for several days. A few evenings since, however, Farmer Jim Addis met with an experience which has satisfied his neighbors as to the true character of the intruder. This is what occurred, as told by himself to the reporter:

"I'd been up in the hills all day plowin', and about dusk I put the team to the wagon and started for home. My off mare was a little lame in one foot and I was drivin' easy. We came down through the lane to the highway, and I stopped and closed up the bars after me. Then I climbed back into my wagon and we headed down into the holler. I was nigh onto the big white oak at the edge o' the swamp when the nigh hoss, Billy, pricked up his ears and took a scent o' the air. He did not seem to like it, and the mare was up to something pesky, too. I naturally looked to see what was wrong, and the first thing I knew we passed within twenty feet of a big ape of some kind. It was just in the edge of the bush and stood on its hind feet, graspin' the limb of a saplin' with one hand. It made a move toward us, and my nigh hoss gosh durn near jumped though his collar. The mare was frightened, too, and they lit out of that holler like they was colts. I wasn't exactly scared, but I looked around and saw the brute watchin' in the middle of the road, and I thought I would let the team git out as quick as they was a mind to. I had two good, square looks at the animal. He stood nigh onto five feet high. His legs was thin up to the knees and then they were quite full. His arms was the same, and he had a little head. He was hair all over, and I didn't see no tail."

This was the story which, connected with the inhuman butchery of sheep and chickens, frightened the quiet village folk. Then the natives began to wonder where the animal had come from, and a party of Sound fishermen was discovered who alleged that a few nights previous a South American trader had sought shelter in the harbor of Port Jefferson, three miles down the coast, and that they had a couple of good-sized gorillas on board. It was further alleged by the fishermen that the animals had escaped while exercising on the deck, and that only one of them had been recaptured. Nobody could be found by the reporter yesterday either in Setauket or Port Jefferson who know who the fishermen were that had told the yarn.

There are many of the villagers of Setauket who have been exercising their imaginations to increase the sensation. A darky named Jerry Woodchuck, a famous hunter, is at present in the lead. He has paralyzed the colored colony by a tale that on Thursday, while hunting for coon in Namakeag [?] Swamp, he came across footprints in the mud which measured twenty-two inches in length. He followed them, so he says, and came across a tremendous gorilla, at least nine feet in height, who stood up to his knees in water and pounded his chest with both fists. Jerry Woodchuck discharged his gun at the beast and fled, or at least that is what he tells his neighbors. Henry Sanford, a farmer, told a grocery crowd at Stoney Brook the other night that the gorilla had stood in the middle of the road and refused to allow him to pass. The animal, he said, slapped its chest violently, producing a sound like a blow on a hollow log. Farmer "Hi" Calkin's son and a schoolboy named Sherman Hawkins each told their playfellows that they had met the gorilla in the woods. Two strange men passed through Setauket on Wednesday, who said they were looking for a gorilla which had escaped from a Brighton Beach museum.

Olean, New York, *Democrat,* November 8, 1888

We thought it was about time for the semi-annual wooly wild man story, and here it comes. The McKean Democrat says that the people in the vicinity of Big Run, Jefferson county, are considerably exercised over the discovery in the woods of tracks about eighteen inches long, which, being unlike those of any known animal, give rise to the belief that they are those of a wild man.

Elmira, New York, *Star-Gazette,* November 26, 1894

IS IT A GORILLA?

WHITE PLAINS COR. NEW YORK HERALD.

There is something loose up Kensico way— something big and brown, with a voice like a calliope; something that is impervious to bird shot fired at short range; something that is not at all nice.

It has scared Kensico folk pretty thoroughly, and has even been accused of peeping in at windows and pursuing belated wayfarers in a hair-raising fashion. It is heard often and seen sometimes in the cranberry woods, a region which includes the hill country above and to the eastward of Kensico Lake. Its presence there is responsible for widespread alarm. Women are afraid to traverse the hill roads at night. Children are kept in the house. The men—when they go abroad at night—carry rifles and shotguns. Indeed, I learned to-day, while investigating the stories of this gorilla-like terror, that many of the inhabitants to the eastward of White Plains have made up hunting parties and scoured the woods of late, armed in many instances with guns, axes and bush scythes.

It is the bush scythe which really gives a proper idea of the state of things in the country about Kensico and N— Hill, for while a story about robbers or ghosts is sufficient to turn out a party armed with guns, it is only since this last apparition announced itself that the community got out its brush scythes and took the trail.

The truth, so far as I could learn it from numerous witnesses during a tour of the country to-day, is that a creature whose shape and voice suggested some member of the gorilla family, has been heard and seen repeatedly, and even shot at, near Kensico Lake during the last month.

John Raven, who runs the Lakeview House, situated between Lake Kensico and the Cranberry Woods, is one of the men who has been hunting the intruder within a few days past. One evening about a week ago he and his wife were called from their house by one of their children, who ran to them in terror and announced that there was a terrible noise in the woods back of the house. They hurried into the yard and heard a series of cries which gave them a sensation of horror in spite of themselves. The Ravens have lived near Cranberry Hill for a long time, and they are familiar with all the voices of the woods. Foxes and owls they know. This was something very different. First they heard a sharp roaring, which seemed to come from a point about 200 yards distant. It was succeeded by a series of piercing shrieks. "Shriek" is the word they use to describe the noise, but they were satisfied that the sound could not have been made by a human being.

Mrs. Raven and the children returned to the house, but her husband and his hired man, armed with guns and accompanied by a dog, started into the woods. The sound was repeated soon, and from its location, the animal seemed to be moving eastward. When they got close to it the dog, which had been growing excited, dashed into a thicket and disappeared. In a few moments the cries were heard again, accompanied by the yelping of the dog and the animal came back on the run. It could not be induced to take the trail again, but followed at the heels of the hunters. The cries became more and more distant after that, and Raven gave up the chase.

One of the hunting parties that set out the following night was made up of Charley and Robert Mosher, Bob Hart and Los Hight. All were armed with guns, and they had with them a coon dog upon whose courage and fighting qualities they could depend.

Plunging into the Cranberry Forest, they traversed the woods in vain until nearly midnight. Charles Mosher had heard the strange cries so often that he had learned to imitate them after a fashion, and when 11 o'clock came and their search had been fruitless, his companions suggested that he call to the "gorilla," as Kensico calls it.

Charles thereupon emitted a tremulous roar and followed it up with a series of piercing shrieks, the peculiarity of which was that the sound seemed to be made by drawing in the breath instead of expelling it. The hunters raised the hammers of their guns and listened. Then, from a spot deep in the thickets by the Cranberry brook, came an answer. They recognized it as the real thing and moved toward it. Mosher signaled again, and again came the answer, much more distinct this time. The dog dashed into the thicket before them, and they could hear him barking wildly, as if circling the enemy.

And then they saw it. Before them was an open space, and as they watched something broke cover on the left and moved into the open. None of them pretends to describe it minutely. Mosher, in telling me about it today, said it walked at one moment and went on all fours at the next, though its forefeet scarcely seemed to touch the ground. When it was in an upright position, he says, it stood about 4½ feet high. The head and neck he could not see plainly. It seemed to be brown or black, and its shape was that of a gorilla. As it paused for an instant, Charles Mosher and Bob Hart fired simultaneously. When the smoke cleared away the creature was gone, and that was the last they saw of it that night.

A careful examination next day, in which all of the parties participated, disclosed curious footprints in the sand where the animal had crossed the old wood road. These Mosher says, were like those which would be made by a human hand, except that the fingers were somewhat indistinct and the thumb mark was widely separated from those of the finger.

The guns used by Mosher and Hart were charged only with bird shot, and even if their aim was true, which is unlikely under the circumstances, the shot was not heavy enough to stop the game.

Charles Mosher and Hart had an even more startling encounter with the creature a night or two afterward, while they were coon hunting. They nearly fell over it, not having been warned by its cries, as usual. The coon dog they had with them attacked it without hesitation. The dog sprang at its throat. They say that the strange creature, instead of biting the dog or running away, simply caught it in a crooked forearm and hurled it against a tree. Mosher and Hart went right home.

New York, New York, *Times,* November 22, 1894

THERE'S NO GORILLA
NEAR WHITE PLAINS

THE STORY OF A ROAMING
APE IS PURELY A "FAKE."

White Plains, N.Y., Nov. 21.—Periodically the people of this vicinity are treated to stories in the newspapers of the appearance of wild animals of different kinds, causing destruction in the outskirts of some of the hamlets in this town, or near by. A few years ago a panther was described as frightening the farmers and killing live stock, but when investigated, the story proved a hoax. Likewise there was a wild man of the woods back of Poundridge, who was described by "eye witnesses," who admitted afterward that they only invented the story for a scare.

The latest in this line is a gorilla, or chimpanzee, which is said to be ranging at large in the vicinity of Kensico Lake, and in the "N— Hills," as a certain locality back of White Plains is called. It is furthermore asserted that a farmer named Mosier, with some others, had seen it and fired with shotguns at it, but diligent inquiry about this village to-day could find no one who ever heard of a farmer named Mosier.

Nor could any one be found who had ever heard of the depredations of the aforesaid gorilla, chimpanzee, et al., and the first they knew that such a dangerous creature was about was in reading of it in the newspapers.

One of the local newspaper men, when asked about the story in the papers this morning, laughed and said: "It is a pure fake. There is nothing in it."

Middletown, New York, *Daily Argus,* July 27, 1895

DELAWARE COUNTY'S WILD MAN.

HE EATS HORSES—DESCRIBED AS A GIANT AND OF HAIRY APPEARANCE—REIGN OF TERROR.

FROM THE WALTON REPORTER.

One night recently, as Peter Thomas was driving along a lonely road, he was startled by seeing a wild-eyed man or ape, whose ferocious appearance frightened him into a state of helplessness. The creature jumped into the road, seized the rear horse, with a single sweep of its long hairy arm tore the harness from the trembling beast, and after breaking the horse's neck with a single deft twist, dragged him into the woods and out of sight. Mr. Thomas was too thoroughly frightened to give a definite description of the creature, but is firm in his declaration that it was a man.

Saturday the excitement was still further increased by the discovery of what had evidently been the camp of the creature. It was run upon by a party of berry pickers in the woods near Rattlesnake hill. A big fire was still smouldering and nearby was a portion of the carcass of Mr. Thomas' horse, and scattered about were the bones and remains of several cows, sheep and other animals. The party left in sudden haste.

Those who have seen this fearful creature agree only in one thing; they would not face the thing for all the wealth of the Vanderbilts. A panic has seized the farmers and lumbermen of that region. While the more courageous are organizing parties to hunt the creature down, the more timid are leaving the neighborhood. It is thought by some that the animal is a chimpanzee that has escaped from some menagerie, while others claim that it is a man, reduced to a state of animal ferocity by long exposure and a demented mind.

Philadelphia, Pennsylvania, *Times,* July 29, 1895

WILD MAN IN THE WOODS.

John Cook, a farmer, heard a terrible rumpus in his piggery the other night and, believing that the pigs had upset a beehive placed temporarily in their sty, he ran out. As he stepped into the shed he was grabbed by the wild man. The fellow looked seven feet high and was quite naked. He was a hairy man and wore a beard as long as a Western free silver man's. From his mouth protruded big teeth like fangs. Farmer Cook is six feet three and very powerful, but he was helpless in the grasp of the wild man, who carried him to the door and hurled him thirty feet. The farmer fell unconscious; when he woke up he found himself lame and bruised. His best pig was gone. A crowbar lay on the ground tied into knots. Farmer Cook says the wild man did this to show his annoyance at being interrupted.

Hartford, Connecticut, *Daily Courant*, August 1, 1895

MARGARETVILLE'S WHAT-IS-IT.

(NEWBURG, N.Y., LETTER TO NEW YORK HERALD.) All Margaretville, a town near here, and its environs are in a state of excitement over the appearance of a ferocious ape-like being, which devours horses, sheep and cattle and splits their bones to get at the marrow. The monster had a hand-to-hand fight with William Cook yesterday, and threw his opponent twenty feet and nearly killed him.

The monster is the most energetic summer man, if he is a man, that has ever visited these parts.

Peter Thomas, who is neither weak-willed nor a doubter, was driving a team of horses along a lonely road near Margaretville, last Friday night, when, he says, a horrible monster hopped out from the underbrush along the road and stood in the middle of the thoroughfare, brandishing a pair of long and hairy arms and uttering a raucous, inarticulate cry. Mr. Thomas is a truthful man, as every one who knows him is willing to vouch. He says that he rolled against the dashboard of his wagon, almost petrified with fear.

Tackles the Horse.

The creature leaped high in the air, and with loud cries landed on the ground, within a foot or two of the wagon. It seized the nigh horse, and, with a faculty which betokened long practice, broke the animal's neck and then divested it of its harness. The monster then tore the harness from the still quivering form of the horse and bore off the carcass to the woods. The other horse broke into a run, and, all steaming and with its body flecked with foam, tore into the village.

Mr. Thomas, pale as a ghost, clung feebly to the dashboard, and with eyes almost popping from their sockets looked behind him at the stretch of dusty roads. He was taken to a house of public entertainment, where, under the stimulus of restoratives, he was able to tell his story. He could give no adequate description of the monster, but said that it seemed to be taller than a man and had sinewy arms covered with hair. The creature, he said, too, was "wild eyed," but he could not describe the face beyond saying that it was devilish in its expression.

The Chase.

Men are scarce at Margaretville. It is a little village, much frequented as a summer resort. However, bands of youths, in duck trousers and blue coats, joined the farmers to hunt the creature to its lair. Several young women inclined to be flippant said that the monster, if a man, would be in great demand if invited to the next hop. Mr. Thomas, who never said "I doubt," led the searching party.

The camp of the creature was discovered on Saturday afternoon, about two miles form Margaretville. It was in a clearing in the woods. In the center of the space there were the smouldering embers of a big fire. Around it were the half gnawed bones of sheep and cattle and part of the remains of Mr. Thomas's unfortunate horse. No trace of the monster could be found in the vicinity. The farmers were horror-stricken. One of them said that never in his forty years as man and boy had he seen anything so "weirdlike" before.

John Cook, a farmer, was a member of the hunting party. He returned alone last evening. He claims to have seen and attacked the mysterious stranger, but says that bullets appeared to have no effect on it. Cook got in close quarters with the creature finally and was thrown twenty feet by it. Cook describes the "wild man" as being about seven feet tall, entirely nude, covered with black hair, with a long beard and with teeth which project from his mouth like fangs. Some of the natives are debating the question whether they should have a right to shoot the "wild man," and are afraid they would be indicted for murder if they did so.

New York, New York, *The World*, September 12, 1900

ARMED FARMERS HUNT WILDMAN
THREE MILES NORTH OF THE
SPRING VALLEY N.Y. AREA.

Mrs. Matt Starr while heading to her pickle patch this morning spotted what she thought was a wild animal on the ground eating her cucumbers, until it rose up on two feet. It was gigantic, with shaggy black hair and small eyes that gleamed evilly. It chased her, gaining at every step until her husband and son came out of the barn, causing it to flee into the woods, howling. Local men loaded up their shotguns and pistols and went off in pursuit. They discovered corn cobs it had eaten and a bed of broken down corn stalks and brush. They vow to hunt it till it's captured.

1909: Bartholomew et al. (2002) noted that in February 1909 strange cries and a strange creature were reported near various Long Island communities.

Seattle, Washington, *Republican,* March 12, 1909

Either a wild man or an ape has been seen in the forest of a [New] York state community. It's doubtless an ape and an envoy from Africa to act as an escort to Teddy Bear to the jungles.

Lake Placid, New York, *News,* September 2, 1921

JUST A BOOTLEGGERS' RUSE

Nearly every officer who found it possible to get away was last week searching for a reported wild man in the region about Skerry, twelve miles southwest of Malone. A new aspect of the case came to pass when a report reached the ears of officials of Franklin county to the effect that it was nothing more than a clever ruse, effected by bootlegger to take advantage of the absence of officers in coming across the border with $5000 worth of liquor.

Danville, Virginia, *Bee*, November 6, 1922

DOG COMES TO RESCUE AS GIANT APE ATTACKS BOY

New York, Nov. 5.—A big baboon, thought to have escaped from a rum-running ship, is being sought in the vicinity of Babylon, on Long Island. Half a dozen persons have seen the animal and one, William Ellinger, was knocked by it during an encounter several days ago.

Young Ellinger, son of the caretaker on the estate of Mrs. W. E. Hawkins, came suddenly upon the baboon as he was walking along the banks of a creek looking after muskrat traps. The boy shouted to frighten the animal, but instead it made for him and knocked him down. The great ape had started to tear the lad's clothing when his German police dog rushed up, only to be knocked back by a sweep of the baboon's long arm. The dog returned to the attack and after a brief encounter the ape fled. Searching parties were formed, after the boy had reported the incident to his father.

Some hunters saw it climb from the third-story window of an abandoned house and lower itself to the ground by the lightning rod. It happened so quickly that none of the hunters were able to fire.

New Castle, Pennsylvania, *News*, June 30, 1931

ROAMING GORILLA
HUNTED BY POLICE

SMALL BOY AT MINEOLA, LONG ISLAND,
TELLS POLICE OF BIG BEAST

New York, June 30—Squads of police and scores of citizens were preparing today to use guns, traps and gas bombs in an effort to capture a roaming gorilla at Mineola, Long Island.

A boy's vivid description of the beast convinced authorities the animal actually was at large.

Footprints of the gorilla were found, police said.

Pittsburgh, Pennsylvania, *Post Gazette*, July 20, 1931

NEW GORILLA SCARE SENDS
THRONGS FOR AID OF POLICE

SPECIAL TO THE PITTSBURGH POST-GAZETTE
AND THE NEW YORK TIMES.

Huntington, L.I., July 19.—Like some strange figment of Edgar Allen Poe's imagination, Long Island's wandering gorilla appeared again today at Huntington to send terrified residents clamoring for help to the police station.

Last reported seen about two weeks ago, the monstrous hairy ape, variously described as from five to eight feet tall, made two reappearances within a few hours.

Shortly after dusk Saturday night trembling witnesses in Oakwood avenue swore they had seen the beast scuttling across a field near some woods. Police could not follow the trail.

Early this morning police were called to the exclusive Fort Hill residential section, where more persons insisted they saw the gorilla swinging across a field. Again the police searched and found nothing.

In previous appearances the awe-inspiring beast has been reported at East Williston and Albertson Park, each a few miles from Huntington. Police say they have no report of a gorilla escaping from any circus or zoo.

"Another Mystery" columnist Whit Wellman wrote (December 5, 1936) that in June and July 1931, a "huge monkey" or "gorilla" was repeatedly seen near Mineola, Long Island, and that "innumerable prints were discovered, but were the prints of only hind feet, the size of a big man's hand."

New York, New York, *Herald Tribune*, September 5, 1934 (from Bartholomew et al. 2002)

MAN, BEAST OR DEMON?

IT'S LOOSE IN AMITYVILLE

MYSTERIOUS APELIKE MARAUDER

RAIDS GARAGE; TOWN ON GUARD

SPECIAL TO THE HERALD TRIBUNE

Amityville, L. I., Sept. 4—The mysterious animal, described by some as a large monkey, which was first seen in this section last week, paid a visit early this morning to the home of Mrs. Alfred

C. Abernathy, of Bennett Place, South Amityville, tore up an old fur coat, ripped several mattresses and clawed an old automobile in the garage. Tonight most of the male residents of the neighborhood are sitting on their porches waiting for the animal with shotguns, rifles, revolvers and garden hoses.

Valparaiso, Indiana, *Vidette-Messenger*, July 25, 1936

GREEN-EYED MONSTER STRIKING TERROR INTO CITIZENS OF NEW YORK TOWN; REMAINS MYSTERY

Wading River, N.Y., July 25. (UP)—Out here in this quiet Long Island community they are talking about organizing a posse to hunt for "it."

"It" goes about shrieking at night, and scaring women out of their wits and making shivers run down the spines of men. About all that is known to date about "it" is that it prowls at night only, has [—] green eyes about a foot from the ground, and, when disturbed, runs helter-skelter through the bush.

Some practical persons have suggested "it" is a monkey. It never has been seen in trees.

Two persons have come face to face with "it." Seldon W. Heatley espied it from a distance of 150 feet in the [—] and said it resembled a dog-faced baboon.

"But I'm not sure," he admitted. "I was walking along the road to the barn when I heard the horrible noise it makes. Horses in the [—] snorted and became unruly. I heard the thing screech near our house at 4 a.m. the other day, picked up a shot gun and, in my nightclothes ran out into the night but I could not find it."

William Meier, returning home about 10 p.m., heard the eerie screech and then saw a pair of furtive eyes, of greenish cast, glare at him. Meier went in one direction, toward home. "It" scampered off in another direction.

William L. Miller, a farmer and justice of the peace, reported that the creature's first cries were heard about six weeks ago. Mrs. Miller described the shriek as "unearthly like a human hurt or frightened."

Rochester, New York, *Democrat and Chronicle,* July 29, 1938

HIKING PREACHER QUIZZED IN SEARCH FOR 'WILD MAN'

Varysburg—With reports fresh in their minds of a "modern Tarzan," who sprang from tree to tree and ate raw fish, farmers and their wives along the 16 miles of U.S. Route 20A in Wyoming County followed a hairy, bewhiskered, barefoot man yesterday with telephone calls to the sheriff's office in Warsaw.

Sheriff Lewis Spring here caught up with the man, who claimed to be a Russian preacher "walking the length and breadth of the nation trying to get people to consecrate themselves to the Lord." . . .

Fishermen, picnickers and farmers in various sections of Wyoming County have reported to Sheriff Spring during the last month they had sighted something described as a hairy wild man, a modern Tarzan and a gorilla. Two small boys fishing near Lamont reported the creature grabbed their fish and ate them raw. Sheriff Spring reported yesterday that thorough investigation had led him to believe that the "creature" was purely imaginary.

Springville, New York, *Journal,* August 4, 1938

GORILLA OR WILD MAN
MYSTERY UNSOLVED

During the past week the subject of conversation seems to center on the report of a "wild man," "Gorilla," or some such beast being at large here abouts. Troopers were notified that the beast was seen on the Dersam farm eating a chicken and frightening some heifers in the pasture lot. Another lady said it was in a berry patch on the Schram farm on the Cowlesville road, it had stripped the patch of berries and trampled down the bushes.

Several persons claimed to have seen it at a distance, described it as being covered with brown hair with face like a gorilla and at times walked erect, but seemingly not frightened and takes its time to disappear.

It was reported that several of our hunters from Alden and Cowlesville searched the wood lots during the past week but failed to solve the mystery.

The mystery beast has caused no particular damage or harmed anyone, it merely is satisfied to appease its hunger and disappears.

It was reported here that mothers have cautioned their children to refrain from going to the wood lots, or swimming, but to date many enjoy the old swimming hole and no harm has come to them.

The mystery is still unsolved but has caused no end of excitement for those who claimed to have seen the beast.—Alden Advertiser.

Margaretville, New York, *Catskill Mountain News,* September 7, 1945

HAD CITY FOLKS IN UPROAR

Quite a bit of excitement prevailed throughout this village on Monday evening when the report came that a strange animal had been seen in the vicinity of the farm of Kenneth Spaulding in West Settlement, which [resembled] an ape and was the size of a man. It is reported that the animal has been in the vicinity for several days and early in the evening begins wandering about in search of food. It has been seen by several people and Monday evening a posse of local men went to the Spaulding farm with searchlights and were unable to find any trace of the

animal which looks like a man and gives out
a horrible screech as it wanders through the
fields.—Prattsville Cor.

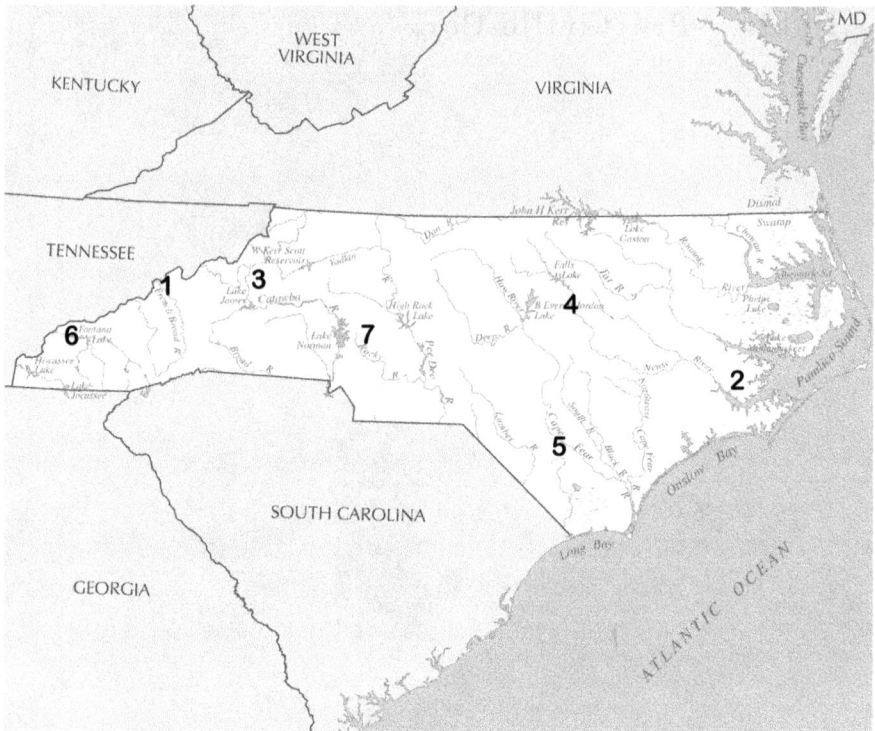

1 Bald Mountains

2 Kit Swamp

3 Globe Valley (Collettsville, Caldwell County)

4 Raleigh (Wake and Durham Counties)

5 Elizabethtown (Bladen County)

6 Yellow Creek (Graham County)

7 Kannapolis (Cabarrus and Rowan Counties)

North Carolina

Annapolis, Maryland, *Gazette,* June 27, 1793

Charleston, May 17.

A gentleman on the South Fork of the Saluda river, in a letter of the 23d ult. Sends his correspondent in this city the following description of an extraordinary animal which has been lately discovered on the Bald Mountain, and on other mountains in the western territory:—

This animal is between twelve and fifteen feet high, and in shape resembling a human being, except the head, which is in equal proportion to its body, and draws in somewhat like a tarapin; its feet are like those of a negro, about two feet long, and hairy, which is of a dark dun colour; its eyes are exceedingly large, and open and shut up and down its face; the hair of its head is about six inches long, stands straight like a negroe's; its nose is like that of the human species, only large, and inclined to what is called Roman.

These animals are bold, and have lately attempted to kill several persons—in which attempts some of them have been shot.

Their principal resort is on the Bald Mountain, where they lie in wait for travelers—but some have been seen in this part of the country. The inhabitants of this place call it Yahoo; the Indians, however, give it the name of Chickly-Cudly.

Petersburg, Virginia, *Index and Appeal*, August 26, 1875

A STRANGE ANIMAL ON THE NORTH CAROLINA COAST

The Newbern *Journal of Commerce* is responsible for the following:

Asa Grandy, a colored resident of Kits Swamp, relates a strange and startling incident that occurred in his immediate neighborhood on Thursday last, and which has occasioned considerable excitement and alarm among the inhabitants thereabouts.— It appears that for some time past a strange looking animal has occasionally been seen, by different parties, lurking on the outskirts of the forests between sundown and dark, but until recently no one had been able to approach the stranger near enough to describe its appearance. From the description given by Asa, we conclude it to be a nondescript which

Barnum the great showman would be glad to possess even at an expense of thousands of dollars. Its face in appearance is quite similar to that of the Wanderoo, having a long snowy beard or mane, while its body closely resembles that of a Baboon, though from the knees down, its feet and limbs are, in shape and form, precisely human.—In height it would measure about five feet, while its volume around the chest would eclipse the Cardiff Giant. Asa states that this nondescript has for several weeks past been preying upon poultry, garden vegetables, and green corn to an alarming extent, when on Thursday morning last while his little girl of five years was at play in the corn crib with a neighbor's child, and himself at work stripping fodder in the field near by, he heard the children screaming, the dogs furiously barking, and his wife loudly crying for assistance, whereupon he swiftly ran towards the point from whence the cries proceeded, and at the edge of the cornfield met face to face this singular being with the children in each paw, making directly towards the woods. At the sudden approach of Asa, the animal, being taken by surprise, halted for a moment, and as it partially turned to change its course, a well directed blow felled it to the earth and the

children were released without injury; but
before its capture could be accomplished it
sprang from the ground and with lightning
rapidity gained the covering of the wood
where all traces of its whereabouts remains
as yet a mystery, though the forests for miles
around have been thoroughly searched. Much
excitement and fear prevails throughout
that section, and no mother will again rest
in peace until this strange intruder is captured and rendered harmless.

Newbern [New Bern], North Carolina, *Weekly Journal of Commerce,* September 11, 1875

THAT STRANGE ANIMAL—

Another Attempt to Kidnap Frustrated—An
Exciting Chase—Capture and Death of the
Nondescript—Perilous Adventure of one of
the Captors—The Inhabitants of Kits Swamp
in Ecstasies.

The inhabitants of Kits Swamp are in ecstasies over the capture and death of a strange
animal which for sometime past has been
prowling about the neighborhood, preying
upon their gardens, poultry, etc., and even
attempting to carry off little children, as
described in a recent (August 21st) of this
journal in which a description of the animal is given. Through Adam Story, a colored

inhabitant of Kits Swamp, we are enabled to publish the gratifying news of the death of this animal, as well as the particulars concerning its capture, which are both startling and interesting.

It appears that our informant Story, in company with two colored neighbors named Eli Sparrow and Frank Hansom have for sometime past been in search for this wily kidnapper, and on Wednesday morning last, for the first time since its attempt to carry off the two children previously mentioned, they espied it lurking on the outskirts of a small clearing owned and worked by a colored woman named Maria Harkley who with her two children, the youngest being a boy about four years of age and the elder a girl some three or four years older, were at the time engaged near the wood, gathering blackberries. Story, who was sitting with his companions upon a large pine log near the clearing was the first to discover the animal which at some distance off was cautiously wending its way towards the little boy then about fifty yards from his mother and in plain view of the men who at the suggestion of Story secreted themselves behind the log upon which they had been sitting and where they could without being observed watch the

movements of the intruder. As the animal
approached the edge of the wood it noiselessly ascended a tree and peered through
the branches toward the clearing for several
minutes then descended and directed its
course towards the little boy who was then in
fair range and within gunshot of the men behind the log with their guns ready to fire at
the proper moment. It was evident that the
animal intended to kidnap the boy, but the
men decided that they would not fire upon
him until they were quite sure of his intention as they desired to capture him alive.
Slowly and stealthily the animal crept along
through the bushes, occasionally raising
himself up to take a survey of the premises,
until he had reached within ten feet of the
boy when, as he arose and was about to spring
upon the little fellow, Hansom and Sparrow,
aiming at his lower extremities, fired; from
the effect of which the animal uttered an
unearthly yell and fell to the ground. The
men rushed towards the wounded creature,
but before they could reach him he was up
and with a running limp swiftly made for the
woods where for a time he eluded his pursuers, though from the blood left behind him
his trail was easily traced, yet owing to thick

bramble bushes and deep morasses it was
with great difficulty followed. However they
kept up the chase for about two hours when
at last they came to a chaparral so dense
that it was impossible to go through it without the aid of an axe, which they of course
did not have with them. Upon examining the
premises carefully, they succeeded in finding a small opening close to the ground and
just large enough to admit the body of a man
by creeping on his hands and knees; this
opening was found to be partially covered by
an old tree stump upon which spots of fresh
blood were plainly distinguished, and showing conclusively that the wounded animal
had passed through the aperture and gained
his place of abode. The question now arose as
to who would venture to crawl through this
opening in search of the fugitive, when Story
volunteered to make the perilous adventure,
and with his gun before him he entered the
dark tunnel not knowing at what moment he
might be attacked from within. After crawling a distance of about twenty feet, the muz-
zle of his gun came in contact with a hard
substance which by a vigorous push he succeeded in removing and found it to be a short
piece of plank about two feet in width which

had been set up edgewise against the inner entrance of the opening and supported by a large pine knot, thus shutting out the light from the tunnel through which he had passed. Upon the removal of this plank he crawled out into an open clearing about three or four yards square, and the first thing that met his gaze was the animal in question. He immediately called to his companions who could now plainly see through the small opening, and they at once started to creep through, but before they could reach the clearing, the animal or nondescript seeing no way of escape, made a spring for Story who had raised his gun in position to fire and as the animal neared him he pulled the trigger and the charge entered its body and fortunately put an end to its existence.

The carcass of this wonderful being was carried to the settlement where hundreds of men, women and children for miles around had an opportunity of viewing it, and much rejoicing was manifested over its capture and death. Story and Hansom brought the skin of the animal to this city on Thursday when it was forwarded through Capt. Hall of the steamer Gary to Baltimore with the view of having it stuffed for exhibition.

Smethport, Pennsylvania, *McKean County Miner,* January 3, 1878

A WILD MAN OF THE MOUNTAINS.

A gentleman who resides near Fairview, Watauga county, says the Statesville (N. C.) Landmark, writes us that in company with several gentlemen, he went out prospecting in a portion of the Globe Valley. While in the heart of the valley, some miles from any place of habitation, their attention was attracted toward a peculiar specimen of humanity, some forty yards distant. They neared the object, or giant as he seemed, until they came within twenty step of him. Then they stopped still, to advise with each other as to whether they should go nearer. While they were consulting, one of the gentlemen gave a yell and jumped toward the wild man, when he started toward the party a few steps, stopped still and began to pound himself in the breast with his ponderous fists. There he stood for two minutes, evincing no power of speech. Suddenly he turned and bounded off with the speed of a deer. The party then repaired to the house of one of the men, secured a gun, pistol, and other articles of warfare, and went in pursuit of this strange being. They searched the balance of the day, but nothing could be seen of the object of their pursuit. During the search they ascended the crags of Blowing Rock and discovered a small cave, in which was found a bed of leaves and many bones, resembling those of the opossum. It is supposed this cave has afforded this wild man a home for many years. Our correspondent describes the wild man as being about six feet five inches tall, with broad shoulders and long apeish arms, smooth face and funnel-shaped head. His body is covered with dark brown hair, near two inches long. His head and a greater portion of his forehead is covered with long, luxuriant, dark red tresses. Our correspondent affirms that this is the first time this wild man has ever been seen or heard of in the neighborhood.

Raleigh, North Carolina, *Signal,* September 1, 1887

WILD MAN OR GORILLA.

A number of people were out on Tuesday last hunting the country over about four miles from Raleigh for the wild man or gorilla said to have been seen in that neighborhood. Some of the hunters had guns, others pitchforks, hoes, sticks, scythe blades and axes. They scoured the woods during the day but found no wild man, bear or gorilla. Mr. Pierce Howell is reported to have seen the "varmint" on his place on Monday last and said that it was a grown gorilla with a young one. Others say it is a large bear, and others say that it is a wild hairy man. The neighborhood is pretty well scared and the women and children keep close in the yards during the day and in the houses as soon as the sun goes down. We are curious to know what the ultimate explanation of this nine days wonder will prove to be. Heretofore when the Editor of The Signal decided to remain out a little late at night he always had as an excuse that there was a masonic meeting and that he had been there with Dr. Eugene Grissom. But since the wild man, bear, or gorilla has been in our neighborhood, this excuse don't pass muster with the wife and children, and we have called upon Dr. Grissom to furnish one that will enable us to stay out now and then a few hours at night. Under these circumstances, if the "varmint" is not captured or killed in a few days, we expect to join in the hunt.

Raleigh, North Carolina, *News and Observer,* September 9, 1887
The "wild man" scare is getting worse. A big hunt is being made for him. It is now reported that he "eats folks" and has eaten one or two people already.

Statesville, North Carolina, *Landmark,* October 6, 1887
Wake county is in the midst of a great sensation on account of a "wild man" in the woods. He is about the size of a bear and runs on

all fours. Numbers of persons have seen him but none have been able to get near him, and nobody knows who he is or how he got there. At this distance from the scene of excitement we cannot be expected to know much about the matter except in a general way, but we do not mind expressing the opinion that the "wild man" is the "Wake county boy preacher," grown up and taken to the woods. This theory is incompatible with the theory advanced by our brethren of the Raleigh press last year that the boy preacher is "inspired," but it is not inconsistent with Dr. Grissom's uncharitable theory that he has epilepsy.

Asheville, North Carolina, *Weekly Citizen*, May 24, 1901

Elizabethtown cor. Clarkton Express: It seems that there is some truth in the gorilla story after all. Calhoun Daniel, a colored man who lives about a mile from town, reports that some kind of a varmint caught one of his children in the yard, on the night of the 6th. The girl tore loose from it, after a terrible struggle, and the print of the beast's paw was still visible on her arm when her father reached her. She says it was about the size of a small man, all hairy over, and had a face somewhat on the order of a human being.

Asheville, North Carolina, *Citizen-Times*, November 16, 1930

COUNTLESS LEGENDS BORN
IN GREAT SMOKY PARK
PRESERVED BY INDIANS

By Lola Love McCoy

Nearly every "bald" and "knob" in the Smokies is the basis for one or more legends. One story tells of a mysterious being who, long years ago, haunted a round knob near the mouth of Yellow creek on Cheowa river. Sometimes, this strange creature, evidently a human being, would walk about on the top of the knob, crying "Yawa! Yawa!" Sounds of unseen guns came from the place as the stranger cried out, and the Indians were afraid to go near. On account of the weird cry of the visitor, the whole region was called "Yawa place," or Yawal.

Kannapolis, North Carolina, *Daily Independent*, September 16, 1956

'CREATURE' SIGHTED

By Bill Maultsby,

Daily Independent Staff Writer

A "mystery monster" in the vicinity of Concord lake had North Kannapolis Police and State Highway Patrolmen scratching their heads last Saturday.

Alternately described as a bear and a "big gray hairy thing" that foams at the mouth, the "monster" reportedly entered the home of John H. Brown on Glenwood street around 4 o'clock Saturday afternoon and pulled a sleeping baby off the bed before fleeing to some nearby woods.

Summoned to the scene by Brown's daughter, Louis Boyce, Officer Otis Chapman and Patrolman Ed LeFurgey rushed to the scene and searched the area around the house—without success.

Mrs. Brown, Louis and another daughter, Christine Wadford, who were washing clothes at a pump several yards from the house, told this story to officers:

The baby was at the house alone, sleeping on a bed, when the women heard a scream in the vicinity of the house. They started in that direction, then stopped short when "The Thing" appeared on the front porch and wandered off into the woods. Louise fainted, and Mrs. Brown hurried into the house to check on the child.

The baby was lying on the floor, apparently unharmed, but with saliva covering its face. There was a wet spot on the bed that Mrs. Brown theorized was saliva from the strange creature.

Mrs. Brown and Mrs. Boyce, the only persons who claimed actually to have seen the alleged intruder, described him as bigger than a man, with grey hair six inches long, and walking on his hind legs with both front paws held in the air.

Both admitted they had never seen a bear, but they said the creature was like they imagined a bear to be.

LeGurgey got a negative reply to his query as to whether the animal staggered—apparently toying with the idea that an unkempt drunk might have been mistaken for a bear by the excited women.

Chapman explored the theory further by asking point blank if "The Thing" could possibly have been a man—but the women insisted that he was "too big to be a man."

Other persons on the scene at the time of the incident, who did not see the intruder, said they saw the bushes moving down in the woods after he had left the house.

Late last night officers were still wondering about the strange tale—but they plan no "bear hunt" unless there are further developments.

Kannapolis, North Carolina, *Daily Independent,* September 17, 1956

'THE THING' SEEN AGAIN

"The thing" continued to plague the John H. Brown family on Glenwood street today, but so far the menace has apparently not spread to neighboring homes.

Alternately described as "a big ape" and a "gray bear" the hairy monster reportedly entered the Brown home first on Saturday afternoon and later fled to some nearby woods after pulling a sleeping baby from a bed.

He was said to have made a second appearance later Saturday night, sparking a hunt in the woods with searchlights and hunting dogs. Mrs. Brown and her two daughters, who were at the house with some small children at the time of the first intrusion, notified North Kannapolis Police. Officers have been unable to find a trace of "the thing."

Officers said this morning the women had reported seeing it again Sunday.

The initial report on the incident said the women, who were washing clothes at a pump near the house, were startled by the baby's scream. When they went toward the house to investigate, they said a hairy monster, bigger than a man, came onto the porch and walked toward the woods—on its hind feet.

They said his face was covered with saliva and that they found saliva on the bed where the baby had been sleeping.

An unconfirmed report this morning said that a man searching the woods Sunday got a glimpse of "the thing" and fired at it but missed. Another report said a dog was killed when two hounds tangled with the creature.

"A band of young hunters" went searching for the creature, but no additional follow-up has been located. ("Hunters search for hairy monster," Wilson, North Carolina, *Daily Times,* September 20, 1956.)

1 Killdeer Mountains

North Dakota

Bord & Bord (2006) noted that around 1900, a group of people in a sleigh near the Killdeer Mountains reported seeing a gorilla-like animal run at them, then run off through the snow, leaving large footprints.

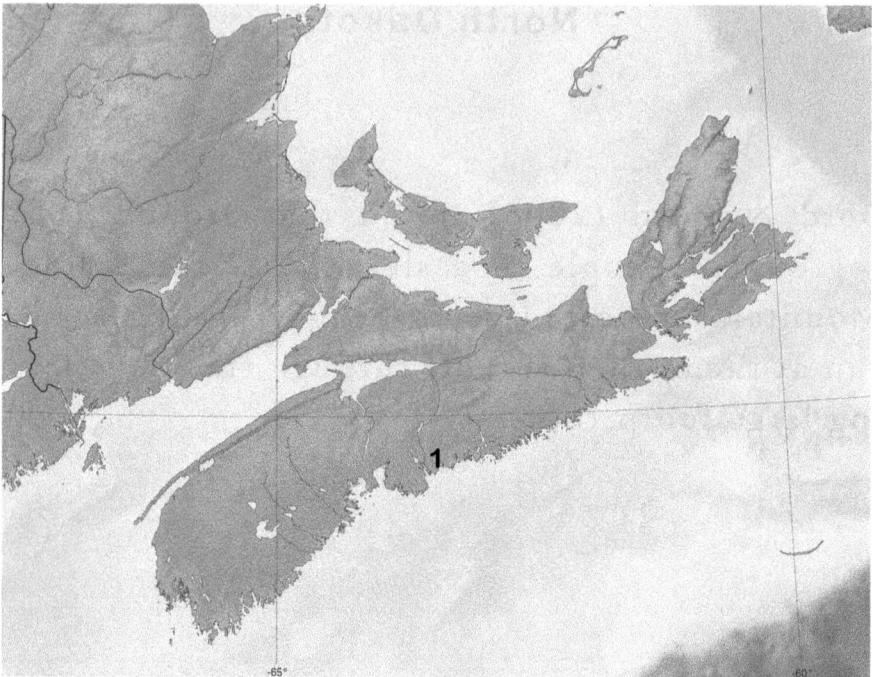

1 Cole Harbor

Nova Scotia

Fort Wayne, Indiana, *Weekly Gazette,* April 14, 1892

The people of Cole Harbor, N. S., were much excited and terrified about a strange animal that, so they say, appeared in the woods near that place. The animal was seven feet high, and looked like a gorilla.

1 Gallipolis (Gallia County)

2 Spruce Vale (Columbiana County)

3 Sycamore (Wyandot County)

4 Holmes County

5 Negee (dead placename; Belmont County)

6 Mapleton (dead placename; Belmont County)

7 Richville (Stark County)

8 Rome (Adams County)

9 Berea (Cuyahoga County)

10 Rockport (Allen County)

Ohio

Mankato, Minnesota, *Weekly Record,* January 23, 1869 (from Schaffner 1997-2006)

A GORILLA IN OHIO

Gallipolis is excited over a wild man, who is reported to haunt the woods near that city. He goes naked, is covered with hair, is gigantic in height, and "his eyes start from their sockets." A carriage, containing a man and daughter, was attacked by him a few days ago. He is said to have bounded at the father, catching him in a grip like that of a vice, hurling him to the earth, falling on him and endeavoring to bite and to scratch like a wild animal. The struggle was long and fearful, rolling and wallowing in the deep mud, have suffocated, sometimes beneath his adversary, whose burning and maniac eyes glared into his own with murderous and savage intensity. Just as he was about to become exhausted from his exertions, his daughter, taking courage at the imminent danger of her parent, snatched up a rock and hurling it at

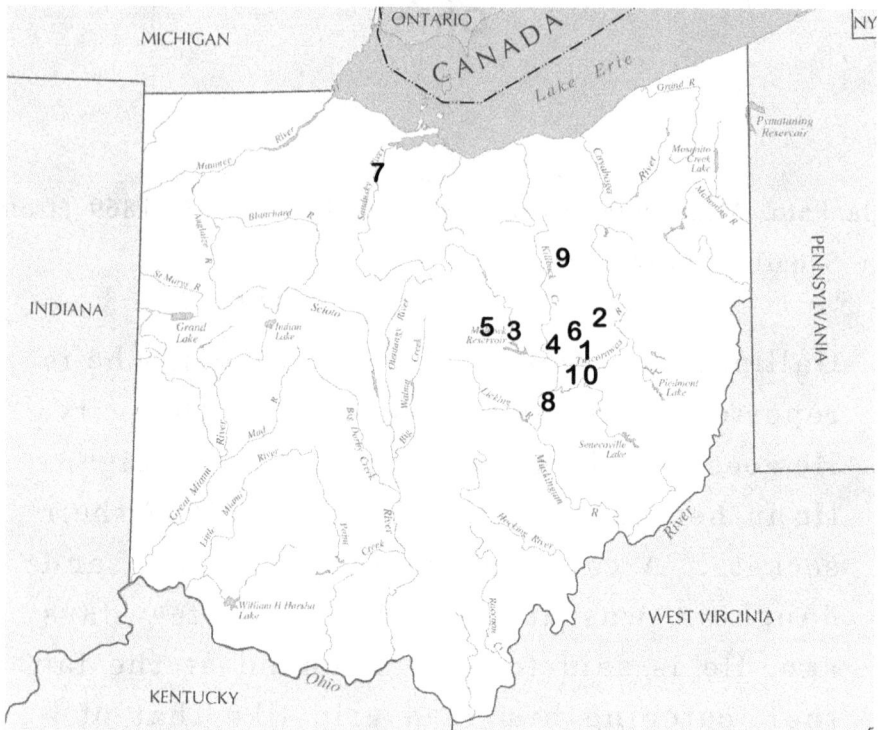

1 North Salem (Guernsey County)

2 New Philadelphia (Tuscarawas County)

3 Walhonding (Coshocton County)

4 Coshocton and Roscoe (Coshocton County)

5 Knox County

6 Postboy (Tuscarawas County)

7 Fremont (Sandusky County)

8 Chandlersville (Muskingum County)

9 Homesville (Holmes County)

10 Cambridge (Guernsey County)

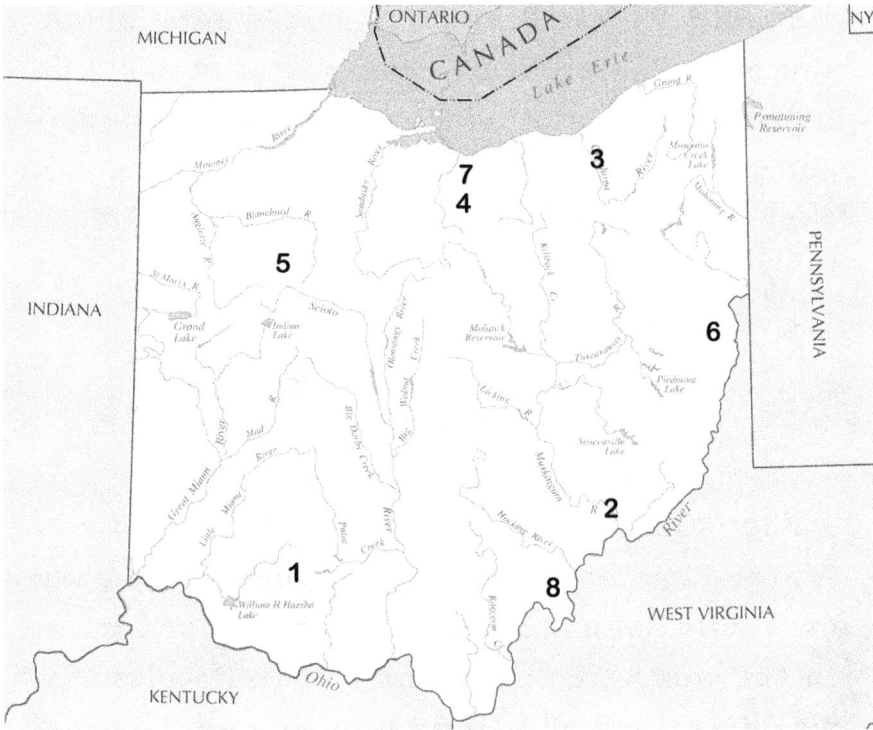

1 Hillsboro (Highland County)

2 Marietta (Washington County)

3 Hudson (Summit County)

4 Richland County

5 Alger (Hardin County)

6 Steubenville and Alikanna (Jefferson County)

7 Norwalk (Huron County)

8 Lock Run (dead placename; Meigs County)

the head of her father's would be murderer, was fortunate enough to put an end to the struggle by striking him somewhere about the ear. The creature was not stunned, but feeling unequal to further exertion, slowly got up and retired into the neighboring copse that skirted the road.

Burlington, Vermont, *Free Press,* January 23, 1869

A WILD MAN.

HIS HORRIBLE APPEARANCE
AND FEROCIOUS ACTIONS.

FROM THE GALLIPOLIS, OHIO BULLETIN, 6TH.

A story has been current for some days past of a wild man having made his appearance in the woods in the vicinity of Gallipolis. He was described as being in quite a nude state, covered with hair, very tall, and with eyes starting from their sockets. Some grown lads who had been gunning back of "Carrel's hill" first brought the news; then some women, whom he had chased along a Chillicothe road and had nearly overtaken, when a wagon coming in sight, he fled to the hills, uttering as he ran loud and discordant yells. Little attention was paid to these tales until one day last week, when some light was thrown on the matter by a gentleman who was returning with his daughter (a pretty and

interesting girl of seventeen) in a buggy
from the country. He states that just before
dark, about five miles from town, he was
obliged, from the state of the road, to get out
of his carriage to rest his horse, leaving his
daughter to guide the animal, and walking
on a few hundred yards in advance. Suddenly
at a place where a turn in the road concealed
the vehicle from his view, he was surprised
by hearing two or three yells and whoops in
his rear, and shortly afterwards the terrified
screams and cries for help in his daughter's
familiar voice. Half distracted at her cries
of distress he rushed with all his speed toward the place whence the noise proceeded
and there behind his child struggling with
something in the shape of a man, which, on
coming up to he found to be a creature of the
human shape indeed, but of such a terrible
and forbidding aspect as to create fear and
dismay in the breast of the most courageous.
Upon perceiving the gentleman's approach he
left the girl and bounded toward the father,
catching him in a grip like that of a vice and
hurling him to the earth, falling on him and
endeavoring to bite and scratch like a wild
animal. The struggle was long and fearful,
rolling and wallowing in the deep mud, half
suffocated sometimes beneath his adversary,

whose burning and maniac eyes glared into his own with murderous and savage intensity. Just as he was about to become exhausted from his exertions the daughter, taking courage at the imminent danger of her parent, snatched up a rock and hurling it at the head of her father's would-be murderer, was fortunate enough to put an end to the struggle by striking him somewhere about the neck or ear, obliging him to desist. The creature was not stunned, however, but feeling unequal to further exertion slowly got up and retired into a neighboring copse that skirted the road. As soon as the gentleman had sufficiently recovered he, with the help of his daughter, continued his journey to the city, where he arrived after dark, exhausted, cut and bleeding from his severe wounds. His description of the wild man's appearance tallies with those who had previously seen him. The young lady luckily escaped without injure farther than the nervous excitement consequent on such a catastrophe.

Fort Wayne, Indiana, *Gazette,* December 11, 1883

A WILD MAN OF THE WOODS.

New Lisbon, Ohio, Dec. 10.—Bob Bradley and Henry Raush, two Columbiana county hunters, while out hunting a few days ago in the woods near Spruce Vale, were pursued by a wild man, covered with hair and looking like a bear. These woods were some years ago the resort of horse-thieves and counterfeiters, and of late have seldom been visited. While in the vicinity of this retreat the hunters saw a huge, hairy object, apparently half man and half beast, spring from behind a cliff and start for the woods, running with great speed. Mistaking it for a wild animal, one of the hunters fired at it. The shot appeared to take effect in the arm, for with a scream of pain the creature halted, tapped the wound, and turning charged its pursuers, who dropped their empty guns and sought safety in flight.

Hartford, Connecticut, *Courant,* December 15, 1883

AN OHIO WILD MAN.

(NEW YORK *SUN.*)

Calcutta, Ohio, Dec. 10.—One day last week Messrs. [H.] Rauch and Robert Bradley left town for a hunt in the woods north of this place. The forest is very dense, and contains a number of rocky hills, precipices and caves. It has long been the hiding place of criminals while eluding arrest. While Rauch and Bradley were walking along the top of a bluff in the thick of these woods they were startled by a peculiar cry. They could at first see nothing, but soon a creature of formidable aspect rushed out from a cleft in the rocks. It was about the average size of a man, and somewhat resembled a gorilla. It stood perfectly erect, and was covered from head to foot with hair.

After staring a few minutes at the hunters the creature gave another cry and jumped away into the woods. Never thinking of consequences, one of the hunters raised his gun and fired, wounding the animal in the arm. It turned with a horrible scream of rage and pursued the hunters, who threw away their guns and ran at the top of their speed. The creature gained on them until they reached a clearing and a fence, over which they jumped. The animal then ran back into the woods.

The hunters declare they would not go back again for a mint of money. A posse of citizens, however, is looking for the animal. It is believed the creature is an escaped lunatic. Some years ago, a young man who had become inane and was confined in the county poorhouse, escaped and took to the woods, where he subsisted by eating berries, nuts, roots and small animals. He has been seen several times. It is thought that he will soon be captured.

Akron, Ohio, *Summit County Beacon,* August 6, 1884

The stories that continue to come from Springfield about the panther and gorilla scare in that locality are enough to disgust anybody.

Napoleon, Ohio, *Democratic Northwest and Henry County News,* August 19, 1886

A WHAT IS IT.

A STRANGE ANIMAL EXCITING THE PEOPLE.

The *News,* published at Sycamore, a small village about twelve or fifteen miles beyond Fostoria, on the Toledo and Ohio Central R., gives the following account of a strange animal seen in that neighborhood:

"There has been a strange animal seen by several different parties, in a piece of woods between Mexico and the Toledo and Ohio Central railroad bridge, near the river. It has been described to us as being about the size of a child four or five years old, when standing erect on his hind feet. It has four legs with feet resembling monkey's. It is covered with short, reddish brown hair about an inch in length. The head resembles that of a child with the nose very wide and flat; ears like a fox. The mouth is very large, and prominently filled with large, fang teeth. When it cries it makes a noise that is unlike anything that has ever been heard before. It is something like the cry of a child and howl of a wolf combined. It stays hid during the night and has only been seen along the river bank in the day time, hunting for frogs, which appear to be his favorite diet. It is very dexterous in catching them, and when caught devours them with a great relish. There are parties trying to capture the thing alive, and if they succeed they will have one of the greatest living curiosities of the age. So far they met with failure as it is very shy and shows considerable sagacity in avoiding all traps and snares that have been set to catch it."

Indiana, Pennsylvania, *Progress*, November 25, 1886

THE WILD MAN OF OHIO.

A Curious Creature Seen Among the Hills of Holmes County.

A party of hunters, who have just returned from a hunt in the hills of Holmes County, Ohio, say they encountered a curious creature on their trip. According to their description, a wild man, or some other strange being, is at large in Holmes County. The party who report seeing this strange creature claim that he or it looked like a man, but acted like a wild beast. The creature was encountered near a brushy thicket and willow copse

near what is known as Big Spring, where
General Buell rested on his march through
Ohio, at a point a short distance south of the
Wayne County line in Holmes County. The
hunters were beating the brush for pheas-
ants when the attention of one of the party
was attracted to an object that suddenly
darted across an opening in the brush. Later
on the object was again seen along the edge
of the brush. By this time the hunters had
reached open ground, and were surprised
to see what they describe as a man, entirely nude, but covered with what appeared to
them to be matted hair. When seen he was
some distance away, but on discovering the
hunters he started toward them on a run and
gave forth queer guttural sounds. On seeing
the strange being moving toward them the
party of hunters, which included four persons, all armed with shot guns, broke and
ran. The strange creature pursued them for
a short distance until the party had reached
a public highway, when he turned back and
was seen to enter the Killbuck Creek, which
he swam, and then disappeared in the brush
again. On approaching the water he dropped
on all fours and plunged in like a dog, swimming in a manner similar to a canine. The
hunters did not have the nerve to return, but

got away from the place as soon as possible. They are emphatic in their assertion that they encountered a wild man and describe him as above, but they are of the impression that he is no relative of the famous wild man of Rockaway.

Salem, Ohio, *Daily News,* August 27, 1891

IS IT WILD MAN OR BEAST?

Martins Ferry, O., Aug. 27.—The farmers near Negee, this county, have organized to hunt down the wild man or animal that has been killing and devouring sheep, hogs, chickens, etc., in that section. Many of the farmers are afraid to work in their fields, go out after their stock or go to sleep at night, fearing they will be killed. The wild man or whatever it is has been seen by Samuel Crow and others. Crow says it is covered with dark reddish hair, has large ears, small eyes, teeth like those of a wild boar, huge mouth and paws, measures about five feet in height and weighs fully 200 pounds. It is said that the animal walks and runs as well on two as four legs, can climb a tree or hill quickly and is seen only in the morning and evening. Farmers and their families in the vicinity are very much frightened.

Pittsburgh, Pennsylvania, *Daily Post,* September 5, 1891

BELMONT COUNTY'S MONSTER.

SPECIAL TO THE PITTSBURGH POST.

Bellaire, O., Sept. 4.—The excitement in Mead township over the man-beast, gorilla or "what-is-it" is still great. It was seen last Wednesday evening by Mrs. Milligan and Mrs. Wagner, near Mapleton. Mrs. Milligan was out looking for the cows when this strange thing raised from the grass a few yards from her. This frightened her so that she cannot describe its appearance except that its eyes were like small balls of fire. It is needless to say that she made all possible speed to a place of safety. It is supposed that Mrs. Wagner saw the same animal on the same evening; but as it was late and she was so badly scared, she cannot describe its appearance.

This caused great excitement in the immediate neighborhood, and the following day 40 or 50 men and boys, armed to the teeth, went in search of the animal. During the hunt some one said: "Look! There it is, in the tree-top!" Bang, bang, bang, went three guns in an instant. Upon a close examination it was found that a black log had received all three shots. Still the search went on, and as evening approached and the weary hunters came in one by one, all reported they had seen no strange animal, but some had seen strange tracks in the mud.

Canton, Ohio, *Stark County Democrat,* January 5, 1893

RICHVILLE LETTER.

Richville, O., Jan. 3.

All Richville and vicinity is greatly excited about reports of a gorilla being seen by different parties. Some say it has horns a foot long; other said it had eyes like tin plates (no doubt some of McKinley's tin). John Deville said he did not believe it at first reports as he never heard or saw anything but the rattling of the leaves, but since Brother Hibbert told him it was after him as he was coming home from Gambrinus church he believes it. Hibbert said he ran till he got out of wind, then he squatted behind some bushes when the gorilla came up to him. He was sure he was a goner but he took courage by patting the gorilla, so the animal licked his hand and then vanished. Bro. John has more faith and told G. S. Brown that he saw tracks in the mud two feet long and ten inches wide. John Hafer, the butcher, says he believes there must be some truth in the above reports as he missed some of the ram's horns that were lying in the yard below—no doubt to be used as weapons of destruction; but since the snow there are no tracks to be seen and no reports. Since the election it is presumable it went with the gorilla as with the g.o.p. He crept into a hole and took the hole along with it.

P. K.

Newark, Ohio, *Daily Advocate,* June 7, 1897

WILD MAN SEEN AGAIN.

HE WEARS NOTHING BUT HAIR,
WHICH IS LONG AND CURLY.

The wild man who created so much terror among the inhabitants near Rome, O., several weeks ago by his strange actions has again been seen. Charles Lukins and Bob Forner, while cutting timber a few miles from Rome, claim they encountered a wild man and after a severe struggle say they were able to drive the gorillalike object into his supposed retreat among the cliffs.

They describe the terror as being about six feet tall and his only covering, apparently, a mat of long, curly hair. From their description of the supposed wild man he is undoubtedly the same seen a number of times several weeks ago.

Women and children are now more thoroughly frightened than ever and are afraid to venture from their homes lest they meet the wild creature. A posse of determined men will scour the country now until the terror is located and captured or killed.—Cleveland *Plain Dealer*.

Lima, Ohio, *Times Democrat,* August 1, 1901
"WILD MAN"
WAS THE INVENTION OF CROWD OF BERRY PICKERS. THEY FOUND A PATCH OF BLACKBERRIES AND WANTED TO KEEP OTHERS AWAY FROM THE PLACE. SPECIAL BY WIRE TO TIMES-DEMOCRAT.

[Berea], O., Aug. 1.—Newspapers of the state have been full of stories about a "wildman" terrorizing the community. It was a scheme of berry pickers who had found a nice patch of black berries and rigged up a wild man to keep others away. Since a posse has been on the trail of the alleged wild man, he has kept under cover.

Delphos, Ohio, *Daily Herald,* April 14, 1902
STRANGE BEING.
TERRORIZES ALLEN COUNTY RESIDENTS NEAR BEAVER DAM.

The person who wrote the following has evidently been sleeping under a crazy quilt, or else he is trying to work the city press for a few stray dimes. Here is what has been sent out from Columbus Grove:

"A strange being, apparently half man, and half beast, is seen in the county round about Rockport and Beaver Dam. The creature puts in an appearance at or near farmhouses.

"For some time the farmers in that vicinity have been troubled by nightly visits, apparently from intruders bent on securing money or other valuables. It was the scheme of the prowler to attempt to open a window or fumble at the door locks, then move on to the rear part of the house, and after giving the gates and such outposts a good shake disappears as quickly as he came. The family of Frank Conkleman left their home because of these visits, and while they were gone the strange being was seen.

"The creature is described as resembling a man, although possesses of features coarse and rough, and is said to be covered with hair. The inhabitants of that staid old country vicinity are half crazed with excitement, and the female portion will not venture outside after nightfall.

"It is firmly believed that the strange creature is an insane person who has been at large for some time. The being is attired in dress peculiar to one of the male sex, although scantily clad. A searching party will be organized to capture the fellow if possible, although his fleetness of foot and abilities at fence jumping almost preclude any idea of so doing."

Xenia, Ohio, *Daily Gazette,* August 10, 1904

WILD MAN AT LARGE.

Akron, O., Aug. 10.—The farmers in the vicinity of Hudson are living in fear of their lives on account of the antics of an alleged wild man, who during the night makes the air resound with hideous yells. Posses have been formed to capture him and he has been seen on several occasions, but is too fleet of foot for his pursuers.

Newark, Ohio, *Advocate,* October 12, 1904

WILD MAN SCARING PEOPLE IN VICINITY OF NEW PHILADELPHIA.

As Big as Goliath, Fleet as the Wind and Lithe as the Deer Is at Large.

New Philadelphia, O., Oct. 12—The people of this community are greatly exercised over stories related by wayfarers that a wild man, who haunts are the woods, is at large. Mothers have warned their boys and girls to keep within calling distance, while their fathers are on the lookout for the creature that has suddenly become a menace to hickory nut parties.

The wild man is said to be a giant in stature and to roam about without a stitch of clothing on his body. As fleet as the wind and lithe as the deer he has so far outdistanced the swiftest hounds that have been put on trail by their masters. Some men all but cornered him Monday night, but were afraid to tackle him. He tore up a handful of grass and munched it while the hunters were in view. Then he ran away.

Coshocton, Ohio, *Tribune,* July 31, 1919

APE, ESCAPED FROM A ZOO, IS SIGHTED IN WALHONDING VICINITY

COSHOCTON MEN SPY WILD ANIMAL IN THICKET NEAR MOHICAN BRIDGE— WAS RECENTLY PURSUED NEAR MT. HEALTHY BY POSSE— THOT TO HAVE ESCAPED AT CLEVELAND ZOO— REWARD FOR CAPTURE—LOCAL POSSE MAY ATTEMPT TO LAND IT.

That a full grown ape is at large in the vicinity of Walhonding is the story vouched for by several local men. Those claiming to have seen and to have knowledge of the animal are C. H. Hood,

R. B. Gauley, John Branfield and family, all of Coshocton. Efforts to organize a posse in Coshocton to go in hunt of the animal were halted by the rain Thursday morning.

The animal was seen recently in the neighborhood of Mt. Healthy, where a posse, headed by J. C. Kyke, were out in search of the ape.

It is thot to have traveled from that neighborhood to its present haunts in the Walhonding vicinity.

The ape is believed to have escaped from a Cleveland zoo. Efforts to get into communication with officials in that city were unavailing late Thursday. It is understood that a reward of $2000 is offered for its capture alive, or $200 for its carcass.

Just how the animal made its way from the vicinity of that city as far south as the neighborhood of Walhonding remains unexplained.

On the strength of the story local officials were preparing to take the matter in hand and render every aid that might lead to its capture. Grave fears are entertained that the animal might have become wild because of its new-found freedom and become a menace to human life.

C. H. Hood and R. B. Gauley made their discovery of the animal while camping near Walhonding. The ape was hiding in a dense thicket not far from the railroad track when they discovered it. In taking a short cut in

their camp along the river, Mr. Hood and
Mr. Gauley suddenly came upon it. According to their story the ape was crouching on
its haunches and eating. Unarmed and taken
completely by surprise the men permitted the
animal to escape, not, however, without following it for a short distance and confirming
their first impression. They went so far as to
throw a rock into the bushes into which the
animal had scampered off, on seeing them,
and were answered with loud, intensified
chattering. Satisfied beyond a doubt that the
animal was an ape, the men made their way
to their camp and later to this city. Because
of the peculiar nature of their adventure,
they were at first uncertain as to whether or
not they would make the affair known. They
made careful and diligent inquiries both in
Walhonding and this city, but were unable
to find anyone to support their statements
until by chance Mr. Gauley told the incident
to John Branfield.

On mentioning the affair, Mr. Gauley was
surprised to learn that Branfield also had
some knowledge of the animal's presence but
like himself had refrained from referring to
it thru fear of ridicule. In the course of their
exchange of confidence it developed that
Paul, the small son of Mr. Branfield, had

seen the animal while the family was visiting with relatives in the Barnhill, O., neighborhood. Like Gauley, Mr. Branfield had
remained quiet concerning the affair but was
determined to investigate at his earliest opportunity. Mr. Ross Hawkins, Barnhill, O.,
is mentioned among other Tuscarawas-co
people who are said to have seen the animal.

Following their talk the two men, together with C. H. Hood, met with Sheriff Cullson
and other local officials preparatory to the
organization of the hunt. Plans were made
to go out Thursday morning but owing to the
heavy rain it was deemed advisable to post-
pone the affair until a more favorable time.

Residents of the Walhonding vicinity were
considerably alarmed by the news and were
making their own preparations for a hunt
Thursday morning.

Word concerning the affair has been widely circulated and the capture of the ape is
thot to be only a matter of time.

WAS IT A GORILLA OR A GROUNDHOG?
Reports, afloat for the past few days that
Rev. C. H. Hood and R. B. Gauley, Coshocton,
saw a strange animal resembling a gorilla or
grisly bear in the vicinity of the lamp black
works above Walhonding, while they were on
a fishing expedition a few days ago had not
been discredited Thursday.

One theory advanced by the skeptics is that it is a big groundhog, but as Levi Kent, the famous trapper, lives in that vicinity it is considered hardly possible that a groundhog would live to attain full growth within a radius of a few miles of Levi's gun.

As the Hornets Nest Camp will be opened in that locality in a short time, the Hornets may succeed in capturing the animal. Gauley and Hood are both men of unquestioned veracity and sobriety, and their report of seeing the animal disappear into the undergrowth and gnash its teeth when they threw a club into the brush, cannot be questioned.

Coshocton, Ohio, *Tribune,* August 1, 1919

REV. HOOD SAYS APE HE SAW WAS ONLY AN ORDINARY GROUNDHOG

MINISTER EXPRESSES SURPRISE THAT INNOCENT PEOPLE SHOULD BE TERRIFIED BY WILD STORY FOR WHICH HE DECLARES THERE IS NO FOUNDATION IN FACT.

Declaring that the statement that he saw an ape near Walhonding or anywhere else, and that the whole story was manufactured out of the whole cloth, Rev. C. H. Hood, of Coshocton, expressed his regret that anything so preposterous should be foisted upon the people of the county, Friday. Mr. Hood returned late Thursday from Byesville where

he attended the funeral of his brother. He
had been gone since Monday.

"It is unfair to the people of the Walhonding community to circulate such a story,"
says Mr. Hood. "People up there are afraid
to let their children get out of their sight
for fear this mysterious animal will capture
them. The whole community is terrified, and
for my part I do not want to be included in
any such group of alarmists. What I saw was
a large groundhog, and I called it that at the
time. At no time have I even intimated that
it was anything else, and obviously I have
taken no part in conferences with the county
officials, having been out of town since Monday.

"I wish you would correct the impression
that I was a party to the circulation of this
wild rumor," he told a reporter. He also stated emphatically that he could not account for
the report given the paper.

The report that an ape had escaped from
a Cleveland zoo and had been sighted in at
least two central Ohio communities, the last
of which was near Walhonging, had its effect. A camping party west of Walhonding
and near the spot where the animal was reported to have been seen, broke camp Friday

morning. People in the neighborhood were sticking close to their homes or going armed. Blackberry picking had ceased for miles around, while the sole topic of conversation was the ape.

Wild stories of a man having been killed near Dennison by the animal, the serious injury of a woman berry picker in Tuscarawas-co, and the capture of the ape near Cavallo sprang up like mushrooms Friday and spread like wildfire. It is doubtful if anything has so stirred the county in months. In many communities and thruout Coshocton groups of men and boys were feverishly discussing means of capturing the animal and claiming the $2000 reward, alleged to have been offered for its return to Cleveland alive.

R. B. Gauley and John Branfield, who told the story in Coshocton, stuck to their original statements Friday. Rev. Hood, who is a partner of Mr. Gauley's in the insurance business said Friday that he was hunting groundhogs when he spied the animal and attempted to stalk it. He said he carried a rifle of .22 caliber, and was too far away to risk a shot. When he started to creep up on his game he declares Mr. Gauley insisted it was not a groundhog. Hood declared he laughed to himself and went on, but was unable to get within gunshot of the animal before it disappeared into the bushes.

"I did throw a stone into the underbrush in an effort to start the groundhog, but there was no 'monkey chattering' reply." Hood asserted. "I naturally dismissed the matter from my mind and thot no more about it, until upon arriving home late Thursday to be confronted with this harrowing tale. People kept my telephone ringing last night until after 11 o'clock, wanting to know all about the 'ape.' I have been forced to leave the house to avoid the continual nuisance," he declares.

Coshocton, Ohio, *Tribune,* August 2, 1919

GAULEY SAYS HOOD MAY BE AFTER $2,000 APE REWARD

DECLARES MINISTER IS UNDECIDED WHAT SORT OF ANIMAL IT WAS BRANFIELD BACKS UP HIS STATEMENT HOOD LEAVES EARLY SAT. "ON BERRY PICKING TRIP," GAULEY LEARNS

That down in his heart the Rev. C. H. Hood knows he is undecided whether or not he saw an ape or a groundhog near Walhonding a few days ago is the contention of R. B. Gauley, who expressed surprise Saturday at the statement made by the minister Friday.

"Mr. Hood went berry picking early to-day," Mr. Gauley said Saturday. "I wouldn't be surprised to learn that he went to Walhonding vicinity in the hope of again sighting the animal and perhaps winning the reward for its capture. When I told him Friday—before the paper came out with his statement that it was only a groundhog—that a reward of $2,000 is offered for the ape's capture he exclaimed, 'I'll bet that's what we saw.'"

That an ape has been at large in Tuscarawas-co and has been unsuccessfully pursued by posses was insisted by John Branfield Saturday. Branfield declares he is not an alarmist and says he can prove his statements in connection with the affair by scores of Tuscarawas-co residents. "Of course I do not know whether the ape has wandered over to Walhonding," he said Saturday, "but I do know that it has been repeatedly sighted near Barnhill."

Branfield said Saturday that James Beach, city had been told by his father, Harry Beach, who is camping near Pomerene, that a strange animal visited the camp a few days ago. William Valentine, local barber, is said to have seen the animal at that time.

Mr. Gauley insists that Rev. Hood concurred with him at the time they saw the animal near Walhonding, that it was not native to this locality. He also declared Saturday that Mr. Hood admitted that no groundhog attains to the proportions of the animal, nor does the woodchuck chatter under ordinary circumstances, as the animal undoubtedly did.

"We don't want to reflect on Mr. Hood's veracity, but we insist that he was somewhat excited about the incident in spite of the effort he has put forth to quiet his terrified parishoners," said Mr. Gauley Saturday.

Referring to the alleged meeting with the sheriff and his deputy, Mr. Gauley said he took the proposition up with Sheriff Cullison for the purpose of learning whether he had received official notice of a reward being offered for the ape's capture. The sheriff had received no such notice, but expressed his willingness to attempt the capture of the animal, according to Mr. Gauley. A trip to Newcomerstown Thursday by the Sheriff interfered with the hunt and it was called off, Gauley declared.

Nor report of the ape having been sighted a second time near Walhonding has reached Coshocton. People in that vicinity are avoiding the vicinity in which the animal was reported to have been seen, it is said.

Judging from the travels of the animal within the past few weeks, extending from Cleveland to Tuscarawas-co and probably to Pomerene, near Walhonding, it is thot that the ape will next be heard from at some point farther south.

Coshocton, Ohio, *Tribune*, August 17, 1919

TUSCARAWAS-CO APE WAS A DEACON ARRAYED IN BUFFALO ROBE AND RED STAGE WHISKERS

[Summary: While trespassing on a neighbor's property to pick blackberries, a Conesville woman encountered a strange figure that scared her away. Her oldest son, hearing about a $2000 reward for the capture of the ape reported roaming the region, grabbed his shotgun. The neighbor, Deacon Smuckfinckle, ended up with a rear full of buckshot, confessing the disguise was intended to keep "them dratted boys out of the berry patch," and that he hadn't taken into account reports of an escaped ape in the area.]

Lima, Ohio, *News,* July 15, 1920

BIG APE ROAMS NEAR MARIETTA

ANIMAL ESCAPED FROM ZOO OR CIRCUS IS HUNTED

Marietta, Ohio.—If the Cincinnati Zoo or any rambling circus that has passed thru Ohio, have lost a first class man-sized ape, disturbed residents of this town and the vicinity of Gravel Bank would like to have representatives come here and inquire into the antecedents of a strange animal that has stirred the quiet folk hereabouts to a high pitch of excitement.

Rumors of what is declared to be a large specimen of the African ape, seen in a heavy woods near Gravel Bank, eight miles below here on the Ohio river, have been confirmed by the weird experience of many people. The animal is declared to have on a number of occasions disputed the right of road with persons walking in the direction of Marietta.

The other night the strange animal is declared by Archie Cassady of Marietta, to have squatted in the road and to have refused to permit Cassady and his party to pass. When the party offered to give the animal the road, the ape calmly moved over in front of them and blocked their passage. They returned later with an armed searching party, but the beast had disappeared. Another posse was organized after the people on a train, returning home, had seen the ape, but tho they found huge tracks in the under brush, the animal evidently, had taken to the trees.

Several persons have fired at the animal, including William Fish, a farmer living near

Gravel Bank. When frightened, those who have seen the animal report that the ape swings into the trees, jumping from branch to branch.

The ape is said to be considerably larger than a man, apparently being seven feet tall. It has not attacked any persons or livestock, and it is believed it hunts human habitation more from a desire for companionship than with the purpose of harm. When last seen the ape appeared to be well fed and at home in the woods he has selected as his habitat.

Reno, Nevada, *State Journal,* May 19, 1921

CUTUP SCARES GIRLS
IN HIS APE MAKE-UP

MYSTERY OF "WILD APE" IS CLEARED UP
AFTER LONG YEAR OF WAITING

Uhrichsville, Ohio, May 18.—The mystery of the "wild ape" has been cleared up.

A year ago, workmen reported seeing a creature resembling an ape in the woods and fields.

One Roanoke woman was badly frightened when the creature played around her, cutting all kinds of capers.

It now develops that the "ape" wasn't an ape at all. It was a young man dressed in a calf skin.

Massillon, Ohio, *Evening Independent*, August 6, 1925

Pomeroy, O. (AP)—A correspondent of a local paper writing in from Lock Run, a rural precinct in the eastern end of Meigs county, says:

"There has been quite a bit of excitement in our community owing to the fact that some of our folks have been disturbed by an animal resembling an ape or gorilla. It was last seen between here and Portland. Many have seen its tracks where it leaped about ten feet at a jump. It is hoped that some brave adventurer will jump in and capture this beast, as it is keeping most of the populace under their respective beds in their homes. If it keeps on annoying us we will be compelled to call for state aid."

Elyria, Ohio, *Chronicle Telegram,* June 6, 1930

APE TERRIFIES NORWALK

Norwalk, O., June 6.—Terrified residents of Norwalk today were barring doors and windows and afraid to leave their homes on the report that a large ape was seen running wild near the Memorial hospital.

Police and deputies began a systematic search for the beast after it was authentically reported that a dog was seen fighting with the animal.

The hospital area is near the Norwalk city limits. It is believed the ape escaped from a circus which showed here about 10 days ago.

The animal was seen last in the garden of John Landoll, just over the corporation line. Many other persons reported seeing the beast in a woods nearby.

A party of Detroit motorists parked along the road yesterday was frightened when the animal appeared near the highway and notified the sheriff's office. A search failed to find any trace of the ape.

Attaches of the hospital also have told police of seeing the animal near the building.

Helena, Montana, *Independent,* June 7, 1930

ESCAPED APE HAS OHIOANS WORRIED

SHERIFF WILL SEEK CIRCUS ANIMAL

Norwalk, O., June 6.—(AP)—An ape, thought to be a chimpanzee or an orang-otang, recently escaped from a circus, which has frightened persons west of the city in the last five days, will be the object of a search by Sheriff Harry D. Smith and a posse of men, he announced late today.

The animal was seen first by three motorists from Detroit, who ran out of gasoline near the home of John Landoll, farmer west of the city. One of the men, badly frightened, ran for a quarter of a mile to a gasoline station, where he told his story to the attendant.

Seen in Garden

Landoll and his wife and two grown sons reported seeing the animal three nights ago in their garden. The next evening persons pacing near the farm also reported seeing it.

It was reported the ape had frightened boys away from the old swimming pool west of the Landoll home.

Elyria, Ohio, *Chronicle Telegram,* June 7, 1930

ORGANIZE HUNT FOR
APE AT NORWALK

Norwalk, O., June 7.—Terrified women and anxious children who have remained behind locked doors in their homes for the past few days, today eagerly awaited the result of the organized search planned for this afternoon for an ape reported roaming the woods on the western outskirts of the city.

That section of the town spent a night of terror when a posse of 100 men and deputies failed to find any trace of the supposed beast in a hunt through the woods about midnight.

John Landoll is the latest person to have reported seeing the beast in the garden at the rear of his home near the city limits. He said his dog had been barking at the animal for several nights and that on investigation he sighted the ape in a crouching position.

Others who have seen the anthropoid include two motorists from Detroit and another party of tourists from Mansfield.

Although Sheriff Harry D. Smith places little credence in the existence of the ape, he has offered the aid of the deputies in finding the beast.

Lima, Ohio, *News,* June 7, 1930

APE HUNTED BY POSSE IN OHIO.

100 ARMED WITH SHOTGUNS AND RIFLES SEARCH WOODS BUT BEAST NOT SEEN

Norwalk, O., June 7—(AP)—Norwalk went ape hunting early today, but found nothing resembling the beast whose reported presence in the vicinity gave women and children a scare.

A posse of 100 men, led by Chief of Police F. R. Remington and armed with shotguns and rifles, started at midnight. They scoured the western edge of the city for three hours, but found nothing that looked like an anthropoid beast.

A number of tourists, truck drivers and John Landoll, a farmer living just outside the city, had declared they saw an ape, or some kind of a lumbering, half-upright creature, in the last few days.

Those believing in the presence of an ape pointed out that one was reported to have escaped some time ago from a circus at Sandusky.

Coshocton, Ohio, *Tribune,* June 7, 1930

ARMY OF APE-HUNTERS SEARCH NORTH OHIO FOR ANTHROPOID

Norwalk, O., June 7.—An army of ape-hunters, a new kind of searching party in Ohio, is combing northern Ohio today for a large anthropoid ape, which is reported to be roaming this section.

Residents in the vicinity of Norwalk are horror-stricken following the many persistent reports of the huge animal's roaming activities.

First reports came from a party of motorists from Detroit. They said they had seen the ape, Monday, near the Norwalk Memorial hospital. Local residents scoffed at the news. Impossible, was the common opinion.

A tourist from Mansfield gave the next report. He said he saw the beast in the outskirts of the city. Many truck drivers and motorists made similar reports. Norwalk citizens still thot someone was "seeing things."

John Landoll, who lives near the city limits, went into his garden to quiet his dog last night. The dog had scented something. Landoll saw the shape of what appeared to be a man.

As the shape lumbered away in true anthropoid fashion, Landoll remembered the rumor about the ape. He didn't wait to see any more.

It was reported several weeks ago that an ape escaped from a circus at Sandusky.

Athens, Ohio, *Messenger*, June 8, 1930

ROAMING APE STILL AT LARGE NEAR NORWALK AS TERRIFIED

RESIDENTS STAY IN HOMES, AWAITING CAPTURE ORGANIZED SEARCH PLANNED OVER WEEK-END FOR BEAST THAT IS REPORTED SEEN BY CITIZEN AND TWO PARTIES OF TOURISTS.

Norwalk, June 7.—(U.P.)—Terrified women and anxious children who have remained behind locked doors in their homes for the past few days, today eagerly awaited the results of the organized search planned over the week-end for an ape reported roaming the woods on the western outskirts of the city.

That section of the town spent a night of terror when a posse of 100 men and deputies failed to find any trace of the supposed beast in a hunt through the woods about midnight.

The young army of hunters carried shotguns, picks, clubs and rifles. Flashlights and lights from autos aided in the search.

The entire west side of the city was in a grip of terror today following the persistent reports that the animal was running wild.

John Landoll is the latest person to have reported seeing the beast in the garden at the rear of his home, near the city limits. He said his dog had been barking at the animal for several nights and that on investigation he sighted the ape in a crouched position.

Others who have seen the anthropoid include two motorists from Detroit and another party of tourists from Mansfield.

Although Sheriff Harry D. Smith places little credence in the existence or the ape, he has offered the aid of deputies in finding the beast.

Washington, D.C., *The Sunday Star,* June 8, 1930

HUGE APE, AT LARGE NEAR CITY, SPREADS FEAR IN OHIO HOMES

HOSPITAL PATIENT AND TWO CHILDREN REPORT SEEING BEAST, HUNTED BY HEAVILY ARMED POSSE. By the Associated Press.

Norwalk, Ohio, June 7.—A renewed hunt for a huge ape was planned here tonight as many

residents in the western part of the city continued to be seriously frightened over reports
that such a beast has been prowling in their
neighborhood.

More reports of citizens who claim to have
seen an ape at large within the past few days,
were received by authorities today.

John Goodsite of Milan, Ohio, patient at
Memorial Hospital, Norwalk, told of hearing
a hoarse scream in the night. He looked out
of the window and saw an ungainly, fur-covered animal ambling into the woods at the
rear of the hospital.

John Remele, janitor at the hospital, reported that some beast of unusual strength,
had broken into a chicken coop at the hospital, twisting posts and wire in its path, and
had killed many chickens.

Hardly 500 feet away from the hospital,
the ape was seen by two children, police
were told. Dolores Grossweller, 13, daughter
of Charles Grossweller, said she saw an ape
about as large as a 10-year-old boy, walking
along Cole Creek. Donald Barman, 10, son of
Carl Barman, saw the animal near the same
place. He said it tried to hide from him in
the grass and that it seemed frightened.

Neither of the children was alarmed seriously because in both cases the animal ran
away from them.

Led by Chief of Police F. R. Remington, a posse of 100 men armed with rifles and shot-guns, searched for the ape several hours last night, but were unable to find it.

Elyria, Ohio, *Chronicle Telegram,* June 9, 1930

LOSE TRACK OF NORWALK APE

Norwalk, O., June 9—Search for a huge ape, believed to be at large near here, was still in progress today though no one had reported seeing the animal since last week.

Carl Landoll, young farmer, discovered tracks, apparently those of the big anthropoid, in the soft mud of the Huron River Valley, to the rear of his home on the old Water Works property a short distance west of the city.

Landoll's father and several other persons reported seeing the animal in that vicinity last week. The valleys of the East Branch of Huron River and Cole Creek are as densely wooded as an African jungle and persons familiar with the country say the ape might have escape there indefinitely.

The city has been greatly interested in the search for the animal which, it is believed, might have escaped from a circus. Hundreds of Sunday motorists visited the sections where the ape was reported seen but no trace of it was found.

Carl Landoll reported that a decayed stump near his home has been torn to pieces. He believes the ape may have dug into it while searching for insects.

The more skeptical are still [inclined] to doubt that there actually is an ape at large.

Coshocton, Ohio, *Tribune,* June 12, 1930

OHIO'S APE IS AGAIN SEEN IN FREMONT VICINITY

Fremont, June 12.—Interest in the "ape mystery," which his gripped this county for the past week, was heightened today when Frank Binder, of Rice tp., near here, reported that he saw the prowling anthropoid.

Posses of farmers and deputies from the county sheriff's office organized immediately and started an intensive search in the district. It was believed the animal is in thickets several miles north of this city.

Binder described the beast as a large gray animal. He declared that he chased it for some distance thru a corn field but finally lost trace of it. The animal had a "peculiar style of running," Binder said.

The strange animal was first reported seen on the western outskirts of Norwalk. A group of tourists from Detroit told city authorities they saw an ape. A motorist from Mansfield made the next report which was followed by numerous stories from truck drivers and tourists.

A thoro search by a large posse last week-end failed to reveal any trace of an ape.

Zanesville, Ohio, *Signal,* June 29, 1930

APE FROM CIRCUS KEEPS VILLAG-ERS AT HOME AT NIGHT

RESIDENTS OF OHIO TOWN TERROR STRICKEN; POSSE TO SEARCH FOR PROWLER

Lima, June 28—(AP)—Panic stricken residents of the village of Alger, 15 miles east of here, formed posses today to search for an ape, supposed to have escaped from a circus at Carey, O.

The animal first appeared in Alger Thursday. Mayor Lyman Clark met it on the edge of a grove, and later it was seen on the porch of the Cooney farm house. Members of the family, thinking their dog might drive the ape away, attempted to coax the dog out of the house, but the animal refused to leave. On Friday the ape appeared in a corn field where Myron Herrick was at work. He fired several shots at it from a shot gun, but the ape escaped into a woods.

For two nights Alger has appeared as a city of the dead—for there are no street lights, and residents have feared to leave their homes after dark.

Elyria, Ohio, *Chronicle Telegram,* July 30, 1930

REPORT APE SEEN
NEAR SANDUSKY

Homeville, O, July 30.—The elusive ape that has left a trail of terror in towns between Sandusky and Norwalk was reported to have entered a dwelling here today and frightened John Rucker and his wife from their home.

Mrs. Rucker was first to see the animal entering the house by a rear door. As she screamed, her husband sighted the ape and grabbing his wife by the hand, fled from the house.

Sheriff John Parker of Sandusky was called, but deputies failed to find the animal. Instructions have been issued by the sheriff to capture the animal if found.

Mr. and Mrs. Rucker assured deputies that the intruder was an ape.

Newark, Ohio, *Advocate,* August 28, 1930

Six Cambridge men claim to have seen an ape Tuesday afternoon, three miles southeast of Cambridge, in a woods, while changing an auto tire. George Cain, Joseph Farley, Charles Curtan, Donald Jirles, Lane Huff, and Allen Moss observed the animal, having the appearance of an ape, moving about in the trees overhead, uttering gutteral roars. They hastily boarded their truck and left the vicinity. It is thought the animal may be the one reported escaped from a circus in Mansfield some time ago.

Cambridge, Ohio, *Jeffersonian,* August 27, 1930 (from Keating 1993)

"SPOOK, SPIKE OR DEVIL"— MONKEY, APE OR GORILLA.

Six Cambridge men claim to have indisputable evidence that an ape or exceptionally large monkey is loose in the woods of Guernsey county, following an experience Tuesday afternoon in the vicinity of High Hill schoolhouse, three miles south west of Cambridge on the Georgetown road.

The men are George Cain, Joseph Farley, Charles Curran, Donald Jirles, Lane Huff and Allen Moss. They left Cambridge in a truck Tuesday afternoon to go to an old sawmill site near High Hill school for sawdust for use in the construction of a miniature golf course. They were enroute back from the pile when one tire on the truck went flat in a hollow. The tire had just been repaired and replaced when all six of the men heard a rumbling roar, which at first was believed to be thunder. No clouds were overhead, however, they continued to consider the noise which was repeated several times as thunder, until Charles Curran, looking up along one side of the hollow saw a strange object moving in a tree.

Calling in his companions they each saw a large animal with every appearance of an ape moving about in a tree. The animal made several loud gutteral sounds which were recognized as the sounds previously believed to have been thunder. The ape or monkey descended from the tree and stood for a short time beneath it beating its fore legs against its chest and continuing to emit the strange sounds. It then disappeared in the woods. All of the men who saw the ape were thoroughly frightened, boarded their truck and drove hastily to Cambridge.

A report was also circulated early Tuesday afternoon that the ape had been seen between Cambridge and Byesville.

Monday night at 10 o'clock a large number of people on south Eleventh street and Morton avenue were attracted by the strange waving of branches in a large elm tree in the City cemetery. There was no wind blowing and the branches swayed and jerked for several minutes. The movements of some animal in the tree could be faintly distinguished in the rays of a nearby street light. Later several men entered the cemetery and investigated but could find nothing. In view of the developments of Tuesday afternoon near High Hill school house it is believed the ape was in the tree in the cemetery and that the movements in the branches were caused when it jumped from limb to limb, although no one saw or could determine the exact cause of the movements.

Several weeks ago news dispatches carried a story that an ape had escaped from a circus near Mansfield. Several people here believe the animal has reached this vicinity and that the one seen near High Hill school house is the same.

Newark, Ohio, *Advocate,* August 30, 1930

An ape, supposed to have escaped from a circus in the north part of the state some two months ago, is believed, from tracks seen by boys here, to have reached Knox county in its travels. Tracks like those of a broad bare foot have been seen in a cornfield near this city. Robert Clements, owner of the cornfield, where the tracks were said to have been seen, made an investigation and could find no tracks, but did find a place where the weeds and undergrowth were trampled down into what appeared to be a bed.

Coshocton, Ohio, *Tribune,* September 12, 1930

APE AT LARGE, REPORT

Rumors were circulated here Thursday that an ape had been seen near the C. and M. railroad tunnel south of here Tuesday. After an investigation it was found that these reports were without foundation.

Several people in the vicinity of North Salem, Guernsey co., reported seeing an ape about a week ago. It is thot that an ape which escaped from a circus at Mansfield sometime ago is running at large somewhere in this section of the country.

Charleston, West Virginia, *Gazette,* July 17, 1931

'APE' IS REVEALED
AS COUNTY'S BOOTLEGGER

Mansfield, O., July 16—(UP)—Residents in the northern section of Richland county may roam the woods at night undisturbed, for the mystery of the "ape" has been exploded.

The sheriff's office was notified last September that a huge ape was roaming at large over the northern section of the county. An investigation followed, and several persons who apparently had a keen sense of imagination, testified that they had seen the creature.

The former county sheriff Aaron Davis, said he had never been really satisfied with the case and, with the hope that something more might be learned about the "monster," continued investigating.

The former sheriff learned the inside story a few days ago. He related it as follows:

"It developed that the huge ape was a man engaged in bootlegging. He was a short, heavy set individual who was in the practice of hiding his wares in the woods. One afternoon, about dusk, he wanted to get some liquor, and, borrowing his wife's fur coat, he started out.

"He became fearful lest he should attract attention from people nearby, and sped from tree to tree as he dodged into the woods. Then he secured his package and escaped."

Aaron said he had been advised that the "ape man" recently had left the county.

Zanesville, Ohio, *Times Recorder,* August 10, 1932

CLAIM BIG APE ROAMING WOODS HARDESTY FARM

SEEN BY RESIDENTS CHANDLERSVILLE AND VICINITY SEVERAL TIMES

A big ape roaming the woods on the Henry Hardesty farm one mile east of Chandlersville is causing fears in the neighborhood and residents of the vicinity are on the watch lest the beast leave his favorite haunts and visit their own barnyards, especially at night.

Hardesty has seen the ape twice at night and heard it crashing around in the woods on another occasion. Neighbors have seen it in the daylight, it is claimed, but none of them have been able to give an accurate description of it other than it is an ape.

Sheriff William Curtis has been notified of the ape's presence in the woods but no organized efforts are now being considered for either capturing or killing it.

Believed to have escaped from a circus the ape has made himself at home in the Hardesty woods and refuses to leave.

Zanesville, Ohio, *Signal*, August 11, 1932

TWO FOX HUNTERS ALSO REPORT SEEING STRANGE ANIMAL IN TREE

While reports of the presence of an ape in the vicinity of the Henry Hardesty farm near Chandlersville were being questioned by some residents and substantiated by others, two fox hunters came forward today with an account of seeing the ape on the William Osborne farm, near Riz Mills some time ago.

Harry Prouty, Green Valley, and Dewey Hughes of near Chandlersville declare that while hunting fox on the Osborne farm, they saw a strange animal in a tree, gripping branches with odd hands and feet and all the while peering at them. They said that as they approached the animal clambered through the tree foliage and disappeared.

Although they wondered at the presence of the strange animal, it seems as though they made but little mention of the incident until reports were made to Sheriff William Curtis by Henry Hardesty a few days ago that an ape was seen in the trees of his farm, some distance from the Osborne tract.

Prouty and Hughes were not armed with a gun and were using only one dog while hunting. They continued on their way and did not investigate.

Until the beast is trapped or shot, residents of the rural area where the ape was reported seen are keeping close to their homes and children and young folk are cautioned not to venture into the fields or forests.

The ape is believed to have escaped from circus or carnival and to have taken refuge in the country which is heavily wooded in sections. It is said to be easily distinguishable by a white ring about its neck. The ape may or may not be vicious but neighbors are planning to organize and search out the beast. No reports have been received of it attacking or killing livestock on the farms.

Athens, Ohio, *Messenger,* August 12, 1932

TIMID SOULS STICK TO
HOMES, APE SCARES 'EM

Chandlersville, O., Aug. 12.—(U.P.)—It may be only the seasonal reappearance of the time-worn "wild man" stories which have sent many a youngster scurrying in terror down the streets of his town.

But the fact remains, the "ape scare" in this vicinity is the basis of real fears.

Persons move about at night in groups. Farmers' wives and children are kept "close to the house."

Henry Hardesty, a prominent farmer, first "saw" the ape. It was a "long gangling, loose-armed creature" that loomed large in the darkness near Hardesty's barn.

The story of its apparently harmless expeditions around neighboring farms has loomed larger. Farmers planned to organize a hunt and take the animal alive if possible. It is believed he may have escaped from a circus which showed at Zanesville recently.

Coshocton, Ohio, *Tribune,* September 16, 1932

PERPETRATOR AT APE HOAX GETS FRACTURED RIB AS BUDDIES FLEE

An "ape" roams the hinterlands in the vicinity of Roscoe. If you don't believe it, interview any of the group which Tuesday night invaded the "ape's" stamping grounds near a vacant cabin in the hills west of Roscoe with the avowed intention of putting a stop to the "silly" rumor.

The Coshoctonites came away in a mad rush, trampling each other underfoot, banging into trees and injuring their leader, George Gutting, Main St. butcher, who was the instigator of the hoax.

The stampede started when a gigantic, hairy figure dropped from the heights of an apple tree in the midst of the skeptical group.

Men scattered in all directions. Harold Brink stepped over small trees and didn't start to jump until he ran into tall timber. He was first away, followed closely by Noah Barrett, Tom Gray, Joe Gallimore, Francis Head, Russ Raymer and Ed Smith.

Gutting, unfortunately, was in the path of the general exodus. Just as he led the group to the spot said to be the habitat of the monster, he tried to lead it away. Less fleet of foot than his comrades, he was caught in a "pocket" and either hurled into a tree or trampled underfoot.

A physician discovered a fractured rib.

Gutting organised the "ape" posse for the purpose of convincing farmers of the vicinity, many of whom swore they had seen the animal, that no such creature existed. A colored confederate in a fur coat took the role of the ape.

Certain members of the group insist it really was an ape and say they wouldn't return to the spot without an escort composed of Battery F, under personal command of Capt. Tom Carton.

At noon today Gutting had not made a complete check on his squad, but it was thot most of its members had returned.

Coshocton, Ohio, *Tribune*, September 20, 1932

WILL ATTEMPT APE'S CAPTURE IN JACKSON TP.

Stories circulating about the ape reputed to be wandering in the western part of the county are substantiated by residents of the district west of Roscoe.

Glenn Adams, who lives about three miles west of Roscoe, was among the first to see the animal. His son returned home about 11 o'clock one night last week and, noticing some animal in an apple tree in the yard, called his father and the two investigated. When they approached the tree the ape swung down from the lower limbs to the ground and stood watching the men. Adams had his police dog with him and attempted to set him on the ape, but the dog was reluctant to tackle the animal. After a few minutes of watchful waiting the ape retreated to the woods.

Homer Goodin, a neighbor of Adams, saw the ape during the day and shot at it, but failed to injure it.

The ape is believed to have escaped from a circus during a recent stand at Zanesville, and is making his home in the dense woods and abandoned farms north of the Adams farm. The animal is said to be about four feet high when erect, and has about six feet of small chain attached to its neck. It seems to have an appetite for wild grapes and sweet corn, as it has several times tried to break into buildings where these are stored. Its great strength is attested to by the residents, who say that wire fences have been literally torn apart by the animal.

If the ape "is not killed or captured soon the community plans to have a "round-up" and either kill or capture it.

Mansfield, Ohio, *News,* September 21, 1932

ESCAPED APE ROAMS
COSHOCTON COUNTY

ANIMAL SPREADS ALARM IN RURAL AREAS

By International News Service

Coshocton, O., Sept. 21—Alarmed by reports that a large ape with powerful strength is on the loose in this section, residents of Coshocton county today announced that a round-up will be conducted in an attempt to capture the animal.

Believed to have escaped from a circus which recently showed at Zanesville, the ape has been seen lumbering about barnyards in the rural districts near Roscoe, O., trying to break into buildings.

The animal's strength is attested by residents of the heavily-wooded section of the county, who declare that it does not climb wire fences but pulls the wires apart and crawls through.

Two or three shots have been fired by persons frightened by the ape's approach. The animal is usually seen at night.

Lima, Ohio, *News,* September 21, 1932

ALARMED BY REPORTS OF
APE AT LARGE, COUNTY
MAPS HUNT FOR ANIMAL

Coshocton, Sept. 21—(INS)—Alarmed by reports that a large ape with powerful strength is on the loose in this section, residents of Coshocton-co today announced that a round-up will be conducted in an attempt to capture the animal.

Believed to have escaped from a circus which recently showed at Zanesville, the ape has been seen lumbering about barnyards in the rural district near Roscoe, O., trying to break into buildings.

The animal's strength is attested by residents of the heavily wooded section of the county, who declare that it does not climb wire fences but pulls the wires apart and crawls thru.

Two or three shots have been fired by persons who were frightened by the ape's approach. The animal is usually seen at night.

Van Wert, Ohio, *Daily Bulletin,* September 22, 1932

Steubenville, O., Sept. 22. (INS).—A large ape reported roaming about Coshocton county yesterday is believed to have transferred its prowling to the hills of Jefferson county, Sheriff William J. Yost said to-day. A miner en route to work told the sheriff that an animal, possibly an ape, leaped at him to-day. Residents of the hill section said they have heard the chattering of an animal or animals recently.

Steubenville, Ohio, *Herald-Star,* September 22, 1932

APE TERRORIZES
ALIKANNA FOLKS

A strange creature, believed by authorities to be an ape which escaped recently from a circus showing in the central part of the state, has been terrorizing residents around the Alikanna district.

The beast, said to be the size of a large shepherd dog, has been seen almost nightly since last Monday, and yesterday chased a Pottery addition resident as he was returning home from work at Weirton.

Sheriff William J. Yost gave little credence to first reports that the ape was at large here, but with continued complaints coming into his office, he ordered an investigation.

Armed deputies, strengthened by a force of the alarmed residents, combed the wooded hills about the Stanton park region last night and early this morning without results.

Numerous shots have been fired at the strange form by persons frightened by its approach. The ape is usually seen at night time, and one of the residents said it climbed trees like "greased lightning and disappears as if by magic."

An ape is thought to have escaped from a circus showing recently . . .

Zanesville, Ohio, *Signal,* September 22, 1932

MUSKINGUM COUNTY'S
MISSING LINK

MAY HAVE MOVED TO STEUBENVILLE

Muskingum county's widely heralded ape, which for several days was the object of a search in the Chandlersville vicinity, seems to have crawled into its hole (if apes live in holes), because nothing has been heard of the animal for a few weeks now.

That is, nothing was heard of it until today when county officials at Steubenville called Sheriff William Curtis long-distance to inquire if the ape might have escaped from the confines of this county and migrated to the north.

Steubenville, it seems, is the latest metropolis to be troubled with the ape "epidemic." A large, hairy animal was seen making its way along the river bank at Steubenville, throwing great fear into those who claimed they saw the jungle beast.

Sheriff Curtis was amazed at the report concerning the ape but felt sure that the Steubenville ape was in no way linked with the Muskingum county ape. If it was, he gave assurance, it must have been the missing link.

The report current in this county for several days about an ape being seen in a woods near Chandlersville never was substantiated, despite persistent efforts on the part of county officers, the dog warden, game protector and public spirited residents of Salt Creek township, to rout the bosom pal of one Mr. Darwin.

Zanesville, Ohio, *Times Recorder,* September 23, 1932

THAT "ZANESVILLE APE" SEEN NEAR STEUBENVILLE

Steubenville, O., Sept. 22—(AP)—An animal "with eyes as big as a dollar and making sounds like an automobile horn," was hunted in the brush at Alikanna near here today.

Although none has gotten a good look at the animal, many believed it was an ape. An ape was reported to have escaped recently from a circus at Zanesville, about 100 miles west of here last week.

The animal first made its appearance last night when it chased a man. He took one fleeting glance and "dug out" for home. His only description was that it had "eyes as big as a dollar."

Other reports of the animal's existence caused deputy sheriffs to take up the hunt.

An all-day search failed to reveal any trace of the animal.

Coshocton, Ohio, *Tribune,* September 23, 1932

MINER REPORTS SEEING
APE IN JEFFERSON CO.

The large ape reported seen in Jackson tp. recently may have transferred its prowling to the hills of Jefferson co., Sheriff William J. Yost said today.

A miner enroute to work told the sheriff that an animal, possibly an ape, leaped at him today. Residents of the hill section said that they have heard the chattering of an animal or animals recently.

Glenn Adams and Homer Goodin, who reside west of Roscoe, reported seeing an ape there during the past few weeks.

Steubenville, Ohio, *Herald-Star,* September 23, 1932

ALIKANNA 'MISSING LINK'
MYSTERY STILL UNSOLVED

The Alikanna ape case continued as deep a mystery as ever today with deputy sheriffs and residents still hoping to glimpse the 'missing link' in daylight.

One woman in the Pottery addition, frightened by the screams of the beast, called for protection about 1 p.m. Thursday, but officials heard nothing more of the animal.

According to them, the ape heads toward the river shore at night, but hides out in the wooded hills during the daytime. It exists on leaves, birds and small game, they believe.

Some of the searchers from the sheriff's office yesterday, who were skeptical about reports of the monkey being at large in these parts, changed their opinions, they said, after finding tracks made in the ground by the ape's feet, and examing trees, bark of which had been torn and damaged by the animal's claws.

Steubenville, Ohio, *Herald-Star,* September 24, 1932

APE BLAMED FOR LOSS OF SHEEP

The Alikanna "ape" was still at large today despite reports, circulated yesterday, that the beast had been chased up trees or trapped in basements and barns in a half-dozen localities.

The ape was supposed to have been trapped once in the cellar of a Shirley Circle home, off West Market street; caught again up a tree along Paddy Mudd's road and penned up in a Knoxville farmer's barn.

Such wasn't the case though for residents in subdivisions north of the city continued to complain in fear of being harmed by the ape.

Twenty sheep on the Bruck farm, four miles back on the Alikanna-Richmond road, are believed to have been killed by the ape

Thursday night. They were found dead in pasture yesterday morning chewed and torn as though by sharp claws.

This was the first report of stock loss since the ape was first sighted Monday. According to information from the sheriff's office, deputies are to team up with Game Protector Jack Gaylord in a weekend search for the strange animal.

Steubenville, Ohio, *Herald-Star,* September 28, 1932

NEW CLUE FOUND
IN APE MYSTERY

County Commisioner James Smith has a new angle on the Alikanna ape mystery.

He claims that footprints of the beast believed to be the missing circus ape were seen today in the locality of Dungeon Hollow, near the headwaters of Island Creek.

And if the "ape" now has his den in the fastness of the hollow, his capture will be difficult and a hazardous undertaking, Commissioner Smith believes.

The hollow is the grand canyon of Jefferson county and is almost impenetrable, the commissioner states. He recalls that several years ago, a wild man by the name of "Red River," who terrorized the farmers in that section for several months before he was finally captured, had his abode in a cleft of rocks in this dungeon.

There was also committed at the southern entrance of the hollow, more than a generation ago, one of the county's most horrible crimes, the murder of a woman known as Jennie Owens, history has it.

Steubenville, Ohio, *Herald-Star,* October 12, 1932

APE NOW IN BELMONT, WOMAN RESIDENT CLAIMS

Apparently leaving Jefferson county more than a week ago for better foraging ground, the "ape" which first gained attention to himself by appearances at Alikanna, later turning up at Fernwood and Richmond, is reported to have transferred his operations to Shadyside, O.

At least that is the story of Mrs. Earl Hill, resident of Route 7, south of Shadyside who claims she opened her kitchen door yesterday to see a large ape standing in the doorway of a nearby garage.

Too frightened to move, Mrs. Hill said she watched the ape while he ambled about, leaped a barbed wire fence and disappeared.

Another report from the Schramm Hollow district claims the ape was seen there by a small boy, Sunday afternoon.

Portsmouth, Ohio, *Times,* October 13, 1932

"APE" IS TRAMP IN FUR COAT, POLICE REPORT

Bellaire, O., Oct. 13—Capt. John Hummel of the Bellaire police department has offered an explanation for the "ape" that has frightened residents of eastern Ohio in recent weeks.

Captain Hummel says it is a tramp, garbed in a discarded fur coat. When last seen the "ape" was on Boggs Island in the Ohio river opposite Bellaire.

Several weeks ago, the "ape" was reported to have chased several residents of a nearby village.

Early 1940s: Keating (1993) recorded the sighting of a man living in Post Boy, Ohio. On a Sunday evening, alone in his house, the man looked up while cleaning a rabbit to see the head of a creature, "half man and half animal" looking through the kitchen window at him. The man's family came home to find him hiding under his bed.

Hillsboro, Ohio, *Press Gazette,* June 18, 1946

POLICE SQUASH WILDCAT RUMORS

The rumors of a strange creature terrorizing the village of Hillsboro was still classed in the category of fiction by police today. The first reports of the creature being seen in the East End were heard by police Thursday night. Since then, the rumors and the size and shape of the strange animal have grown proportionately large. It was first reported to be a wildcat. Subsequently it was tagged as an ape, wild man, and various other weird beings.

Despite the seeming levity of the situation, police added a serious note when they reported that some of the colored persons in town had been shooting at "things in the night." This is a serious offense and some innocent person might be seriously injured, police warned.

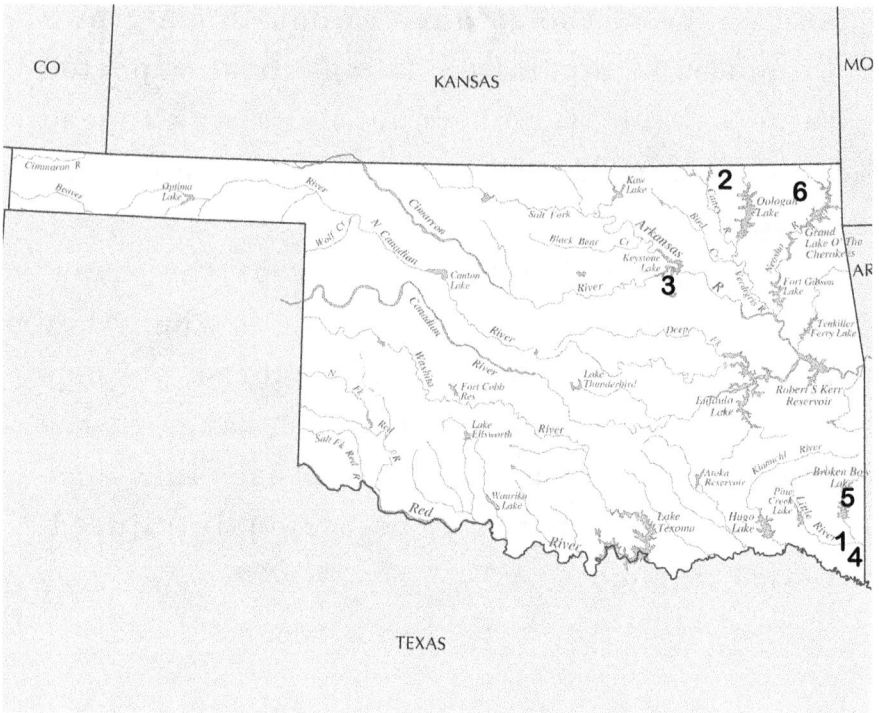

1 McCurtain County

2 Wann (Nowata County)

3 Slick (Creek County)

4 Goodwater (McCurtain County)

5 Mountain Fork of the Little River

6 Vinita (Craig County)

Oklahoma

1849: Bord & Bord (2006) noted the report of a "strange critter" that apparently matched that of a hairy primate, seen by a hunter in the swamps of McCurtain County.

1856: A young white girl was exhibited as a "wild woman" supposedly captured in the Wichita Mountains of Comanche country. This was soon exposed as a hoax. They had originally planned to coat the girl with a bearskin, but were unable to successfully attain a reasonable likeness, so decided to just run with the story (Buffalo, New York, *Morning Express*, August 4, 1856).

c. 1915: Bord & Bord (2006) noted a report by Crum King who saw a hairy manlike creature standing near the gate to his home near Wann, Oklahoma.

Bartlesville, Oklahoma, *Daily Enterprise*, August 20, 1921
"GORILLA" PROVES TO BE HOG.
Miami, Okla., Aug. 20.—Joe Hagan, marshal of Slick, who was in Miami this week,

said that the "8-foot gorilla" reported in the neighborhood of Slick, was found to be a wild hog, which escaped from a show there several days ago.

A hunter had two dogs chewed up, Mr. Hagan said, when they ran on the hog in the woods and reported that a monster had whipped his fighting hounds.

Mr. Hagan said the hog was lassoed later and found to weigh less than a hundred pounds.

1926: Bord & Bord (2006) noted a report from the Goodwater area by a doctor who saw a "thing" run across the road in front of his Model T Ford.

1926: Bord & Bord (2006) noted the report by two hunters in the Mountain Fork River region who saw a "manbeast," which later killed their dog.

Oklahoma City, Oklahoma, *Daily Oklahoman,* July 6, 1929
VINITA'S 'GORILLA' APPEARS AGAIN
Vinita, July 5.—(Special.)—The "gorilla" which terrorized Shanahan community several nights ago, and which caused several posses to go out from Vinita in vain attempt to kill it, disappeared and was not seen for two weeks, until Wednesday morning. As two farmers were driving to town it crossed the road

in front of them. They passed it and saw that it had stopped in the ditch beside the road.

The men stopped their car and started toward it but when it started for them they made a wild dash for the car and fled.

Several men from Vinita searched for it Thursday, but in vain. It had again "disappeared."

Vinita, Oklahoma, *Leader*, July 25, 1929

'GORILLA' REMOVES TROUSER LEG FOR KELSO YOUTH, SAID

Stories of the "gorilla" which is running wild in Craig county are beginning to stir all sorts of imaginative "terrors" among the minds of the late traveler, who happens to be in timbered sections in the moonlight night when just the right amount of shadow is cast to keep one's nerves continuously jerking.

But it was not a "shadow" that Oscar White, of Kelso, grabbed Sunday evening, according to reports given at the meeting of the members of the 4-H club representatives of Craig county, which met here last evening.

Oscar, according to the story, told at the meeting, had been visiting friends until a late hour, and on his way home, he suddenly became aware of a chain rattling near him. He looked around and saw a large animal going down the road on all fours, the chain dragging along after it. Oscar determined at once to capture the "gorilla" which has been causing so much comment, but is seldom seen at such close quarters.

He grabbed the chain. Thinking it might have escaped, and be used to obeying commands, Oscar is reported to have yelled at it. But the "gorilla" (for that was what Oscar was sure it was), did not like being yelled at. It turned and started after him. And Oscar arrived home minus part of a trouser leg, which the animal had removed in the flight. It was probably the removal of the pant leg that enabled Oscar to get up such speed as he outran the animal, but anyway, he escaped.

Edgar Berry was said to have encountered the same animal, when he heard it in his yard the same evening, but Edgar did not investigate as did his friend Oscar. He (Edgar) simply tore down a couple of fences and escaped before it had a chance to remove his trouser leg.

The boys were sure they had a good story, but it was all upset Monday, when they learned their "gorilla" was a large dog, which had escaped from its owner and was dragging a chain after it.

McAlester, Oklahoma, *News-Capital and Democrat*, August 1, 1929

One of the gorillas which recently escaped from the zoo at Nowatta was reported as having been seen near the Churchill farm at Vinita. A group of Vinita men formed a posse and searched for the animal but failed to find him. A reward of $50 has been offered for the return of each animal, either dead or alive.—State Exchange.

Vinita, Oklahoma, *Leader*, August 1, 1929

CLAIM TO SEE "WILD GORILLA"

Eleven Vinita youths went in search of the "wild gorilla" last evening according to a story on the streets this morning.

The party was organized by R. C. King, and was composed of the following: Cliff Elliot, Ray Sippy, Dale Lomax, Ray Lomax, Elbert Elder, Pete and Tige Terrell, Mike Galvin, Milton Ficklin, Joe Durbin and one other whose name was forgotten in the mad rush to get home after the carbide lamp was thrown away by King, who was leading in the pursuit of the supposed gorilla.

All the boys but Pete Terrell and Clifford Elliot claim to have seen the animal. These two admit they were too far in the lead to see anything which might have been following them.

The party said they ran onto the animal just west of town, at the bridge across Big Cabin west of Churchill's place. They followed it to Pawpaw creek where it turned and started after them. R. C. threw his light away and the riot to reach home began. The party arrived in Vinita about eleven last evening.

Vinita, Oklahoma, *Craig County Democrat,* February 20, 1936

A corpse, six years dead, is beginning to show signs of a return to life. Six years ago, a fearsome thing of flesh and blood, at least, according to certain citizens, roamed the summer jungles of Big Cabin and Locust creeks. Blood-curdling and chill-blains-producing howls, grunts and roars froze the marrow in the citizenry's bones as that thing, a seven-foot gorilla, searched for its prey. Those roars were echoed from many a front page printed in many a big city.

The existence of the animal was first reported by the young bloods who roamed along the creek banks after night. Many a childish necking party along the highways and byways was rudely interrupted as one or the other of the parties recalled the stories connected with the brute. . . .

Ontario

From *The Beaver* (National History Society, Canada), September 1942, reprinted in Wyman (1969).

THE MERMAID OF LAKE SUPERIOR

On November 13, 1812 there appeared before the Court of King's Bench in Montreal, a respectable fur-trader and merchant, Venant St. Germain, who made the following deposition under oath relative to the Lake Superior mermaid which he had once observed:

"That in the year 1782, on the 3d of May, when on his return to Michilimackinac from the Grand Portage, he arrived at the south end of the Isle Pate (Pie Island, near Fort William), where he formed his encampment to stop for the night. That a little before sunset, the evening being clear and serene, deponent was returning from setting his nets, and reached his encampment a short time after the sun went down. That on disembarking, the deponent happened to turn towards the lake, when he observed, about an acre or three quarters of an acre distant from the

1 Pie Island

2 Pembroke

3 Pretties Island

4 Orangeville

5 Cobalt

bank where he stood, an animal in the water,
which appeared to him to have the upper part
of its body, above the waist, formed exactly
like that of a human being. It had the half
of its body out of the water, and the novelty
of so extraordinary a spectacle excited his
attention, and led him to examine it carefully. That the body of the animal seemed to
him about the size of that of a child of seven
or eight years of age, with one of its arms
extended and elevated in the air. The hand
appeared to be composed of fingers exactly
similar to those of a man: and the right arm
was kept in an elevated position, while the
left seemed to rest upon the hip, but the deponent did not see the latter, it being kept
under the water. The deponent distinctly
saw the features of the countenance, which
bore an exact resemblance to those of the
human face. The eyes were extremely bril-
liant; the nose small but handsomely shaped;
the mouth proportionate to the rest of the
face; the complexion of a brownish hue, somewhat similar to that of a young negro; the
ears well formed, and corresponding to the
other parts of the figure. He did not discover
that the animal had any hair, but in the place
of it he observed that wooly substance about
an inch long, on top of the head, somewhat

similar to that which grows on the heads of negroes. The animal looked the deponent in the face, with an aspect indicating uneasiness, but at the same time with a mixture of curiosity. And the deponent, along with three other men who were with him at the time, and an old Indian woman to whom he had given a passage in his canoe, attentively examined the animal for the space of three or four minutes.

"The deponent formed the design of getting possession of the animal if possible, and for this purpose endeavoured to get hold of his gun, which was loaded at the time, with the intention of shooting it; but the Indian woman, who was near at the time, ran up to the deponent, and seizing him by the clothes, by her violent struggles, prevented his taking aim. During the time which he was occupied in this, the animal sunk under water without changing its attitude, and disappearing, was seen no more.

"The woman appeared highly indignant at the audacity of the deponent in offering to fire upon what she termed the God of the Water and Lakes; and vented her anger in bitter reproaches, saying they would all infallibly perish, for the God of the Waters would raise such a tempest as would dash them to pieces upon the rocks; saying that for her own part, she would fly the danger, and proceeded to ascend the bank, which happened to be steep in that part. The deponent, despising her threats, remained quietly where he had fixed his encampment. That at about ten or eleven at night, they heard the dashing of the waves, accompanied with such a violent gale of wind, so as to render it necessary for them to drag their canoe higher up on the beach; and the deponent, accompanied by his amen, was obliged to seek shelter from the violent storm, which continued for three days, unabated.

"That it is in the knowledge of the deponent, that there exists a general belief diffused among the Indians who inhabit the country around this island, that it is the residence of the God of the Waters and of the Lakes, whom in their language they call Manitou Niba Nabais, and that he had often heard that this belief was peculiar to the Sauteux (Chippewa) Indians. He farther learned from another voyageur, that an animal exactly similar to that which deponent described, had been seen by him on another occasion when passing from Pâté to Tonnerre, and the deponent thinks the frequent appearance of this extraordinary animal in this spot has given rise to the superstitious belief among the Indians, that the God of the Waters had fixed upon this for his residence.

"That the deponent, in speaking of the storm which followed the threats of the Indian woman, merely remarked it as a strange circumstance which coincided with the time, without attributing it to any other cause than what naturally produces such an effect, and which is a well known occurrence to voyageurs; that fish in general appear most numerous near the surface, and are most apt to show themselves above water on the approach of a storm.

"And further the deponent saith not.
Signed VENANT ST. GERMAIN
"Sworn before us, 13th November, 1812
Signed,
"P. L. Panet, J.K.B.
"I. Ogden, J.K.B."

Newark, Ohio, *Daily Advocate,* August 1, 1883
MAN OR GORILLA?
THE EXTRAORDINARY CHARACTER
WHO IS SCARING CANUCKS.
Ottawa, Ont., Aug. 1.—Pembroke, about one hundred miles north of Ottawa, has a lively sensation in the shape of a wild man eight feet high and covered with hair. His haunts are on Prettis Island, a short distance from

the town, and the people are so terrified that no one has dared to venture on this island for several weeks. Two raftsmen named Toughey and Sallman, armed with weapons, plucked up sufficient courage to scour the woods in hope of seeing the monster. About 3 o'clock in the afternoon their curiosity was rewarded. He emerged from a thicket having in one hand a tomahawk made of stone and in the other a bludgeon. His appearance struck such terror to the hearts of the raftsmen that they made tracks for the boat which was moored by the beach. The giant followed them, uttering demoniacal yells and gesticulating wildly. They had barely time to get into the boat and pull a short distance out into the stream when he hurled the tomahawk after them, striking Toughey in the arm and fracturing it. Sallman fired two shots, but neither took effect, the giant retreating hurriedly at the first shot of firearms. It is more than probable that the townspeople will arrange an expedition to capture, if possible, what Toughey describes as a man who looks like a gorilla, wandering about in a perfectly nude condition, and, with the exception of the face, completely covered with a thick growth of black hair.

Renfrew, Ontario, *Mercury,* August 3, 1883

ONTARIO WILD MAN

A citizen and family went up the lake to Pretty's Island on Saturday evening to camp out. The husband brought back the report that on the first evening a plague of mosquitoes having fallen upon them and deprived them of power to sleep, he was sitting in the tent when suddenly upon the foreground of the shadows produced by the departing fire he distinctly saw the outlines of a man appear whose height was about eight feet. His hair was long and shaggy, and hung about his face he had a vest but no sleeves to his coat, knickerbocker pants, with hairy legs and arms. He stood still at the threshold of the brightness and was questioned, whence and whither. There came no response, whereupon the citizen picked up a large stone and hurling it with all his force struck the strange object amidships and it fell with a splash into the water. Hastening to the spot, he saw the stranger arise and depart swiftly, and though he searched for many hours there came no reward. So far as we are concerned we give as we receive. Possibly the wild man is somewhat of an offset to the sea serpent sensation of other streams so that the Mississippi may not be behind the times. The person who camped and saw is a well known river driver in the service of Mr. Peter Mc-Laren.

Victoria, British Columbia, *Daily Colonist,* August 18, 1887

Reports come from Orangeville of a wild, hairy man seen running about in some woods near there.

North Bay, Ontario, *Nugget,* July 27, 1923 (from Green 1978)

Cobalt—July 27, 1923—Mr. J. A. MacAuley and Mr. Lorne Wilson claim they have seen the PreCambrian Shield Man while working on their mining claims North and East of the Wettlaufer Mine near Cobalt. This is the second time in seventeen years that a hairy apelike creature nicknamed "Yellow Top" because of a light-colored "mane" has been seen in the district.

The two prospectors said they were taking test samples from their . . . property when they saw what looked like a bear picking at a blueberry patch. Mr. Wilson said he threw a stone at the creature.

"It kind of stood up and growled at us. Then it ran away. It sure was like no bear that I have ever seen. Its head was kind of yellow and the rest of it was black like a bear, all covered with hair.

The first report of the creature was made in September, 1906, by a group of men building the headframe at the Violet Mine, east of Cobalt. It has not been seen since that time.

North Bay, Ontario, *Nugget,* April 16, 1946 (from Green 1978)

Cobalt—April 16, 1946—Old Yellow Top, the half man, half beast that is supposed to be roaming the wilds around the Cobalt Mining Camp was reportedly seen again, this time by a woman and her son, who live near Gillies Depot, while they were walking the tracks into Cobalt.

The woman, who did not want her name made public, said that she spotted a dark, hairy animal with a "light" head ambling off the tracks into the bush near Gillies Lake. She said she did not get a clear look at the thing but said it walked almost like a man.

The sighting is the second such report to be made since 1906 or 1907. A search party may be formed to try and find "Old Yellow Top."

Oregon

1810: David Thompson, an agent with the North-west Fur and Trading Company, found tracks in the Rockies of large footprints, about fourteen inches in length, resembling the pawprint of a large bear, but with short claws (Byrne 1976). His Native American guides told him they were made by a "Mammoth." It is unknown which animal the guides were referring to, (certainly not the fossil elephant), and there is some doubt among current researchers as to whether this track has relevance to Bigfoot. It may just have been a large bear, though why the guides didn't recognize it as such is unknown.

Vincent (1947) told the story of "Nugget" Tom, who in 1871 went exploring up Star Mountain near the headwaters of the Sixes river (Curry county), in search of a ledge that might be the source of his placer gold claim. After locating a shelf with gold-rich quartz, Tom was knocked off a cliff by an unknown assailant. After recovering from the accident, Tom spent four years unsuccessfully

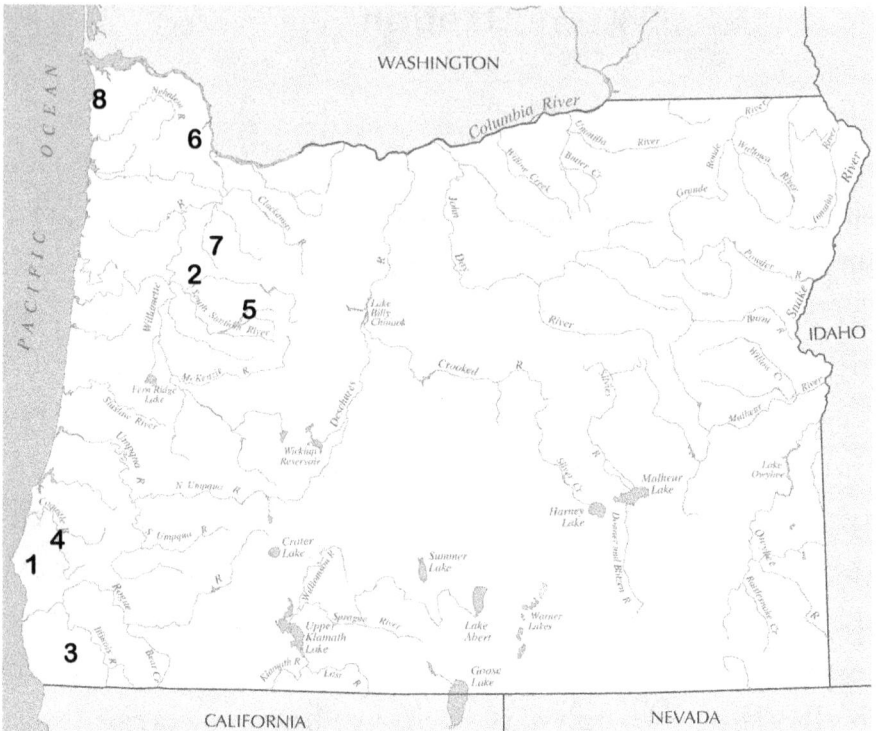

1 Sixes River (Curry County)

2 Lebanon (Linn County)

3 Chetco River

4 Myrtle Point (Coos County)

5 Bald Peter Mountain

6 Yankton (Columbia County)

7 Marion County

8 Tillamook Head

trying to relocate the ledge. In 1899, two more prospectors decided to search for Tom's lost gold ledge. They managed to locate it, and began working. After stopping for lunch, they returned to the ledge to find a large creature, erect and covered with yellow fur, throwing their gear off the cliff. They tried to shoot it, but it took off and disappeared. Naming their mine "The Wild Man," they sold it. By this time, several men in the area were known to have died mysterious deaths. One man, "Doc" Elgin, claimed to have seen such a creature one autumn morning as he took a pail to collect water from a stream. It left tracks sixteen inches in length and eight inches across at the toes.

Olympia, Washington Territory, *Washington Standard*, August 27, 1880

A VERITABLE MONSTROSITY.

Long years ago, when the first settlers came to Oregon, there were stories told to new-comers of the existence of a monster that had been seen in the wilds of the Coast range. He wandered over every part of the vast domain between the mouth of Rogue river and the Columbia, going as far east as the Williamette river and the boundless ocean on the west. When the people began to settle the rich fields and vales of this part this monster went deeper and deeper into

the wilderness, and was only seen at long
intervals as some venturesome hunter would
suddenly come across him in the mighty jungle of forests that covered his vast range.
His appearance, frightful in the extreme,
would so in spire his beholder with terror
that in his fear he would make all haste to
leave that spot of horror with only an indistinct remembrance of the vision he had beheld of the greatest monster on earth. His
story told by the campfire on his return to
his comrades would only be hooted at, and
he would retire amid their derision for being such a coward. This fearful fiend would
sometimes venture near the settlements, and
in the night would commit such depredation
that would bring out the hunters and their
dogs for a chase, but after several hours the
hounds would come back dragging their tails
in terror and slink crouching to their masters' feet. For years this demon monarch
held his sway of the forest, and his fame
grew from the north and south, from east to
west, and many would start out to meet and
conquer him. Some came back regarding him
as myth, others with fear written over each
lineament of their features, and others went
out and never returned. Those who had seen
him were unmanned forever, and their skill

as hunters gone; nor could they ever be induced to go beyond the settlements again to
seek the bear or elk for fear of an encounter with this inhuman monster. It was re-
served for a party of tourists and hunters
from California to meet him face to face, and
to them we are indebted for the tale of their
adventure. Two weeks ago a party of four,
renowned as might hunters of the grizzly in
the Sierras, came ashore from the *Oregon*
and took the boat for Nehalem valley. Intent
upon being the first to tread many portions
of this wild country they went on and on deep
into the wilderness. One day last week, when
far from the mighty Columbia, they sent out
their dogs to chase the game, and each took
a stand by a "run." One, more full of curiosity and adventure than the rest, began to
look around, and soon he saw in the soft mud
near the spring the prints of a monster foot;
but one track was visible, but its size, its resemblance to a human foot, made him start
back in horror and clench his trusty gun as
he held his bated breath. He remembered the
stories he had heard, and called his companions and hounds around him. They decided
to give the monster chase, nor rest until he
had been brought to bay. The track in the
mud was shown to the dogs, and soon their

deep baying betokened that they had found
their quarry. On through the tangled woods
rushed the men, and soon they were face to
face with the horrible form that had haunted
this place for years. Of giant height, with
hair falling in grizzled locks, his arms of the
size of saplings, and covered with a coarse
red hair all over his body, he stood facing the
men with an expression of hate and ferocity.
His teeth were set, and two long tusks on
each side showed that life would be of little
worth to anything into which they might be
set, and with a sweep of his long arm one of
the baying hounds was caught up and those
fearful tusks sent crushing through its quivering brain. The men stood awed with horror.
The remaining dogs, seeing the fate of their
comrade, drew back, and this horrible figure, throwing the dog from him, moved away,
and then they saw what they had not noticed
before—that one foot was backward and the
other forward, and that he could run one way
as well as the other. Fleet of foot, he could
dodge first one way and then the other, and
springing by the mighty trees of the forest,
he was soon lost to view. His track was measured and found to be twenty-seven inches
in length. His height was estimated by measuring a small tree near which he stood, and

found to be eleven feet and five inches. His
terrible eyes and ferocious teeth, that grinning mouth and the swelling muscles of his
body so inspired the hunters with a whole-
some fear that they returned to the city, and
on last Wednesday morning returned to their
own State, content to hunt the grizzly and
mountain sheep amid the hills and rocks of
the Sierra Nevadas.

Winnipeg, Manitoba, *Daily Free Press,* December 31, 1885
HUNTING A WILD MAN.

Portland, Or., Dec. 30—At Lebanon, Linn
county, Oregon, great excitement prevails
over the discovery of a wild man in the mountains near that place, who is supposed to be
the long lost John Mackentire. About four
years ago John Mackentire of Lebanon, while
out hunting in the mountains, mysteriously
disappeared and no trace has ever been found
of him since. A few days ago, two well-known
reliable citizens of Lebanon, while out hunting in the mountains, discovered a man who
very strongly resembles Mackentire. The
man was entirely destitute of clothing and
his body was covered with long hair like
an animal's. When first seen the man was
voraciously devouring raw flesh of a deer.
The hunters approached within a few yards

before being discovered, when the wild man fled into the mountains with the swiftness of the wind as soon as he saw the hunters. The men who saw him claim he looks very much like Mackentire and willingly made affadavits to their statements. A party is now being organized to search for and capture the wild man. Several other responsible citizens assert they have also recently seen the strange human being.

1890: Sanderson (1961) noted that a mining camp along the Chetco river near the California border was harassed by something that left large footprints and moved large objects. After a posse failed to track the animal down, two men on watch were found dead, "apparently by being picked up and slammed repeatedly onto the ground so that they looked as if they had fallen off a high cliff onto rocks." The creature was tracked into the Siskiyous by Native American trackers before being lost. It is unknown where Sanderson got this report.

Roseburg, Oregon, *Daily Review,* December 24, 1900 (from Green 1978)

A Kangaroo Man—The Sixes mining district in Curry county has for the past 30 years gloried in the exclusive possession of a "kangaroo man". Recently while Wm. Page and

Johnnie McCullock, who are mining there, went out hunting McCulloch saw the strange animal-man come down to a stream to drink. In calling Page's attention to the strange being it became frightened, and with cat-like agility, which has always been a leading characteristic, with a few bounds was out of sight.

The appearance of this animal is almost enough to terrorize the rugged mountain sides themselves. He is described as having the appearance of a man—a very good looking man—is nine feet in height with low forehead, hair hanging down near his eyes, and his body covered with a prolific growth of hair which nature has provided for his protection. Its hands reach almost to the ground and when its tracks were measured its feet were found to be 18 inches in length with five well formed toes. Whether this is a devil, some strange animal or a wild man is what Messrs. Page and McCulloch would like to know, says the Myrtle Point Enterprise.

Port Orford, Oregon, *Tribune,* January 29, 1901 (from Crowe 1993)

The boogy man has been sighted in western Oregon. They call it the Kangaroo Man. They say that the creature has the shape of a man but is of enormous size and covered with hair. He is supposed to eat miners raw without salt, and has been seen to jump from one mountain peak to another, all the while emitting blood-curdling yells, and spouting sulfurous flames from his nostrils. What kind of whiskey do they sell over in that country, anyhow?

Medford, Oregon, *Mail,* December 13, 1901

We are informed that a determined effort is being made to capture the "Kangaroo man" who is supposed to be roaming in the wilds of the Sixes River country, terrorizing the tenderfoot prospectors in that region and destroying the game supply to satisfy his insatiable desire for spilling blood, tells the Coos Bay News. An Eastern man, who has handled freaks in the show business for a number of years, was in town last week, and gained much information from Levi and Al Smith regarding the wild man; his habits, his appetite for lone prospectors, and the probable location of the cave which he makes his winter quarters. A hunting party is to be organized in the near future and should they succeed in capturing him he will be exhibited in the principal cities of the United States and European countries.

Portland, Oregon, *Daily Journal*, March 19, 1904

Coos Bay News: Stories of the Sixes River wild man are coming in early this year. The Myrtle Point Enterprise learns that the Kangaroo man was seen three times since the 10th of last month. Two men, Ward and Burlison, saw the monster plainly and took a shot at him, but failed to bag him. At last accounts he was still roaming the wilds of the mining region, ready to gobble up tenderfoot prospectors, whom, it is presumed, he eats without salt.

Cottage Grove, Oregon, *Lane County Leader,* April 7, 1904 (from Byrne 1976)

SIXES WILD MAN AGAIN.

VISITS THE CABINS OF MINERS
AND FRIGHTENS THE PROSPECTORS.

At repeated intervals during the past ten years thrilling stories have come from the rugged Sixes mining district in Coos County, Oregon, near Myrtle Point, regarding a wild man or a queer and terrible monster which walks erect and which has been seen by scores of miners and prospectors. The latest freaks of the wild man is related as follows in the last issue of the Myrtle Point Enterprise: The appearance again of the "Wild Man" of the Sixes has thrown some of the miners into a state of excitement and fear. A report says the wild man has been seen three times since the 10th of last month. The first appearance occurred on "Thompson Flat." Wm. Ward and a young man by the name of Burlison were sitting by the fire of their cabin one night when they heard something walking around the cabin which resembled a man walking and when it came to the corner of the cabin it took hold of the corner and gave the building a vigorous shake and kept up a frightful noise all the time—the same noise that has so many times warned the venturesome miners of the approach of the hairy man and caused them to flee in abject fear. Mr. Ward walked to the cabin door and could see the monster plainly as it walked away, and took a shot at it with his rifle, but the bullet went wild of its mark. The last appearance of the animal was at the Harrison cabin only a few days ago. Mr. Ward was at the Harrison cabin this time and again figured in the excitement. About five o'clock in the morning the wild man gave the door of the cabin a vigorous shaking which aroused Ward and one of the Harrison boys who took their guns and started in to do the intruder. Ward fired at the man and he answered by sending a four pound rock at Ward's head, but his aim was a little too high. He then disappeared in the brush.

Many of the miners avow that the "wild man" is a reality. They have seen him and know whereof they speak. They say he is something after the fashion of a gorilla and unlike anything else either in appearance or action. He can outrun or jump anything else that has ever been known; and not only that but he can throw rocks with wonderful force and accuracy. He is about seven feet high, has broad hands and feet and his body is covered by a prolific growth of hair. In short he looks like the very devil.

Albany, Oregon, *Evening Herald,* July 21, 1924

MAN APE TALE IS OLD STUFF; ONE IN LINN YEARS AGO

That the man-gorilla who is reported to have molested the Kelso miners in their lonely cabin near Spirit Lake, Wash., was not a fiction of the imagination but may be a descendant of ape-men who infested the Cascade range years ago was brought to light here yesterday by Henry Wallace, former Albany man who now is engaged in the sawmill business near Monroe.

According to Wallace, the miners' story is old stuff, or, he avers, a prospector named

"Bud" Uhmanhaufer saw a being of the Spirit Lake genus 30 years ago near Bald Peter mountain in McDowell creek.

And to show that he is not "spoofing," Wallace refers the readers of this article to Mr. Uhmanhaufer himself, who is still alive and hearty and who lives in Talent, Or. Uhmanhaufer, says Wallace, is a man of known veracity, an old hunter, honest and a church man. Uhmanhaufer is now about 60 years of age.

One day about three decades ago, Uhmanhaufer and his partner, Link Fitzgerald, started out to hunt in the vicinity of Bald Peter. The two men separated. As Uhmanhaufer pursued his quest for game, there arose suddenly before him a big hairy giant. The wild being stood for a moment and looked at Uhmanhaufer. For several minutes the two stared at one another. Then the wild man suddenly turned, caught hold of a bent vine maple, jumped over its top and landed 20 feet away.

Uhmanhaufer was too surprised to act quickly. As he saw the strange being hurtling his way through the underbrush with giant strides, he resolved to go to the nearest settlement, organize a party and search for him.

Mike Fitgerald, a brother of Link, was the only man available and he and Uhmanhaufer set out for the scene of the strange meeting. When they arrived at the place, they met Link, who had just returned form his expedition. The three then made an investigation of the tracks of the giant. They followed them for some little distance after difficulty, for they were more than 15 feet apart, large and similar to human footprints.

However, Link was skeptical. He and Uhmanhaufer almost came to blows, and Link made sport of "Bud's" story. In spite of the fact that the tracks were similar to a man's Link insisted that his partner had seen a bear.

However, the three men continued the search, but unsuccessfully. Bud to this day, Wallace says, has been puzzled by the appearance of the hairy giant and was much downcast by the unbelief of his comrade.

1926: Bord & Bord (2006) noted that several sightings with multiple witnesses occurred in the Yankton region.

Salem, Oregon, *Statesman Journal,* August 31, 1927

"A hairy wild man is at large in Marion county. That will beat the oligocene bones

of Deschutes or the white metal mystery in
Southern Oregon. Marion county against the
world!"—Portland Telegram. (Correct you
are. Thanks!)

Modesto, California, *Bee and News-Herald,* August 19, 1933
THREE SEE 'ANIMAL-LIKE HUMAN'
IN OREGON WILDS

Seaside, Ore., Aug. 19—(UP)—A "wild man"
was hunted by a party of veteran woodsmen
in the scrub pine and manzanita of Tillamook
Head to-day.

Three persons who saw the wild man said
he was a "shaggy-appearing human," with an
animal-like face, who bounded away when
observed.

At last report the creature, whether lunatic, hermit or figment of imagination, had
eluded his pursuers and had left no trace.
Searching parties sent out recently to find
lost vacationists in the wild region which
overlooks the sea reported the wild man.

Irving C. Allen, city attorney of Seaside,
said:

"I happened to lag behind the searching
party of Bald Mountain. I glanced behind
me, and there it was. It looked like a shaggy
beast, yet human. It was growing dark, and I
couldn't see it plainly.

As I stood watching, it turned and fled into the darkness."

Clement King, member of another search party a few days later, said:

"We were hunting near the 'death trap.' I looked up a cliff and saw an animal-like human peering down at me. I watched the creature, which was at a considerable distance, and it bounded away."

William Laighton, who knows every animal trail and crag on Tillamook Head, was reported to have seen the wild man. "Well, I saw something queer," Laighton said when questioned. He refused to say more.

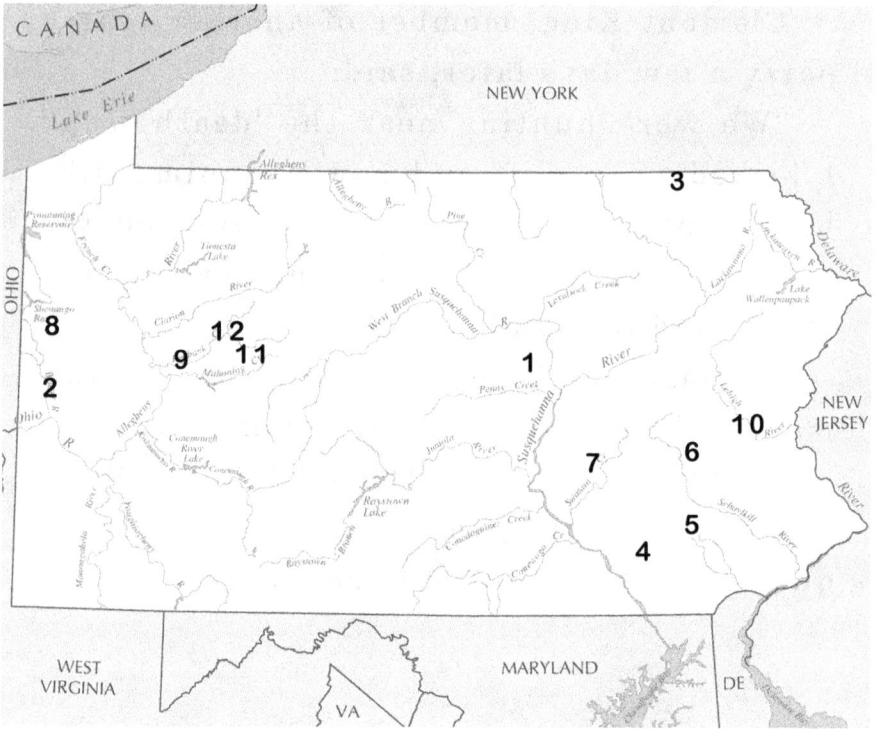

1 Northumberland (Northumberland County)

2 Bridgewater (Beaver County)

3 Silver Lake township (Susquehanna County)

4 Lancaster (Lancaster County)

5 Morgantown (Berks County)

6 Hamburg (Berks County)

7 Swatara Gap (Lebanon County)

8 New Castle (Lawrence County)

9 Armstrong County

10 Lehigh Mountain

11 Mehaffey (now Mahaffey; Clearfield County)

12 Big Run (Jefferson County)

Pennsylvania

Windham, Connecticut, *Herald*, October 15, 1801

Harrisburg, (Penn.) Sept. 7.—A singular non-descript animal has since a few weeks several times made its appearance, near Northumberland town, in this state, which has been the subject of much speculative enquiry in these parts. The extraordinary formation of this wonderful creature, as represented by a number of respectable inhabitants of that place, who have seen it, is certainly astonishing to every one, particularly to those acquainted with natural history, and furnishes the mind with a variety of conjectures, some of which perhaps not very favorable to the human species. It is said to be about five feet in height, and moves erect; it has a more perfect human face than any other animal of the brute creation hitherto spoken of. The head is crowned with hair, which falls regular over the forehead, near to the eye brows; its neck and breast are bare, but downwards it is covered entirely with hair of a reddish

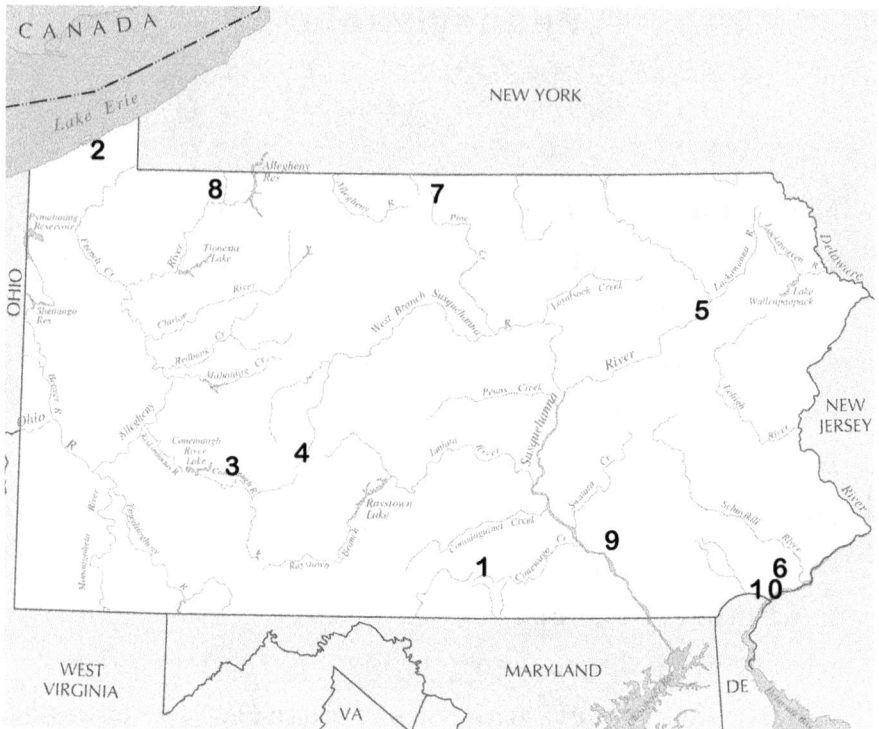

1 South Mountain

2 Erie (Erie County)

3 Bolivar (Westmoreland County)

4 Blair County

5 Laurel Run (Luzerne County)

6 Morton and Springfield (Delaware County)

7 Westfield (Tioga County)

8 Putnamville (Clarion County)

9 Marietta (Lancaster County)

10 Leiperville (Crum Lynne, Delaware County)

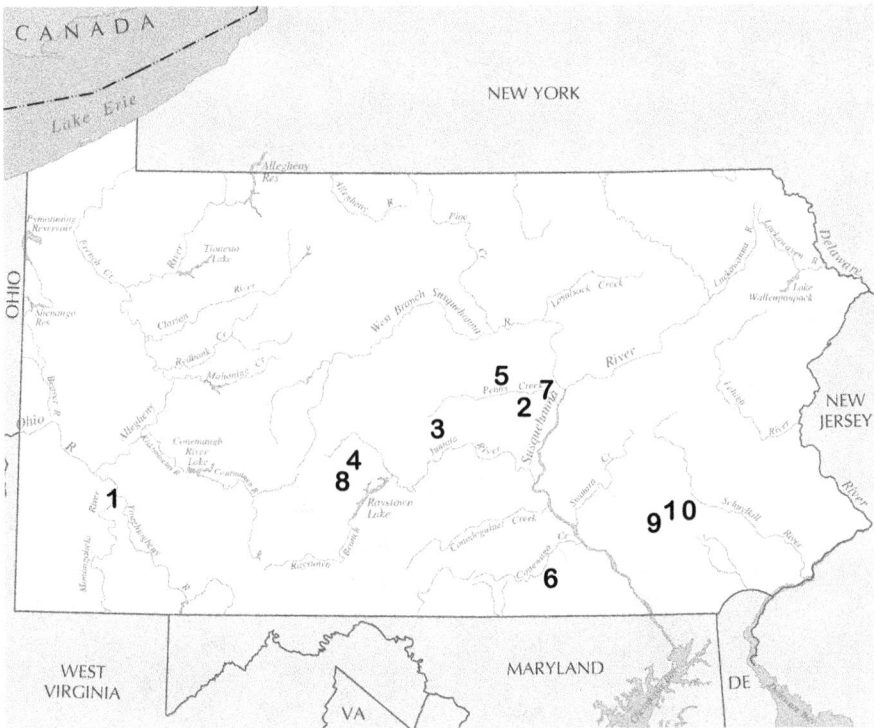

1 New Homestead (Allegheny County)

2 Meiserville (Snyder County)

3 Lewistown (Mifflin County)

4 Canoe Creek (Blair County)

5 Middleburg (Snyder County)

6 Cross Keys (Adams County)

7 Selinsgrove (Snyder County)

8 Kladder station (Hollidaysburg, Blair County)

9 Bareville (Lancaster County)

10 Farmersville (Lancaster County)

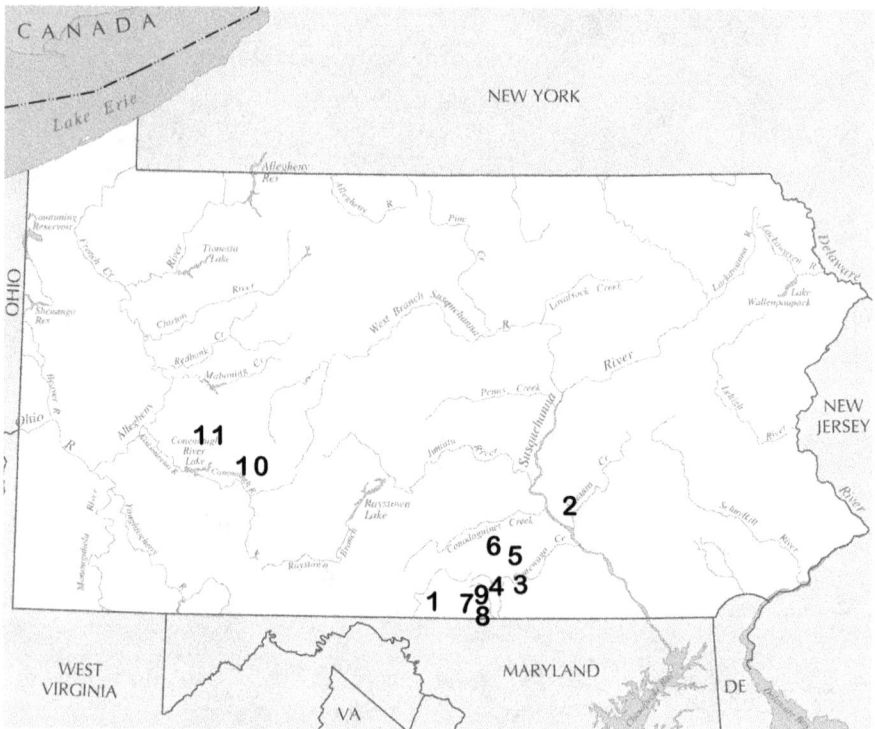

1 Waynesboro (Franklin County)

2 Dauphin County

3 Mount Rock (dead placename; Adams County)

4 Gettysburg (Adams County)

5 York Springs (Adams County)

6 Idaville (Adams County)

7 Rouzerville (Franklin County)

8 Pen Mar (Franklin County)

9 Fairfield (Adams County)

10 Summerhill (Cambria County)

11 Lucerne (mining town above Homer City; Indiana
   County)

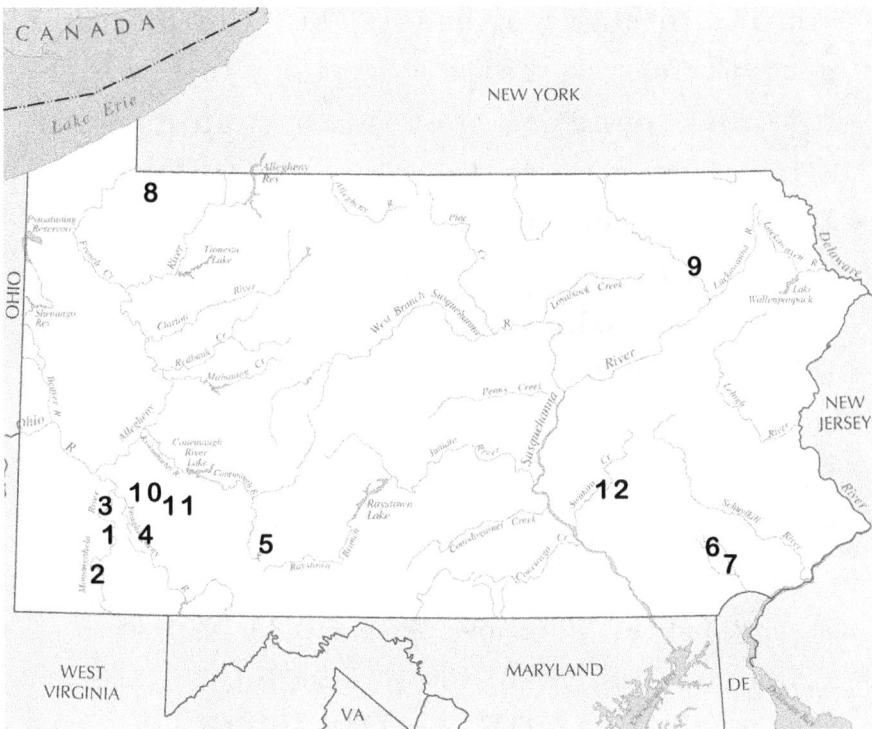

1 Brier Hill (Fayette County)

2 Masontown (Fayette County)

3 Webster (Westmoreland County)

4 Indian Head (Fayette County)

5 Tatesville (Bedford County)

6 Lyndell (Chester County)

7 Downington (Chester County)

8 Corry (Erie County)

9 Shavertown (Luzerne County)

10 Crabtree (Westmoreland County)

11 Latrobe (Westmoreland County)

12 Lebanon (Lebanon County)

cast. Its arms and hands appear perfect like those of a man, excepting the nails which are similar to claws of beasts; but the feet appear perfect. It has a very long tail, which it winds round its body when running.—An attempt was made to catch it a short time since, by three gentlemen on horseback; one of them was near enough to strike with the lash of his whip, but taking down a steep hill, the gentlemen were obliged to dismount to pursue it, when it made its escape. We hear a thousand dollars is offered for this animal alive.

Logansport, Indiana, *Telegraph,* September 15, 1838

From the Montrose, Pennsylvania, *Spectator*

STRANGE ANIMAL, OR
FOOD FOR THE MARVELLOUS

Something like a year ago, there was considerable talk about a strange animal, said to have been seen in the southwestern part of Bridgewater. Although the individual who described the animal persisted in declaring that he had seen it, and was at first considerably frightened by it, the story was heard and looked upon more as food for the marvellous, than as having any foundation in fact. He represented the animal as we have it through a third person, as having the appearance of a child seven or eight years old though somewhat slimmer and covered entirely with hair.

He saw it, while picking berries, walking towards him erect and whistling like a person. After recovering from his fright, he is said to have pursued it, but it ran off with such speed, whistling as it went, that he could not catch it. He said it ran like the 'devil', and continued to call it after that name.

The same or similar looking animal was seen in Silver Lake township about two weeks since, by a boy some sixteen years old. We had the story from the father of the boy, in his absence, and afterward from the boy himself. The boy was sent to work in the backwoods near the New York state line. He took with him a gun, and was told by his father to shoot anything he might see except persons or cattle. After working a while, he heard some person, a little brother as he supposed, coming toward him whistling quite merrily. It came within a few rods of him and stopped.

He said it looked like a human being, covered with black hair, about the size of his brother, who was six or seven years old. His gun was some little distance off, and he was very much frightened. He, however, got his gun and shot at the animal, but trembled so that he could not hold it still. The strange animal, just as his gun "went off," stepped behind a tree, and then ran off, whistling as before. The father said the boy came home very much frightened, and that a number of times during the afternoon, when thinking about the animal he had seen he would, to use his own words, "burst out crying."

Making due allowance for frights and consequent exaggeration, an animal of singular appearance has doubtless been seen. What it is, or whence it came, is of course yet a mystery. From the description, if an ourang outang were known to be in the country we might think this to be it. As no such animal is known (without vouching for the correctness of the story) we shall leave the reader to conjecture, or guess for himself, what it is. For the sake of a name, however, we will call the "strange animal," The Whistling Wild Boy of the Woods.

Why is not this story as good as that copied into the Volunteer of a week before last, relative to the wild boy of Indiana? We acknowledge that the story has excited somewhat our propensity for the marvellous and we give it, as much as anything, to gratify the same propensity in others.

Grand Traverse, Michigan, *Herald,* December 17, 1858

Wild People.—In Lancaster, Pa., a thing like a man, but hairy as a bear, has been seen by the people. It was very wild and strong. It was once seen in a pen, sucking the cows, and when discovered it started as if about to fight, and then turned and fled, bounding like a deer. It walks upright and is supposed to be a wild man.

Kokomo, Indiana, *Tribune,* August 15, 1871

A prevailing superstition amongst the Dutch is that of the "Hairy man," the wild man of the mountains, a being without any other clothing than hirsute abundance, who climbs lofty trees, afflicts children and stock, and defies pursuit and capture. Only last week this ancient adventurer was reported in the Reading papers as having been seen on the Welsh Mountain, and the sagacious editor added: "It is high time that this formidable monster was brought to terms and put under durance."

Portland, Oregon, *Oregonian,* August 26, 1871

WILD MAN OF THE MOUNTAINS.

A wild man in the Welsh Mountain, near Morgantown, Berks county, seems to be creating much excitement among the natives.

About two weeks ago a man presenting the appearance of a huge overgrown bear, made his appearance on the Welsh Mountain, directly opposite the village of Morgantown, and made the night hideous with his beast-like howling. The citizens becoming alarmed concluded to catch him if possible, and with this object in view a number of the neighbors assembled, armed with guns, clubs, &c., and started for the mountain. The men were deployed in squads, and at times the yells from this half man and half beast were so close to them, they thought it impossible for him to escape, yet when the morning dawned the object of their search was nowhere to be found. Night after night, the same doleful howlings have been re-echoed through the valley bordering on the mountain. A few days since he was seen in a field back of the village, and a number of the citizens started in pursuit and overtook him. He was captured and brought to the hotel of Mr. D. K. Plank. When caught he was very nearly in a nude state, having but a few rags hanging to his back; his face is very nearly covered with long bushy hair, giving him the appearance of a gorilla more than of a human being. To questions put to him he said that he was a native of Ireland, and had lived in the State of Connecticut for a long time. He gives his name as Thomas Foley, and says he has been roaming in the woods for two years. A good suit of clothes was put upon him, and he immediately started for the mountains, tearing his clothes in strips as he moved along. The horses and cattle belonging to farmers along the mountain run and gallop through the fields continually, as if frightened for some unknown cause; the dogs howl and cry as soon as night approaches; in fact, the community is in a terrible state of excitement. Crowds have gone out at night to capture him, but up to this time have not succeeded. At times he is seen on his hands and feet, moving along with the fleetness of a wild tiger.

Reading, Pennsylvania, *Times,* July 23, 1873

LETTER FROM HAMBURG.

[CORRESPONDENCE TIMES AND DISPATCH.]

HAMBURG, JULY 22, 1873.

A wild man is said to have been seen on the Blue Mountain, in Upper Bern township, last week, by a man who drove his cattle on the mountain. He says that the man is in a nude condition, and that his entire body is covered with hair about three inches in length. After the man had driven his cattle to the desired place he went home and got some neighbors to go along up the mountain to catch the "critter," but he had disappeared, and their search was unsuccessful. Some think that the whole thing is a hoax, while other think otherwise.

Williamsport, Pennsylvania, *Sun Gazette,* September 20, 1874 (courtesy Gary Mangiacopra).

THE WILD MAN, THE WILD BEAST, AND THE BIG SNAKE.

Every year about this time Morgantown, situated on the confines of Lancaster, Berks and Chester counties, becomes excited over a wild man of immense stature and aspect, who haunts the mountains in the vicinity of that thriving village. Latter in the season they are usually troubled with a wild beast, of unknown species, which strikes terror into the hearts of the inhabitants. During the summer the scourge of the neighborhood is a large serpent, varying in length from fifteen to thirty feet, and whose chief delight seems to be to frighten women and children away from the blackberry and whortleberry patches for which that vicinity is so noted. The snake story is a very good one, and deserves a very good purpose in keeping timid people out of the woods, and thus permitting the professional berry gatherers to reap the harvest unmolested by juvenile competition; but for the life of us we cannot see the expediency of starting out the wild man every fall and the wild beast every winter.

What good purpose can they possibly serve the Morgantowners that they are thus remorsely compelled to walk along the "ragged edge" of the ridge all the way from Adamstown to Parkersburg? And yet the wild man has already been trotted out. He is, according to the statements of those who have seen him, nearly seven feet high, and weighs over two hundred and fifty pounds; he walks generally on all fours, is almost covered with hair, gives unearthly yells and makes all kinds of gestures. His hands and feet are double the size of an ordinary man's, and he presents altogether a horrible appearance. He approaches the cabins of the settlers in the mountains, carries off their pigs and sheep, and with a demoniac laugh, disappears in the dense forests. The brave spirits of the neighborhood go gunning for him, but whenever they come in sight the monster gives a yell and a jump, and before the hunters have time to pull trigger, he is gone.

Now of what use to the Morgantowners is that wild man? They certainly do not trot him out for nothing. They must have an

object in view, but what it is we are at a loss
to determine. Won't somebody enlighten us
as to the use of this monster as also to the
use of this wild species, which haunt the forest every winter?

Since the above was written intelligence
reaches us that the beast is already on its
travels. It has put in an appearance near
Parkesburg; has been seen by several persons, none of whom can describe either its
appearance or the unearthly tones of its
voice. It is simply terrible and of ferocious
aspect. We await with much interest its
appearance at Morgantown.—Lancaster Intelligencer.

Altoona, Pennsylvania, *Tribune,* October 1, 1874

A MONSTER IN THE MOUNTAIN.

Our readers will remember that about two
years since, a wild man was seen on the
Welsh mountains, near Morgantown, in this
county, and created quite an excitement at
the time. A correspondent from Bethel township sends us the following description of
one of the most hideous monsters in human
shape ever seen in that section. It is written
by a reliable gentleman, and the story seems
to have the foundation of truth.

On Sunday last while three young men
were out on the Blue Mountains, near

Swatara Gap, they met an old gentleman named Jos. Feshter, who resides in a small hut near the mountains. He informed the party that about an hour before a monster nearly seven feet high, and weighing over two hundred and fifty pounds, came within twenty yards of his cabin, and gave an unearthly yell, when Feshter looked out and saw the creature on all fours, in the middle of the road making all kinds of gestures. His hair on his head was very long, and his face literally covered with hair. His hands and feet were to all appearances double the size of ordinary hands and feet, and altogether he presented a horrible appearance. Feshter asked him what he wanted, and received merely a grunt for an answer.

He says that he heard a noise on Saturday evening about midnight, in the rear of his hut, but paid little attention to it. In the morning when he got up he found that two pigs about ten weeks old, had been taken away, and also three lambs. He could not imagine what became of them, as he has not neighbors within three miles.

The monster, after sitting in the road a few minutes, gave another yell and a maniac laugh and leaped some ten feet on his hands and feet near him, when Feshter became uneasy and ran down the road. He returned and found that two more of his lambs were gone, and the stove in the cabin overturned, and the fire burning the floor. He put the fire out and locked the cabin, and then started for his nearest neighbor for assistance, when he met the three men, one of whom was your correspondent. We all went to a house two miles distant and procured two guns and other weapons. We searched the mountains until five o'clock in the afternoon, when we were about to return to the cabin, and when within a mile of it, and passing through a deep ravine, we heard some noise upon the bank, and in looking up discovered the monster grinning like a wild beast, and before we had time to take a second thought he gave one yell and a jump, and when we reached the top of the bank, nothing could be seen of him. A party of some twelve are going out on Tuesday, and will remain until the brute is captured.—Reading Eagle.

Providence, Rhode Island, *Press,* October 10, 1874

The Pennsylvania wild man, who haunts the mountains in the neighborhood of Swatara Gap, has been seen again. He is said to be over seven feet high, with face and body covered with long hair, walks on his hands and feet like a dog, and jumps ten feet at a time with apparent ease.

Canton, Ohio, *The Stark County Democrat*, Feb. 3, 1876

NEW CASTLE, PA., JAN. 22, 1876.

Mr. McGregor & Son:

Gents: The enclosed narrative I cut from one of the New Castle papers. Whether it is a hoax or true, you can believe as much as you like and take it for granted for the balance, and if you print it in your valuable paper you can do likewise; at least it is well gotten up. Yours respectfully,

H. D. McCrea.

N. B.—Afterward there was a posse of men captured the "Gorilla" and paraded him through the streets in a crockery crate on a wagon. Having seen this myself, I can testify to the truth of this part of it. Yours, &c., Mc.

"WHAT IS IT?"

A WILD MAN SEEN ON NESHANNOCK CREEK— THE WONDERFUL ADVENTURE OF JOHN NEMO, OF NESHANNOCK TOWNSHIP.

Editor Holiday Advertiser;

Sir: On Monday, December 20th, a singular adventure happened to me, which has ever since been so painfully impressed on my mind that I have resolved to give it to your paper for publication. Early in the morning of the day named above, accompanied by a small dog, I started to visit some musk-rat traps which I had set along the banks of the Neshannock some distance below Reynolds's

mill. I was making my way through the underbrush near the creek, about three-quarters
of a mile from the mill in the direction of
New Castle, when my attention was attracted by a peculiar-looking foot-print imbed-
ded in the snow that had drifted around the
pine bushes. It was a very broad track, some
thirteen inches in length, and was different from anything I had ever seen. It had
five toes, the first being spread out from the
others, giving the track the appearance of
having been made by a gigantic hand, with
the thumb extended. This discovery startled
me, and it also affected the dog very much,
as he ran around among the underbrush,
howling dismally all the while. I got over my
fright in a degree and started for my traps
once more. I had gotten but a short distance
from the spot where I had discovered the
footprints when my ears were saluted by the
most terrible roar I ever heard in my life,
the bushes were parted about thirty yards in
front of me, and the most singularly-looking
man I ever beheld appeared to view. He was
covered all over with grayish colored hair,
with the exception of his face and breast,
the latter being covered with a dark, parch-
ment-like skin. His height was about six feet;
his arms had a spread of near seven feet, and

seemed like cables of twisted wire, so muscular looking were they. His chest must have
measured seven feet around, and he was all
in all, the impersonification of strength. To
my inexpressible horror he advanced rapidly
toward me, beating his breast with his muscular arms, producing a sound like the drum-
ming of a pheasant on a hollow log, but much
louder and deeper. When he had approached
to within ft distance of twenty feet I could
plainly see his ferocious face. It was very
black, and was ornamented with large teeth,
which protruded from an immense mouth.
His countenance was distorted with rage;
his huge teeth were ground against each other, so that I could plainly hear the sound:
the skin of his forehead was drawn forward
rapidly, which made his hair move up and
down, and gave a truly devilish expression
to his face. Once more he gave out a roar
which seemed to shake the woods like thunder; I could feel the earth trembling under
my feet. The monster was looking me in the
eyes and advancing rapidly, and beating his
breast, was spell-bound and paralyzed, and
had it not been for a fortunate intervention I
should have been undoubtedly crushed in his
long arms. The little dog that was with me
darted forward and sunk his teeth in one of
the lower limbs of the wild man and drew his

attention from me. He stooped down, grabbed the animal by the hind legs with both of his hands, whirled him with lightning rapidity around his head half a dozen times, loosened his grip, and the poor dog went through the air like rocket for thirty yards, struck head first against a large sycamore tree, and then fell to the ground dead, crushed to jelly-like mass. Overcome with horror, I lost all consciousness. When I came to myself, about two hours afterward, the man was gone.

I have been confined to my bed ever since from the effects of the adventure, and am unable to be around: but as soon as I am able my sons and I intend, with guns and dogs, taking a hunt for the wild man, and we may have something further to report, as we are determined to capture him if possible. The whole of Neshannock township is excited over the matter, and there is scarcely a night passes but what corn, chickens, and other produce are taken from the farms in the vicinity, and no clue left as to the perpetrator, except peculiar-looking foot-prints in the snow or mud. The place where I saw him was about three-quarters of a mile from the farm of Thos. McCreary, in sight of Neshannock creek, and about three and one half miles from New Castle.

Yours truly, John Nemo.

Neshannock, Tp., Dec. 24, 1875.

(We submit Mr. Nemo's singular narrative without any further comment than that from the description given of the stranger it must have been a full-grown gorilla, instead of a wild man, But why a gorilla should roam around in this cold country we cannot fathom.—Ed.)

Indiana, Pennsylvania, *Progress*, October 16, 1879

A WHAT-IS-IT.

Quite a large searching party has been organized in eastern Berks County, Pa., for the purpose of scouring Muhlenberg and Ruscombmanor townships to hunt up and capture, if possible, one of the strangest looking beasts ever heard of within the borders of the county. What gives emphasis to the sincerity of the people engaged is the fact that responsible and reliable parties were first to report having seen the so-called monster. A son of Prison Inspector Schmehl was first to bring the intelligence to Topton Station. O. H. Hinnershitz, proprietor of the leading hotel there, and a number of others went in pursuit of what Schmehl had described. The monster had been reported on previous occasions, and when Mr. Schmehl saw it it was lying near a gate entrance to a field through which he was about driving a lot of cattle. The "what-is-it" is represented to be about four feet tall, long arms, with but two talon-like fingers on each paw; feet without toes, furrows on its head, body smooth and naked, quite yellow, looks as if it had been wallowing in clay. Jared Rissmiller heard of the animal. It had run up towards Schmehl with extended paws, and then darted into a corn field and was lost to view. The two men then went in search, and discovered the animal on the other side of the field lying near the fence. It reared up on its hind legs like a man. Rissmiller says it is yellowish brown in color, has no hair, small eyes and face, arms about fourteen inches long, legs somewhat longer, the hands and feet resembling those of a human being, and has two horns on the top of the head. The young men made a raid on the monster, when they say it darted toward the forest, and was soon lost in the foliage. A Mr. Heckman, also residing near there, is reported to have seen the beast, and he is inclined to believe that it is a large-sized ape, that may have escaped from some traveling menagerie. Every cornfield is to be searched, together with the neighboring swamps for the purpose of ascertaining what the young men have really seen. After the recent rains the farmers plainly saw very strange looking tracks in the sand on the road-side. They have also heard very unusual howls at night and the dogs of the neighborhood have been trying to hunt down the beast without success.

Mifflintown, Pennsylvania, *Juniata Sentinel and Republican*, January 12, 1881

STATE ITEMS

A monster gorilla is reported to have made its appearance on Jimmy Brunt's farm, Valley township, Armstrong county. The other night the animal visited the house of John Emory and captured a dog, which he carried away into the woods. Subsequently, it is said, the animal attacked and badly wounded a gigantic hound belonging to Mr. Con Nulton. A party is organizing to effect his capture.

Reading, Pennsylvania, *Times*, January 21, 1881

A WELSH MOUNTAIN STORY.

A gentleman living near Morgantown, Berks county, was in town the other day, and tells another "Wild Man of the Woods" story about New California hills, a portion of the Welsh Mountain range. He says a party of young gentlemen were out sleighing with their ladies, and while driving through a pass in the hills the foremost horse suddenly became unmanageable and evinced all the signs of great terror. At the same time a wild cry came from the thicket, causing the horse to turn around, and all efforts to make him pass the place were unavailing. The young men remained near the hills for some minutes, and heard the noise a number of times. The same gentleman says that the farmers in the vicinity have suffered from the depredations of some animal, which makes peculiar foot-prints in the snow, but up to this time have not been able to discover it, though the hills have been scoured by armed men with dogs a number of times. Some think the animal is a catamount or an animal of its species. Whether there is anything in the story or not we do not know, but we give it for what it is worth.—*Pottstown Ledger.*

Reading, Pennsylvania, *Times,* June 6, 1885

A WILD MAN OF THE WOODS.

A wild man is reported on the Lehigh Mountain, near Allentown. He leaves his hiding place between 9 and 10 o'clock nightly and keep up an unearthly howling nearly all night. He is supposed to be an escaped lunatic.

Indiana, Pennsylvania, *Weekly Messenger,* August 1, 1888

Some persons who have been drinking mountain dew, manufactured in the neighborhood of Nicktown, report that they met a wild man in the neighborhood of Mehaffey. They report him as being ten feet high, and covered with hair and his tracks in the sand measure 16 inches. That Nicktown whiskey must be terrible stuff. We imagine the men who originated the story are in training for campaign liars for Democratic newspapers. If they would take a few lessons from the editor of the Indiana Democrat, they might get situations promptly.

Indiana, Pennsylvania, *Weekly Messenger*, October 3, 1888

"For the past several days wild rumors have been floating about to the effect that some gigantic animal resembling a gorilla is running at large through the forests near Big Run. Several parties had reported seeing strange tracks in the mud at various places. At first no account was taken of it, but the reports came in so thickly that several prominent citizens of Big Run finally concluded to investigate the matter. Going to the places designated they were surprised to find the tracks more peculiar and gigantic than had been reported. They measured one of them and it proved to be a trifle over sixteen inches in length. It was wide at the toes and narrowed gradually toward the heel. Distinct marks of toes with long nails or claws were

visible, suggesting the idea of a gorilla. The
animal has not yet been sighted, but the oldest
hunters acknowledge themselves completely
at a loss to know to what species of created
beings that wonderful foot belongs."—*Spirit*

Altoona, Pennsylvania, *Tribune,* August 3, 1891
SAW A WILD WOMAN.
Womelsdorf, Pa., August 2.—The wild woman
who roamed over South mountain near this
place years ago, it is reported, has made her
appearance again. One of the party from this
place while picking huckleberries says he saw
her. "While going through a ravine," he said,
"our attention was drawn to a peculiar noise
on the incline above. We ventured near the
spot and saw to our amazement a woman with
long hair growing over her face and body and
one arm and leg shorter than the others. She
was hanging on a vine suspended from a large
tree, swinging to and fro, and as if humming a
lullaby. Upon seeing us she leaped from tree
to tree and was soon lost to sight, chattering
to herself as she disappeared." The affair has
caused considerable talk here, and the matter
will be further investigated.

Olean, New York, *Democrat,* August 6, 1891
The city of Erie, Pa., and the surrounding country is said to be infested by a wild

creature, half man and half beast, which visits the hen roosts at night and kills the fowls, sucking their blood and leaving their carcasses on the ground. His record is between 500 and 600 dead fowls up to date.

Olean, New York, *Democrat*, August 14, 1894

POTTER COUNTY ROMANCE

GIANT WILD MAN SAID TO BE ROAMING THE WILDS

The Gazette of Galeton, Potter county, Pa., is responsible for the following story, which certainly beats the most inspired efforts of any New York state newspaper liars: Last Sunday afternoon Jud Burrows' boys whose home is in Dry Hollow, five miles west of this place, received a scare that will not leave their memory while they breathe the air of life. After breakfast the boys went to pick some blackberries for their mother, accompanied by the family dog. They were picking away unconcernedly near the edge of a piece of thick woods not far from the house and but a short distance from a high bank at the river's edge, when they were suddenly startled by the awfulest yells, mingled with cries of pain from their dog, that they had ever heard. Wondering what was the matter they rushed out of briers to a spot of clear ground, when, on looking up, they beheld a sight that temporarily froze their blood and struck their limbs with palsy. For a few seconds they were rooted to the spot, bereft of the sense of speech and the means of locomotion. The fearful sight that met their eyes was a giant about seven feet in height, from whose nude body, from feet to head, grew long, matted hair. In one hand at arm's length he held the large dog as easily as a boy could hold a stick of candy. Luckily for the boys the dog's cries of pain restored to them the use of their legs and lungs, and they hallooed loud for help as they fled toward home.

With an indescribable screech that raised the echoes for three miles distant, the wild man flung the dog after the retreating boys, rushed toward the river, and in two bounds from the 20-feet-high bank, cleared the stream and disappeared. In the afternoon a party of armed settlers started in search of the wild man but, though his trail was plain, they failed to find him. Monday of this week several men got a glimpse of him from a distance, but did not attempt to molest him. He is described as a giant in size, with high broad shoulders, extraordinarily long arms, large head, and his whole body covered with thick, dark hair. He is probably the same wild man that was reported as having been seen over near Hull's last spring. His appearance has set this part of the country in a commotion. Mr. Burrows' dog was found in a pretty dilapidated condition. Several of his ribs were broken in the giant's grasp, and his hide is fearfully punctured from the wild man's finger nails.

Wellsboro, Pennsylvania, *Gazette,* Aug. 22, 1894

There is considerable excitement along the West branch over a wild man who has been seen by a dozen persons. He is described as being about seven feet tall and covered with hair. He has made several raids in that vicinity, and last week Sunday he came out of the woods into Walter Thompson's field and gazed on the house for a long time. Mrs. Thompson and her three daughters stood watching him, trembling with fear; the men being away from home. This chap may turn out to be the "wild man of Borneo."

Smethport, Pennsylvania, *McKean County Miner,* August 24, 1894

Some people near Galeton, about ten days since, were frightened by what they supposed was a wild man of immense stature all covered with hair. It has since transpired that the supposed wild man was a large bear walking on its hind feet as they frequently do. Tom Harrington's fertile brain and ready pen will make Galeton and vicinity noted for its many curiosities.

THE HISTORICAL BIGFOOT

Coudersport, Pennsylvania, *Potter Enterprise,* September 5, 1894

HERE'S THE STORY.

The Wellsboro Republican Advocate tells the tale which this paper intended to tell. Here it is: The "giant" wild man is no mith, but reality. He lives near the Cross Fork, in Clinton county, not far from the post office, in Leidy township. His name is Bodine Brooks, aged about 45 years. For 28 years he has been kept in a log and board pen. His food consists of the leavings of the table of the family and is fed to him in a pan shoved through a small opening in the pen. He hasn't a shred of clothing on, nor has he had but once in that time. An old blanket in the corner is [his] only covering. As people pass along the road he sets up series of yells that are anything but human, and cries and screeches like a panther. He knows his name and responds to it and can articulate a few words. He has a great fondness for tobacco and grabs it like a dog would a piece of meat, and either eats it down, or trots off to the pen and hides it and watches to see that it don't get away.

Within a few feet of the pen is said to reside his brothers and sisters, his parents being dead. The survivors are well-to-do people and own a fine farm, of which he is a part owner as one of the heirs. Brooks instead

of being seven or eight feet in height, if he
stood erect would be less than six feet. He is
very much stooped, said to have been caused
by cuddling to himself, trying to keep warm.
His body is covered with hair, likewise his
face. His hair falls over his shoulders in a
tangling and matted mass from his head.

The pen in which he has been confined
was securely locked, but Bodine broke the
fastenings and is now enjoying unrestricted
freedom. He is undoubtedly the "giant wild
man" who is terrorizing the inhabitants of
the West Branch.

For the past few years he has become ugly
and unmanageable. The family has been offered large sums of money for this "wild man"
by the proprietors of circuses, but has stead-
fastly refused. Several years ago Brooks escaped, in the winter, and was traced by the
pieces of green bark, which he had torn off
the trees to stand on while resting. A few
days ago, a party of braves surrounded a
barn in the West Branch valley, in which the
"giant" lay asleep, and when he awakened
and saw the assembled multitude, he gave
one of those demoniac yells, and the crowd
fled precipitately. At last accounts he is still
at large and the family has made no effort to
recapture him. We have communicated with

the State Board of Charities concerning the matter and he will undoubtedly be cared for as he ought. It seems almost impossible that such a condition of affairs exists in this enlightened age, but the fact that the Brookes lived in the heart of an almost unbroken wilderness may account for it.

Tionesta, Pennsylvania, *Forest Republican*, September 12, 1894

The giant wild man of Potter County is said to have been captured by a posse of nearly 100 men. The man was first discovered by some women while berrying. He was not afraid of women but would flee at the presence of man. Wonderful stories are told about the marvelous strength of the captured man. He is said to be nearly seven feet in height and his body is covered with long hair. Flowing locks, two feet in length, hang down his back and his hands are said to resemble long bird-like claws. The scene of his capture is laid near Westfield.

A reminiscence of Potter county newspaper man Tom Harrington noted that this 1894 series of "wild man" reports was the product of Harrington's imagination. "An inimitable humorist his writings took a quaint turn at the most unexpected moments. Some years ago in one of his lighter moods he wrote an account of an imaginary wild man for one of the Coudersport papers and the article was received with such acclaim that further chronicles of the mythical wild man simply had to follow. While readers in this part of the country accepted the articles at their face value and knew that the mysterious creature described had never existed, it was different further away from home where the stories were copied accorded doubting but fascinating belief. Finally a great New York newspaper sent one of its most skillful writers into the wilds of Potter county to investigate and the myth was exploded while half of the nation laughed with Tom Harrington. ("Just Jottings," by R. K. Knapp, Smethport, Pennsylvania, *McKean Democrat,* December 16, 1920.)

Warren, Pennsylvania, *Ledger,* November 15, 1895

A wild man in the woods is terrorizing the natives of Bolivar and vicinity.

Philadelphia, Pennsylvania, *Inquirer,* Feb. 28, 1901

WILD MAN WHO LOOKS LIKE GORILLA MADE CRAZY BY JOHNSTOWN FLOOD

Hollidaysburg, Pa., Feb. 27.—Blair county has a wild man. He was made crazy by the Johnstown flood, and has been living ever since in the woods and amid rocks. Only recently he came into public notice at Blue Kob, a county hamlet, located among the peaks of the Alleghenies.

In accordance with the theory of evolution, this strange creature, who has forgotten even his own name, looks, by this time, very much like a wild animal or gorilla. Farmers and their families along the mountain side are frequently terrified by his unexpected appearances before them in unfrequented places.

Newark, Ohio, *Advocate,* July 21, 1906

WILD MAN

Fought the Captors and Made His Escape After One Had Been Badly Bitten.

Pittsburg, Pa., July 21—The wild man, supposed to be an escaped patient from Dixmont, who has been terrorizing the boroughs of Ben Avon, Avalon, and Elmsworth, was caught by a party of Ben Avon citizens, but made his escape later.

J. S. Wagoner, Charles and Robert Crawford and John Trust, while returning home, were accosted by a man with long hair all over his body and who had the appearance of a full grown gorilla.

Mr. Wagoner, as well as Charles Crawford, immediately gave battle, and with the assistance of Robert Crawford succeeded in getting the supposed wild man down on the ground. Mr. Trust took his handkerchief and bound the wild man's wrists behind his back, but when they allowed him to arise the lunatic began kicking and biting in such a manner that all parties concerned were only too glad to let him go. Straining his wrists he managed to get his hands free, and he ran to a near-by tree and went up with the agility of a cat.

Wagoner and Trust were left to watch while the Crawford brothers went home and secured lanterns and additional help, but when they returned they could find no signs of Wagoner and Trust or the supposed wild man. They searched the locality and found no signs of either. Then they started home and when near Crawford's farm caught up with the watchers, who gave an exciting account of their experiences, stating that the wild man came down the tree and gave them a fierce battle, in which Wagoner was badly bitten and scratched and his clothing badly torn.

Scranton, Pennsylvania, *Republican*, October 28, 1906

GORILLA AT LARGE

A wild story comes from Wilkes-Barre to the effect that a gorilla is loose on the mountains back of Georgetown and Laurel Run. People in the vicinity are greatly excited over

reports of the animal being at large. Several
profess to have seen the gorilla and to have
been greatly frightened by it.

Several seem to be of the impression that
the wild animal is a bear, but the general
opinion is that it resembles a gorilla. Two
young women on their way home from Laurel
Run appear to have been the first to see the
gorilla. So far as they know it did not pursue
them.

Scranton, Pennsylvania, *Republican,* November 1, 1906
MORTON'S GORILLA STIRS 'EM
FOLKS WHO DON'T DRINK,
LIKE THOSE WHO DO, SEE HIM.

Chester, Pa., Oct. 31.—The negroes residing
in and about Morton and Springfield are still
being terrorized by the monstrosity, which,
it is said, resembles a gorilla, and which has
been roaming about with the speed of a deer.
Many persons who are compelled to travel by
the lonely road at night have armed themselves with revolvers.

Charles Dotts, a white farmer, declares
that he saw the strange beast and that he
shot it several times, but the bullets did not
appear to have any effect except that the
animal snorted, tore up several small trees
and scampered off.

Harry Batty, a butcher, attributes his loss of fifty chickens on Monday night to the strange animal, which ate the entrails of the fowls and left the carcasses on the ground.

Daniel Norris is willing to make affidavit that he has frequently seen the freak and that the last time he saw it the animal was enjoying a bath in Whiskey Run, a small stream in Morton.

While driving to his home in Springfield last evening William Holliday says he saw a strange object some distance ahead of him, and that when he reached the top of the hill, on Woodland avenue, the animal, which looked like a gorilla, disappeared in a clump of bushes.

Others who declare they saw the mysterious animal are H. J. Mason, Frank Toland, Elwood Powell and Joseph Johnson.

Many of the negroes are going around armed to the teeth, in readiness to meet the strange wonder.

Oakland, California, *Tribune*, November 9, 1906

NEGROES SCARED BY GORILLA-LIKE GHOST

Philadelphia, Nov. 9.—Negro residents of Springfield township and Morton are tremendously agitated over a wild and uncanny thing, resembling a gorilla, which, they say, is wandering about the neighborhood at night.

It walks on its hind legs and makes its appearance about dusk. Apparently it manifests itself only to persons of African descent, for none of the white citizens have seen it as yet.

One negro says it growled at him a few nights ago, and that the growl was sufficient inducement to him to run all the way home.

Another asserts that he shot the beast, but that the bullet bounded off as though it had struck a chunk of armor plate.

Philadelphia, Pennsylvania, *Inquirer*, Nov. 25, 1906

APE-LIKE ANIMAL SCARES PEOPLE IN DELAWARE COUNTY

TRAP SET FOR IT PULLED UP BY ROOTS AND WIRES AND CHAINS SNAPPED

Darby, Pa., Nov. 24.—All Delaware county is exercised over the antics of a strange, gorilla-like animal, which has been frightening belated pedestrians almost out of their wits in widely separated parts of the county within the last two weeks. One night it was seen near Chester, another night it was seen prowling near Media, and again it was seen running along the roads on all fours in Morton.

Runs Like Race Horse

Walking sometimes upright like a man, or else running along at race horse speed on all fours, with a peculiar leaping stride, and covered with a heavy coat of hair, the animal is differently described by those who see it. The negroes have become terrorized, and in many sections of the county cannot be induced to pass certain localities after dark where the animal has been seen. Others have stocked themselves with all manner of weapons to put an end to the freak and still have fled.

Some are of the opinion that it is an escaped ape from the Zoo, which is strengthened by the fact that a representative from the Zoological Gardens was making inquiries in Springfield township a few days ago concerning it. Traps have been set for it, only to be pulled up by the roots and the heavy wires and chains snapped like sugar-twine.

Bear Traps Too Weak

Frank Carr, of Springfield, aided by several of his neighbors, last Tuesday week got out two heavy steel bear traps, baited and set them. The strange animal had been seen lurking in the woods nearby at nights, and it was determined to capture it. The traps were set in an inclosure in the back of Mr. Carr's house, but the next morning both were sprung, the bait eaten off, and a section of heavy telegraph wire, with which they were fastened to a big oak tree, was snapped like thread. The ground was clawed up as if newly furrowed, and the traps were found several rods away, as if carried that distance before the animal released itself. It was reported last Saturday night as having been seen in Media, on Washington street, near the residence of United States Marshal John B. Robinson, but it disappeared in the darkness.

Philadelphia, Pennsylvania, *Inquirer*, November 29, 1906

GORILLA SEEN AGAIN

Darby, Pa., Nov. 28.—Apparently emboldened by the excited attitude of the people towards it, the gorilla-like being which, according to reports, has been causing all kinds of excitement in various parts of Delaware county the past two weeks, turned up again, so it is asserted, in several places early this morning, long enough in one to be shot at three times by a policeman, near Clifton Heights.

"Spot" Evans, a colored man, who lives on Hook road, on the outskirts of Sharon Hill, says that when on his way home from Darby early this morning, and half a mile up Chester pike, he heard something running after him. He turned and saw a big wooly object, which followed him to his home. Evans was so frightened that he got his gun, but by the time he reached the second-story to shoot it from the window it had slunk away in the woods. . . .

Wilkes-Barre, Pennsylvania, *Times*, Nov. 30, 1906

DARBY'S "GORILLA" PROVES TO BE A DOG

Darby, Pa., Nov. 30.—The "arrest" of a big brown-haired dog with an enormous head and an exceptionally long body last night by Policeman Clark, is believed to have solved Delaware county's mysterious gorilla-like bugaboo, which has been terrorizing belated pedestrians.

Clark came across the animal on Main street, and, drawing his gun, he made his way cautiously toward it, step by step. When he came within a few yards it turned and ran, with a peculiar leaping motion and its long matted hair, which flew out, gave it an aspect like that of the much-talked of "gorilla."

After a chase of a square in the darkness Clark threw his arms around the fleeing mystery, threatened to shoot if it showed fight and found that it was a dog.

Thinking that its presence would explain the gorilla-man mystery, he took it to the station house and locked it up. Hundreds of people journeyed to the jail and had a look at the animal, although many negroes would not venture near it, fearing that it might break out.

Syracuse, New York, *Herald,* December 2, 1906

PENNSYLVANIA'S STRANGE BEAST

Residents of Georgetown and Laurel Run, on the mountain near Wilkes-Barre, have been frightened by some strange animal during the last few days, which they say has appeared from the brush along the mountain road between the two places. Opinions as to what it is differ.

Some say it is an enormous ape and others say that it is a bear which has wandered down from the Bear creek district, where they are plentiful.

Those who have seen it have not waited to make any investigation, but have fled as fast as they could.—Philadelphia *Press.*

Eureka, Utah, *Reporter,* December 7, 1906

STRANGE ANIMAL IS SEEN

Wilkesbarre, Pa—Several parties living near the Wilkesbarre mountain report that within the last few days they have seen a strange animal in the woods resembling a gorilla. At first it was thought that it might be a bear but two hunters who saw the strange creature the other day claim it climbs trees like a monkey and goes into hiding upon the approach of men.

Tooele, Utah, *Transcript Bulletin*, December 28, 1906

STRANGE MONSTER
SCARES CITIZENS.

WEIRD BABOON LIKE CREATURE
SEEN NEAR DARBY, PA.

Darby, Pa—All Delaware County has stirred up over the supposed antics of an alleged wild animal which is asserted to look like a gorilla and to have frightened belated wayfarers almost out of their wits in various parts of the county. While it is believed by most persons that the whole thing is a practical joke on the part of some one who is literally making a monkey out of himself, still many of the more timid class are thoroughly alarmed and fully believe all the tales that are told about the creature.

Those professing to have seen the wonderful animal assert that it sometimes goes upright like a man and then dashes along on all fours with marvellous speed maintaining a queer galloping gait. They furthermore feel certain that it has a coat of dark hair but that is not considered remarkable as the weather is cool. Their stories of how they almost encountered the strange beast have been so thrilling that many of the negroes in the county cannot be induced to pass the spots where it is said to have been seen. Others have purchased pistols and go about armed, fully resolved to sell their lives dearly should they encounter the mythical monster in any of its hypothetical haunts.

Others take the thing seriously without being unduly alarmed and they try to explain the matter. That it is an ape escaped from some zoological collection is the most commonly accepted theory. This was strengthened by a rumor that the authorities of the Zoological Gardens of Philadelphia were out looking for a lost simian in Delaware county. But a telephone message to the zoo exploded the story. All the Philadelphia monkeys are safe in their cages. Their keeper respectfully suggested that the animal down by Darby is probably a monkey of native Delaware county stock.

Nevertheless several persons in Springfield township are so convinced that there is a strange animal prowling about that they have set traps for it. Frank Carr is one of them, and he set a number of traps in an enclosure in the rear of his house near some woods where the reputed creature was reported to have been seen. It is now stated that the traps were found broken, the bait devoured and all evidences on hand of a struggle made by some animal.

The practical joker who is working the scare, if such is the case, has succeeded to an extent which may work his own harm. For there are a number of Delaware county citizens who while not getting in hysterics about the matter have quietly placed big guns in their hip pockets and are waiting for a chance to pot anything that looks like a baboon.

Los Angeles, California, *Daily Herald,* April 14, 1907

"GORILLA" DEMON
ONLY CRAZY NEGRO

Sharon Hill, April 13.—The mystery of Delaware county's strange ape-like creature, that for the past fortnight has been prowling from village to village, terrorizing scores of men, women and children, has been solved, according to Charles Wagner, a detective of Philadelphia.

From the investigation which he and another operator carried on several nights ago in the vicinity of Darby, he learned that the wild-eyed demon was none other than a crazed negro, who makes his home in a shanty in a woods on the outskirts of this town.

With a rug of bearskin thrown over his body and his hair daubed with phosphorus, the negro, the sleuth asserts, stalked about the county roads, and on several occasions ventured to secret himself at an extremity of a town.

Jumping and yelling as pedestrians passed, the demented man caused much excitement. Stories circulated about him increased the fear of the farmers and soon it was gossiped around that a "gorilla" was at large.

Detective Wagner has placed the man under surveillance. Means will be taken at once to have him removed to some institution.

Wellsboro, Pennsylvania, *Agitator,* June 23, 1909

A Westfield correspodent says: "There has been much discussion recently in regard to the wild man or animal which several people have seen on Mill creek, on the Broughton Hollow and on the Jameson. Some think it may be a bear but those who have seen it report that, though it sometimes stands on all fours, it raises itself upon its hind legs to travel and gets itself along at a very good pace. It is reported to have chased one man and also at another time to have turned and ran away when it received a charge of bird shot in the face, from a gun in the hands of a boy. It is said to have more the resemblance of a wild man or gorilla than a bear. Some hunters have made a pretence at least of endeavoring to hunt it down, but without success."

Wellsville, New York, *Allegany County Reporter,* June 29, 1909

WILD MAN NOT GONE

(FROM THE WESTFIELD FREE PRESS.)

In view of the publicity given the mysterious wild man which has been spreading terror throughout Clymer Township, it was believed that nothing further would be heard from the animal, but disapproval and press notices do not make this hairy monster [vamoose]. It bobs up serenely and holds to its fame just when the public thinks it has gone into retirement.

It is a discouraging business, this seeing a wild man. With all the requirements for a thrilling tale, the narrator is obliged to go easy and minimize facts to obtain any sort of credence. Those who have seen this quaintly curious monster say it is six feet tall, but will allowance for the desire of being believed, who knows but the ones who saw it are firm in the belief that it is eight feet tall. It is also a sad task for the natural history editor to set out the peculiarities of the creature to an unbelieving world.

Howsomever to proceed with the narrative, a boy was rusticating at Eldridge Pond the other evening and listening to what the wild waves were saying when the hairy biped intruded itself on the peaceful pastoral scene and acted as a starter for the first country run which has been held in Clymer this year. The boy made Mercury, the gent that wore wings on his heels, look like a tortoise on a warm, lazy day and if that gorilla was making observations of the genus homo it did not require much information that evening.

The boy says that the beast was six feet tall, had long arms, walked on its hind legs, wore its hair in an inverted pompadour and was altogether unlovely.

Here is also a letter from Sabinsville, dated June 21st:

Sabinsville, Pa.,
June 21, 1909.

Editor Free Press,

The stories with regard to the wild man or gorilla are perfectly true. I was visiting my sister, Chloe Dickens, near Sanderinville, Thursday, June 17th. I was sitting in the house, when she called me to the door and said look at that animal. I looked and saw, about forty or fifty rods from the house, in the meadow, a large animal which was lying on the grass. I shouted at it and it raised upon its hind legs and looked towards me. I went in the house after a gun but could find not shots and went back to the porch and the animal, whatever it was, was walking upright. . . . *[Rest of text illegible.]*

Warren, Pennsylvania, *Evening Mirror,* July 13, 1911

An Unknown Monster—The report is current in Russell that a large animal of an unknown species has taken up its abode in the woods between Porter's Point and Putnamville. Several persons claim to have seen it on different occasions. It is described as being tall, somewhat like a man with large fiery eyes and gives vent to blood curdling shrieks when approached. The appearance of the monster in that quiet neighborhood is causing a great deal of comment and speculation.

Frederick, Maryland, *News,* November 2, 1912

NEW MYSTERY IN MARIETTA
WILD BEAST DEVOURS TWO
DOGS CHAINED IN KENNEL.

Marietta, Pa., Nov. 2—The community is excited over the supposed appearance of a wild beast.

A. R. McKain, upon returning with his three brothers from a gunning trip, found that his two valuable beagle dogs, which he had left tied in the kennel, were gone. He went gunning without seeing the dogs, telling his wile to give them breakfast. She found the collars empty with chains attached and bones were lying around.

It is supposed that a bear, which found its way along the Susquehanna river, visited the McKain home, which is close to the stream, and the rain which fell hid the tracks.

Some time ago a wild man was seen at Kinder Hook, several miles east, and this, with the hole and automobile mystery at Maytown a few weeks ago, has caused considerable excitement. Men are armed and on watch.

Philadelphia, Pennsylvania, *Inquirer,* September 4, 1919

HAIRY WILD MAN LOOSE IN LEIPERVILLE SECTION, CRIES OO-OO! AND MAG MAG!

Chester, Pa., Sept. 3.—A wild man is roaming around in the section of Delaware county adjacent to Leiperville and through Ridley township, according to the story brought into the village this morning by Hugh Duffy, John Wiley, Mike Dillon and Lawrence Scott, a quartette of fishermen who took a day off to angle for carp in Ridley Creek, near Avondale.

The four men tell the same story in the same way about the strange creature they saw hopping around on all-fours, pawing the earth and going through pantomimic antics. He gives vent to a piteous "oo-oo" and cries out in a guttural, but loud and distinct voice, "Mag-Mag-Mag." These are the only two sounds he makes.

Duffy, Wiley, Dillon and Scott are employed at the Eddystone plant of the Baldwin Locomotive Works, and have lived in Leipersville for a number of years. All are known to be truthful, sober men. One by one the perturbed anglers gave an account of their experiences, and so great was the thrill and sensation thrown into the villagers, that many of them declared they would put double locks and stronger bars upon their doors and windows before going to bed tonight.

The women folks are especially worked up over the stories of the returning fishermen, and are more susceptible to the hair-bristling accounts of the wild man than are the men, who organized a hunting party this afternoon and went to look for the strange creature. At nightfall they had not found him.

Anyone having felt the blood-curdling effect of the awful "oo-oo" will never want to hear it again, aver both Wiley and Duffy, but the pronunciation of his second call, that of "Mag-Mag," is still more ghostly and ominous as the strange being keeps hopping about the bushes and tall grasses. The name "Mag" is believed to be that of a woman for

whom either in fact or in fancy the wild man
is looking.

Lawrence Scott says he was so badly rat-
tled that he was speechless.

"Of all the hideous animals, it was that
wild man," declared Wiley. "He had hair all
over his face and it hung a foot from his chin,
and he went jumping among the rocks just
like a bear, and every minute he would poke
his devilish head above the bushes and yell
'oo-oo.' Then we would lose sight of the old
fellow, when he would suddenly pop up his
head and yell 'Mag-Mag.' Why, the cries were
so pitiful they went clean through me."

Some believe the strange creature is a man
who has escaped from some institution. As for
the four men who claim they saw the "Wild
Man," they cannot be shaken in their story
and are firm in their belief that the frightful being is wandering through the country in
search of an old sweetheart, maybe, who probably spurned his love and drove him crazy.

Pittsburgh, Pennsylvania, *Press,* August 21, 1920

GORILLA HUNT BEING
WAGED IN MIFFLIN TWP.

Electric searchlights will be used by residents of Mifflin township today to explore
the abandoned mine near New Homestead

in which it is reported a gorilla or ape has taken up his abode, sallying forth from time to time for food.

Boys and men armed with rifles and shotguns have been watching the mine entrance since yesterday to trap the animal.

Nich Broeski entered the mine late last night in a search for the gorilla. He could not find it but brought out the torn body of an animal thought to be a sheep.

Women and children in the neighborhood are terrorized and to definitely determine whether there is a gorilla in the mine a posse will enter the workings this evening with searchlights and rifles.

Pittsburgh, Pennsylvania, *Post,* August 21, 1920

GORILLA CAUSES
TERROR IN TOWNS

New Homestead and Doerr Terrace in Mifflin township were the scenes of much excitement yesterday over the rumor that a gorilla or large ape had taken up its abode in an abandoned coal mine on the hillside in Doerr Terrace. The animal was first reported to have been seen Tuesday evening by Mrs. William Jenkins and Walter West of Doerr Terrace.

It has caused a number of scares to persons in the district, at night, at which time, it is said, it leaves the abandoned mine and saunters about in search of food. Homer Wozley, of Mifflin township, reported that the animal followed him Thursday night almost to the doorstep of his home.

Charleston, West Virginia, *Daily Mail,* August 22, 1920

SEARCH FOR MONKEY.

Pittsburgh, Pa., August 21.—A little group of drowsy men were still waiting tonight at the mouth of an abandoned mine on the outskirts of Homestead near here, for the appearance of an ape reported to have been "terrorizing farmers and milking cows" for the past two weeks. Many farmers allege their cows are being milked dry by a mysterious prowler.

The ape has been reported seen in many sections of Westmoreland and Alleghany counties. A friendly poker game was said to have broken up when the animal dropped from an overhanging branch in to the ante. The players fled leaving the ape in possessions of the money and cards.

Pittsburgh, Pennsylvania, *Press,* August 22, 1920

MYSTERIOUS GORILLA IN MIFFLIN TOWNSHIP MILKS EIGHT COWS!

Not content with a diet of fruit and vegetables stolen from gardens in the West Homestead and Mifflin township district, the big gorilla which has been terrorizing Negroes in that district is thought to have sallied forth from his supposed hiding place in an abandoned mine yesterday afternoon, and milked eight cows pasturing in the vicinity. No one actually saw the animal in the act, as far as is known, but the farmers to whom the cows belong are reported to place the blame for the theft of the milk on the simian marauder and have joined the gorilla hunt.

How the animal escaped from the mine yesterday except by some side entry, it is believed by Nick Proto and Peter Delanto, members of the posse who kept an all-day vigil with loaded rifles at the mouth of the mine yesterday while others explored the accessible parts with electric searchlights. It is believed the activities of the searching party around the mouth of the mine and the shooting by several foreigners Friday night when they imagined they saw the gorilla caused it to slink back into some remote part of the mine and find another way to escape.

Several of the farmers whose cows came home milkless and who were forced to drink their coffee black last night expressed their intention of keeping their cows under observation today for the purpose of determining just how a gorilla goes about the operation of milking a cow.

Pittsburgh, Pennsylvania, *Press,* August 23, 1920

SHOOTING ON "SUSPICION."

GORILLA NOT EXACTLY SEEN,

BUT SHOTS ARE FIRED

Shots were fired again last night in Mifflin township's "gorilla chase." Excited guards watching cattle and sheep are said to have fired the shots on "suspicion."

Many persons were out until late last night in hopes of glimpsing the gorilla which is reported to have been prowling about for several days, but none reported having seen it. Excitement over the affair is gradually dying out and today residents of the district are beginning to look upon the matter as a hoax.

Pittsburgh, Pennsylvania, *Daily Post,* August 24, 1920

SCARECROWS FAIL TO FRIGHTEN CROP THIEVES, BUT GORILLA YARN, HOAX OF FARMERS DOES WORK

PLUNDERING CEASES ABRUPTLY WITH FIRST STORY

Mifflin township not only produces fine farm and garden products, but good farmers, and wise ones at that. For farmers in that district have pulled a real stunt—one that would make the wildest press agent turn green with envy, and one that promises to keep the township before the public for many weeks.

Mifflin township has a gorilla—a wild, ferocious animal that milks cows, chases women and children and, in fact, terrorizes the entire neighborhood. But the gorilla is only an imaginary one—the product or brain child as they call them of one of the wise farmers of the district, started in an effort to protect the farms of the neighborhood.

For years the foreign residents of Homestead and Munhall have swept down on the farms of Mifflin township plundering them of fruits, berries and everything eatable. Trees in the orchards were destroyed, and vegetables of all kinds were trampled or stolen. Every effort was made to prevent the plundering, but without results.

Then along came prohibition and the instillation of stills for the making of home brews. The berries never even had a chance to ripen. The thirsty horde just marched in and swept through the farms. Everything that could possibly give a kick was either stolen or destroyed.

It's Scarecrow Idea

Early this year the mighty horde again swept down on the farms in Mifflin township, plundering the places. The farmers did everything possible to keep back the army of thirsty souls but without avail, for they cleaned things up and hurried to their stills and wine presses.

About this time reports of a wild gorilla in the hills of West Virginia reached the daily papers. The farmers were talking about it in a short time. And right then and there the idea struck one of the younger farmers.

Why couldn't that gorilla appear out in Mifflin township?

It would be a good stunt to keep the thirsty natives of Munhall and Homestead off their farms. Soon the word was passed around the district and in a few hours talk of the gorilla had been spread broadcast.

Men told their wives of seeing a furry animal trying to milk the cows in the pasture. The wives told the neighbors, and the children told strangers. The strangers told others and soon the word was passed along that a wild gorilla was roaming about in the hills, terrorizing the district.

But the scheme would not be complete unless it reached the newspapers. So they decided to get the yarn in print. A reported was tipped off to the story and gave all the details, all night searching parties, guns, search lights, candles, torches, and everything.

The story was printed and soon became the talk of the town. Other reporters called and were given additional details of how the gorilla had chased so and so's wife, children, milked this farmer's cow, and how they had searched such and such a mine.

In fact they talked so much of the gorilla and gave out so many stories that many of the natives soon started believing that there really was a gorilla loose. But the stories did the work, and the thirsty army passed Mifflin township by in the search of material for their home brew.

Children Unafraid

A number of the farmers of Mifflin township were visited yesterday and many were the queer stories that were told. Some believed the yard, while others just smiled and talked about the crops and the recent cool spell.

"There ain't no such animal. Only place they have 'em is in the circus," was the way James V. Boland, a farmer, answered questions about the gorilla.

"I ain't never seen a circus, even if I am 68 years old, nor a gorilla 'cept in a picture book one time. Might be one of them animals around here, but he ain't never come near my farm," he smiled, as he walked away toward the corn field.

Boland's three children didn't appear frightened over the gorilla and romped and played about in the field near their father.

Robert Charles Dunsey, a neighbor, appeared to be in earnest over the gorilla. He announced when questioned that he really believed in the story, but had never aided in the hunt for the wild animal. "Been hearing kinda funny noises around the house at night. Don't know—it might be that animal." Dunsey smiled as he pulled a bucket of water out of the old well. "Lots of berries around here you know; he might like them, still I ain't botherin' much."

George Metz, a farmer of the Dravosburg road, smilingly told of his experience in the gorilla chase. "I ain't never seen the animal, but heard a lot about it. I guess folks around here are drinking a little too much corn whiskey—what do you think?" When questioned further about his berries, Metz just smiled and said, "Lots of berries and apples, we farmers have to make hay while the sun shines you know."

All along the country roads in the district children romped and played throughout the day. They did not fear the gorilla and to show that they knew it was a joke visited the spots where the man-eating animal was supposed to be hiding.

Some Believe it?

The story of how the cows were being milked by the gorilla was told to Silas B. Thompson, a farmer. Thompson appeared indignant over the matter and promptly replied that nothing ever milked his cows.

"Why I have been milking my own cows for over 12 years and no animals are going to do it if I can help it." When further questioned about the gorilla, Thompson smilingly told of how he had seen a gorilla in the movies several weeks ago.

"Went to town to do some shopping. Stopped in one of them picture shows. They had a picture of a gorilla fighting a man. Darned if I would want that job or any part of it; bad enough to have to work on the farm. You can tell them all that if that gorilla is around here that they can count me out of the hunt or fight with him; they had better get that man in the pictures to fight him."

On and on through the district the story is the same. Farmers, their wives and children smile and jeer at the yarn. Still there are a few who believe the story and they are the ones with the finest farms and the ones nearest the road. As far as they are concerned the gorilla can stay there, because as long as it is running around, the thirsty horde from the

city will pass up their farms in their search
for material for the home brew.

Philadelphia, Pennsylvania, *Inquirer*, August 26, 1920

'APE' THAT TERRORIZED
COUNTRYSIDE CAPTURED

HALF CLAD, UNKEMPT AND HAIRY, WILD MAN
PROWLED WOODS LIKE HUGE SIMIAN

Pittsburgh, Aug. 25.—The ape-man who has
terrorized the countryside between Greensburg and Homestead for two weeks was captured today in a heavily wooded thicket near
the Glassrun road, Baldwin township, and
put behind bars in the police station.

His body nearly nude, and the matted
hair on his face and head six inches long,
the man so closely resembles his Simian an-
cestor that the officers who came upon him
unawares were in doubt for several minutes
how to class him.

When captured, the man was sleeping beside a fire. On being awakened he sprang at
Constable Risenbarth and attempted to stran-
gle him. It took hard work to subdue him.

Apparently unable or unwilling to speak,
the captive sat moaning in his cell in the
police station, occasionally giving utterance
to deep guttural sounds.

County officials and officers of Mifflin township and Hays borough who have seen the man

declare that it would be hard at a distance, especially in a heavily wooded thicket, to distinguish the prisoner from a big hairy ape.

Pittsburgh, Pennsylvania, *Press,* August 26, 1920

TONY NOT GORILLA MAN, GIRLS ATTACKED SAY

Tony Ruzicka, aged 35, thought by some to have been the "gorilla" which has caused apprehension in Mifflin and Baldwin townships, last night was acquitted of a charge of vagrancy, at a hearing before Justice of the Peace Walter Terrill of Hays. Ruzicka agreed to leave the district.

An attempt was made to connect the man with an attack Monday on Miss Anna Shaffer, aged 21, of Baldwin township. Miss Shaffer and her younger sister, confronting Ruzicka, said he was not the man who accosted them.

Ruzicka told the authorities he had walked most of the way from New York, arriving in Baldwin township yesterday. He was arrested in a wood near Glass Run rd.

Pittsburgh, Pennsylvania, *Daily Post,* August 27, 1920

"GORILLA" OUT AGAIN

A "gorilla" hoax broke up a picnic and a ball game in Mifflin township yesterday, and a hunt for the simian ended when farmers told of seeing it changing its clothes in an automobile parked beside a road.

Business and professional men had made up two ball teams, the Tigers and Cubs, for a game in the township grounds.

Disguised as a gorilla, an overseas veteran perched in advance in a tree in right field. In the fourth inning, with the Cubs leading 3 to 2, Righfielder H. A. Stober sighted the gorilla while trying to field a ball, and promptly decided he had urgent business somewhere else.

While a hurried council of war was being held, the gorilla disappeared over a hill.

Lewisburg, Pennsylvania, *Journal,* October 29, 1920

APE-MAN'S REIGN OF TERROR ENDS

Pittsburgh, Pa.—The "ape-man" who has terrorized the countryside between Greensburg and Homestead for two weeks has been captured in a heavily wooded thicket in Baldwin township and lodged in the Hays police station. His body, nearly nude, a fearsome, grimy sight, and the matted hair on his face and head six inches long, the ape-man so closely resembled his simian ancestors that the officers who came on him unawares were in doubt for several minutes whether he was man or beast.

When captured the ape-man was sleeping beside a fire. On being awakened he sprang at Constable Risenbarth and attempted to sink his fangs in the officer's throat. He was subdued after a struggle lasting several minutes. . . .

[This is the Tony Ruzicka case, above, sensationalized.]

Lewistown, Pennsylvania, *Daily Sentinel,* December 14, 1920

SNYDER COUNTY BOY CLAIMS A HUGE GORILLA ATTACKED HIM

YOUNG BOLIG, ROUGHLY HANDLED BY SOME FEROCIOUS ANIMAL, IS POSITIVE

IT WAS A BIG APE

At 2 o'clock this afternoon Charles Bolig of near Meiser, Snyder county, came into the news rooms of The Sentinel, to verify the story that his son had been [attacked] by a huge ape, supposedly an escaped gorilla from a carnival company, that has been roaming about the woods near Meiser for at least several weeks.

Mr. Bolig in his graphic account of the affair said that his twin children, Samuel and Margaret, aged 15 years, first saw the ape three weeks ago when they heard a peculiar noise near the Bolig wood pile. Securing a searchlight they investigated and plainly saw the uncouth form of a giant ape. They looked at the animal in open mouth amazement and after staring at them on its hind legs for a few moments, the animal dropped upon its four legs and scurried away into the nearby woods.

The animal's cries were heard nightly for a week after that, but no sign of the brute was seen until a week later when young Sam Bolig saw him standing in a corn field on the Bolig farm. The youth had a 22 calibre rifle with him and raising the slight gun took careful aim at the beast's breast, pulled the trigger and fired. The animal fell to its feet, rolled over as if in agony and then managed to again scamper away. He was tracked by a trail of blood into the woods.

The third encounter occurred last Friday evening between 7 and 8 o'clock while Mr. Bolig was chopping wood. The Bolig twins in the house heard the peculiar throated noise made by the gorilla and Samuel armed himself with a 32 caliber revolver, went to investigate, followed by his sister. They saw the animal standing upright under an apple tree not more than ten feet from the house. The boy raised his arm to fire, but before he could pull the trigger the ape leaped upon him and smote him to the ground. In response to his

son's and daughter's terrified calls for help,
Mr. Bolig, armed with an axe, rushed to the
scene. The brute saw him coming and fled.

Mr. Bolig declares that fully 100 armed
men are today scouring the vicinity of his
home in the hope of meeting up with the
animal, which is generally believed to be the
gorilla that escaped from a carnival company
early last summer at Williamsport.

Color to the persistent rumors that a full
grown gorilla, or some other gigantic member of the monkey family is at large in Snyder county and has been roaming through
the woods there since last summer, when the
animal is alleged to have escaped from a carnival showing at Williamsport, has been provided coming in the form of a savage attack
upon a fifteen year old boy named Bolig, who
resides along the mountain a mile and a half
from Meiser, along the Sunbury line.

For several months reports have been
filtering into Snyder and Northumberland
county towns that a huge ape has been seen
in isolated woody sections, but these reports
could never be verified and were generally
discredited, but now the unfortunate lad's
story has set the whole community agog with
excitement and talk of armed searching parties being formed is rife.

Charles Bolig resides one and a half miles south of Meiser, between Middleburg and Kreamer, along the mountain. Mr. Bolig has a fifteen year old son, who with his father, were chopping wood at their home at the mountainside by night. They had a burning lantern by their side. The boy relates the following story of his encounter with an animal that he called a gorilla: "The gorilla standing upon its hind legs appeared to be seven feet high. After its attack upon me it ran away before my father had an opportunity to see it. When the gorilla sprang away it did not seem to be such a big animal."

The boy's father came to Kreamer and to Lewistown yesterday and told his friends the boy's story of the encounter with the animal. Harry Faux of Lewistown passing through Middleburg yesterday met Mr. Bolig who narrated the lad's experience to Mr. Faux.

This morning it was reported that the gorilla had appeared along the mountain sides of Lewistown Narrows where some travelers alleged they saw the animal last night.

Reports from Meiser today were that the Bolig boy was knocked unconscious by his assailant, the gorilla, and that the lad is confined to his bed, in a semi-conscious

condition with a broken arm and badly
bruised places on his body.

It is reported that a circus or carnival
train was wrecked near Williamsport last
summer, and that a gorilla escaped from a
car at that time, and that the animal was not
captured. It is believed that the ape roamed
over the mountains in the vicinity of Sunbury and Northumberland until it came to
the Bolig residence where it attacked the boy
several days ago.

Telephone wires to Kreamer and Meiser were not working well this morning and
The Sentinel reporters quickly resorted to
interviews with Lewistown persons who had
talked with persons to whom Mr. Bolig related the thrilling experience of his son, as
described above.

Mr. Bolig who was in Lewistown yesterday visited the Charles Gilbert family, South
Spruce street, and related the story of his
son's attack by the animal thought by the lad
to be a gorilla.

Mr. Bolig came to the railroad station
at Kreamer where he narrated the story of
the appearance of the gorilla and its assault
upon the boy, as told by the boy himself.

THE HISTORICAL BIGFOOT

Lewistown, Pennsylvania, *Daily Sentinel,* December 15, 1920

$500 DEAD OR $1,000 ALIVE FOR GORILLA SAYS BOLIG

FATHER OF BOY ATTACKED BY CREATURE DECLARES CARNIVAL COMPANY HAS OFFERED THAT AMOUNT OF REWARD

Charles Bolig of near Meiser, Snyder county, whose fourteen year old son Samuel was attacked by an animal said to be a gorilla, a few days ago, is a guest of his brother-in-law, Charles Gilbert, 216 South Spruce street, Lewistown. Mr. Bolig is in Lewistown, awaiting the return of John H. Miller from Philadelphia. The two men intend to make a trip to Mr. Miller's coal mines in Huntingdon county.

Mr. Bolig is besieged by persons who come to him, desiring to secure information about the gorilla or ape that attacked his son, Samuel, a few nights ago, at the Bolig residence, along the mountain, one and a half miles south of Meiser.

Mr. Bolig today entertained many Lewistown persons as he related the thrilling story of the gorilla's three appearances at the Bolig home. The father declares that he himself has not been able to get a view of the mysterious animal that is terrorizing Snyder county.

Today Mr. Bolig reiterated his description of the three visits of the gorilla to his home, saying that the beast made its first appearance three weeks ago. A week later it came back and his son shot at it with his 22 calibre rifle, the ball hitting the animal upon its breast, causing it to reel and bleed from the wound. Upon its third appearance the boy Samuel attempted to shoot it with his revolver. He snapped the trigger three times, each time the weapon refusing to discharge its load, with the gorilla only ten feet away from the lad.

The gorilla becoming enraged by the boy's actions assaulted the lad throwing him to the ground and tearing most of his clothing from his body and almost strangling him to death. For two days the boy was confined to his bed. He is now able to be up and around. Claw marks and skin abrasions made by the gorilla, cover the boy's form from face to feet.

Samuel described the animal as having a color between black and brown, a human-like face and large lips. It walked upon its two hind legs and was at least, says the boy, seven feet high. When it ran away it moved upon its four legs.

Mr. Bolig discovered blood on the ground, after his son had shot and wounded the gorilla on its second visit to the Bolig residence. The trail of blood was lost in the leaves of trees.

Articles of food disappeared from the cellar of the Bolig home and it is believed that the gorilla in search of something to eat has been making nocturnal visits to the cellar. Apples partly eaten were found just outside the apple bin where a night prowler evidently has been making his regular visits.

None of the members of the Bolig family venture outside of their home without being armed. More than a hundred people visited the Bolig residence last Sunday, attracted there by a desire to get a description of the strange animal and to discover some clue that will lead to its capture.

Mr. Bolig stated yesterday that rewards have been offered for the capture of the gorilla, $500 if captured dead and $1,000 if caught alive. He claims these rewards have been offered by the carnival company from whom the animal is said to have escaped.

Skilled hunters are confident that the gorilla will be captured when the first snow fall comes and the animal will leave its tracks in the snow. There are extensive caves and mines in close proximity to the Bolig home and it is believed that the gorilla has established his habitat in one of the underground passage ways.

Harrisburg, Pennsylvania, *Patriot*, December 15, 1920

MIFFLIN COUNTY ON HUNT FOR 'MYSTERY ANIMAL' IN WOODS

The appearance of a strange animal in the vicinity of Lewistown, Mifflin County, which is said closely to resemble an ape, and which has attacked and injured one boy, has aroused that entire community.

The animal has been seen on several occasions, but usually at night and not distinctly enough for anyone to give a complete description.

Yesterday at least a hundred men, heavily armed, were scouring the countryside in search of the beast.

The supposed ape was seen for the first time about three weeks ago by Samuel Bolig, 15-year-old son of Charles Bolig, at his home in Meiserville, just over the Snyder County line.

On this occasion the boy had gone to a woodpile close to his home at night and with the aid of a pocket searchlight was gathering up kindling wood.

Boy Shoots at It

The beast appeared then in the rays of the light. The boy, frightened, grabbed up his little sister who had accompanied him and fled into his home. A further search by members of the family revealed nothing, and little credence was given the story that he told.

A few days afterward the boy came upon the animal again in the daytime. This time, the story goes, he was armed with a 32-caliber rifle. He shot at it as it was running through a cornfield. The shot took effect and he was able to trail the beast for some distance by the trail of blood until it reached a wooded district where the trail was lost.

Nothing further was seen of the animal until last Sunday night when it appeared again at the Bolig home. The Bolig boy and his father were gathering kindling on the same woodpile when the beast came into the rays of the searchlight.

Father Also See It

As the father held the animal at bay the boy ran to his home and secured a revolver. He returned and walked up to the beast to get a good shot When it leaped upon him. The gun was knocked from his hand and he was thrown to the ground, breaking his arm. The father of the boy swung at the animal with an axe but missed it. It then disappeared.

This story was verified yesterday in Lewistown by the father of the boy, Charles Bolig.

When these reports were confirmed yesterday afternoon by Bolig, excitement gripped the whole community. Outside of the towns parents refused to allow their children to go far from their homes. Gunning parties have been sent out to kill the beast.

It was reported yesterday that it was seen in the mountains of the Lewistown narrows.

Various stores are in circulation as to just what kind of an animal has been creating the disturbance. The boy declares that it resembles a giant monkey.

Others think that it is a gorilla, one that is said to have escaped from a circus that was showing at Williamsport last Summer. Some think that it is a bear.

Harrisburg, Pennsylvania, *Patriot,* December 17, 1920

BELIEVE 'ANIMAL'
HIDES IN A CAVE

The "mystery animal" which on three occasions appeared at the home of Charles Bolig, of near Meiser, Snyder County, once attacking and injuring a 14-year-old boy, is believed to be living in a cave near the Bolig home.

This theory was advanced yesterday by Mr. Bolig who was visiting Lewistown relatives. During his stay in Lewistown Mr. Bolig received scores of callers who wanted to hear his thrilling story of the strange animal that made nightly visits to his home.

Although Mr. Bolig said that he himself had not been able to get a distinct view of the animal that is terrorizing Snyder and Mifflin Counties, he said that his son Samuel, who has seen it on three occasions and was attached by it describes it as being shaped like an ape or gorilla. In color it is between a black and brown, has a human-like face with very large lips.

When standing on its hind legs the boy says that it is at least seven feet tall. When running it travels on all fours.

Wait for Tracking Snow

Although hunting parties have scoured the section where the animal was seen they have found no trace of it. Some of the skilled hunters are anxiously awaiting the first "tracking" snow, when they say they will be able to run the animal and kill it

Mr. Bolig said yesterday that he believed that the animal had made visits to his home, although it was seen only three times. The visits were made at night, he thinks, when it prowled around his home, eating anything that was left outside of the house and entering the cellar in search of something to eat.

Almost nightly articles of food have disappeared from the premises, and apples are found in the morning lying about the ground partly eaten, Mr. Bolig said.

Family Is Armed

No members of the Bolig family, he said, leave their home unless they are armed, either at night or in the daytime, as on one occasion the animal visited the place in the middle of the day. On this occasion it was shot and wounded by the son and was traced for some distance by spots of blood that were left on the ground.

One day this week more than a hundred persons visited the Bolig home to hear the story of the visits of the strange animal. Some of them wore seeking clues that might lead to the capture of the animal.

The beast first made its appearance at the Bolig home about three weeks ago. At that time it came at night and was discovered by the son when it jumped into the rays of his searchlight as he was out gathering wood. Another time it appeared in the daytime and was wounded by a shot.

The last visit, was made a few nights ago. This time the father and son saw it indistinctly in the light of a searchlight. The son was standing within ten feet of it with a 32-caliber revolver and tried to shoot. As he did the weapon failed to fire and while he snapped it three times the animal sprang upon him, threw him to the ground and inflicted a number of scratches and bruises. The boy was confined to his bed for several days.

Hear of Reward Offered

Near to the Bolig home, which is located along a mountain, just across the Snyder County line, there are a number of caves. It is thought that the animal is making its home in one of these underground passageways and that it ventures forth only at night in search of food.

There have been many theories advanced by residents of the section as to the identity of the animal. Members of the Bolig family are convinced that it is some kind of an ape or gorilla that has escaped from some circus or carnival company.

It is said that a gorilla escaped last Summer from a circus that was showing at Williamsport, and some believe that this is the animal. It is said also that that company has offered a reward of $500 for the capture of the animal dead, and $1000 if it is returned to them alive. Mr. Bolig stated yesterday that he has heard of these rewards being offered.

Lewistown, Pennsylvania, *Sentinel*, December 17, 1920

GORILLA SOME TRAVELER, APE SEEN IN BLAIR COUNTY, PEOPLE SCARED

The following is taken from today's issue of the Altoona Times-Tribune:

A good many Blair county people when reading of the escapades of the wild ape in Snyder county, thought perhaps the brand of the beverage consumed may have had something to do with the inception of the story, but truth is stranger than fiction. Blair county has a story which is a top notcher, compared with the Snyder county story, while similar in many respects.

When Samuel Brannen, a Canoe creek resident came home from work on Tuesday he observed that his 12 year old son, Chalmer, had neglected to get in kindling for the starting of the morning fire in the kitchen range. The youth lighted a lantern and went out to the wood pile to gather some chips. There is a high wire fence between the wood pile and the road.

Looking up from his work, young Brannen was startled at seeing a brownish form, resembling as nearly as he could describe when he recovered from his fright, an ape. The thing ran toward him, but coming in contact with the wire fence, was knocked backward. The youth ran into the house and summoned his father and mother.

When they came out, seeing what confronted them, Mr. Brannen went into the house for the gun. When he returned the thing was gone. A peculiar coincidence in connection with this is that the same night something entered the smoke house on the George Mattern farm, nearby, and took two pieces of meat.

There was no lock on the door of the smoke house, but a button held the door shut. Whatever or whoever entered, did not turn the button, but pulled it off. One piece of meat partly eaten, was subsequently found, no trace has been found of the other.

The same night, Mike Sutlige, an Austrian, who lives nearby, was going to the post office. Mike met the same thing on the road. He was scared and ran like a deer. He came to the home of a neighbor. He did not stop to knock, or even turn the door knob. He just burst into the house. His description of the thing was so badly mixed between Austrian, English and profane language, that it is unprintable, even if accessible.

The latest report from the scene of the curious nocturnal visitor is that a posse is being recruited to make a hunt of the neighborhood for it.

Altoona, Pennsylvania, *Tribune,* December 20, 1920

APE STILL AT LARGE

The ape, gorilla, or whatever sort of animal or freak it may be, which was seen at Canoe

Creek last week by Chalmer Brannen and Mike Sutlige, is still at large, so far as the public in general knows, for despite the fact that a still hunt has been made throughout the community, not a single trace of it has been found.

Lewistown, Pennsylvania, *Sentinel,* December 20, 1920

SAY BEAST LEAPED AT CAR

Middleburg, Pa, Dec. 20—While Mr. and Mrs. Bruce P. Yeager were driving along a dark road near here early Saturday, a huge animal that looked to be seven feet high and to have arms and legs like telephone poles jumped at their car, missed it and fell sprawling on the road. Yeager fired two shots at it but the animal made off into the woods and has not been seen since.

Yeager thinks it was the same animal that attacked a boy near Meiser last week, although the spot where it attacked the Yeagers is four miles from where the boy lives. It is believed the animal is an ape that escaped from a carnival company at Sunbury last summer.

Altoona, PA, *Tribune,* December 21, 1920

MORE EVIDENCE SHOWS SUPPOSED GIANT SIMIAN STILL ACTIVE IN REGION

Manning Farm Residents Find
Imprint on Coop Floor
Gobbled Up Hens

Hollidaysburg, Dec. 20.—The escaped gorilla that has been prowling about Hollidaysburg and vicinity for the past several days, has a great fondness for chicken, as is evidenced by the fact that it has invaded several coops at night and feasted to its heart's content on the tender juicy meat. The big animal visited the Manning farm at the west end of Chimney Rocks, on Sunday night and broke into the chicken coop, where it enjoyed a royal feast on fifteen fine hens, afterwards taking a siesta on a pile of straw. In the morning when a member of the family visited the coop, the place was found to be littered with feathers and blood, and on the straw was a depression where the ape man had slept.

At Roselawn, the beast's footprints were seen the latter part of last week, in the soft mud near the Brush Run and it was at first supposed to be a bear but was later seen by several persons, who declare it was of the shape of a huge ape. It broke into the chicken coop of George Brenner and Mike Wiseman, and feasted on a number of choice fowls. . . .

Eldorado Young Men See Gorilla
Pass Great Ape in Road near Cross Keys

Hearing a slight noise on the road ahead, as though something or someone was coming through the bushes into the road, Lester Bucher and Charles Fink of Eldorado, who were coming down the long hill from Duncansville to Cross Keys at 10 o'clock last night in Fink's automobile, sounded the horn and gazed to the side of the road as they passed the object, only to be horrified as the spotlight crossed the thing to find it a brown colored animal, between six and seven feet tall and standing erect beside the road facing them.

Almost senseless with fear, Fink shoved the gears into high and the car rapidly left the supposed jungle denizen behind. As the automobile got a few feet beyond the thing it emitted a horrid yell, which the young men describe as "loud and coarse." Neither had a gun and for this reason no further attempt at investigation was made. Talking of the incident later, young Bucher stated that they both got a good luck at the thing as the light played on it and they have no doubt but that it was a gorilla or an animal closely resembling it.

NARROWS TOWER MAN WITH
MEGAPHONE GETS ANSWER

Lewistown, Dec. 20.—Canoe Creek, Blair county, may have imported an alien gorilla or ape-man for its own convenience, but it can't take any of the lustre from Snyder and Mifflin counties which have a prior claim by right of original discovery. All of Saturday night the wild cries of the ape-man that attacked little Samm Bolig near his home along the mountains near Meiser one week ago and beat him into insensibility echoed from the knob that forms the eastern bank of Macedonia Hollow on the state road side of the Lewistown Narrows. A score or more of railroad men who work in the Denholm yards of the Pennsylvania railroad listened to the cries for hours and vowed that nothing akin to it had ever been heard in the mountains in that section.

They describe the cry as being a cross between that of a child in distress, magnified a thousand fold and that of Dante's description of the wail of a lost soul. Its volume is something wonderful, the cries being echoed for miles across the mountains.

The cries at first were heard just across the Juniata river from MI signal tower and receded as if the animal was traveling across the knob in the direction of Middlesburg. When on the eve of disappearing, M. C. Hack, a signalman, obtained a megaphone and gave the far-famed "call of the wilds" as known to the mountain folk in the valley, the animal immediately answered by a shrill scream. Hack continued to call and the animal to answer until it reached a point almost at the foot of the mountain. The passion in the cries made old-timers, men who have braved the dangers of half a century on the rail, quake in their boots.

The "missing link" hovered about the water's edge for some time, when its cries again showed that it was climbing the knob. The course of the animal could be followed by its wails until they died almost to a whisper in the great distance when one old veteran heaved a sigh and remarked, "It's Satan, unchained and abroad. No human animal ever made that noise, leastwise I have never heard it and I have been here nigh onto eighty years." . . .

Waynesboro, Pennsylvania, *Record-Herald,* December 21, 1920

MOUNTAIN FOLK IN PANIC
OVER 'MISSING LINK'

. . . Although many have accepted the theory that it is an escaped gorilla that broke away from a carnival company at Williamsport last summer, many others doubt this. Residents of the terrorized section have nicknamed the animal the "missing link."

Regardless of what it is few residents of the rural districts will leave their homes unless they are heavily armed. . . .

Reports from Canoe Creek, Blair county, say that a similar animal has been seen there during the past week. Samuel Brennan, of that place, is reported to have seen a strange animal resembling an ape near his home, but it disappeared when he went for his shotgun. It had previously scared his son.

The same night, Mike Sutlige, an Austrian, who lives nearby, met the creature on a dark road and raced to the home of a neighbor, not stopping to open the door, but just burst into the house. Two pieces of meat were taken from the smokehouse on George Mattern's farm in that vicinity. One piece partially eaten, was found not far away.

Lewisburg, Pennsylvania, *Journal,* December 24, 1920

GORILLA STILL IN SNYDER COUNTY

New stories concerning the mysterious animal that looks like a gorilla and makes a noise like a horse, which has been seen in the lower end of Snyder County during the past month, are in circulation every hour of the day here with the tales of an alleged attack upon an autoist south of Selinsgrove Friday night as today's best tale.

The gorilla, or whatever the animal terror may turn out to be leaped upon an autoist traveling toward Selinsgrove. So the story goes, and he would no doubt have been badly done up, but for resistance with a small pen-knife, which was the only weapon on hand.

When the fight was at its height, according to the story, another autoist came along and joined in the fray, the two automobile drivers succeeding in beating off the animal's attack.

Exhaustive investigations failed to reveal the names of the autoists or other particulars of the incident.

Altoona, Pennsylvania, *Tribune,* December 27, 1920

DRY GAP MAN IS CERTAIN IT'S APE

"The gorilla is not dead," was the statement of a Dry Gap resident who drove to Hollidaysburg yesterday morning for medicine for his sick child—a trip that had been suddenly postponed Christmas night when the same individual started down the lonely mountain road, toward Kladder station, past the Gaysport borough water works.

According to this man, giving his name as Samuel Nedrow, one of his children became ill Saturday afternoon and he decided to come to Kladder, board the 5 o'clock train for Hollidaysburg, get the medicine and return that far on the outgoing train at 7, walking the distance between his humble mountain home and the station.

He declared that as he neared the Gaysport water works, he heard a barking noise that made his blood run cold. He had never heard anything like it. It was just twilight, and he stopped for an instant to get his bearings. Then again he heard the barking noise. Satisfied the sound was coming from the direction of the reservoir, he started back up the mountain trail.

The racket caused by his running evidently intensified the animal that possessed the barking voice, for he then declared that it turned into a terrific roar. Looking back, Nedrow saw the animal scramble through the bushes, onto the road. He declares he plainly saw a hairy face, practically bare breast, immensely long arms, broad shoulders, but with hind legs very short.

He made no further attempt at investigation. He was unarmed. He had not heard of a gorilla being reported at large, until he came to town and related his experiences, whereupon he declared he must certainly have seen it. He declares it could not have been a man, and because it stalked on its hind legs, could not have been a bear or any other animal, wild or tame, likely to be found in this climate.

He is of the opinion that it was drinking from the reservoir when it heard him and barked and fumed because disturbed. Nedrow carried a high powered rifle yesterday and if the gorilla should happen on his path, he gives assurance he will make this climate hot enough for him, although it is alleged a gorilla could not live in this climate.

Mount Carmel, Pennsylvania, *Item*, December 30, 1920

END OF THE SNYDER CO GORILLA

Neighbors of Frank Bolig, of near Meiser, Snyder County, whose son, Samuel, a boy of about 14 years, was the first person to see the "gorilla," mere mention of which has sent the goose flesh creeping up the backs of residents of four or five counties for the past several weeks, are convinced today that the supposed animal terror has existed only in the mind of the Bolig boy himself.

Although some persons, influenced by stories of reputable persons that the tracks of a strange animal had been seen in the vicinity of Middleburg, believed the story of the Bolig boy that he was attacked by the "gorilla" near his father's home, the skeptics have been in the majority and several of these have made several tests with the boy which convinced them that he is either not addicted to the truth or else possesses an overworked imagination.

The boy was taken out near his father's home a few nights ago by Francis Kratzer and a brother, who live nearby, and was told to walk ahead, yelling if he saw any trace of the animal which he claimed attacked him. The lad started out ahead of his companions and after a while screamed with terror, telling his companions when they caught up to him that he had seen the "gorilla" a short distance away. A thorough search failed to reveal any trace of the animal. The same test was repeated a few nights later and the boy again shrieked out in terror without his friends being able to find anything.

Young Bolig, at the time he told the thrilling story of how he was seized by a "long, hairy animal, seven feet high, that looked like a gorilla," had only a badly lacerated knee and a torn trouser leg. He declared that the animal which attacked him seized only his one leg.

Neighbors, fully convinced that the "gorilla" is a myth pure and simple, believe that Sammie tore his trousers and lacerated his leg on a barbed wire fence and told the "gorilla" story to save himself from the wrath of his father.

At any rate, the "gorilla" is dead. Unless some industrious and not altogether truthful scribe succeeds in injecting life into his badly shattered remains.

Lock Haven, Pennsylvania, *Express,* January 12, 1921

GORILLA STORY A MYTH.

A report has been in circulation for a day or two that a number of calves and lambs on the T. B. Bridgens farm above Flemington, and on other farms in that section, had been killed and carried away by a wild animal supposed to be a gorilla, according to those who it is said, caught a glimpse of the animal. When asked about the rumors today, Mr. Bridgens and his tenant farmer declare there is absolutely no truth in the report.

Clearfield, Pennsylvania, *Progress,* January 14, 1921

Several weeks ago a Snyder county newspaper correspondent, who needed the money, sent a special to the Philadelphia newspapers detailing the hair-raising experiences of several Snyder county farmers with a gorilla or ape-man which had escaped from a New York city zoo and made his way through the mountains to that vicinity. That story

furnished a productive lead to several other
fellows in different sections of the state who
"lie about their neighbors for a living," and
soon the gorilla was reported from these several different sections of the state. He appeared for four or five dollars worth around
Patton and northern Cambria county with
the result that veracious natives are now
running into him everywhere.

It remained for a West Side citizen to
land the ape-man close to home. This man
approached Mayor Chase this morning and
asked that vigilant guardian of the welfare
and morals of the community what provision
he had made to protect our citizens from a
possible visit from the gorilla. The mayor
said "Goshang it, I hain't never heard of
him." Then the West Sider broke the news
of the depredations of the hairy monster.
He cited the numerous instances of the
ape-man's appearance as given in the daily
papers from time to time and then knocked
the mayor stiff with the story that the huge
gorilla had appeared last night at Wallaceton, that he had killed and half eaten a farmer's calf in a barn yard handy to the town,
that help had been asked of the Wallaceton
people and a posse raised by the blowing of
the backyard whistle. Fifty men started out

to round up the beast but that Jim Barron, superintendent at the brick works, had run into him and the beast picked up a club and ran Jim half a mile before he succeeded in swatting him with the club. Two blows of the club was said to have stretched Jim on the ground and when assistance arrived the animal beat it through the red brush in the direction of Morrisdale.

The mayor's informant said Jim was being brought to the Clearfield Hospital on the 11:15 Piney train, but he didn't come, and therefore we are satisfied some fellow filled our West Side friend with sawdust; that the gorilla did not appear and that it is the same ape-man that has not appeared anywhere else of the many places mentioned in the state papers the past few weeks.

Lancaster, Pennsylvania, *Intelligencer Journal,* January 15, 1921

GORILLA AT LARGE TERRORIZING FOLK OF TWO TOWNSHIPS

A man-killing gorilla is at large, it is said, somewhere in Upper Leacock or West Earl townships. People of the district today are terror-stricken, and for two days have been afraid to leave their homes at night. It is claimed that the beast was seen by a number of people. Although those who saw it, are unable to give a correct description, they agree that it is "an ape that is bigger than a man."

Yesterday the animal was seen on the Thomas Singer farm near Bareville and Farmersville, where he is said to have been hidden in a straw stack. The farmer states that he was securing straw to bed his horses shortly before dark when the huge "ape" jumped from the top of the stack and disappeared in the shadows.

Another man declares that he saw a dark object in his orchard and when he went to investigate, it disappeared in a tree. He says he thought it was a bear, but when he got to the tree there was no sign of the beast. School children also have reported seeing a strange animal, near Bareville, in the evenings.

Apparently, the gorilla is sticking near barns, because of the cold weather. Although thus far there have been no depredations, the ferocity of the beast is so well known that the people of the district are living in dread and the men folks who go out of evenings are carrying arms.

It is generally presumed that the animal escaped from some circus which is quartered in the east. The Welsh Shows have their winter quarters at Oxford and the Walter Main shows are located at Havre de Grace.

Village Aroused by Beast

The story of a strange beast being seen was reported yesterday afternoon to William Hoshower, manager of the Bareville Hardware Company, by a number of people, and it was the talk of the village last evening. No subsequent reports of its appearance was made this morning, despite the fact that everybody was on the alert.

Investigation today showed that a gorilla of about the size of the beast seen in the eastern end did escape from the Robinson circus at Sunbury, during the latter part of the summer and the killing of calves and dogs in Northumberland county were attributed to it.

Middletown, Delaware, *Transcript*, January 15, 1921

GORILLA SHIFTS RANGE.

Waynesboro, Pa.—South Penn trainsmen report that the gorilla ape, baboon, or whatnot, that has been terrorizing the inhabitants near Altoona and other parts of the State, has migrated from the Allegheny Mountains and is now roving the Big Cove Range. Rumor says that a cow was killed a few nights ago not far from Richmond Furnace.

Lancaster, Pennsylvania, *News-Journal*, January 18, 1921

BAREVILLE 'GORILLA' BORN OF NEGRO'S FOOT AND CIDER

FAR FLUNG HOAX ORIGINATED IN MARYLAND TO STOP THEFTS OF TREES—BAREFOOT TRACKS, HOME BREW AND IMAGINATION FINISH WORK

Cumberland, Md., Jan. 17—The origin of the "gorilla" story belongs to this railroad valley town.

After going the rounds of many villages and towns in Maryland and Pennsylvania towns, the story now crops anew in Bareville, Lancaster county, one hundred and fifty miles from its source. The story of the man-eating, hairy monster of African jungles, who frightens children and causes farmers to carry arms is a myth born of a jug of hard cider and a negro's footprints.

Dame rumor has had the "gorilla" appear in woods, farmlands, before school windows and chasing cows from barns; has caused strong men to take a drink and weak men to carry shotguns. Newspapers in all sections of Maryland have carried the story of the "gorilla" and his escapades adding to the effect by publishing interviews with those who have seen the animal in action.

When the story reached Lancaster county the perpetrators of the hoax believed the truth should be known.

According to the information given out by a group of Alleghany county, Maryland, farmers, in whose locality an enormous amount of fir and cedar trees abound, the story started from an attempt to prevent peddlers of Christmas trees from carrying off too many of the trees.

Many means had been taken, it is said, until a group of farmers hired a big negro of Cumberland to walk barefoot about several trees. His footprints resembled those of a gorilla or huge bear.

When tree choppers arrived on the scene, late at night, they were greeted by these enormous footprints. It caused them to raise the cry of bear or gorilla. The farmers, hiding in trees, began to moan and the men took to the wagons awaiting in the bypaths.

It is presumed when the men reached their various destinations a couple of swigs of home-brew was necessary, and a flight of imagination soon followed.

They can't explain, however, how the animal could have been "seen" in Lancaster county, too.

People who live around Bareville are still alarmed over the report of the "gorilla" being at large in the district. While some of the people of the district show a tendency to scoff at the story and say they think it was manufactured by children, others give it credence. A few men are carrying arms while going about their work or at night.

This morning one man told that a West Earl farmer had seen a beast the size of a gorilla running on "all fours" at his barnyard.

The state police have men on duty in the vicinity but none of them have seen the strange "beast."

Lancaster, Pennsylvania, *New Era,* January 18, 1921

ESCAPED APE SCARES RESIDENTS IN VICINITY OF FARMERSVILLE

Several persons in Upper Leacock and West Earl townships have reported seeing an animal believed to be an ape running through the fields. The strange animal was seen on Thursday afternoon by children returning from the Good school near Bareville. On Friday morning Augustus Miller reported that he saw the animal running across the farm of Charles Wise near Farmersville. The school children say that it was as tall as a fence post. . . .

Some weeks ago a report was circulated in Dauphin county that a man-size animal was seen in several sections. Railroaders report seeing such a beast. It became frightened at the approach of the men and sought shelter in the woods. Its calls could be plainly heard during the night. It may be possible that the animal has found its way to this section.

Gettysburg, Pennsylvania, *Times,* January 20, 1921

THOUGHT THEY SAW GORILLA

One of the wildest of the many wild rumors that circulate throughout Adams county reached Gettysburg today. According to this unfounded report a huge gorilla was spied sitting on a rock near Mount Rock Wednesday afternoon. When the monstrous animal saw that it was discovered by some Mount Rock citizens it arose, stretched itself, and disappeared into a nearby wood, according to the report.

When told this story one Gettysburg citizen said, "It is evident that some of my Mount Rock friends are seeing more peculiar visions now than they did before the advent of the Eighteenth Amendment."

Lancaster, Pennsylvania, *News-Journal,* January 25, 1921

GORILLA SCARE INVADES ADAMS COUNTY; MAYBE IT'S KANGAROO

Disappearing for the time being from the vicinity of Bareville and Farmersville the "gorilla" which kept farmers on the alert in that section for several days has made its appearance in Adams county, according to reports. And he is every bit as big and elusive.

When reports of his appearance here went the rounds some farmers got out their best guns and kept a wary eye on strange shadows while others viewed the rumor as having been brewed with the rest of the homemade "Hootch." Not so in Adams county, however.

First reports of his arrival there came from Mt. Rock in the northern end of the county. Idaville residents and farmers gave chase to the dangerous creature. Last reports have the gorilla being chased over the line into Cumberland county. The report says that it was reported by some as a huge gorilla and by others as a kangaroo. It is said that this may depend upon the percentage of alcohol in the brew.

Just before the animal escaped into another county fifty men gave chase when it was seen near York Springs but failed in an attempt to capture or shoot it. During its stay in Adams county there were few places in which it has not been seen.

Gettysburg, Pennsylvania, *Times*, January 27, 1921

SEE "GORILLA" AGAIN

The "gorilla," visions of which have been reported in this county, and which has

HONORABLE MENTION

DRAWN BY LIDA MUSSELMAN, 16, BAREVILLE, R. F. D. NO. 1.
This drawing was submitted during the excitement of the "gorilla" scare and the young artist has aptly caught the idea to incorporate it in her drawing.

Gorilla rumors sparked local imaginations.

(Lancaster, PA, INTELLIGENCER, January 25, 1921)

furnished new stories from various sections of the state, has been seen in Waynesboro, it is said.

Harry Shindledecker, an employe of the trolley company in Waynesboro, was on his way to work Wednesday morning and while passing the baseball grounds saw something he took to be the animal. He arrived at the car barn in an excited condition. He said the animal was about the height of a man.

Gettysburg, Pennsylvania, *Times,* January 28, 1921

CHASE GORILLA TO MOUNTAINS

"Gorilla" warfare which was started last week in the vicinity of Idaville when Adams county residents, well armed, pursued what is believed to be an animal that escaped from a circus car when it was wrecked, not long ago, was renewed by citizens of Rouzerville Wednesday night when an armed posse scoured the Blue Ridge slopes in the hope of getting a shot at the beast.

The animal was discovered in an alley just as dusk was falling on the village. The word was quickly spread and the members of the Rouzerville deer camp and every one else that had a rifle soon turned out for the hunt. After the mobilization of marksmen was completed, the attackers in battle formation started up the mountain.

Gorilla Chased Out

They had barely gotten underway when the animal was chased out. Although a number of shots were fired the chimpanzee kept on bounding toward the thicker brush of the slope. It was then that an elaborate campaign was decided on and a messenger was sent for reinforcements. The firing in the mountain was heard in the village and the town was soon in an uproar. It was decided to form a great circle around the foothill where the animal was last seen. Deployed in this fashion the grizzled hunters and young marksmen moved into the woodland.

Dog Pays Penalty

They scoured the mountain slope half way to Pen Mar but found no trace of the gorilla. A black dog running through the underbrush paid the death penalty when an excited hunter mistook it for the ape. When the hunters returned from the mountains, reports say, the town was in a turmoil—the animal had been seen there while the hunt was on. Young women who happened to be on the streets when the "panic" started were afraid to go home and escorts had to be provided.

Since the Rouzerville affair, the gorilla was seen at Monterey by two young men who were on their way home from a party. As they neared the Monterey golf links, they saw what they thought was a man approaching on all fours. When they called the animal rose on its hind legs and came toward them making gurgling sounds. The young men did not investigate any further.

Gettysburg, Pennsylvania, *Times*, February 1, 1921

SAW GORILLA IN DAYLIGHT

ANIMAL HAS HAUNT IN MOUNTAIN, ACCORDING TO REPORTS

The big gorilla, which has been wandering in the mountains of southern Pennsylvania for some weeks, has turned up again near Pen Mar, according to reports from that section.

The big ape was seen by John Simmons, who resides between Pen Mar and Rouzerville, Saturday afternoon, while the light of the sun was so bright it could leave no doubt upon the mind or vision. Simmons was going through a field near his home, when he saw a strange, unlikely object, which be at once connected with the "gorilla," from descriptions he had read in the newspapers.

At the time he saw the strange animal, Simmons was not armed and he was not in the mood to enter combat with the gorilla.

Harrisburg, Pennsylvania, *Evening News*, March 21, 1921

COON CAUGHT IN TRAP
SOLVES GORILLA MYSTERY

Milroy, March 21.—The last remnants of the gorilla story that was far better than an organized curfew in keeping those of tender years at their home nights in the country districts disappeared yesterday when "Bill" Bargo found a raccoon in a corn field along the foot of the Seven Mountains toting a bear trap supposed to have been stolen from Will John Henry by the gorilla more than two months ago. The coon was in a pitiful condition, nothing but skin and bone from the irritating wound and the effort of continually dragging the big trap, but it cleared up the mysterious disappearance of the trap and in consideration of this fact, and in fact that neither its pelt or flesh was good, the animal was given its liberty and gobbled off into the wild.

Gettysburg, Pennsylvania, *Star and Sentinel,* August 13, 1921

TOWN RESIDENTS SEE "GORILLA"

It's in again.

After having passed out of the limelight several months ago, the well known "gorilla" is back. It was in Gettysburg several nights ago, according to information from well informed circles.

It was not only seen but shot at.

Whether or not it was wounded is not known, but it departed hurriedly from lower York street in the direction of Biglerville.

Not long ago a woman residing on York Street saw a strange object about four feet high moving along the fence in rear of her house, it is said, and being alone, she rushed to the place next door seeking help. The man of the house secured a shot gun. He too saw the beast. He fired. The gorilla dropped to the ground.

Thinking he had bagged his game the gunner went toward the fallen animal. When only a few feet away the beast jumped to its hind legs and chased the man into the house, residents of that part of town declare. Those who ventured to look out say the animal disappeared in the direction of Biglerville. In fact, they declare an examination of the ground in a field nearby revealed foot prints of a strange beast.

A number of York street residents have oiled shot guns long obscured and a second visit by the beast to that part of town would probably result fatally for it. Others believe the animal by this time has returned to the fastnesses of the mountains.

Gettysburg, Pennsylvania, *Star and Sentinel,* August 20, 1921

GORILLA SPIED ALONG HIGHWAY

ELUSIVE ANIMAL SEEN SQUATTING
NEAR FORT LOUDEN IN THE MOONLIGHT.

Fleeter of foot than Paddock the great California sprinter, more strongly built for endurance than Jack Dempsey, the heavy-weight champion, and far more elusive than a bootlegger to would be captors is the one and only Gorilla.

Miles are nothing in the life of this animal whose fame has spread throughout southern Pennsylvania and northern Maryland. One night he is seen cavorting over the hill-sides between York Springs and Gardners in northern Adams county. The next night he looms up in Biglerville, then Gettysburg and ere a week flits by he is seen in the hills of Franklin county or Maryland. What an asset to a football coach planning for a success-ful season would be this never weary animal who flits from mountain top to mountain.

Friday night he was seen again.

Just a short time ago a York street res-ident in Gettysburg fired a load of shot at the rapidly disappearing figure of this noted beast. Since leaving here in the direction of Biglerville the gorilla evidently has made a semi-circular jaunt for he was seen Friday night near Fort Louden.

While coming home from Pittsburgh where he attended a meeting of Lincoln Highway officials, Howard C. Mitinger, of Gettysburg, saw the gorilla sitting on a stump along the highway a short distance west of Fort Louden.

"He was plainly discernible in the moonlight," said the secretary.

To corroborate his statements, Mr. Mitinger has his sister-in-law Mrs. George Ramsey, of Huntington; her daughter, Miss Jean Ramsey; and Robert Mathias, steward of the Hoffman hotel, who were with him in the car at the time.

Gettysburg, Pennsylvania, *Star and Sentinel,* August 27, 1921

WHO LEFT THE DOOR OPEN?

ONLY ORIGINAL GORILLA
SEEN IN COUNTY AGAIN.

The only original Adams county gorilla which occasionally flits across the mountains into Franklin county is in the vicinity of Fairfield if reports from that section are to be relied on.

Sunday evening while driving along the Fairfield road, Ray Weikert saw the animal plainly as it crossed the road not many feet in front of his horse, according to reports from that region. Not only did the young man see the beast, but the horse as well, and it was with difficulty it was kept from running away. The animal crossed the road leisurely, walking on its hind legs, climbed the fence and disappeared in the underbrush. It was described as being about five feet tall.

Lancaster, Pennsylvania, *News Journal,* July 5, 1926

TOWN HAS GORILLA SCARE

Summerhill, Pa., July 4.—A gorilla, about five feet tall, reported recently near here, has caused considerable alarm in this community. A dog on the farm chased the gorilla, but was beaten off. A farm laborer was attracted by the barks of the dog and saw the gorilla running into the woods.

Indiana, Pennsylvania, *Evening Gazette,* August 19, 1926

TIGER SCARES IN NEW JERSEY
"APE" TERRORIZES IN HOMER CITY

Homer City, Aug. 19.—A real ape at large in the hills above Lucerne. A hunt by a half dozen citizens of town. The ape is still at large.

Some few days ago some children picking berries above Lucerne were frightened by what they claimed was a "big ape." They told their stories and on Tuesday a couple of curious men went up to where they had been scared and searching around the saw a real, live ape and it was a pretty big one. They came back and told their story and yesterday morning a half dozen men, armed with shot guns left here in a truck for the scene. They searched in vain for the animal, but found plenty of tracks to show that it had been there and where it had been climbing on small trees.

If we are informed right, an ape escaped from a circus in Johnstown some time ago, and this is thought to be the animal. Until it is definitely located and captured there will be some uneasiness among those living in this locality.

Uniontown, Pennsylvania, *Morning Herald*, October 13, 1926
GORILLA STIRS BRIER HILL
Visions of being caught by a gorilla are passing through the minds of residents of Brier Hill as the result of many reports in that district of the escape of a gorilla from a circus at Brownsville recently. The animal is reported to have been seen by telephone linemen and only recently Officer Harry O'Connors of Brier Hill reported that he fired three shots at the animal which he claims to have seen in the neighborhood of Redstone Park.

As a result of these reports, residents in the neighborhood are cleaning their guns, preparatory to shooting at the beast should it be seen in the vicinity again.

Uniontown, Pennsylvania, *Morning Herald*, October 19, 1926
GORILLA PROWLS AT GRIFFIN MINE
Brier Hill's gorilla scare has moved across country to Griffin Mine No, of the Banner

Coal and Coke Company, near Masontown,
according to reports emanating from that
section last night. Employes at Griffin claim
to have seen the animal at 2:30 o'clock Monday morning and, when they made efforts to
get near it, the animal swung off into the
darkness.

Charleroi, Pennsylvania, *Mail*, October 20, 1926

MASONTOWN DISTRICT HAS
ALARMING GORILLA SCARE
As Farmers Find Animals
and Fowls Slaughtered.

Posses are scouring the woods today in the
vicinity of Masontown and Brier Hill for what
is believed to be an escaped gorilla after the
finding last night of a cow and a horse dis-
emboweled, and showing the evidence of a
terrible struggle with some huge animal, on
a farm two miles from Masontown. Hundreds
of chickens and pigs have been slaughtered
by the marauder. The anger of many farmers
has turned to genuine alarm as the report
is spread than an escaped circus gorilla is
prowling the district.

The depredations began about two weeks
ago, when, according to a Brownsville rumor,
a gorilla escaped from a circus train while
passing near Brownsville. Scores of chickens
have been killed by the supposed brute while

pig-stys, broken into have been the scene of a number of killings. The animal, in practically every instance has literally torn its victim to pieces with apparent great strength.

Parents won't allow their children to venture from their homes after dark and even some grown-ups prefer to spend their evenings indoors.

The sureness of the identity of the animal is not positive, but farmers say the slaughter of their barn-yard stocks is the work of a giant creature.

Bloody trails were followed from one barnyard to a point in a woodland section back of Brier Hill last Saturday night, after a number of chickens were killed and partly devoured.

Posses, searching the woods about Masontown have found little trace of the mysterious marauder, which has successfully hidden itself in some unknown lair.

Cumberland, Maryland, *Sunday Times,* October 24, 1926

GORILLA AT LARGE IN NEARBY PENNSYLVANIA

Connellsville, Pa., Oct. 23.—With the finding of a dead horse near the Bessemer coke ovens yesterday, the body badly clawed with wounds on the animal's flanks and belly, the story of a gorilla at large in the vicinity of Masontown is given more credence. The gorilla is said to have escaped from a circus train that passed through Brownsville some time ago.

To the appearance of the gorilla goes the blame of the disappearance of pigs and chickens that have been killed lately. The people in that neighborhood refuse to let their children out of the homes after dark.

Two children came home screaming one night recently and said that they had been chased by a large hairy animal that was hid behind a tree.

Monongahela, Pennsylvania, *Daily Republican,* October 26, 1926

WEBSTER STIRRED BY GORILLA SCARE; ESCORTS IN DEMAND

Considerable excitement was caused, and escorts were in demand, when a gorilla, which is said to have escaped from a circus train near Brownsville and to be roaming the valley, was reported seen on the hills near Webster.

A posse was quickly formed, and went in chase of the alleged denizen of the jungle, but no trace was found. It is now believed that the report originated in the vivid imagination of some person.

Brownsville has not altogether recovered from the gorilla scare and police have been kept busy denying the report that an animal is running loose there. The story has spread far and wild within a few days. Unfounded as the story is, hundreds of instances of depredations on the farms in Washington and Fayette counties are being blamed on the gorilla.

Monongahela, Pennsylvania, *Daily Republican,* October 27, 1926

GORILLA SCARE IN UPPER VALLEY LAID TO JOKERS AND BLUNDER

The gorilla scare that has caused quite a little excitement in the upper valley is believed to have been solved, and the blame has been placed on practical jokers and an oversight on the part of a reporter.

Early last week, Hallow'en celebrants in West Virginia caused some property damage. A paper commented editorially on the affair and declared it the work of "abandonned guerrillas."

The story drifted over to the Monongahela valley, and "abandonned" became escaped and "guerrilla" became gorilla.

A farmer's horse died, a cow passed away and a cat had fits. Someone suggested it might have been the work of the "escaped gorilla." And the "Gorilla" story was launched.

Housewives in Brownsville, Webster and Monessen have been terrorfied by reports of practical jokers that gorilla had been seen. Doors were barricaded and windows locked. Even the assurance of officers that the scare is unfounded has failed to relieve some of the weak-hearted.

Others, however, have forgotten about the ape to protect their property from the original "Hallowe'en guerrillas."

Lebanon, Pennsylvania, *Daily News and Daily Times*, February 2, 1927

GORILLA SEEN IN WOODS IN ADAMS CO., SUNDAY

Gettysburg, today—Motorists who arrived in Gettysburg Tuesday from Iron Springs in the mountains of the western part of Adams County, reported that on Sunday a gorilla jumped over their automobile as they drove over a bridge.

They say that the animal was sitting on the arch of the bridge and as they drove past jumped from one side to the other. They were afraid the animal would fall into the car, they said. According to their story, the animal disappeared in a pine grove nearby and is [now] believed to be on Jacks Mountain.

1931: Berry (1993) noted a report collected by Stan Gordon, from a woman who claimed multiple sightings of a hairy manlike creature near Indian Head, Fayette County.

Everett, Pennsylvania, *Press*, February 13, 1931

RUMORS OF GORILLA SEEN IN THE VICINITY OF TATESVILLE FALSE

SEARCH BY MEN OF COMMUNITY REVEAL
NO TRACKS OR EVIDENCE OF GIANT APE

Rumors of a gorilla in Bedford county woods took a representative of The Press to Tatesville this week with hopes of getting a specimen for the starting of a community zoo. Investigation revealed the fact that some folks must have seen too many motion pictures of the Tarzan type or they must have highly developed imaginations.

Two young men, as the story is told, were returning to their homes in the vicinity of Tatesville late Sunday night, February 1. They had been calling up on their "girl friends." As they traveled along the ridge near Tatesville, they suddenly heard something walking heavily in the woods.

The young men ran and ran very fast, it is said. Later, in telling the story, one of them stated that he glanced over his shoulder and saw something chasing them that resembled a gorilla.

Since that night there have been stories of men employed at the sand bank being frightened at their work by the gorilla. A young lady going home one night in her car saw something large and black standing beside the road, and she thought it was surely "the gorilla."

Another version was given by a man who on his way home from work saw "the gorilla" standing beside the road and, according to his story, he drove within a few feet of it. In fact part of the population of Tatesville and vicinity think that every large shadow is a gorilla.

On the other hand, the more sensible residents give no credence to the story and believe that the story started by two young men has been misquoted by imaginative folks. One story told was that the huge ape had looked in the window of the store of Mrs. Nellie Plummer last week. Mrs. Plummer told the Press representative that no such thing had occurred and that she has seen nothing that even resembles a gorilla.

Several nights last week, groups of men from Tatesville and the vicinity hunted through the woods and watched for the jungle animal, but their search was fruitless. No tracks or other evidence has been found indicating the presence of an ape in the vicinity.

It is though that a dog was possibly the animal that frightened the men on February 1. By their weird story they set to work the imaginations of others, started folks jumping at shadows and put the community as a whole on "needles and pins."

No gorilla could last very long in this cold climate. Besides one could not get in this section unless it had escaped from a show or zoo, and if that was the case, the loss of the animal would have been advertised long ago.

Chester, Pennsylvania, *Times*, January 22, 1932

WILL BEGIN SEARCH FOR STRANGE CREATURE

John McCandless, of Swarthmore, with eight other men; all armed, will begin a man hunt near Lyndell, five miles north of Downingtown, today. The object of the hunt, believed to be a maniac, was seen by McCandless and a companion in the locality last Tuesday.

According to McCandless, who is employed at the Upper Bank Nurseries, near Media, the creature crawls on all fours like an animal, but otherwise has the appearance of a human being of unusually large build. McCandless and a friend, Lee Yeager, of Media, saw the strange creature last Tuesday, prowling about among the pines when a group of men from the nursery were digging trees in the vicinity of Lyndell.

"I couldn't get a clear glimpse of the body," said McCandless yesterday, "but I know that it was not hairy, like an animal's body would have been. I saw the hands very clearly, however, and they were just like human hands, only unusually large."

He said the strange creature lunged at him uttering a series of sounds like groans. He did not have a weapon and did not wait to see what the creature would do. Later on, he said, boys living in the neighborhood discovered footprints like those of a man, but exceptionally larger, but did not find any traces of the creature itself.

Shamokin, Pennsylvania, *News Dispatch,* January 23, 1932

MONSTER CAUSE OF EXCITEMENT IN NEW JERSEY

Philadelphia, Jan. 23 (INS)—Residents of the Pine Belt region in the vicinity of Downingtown laughed today over reports "a Jersey madman" is loose in the district.

"It's the Jersey devil," commented one scoffer. "It's a deer," said another.

Anyhow there is little credence given the highly excited report of John McCandless, Swarthmore gardener, that a monstrous creature is at large in the timbered creek road district near Downingtown.

The gardener espied the "devil," which he described as "looking like a man, acting like a man, and covered with long hair," Wednesday afternoon. The strange creature emitted weird moans, said McCandless. Harry Eppenheimer, 10, living near the spot where the Swarthmore man said he saw the "devil," claims he saw the strange man or beast yesterday morning.

Some of the more excitable persons in the section fear a madman may be hiding in the woods.

Those believing the "monster" is a deer also assert the queer moans heard by Mc-Candless was just a deer wailing. "That cry is as familiar to us as the honk of a horn is to you city fellows," said one of the doubting residents.

The original "Jersey devil" was the brain-child of a former operator at the old Dime Museum in Philadelphia. He took a kanga-roo, painted it with red and white stripes and attached a pair of wings. Then it was turned loose in the south Jersey pines and promptly recaptured. Brought to Philadelphia and ballyhooed as "The Jersey Devil," the museum operator collected hundreds of dollars from curious spectators.

Charleroi, Pennsylvania, *Mail,* September 23, 1938

'HAIRY APE' SCARE LOSES OUT IN WOODLAND WILDS AT CORRY

Corry, Pa., Sept. 23—Fears of a "furry thing resembling an ape" subsided today in this Erie County community after a posse of farmers failed to locate the mysterious animal in a 48-hour search.

The "thing" popped up Sunday at the edge of a woods three miles south of Corry and sent Rose Marie Clabbatz, 13, and two smaller children of Howard Clabbatz, scurrying across fields to their father.

Clabbatz listened to their breathless story about an animal that "started chasing us" and organized a hunting part of 50 persons, many with guns.

Yesterday Frank Ross and Fred Lindstrom said they spied the beast ambling near their farms, on the edge of a woods. Ross said "it" appeared to be four feet tall and "resembled an ape."

Cabbatz said he believed the animal left the vicinity and now "the women folk and kids dare to go out again." Some discounted the ape story, saying the mysterious animal probably was a bear cub walking on its hind legs.

Oil City, Pennsylvania, *Derrick,* October 14, 1938

APE-LIKE ANIMAL
IS SIGHTED AGAIN

Corry, Oct. 13.—(AP)—An animal "resembling an ape," which several days ago frightened two children and became the object of an intensive search by armed farmers, was reported seen again today.

Carl Kighlinger, 26-year-old worker on Charles Swan's farm five miles northwest of Corry, said he was walking through the fields today when:

"I heard something squeal and saw a furry animal sitting on its hind legs under a tree about 500 feet away.

"I ran and my view was cut plenty short. I glanced over my shoulder and saw an animal, which seemed to be about five feet tall, swinging along in a stooped animal manner, in the opposite direction with only its furry back visible." . . .

Wilkes-Barre, Pennsylvania, *Times Leader,* November 28, 1942

SHAVERTOWN RELAXES AGAIN
AS ARMED YOUTHS GIVE UP
SEARCH FOR 'GORILLA MAN'

Having passed through "a week of nerves,"
residents of the Shavertown area and particularly the women, young and old, heaved a
genuine sigh of relief today when it was reported by reputable citizens of the town that
the gorilla-man scare spread a week or so
ago was nothing more than a myth.

They were unable to explain the source of
the rumor which kept women and children
indoors after dark except when accompanied
by a male escort but stated that the whole
thing was the result of an overworked imagination.

Their relief today was all the more genuine because of the fact that most of the
backmountain residents were more afraid
of being shot than of seeing the mysterious
gorilla-man.

When the report was circulated first, a
week ago, it sent squads of men and boys
on the highways and byways bristling for
action and declaring it wouldn't be well for
the gorilla-man to cross their paths. Some of
the groups were reported made up largely of
youths and, according to businessmen, it was

"only a miracle" that saved some pedestrian from being shot. No shots were fired, as far as can be learned.

At any rate the mystery appears to have vanished in thin air and the highways once more are safe for travel.

Connellsville, Pennsylvania, *Daily Courier*, August 18, 1945

BABOON REPORTED ON LOOSE IN WESTMORELAND WOODLAND

The story:

Robert Reed of Latrobe, Westmoreland county game protector, received a call recently from several persons at Crabtree, who said they saw an animal resembling an ape or a baboon was on the loose in the woods near Crabtree and was frightening people.

Mr. Reed went to Crabtree to investigate. His report is not yet it.

Connellsville, Pennsylvania, *Daily Courier*, August 27, 1945

MONKEY, IF THERE IS ONE, STILL ELUDES FOLKS OF THE LATROBE REGION

State game officials, firemen and veteran hunters participated this week in a fruitless search through open and wooded country in the region about Latrobe following repeated reports a monkey or some animal resembling a simian had been seen.

The mysterious creature was first reported in the Greenwald-Crabtree area, where several persons said they had seen it. Then it disappeared and nothing was heard of it for two or three days, when six-year-old Jerry Nolan of Lloydsville came running into his home, crying he had been chased by a "monkey" while he was playing in a field. He was not sure whether the animal wanted to play with him or meant him harm.

To cap it all, Mrs. Delbert Nolan, hearing the family dog barking furiously, rushed to a window to see what the excitement was about. She said she could see the dog under a grapevine near a tree. She got a glimpse of what she thought was a monkey striking at the dog. Then the mystery animal turned tail and ran, leaping over a four-foot garden fence.

The matter reported to the Latrobe police, Game Protector Robert Reed was summoned. He enlisted the services of John Horne, veteran Latrobe hunter. They and others went to Lloydsville and organized the hunt. Much of the night was given over to scouring the area, but without result.

Camden, New Jersey, *Courier-Post,* September 7, 1945

WILD APE SCARES WILDCAT HOLLOW; SCHOOL IS CLOSED

Latrobe, Pa., Sept. 7 (UP)—The wild ape of Wildcat Hollow was the object of a search by State Police and an armed posse today after raids by the animal forced the closing of the Reed school, near here.

Believed to have escaped from a circus which played in the vicinity six weeks ago, the animal has been seen in various sections of Westmoreland county.

The animal has been variously identified as a large rhesus monkey or a chimpanzee.

A corn roast at the school Wednesday night was suddenly broken up when the animal leaped boldly into the crowd, snatched two ears of corn and disappeared into the bushes.

The animal is believed to hide by day in abandoned mines, coming out at night to forage.

Paul Claycomb, a farmer of near Marietta, saw the animal at a distance of about 100 feet and said it weighed about 100 pounds. The monkey broke his chicken-house door and made off with a hen. Claycomb's large dog was frightened by the animal.

Indiana, Pennsylvania, *Evening Gazette,* September 8, 1945

"THE MONK" IS STILL
ON THE RAMPAGE

Latrobe, Pa., Sept. 8.—(AP)—That fleeting monkey, chimpanzee or whatever it is on the loose in Wildcat Hollow was seen again last night by two boys who were walking with their dogs.

And from the report they made to Game Protector William Mathews he figures the animal must be "about four feet tall and weighing 100 pounds."

For several weeks residents have been reporting something cavorting in a beastly manner, but nobody could lay hands on it, or didn't want to, even when it interrupted a corn roast earlier this week by leaping into the center of things and grabbing two ears of corn.

There might even be two monkeys, instead of one. Mathews said this possibility shouldn't be overlooked. The theory is that something escaped from a circus which played here six weeks ago, "and," says Mathews, "if one animal can get through the bars, another one certainly can."

The animal was seen last night by Norman White and Joseph Seville, who live in Norvel.

Mathews said that upon hearing their dogs growl the youths flashed their lights upon a tree and spotted it on Seville's lawn. A posse was formed but got nowhere.

Connellsville, Pennsylvania, *Daily Courier,* September 15, 1945

MONKEY TALES HOAX?

A considerable number of Westmoreland county folks resident with in the area about Latrobe will have to conclude they can't believe what they see, if what Captain Andrew J. Hudock of the State Police at Greensburg says is true. He brands the stories that have circulated for weeks about a monkey or some other animal of the species at large as a hoax.

The trooper captain speaks after what he thinks is a thorough investigation of the numerous tales coming to him and other officers. He includes that of James Poole of Greensburg, who says a simian dropped from a tree, landed on his back and bit him on the neck and hands. The alleged bites were treated by a physician.

Perhaps a score of persons at Crabtree, Lloydsville and Wilpen were quoted as having said they saw the animal at divers times and places. At Wilpen, for example, the allegation was the monkey dashed into the midst of children enjoying a corn roast, grabbed two ears of corn and raced back into the bushes.

Will the trooper's denunciation still the controversy? Many of these people convinced against their wills, if they can be, will be of their "own opinions still."

The theory has been the monkey escaped from a carnival.

1946: Berry (1993) noted a report from Lebanon, when a farmer shot at a tall, hairy, man-like creature that was feeding on a dead cow. It disappeared into the woods.

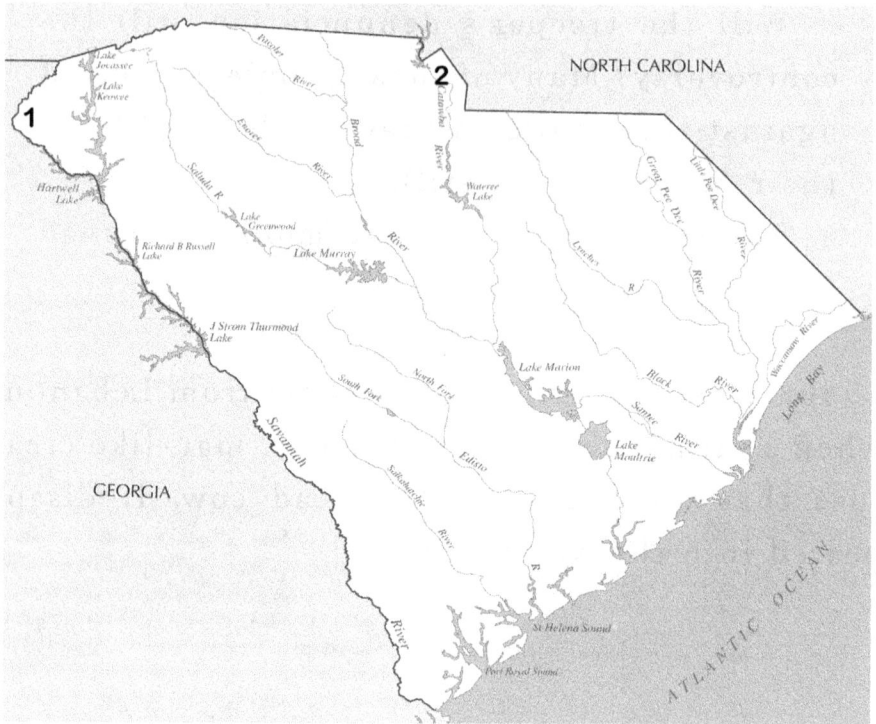

1 Oconee County

2 Rock Hill (York County)

South Carolina

Berry (1993) noted old reports of a hairy, manlike creature, known as "Red-Eye," in the Black River region.

Dunkirk, New York, *Observer-Journal,* July 16, 1889

A MONSTER ANIMAL.

HE WAS SEVEN FEET HIGH, COVERED WITH HAIR AND WALKED ERECT.

During the time the Indians were in the South, a hunting party established a camp east of Tugalo river, in what is now Oconee County, S. C., says the Clarksville (Ga.) Advertiser. One day they all went hunting, leaving a deer they had killed the evening previous at the camp. At night when the Indians returned to the camp the deer was gone, and the next day the same thing was repeated, when they concluded to leave an old Indian to guard the camp and see what went with their deer. That day the old Indian saw a monster animal come and carry

off the deer, and was afraid to make any
attempt to kill the monster, which was about
seven feet high and walked erect like a man,
hairy all over, and its mouth was in the chin
and great claws on the fingers and toes. The
next day all seven of the Indians stayed at
the camp, and, as usual, the monster came,
gathered up the deer and started off, when
one of them fired at it, the ball taking effect
in the back. The animal dropped the deer and
turned and started toward them, when the
other six poured a volley into its breast and
it fell dead. About three hours after that the
Indians heard a noise like some one hallooing about a mile distant: "Yaho, yaho, yaho!"
The Indians left the camp and called on the
posse comitatus for protection, when a party
of whites on horses, with all the dogs they
could get, went in search of the other animal
and found it. It was like the one the Indians
killed, and they put the dogs after it. When
the men appeared in sight the animal would
run, but it could whip every dog they could
get after it. The party pursued it to the river
and at jumps it went across the river over
into Habersham County, and was shot by a
party soon after it crossed the river.

Greenville, South Carolina, *News,* July 31, 1925

GORILLA SCARE IS GONE AND EASLEY FOLK HAVE LAUGH

FACETIOUSLY INCLINED FELLOW GIVES FELLOW TOWNSMEN GENUINE 'GORILLAITIS.'

CASE OF WOLF! WOLF!

The epidemic of "gorillaitis," which swept over Easley and vicinity several days ago and filled weak hearts with stark terror, seems to have abated. Normalcy reigns again and old and young have resumed their habits of staying outdoors or indoors at night whenever and wherever they please.

The gorilla wasn't a gorilla after all: the "gorillaitis" was genuine, however. Most everybody was scared.

Some weeks ago a carnival company visited Central, the prosperous little community along the main line of the Southern just west of Easley. It was reported that a large and ferocious gorilla escaped from the show company while doing its stuff at Central. Terror spread through all the land round about.

Gorilla at Large.

Now these gorillas, or troglodytes or anthropithecus as Darwin and his ilk knew them, have a way of eating people alive, tearing down houses and raising the proverbial brother of Abel in sundry and summary fashion. The good people of Central knew all this. However, the gorilla, if he escaped the carnival, did a good job of it. He was not seen or heard of in that neck of map again.

Things picked up in Easley a few days later, however. A gorilla was seen, or alleged to have been seen, or perhaps said to have been seen in that vicinity. Tracks were there, pieces of dead chickens were picked up out of front yards, fences were torn down, et cetera. Cats became obviously scarce and dogs ran under houses and howled loud and long during the nocturnal hours.

The situation became unbearable and the other day men, a large crowd of them—an Easley citizen says 40 of them—shouldered their guns and took to the open about Easley to find the gorilla which had been eating chickens, chasing vagrant canines under houses and otherwise playing the very heck. They trailed and trailed and found pieces of dead chickens, broken fences, down trodden peach trees and other signs and indications of depredations by Brother Troglodytes, but no gorilla rewarded their efforts.

Finally the hunt was suddenly brought to a close. The "brother" of the gorilla had spilled the beans.

Case of Wolf! Wolf!

Briefly, here's what happened, according to reports from the good city across the Saluda! A certain man hearing of the escaped gorilla at Central took two pieces of board and cut the impressions of gigantic gorilla-like feet from them. The toes were made plainly and on the heels he tacked rounded pieces of rubber to give the proper effect to the track. It worked marvels after he nailed the "gorilla feet" to his own shoes. This modern fun maker proceeded to tramp all over the community on several nights, tossing chicken feathers here and there, tearing down a garden fence here and throwing dismembered biddies about. The effect was ideal. The natives fairly went cuckoo over it all. And no wonder.

The gorilla wasn't a gorilla after all: the "gorillaitis" was genuine, however. Most everybody was scared.

The gorilla's name? you say. Well, it hasn't been officially made public, but it is said there were thousands by that name in the American army during the world war. Forty-five hundred of them used John for a first name.

Greenville, Mississippi, *Delta Democrat-Times*, February 6, 1938

DISTANT RELATIVE OF
MOBILE'S MONSTER REPORTED

Rockhill, S.C., Feb. 5 (UP). "The Monster of Marmotte Street" which has terrorized the negro population of Mobile, Ala., was reported tonight to have a distant relative operating among the dusky folk of Rockhill.

The mysterious beast here was called the "African Udilacus," said to resemble a gorilla.

Two frightened negro men told police that a fierce, fur-covered animal accosted them on a lonely, dimly-lit street last night. Another negro reported that the beast had attacked him and ripped off his clothing before he managed to escape its "awful" clutch.

Police, who were without a theory as to the identity of the weird animal, also received a report that the African Udilacus had killed a large calf on the edge of this small South Carolina town and eaten away much of the carcass.

A check was made at a circus wintering near here, but they reported all their animals present and accounted for in their cages.

Police at Mobile, Ala., after spending a hectic week investigating fantastic reports in the colored district, decided the "Monster of Marmotte Street" had slunk back to the swamp bordering the colored residential district.

The Mobile monster was described in various ways—all horrible. Police never were able to secure more tangible evidence concerning the beasts other than wild rumors. The same situation existed in Rockhill.

The Udilacus was first reported in a cotton mill section on the outskirts of Rockhill.

John White, a "dark town" resident, furnished the details:

"It was standing in the water. It was black and tall as a man. I threw a rock at it, but it snarled and started after me.

"I ran."

Bruce Neal, who was with White when the Udilacus appeared, said the animal ran on two legs as it chased them.

"After it chased us a little ways, it dropped down on all fours," Neal explained.

Neal also said the monster "smelled terrible."

Columbus, Nebraska, *Telegram,* February 7, 1938
"AFRICAN UDILICUS"
FEARED BY NEGROES

Rock Hill, S.C., Feb. 7 (UP)—Negro dwellers for miles around carried clubs today as protection against the "African udilacus," a "huge, shambling beast with long hair."

The creature has killed two dogs and mauled "not less than a dozen," according to reports from the Willowbrook section of Rock Hill where the creature has concentrated its nocturnal activity.

Sam Watts, negro, asserted he was chased through the woods by "something hairy, making grunting noises."

Constable Carl Hovis said he shot twice [at] "some kind of shambling beast," and said it may have been the menace described by the negroes.

The negroes are certain the animal is the "African udilacus."

Pulaski, Virginia, *Southwest Times,* February 9, 1938

AFRICAN UDILACUS DEPARTS CAROLINA AFTER WILD SPREE

Rock Hill, S.C. (UP)—The "African udilacus" supposedly strange animal that attacked dogs and frightened men, today mysteriously disappeared and negroes reported the "thing" had gone to visit the "monster of Marmotte street" which frightened the colored section of Mobile, Ala.

Others who claimed to know all about the udilacus, but did not know where or how the name originated, said the Rock Hill monster had gone into hibernation for 10 years for it only appears once a decade.

Authorities who investigated the mystery said the "thing" may have been one of the [hamadryad] or sacred baboons being trained by Tommy Burns, at York, S.C. Burns, a circus animal trainer, said he did not believe any of his animals were loose but sometimes the monkeys got out and ran free.

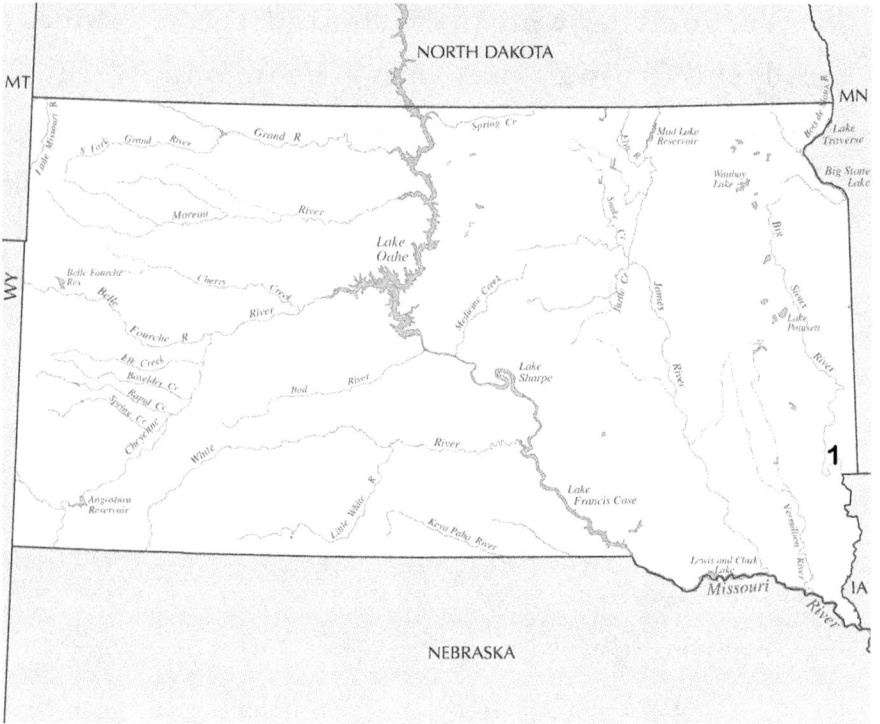

NORTH DAKOTA

MT

MN

Lake Missouri R

S Fork Grand River

Grand R

Spring Cr

Mud Lake Reservoir

Lake Traverse

Moreau

River

Lake Oahe

Winbury Lake

Big Stone Lake

WY

Belle Fourche Res

Cherry Creek

Medicine Creck

South Cr

James

Big

Siour Lake Poinsett

Belle

Fourche R

River

Elk Creek Boxelder Cr Rapid Cr Spring Cr Creek Cheyenne

Bad River

Lake Sharpe

River

White

River

Angostura Reservoir

Little White R

Keya Paha River

Lake Francis Case

River

Vermont River

1

Lewis and Clark Lake

Missouri

IA

River

NEBRASKA

1 Big Sioux River

South Dakota

Fort Wayne, Indiana, *Daily Democrat*, December 11, 1869

A WILD MAN IN DAKOTA.

[FROM THE SIOUX CITY *TIMES*, DEC. 1.]

We are indebted to Mr. Thompson, who resides on the Dakota side of the Big Sioux,
about fifteen miles northwest of this city,
for the particulars of the facts which we are
about to narrate:

About one month since, a farmer named
Evans, who resides a few miles north of Mr.
Thompson, was engaged in hauling firewood
from the timber of the Big Sioux, when he
was startled by seeing what at first glance
appeared to be some wild animal, bound out
from a hollow log but a few yards from where
he was standing. A close observation of the
object while it was decamping, satisfied Mr.
Evans that it was a wild man; he immediately
made pursuit, but the rapidity with which
the wild man ran, added to the thickness of
the woods, soon put him out of either sight or
reach. Mr. Evans shortly afterward returned

home, and informed his neighbors of his adventure and what he had seen. A small party of well-mounted men started the next day on the trail of the wild man. The party first ransacked the woods in the neighborhood. In a secluded spot, entirely obscured from ordinary observation by the thickness of the underbrush, they discovered a fissure between two rocks. This fissure penetrated into the rocks about eight feet; on the top was a large lot of underbrush, limbs of trees, and several pieces of portions of hides of animals. There were no indications that there had been a fire kindled anywhere near the place, but from the pieces of [rags], long grass, and other matter found on the ground, they were satisfied that it was the habitation of the wild man. Not being able to see any thing of the object of their search they went to their homes.

A few days afterward another party of horsemen started out, on the same mission as their predecessors, and with more satisfactory results. About three o'clock in the afternoon, while following up a ravine, a few miles from the place where the strange being was first discovered, the party was attracted by the barking of one of their dogs. Immediately afterward the wild man crossed

an open space, closely followed by two of
the dogs. The men put spurs to their horses,
and for a short distance gained rapidly on
the object of their search; but, coming to a
deep ravine or gully, skirted on either side
by underbrush, their progress was impeded,
and during the delay caused by getting out of
their situation, the man escaped. Since that
time he has not been seen.

We understand that a party of gentlemen
from this city propose starting out in a few
days for the purpose of catching this man, or
rather, nondescript, dead or alive. We hope
that no effort will be spared to take him alive
and uninjured. From a conversation with Mr.
Thompson, we learn that this singular being
is entirely covered with a seemingly heavy
coat of dark colored hair; that he is as agile
as a cat, and as fleet as a deer. Old settlers
in the region where the wild man has been
seen state that about twenty-three years
since a Frenchman, with his wife and three
children, settled upon a piece of land on the
banks of the Big Sioux. At that time the only
occupants of this section consisted of the
Indians, who were the sole owners of Dakota,
some half-breeds and a few French settlers,
most of whom took squaws for their wives;
it is related that the Frenchman we have

alluded to did not live agreeably with his family; that his affections were lavished upon the dusky daughter of an Indian Chief; that the white wife, learning of this, upbraided her husband for the symptoms of his waning affections, and that one morning a friendly Indian, visiting the claim of the Frenchman, discovered the dead bodies of the wife and children lying on the floor. An examination discovered the fact that the throat of the woman had been cut from ear to ear, and that the children had been clubbed to death by blows on the head with the stock of a gun or some similar weapon. No clue to the murderer was ever discovered.

The Frenchman has never been seen in the country since. The supposition now is that he committed a triple murder; that, reflecting on the horror of his crime, he became insane, took to the woods, and resided there since, and that the wild man that has lately been seen and the French settler of twenty-seven years since, is one and the same person. It is well-known that many years since the majority of the Indians who resided in the Big Sioux Valley, were, on account of the scarcity of game, compelled to go further west, and as it is only within the last few years that the section of country alluded to has become settled, it was very possible for a man to live there without being discovered, or any person knowing his whereabouts. The whole affair is wrapped up in such a singular mystery that we refrain from comment or surmise until we can speak intelligently on the subject.

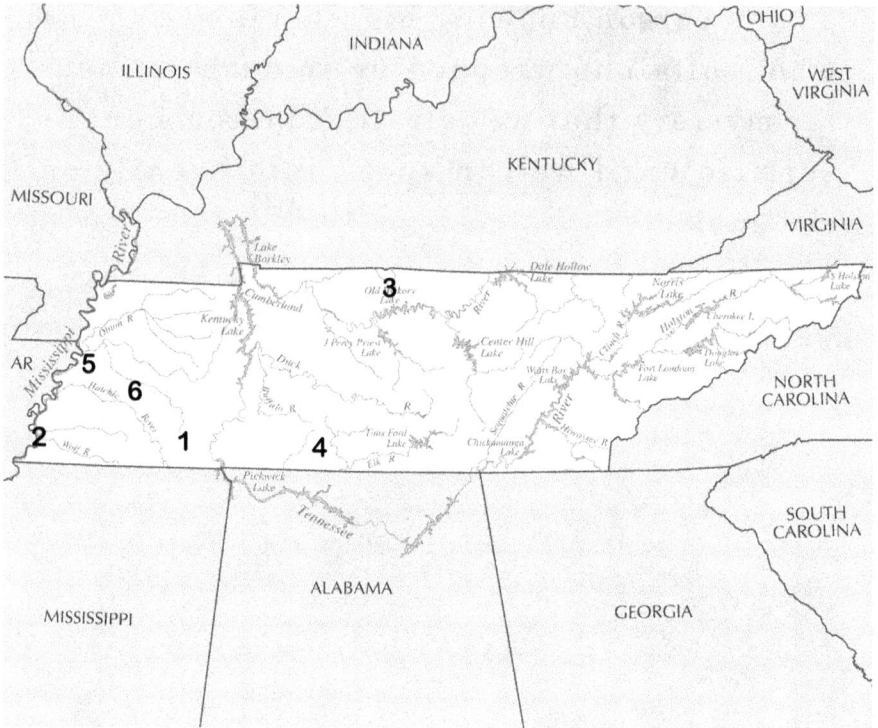

1 McNairy County

2 Memphis (Shelby County)

3 Gallatin (Sumner County)

4 Minor Hill (Giles County)

5 Arp (Lauderdale County)

6 Jackson (Madison County)

Tennessee

Philadelphia, Pennsylvania, *Democratic Press,* May 4, 1871
THE TENNESSEE WILD MAN.

The Jackson Tennessee Whig, of the 15th inst., says: We learn that between Sobby and Crainsville, on what is called Piney, in McNairy county, a strange and frightful being has been observed for several weeks. He is said to be seven feet high, and possessed of great muscular power.—His eyes are unusually large and fiery red; his hair hangs in a tangled and matted mass of jet below his waist, and his beard reaches below his middle, his entire body is covered with hair and his whole aspect is most frightful. He shuns the sight of men, but approaches with wild and horrid delight every woman who is unaccompanied by a man. He sometimes with great caution approaches houses; and should he see a man he runs away with astonishing swiftness, leaping the tallest fences with the ease of a deer, defying alike the pursuit of men and dogs. He has frightened several women by attempting to carry them off, as well as by his horrid aspect, and the whole country around Sobby is in consternation.— The citizens are now scouring the woods, and are determined either to capture or drive off the monster.

1878: The following case is a prime example of showman's exhibition hype. The extensive descriptive background narrative was created to stimulate wide interest, drawing crowds and their money. This type of hoax needs to be considered a possibility whenever a classic case involving an exhibition is found. Does the article appear designed to attract visitors? If so, caution is warranted. Shoemaker (1990) provided some details regarding this form of ichthyosis, and I've included the report of another doctor who examined the "wild man." I'm not certain why Shoemaker stated that a showman's hoax was precluded in this case (by independent news reports and examination by physicians), while noting that the background story was fabricated; perhaps he misunderstood the intent. A showman had little to lose by allowing doctors to examine the "wild man," even if they recognized the disease. Publicity sells.

Galveston, Texas, *Daily News,* November 2, 1878

WILD MAN OF THE WOODS.

A FEARFUL PRODIGY CAPTURED IN THE
WILDS OF TENNESSEE AND BROUGHT TO
LOUISVILLE FOR EXHIBITION—
ITS BODY COVERED WITH FISH-SCALES.
[FROM THE LOUISVILLE COURIER-JOURNAL.]

The wild man brought to the city yesterday
by Dr. G. C. Broyler, of Sparta, Tenn., is truly a mysterious and wonderful creature. He
will be exhibited throughout the country by
manager Whallen, of the Metropolitan, who
is a third owner in this remarkable being,
who promises to successfully baffle all scientists who desire to give a satisfactory explanation of his unnatural appearance. Before entering into the details of his capture,
which forms quite a thrilling and interesting
episode, a description of the curiosity, which
promises to excite more attention than Barnum's "What is it?" will be given. At a distance the general outline of his figure would
indicate that he is only an ordinary man.
Close inspection shows that his whole body
is covered with a layer of scales, which drop
off at regular periods, in the spring and fall,
like the skin of a rattlesnake. He has a heavy
growth of hair on his head and a dark reddish

beard about six inches long. His eyes present a frightful appearance, being at least twice the size of the average-sized eye. Some of his toes are formed together, which give his feet a strange appearance, and his height, when standing perfectly erect, is about six feet five inches. A nervous twitching of his muscles shows a desire to escape, and he is constantly looking in the direction of the door through which he entered. His entire body must be wet at intervals, and, should this be neglected, he begins immediately to manifest great uneasiness, his flesh becomes feverish, and his sufferings can not be alleviated until the water is applied. At times he is dangerous, and yesterday morning, when Mr. Whallen attempted to place him in a wagon, in which he intended to bring him to the theater, it occupied some time. The strange creature acted in the most mysterious manner, refusing obstinately for some time to get into the wagon. He has quite a sharp appetite, having eaten a meal yesterday morning that would have fully satisfied at least four men. With the exception of fish, his meals are all prepared in the ordinary way, but the fish is eaten entirely raw. Dr. Broyler says that when alone he will sometimes mutter an unintelligible jargon, which it would be impossible for any one to understand, but that in the presence of visitors he remains perfectly silent. Yesterday afternoon, from 1 to 4, a private exhibition was given, and a number of physicians were present, among them Drs. Brady and Cary Blackburn, who said he was a great curiosity. Dr. Blackburn said that his scaly condition could not be attributed to any skin disease, but undoubtedly he was born in that condition. He will be on exhibition in one of the private rooms of the Metropolitan theater this afternoon and to-morrow between the hours of one and four o'clock. Only physicians and those specially invited will be allowed admission. His exact age is not known, but for the last eighteen years he has been running wild in the Cumberland mountains of Tennessee, near the Carey fork and Big Bone creek. He has been the constant terror of the community, although he was never known to attack any one until the day of his capture. Dr. O. G. Broyler, of Sparta, Tennessee, says that since the surrender of the confederate army it has been his intention to capture this creature and exhibit him throughout the country. The doctor says the parents of the wild man are respectable citizens of North Carolina, named Croslin. That their son is unquestionably a mysterious freak of nature they do not deny, but they could not account for his scaly skin. At the tender age of five years, having always been possessed with a roving disposition, he left his home and plunged immediately into the mountainous region of Tennessee. Here he lived as best he could, subsisting on the produce of the country, such as roots and herbs, and small animals that he could capture. When in the water he was in his element. He would dive down into the depth of the inland lakes, remaining underwater for a considerable length of time, and finally emerge with both hands filled with small fish, which he would devour at once in the raw state. Dr. Broyler says that until about eighteen months ago he had not attempted the capture, although he had been watching the creature's actions for the past twelve years. About the 15th of September he started into the mountains, fully determined to succeed in the capture.

The Wild Man of the Woods, as he was termed by the people of the vicinity, was unusually fleet of foot and possessed of a great deal of agility, bounding over the mountain regions in the most fearless manner. During the chase they kept the wild man constantly in sight, and their plan was to tire him out, in which they finally succeeded. He was pursued over the wild, mountainous country, over lakes and precipices, until his pursuers almost despaired of success, and then a kind of net was formed, into which he was decoyed and captured. He ran fearlessly into the net and became entangled in the meshes. Captured, but not conquered, a struggle ensued, in which Dr. Broyler was seriously wounded. The wild man fought with his hands, after the fashion of a bear, and scratched the doctor in a frightful manner. At last they quieted their unwilling victim and brought him to Sparta. The doctor immediately telegraphed to Mr. Whallen, who purchased a third interest in the wonder, and had him brought to Louisville yesterday morning. The presence of this wild man in Louisville has excited considerable attention among the doctors, and also a large crowd of curious persons, who are anxious to see the wonderful creature. There will be only one public exhibition in this city, which takes place at the Metropolitan theater Saturday afternoon.

Placerville, California, *Mountain Democrat*, February 1, 1879

"A MAN FISH."

A short time since the Tennessee and Kentucky newspapers contained a startling account of a wild man lately captured, with great difficulty, in the Cumberland mountains. He was six feet ten inches high, extraordinarily fleet of foot, and excessively savage. He fed chiefly on raw fish, which he captured without artificial aid. He spent much of his time in the water, and after being captured he had to be frequently bathed. He was covered with shining scales, like those of a fish. His hands and feet were webbed like the feet of water-fowls—so the newspaper accounts, with many embellishments, ran. It is scarcely necessary to say that much of this story was only showman's talk, uttered to attract the attention of the curious and credulous public.

The physicians of Louisville were invited to visit the monster upon his arrival in the city prior to his general exhibition. Among others I visited the merman; but before seeing the case I had diagnosed it as one of icthyosis, and a single glance was sufficient to verify the correctness of my conjecture. The man-fish presents a most magnificent example of the form of icthyosis or fish skin disease, called icthyosis [serpentina] or serpent disease; and his general effect is more that of a serpent than of a fish. But upon different parts of his body may be found nearly all the varieties of icthyosis. The resemblance of this man's skin to the shed skin of a boa constrictor, lately brought me by a friend from the zoological garden in London, is almost perfect. About his joints the skin is loose and wrinkled, hanging in folds, and the scales are large, suggesting the skin of a lizard or alligator about their limbs and belly. His arms and legs remind one of the skin of the buffalo perch, the carp, or other large fish. The cuticle everywhere is dry and harsh, and never perspires. There seems to be an absolute absence of fat, and the man is shrunken and withered, of a dead ashen-gray appearance, except here and there, where he is brownish or blackish. Though only of about fifty years of age, he impresses one as a very old man. The skin of the face is red and shining, and tightly drawn about the cheeks, pulling the lower lids down to such an extent as to perfectly avert them, making a horrid case of ectropion. In some places his scales are silvery, in others dark, and again in others are small and branny. His hair is very thin and dead looking. The backs of his hands are fissured, and on his palms and soles the cuticle is greatly thickened. The fingers and toes seem shorter than natural, and the skin is drawn tightly back over both feet and hands. The septum between the fingers and toes seem to extend much further down than usual, thus suggesting the webbed appearance before alluded to. He is considerably over six feet in height, and is a man of a low order of intelligence. He is married, and is the father of several children, none of whom, fortunately, inherit his malady; and as icthyosis is almost if not always a congenial disease, they are not likely to have it. The fishman fails to present but a single variety of icthyosis and that is the porcupine disease, as it is called. In this, spines, formed by hardened sebaceous material, protrude from the skin, closely packed together. Wilson states that he has observed them an inch in length. I have never seen them longer than an eight of an inch. Many years ago two brothers, in England, having this form of icthyosis, were exhibited in the shows as porcupine men.

Icthyosis is one of the rarest of skin diseases. I am under the impression that it is more frequent in Europe than in this country. In ten years I have seen less than a dozen cases. Its cause, as I have stated in my report to the American Dermatological Association, in 1877, is scrofula, according to observation and experience. It is found in all the walks of life. I have encountered it with equal frequency among the rich and the poor. It is commonly considered incurable, and only temporarily and partially mitigable.

The treatment which I have found successful in permanently removing ichthyosis, in more than one case, consists in the use of the constructives, i.e. codliver oil, extract of malt, syrup of the iodide of iron, syrup of the hypophosphites, &c.; attention to the digestive organs, and by giving the richest and best fat producing foods, such as cream, butter, hog meat fresh or cured, sugar and other sweets. A careful and thorough daily anointing with some oleaginous substance is of great value, and prolonged vapor or hot water baths should be employed frequently. —L. P. Vandell, M. D. in Louisville Medical News.

Philadelphia, Pennsylvania, *Times,* April 3, 1889

The "Bear Man" of Memphis: The negroes of Memphis are in a great state of excitement over the appearance in their midst of a strange monster known as the bear man. The bear man, who is described as an immense grizzly with a human voice, enters houses, frightens the occupants and in the confusion steals anything he can lay his hands on. The authorities think that he is a negro who by some means has come into possession of a masquerade costume and takes this means of robbing his fellow-d—s. Every negro in

Memphis now carries a club or a razor in hope of meeting the bear man, but thus far he has escaped any injury.

Richmond, Ohio, *Gazette*, March 9, 1893

The dead body of a giant wild man was found in the big woods near Gallatin, Tenn. He was seven feet high and weighed 300 pounds.

Athens, Alabama, *Limestone Democrat,* April 28, 1949

MINOR HILL SECTION MYSTIFIED BY PRINTS

The placid calm of Minor Hill and vicinity, southwest of Pulaski, has been changed into a state of alertness with the entire population on the lookout for an animal to match footprints which some believe to be those of a bear or gorilla.

A. E. Fox, who lives six miles south of Minor Hill, reported he first saw the tracks near a branch in Thompson's Hollow last Sunday. He saw them again Tuesday, this time in his back yard. Dogs have been frightened and hunters have reported hearing strange grunting sounds, but no evidence of anyone seeing the creature has been reported.

Fox and five neighbors awaited the supposed animal Tuesday night with loaded shotguns but nothing appeared. The footprints have been preserved and are attracting visitors daily.

If the mysterious prowler is a gorilla or a bear, residents of the area may well wonder where it came from. No carnival or circus has been in the county in recent months.

Kingsport, Tennessee, *Times,* July 10, 1953
HAIRY, APE-LIKE 'BEAST' REPORTED IN W. TENNESSEE

Arp, Tenn. (AP)—That "hairy beast with an ape-like shuffle" still stalks this Mississippi Riverside country and the sale of shotguns and shells in booming.

A lot of folks think the beast is nothing but a wandering bear, a rare animal in West Tennessee nowadays. This theory will get you an argument, however, and nobody is taking chances.

The latest report of the beast comes from a tenant farmer. He says "something" ripped a window screen from his home the other night.

Wilbert Boddie, who farms near Mack, said a 4-year-old child was sleeping inches from the window, three other children nearby.

Boddie said he nailed roofing tin over the hole and, two hours later, heard the "something" panting and scratching on the metal.

Farm owner William Hutcheson said he tracked the beast over a mile but couldn't tell what sort of animal made the tracks.

The beast was first reported last week by Thelma Graham, who was awakened by a crunching on the gravel outside.

"I thought it was a man at first," she said. "It was about a man's height but stooped over and walking very slowly.

"It was hard to see well, but I made out finally that it wasn't a man—no sir! That thing was covered with shaggy hair, nothing else. It moved away into the weeds and woods."

A Memphis zoo superintendent looked at photos of tracks from "Arp's Ape," and declared them bear tracks. Four local hunters went into the bottomlands in search of the creature, but evidently found nothing, as no further news was located. ("W. Tenn. 'Beast' is likely a bear," Kingsport, Tennessee, *Times*, July 13, 1953; "4 men hunt hairy beast near Jackson," Kingsport, Tennessee, *Times*, July 16, 1953.)

1957: Ivan T. Sanderson (1961) received a letter from a young man who, three years earlier, had seen a small apelike creature with reddish-orange hair in a marsh near Jackson, Tennessee. It had no tail, and swung by its arms in the trees. He shot at it repeatedly with a .22 rifle, to no effect.

Texas

The next three articles relate, chronologically, the story of the Wild Woman of the Navidad. This will occasionally crop up in Bigfoot literature. This case does show that eyewitness reports are not always trustworthy, particularly in historical situations.

Gettysburg, Pennsylvania, *Star and Banner*, March 23, 1849

A WILD WOMAN.

[FROM THE VICTORIA (TEXAS) ADVOCATE.]

We know not but our reputation for veracity may suffer by the following statement, but as we have been laying off for the last two years to give it, we think there is no use of waiting any longer. It will require some credulity to believe the story, but we can assure the reader that what we shall state could be established by the testimony of some of the oldest and most respectable citizens of our neighboring county of Jackson.

For the last ten years there has lived and inhabited the thickets of the Navidad

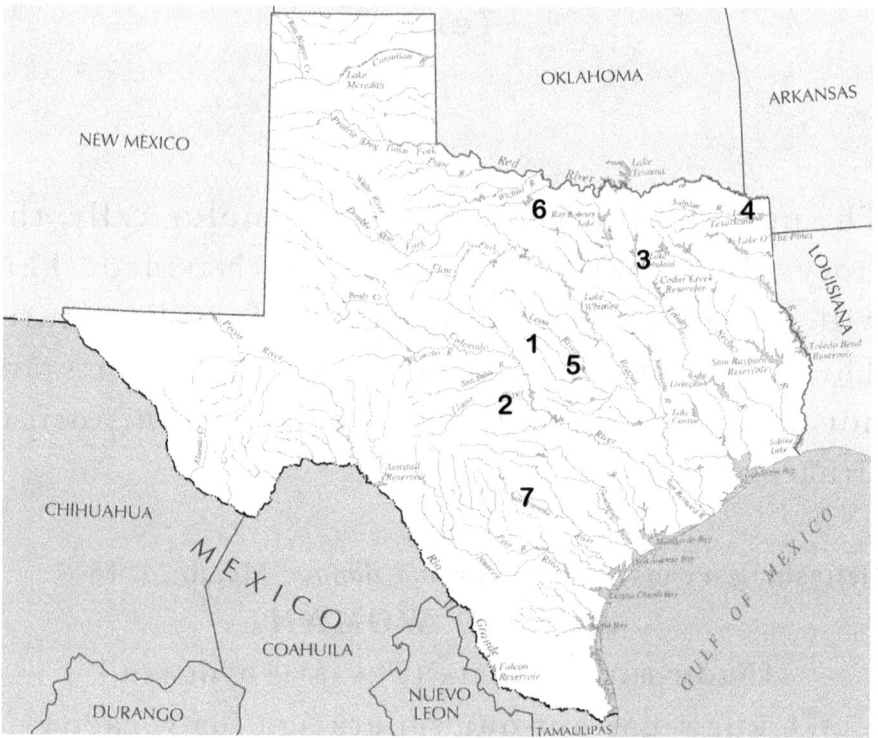

1 Gatesville (Coryell County)

2 Cherokee (San Saba County)

3 Kaufman County

4 Red Bank (Bowie County)

5 Temple (Bell County)

6 Paradise (Wise County)

7 San Antonio (Bexar, Medina, and Comal Counties)

bottoms in Jackson county, an animal universally believed to he a woman; and though diligent search has frequently been made, not a living soul has ever been able to see it; though on one occasion, several years ago, a party driving cows through the bottom, came so close upon its camp or den, as to compel it to drop a kind of basket or trunk, which upon examination, was found to be a perfect curiosity, containing a most astonishing variety of little trinkets, such as pins, needles, knives, brushes, and several articles whose uses were entirely unknown, and all of the most ingenious and exquisite workmanship, and also a pocket Bible, with "New York" written in it in a small beautiful hand writing, together with two guns, one of which it had stocked—having stolen an old gun barrel from the settlements.

The principal reason for believing it to be a woman arises from its track, which has often been seen, and which resembles exactly that of a delicate female. It frequently visits the neighboring houses of nights for the purpose of picking up such articles as it can lay its hands on—clothing in particular, of which it is supposed, from the quantity missing from time to time, it has enough to setup a respectable milinery shop and clothing store.

About a year ago, it went into the house of Sam A. Rodgers, when he was absent, opened his medicine chest, took a portion of all the medicines in it, carefully putting back the stoppers, and committing no other damage beside that of taking several articles of clothing, which after going to the edge of the bottom, it appears to have sorted out—and left such articles hanging about a stick as it did not seem to require. It also came to Mr. Rodgers's place recently and brought back a wooden bowl taken about a year since, and a trace chain that had been missing for eight years.—These are but a tithe of the many eccentricities of the man, woman or animal; but they serve as a specimen.

So sure are the people on the Navidad that it is a wild human being, that we understand a reward of forty cows and calves has been offered to any one who would capture it. It is supposed by some that there was once a man and woman, but that the man had died. How true this conjecture is, we cannot say; but there can hardly be a doubt but a wild man or woman has inhabited the Navidad Mustang bottoms, near Texana, for many years. It cannot be a negro, male or female, because the track forbids the conclusion. We incline to think it a Mexican woman.

Sandusky, Ohio, *Daily Sanduskian,* February 12, 1850

THE WILD WOMAN OF THE NAVIDAD.

FROM THE HOUSTON (TEXAS) TELEGRAPH.

About a year since an account was published
in the Victoria Advocate respecting a strange
creature, whose tracks had been discovered
on the bank of the Navidad, near Texana.
The footmarks of this creature resembled
those of a woman, and a report was circulated to the effect that a wild woman had
made her retreat in the forests of the Navidad. Within a few weeks several attempts
have been made to capture this singular being. Mr. Glascock pursued it for several days
with dogs, and at one time approached so
near it as to cast a lasso upon its shoulders.
It, however, with great adroitness eluded the
snare, and fled to a dense thicket, where it
could not be traced. Mr. Glascock states that
he was near a small prairy enclosed by the
border forests of the river, when the creature emerged from the woods, and ran across
the prairy in full view. It was about five feet
high. resembling a human being, but covered
with hair of reddish brown color. In its hand
it held a stick about six feet long, which it
flourished from side to side, as if to regulate
its motions, and aid it when running at full
speed. Its head and neck are covered with

very long hair; which streamed backward in the wind. It ran with the speed of a deer, and was soon out of sight. The dogs pursued it, and came so close upon it at a small creek, that it was compelled to drop its stick, which was taken by its pursuers.

This stick is about six feet long, straight and smooth as if polished with glass. Several other persons have repeatedly seen the creature, and they all concur in representing it as a human being, but so covered with shaggy hair as to resemble an ourang outang. It has frequently approached the houses of the settlers in that neighborhood during the night, and stole various articles—among other things it carried off a quantity of towels, one or two books, and has also taken several pigs. One of its nests was found in the forest, in which were several napkins, folded up just as they were taken from the house, and a bible, marked J. J. Wright.—A bill for washing was also enclosed in the Bible. The foot-marks of this strange being have often been traced in the bottom of the Navidad, but it has eluded all attempts to capture it. The old settlers in that section say that these foot-marks have been noticed for ten or twelve years, and that several years ago there were other foot-marks, indicating that three of these creatures were in company. Within the last year the foot-marks of only one have been noticed. Mr. Glascock intends to collect a pack of good hounds and resume the pursuit, and he is confident that he will succeed in capturing it. He has incurred considerable expense, and has exposed himself to great hardships and danger to secure it, thus evincing the full belief in the identity of this mysterious being. It is not improbable that during the war of the Revolution when people of that section were driven from their homes by the victorious army of Urrea, some children might have been secreted in the woods or left there, and their relations never returning, have become like wild beasts, clothed with hair, and feeding upon herbs and such small animals as they can capture or pilfer from the settlers.

Gettysburg, Pennsylvania, *Adams Sentinel and General Advertiser,* March 17, 1851

The Wild Woman Caught.—We learn from the Houston (Texas) Telegraph that the famous wild woman of the Navidad has been caught. A party of hunters, who were out hunting deer, accidentally came upon the camp of this singular creature and captured her.

She is an African negress, who fled to these wilds when the settlements were deserted just after Fannin's defeat, and she has been wandering about for a period of about fifteen years. Her food during that period has consisted of acorns, nuts, and other wild fruits, with such other food as she could occasionally steal from the neighboring settlements. She cannot speak any English, but converses freely with the Africans on the neighboring plantations.—Thus is solved the mystery that has hitherto given a romantic interest to the story of the wild woman of Navidad.

Ann Arbor, Michigan, *Michigan Argus,* September 1, 1871

A Texan Orang Outang.—Gatesville, Texas, is excited over the appearance of an immense orang outang in its vicinity. The animal is described as being about seven feet high and covered from head to foot with a thick coating of hair. Its eyes shine like fire and it boasts of a double row of murderous looking teeth. When last seen it had in one hand a large crooked stick, and under the other arm a young calf apparently just killed. A hunting party has been organized to capture or kill the monster.

Fort Worth, Texas, *Gazette*, October 2, 1895

MAN OR GORILLA?

A STRANGE CREATURE

DISCOVERED NEAR COMANCHE

Cherokee Tex., Oct. 1.—(Special)—What is it? Wild man, ape or gorilla? Cherokee creek, San Saba county, runs through a hilly country covered with live oaks in some places, but mostly with cedar, especially the country near the mouth of the creek and for twelve or fifteen miles up the stream. The valleys on the creek are narrow, very fertile and mostly in farms.

The local papers last week contained an account of a Mexican lion chasing some boys on Cherokee creek, where it runs through cedar brakes. S. G. McLean, the mail contractor and mail carrier between the town of San Saba and the village of Cherokee, says the account in the papers is incorrect. He was in that locality a few days since and the people report that the animal seen was undoubtedly a wild man, ape or gorilla. A young man by the name of David Henry saw the animal sitting down like a man and thought it was a negro or a Mexican.

The animal got up and approached him. He did not like the looks of it and took to his heels. The animal followed rapidly, running on all fours like a dog. Young Henry, seeing that he would he caught, picked up a rock, faced about and struck the animal over the eye. It turned, ran up a stooping live oak tree and commenced biting the bark off. The young man summoned some neighbors and returned. He found the marks of the teeth on the tree and examined the tracks. They resembled a bear's track. The paws or hands resembled, so Henry says, a man's hand, only longer. He also says that the animal was covered over with dark brown hair.

Another young man, Ben Harrell, also saw the beast. Has any circus or menagerie lost any of the monkey tribe?

Biloxi, Mississippi, *Daily Herald,* May 19, 1901

CARRIED OFF A GIRL.

LAST DEPREDATION OF THE
"GREAT BEAR MAN" OF TEXAS.

A young lady out in Marble Falls, Tex., was carried off by a "bear man" and returned home unhurt to tell the tale.

The Kickapoo Indians of this region have long believed in a great "bear man" who rules all the bears of the mountains. Miss Ramie Arland, the heroine of this thrilling adventure, believes her encounter was with the chief bear himself.

Ramie Arland is a pretty girl and the acknowledged belle of Marble Falls. She has always been a skeptic as to the existence of the "bear man." The remarkable story she tells has, however, gone far to convince the most skeptical.

The "bear man" in this case ventured almost to the back door of the Arlands, says the San Francisco Chronicle. Ramie went out recently early one evening to gather her flock of sheep, which were grazing near by. This was a common occurrence and her absence was not noticed by the family until her mother heard her daughter scream wildly a short distance from the house. She rush to the door. The screams were repeated, but this time accompanied by the scream of a panther.

The mother seized a gun and rushed into the woods, but could find no trace of her daughter. She returned to the house and, collecting a hunting party, searched the woods all night. No trace of the missing girl could be found.

It was not until the next day that a hunter, wandering in the woods several miles from Marble Falls, found Ramie Arland aimlessly walking about. He helped her home where she quickly recovered from her experience.

"I was walking along a narrow trail," she says, in telling her story, "when a large black bear suddenly appeared in front of me. He quickly turned to run away, when a curious-looking animal, running on four feet, sprang out of the chaparral into the trail. I saw at a glance that the monster in some way resembled a human being, and it flashed across my mind that I was confronted by the 'bear king' of the Kickapoos. It threw one of its long arms about my neck, glared into my eyes, and uttered a horrible sound. I expected to be torn to fragments. The creature seized me and ran towards the mountains.

"It reached the cave at last and then left me lying on the ground. I tried to escape at once, but the creature struck me repeatedly on the head when I did so. I gave myself up for lost. Finally, however, he lay down to sleep. I waited fully an hour before attempting to steal away."

When the settlers and cowboys heard this strange story they at once set out in the direction of the Moon mountains for the purpose of destroying the monster.

It ground its teeth together, and, while pounding its breast, it would roar and scream like a panther. It was now so apparent to the hunters that the thing was at least human in shape that they hesitated to fire upon it. While they were deliberating it suddenly bounded with rage straight toward the astounded hunters. They were compelled to kill it in self-defense.

Both this last account and a second variation on this story were published in newspapers across the country. The second story (e.g., "Stolen by a Mexican man bear," Coudersport, Pennsylvania, *Potter Enterprise,* February 20, 1901) doesn't mention Marble Falls, rather indicating that this is a Mexican tale. Ramie Arland, it was initially said, "had made herself conspicuous as an unbeliever

ON THE BACK OF A BEAR MAN.

in the bear man." After Ramie disappeared, Mr. and Mrs. Arland searched for her, finally discovering she had been found wandering by a local man, Buck Seymore. Ramie said she had been taken by the creature to a cave it shared with an old bear with several cubs. She waited until they all fell asleep before escaping. (There is no mention of hunters finally killing the creature.) There are notable problems with either story, particularly in geography, so this is likely newspaper fiction rather than embellishment of an actual tale.

The following story appears to be outright plagiarism of the January 1902 Idaho "wild man" story published in the DESERET NEWS.

Ardmore, Texas, *Daily Ardmoreite,* February 11, 1902

WILD HAIRY MONSTER.

HUMAN IN SHAPE, EIGHT FEET TALL
ATTACKS A PLEASURE PARTY.

Austin, Tex., Feb. 10.—The residents west of the Colorado river between Mount Bonnell and Bee Cave, an almost isolated neighborhood known as Pantherpath, are greatly excited over the appearance in that vicinity of an eight-foot, hair-covered human monster. He was first seen yesterday afternoon when he appeared among a party of young people who were hunting and fishing on the river several miles above the site of Austin dam. The creature showed fight and flourished a large club, uttering a series of yells, started to attack the pleasure-seekers, who managed to reach their wagons and get away in safety. They declared that the monster followed them some distance, but finally abandoned the chase and disappeared in a large canyon.

Measurements of the tracks of the strange creature showed its feet to be twenty-two inches long and seven broad, with the imprint of only four toes on each foot. Hunters report having seen this track along the range south of the river several times, but declare that they were always at a loss to understand what kind of monster it could be.

A number of citizens residing in the vicinity where the creature was seen have organized a posse and are endeavoring to capture it, dead or alive.

Galveston, Texas, *Daily News,* September 16, 1903

A wild and hairy man has been seen near Red Bank in Trinity Bottom, in Kaufman County. Why not capture him and have him at the Texas State Fair?

Commerce, Texas, *Journal,* September 18, 1903

WILD MAN NEAR RED BANK.

Tall Negro, One-Eyed, Nude and Covered With Hair.

Terrell, Tex., Sept. 14.—It is reported that a wild man has been seen in the Trinity River bottom near Red Bank. He is described as being a tall negro, one-eyed, nude and hairy all over. When seen the wild man run and so did the party who saw him. The point where the stranger was seen is in the southern part of this county. The story of the wild man has had the effect, it is said, of keeping all negroes out of the bottoms.

Washington, D.C., *Post,* November 24, 1914

BABOON CAPTURED IN TEXAS

Animal Thought to Have Escaped from a Traveling Show

Temple (Tex.) Dispatch to Galveston News. While crossing Leon River about ten miles southwest of Temple, A. L. Miller, of this city, and a companion, L. W. Weaver, were attracted to a curious looking animal taking a drink from the stream. Closer investigation showed that it was a baboon, and the two men decided to attempt its capture. This they succeeded in doing after a severe struggle in which they suffered considerable damage to clothing and cuticle. The animal

was brought to Temple, where it is being confined. It is thought to have escaped from a
show that exhibited at Belton a short time ago.

Victoria, Texas, *Advocate,* February 23, 1926

QUEER ANIMAL THAT RUNS ON HIND LEGS REPORTED IN TEXAS

INTERNATIONAL NEWS SERVICE.

Austin, Texas, Feb. 23.—According to a letter
received by the State Oyster, Fish and Game
Commission from N. E. Stewart an animal
has been seen near Paradise that runs on its
hind legs, screams like a wildcat and is destroying stock.

Stewart's letter said a party was organized to hunt down the animal and it routed
the dogs and then attacked the hunters, who,
the letter says, "were lucky to escape with
their lives." Their clothes and flesh were
torn by the animal.

The letter was turned over to the snake king
of Brownsville, a dealer in wild animals, and
he is here today seeking further information.

San Antonio, Texas, *Light,* May 28, 1930

SEEK WEIRD BEAST IN HEIGHTS

Lurking in the wilds and caves of Olimos
creek valley in the vicinity of the West Texas
Military academy and the Jones-Maltzberger
road, a huge beast resembling a gorilla

which has eluded two searching parties after frightening workmen in a rock quarry four days ago, was the object of a third big game hunt Wednesday.

Parker Spence, assistant city marshal in Alamo Heights, and J. J. Caperton, San Antonio police officer, were preparing to lead the third expedition into the beast's hiding grounds.

The beast, which has been variously described by the several persons who saw it as being between four and five feet in height, was first seen Saturday in a rock quarry back of the West Texas Military academy.

Workmen Frightened.

A small group of Mexican workmen were digging in a cut-off wing of the Colglazier Hoff quarry when one of them, who was a little apart from the rest, looked up to see the shaggy giant, growling ferociously, waddling down the slope toward him.

The frightened workman screamed and ran toward the others, who all looked and saw the strange animal stop his lumbering gait, study them for a moment, and then whirl in his tracks and disappear into the brush which lines the quarry.

Spence, who is assistant to Paul Villaret, was notified and he and Caperton went to the scene Monday.

Sees Animal.

Caperton succeeded in seeing the animal, but the beast disappeared in the thick brush and was lost before the officer could fire. Spence, who was near, heard the sound of the animal as he raced through the thickly-grown little valley toward the high cliffs on the west side of the creek.

Jim Jiminez, who lives near the animal's lair, told authorities that he and his wife heard the blood-curdling cries early Wednesday.

The animal's tracks were found by Spence and Caperton. Bits of fur and bones of small animals in which the section abounds were also found by the searchers.

The two returned and searched the vicinity again Tuesday without success.

The third search was to be made Wednesday.

1933: Newspapers reported organized hunts for "modern day Tarzans," or long-haired, bearded wild men, living in the wild. One was in the wooded hills of the Bowie region, and another was along the Brazos river near DeWalt. Both cases appear more hermit-like than Bigfoot-related. ("Texas 'Tarzan' is living alone in cave," Port Arthur, Texas, *News*, February 9, 1933; "Hunt ape man in Brazos area," Mexia, Texas, *Weekly Herald*, April 7, 1933.)

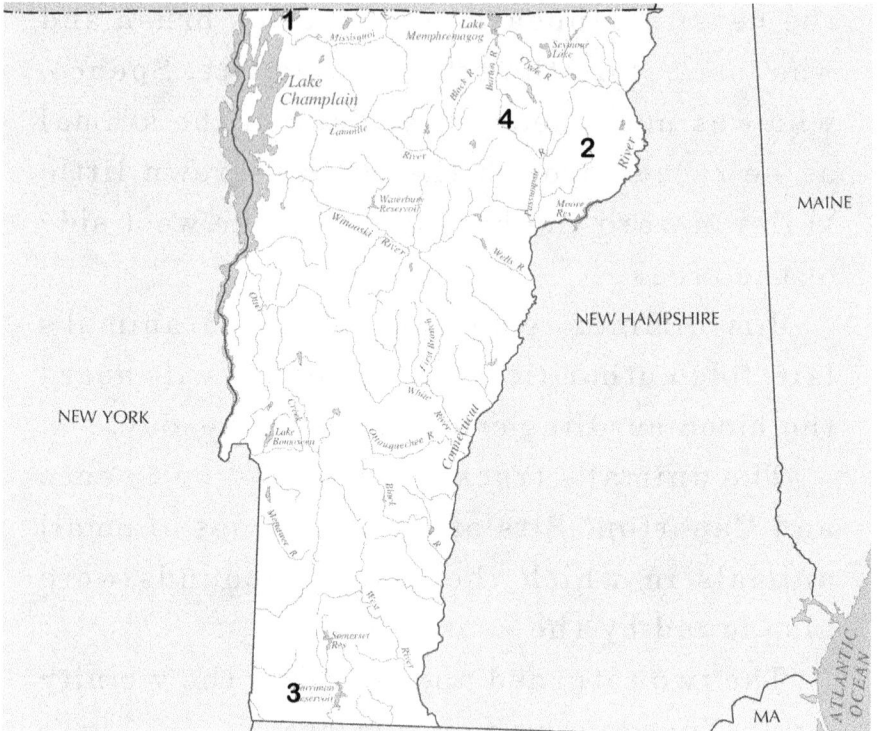

1 Missisquoi Bay

2 Victory, Lemington, Maidstone, and Morgan townships (Essex and Orleans Counties)

3 Stamford (Bennington County)

4 Stannard (Caledonia County)

Vermont

Rayno (1975) noted: "During the French and Indian War, in 1759, Major Robert Rogers and his Rangers left Crown Point, sailed up Champlain to 'Missisquoi Bay' and went overland to attack the Indian village at St. Francis. . . . Rogers and most of his men returned by way of the upper Connecticut River, but one small party, led by the scout 'Duluth,' came back the way they went. His account reads that as they made their way south from Missisquoi Bay, they 'were ever being annoyed, for naught reason, by a large black bear, who would throw large pine cones and nuts downe upon us from trees and leges; the Indians also bein disgusted, and knowe him, and call him Wejuk, or Wet Skine.'"

Rayno noted that "Wet Skin" became "Slippryskin," though Watt (1968) suggested that settlers referred to the creature as "Slippryskin" because it managed to elude every trap they set. Rayno noted that there are abundant records in early histories of Vemont, particularly in Victory, Lemington, Maidstone, and Morgan townships, of such a creature terrorizing the settlers. It "ripped up fences and gardens, chased cows and sheep, dragged trees through cornfields and other crops, threw stones at school children and terrified hunters. It robbed smoke-houses, pushed over haystacks, filled sap buckets with stones, placed barbed wire into hay-rakes and mowing machines, kicked over manure piles and dragged huge rocks into farm machinery which were almost impossible to remove." It was cunning, of enormous size, had legs like "spruce logs," and seemed to enjoy scaring people. It "always ran on his hind legs and never on all fours." It would backtrack its own prints in order to fool hunters. Vermont Governor Jonas Galusha ran for re-election by stating he would catch "old Slippryskin." Galusha doused himself with "scent of female bear," and stalked into the woods, only to return later at a run, with the creature on his heels. The hunting party scattered without a shot at the beast. Another hunting party from Morgan, Vermont, tried to track the animal, but found themselves ambushed as it rolled a huge tree stump down the mountain after them.

The following account was mistakenly given as being from Stamford, Connecticut, in certain newspapers.

St. Albans, Vermont, *Daily Messenger,* August 13, 1861

A STRANGE BEING.

The Bennington Banner gives an account of a mysterious being that is wandering about Stamford and vicinity. This strange creature was first discovered by Charles Wilbur, who, in company with two Pierce brothers, hearing strange yells in the woods, set out to discover their origin. They had not gone far before they encountered a creature all of six feet high, shaped like a man, and completely covered with long black hair from head to foot. One of the Pierce boys fired at the animal, but the shot fell far wide of its mark.— Being all frightened they ran with all their might for home.

One night a man was awoke by continued knocking at his door. He shouted to his visitor, who skulked off, and at a distance very much resembled the strange being. A berrying party was also put to flight, as also was a school mistress in Pownal. Sixteen men gave the creature chase, and one of them overtaking him was so paralyzed at the sight as to keep him from attempting his capture. It is also said that a small cave has been found, thought to be the abode of the creature, and bones found thereabouts are to be sent to

Amherst and Williams College for examination. Quite a number of sheep are missing in the mountain pastures, and some of the farmers say their cows have been milked in the night-time by some unknown person.

The *Banner* says many treat the matter as a humbug, but considering the number of persons who tell the story, it is inclined to believe it. We should think a few "sharp shooters" might find out the mystery without much trouble. The experiment at any rate is worth trying.

Worcester, Massachusetts, *Massachusetts Spy,* August 14, 1861

Was It a Gorilla?—A Sportsman Astonished.—De Chaillu is wanted in this country just now, to ascertain whether the woods near Stamford, Conn., are inhabited by his famous gorillas. One day last week, while Mr. Cortis Wilbur, a sporting citizen of Stamford, was hunting in the aforesaid woods, he came suddenly upon what he supposed to be a large animal, digging roots. Carefully raising his gun, he took steady aim, and pulled trigger, but the weapon missed fire; whereupon the said animal straightened up, to the size and stature of a seven foot man, covered from head to foot with matted hair, and, with an unearthly yell darted deep into the woods, at a speed more than human. As soon as Wilbur recovered from the shock inflicted upon his nerves by the horrible apparition, he turned toward home, and made for the bosom of his family at double-quick, convinced it was a gorilla or the devil. His story was quickly bandied from mouth to mouth; and on the following day, several who had heard strange cries from the woods, during the night, volunteered to lead a party in pursuit of the wild man. A party was quickly made up; and, with Wilbur as a guide, they started on their errand—taking guns for protection, in case the sylvan gentleman should prove to be a secessionist. They soon discovered footprints similar to those left by a man's bare feet, which led directly from the place where the hunter had first seen the strange creature to a very dense thicket. All search for the "gorilla," however, proved useless; though they could distinctly hear its yells in response to their shouts. The matter-of-fact people in the vicinity believe the "gorilla" to be nothing more than a poor lunatic; and the authorities have taken measures to lure him from his forest fastnesses, and return him to his keepers.

Montpelier, Vermont, *Green Mountain Freeman,* August 17, 1861

It seems that "the wild man of the woods," whose appearance has created so much consternation in this State, turns out to be a student at Williamstown, Mass., who assumed the gorilla guise in a frolic which might have cost him his life. He was pursued with guns, but so frightened his pursuers by his hideous appearance that they could not shoot straight, and he escaped harm.

St. Johnsbury, Vermont, *Caledonian,* November 2, 1877
STANNARD.

A Wild Man—or Story.—Quite an excitement was created the first of the week by the report that a wild man had been seen in town. The story is told that Amasa Hutchins and wife went to church and left two boys at home. They soon became uneasy and went into the field to amuse themselves, and while jumping and rolling, a strange object came out of the woods and began to imitate their movements, which frightened them so much that they ran to Mr. Low's near by and got him and his hired man to go in pursuit. They returned to the place where he had disappeared, but searched in vain for some time, but while standing near a fallen tree, he leaped out from beneath it giving an unearthly yell, leaping twenty or thirty feet into the bushes, and was lost to sight. They describe him as three or four feet high and covered with hair, while the hair on his head was fire red and hung over his shoulders. [Our readers may believe just as much of the above story as they please; as for us—well, please excuse us.]

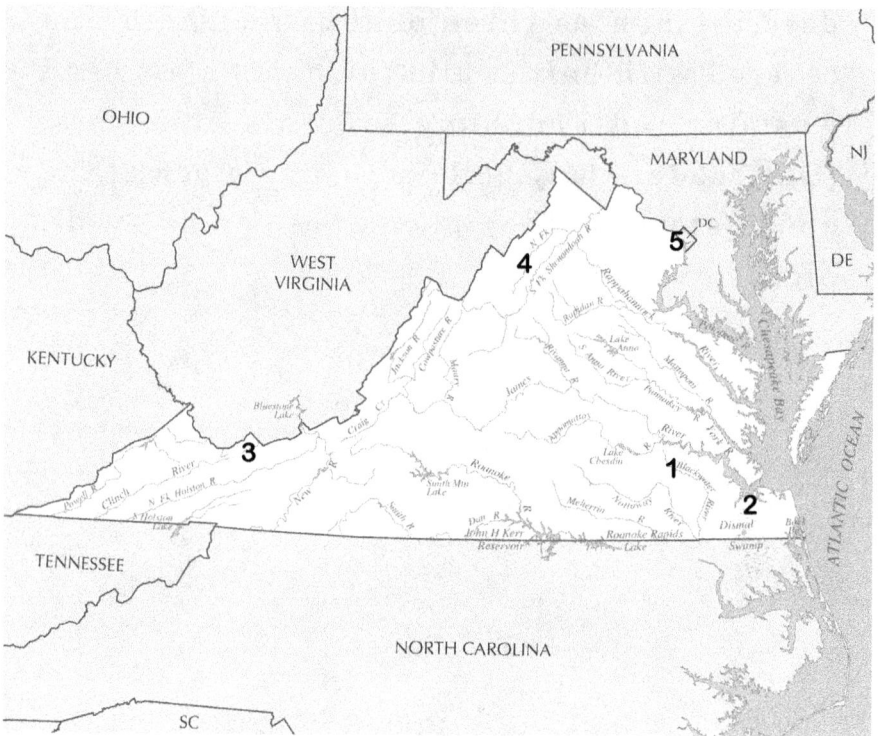

1 Petersburg

2 Cradock (Portsmouth)

3 Boissevan (Tazewell County)

4 Luray (Page County)

5 Arlington (Arlington County)

Virginia

Louisville, Kentucky, *Courier Journal*, September 22, 1882

The Petersburg (Va.) Index-Appeal tells of a strange animal, half man and half sheep in appearance, and which walks as well on its hind legs as on all fours, that is frightening the natives in the country adjacent to Petersburg.

Wise (1911): "'The Bogey of Cradock Marsh,' is one of the earliest traditions, and is to-day one of the best known. This bogey, whatever it may be, whether man or beast, has been sought by armed hunting parties for several centuries. By day and by torchlight, its trail of foot-tracks has been followed only to be lost as the weird cry of 'Yahoo! Yahoo!' resounds through the dismal wastes of marsh to warn the curious of the futility of their quest, and to make the blood of the half-hearted searchers run cold."

Beckley, West Virginia, *Raleigh Register*, December 16, 1921

THE APE ABROAD AGAIN

Readers will recall the stories circulated last

winter of the appearance of an ape or other strange wild creature of the woods in some sections of the country. A Pocahontas, Va., boy starts a tale of having seen a new terror of the woods. The Pocahontas lad is said to have been considerably frightened when an unknown monster followed his trail thru the darkness of the night in the vicinity of Boissevan, and a correspondent of the Graham, Va., News expresses the belief and fear that this dangerous ape is back in our midst and warning is issued to hunters and night travelers to be on the lookout for the animal. The theory has been advanced, by some that the animal may have been summering in one of the abandoned manganese mines near Tip Top and has only recently come out into the open to terrorize the community, and send that creepy feeling down the spinal column of those unfortunate enough to cross its shadow during the stillness of the night.—W. Va., *News*.

Richmond, Virginia, *Times Dispatch,* November 26, 1925

BLUE RIDGE CITIZENS
TERRORIZED BY BEAST
[SPECIAL TO THE TIMES-DISPATCH.]

Luray, Va., Nov. 25.—A wild animal—possibly an ape or gorilla—supposed to have recently escaped from a circus near the line between this state and West Virginia, has been causing consternation to citizens living in the Blue Ridge of this and Madison Counties. The animal was recently seen ear what is known as "Dark Hollow," a wild and isolated section of the Blue Ridge, eighteen miles southeast of Luray. It has brought trouble to men, women, boys and girls. So far only a few have gotten a glimpse of the untamed animal. Hurley and Peter Mallory, of Madison County, recently encountered the animal when they went to their rabbit boxes a few mornings ago. This was the best glimpse gotten of the animal in that county, though Brooking Smith, of that county, two days after the Mallory boys had had their experience, saw the ape or gorilla in the barnyard of G. N. Thrift.

Baltimore, Maryland, *Sun,* June 3, 1949

APELIKE BEAST HUNTED
AFTER DOG IS MANGLED

Arlington, Va., June 2 (AP)—A wild, apelike animal, believed to have mangled a pet dog to death Tuesday night, is being sought by Arlington police.

The dog belonged to Mrs. J. Krug McCloskey. Residents of the area in which the dog

1008 THE HISTORICAL BIGFOOT

was attacked said the animal has been seen several times.

William Holt told police he saw the beast about three weeks ago. He described it as about waist high and running on its hind legs.

Washington

1840: Elkanah Walker, missionary, wrote a letter mentioning nocturnal giants (Green 1978; Byrne 1976) reported by the Spokane Indians. These giants were said to kidnap people—"They come to the people's lodges in the night when people are asleep and take them, and put them under their skins and take them to their place of abode without even waking." Their track was about 18 inches long, and they could "carry two or three beams upon their back at once." They would steal salmon, eating the fish raw. They had a strong, intolerable smell, whistled in the night, and threw stones at the peoples' homes.

1800s: Green (1978) noted a brief sighting by "Grandpa Ducheney" near Mount St. Helens.

1847: Hunter and Dahinden (1973) noted that early explorer and artist Paul Kane logged in his journal for March 26 that there were Native American stories of cannibalistic "skoocooms" living on Mt. St. Helens.

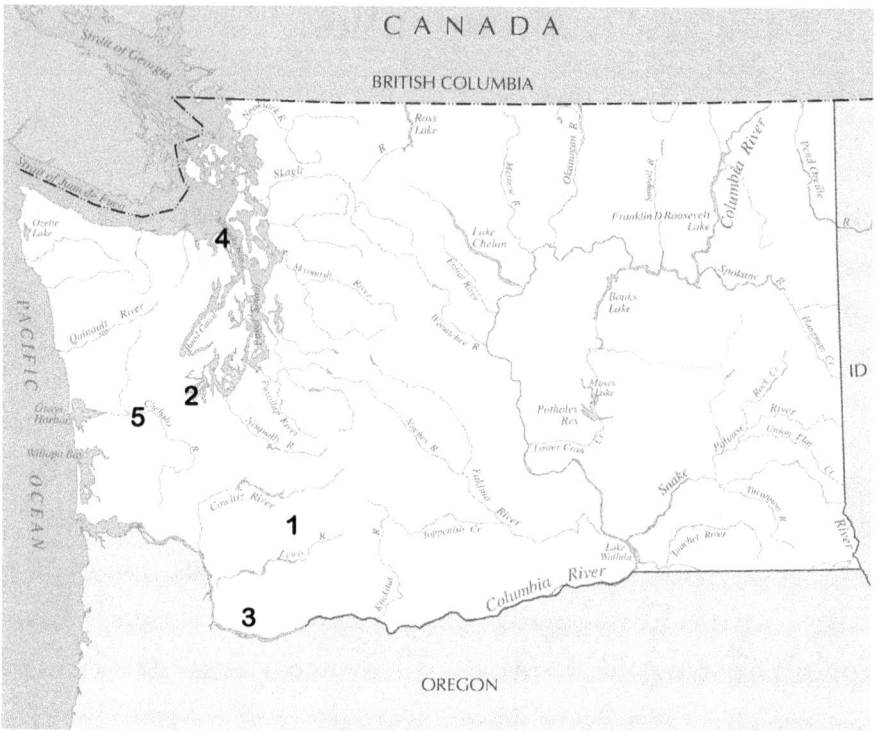

1 Mount St. Helens

2 Olympia (Thurston County)

3 Vancouver (Clark County)

4 Port Townsend (Jefferson County)

5 Oakville (Grays Harbor County)

Portland, Oregon, *Oregonian*, November 11, 1876

R. W. Hall writes as follows to the *Echo* concerning what is called a "mysterious wild person" in the woods near Olympia. Mr. Hall says: "On Saturday, the 4th of November, while I was rowing a boat up Woodward's Bay—which is a branch of South Bay—I saw that something was moving the grass on the beach. Its back, covered with light hair about one inch and a half long, was in sight. I thought it was a fox or coon. The tide was high, and I turned my boat toward the bank. As I neared the shore, and laid down one oar, preparatory to striking the animal with the other, it stood erect, like a man, and looked at me a moment over its shoulder. I was surprised and dropped my oar in amazement. Its body was covered with light, short hair, while longer and lighter tresses hung heavily from its head. Its arms were quite small; lower limbs strong and muscular; stood about three feet high; and face like a child's, with piercing, light blue eyes. It sprang into the brush, jumped over a log, and hid. I found it, and stood within a few feet of it, wondering how to make its capture. Without turning its eyes from me, the strange creature laid under the log till my hands were within a few inches of its body, then it passed under the tree and ran away with such speed that I could not keep it in view. I am sure that it is a white person—young or old; and while its visage is impressed upon my memory, I shall never, never, believe that it is anything else." Indians say the same object has been seen by them twice before.

Albany, Oregon, *Evening Herald,* August 11, 1923

MYSTERIOUS FOOTPRINTS
ARE SOLVED AT VANCOUVER

Vancouver, Wash., Aug. 11.—Mysterious footprints which have terrorized residents in the eastern part of the county, have been identified. Frank Cashmer, believed inane, is under arrest as a "wild man" of the woods. He had wrapped bandages around each toe and instep, leaving footprints resembling those of a grotesque animal.

Portland, Oregon, *Oregonian,* July 13, 1924 (from Green 1978)

FIGHT WITH BIG APES
REPORTED BY MINERS

FABLED BEASTS ARE SAID TO
HAVE BOMBARDED CABIN
ONE OF ANIMALS, SAID TO APPEAR LIKE
HUGE GORILLA, IS KILLED BY PARTY

Kelso, Wash., July 12—(Special) The strangest story to come from the Cascade mountains was brought to Kelso today by Marion Smith, his son Roy Smith, Fred Beck, Gabe Lefever and John Peterson, who encountered the fabled "mountain devils" or mountain gorillas of Mount St. Helens this week, shooting one of them and being attacked throughout the night by rock bombardments of the beasts.

The men had been prospecting a claim on the Muddy, a branch of the Lewis River about eight miles from Spirit Lake, 46 miles from Castle Rock. They declared that they saw four of the huge animals, which were about 400 pounds and walked erect. Smith and his companions declared that they had seen the tracks of the animals several times in the last six years and Indians have told of the "mountain devils" for 60 years, But none of the animals ever has been seen before.

Smith met with one of the animals and fired at it with a revolver, he said. Thursday Fred Beck, it is said, shot one, the body falling over a precipice. That night the animals bombarded the cabin where the men were stopping with showers of rocks, many of them large ones, knocking chunks out of the log cabin, according to the prospectors. Many of the rocks fell through a hole in the roof and two of the rocks struck Beck, one of them rendering him unconscious for nearly two hours.

The animals were said to have the appearance of huge gorillas. They are covered with long, black hair. Their ears are about four inches long and stick straight up. They have four toes, short and stubby. The tracks are 13 to 14 inches long. These tracks have been seen by forest rangers and prospectors for years.

The prospectors built a new cabin this year and it is believed it is close to the cave thought to be occupied by the animals. Mr. Smith believes he knows the location of the cave.

Modesto, California, *Evening News,* July 14, 1924

POSSES SEARCH FOR 'MOUNTAIN DEVILS'

Kelso, Wash., July 11.—Led by Forest Ranger C. Parker, an expedition started from here this morning into the heart of the Spirit Lake country to search for the 'mountain devils," a hand of giant gorillas which five badly-frightened prospectors said had chased them from the woods after an intermittent three-day battle.

With Parker are Frank Helm and F. S. Bailey.

The men are armed for big game and also carry photographic equipment.

The prospectors, all veterans of this district, are Marion and Roy Smith, J. Peterson and Fred Beck. According to their story, they were attacked several times by the weird beasts, succeeded in killing one and wounding several, and finally fled from the woods themselves after they had been held prisoners an entire night by a cordon of thirty gorillas.

According to the men, their cabin was bombarded with heavy rocks throughout the night. More than 200 rocks crashed through the roof to the floor of the shack, they asserted.

Modesto, California, *Evening News,* July 15, 1924

SAYS STORY OF 'DEVILS' IS ALL BUNK

Woodland, Wa., July 15.—Deputy Game Warden Justus Murk, who has spent 20 years in the Spirit Lake district, where the "mountain devils," or gorilla like animals were reported in having attacked a prospecting party, terms the reported discovery as "all bunk." Murk said he has never seen signs of such animals nor has he ever heard of them.

Stick to Story

Kelso, Wa., July 15.— "We expected that people would disbelieve us. But we ran into the beast—whatever it was—four times and finally packed up and left a perfectly good mine to get away from it."

This is the statement today by Roy Smith, Fred Beck and Gabe LeFevre, three of the party of five prospectors whose reported encounters with the "mountain devils," gorrillas, or wild men of Spirit lake has already sent an investigating expeditionary force up the slopes of Mount St. Helens.

Beck denied the reports that were current here of spiritualistic seances held by the prospectors during the long winter evenings in their cabin.

He had, however, seen the "mountain devil," he declared, on four different occasions.

It was about July 1, Beck says—it's hard for a prospector to keep track of the exact date—when he and Marion Smith had gone to the springs for water. Smith was walking ahead on the trail and as they came to a precipitous pitch Beck stood on the edge while Smith descended.

As he stood on top of the slope Beck saw a huge black shape moving among the trees on the opposite side of the canyon, but sixty feet away.

"Look, there is the thing," Beck called to Smith, and raising his gun, fired. The "mountain devil" dodged behind a tree and stared at the two men, only its huge head in sight. The flatnosed face was surrounded by an encircling halo of black hair, mixed with white, and the ears were huge, capped and pointed, said Beck today, in giving the impression he had received of the beast at the first encounter.

None of the prospectors seemed perturbed because of the scoffing with which the tale had been received, as the prospectors themselves had scouted the same stories as they have heard them during the past fifteen years.

Spirit lake, the asserted habitat of the "devils," got its name from the old Indian legends which placed the "devils" there.

Modesto, California, *Evening News,* July 16, 1924

HUNT MOUNTAIN 'DEVILS' IN WASHINGTON

Kelso, Wash., July 16—Although no report has been received from the expeditionary force which Monday went into the hills to hunt the "mountain devils," individuals who returned today from trips to the cabin of the five prospectors partially confirm the story of the members of the Smith-Beck party, who claimed to have been bombarded with big rocks hurled into their cabin during the night, supposedly by the "hairy apes."

The rocks are still inside the cabin, according to these returned investigators, but no footprints of mysterious men or beasts were to be found in the vicinity.

Four new expeditions have outfitted and are on their way to Spirit Lake today. One is composed of local hunters, two other parties . . . , while Chief of Police George Miller of Kelso and County Game Warden Chester Leichhardt have taken their families for an outing and while there will try to find traces of the "mountain devils."

Bismarck, North Dakota, *Tribune,* July 17, 1924

TRIBE OF "APE INDIANS" REPORTED FOUND IN PACIFIC NORTHWEST

SEVERAL PARTIES LEAVE IN SEARCH OF VERIFICATION OF EXISTENCE OF TRIBE IN WILDERNESS WHO ATTACKED BAND OF PROSPECTORS

Kelso, Washington, July 17 (By the AP)— While awaiting reports from parties who have gone to the vicinity of Spirit Lake on Mount St. Helens, in quest of verification of a story told by trappers that they encountered a band of ape men there last week, residents today were interested in statements attributed to George Totsgi of the Clallam Indian tribe that ape men are members of a tribe of Indians known as the Seeahtik tribe.

The trappers reported their cabin was bombarded by the ape men during the night. Totsgi was quoted as saying that members of the Seeahtik tribe are huge in stature. These Indians, he said, talked the Clallam language and are adept at imitating the sounds of birds.

The Seeahtik were last heard of by the Clallam Indians about 15 years ago and it was believed by the present Indians that they had become extinct, said Totsgi.

"The Seeahtiks made their home in the heart of the wilderness on Vancouver Island and on the Olympic range."

Totsgi declared that his tale had been corroborated by Henry Napolean, Clallam tribe, who met one of the Seeahtik Indians while hunting on Vancouver Island recently.

Although no reports have been received from several parties who left here to search for the Indians Monday, individuals who returned today from the cabins of the five prospectors partially confirmed the story of being bombarded by rocks in their cabin by "mountain devils." Rocks were found inside the cabin. No tracks were discovered, however.

Oakland, California, *Tribune,* July 17, 1924

RANGERS REPORT NO 'GORILLA MEN' ATTACKED MINERS

Kelso, Wash., July 17.—The story of the seven-foot tall "Gorilla men," who last week, it is related attacked Marion Smith and his party of gold hunters from Kelso and routed them from their cabin in the mountains near here, today is declared a myth.

Two of Uncle Sam's forest rangers, J. H. Huffman and W. M. Welch, after a personal investigation at the scene of the reported activities of the "ape men," told a Post-Intelligencer staff correspondent that they had found nothing whatever to substantiate the prospector's tale.

True, they found a purported foot print of one of the "animals." Huffman, however, with his knuckles and palm of his right hand, duplicated the imprint perfectly with the statement: "They were made that way."

Welch, accompanied by Fred Beck, one of the members of the prospecting party, went to the edge of the abyss into which one of the "gorillas" is said to have toppled when wounded by one of the party. The ranger scrambled down into the supposedly inaccessible canyon and found—nothing.

Chehalis, Washington, *Bee Nugget,* July 18, 1924

GORILLA STORY RECALLS ONE

The weird story related by the party of Kelso hunters who claim to have seen and combated a drove of huge gorillas near Mt. St. Helens recently has nothing on a fascinating tale brought into Chehalis 24 years ago by a man named J. S. Forrest. The latter's remarkable find was a mysterious cave which he claimed he had discovered by chance, also near Mount St. Helens, the contents of which outrivaled the wonderful beauties and belongings that had been described in the story "King Solomon's Mines," from a careful reading of which doubtless he had become obsessed. . . .

Referring back to the gorilla story, there are a number of men in Chehalis who thirty years ago and since prospected all through the St. Helens section looking for gold. One man who spent twelve summers there and has visited the place since and who knows the district like a book jokingly regards the story of the Kelso men. As the farmer said, when looking at the giraffe, he remarks, "Oh, hell, there ain't no such animals" there or thereabouts.

Bridgeport, Connecticut, *Telegram,* September 2, 1924

MAN AND SUPERNATURAL
LINKED IN INDIAN LEGEND
OF NUNG-NUNGS

Some persons confess they never board a train or a ship—however dull their errand—without feeling that they are embarking on high adventure, Wallace Smith explains in the New York Times.

But prosaic trains reach their destination approximately in time for the snappy business appointment. Ships sidle to their docks and the tourist agent clucks his excited charges under his wing.

We have just been on a gorilla hunt and wild Indian chase in the Spirit Lake country in Washington. It is not our fault that our overcoats will not have collars of gorilla fur this winter or that no ruddy scalp dries on the lodge pole of our wicki-up. Nor can we be justly blamed that this modern record has not a fitting climax.

The hunt began with the story of three prospectors who rode excitedly into Kelso and swore they had been attacked in their Spirit Lake cabin by gorillas seven feet tall, that beat their breasts and tossed rocks through the roof of the shack. The gorillas only quit, the prospectors declared, after one of them had been shot and pitched over a 300-foot precipice.

The story of the prospectors was a sensation. For many days one of the most conservative newspapers in the Pacific Northwest carried front-page columns of it—telegraph dispatches, bulletins, interviews and, of course, letters to the editor. War correspondents hurried to the Spirit Lake front. The gorillas became ten feet tall and extremely hairy. Then they changed into the posterity of an old Indian bad man driven into the hills almost a century ago.

Maverick Tod's unconcerned familiarity with the mystery that had aroused the countryside excited a patter of questions from us. But he leisurely rolled a brown paper "cigareet," dragged slow, thoughtful puffs from it and forecast more rain before he answered our curiosity.

Tale of the Nung-Nungs

"I can orate on this here subject eloquent because not only do I hole up a whole winter with the Ogallalas but I get this Indian lore and pastimes sawed off on me by Nisqually Joe, which is an Indian of the Squallymish tribe who reforms and gives up his evil ways and gets to be top roper on the old Big Spade Ranch. And a very good amigo of mine.

"Myself, I do not warm up regardless to Indian legends since that time a lost and unregenerate Sioux traded me the secret of a lost gold mine for two iron pesos and a quart o' liquor. But Nisqually Joe is a different Indian that way and you can trust him, at least as far as you can throw a chuck-wagon. Which is further than I trust the ordinary buck by exactly one chuck-wagon.

"Well, sir, accordin' to what Nisqually Joe tells me in them good old days, these prospectors actually seen like they claim. Only what they put down for gorillas ain't gorillas, at all, but only Nung-Nungs. Yes, sir, Nung-Nungs is what these were—although sometimes the Indians also call them Tyapish or even See-Ah-Tiks. Which is their business and whatever's in a name anyway, like this here feller Shakespear says.

"For that matter, these Nung-Nungs also are called Brothers of the Noseless. One and that's where old Shakespeare is high-carded outen that wise riddle he makes up. Because when an Indian says you are kin to the Noseless One he is gettin' personal and definite a heap in his simple, aboriginal way.

"Anyway, this is a plumb natural mistake these prospectors make in the dark, bein' unable to read brands or ear-notches at that hour. These here Nung-Nungs stand a average of about eight feet high. They run as high as ten and young ones grade down to seven. Also, they are hairy like the front end of a buffalo or a sheepherder before the spring chinook.

An Ingrown Resentment.

"Indians lay it down were the Nung-Nungs are the result of an all-wise Providence gettin' a little absent-minded about second-drink time in the afternoon. When changin' animals into Indians, Providence falters a whole lot with the Nung-Nung ancestors and they are left kind of betwixt and between, like a lawyer's argument. Which makes them very low-grade and other Indians don't send them no invitation when the tribe throws a roast dog banquet or a quadrille.

"This makes the Nung-Nungs some resentful and onery till you can't rest. They go in for low practical jokes to get even—so low that it makes even a Indian blush like a can of tomatoes to talk about 'em.

"Otherwise, the Nung-Nungs crave to be left alone by theirselves a whole lot. Now and then some Indian made valorous a heap by a pint of vintage bay rum, will start on the trail of a Nung-Nung which he figures had done him wrong, like runnin' off with his squaw, or somethin'. One of these braves went after a Nung-Nung which he suspicioned was monkeying around his pet bear-trap. He crossed the Nung-Nung's trail. The Nung-Nung was toting the bear trap under one arm and a bear under the other. The Indian trapper decided not to molest the Nung-Nung any, but went home and resolved to lead a better life.

"Sometimes the Nung-Nungs are very sentimental. Like they always leave a twig of cedar on whatever party whose mortal coil they have shoved off. Although it's hard to figure where they find enough of the deceased's remains to decorate this way because their method of imparting death is sure thorough and devastating and guaranteed to scatter the late lamented over ten acres.

"The Nung-Nungs got one other fetchin' habit. If one of 'em is killed or hurt or even his feelings ruffled, a round dozen Indians got to be pointed over the High Divide to comfort the Nung-Nung tribe. Last time this happened the Nung-Nungs got plumb hostile toward the Dowamish tribe because a Dowamish had murmured a complaint where his squaw had been stole."

Late 1920s: Green (1978) collected a report from Jim Attwell, who found a series of unusual bare foot tracks near Port Townsend. They emerged from heavy timber to follow an exposed water main. While the stride was not overly large, the agility and a great leap seen in the trackway greatly impressed the witness.

Klamath Falls, Oregon, *Evening Herald,* August 7, 1926

> A fifteen-foot monster with a head like a sheep is reported to be terrorizing natives in the vicinity of Okanogan Lake, British Columbia. The Eugene Guard suggests an expedition of Cowlitz county hairy ape-men to be organized to get the varmint.

1933: Green (1978) collected a report from Mrs. Callie Lund. She stated that, as a young girl on a ranch in Oakville, she heard strange cries that her mother identified as coming from an apelike creature. Her mother had seen the animal back in 1912, but had been ridiculed after telling her family, so had not mentioned it again until that last incident.

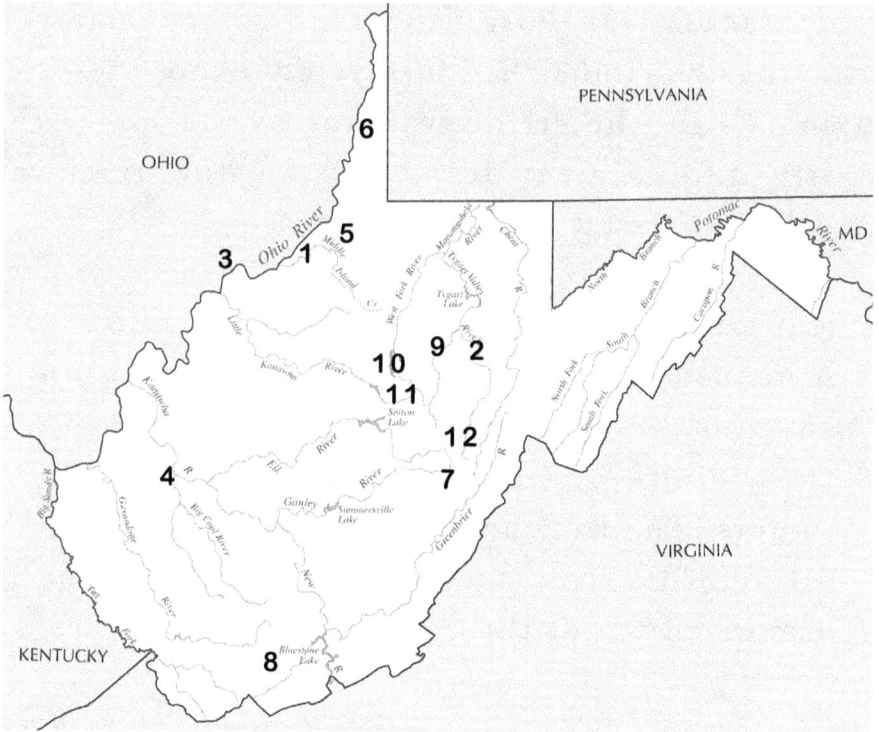

1 Calcutta (Pleasants County)

2 Elkins (Randolph County)

3 Gravel Bank, Ohio

4 Charleston (Kanawha County)

5 Tyler County

6 Roney's Point (Ohio County)

7 Black Mountain

8 Flat Top Mountain

9 Tenmile (Upshur County)

10 Falls Mills (Braxton County)

11 Diana (Webster County)

12 Gauley Mountain

West Virginia

Leadville, Colorado, *Daily Herald,* March 19, 1884

A desperate-looking creature, supposed to be a wild man of the forest, is terrifying the citizens of and around Calcutta, [W.] Va. The animal, or whatever it is, is described as tall as an ordinary-sized man, stands erect, and is covered with long, shaggy hair. The "missing link" was seen, it is claimed, by two men who were out hunting a short time ago, in the vicinity of a high bluff, where they were startled by hearing a peculiar, screaming noise, and on turning around they were horrified by seeing a monstrous looking object, that resembled both man and gorilla, rush out from a cleft in the bluff. The animal with its glaring eyes surveyed the terror-stricken men for a second, and then, with a wild scream, darted off into the woods at a frightful speed. One of the hunters, taking courage from the monstrosity's flight, shot and hit the object in the arm, whereupon the savage creature turned on the men and began pursuing them. Both hunters fled at the approach of the creature, who pursued them until the end of the woods was reached, when it suddenly turned and retraced its steps to the interior of the forest.

Clarksburg, West Virginia, *Telegram,* June 18, 1897

Some farmers near Elkins have seen a wild woman in the woods. She leaps fences like a deer, and at night can be heard making the most hideous noises.

Cumberland, Maryland, *Evening Times*, July 15, 1920

APE CROSSES RIVER
INTO WEST VIRGINIA

Parkersburg, W. Va., July 15.—Here's some more ape information. Two fellows started on an expedition yesterday to Gravel Bank, Ohio, where the famous ape hangs out and here's the story they brought back. On their way to Gravel Bank they stopped a man in a machine to ask him for a lift. The man started talking about the ape and said that while he was on his way from Marietta Sunday night he was passing the thicket at Gravel Bank when suddenly an ape ran across the road in front of his machine. He stopped and saw the ape run up a hill and disappear in the woods. The two ape hunters then decided not to go any further and started through a wheat field. They came to a group of oil men who were drilling a well. The men said they saw the ape on the West Virginia side Saturday evening and when they walked towards it, it disappeared in a thicket. They said the ape was a large one, bigger than an ordinary man.

The story sounds kind 'o fishy but it came from reliable sources. The parties that went up yesterday are going to explore the thicket and a newspaper man is going with them to see if all the stuff that has been spread about the ape is true.

Charleston, West Virginia, *Daily Mail*, August 1, 1920

APE VISITS THE CITY

An ape, believed to have escaped from a circus, has been seen several times in the surrounding community. Last Tuesday night the ape visited the homes near the depot and it is thought that he came as far as the schoolhouse on Sixth Street.

Syracuse, New York, *Herald*, August 18, 1920

ANIMAL, THOUGHT APE, ATTACKS BOY OF 9

Sisterville, W. Va., Aug. 18.—A mysterious animal described as an ape has been terrorizing Tyler county for ten days and although searching parties have scoured the hills since its first appearance. It is still at large.

The animal of mystery has been seen a score of times. It attacked a boy, 9, on a lonely trail half a mile from his home.

Charleston, West Virginia, *Daily Mail*, August 29, 1920

Wheeling—The full-grown ape which is supposed to have escaped from the Cincinnati Zoo, and which was last heard of on the river road north of New Martinsvllle, heading this way, was seen crossing the National Road just beyond Roneys Point. An automobile owned by J. W. Neidhart, of 604 Main street, and occupied by some ladies and children, was being driven along the road in this section when they saw the strange animal leap down from the B. & O. tracks, jump over the street car tracks and cross the road, disappearing into the bush beyond.

Shepherdstown, West Virginia, *Register*, October 28, 1920

THE HORROR OF THE WOODS

Following the accounts that have persisted for some months the ape, babboon, gorilla, wild man, or terror that has been reported at various points from Pittsburg south, has appeared and taken his habitation in the dismal fastness of Black Mountain and there is something approaching a panic in that part of the county, to say nothing of the fearsome thing appealing strongly to the imagination of every school child in this city. Those who wander through the beautiful woods surrounding this town are not wholly at ease by reason of the reports that come in.

We have made some investigation and we hear that a hunter saw the beast some weeks ago in a blackberry patch on Black Mountain near the mouth of Day's Run. He makes no mystery about it, and says that it is no more or less than some apelike animal escaped from a show and that it has been hanging around the bountiful berry patches of Williams River for food. He does not seem to have been particularly afraid of it, and succeeded in finding its nest and he said that the beast had collected a lot of railway spikes from the old abandoned railroad at the Campbell Lumber Company.

This carries out the theory of a half tame gorilla.

The next clear sight of the animal was by a woman who lives near the mouth of Day's Run and she had a bad scare. She was a distance from her house and the thing pursued her. She ran home and slammed the door in its face and called on two watch dogs to drive the brute off. The animal waited until the dogs came up and seized and choked them to death one after the other in a few moments.

Repeated calls have come from that section for the State Police to come and capture or kill it. The appeal has even reached Elkins, the headquarters of the force stationed in this part of the State. The local force is preparing to go to the mouth of Day's Run to investigate the matter one day this week.—Pocahontas Times.

Bluefield, West Virginia, *Daily Telegraph,* December 14, 1920
BIG APE AT LARGE.

Citizens of Flat Top Mountain section report a big ape at large in that section, and if we can get the gorilla over in East River Mountain by Christmas, there will be something going on. Eb. Houtchins, a telegraph operator, saw the animal the other day and shot at it, but the ape made its getaway and disappeared down the railroad track. Both the Alderson Advertiser and the Monroe Watchman carry stories of the ape, and it is entirely probable the stranger may decide to ford or swim New River and make its way into East River Mountain, where a warm reception will await the thing.

Charleston, West Virginia, *Daily Mail*, July 16, 1923

TYLER COUNTY APE
NOW HAS A FAMILY

Sistersville, July 16.—The Tyler county ape story, buried two years ago, has been revived. The mysterious brute which stalked through dark spaces in the wilder sections of West Virginia, Ohio and Pennsylvania, is still stalking, two local citizens say.

The yarn comes from the heart of Tyler county, in the region of Muddy creek. Two men, C. C. Clarke and John Ferrell, of the Manufacturers Light and Heat company, saw the sight which made their hair stand on end and declare the story is "gospel" true.

Clarke and Ferrell told how they were rigging up a bailing machine at a well close to a thicket. Suddenly their attention was attracted to the edge of a precipice by frenzied screams. The men looked. They saw a mother ape with six little ones clinging to her side while in her mouth was another dangling over the edge of the cliff.

Dropping their tools and shutting down the well, the men ran. They ran until they reached their foreman, M. G. Sherwood. With James Henderson as their leader, a posse was formed and went in search of the ape. No trace of the animal could be found, however, but footprints were in evidence on top of the cliff.

Latest reports from the posse are that the ape is still evading capture.

Uniontown, Pennsylvania, *Morning Herald*, September 2, 1925

OFFERS REWARD FOR
CAPTURE OF HUGE APE ALIVE

Buckhannon, W. Va., Sept. 1.—A reward of $250 was offered today by R. S. Reid, newspaper editor, for the capture of an ape that has been frightening residents of Ten Mile, Hesper and Sago near here. The offer states that the animal must be taken alive.

The ape was reported at large several weeks ago in the southern part of Upshur county and recently was seen near Ten Mile. The animal is said to be as large as a small man and has been encountered frequently in orchards eating fruit.

Charleston, West Virginia, *Gazette,* September 6, 1925

[BUCKHANNON:] The report last week that a wild ape was roaming the country near the Wesleyan camp proved to be an exciting subject for the footballers; but when a party was suggested to be formed including some of the squad, to capture the ape, Coach Russ put an end to the monkey business.

Bluefield, West Virginia, *Daily Telegraph*, February 25, 1933

OTHERS SPY TRACK OF
STRANGE WILD BEAST

The presence of some unidentified powerful wild animal in the Falls Mills and Mudfork section is no joke, avers Fred Green and his mother, Mrs. H. A. Green, of Falls Mills, who were here to attend the George Washington celebration Thursday evening. Mr. Green is among those who have seen the animal's track, but like Mr. Hereford and others, Mr. Green is puzzled over the identity of the beast, but believes it to be a prowling gorilla, perhaps lost from a circus and living in this section.

The animal appears to have a liking for crossing fallen trees, where its track have been seen in several places.

The track is described as about as large as a man's foot that would require a No. 10 shoe, with a peculiar looking heel, similar to the ape or gorilla.

The strange track was first seen during the recent snow, when it was plainly visible.

Bluefield, West Virginia, *Daily Telegraph*, February 26, 1933

STRANGE ANIMAL
ROAMING SECTION

That the strange animal roaming the Falls Mills-Mudfork section could possibly be a

stray vicuna, is one suggestion that comes
from a prominent Falls Mill woman, who
[has] been hearing and reading of the beast's
tracks.

The vicuna is described as being peculiar
to the Andes and Ecuador. It makes a queer
track with a sort of twist or tango step but
not so large as a full grown gorilla.

The vicuna resembles more the goat family than the monkey. It goes with its ears laid
back as though it was made and ready for an
attack, but is said to be peaceful unless molested, then it becomes very vicious.

But how could a wild best from the far-
away Andes find its way into Virginia? The
only explanation might be that it had escaped from a zoo or circus, and in its wanderings had made its way into the Falls Mills
vicinity.

Both men and boys, heavily armed and
with dogs, were reported Saturday scouring
the Big Branch country in the hope of getting
a shot at the prowling ruinant.

Should it be a powerful gorilla live stock
in the vicinity would be menaced, as well as
human beings, since the gorilla is vicious
and man-eating.

A mud imprint of the huge tracks was lifted with a shovel and brought to the Daily

Telegraph display window yesterday afternoon, where it attracted considerable attention. The impression made by the beast's claws is easily discernable in the print.

The following "Blue Devil" accounts are not necessarily Bigfoot related. The Blue Devil is a nondescript, a creature not described clearly enough to make a systematic determination. The name is intriguing, though, given reports of blue-haired Wild Men from early Arkansas and Georgia. (One note on the tongue-in-cheek explanation of the Blue Devil as a giant mole—the animal the editor is referring to is a shrew, not a mole.)

Charleston, West Virginia, *Daily Mail,* December 8, 1939

'BLUE DEVIL' STILL EVADES TRAPS, WEBSTER GUNS

Webster Springs, Dec. 8. (AP).—The hunt continues for Webster county's famed "horse-faced blue devil," but scores of hunters admitted today that they had not located the mysterious animal "with a yell like a banshee."

Last physical report of any sign of the "blue devil" came from Mrs. V. S. Cutlip of Diana, who said she heard "a wild inhuman scream" near her home.

But residents of the Diana-Grassy Creek section, where the strange creature is said to make its home, firmly insist that there is a "blue devil." But that he is too smart to be caught in the scores of bear traps that have been set for him and knows enough to stay hidden when he sees a high-powered rifle.

One of the several groups of hunters searching for the beast plans to trap it alive, if possible.

In the meantime, credulous folk in the sparsely settled Webster section are very careful about going out at night without a lantern and gun.

Charleston, West Virginia, *Daily Mail,* December 13, 1939

'BLUE DEVIL' MYSTERY GROWS AS STRANGE BEAST KILLS DOG

Webster Springs, Dec. 13. (AP).—Still puzzled by the mystery of their "dog-faced blue devil," Webster Springs citizens today considered asking the state conservation commission to rid the forest of the Grassy Creek and Jumbo sections of the "blue devil," or to conduct a search which will convince residents of those areas that no such animal exists.

Proposals for this action came following the death of a valuable hunting dog owned by John Clevenger of Jumbo, which was said to have been attacked last week while trailing the "blue devil." Ernest Cogar, also of Jumbo, said sheep and cattle were milling about restlessly in that section every night and that one of his cattle and a sheep had been attacked by some wild animal and wounded.

Hunting parties from Charleston, Buckhannon and Webster Springs have failed to find the "blue devil." Two bear hunters from New York City claimed their dogs trailed some kind of an animal in the Jumbo section shortly after midnight but after a short time came slinking back, refusing to trail the scent any longer.

H. A. Anderson, farmer of the Hacker valley section, said he heard a strange scream Monday morning on the hillside near his home. He said it sounded like a panther.

Glen Fisher, of the Bill Fisher hollow section, is convinced the "blue devil" is dead. He said he shot some kind of an animal two weeks ago and saw it jump in the air as the bullet struck. He said he waited until morning to see what he had shot, but that the animal disappeared. Since then, he said, the blue devil has not been seen in the Grassy Creek section.

Charleston, West Virginia, *Gazette*, December 24, 1939

For some time a great voracious animal has been roaming in the vicinity of Webster

Springs. Some call it the 'Blue Devil'. Many have described it minutely though no one has been found who confesses that he has seen it himself. Always one knows a "feller who talked to a feller who seen the thing."

It took the Clarksburg Telegram editor to figure out just what the animal is. How he did it at that distance the editor doesn't explain but he is quite positive that the animal is really a gigantic mole. Here's how he explains it all:

"For weeks stories have been coming from Webster Springs about the 'Blue Devil', a mysterious, animal. Now one begins to wonder whether it is 'The Big Bad Wolf' or the offspring of a mole. We've never heard a mole make a noise but after reading the stories from Webster Springs it begins to look like the 'Blue Devil' might be an overgrown relation of the small animal known as the mole.

"The mole is one of the most voracious animals on earth. If the tiny creature were the size of a lion or tiger it would be by far the most terrible creature imaginable, for its fierceness is proverbial and its insatiable appetite constantly demands food.

"In a test conducted In West Virginia, a mole ate 132 percent its own weight in food in 24 hours. In another test, a mole given two-thirds of a pint of worms in one day, was found the next morning, apparently starved to death."

Charleston, West Virginia, *Gazette,* January 30, 1940

IT'S A HARD LIFE

The life of the sheep raiser here in the highlands is no bed of roses.

If it's not sheep-killing dogs, it's Ol' Man Bruin who devastates the flocks and brings woe to the mountain shepherds. And as if these varmints were not enough, along comes some strange critter in the Gauley mountain section along the Randolph-Pocahontas county line to lay waste among the flocks and bring further trial and tribulation to their owners.

It's not a bear. We have the word of no less an authority than Wayne Stalnaker, deputy game protector and a man of broad knowledge of the woods and their inhabitants and of impeccable veracity, for that. He's seen the tracks.

The possibility arises, of course, that Webster county's famed "blue-devil" may be on the loose in Randolph county.

We had hoped when we first heard of this strange beast that it would prove to be one of the many painter cats which range the wilds of Cal Price's Pocahontas county hunting grounds.

We've been awaiting these many years definite and incontrovertable evidence that panthers do roam these forests. Not that we need further proof ourselves, having long been convinced by the weight of evidence as ably presented in Cal's Pocahontas Times. There are however, unconvinced souls and Doubting Thomases who refuse to be convinced by either the preponderance of testimony or the rule of reason.

It seems, however, in this instance, that despite our fondest hopes such is not to be the case, that it cannot be said with assurance that a panther is really at large.

On second thought, however, we recall that, the varmint is at large along the Pocahontas county line. We'd like some student of the wilds to take a second look at them tracks.—Elkins Inter-Mountain.

Wisconsin

Milwaukee, Wisconsin, *Daily Free Democrat*, March 14, 1856

Wild Man in the Woods.—The Waupaca Ledger of the 4th inst. says: We hear that a wild man has been discovered in the woods near Jenny Bull Falls, Marathon county. He is described as being completely covered with a coat of reddish hair, and so fleet as to render all attempts at capture abortive. Several times during the severest weather, he was seen browsing in the tops of trees, and on being discovered, made off with the speed of the wind; in one instance he made a side jump of fifteen feet. The inhabitants in that vicinity think it is an escaped lunatic who has been wandering about the country for some years.

A 1926 article ("The Wild Man Scare of old Pinery Days," Stevens Point, Wisconsin, *Journal*, July 17, 1926) explains the 1856 wild man report as a hoax instigated by logging camp cook who made himself up as a wild man to frighten his co-workers. Once over the initial scare, they

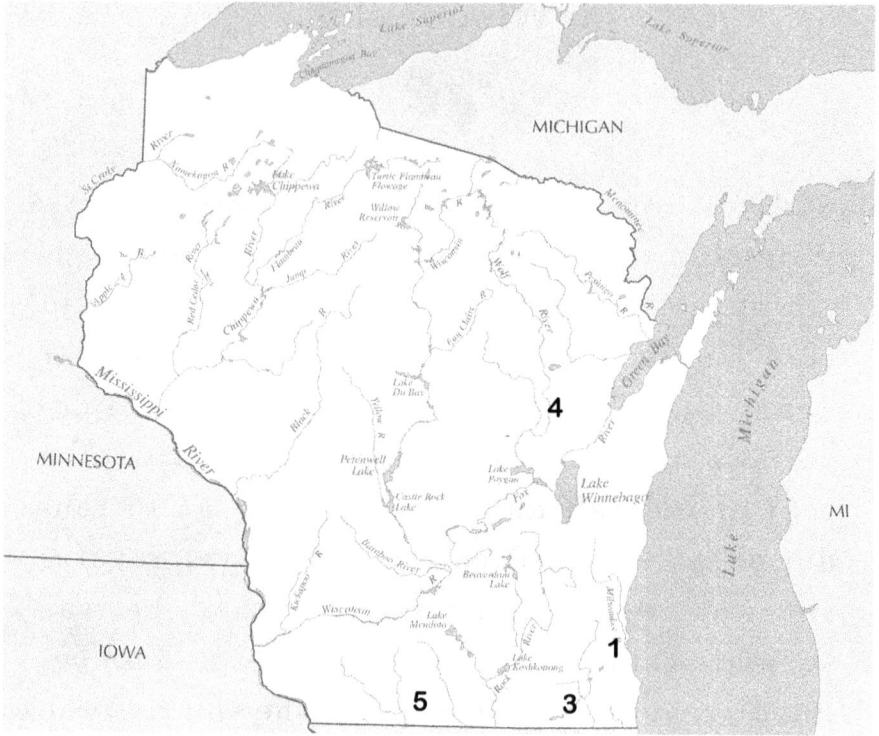

1 Oak Creek (Milwaukee County)

2 Ekerty: Unknown location (possibly intended
  Eckerty, Indiana?)

3 Silver Lake (Kenosha County)

4 Hortonville (Outagamie County)

5 Green County

entered into the spirit of the fun by telling stories to lumberjacks in other camps, and eventually the stories made it into print.

San Francisco, California, *Bulletin*, September 21, 1867

THE LAST SENSATION
IN MILWAUKEE—
THE WOODS HAUNTED
BY A WILD MAN

The *Sentinel* of August 17th, has the following:

We have just learned the particulars of a most singular affair, which is, as yet, in mystery. It seems that for some months past the farmers in the vicinity of Oak Creek, in this county, have been troubled with what they supposed to be minks or foxes, that have entered their hen coops and often almost entirely stripped the hen roosts. All precautions to keep out depredators have proved futile, doors which were latched being opened with apparent ease and the hens taken from their roosts. Occasionally even lambs have disappeared, and traces of their having been destroyed were afterwards found. The supposition that the animals and fowls were stolen was untenable, as the evidences that they had been devoured by some carnivorous animal was too strong. One person, who had been particularly aggrieved by the disappearance of his property, resolved to keep watch—and, if possible, discover his enemy and put him out of existence. Armed with his rifle, he stationed himself one night this week near his hennery and awaited developments. About 11 o'clock he heard a stealthy step approaching, and, peering through the darkness, discovered an object approaching. It crept cautiously to the hennery, now walking on all-fours and again standing erect as a man. The watcher was at a loss to distinguish what the animal or being could be, but resolving to penetrate the mystery, took aim and fired. A piercing shriek arose as of a boy of twelve years of age in terrible pain, and the object bounded off on all-fours, uttering meanwhile a plaintive moan or wail, which could proceed from no animal but a human being. It made its way to the adjacent woods and was soon lost to both sound and sight. The gentleman returned to his house and related what had occurred, fully convinced that he had wounded a human being who had attempted to rob his hen roost. But the fact that the object had gone off like an animal somewhat staggered his belief, and he resolved to fathom the mystery still farther if possible.

The next day, with his rifle on his shoulder, he sallied out into the woods in the direction of the object had taken. He traced it some distance by pools of blood where it had evidently lain down to rest, but soon lost track of it as these disappeared. He found his way into a marsh near by, and when about half way through was startled by the appearance of an animal or being with a distinct human face looking at him from a short distance. As soon as he made a movement, however, the singular creature started off with great swiftness and was soon lost to sight among the tall grass. Going to the place where he had first discovered the animal—for we will call it an animal at present—he distinctly traced in the mire the marks of human feet and hands, somewhat distorted, it is true, and with enormous claws, but sufficiently displayed to remove all doubts as to the matter. Filled with wonder, and not devoid of fear, the gentleman retraced his steps home.

Coming to this city on Thursday, the gentleman related his experience to Lieut. Kendrick of that police force. Of course the story smacked so strongly of the improbable that the Lieutenant regarded it as a hoax: but when he saw that his informant was evidently sincere in his narrative, he resolved to solve the mystery if possible. Making all necessary preparations, he started in company with the farmer for the scene of the affair.

Arrived at the farmer's house, they started forth. Going to the swamp, they searched for some time, but without discovering anything. When they were about to give up the search, on account of the near approach of night, they heard a rustling among the grass near them. On turning, they beheld a sight which startled them. It was without question a human face, but resembled that of a brute so closely as to be almost unrecognizable as such. They made a movement as if to approach it, when it darted off, leaping like a wild cat. As it receded they could obtain a good view of the creature's body, which was covered with hair, but at the same time appeared altogether different from that of any animal in existence, the shape resembled most closely that of a human being in the act of running or leaping on all fours. The twain attempted pursuit, but the creature was soon lost in the dim shades of the woods. They returned wondering, and well they might, in regard to the strange sight they had seen.

This story is almost too incredible for belief, and would be entirely discredited but for the fact that the creature has been seen by two unimpeachable witnesses.

Leavenworth, Kansas, *Times,* September 27, 1889

A naked, hairy creature, which, from descriptions given by reliable persons who have seen him, must be a young gorilla, was seen recently by various persons in the woods near Ekerty, Wis. It is supposed that the beast escaped from a traveling circus.

Janesville, Wisconsin, *Daily Gazette,* November 16, 1889

Palmyra is greatly excited over the appearance of a supposed gorilla that has been seen among the bluffs and about the cheese factory two miles west of the village.

Waukesha, Wisconsin, *Freeman,* November 21, 1889

PALMYRA INFESTED BY GORILLAS

Milwaukee Journal: A reward of $1,000 for the capture of the living gorilla supposed to have escaped from the show quartered at Janesville, or $500 for the carcass, has been offered. Large parties are scouring the woods and bluffs, hoping to secure the prize. It is said the animal was found yesterday in a tree by three men who were frightened and fled. Farmers report the loss of cattle and sheep in a mysterious manner, in some instance their bodies being partially devoured or the blood only drawn from them. Many report having seen a strange animal in their fields, sometimes walking on two feet, then on all fours, the like of which they had never seen or heard of before; and have been terribly alarmed by unearthly and unaccountable noises at night. Villagers on the outskirts of the place have been frightened by these noises. What was at first supposed to be humbug, seems to contain more truth than fiction, and it is certain some uncommon beast roams at large.

Council Bluffs, Iowa, *Daily Nonpareil,* November 23, 1889

A JOLLY GERMAN GORILLA.

Palmyra, Wis., Nov. 22.—The wild and woolly gorilla reported to have escaped from a menagerie at Janesville and to have taken up its abode in Palmyra bluffs, has been captured—in fact, he gave himself up. The "animal" was no less than a jolly German, who indulged his propensity for practical joking by scaring his neighbors. He crossed and recrossed the road with his wooden shoes on and pawed the earth with his fingers on each side of his foot marks. He then called his neighbors' attention to the signs and told about a wonderful animal that he had seen roaming the woods. Many young people suffered greatly from fright in consequence, remaining at home after dark, or, if compelled to go out, arming themselves with clubs, garden tools, pitchforks, or anything that came handy.

Fort Wayne, Indiana, *Sentinel,* December 24, 1902

SEE WILD MAN IN MARSH.

Waukesha, Wis., Dec. 24.—Charles Jackson, accompanied by a small boy, when hunting in the marshes near Silver lake on Saturday, heard a queer sound, which appeared to come from the rear of a pile of underbrush. Upon going to the spot a shaggy creature, apparently a man, jumped from the ground and darted between the trees, disappearing in the thick underbrush. The hunters gave chase, but were outdistanced. Residents of the vicinity of the Mojris farm think that it is a demented man who escaped from the Elkhorn asylum some years ago and was never found.

Racine, Wisconsin, *Journal Times,* December 5, 1939

HUNTERS CAPTURE BABOON WHILE IN QUEST FOR DEER

This is a deer-hunting story that winds up with a monkey in the principal role.

Ten Union Grove men, headed by Village President Ben Jerred, went north after deer. But they had another animal—the monkey.

They didn't shoot it. On the contrary, it's still alive and healthy, although very much in captivity on Ben Jerred's game farm. It has to be kept very much in captivity because its disposition is the opposite of sweet, and it has extremely large and sharp teeth.

Not Sure What Kind.

Neither the hunters, nor others who observed the beast (including Game Warden Arthur Peterson), are sure just what kind of a monkey it is. However, it's a large one, and could be a baboon, chimpanzee or orang-outang.

But that's a small part of the mystery. Where did they get it? That is the question. And questioners haven't been able to get a satisfactory answer.

Several Theories.

There are several theories. One is that some northern amusement park is minus one monkey. Another is that while stopping for a bottle of pop, some member of the expedition took the animal from a tavern. Few believe it was actually captured in the woods, because baboons, chimpanzees and orang-outangs do not often run at large in northern Wisconsin forests.

In the meantime, Game Warden Peterson is pouring through the statutes to see if there are any laws against monkey-hunting in Wisconsin.

Wisconsin Rapids, Wisconsin, *Daily Tribune,* September 7, 1946

'APE' STORY KEEPS
TOWN IN TURMOIL

Hortonville, Wis.—(AP)—An "ape" scare has kept this community in a turmoil for the last 48 hours.

It started when someone told someone else, who passed it along to another person, that an "ape" had escaped from some nearby fairgrounds and was on the loose in this vicinity.

Police were deluged with inquiries. One report said the animal had been seen jumping from limb to limb in trees on the outskirts of town. One schoolboy was said to have informed his wide-eyed fellow students that "the thing was halfway through our window and my dad knocked it outside again." Actually, police haven't found anyone who will say definitely they have seen the "ape."

Police contacted both Winnebago and Calumet county authorities but learned nothing of an escaped ape. "We figure folks'll get tired of talking about it eventually," an officer said.

Madison, Wisconsin, *State Journal,* August 20, 1958

GREEN COUNTY 'BEAR
OR APE' REPORTED SEEN

Monroe—The Green county sheriff's department here is investigating reports of a large creature resembling a bear or gorilla that walks on its hind legs.

It first was seen Friday night near the Michael school, 8 miles east of here, by two fishermen who were walking back to their car from Zanders lake.

Seen 2nd Time

The frightened pair told authorities that the beast stood some 10 feet tall when it stood on its hind legs. It walked part of the time on all fours, they said. They saw it in rough brush and timber.

It was seen the same night by farmer Melvin Blum, who spotted the creature between the schoolhouse and an adjacent cemetery. It stood in a field of oat stubble, he and his companion said.

The next day, Blum found a patch of burdocks which had been rolled in, but it is thought hogs might have flattened the plants.

Possible Escapee

Authorities said the creature might be either a bear or a large ape escaped from a circus. They said no bears have been seen in the neighborhood for many years.

However, a farmer living 5 miles north of Monroe reported Monday that he saw something resembling a bear. But his farm is quite far from where the beast was first seen.

Authorities have been unable to find tracks of the creature, so far. They said the brush and trees in the area are ideal cover for any animal. It apparently had not attacked any farm animals by Tuesday night.

Madison, Wisconsin, *State Journal,* August 21, 1958

GREEN COUNTY BEAST SAID TO BE BEAR CUB

Monroe—Green county's monster is believed by some to be a bear cub weighing about 100 pounds.

Merlyn Erb, a farmer living 5 miles north of Monroe, told authorities Wednesday that he saw the cub Monday night. He said he saw the bear's tracks too, and sent his dog after the animal. The dog disappeared and hasn't returned, Erb said.

He said the bear had "helped itself to corn" several times this summer. However, no sign of a mother bear has been found.

For the past several days rumors have been flying in the area of a 7-foot bear or ape-like creature. The Green county sheriff's office reported earlier Wednesday that it suspected that the "monster" stories were based on a hoax.

Undersheriff Howard Schucht and Arley Roderick, of the Civil Defense auxiliary police, reported a medium-sized black bear near Zander's Lake the following Saturday evening. It was seen near midnight in an open field, via spotlight. ("See 'Mystery Animal': Deputies confirm area bear report," Monroe, Wisconsin, *Evening Times,* August 25, 1958.)

Appendix:
C. A. Stephens and the Pomoola

In 1873, prolific writer Charles Asbury Stephens published *Camping Out*, (Philadelphia: John C. Winston Co.), the fictional adventures of a group of boys camping, hunting, and fishing in the deep woods of Maine. Stephens was born in Norway, Maine, in 1844, and used his knowledge of the region and its lore in his writings. In *Camping Out*, Stephens relates an old guide's tale of an "Indian devil," Pomoola, which certainly relates to the Wild Man stories as we have examined them. In other historical sources from Maine that I've seen, both names are used for the mountain lion. So how did Stephens come to use it for something very different? This could be an interesting project for someone in that region. Bowdoin College of Brunswick, Maine, holds his papers in their library's archives, and it might be worth looking through Stephens' other published material. For now, here is a reprint of Chapter 10 from *Camping Out*.

"OLD CLUEY" AND HIS STRANGE
TALE OF THE POMOOLA

During the evening we explained to Cluey the object of our expedition. He had heard the "lead story."

"Were you ever on Mount Katahdin?" asked Raed.

"I never clomb to the tip-top," said Cluey; "but I've tramped all round it after moose and caribou."

"We would like to have you go with us," said Raed. "We will give you two dollars per day to go with us as hunter and help carry the luggage."

Cluey said he would take till morning to consider the matter.

"Do you ever see any thing of the Indian devil here?" Wash asked.

"The Ingin dav'l!" exclaimed Cluey. "Where'd ever ye hear any thing about the Ingin dav'l, yonker?"

"Oh! I've heard that he lives in this vicinity," said Wash, laughing.

Old Cluey shook his head.

"We've often heard stories of the Indian devil," said I. "Can't you give us one?"

"Do ye know what the Ingins say about the tip-top of Mount Katahdin, yonker?" demanded Cluey, suddenly turning to me.

"Oh, yes! they say that Pomoola will destroy every one who seeks to reach the summit. But that does not apply to white men."

"'Ow do you know that ar?"

"Dr. Jackson ascended it without any inconvenience in 1838; so did Mr. Bowditch; and so also did Dr. Holmes and party."

"Be ye sartin that they went to the tip-top? Thar ar' three or four different peeks."

"They reached the highest point on the Katahdin ridge, if we may believe their statement; and there is no reason why we should not," I added, seeing that Cluey still looked a little doubtful.

"What made you shake your head when I asked you about the Indian devil?" queried Wash. "Do you believe in it?"

"Wal," said Cluey, fairly cornered, "I don't myself; but thar's plenty as do. An' they do tell some cur'us yarns about it,—mighty cur'us."

"But did ever you see any thing of the sort yourself,—any thing that looked diabolical?" persisted Wash, determined to pin at least one of these singular tales.

"Wal," began the old man, after hesitating considerably, "I did see suthin ruther cur'us wunst. I did, no mistake."

"Ah, you did!" exclaimed Wash. "Tell us about it, please."

"Yes, tell us about that," we all put in.

Thus brought to book, Cluey related the following incident. Wash has straightened out his English, and fixed it up fit for perusal. The story is Cluey's in Wash's words, as recorded at the time in his note-book, from which I extract it. Wash entitled it,—

Old Cluey's Indian-Devil Story.

"'Twas years ago," said old Cluey Robbins. "I was nothing but a youngster then. My brother Zeke and I used to hunt in company with an old woodsman named Hughy Watson. This was either our first or second trip with him up to the lakes. After a tramp of five days through the woods from Norridgewock, our native town, we had come out on the shore of a wild-looking sheet of water, now called 'Ragged Pond.' Its notched, scraggy, and craggy shores might well have suggested the name. Near us a noisy brook came rattling down into it; and, not more than a quarter of a mile farther on, the outlet comes out in a parallel direction with equal noise and foam. Some idea may be obtained, from this circumstance, of the rough surface of the country about us.

"'It ought to be a clever place for mink,' said Hughy; 'and we may find a family of beaver up this brook. I never was on these waters before.'

"We made up an open camp, Indian fashion, under some large spruces; and just at dusk we had the good fortune to see and shoot a caribou. It was cloudy, and came on very dark. I never, before nor since, heard such a serenade from owls as our fire drew around us. Screeches and the most dismal hoots blended in horrible concert. Round and round us they glided in noiseless circles. There were scores of them. It was utterly impossible to sleep; and the frequent discharge of our guns failed to disperse them. But in the morning the merry notes of the king-fisher told us there were plenty of trout in the stream we were on; and, where there are trout, there are always mink: so we fell to lining the banks with 'figure-four' traps, which occupied us during the whole of the following day. There were no indications that the stream had ever been trapped before; and we anticipated a full pack of fur.

"'This is what I call freedom,' said Hughey as we sat round our fire that night. 'Every thing just as old Mother Nature made it; and she made it pretty rough and wild too,' continued the old fellow, gazing off at the black spruce-clad peaks of Katahdin far to the eastward, where the 'hunter's moon' was looming up over that desolate ridge. 'Like enough we are the first white folks ever in here. The lumber-men wouldn't come into such a region as this. We crossed their old trail ten miles below.'

"Likely enough we were; at least, we had no reason to complain of the trapping-ground we

had thus stumbled upon. We began to reap a fine
harvest of fur ere the first three days had passed;
and for boys of sixteen, like Zeke and I, no better
entertainment could have been got up.

"But, as days passed, we began to notice that
Hughy seemed uneasy and watchful.

"'What can ail the old man?' asked Zeke as we
were making the round of the traps one day. 'He
don't act at all as he did the first few days we were
in here. Haven't you noticed it?'

"Yes. I had noticed it; and we agreed to rally
the old chap a little when we got back. Well,
after supper that night, seeing Hughy looking
sulky and absent, I asked all at once,

"'What is it, Hughy? Aren't things going on
right here?'

"The old man turned and looked at us a moment, as if not certain what he should answer.
Then he said,

"I never like to be laughed at, especially by
boys. I thought, at first, we'd struck a fine stream:
and perhaps it's all fancy; for I haven't seen or
heard a single thing wrong yet. But I've been feeling for several days just as if there was something,
either man or beast, hanging round us here. It
may be a catamount; or it may be some mean thief
of a river-driver, sneaking about for a chance to
steal our fur; or some Indian who hunts here,
and would be glad to be rid of us. Can't tell. And

perhaps it's all my notion; but I can't get rid of it. I remember, once when I was up at the Telos Lake, I felt just so several days; and finally one night I hid in a clump of hemlocks a little ways from my camp, and didn't go to it at all. Along in the night I heard a noise about it, and saw what I took for men there. I didn't speak, or fire on them. Things were upset round the next morning; but I had moved my fur the day before. And, another time, I was up beyond Katahdin; and, several days before I had seen any signs, I began to feel that something was watching me. A night or two after, I waked up, and saw a catamount glaring at me from a tree-top. I suppose he had been prowling round, but had kept out of sight. And I think we shall find that there's something unusual lurking round us now.'

"Old Hughy's presentiments served to keep us wakeful and vigilant; but several days passed without the least sign of any one's being near us, and we were beginning to forget it, when one evening I saw what certainly justified Hughy's suspicions. I had left the fire to bring some water from the brook, which was within a few rods of us. I had stooped to dip it up, when, as I rose, I caught a glimpse of what I took to be a man, standing at a little distance. In an instant it vanished behind a shrubby fir. I felt quite positive; yet it was so dark, and whatever I had seen was out of sight so quick, that I knew I was very liable to have been mistaken. Checking my first impulse to run to the camp and give an alarm, I decided to say nothing at present, but watch.

"The evening passed. By nine o'clock, Hughy and Zeke were both asleep. I lay down, but kept awake.

"Hour after hour went by. At length, the moon rose. It was one of those still, late autumn nights when frogs are silent, and birds and insects are gone; when only the larger beasts of prey are abroad. There were no owls that night. The leaves had fallen, and covered the ground with a dry and rustling carpet.

"After a while I began to distinguish footsteps among them at a distance. They were faint and stealthy; and I was somewhat in doubt whether it were not my fancy, till the sharp snap of a twig convinced me. It might easily have been a 'luci-vee,' or a 'fisher,' or a bear; but somehow I at once connected it with what I had seen in the evening.

"I listened breathlessly.

"The steps were coming nearer. But it was very dark under the thick spruce-boughs. Suddenly the steps ceased; and for a few moments all was still. Then I saw a dark shadow pass a narrow vista where the moonlight fell through the black tree-tops. It had the shape of a man. The steps went on as if the creature, or whatever it was, were passing around us, keeping at about the same distance. Gradually it came around to the point where I had first heard it. There was another pause; and again I saw it cross the moonlit line, to continue its walk around our camp. I wasn't much scared; but its movements gave me a strange sort of feeling. I remember thinking it was no use to wake Zeke, or Hughy, who was snoring away at a great rate. So, cocking my gun, I crept noiselessly down the path we had beaten to the brook, to get nearer the place where I had seen the shadow in the moonlight. Creeping up within two or three rods, I crouched at the root of a fallen tree, and waited. The footsteps were again approaching in their circuit. There was the same pause as before; and again the form stepped into the moonlight a moment, and was again in the shadow. But the moon was pouring down brightly; and I distinctly saw its shape,—the figure of a man, looking brown and naked, save where a hairy outline showed against the light. A feeling of sickness or of horror came over me. The idea of using my gun did not even present itself. I crept back as silently as I came down. I heard the steps come round again; then they grew fainter and fainter as the walker moved off into the forest.

"It was getting toward morning. I sat down to think the matter over. Presently Hughy woke.

"'You up?' said he. Whereupon I told him what I had seen. He listened without a word, till I was describing how it looked as I last saw it; when he exclaimed,

"'It's an Indian devil! It's old Pomoola! That's just as I've heard the Oldtown Indians describe it a hundred times; but I always thought it was all a lie. They always left a place as soon as they'd seen one of these things; and I reckon we'd better.'

"But we didn't leave; and our good luck with our traps continued, despite Hughy's hints at Indian superstitions. We were pretty cautious, however, and kept together a good deal. It was not that we were particularly afraid of it as a beast; but its singular movements had given us a sort of dread of it.

"Nothing further was seen for some time. We had begun to fish in the lake for trout. It was alive with them too,—splendid fellows. We frequently caught them as heavy as ten pounds; and one day Zeke caught a togue which must have weighed twenty or twenty-five pounds. He fairly drew our canoe after him when he was hooked, and it took all our skill to land him.

"I remember we were up near the head of the lake that afternoon. Our camp was at the foot, or lower end. It was getting dusk as we paddled back along. There were several islands in the lake, nearly all of them craggy and high. Just as we were passing the lower one we heard a curious noise,—a sort of 'Waugh, waugh!' and, looking round to the island, we saw a strange, manlike creature standing upright on a rock overlooking the water. We were not more than eight rods off, and it was not so dark but that we could see it plainly enough. As we stopped paddling, it uttered the same sound again,—a noise between a grunt and a bark.

"I knew at once it was the same creature I had seen before, and told them so. It must have swum half a mile to get up on the island. If we hadn't been fools we should have gone up, and found out then and there what it was, and so solved the mystery; for the island was small, and we should have had it completely penned up, and at our mercy. But we were boys then, with our heads full of Hughy's big stories; and as for Hughy himself, all the fur in Maine wouldn't have hired him to go a stroke nearer. Zeke hallooed at it: whereupon it raised its fore-paws, or arms, and swung them about like a drunken man, making the same noise as before. It was growing dark; and we came off and left it.

"The next day we went down round the island; but it wasn't there. It had gone away during the night.

"It was now November; and one morning we woke up to find the ground white and a smart snow coming. Towards night it cleared up cold and wintry. Our open camp wasn't very comfortable that night. We waked up shivering. Hughy was wincing under twinges of his old foe the 'rheumatiz.'

"'We must get out of this, boys,' said he. 'Winter's coming.'

"During the day we took up our traps, and prepared for our long tramp southward. We packed our fur in bundles; for we had to back it out for the first forty miles. It was to be our last night there; and we sat about our fire talking over home-matters, and thinking of what might have happened since we left. All at once, Hughy remembered our canoe.

"'We may come here again,' said he; 'and its some work to make one. You go down, Cluey, and pull it up out of the lake, and hide it in that little clump of cedars close to the water. It'll keep sound there two or three years.'

"So I ran down to the lake. It wasn't more than a hundred rods. Drawing the canoe out of the water, I stowed it away, bottom up, among the cedars at the foot of a low crag which overhung the lake.

"I was just coming away, when I heard behind me the same queer sound we had heard at the island, and, looking up, saw the beast-man again, standing at the top of the crag. He wasn't more than a hundred feet off: so I had a pretty good view of him as he stood out against the clear sunset sky. It was the same form and shape as before, fully a tall as a man; and I could now see his face. Perhaps it was partly fear; but I did think it had a devilish look. There was a tuft of thick hair on the head, which lent a frightful expression to the face.

"If this was what the Indians used to see, I don't wonder they thought it was the Devil. I had my gun, and slowly raised it as if to take aim. The creature raised its arm in the same way. But I had no thoughts of firing; I didn't dare to: and, when I lowered my gun, the creature dropped its arm with another 'Waugh, waugh!'

"I know I was frightened; yet I saw it plainly enough, and could have sworn to its identity anywhere.

"I don't know how long we stood staring at each other: but I saw it was growing darker; and, stepping backward till I was out of sight behind a cedar, I went into camp about as fast as my legs would carry me.

"Zeke was for going down all together, and shooting at it; but Hughy wouldn't hear of it. He was pretty strongly tinged with the old Indian whims concerning Pomoola, the demon of the mountain near us.

"'We'd no business with it,' he said; 'and he'd have nothing to do with it whatever, unless he was obliged to.'

"The next day we started for the settlements. That was the last we saw of it. Of course, Zeke and I told our story after getting home; and I presume it never increased our reputation for veracity among our neighbors. Hughy showed an old hunter's wisdom by keeping still about it. When persons who had heard us asked him, he merely said that we did see something rather queer; and that was all they could get out of him. Zeke and I pitched into him once for not substantiating our account better.

"'No use, no use at all,' said the old man; 'and I ain't going to get laughed at for nothing.'

"I've thought about it a great deal since; but I never could satisfy myself what it was we saw. I've heard of wild men, of children carried off and reared by wild beasts; and the Indians were always telling of Pomoola: but I never could settle it in my mind. I know there are a great many things in the Northern wilderness which the 'scientific men' would laugh at a person for seeing or trying to describe.

"Put here's my story. You can take it for what it is worth; and so must the reader. But we record it as a very fair specimen of hundreds of similar 'yarns' common among the lumber-men and Indians, concerning the fabulous being or demon of the Katahdin region. My opinion is that it is all pure bosh, not only this story of Cluey's, but the whole batch of them."

I heartily concur with Wash; though it does seem strange that there should be so many stories with no foundation whatever in fact.

Reference Material

Arment, Chad. 2006. *The Historical Bigfoot*. Landisville, PA: Coachwhip.

—. 2011. The historical Bigfoot: a supplement. *BioFortean Notes*. Vol. 2. http://www.strangeark.com/biofortean-notes

—. 2013. Trinity River baboons. *BioFortean Notes*. Vol. 3. http://www.strangeark.com/biofortean-notes

Baer, John. 1982. The great cocktail hoax. Baltimore, Maryland, *Sun Magazine* (January 17): 7+.

Bartholomew, Paul, et al. 1992. *Monsters of the Northwoods*. Second Printing. Whitehall, NY: Bartholomew et al.

Berry, Rick. 1993. *Bigfoot on the East Coast*. Stuarts Draft, VA: Berry.

Bode, Carl. 1991. Mencken's fakery. Baltimore, Maryland, *Sun* (January 31). https://www.baltimoresun.com/news/bs-xpm-1991-01-31-1991031124-story.html

Bord, Janet, and Colin Bord. 2006. *Bigfoot Casebook Updated*. Enumclaw, WA: Pine Winds Press.

Burns, J. W. 1929. Introducing B.C.'s hairy giants. *MacLean's Magazine* (April 1): 9+.

Byrne, Peter. 1976. *The Search for Big Foot: Monster, Myth or Man?* New York: Pocket Books.

Champlain, Samuel de. 1922. *The Voyages and Explorations of Samuel de Champlain, 1604-1616.* Vol. II. Bourne, Annie Nettleton, trans. Bourne, Edward Gaylord, ed. New York: Allerton Book Co.

Chorvinsky, Mark. 1990. The "mystery photograph" solution: anatomy of an investigation. *Strange Magazine* 5: 5-10.

Cobb, Norma, and Charles W. Sasser. 2000. *Arctic Homestead.* New York: St. Martin's Press.

Coleman, Loren. 2001. *Mysterious America.* Revised edition. New York: Paraview Press.

Colp, Harry D. 1953. *The Strangest Story Ever Told.* New York: Exposition Press. (Online at https://babel. hathitrust.org/cgi/pt?id=uc1.31822043018795& view=2up&seq=1)

Crowe, Ray. 1993. Historic accounts of Bigfoot sightings. *INFO Journal* (69): 12-13, 41.

Davis, Don. n.d. Bigfoot at Tonto Creek. *Bigfoot Encounters.* http://www.bigfootencounters.com/stories/ dondavis.htm

Gerstäcker, Frederick. 1864. *Western Lands and Western Waters.* London: S. O. Beeton.

Green, John. 1978. (1981 edition.) *Sasquatch: The Apes Among Us.* North Vancouver, B.C.: Hancock House.

—, and Sabine W. Sanderson. 1975. Alas, poor Jacko. *Pursuit* 8(1): 18-19.

Hall, Mark A. 1993. The Yeti. *Wonders* 2(4): 75-95.

—. 1999. *Living Fossils*. Minneapolis, MN: MAHP.

Hallan, Pamela. 1987. Curio. Santa Ana, California, *Orange County Register* (December 3): B2.

Hand, Bill. 2017. Did Bigfoot live in Kit Swamp? New Bern, NC, *Sun Journal* (June 25). http://www.new-bernsj.com/news/20170625/did-bigfoot-live-in-kit-swamp

Hunter, Don, and René Dahinden. 1973. *Sasquatch*. New York: Signet.

Keating, Don. 1993. *The Buckeye Bigfoot*. Newcomer-stown, OH: Keating.

Kinne, Russ. 1976. Jacko reconsidered. *Pursuit* 9(2): 42-43.

Krantz, Grover S. 1992. *Big Footprints*. Boulder, CO: Johnson Books.

Leonard, Larry. 1975. Illinois: Something hairy hunted Lepton. Mount Carmel, Illinois, *Daily Republican-Register* (July 11): 1.

Lincoln, K. J. 2018. Nunivak Island Bigfoot. Bethel, Alaska, *Delta Discovery* (July 25, 2018). https://deltadiscovery.com/nunivak-island-bigfoot/

Mangiacopra, Gary S., and Dwight G. Smith. 2002. Wild men and mountain gorillas: A historical retrospective of 19th century Sasquatchery encounters as recorded in North American newspapers. Heinselman, Craig, ed. *CRYPTO Hominology*, Special Number II: 40-47.

—. 2006. A pre-Civil War immature Bigfoot report? *North American BioFortean Review* 8(1): 5-7.

Matthews, Mychel. 2017. The wild hairy man from Birch Creek. Twin Falls, Idaho, *Times-News* (February 2): A2.

O'Brien, Joseph. 1991. Winsted wonders: The world read in awe the hometown tales reported by Louis T. Stone. Hartford, Connecticut, *Courant* (October 20): H1+.

Opsasnick, Mark. 2004. *The Maryland Bigfoot Digest.* (Revised edition.) Xlibris.

Peck, Chris. 1977. King Kong has a problem. Twin Falls, Idaho, *Times-News* (January 2): 5.

Quast, Mike. 1990. *The Sasquatch in Minnesota.* Fargo, ND: Mike Quast.

—. 2019. Bigfoot Chronicle. Moorhead, MN: Mike Quast.

Rayno, Paul. Pioneers and patriots: He lost Old Slippryskin—and election. Glen Falls, New York, *Post-Star* (March 26): 10.

Ricker, Nok-Noi. 2013. Bigfoot in Maine? 10-foot-tall 'wild man' was killed in 1886, newspapers reported. *Bangor Daily News* (Oct. 27). https://bangordaily-news.com/2013/10/27/news/state/bigfoot-in-maine-10-foot-tall-wild-man-was-killed-in-1886-newspapers-reported/

Roberts, Leonard. 1957. Notes and queries: Curious legend of the Kentucky mountains. *Western Folklore* 16(1): 48-51.

Roosevelt, Theodore. 1893. *The Wilderness Hunter.* New York: G. P. Putnam's Sons.

Ross, Margaret. 1971. The Fouke 'Monster' had look alikes. *Arkansas Gazette* (June 27): 5E.

Sanderson, Ivan T. 1961. *Abominable Snowmen: Legend Come to Life*. Philadelphia: Chilton.

—. 1967. *Things*. New York: Pyramid.

Schaffner, Ron. 1997-2006. *Creature Chronicles*. (See http://blakemathys.com/creaturechronicles.html for many issues)

Shoemaker, Michael T. 1990. Searching for the historical Bigfoot. *Strange Magazine* 5: 18-23, 57-62.

—. 1993. The Winsted Wild Man revisited. *Strange Magazine* 11: 30-31, 59.

Smith, Dwight G., and Gary S. Mangiacopra. 2003. What the readers wrote in: Secondary Bigfoot sources. . . . *North American BioFortean Review* 5(4): 19-31.

—. 2005. Canada's "ape-men" of Labrador. *North American BioFortean Review* 7(1): 18-21.

Standwood, Larry. Swiss Alpinist hunts Sasquatch. Victoria, British Columbia, *Daily Times* (April 12): 23.

Taft, Michael. 1980. Sasquatch-like creatures in Newfoundland: a study in the problems of belief, perception, and reportage. in, Halpin, Marjorie M., and Michael M. Ames, eds. *Manlike Monsters on Trial: Early Records and Modern Evidence*. Vancouver: University of British Columbia Press.

Varley, James. 2010. Wildmen of the Big Wood River. Twin Falls, Idaho, *Times-News* (November 25): Opinion 1, 7.

Vincent, Dale. 1947. Vincent tells story of rich gold find guarded by Star Gulch wild man. Medford, Oregon, *Mail Tribune* (November 9).

W., A. 1934. The wolf-man of B.C. Vancouver, British Columbia, *Province* (March 3): 2.

Watt, Lynn. 1968. This'n that from here'n there. Burlington, Vermont, *Free Press* (April 1): 12.

Wise, Jennings Cropper. 1911. *Ye Kingdome of Accawmacke or the Eastern Shore of Virginia in the Seventeenth Century.* Richmond, VA: Bell Book and Stationery Co.

Woollacott, Arthur P. 1944. Wild men of B.C.? Vancouver, British Columbia, *Province* (January 15): 3.

Zheutlin, Peter. 2005. The mystery of the New York reporter and the Massachusetts "wild man." *The New England Quarterly* 78(4): 617-630.

COACHWHIP PUBLICATIONS
CoachwhipBooks.com

VARMINTS
CHAD ARMENT

MYSTERY CARNIVORES
OF NORTH AMERICA

A survey of black panthers, strange bears, mysterious canines, and other carnivorous enigmas in North America . . .

COACHWHIP PUBLICATIONS

CoachwhipBooks.com

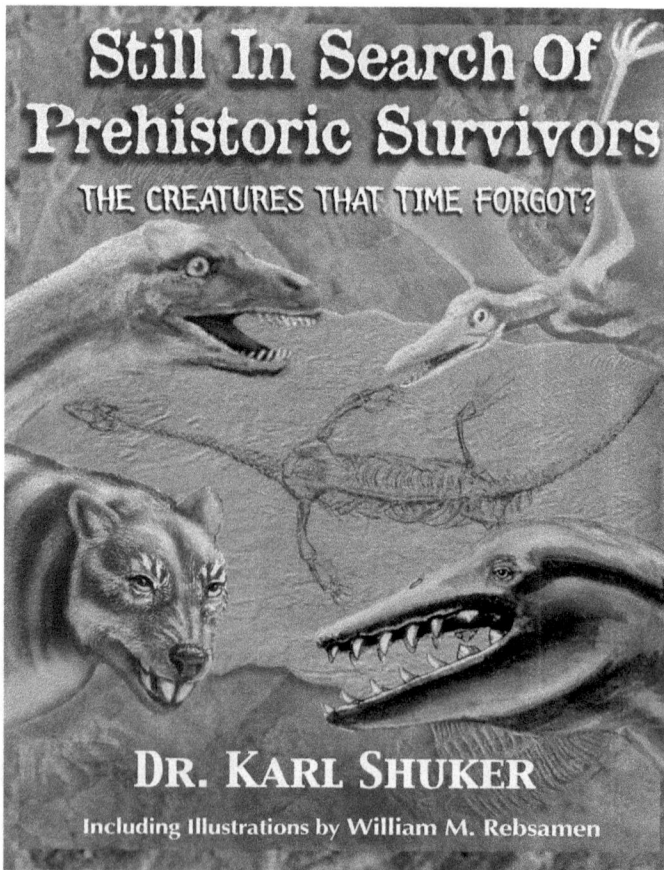

Still In Search Of Prehistoric Survivors

THE CREATURES THAT TIME FORGOT?

DR. KARL SHUKER

Including Illustrations by William M. Rebsamen

Dr. Karl Shuker investigates stories of creatures thought to be extinct, allegedly showing up in the modern world. . . .

COACHWHIP PUBLICATIONS
CoachwhipBooks.com

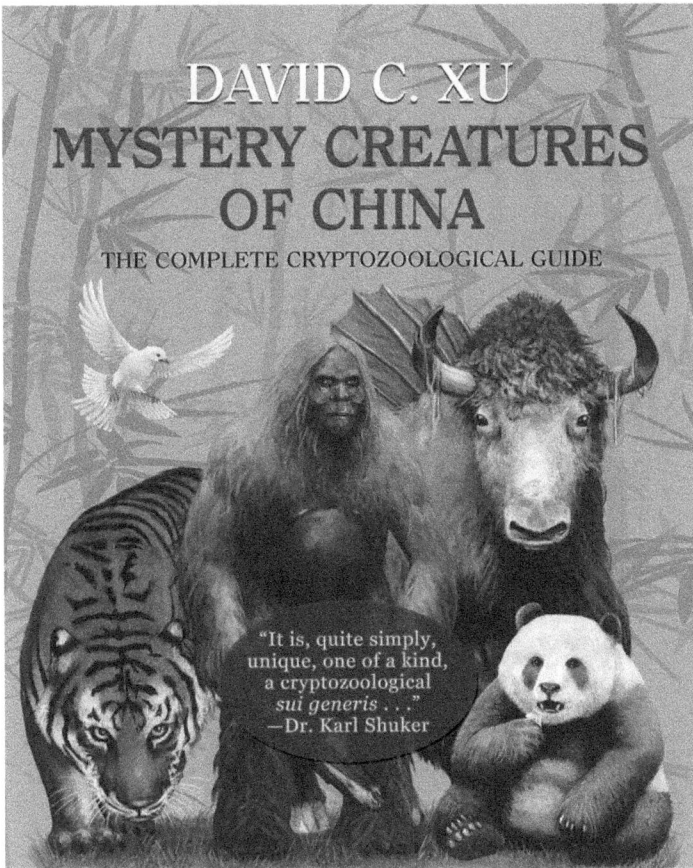

DAVID C. XU
MYSTERY CREATURES
OF CHINA
THE COMPLETE CRYPTOZOOLOGICAL GUIDE

"It is, quite simply, unique, one of a kind, a cryptozoological *sui generis* . . ."
—Dr. Karl Shuker

David Xu opens up the cryptozoological landscape of China, from hairy giants to mysterious cats, lake monsters to flying beasts. . . .

COACHWHIP PUBLICATIONS
CoachwhipBooks.com

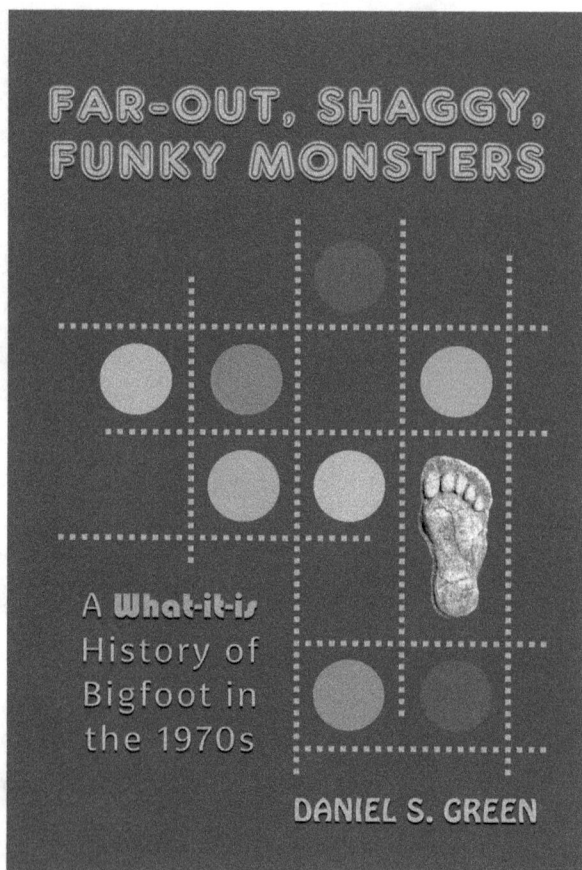

FAR-OUT, SHAGGY, FUNKY MONSTERS

A *What-it-is* History of Bigfoot in the 1970s

DANIEL S. GREEN

Daniel Green delves into the 1970s, showing the cultural history of Bigfoot as it developed from a regional oddity to a national phenomenon. . . .

COACHWHIP PUBLICATIONS
CoachwhipBooks.com

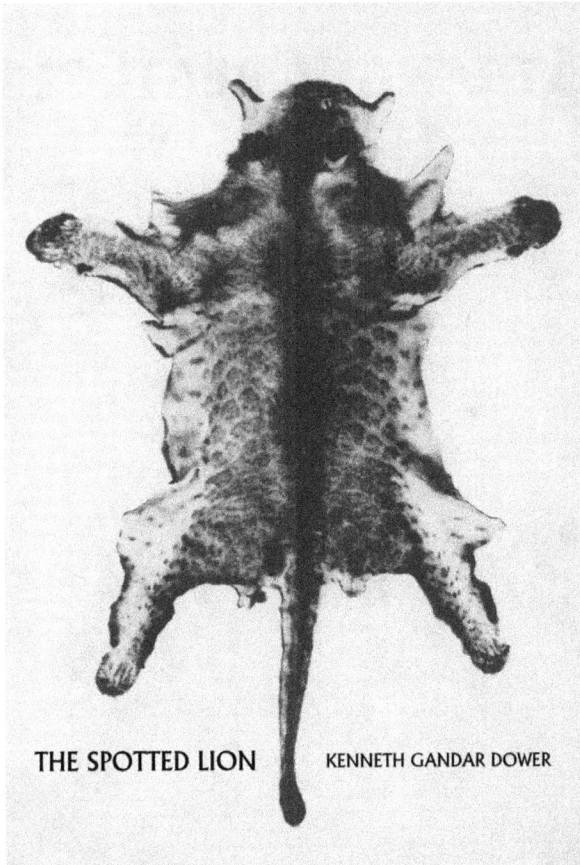

THE SPOTTED LION   KENNETH GANDAR DOWER

The expedition in search of a mystery feline in Africa . . .

COACHWHIP PUBLICATIONS
CoachwhipBooks.com

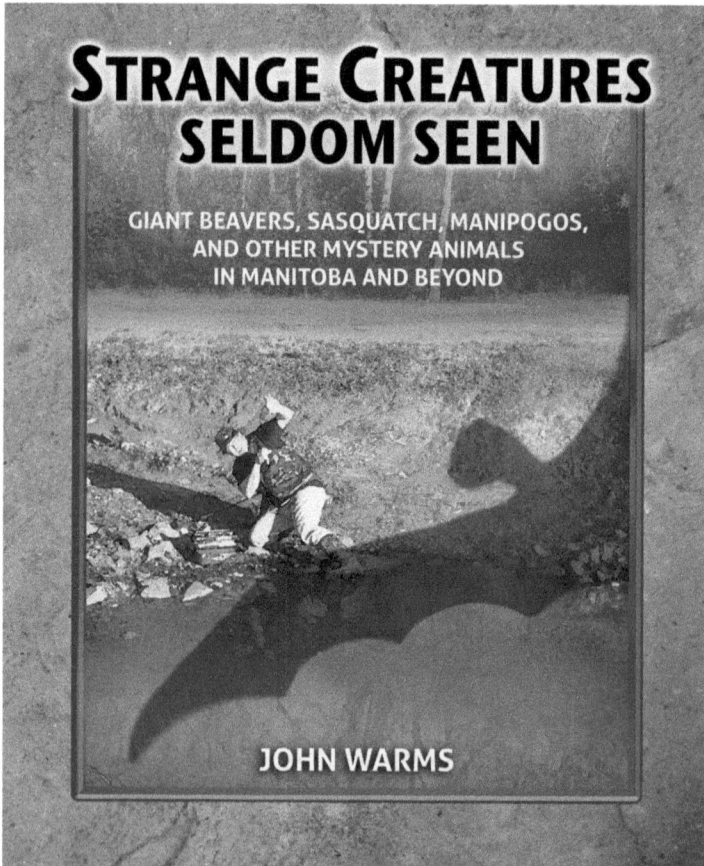

STRANGE CREATURES
SELDOM SEEN

GIANT BEAVERS, SASQUATCH, MANIPOGOS,
AND OTHER MYSTERY ANIMALS
IN MANITOBA AND BEYOND

JOHN WARMS

John Warms has interviewed witnesses all over Manitoba who believe they have seen Bigfoot, giant beavers, flying monsters, and other strange creatures. . . .

COACHWHIP PUBLICATIONS
COACHWHIPBOOKS.COM

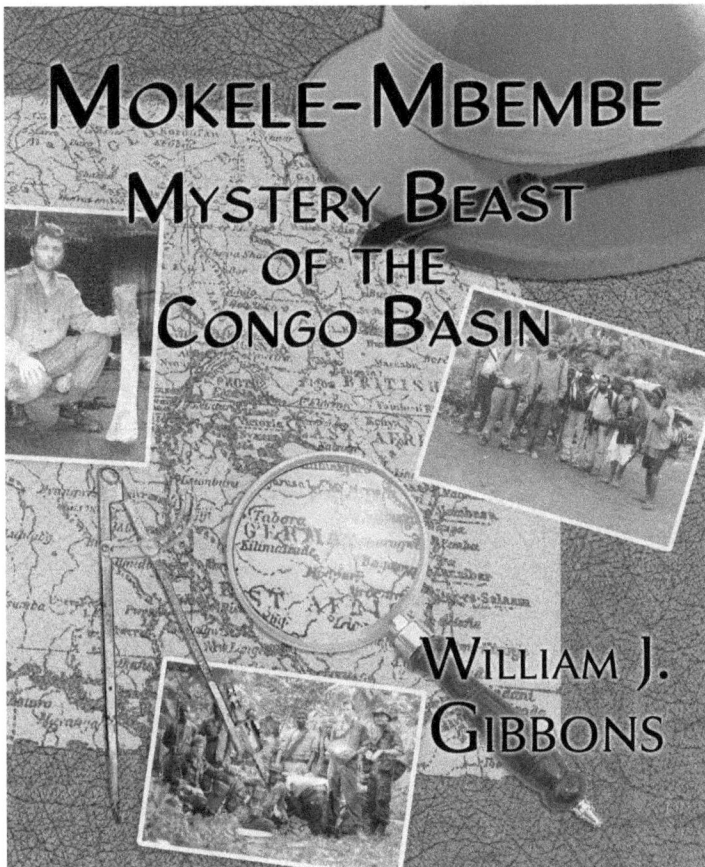

MOKELE-MBEMBE
MYSTERY BEAST
OF THE
CONGO BASIN

WILLIAM J.
GIBBONS

Bill Gibbons takes us on expeditions for a living dinosaur in the Congo and Cameroon. . . .

COACHWHIP PUBLICATIONS
CoachwhipBooks.com

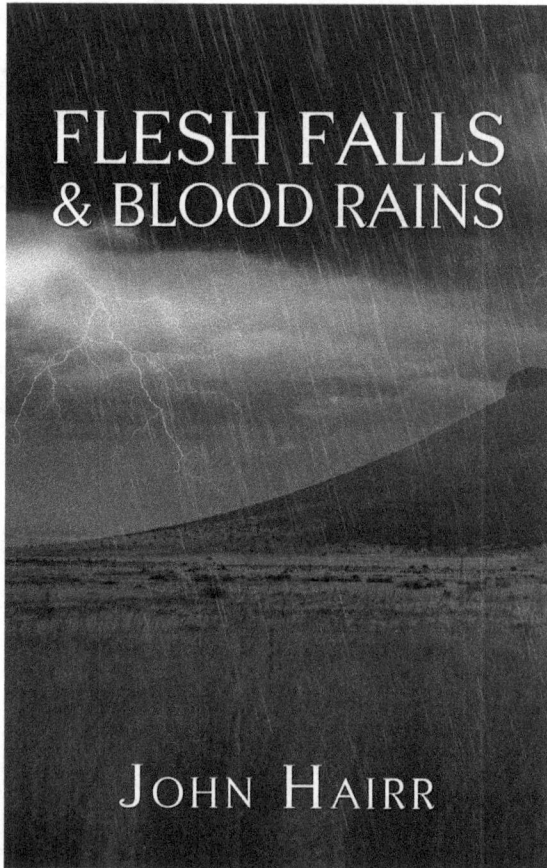

FLESH FALLS
& BLOOD RAINS

JOHN HAIRR

John Hairr looks into strange reports of flesh and blood falling from the sky. . . .

COACHWHIP PUBLICATIONS
COACHWHIPBOOKS.COM

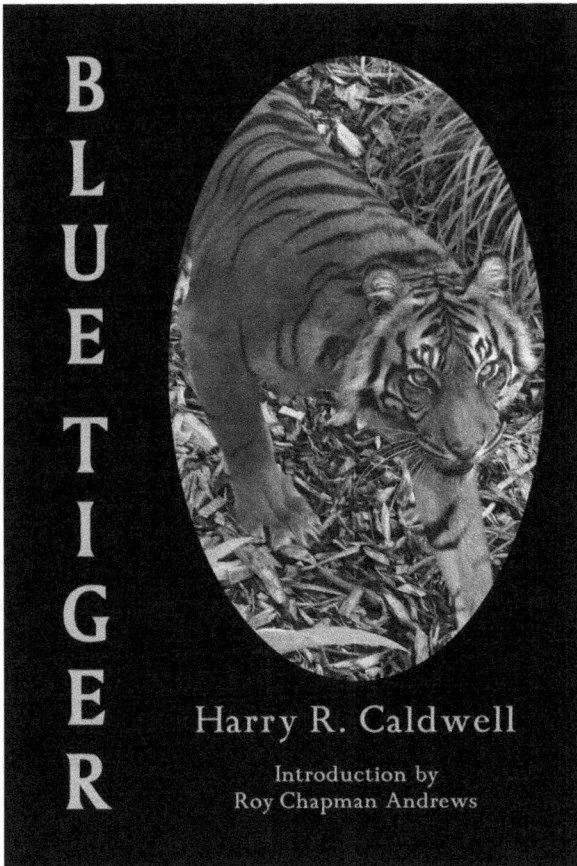

BLUE TIGER

Harry R. Caldwell

Introduction by
Roy Chapman Andrews

A classic zoological mystery: searching for a reported blue tiger in China . . .

COACHWHIP PUBLICATIONS
CoachwhipBooks.com

DR. KARL P.N. SHUKER

DRAGONS
IN ZOOLOGY, CRYPTOZOOLOGY,
AND CULTURE

*Culture and cryptozoology collide as
Dr. Karl Shuker focuses on dragons . . .*

COACHWHIP PUBLICATIONS

CoachwhipBooks.com

A compendium of weird and wonderful wildlife from Dr. Karl Shuker's popular blog posts . . .

BioFortean Reprint

Sculptured Anthropoid
Ape Heads Found In or Near
the Valley of the John Day
River, a Tributary of the
Columbia River, Oregon

James Terry

*An archaeological reprint: ape-like heads
found in Oregon . . .*

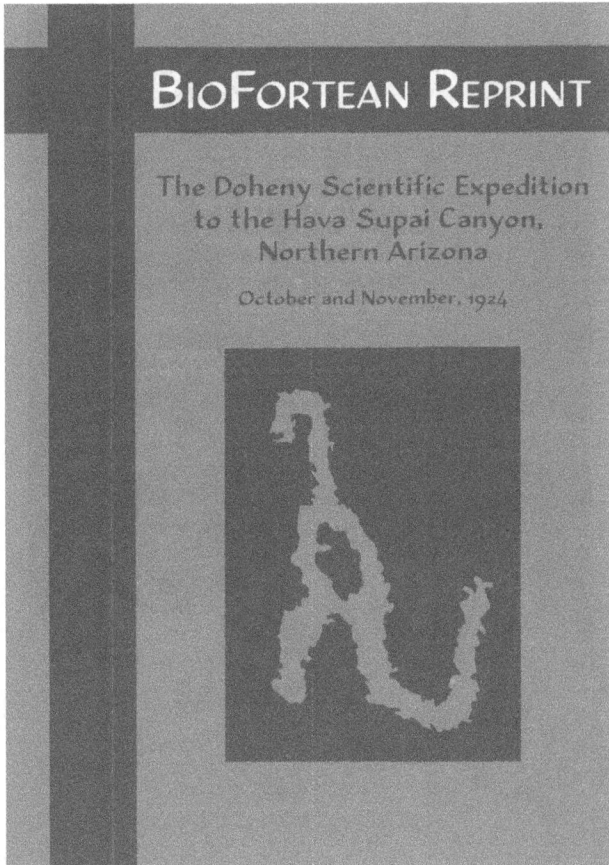

BioFortean Reprint

The Doheny Scientific Expedition to the Hava Supai Canyon, Northern Arizona

October and November, 1924

An archaeological reprint: strange petroglyphs in northern Arizona . . .

ALASKAN
TEN
FOOTED
BEAR

AND OTHER LEGENDS

Compiled by RUTH McCORKLE
Illustrated by WILBUR WALLUK

A folkloric reprint: stories of beasts and beings from the Far North . . .

COACHWHIP PUBLICATIONS
CoachwhipBooks.com

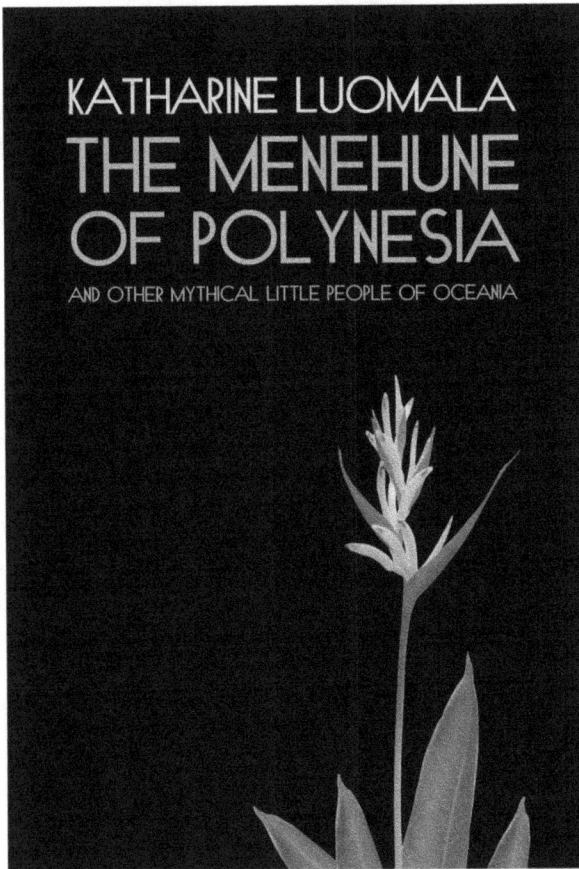

An anthropological reprint: stories of little people from Polynesian islands . . .

THE LAST
MAMMOTH

Manly Wade
WELLMAN

A boy's adventure novel from popular American fantasty writer Manly Wade Wellman . . .

COACHWHIP PUBLICATIONS
CoachwhipBooks.com

Bestiarium Cryptozoologicum

*Mystery Animals and Unknown Species
in Classic Science Fiction and Fantasy*

Short stories of strange beasts, undiscovered species, and cryptozoological monsters . . .

COACHWHIP PUBLICATIONS
CoachwhipBooks.com

Short stories of fantastic creatures and mysterious monsters . . .

COACHWHIP PUBLICATIONS
CoachwhipBooks.com

SAURIA MONSTRA

Dinosaurs, Pterosaurs, and Other
Fossil Saurians in Classic
Science Fiction and Fantasy

*Short stories of living dinosaurs, ptero-
saurs, and other prehistoric reptiles . . .*

www.ingramcontent.com/pod-product-compliance
Lightning Source LLC
Chambersburg PA
CBHW071350290326
41932CB00045B/1268